Design, Adoption, and Impact of Human-Centered Technologies

Sihem ben Saad
https://orcid.org/0000-0003-3034-9206
University of Manouba, Tunisia

IGI Global Scientific Publishing
Publishing Tomorrow's Research Today

Vice President of Editorial	Melissa Wagner
Director of Acquisitions	Mikaela Felty
Director of Book Development	Jocelynn Hessler
Production Manager	Mike Brehm
Cover Design	Jose Rosado

Published in the United States of America by
IGI Global Scientific Publishing
701 East Chocolate Avenue
Hershey, PA, 17033, USA
Tel: 717-533-8845 | Fax: 717-533-7115
Website: https://www.igi-global.com E-mail: cust@igi-global.com

Library of Congress Cataloging-in-Publication Data

(CIP Data Pending)
ISBN13: 9798337399584
Isbn13Softcover: 9798337399591
EISBN13: 9798337399607
British Cataloguing in Publication Data
A Cataloguing in Publication record for this book is available from the British Library.

Table of Contents

Detailed Table of Contents

Our paper evaluates lightweight Federated Learning (FL) models for privacy-preserving Arabic sentiment analysis. We propose a CPU-efficient FL framework using classical models (SVM, Random Forest, Logistic Regression, etc.) as a practical alternative to resource-intensive transformers. tested on Arabic tweet datasets (ArSAS, ASTC, SS2030), Federated SVM achieved top accuracy (e.g., ~90% on ArSAS), while Logistic Regression offered an optimal balance of high performance and minimal execution time. Results confirm FL provides comparable accuracy to centralized training with no significant performance trade-off, while ensuring data privacy, low communication costs, and scalability, making it ideal for edge devices.

Information systems and technologies have become indispensable organizational tools for achieving strategic objectives. This critical role has driven the development of numerous technology acceptance theories, among which TAM has emerged as a fruitful research domain. Being one of the most widely applied models in information systems research, TAM seeks to explain and predict user acceptance and adoption of technologies The model's robustness is evidenced by its extensive application across diverse technologies, cultural contexts, and organizational scales worldwide. However, despite its empirical validation, TAM faces growing enquiry regarding its continued relevance in light of rapidly evolving technological landscapes. This chapter presents a critical examination of TAM, addressing its origin, evolution, main extensions and both its enduring strengths and inherent limitations. Building on this analysis, we propose strategic future directions for the model's evolution,

and VOSviewer, 156 documents were analyzed through performance analysis, co-word mapping, bibliographic coupling, and thematic evolution. The findings reveal (1) the growing convergence between ethical AI, CSR, and sustainability, (2) the emergence of "responsible innovation" as a conceptual bridge linking technological and societal value creation, and (3) evolving clusters around AI ethics, stakeholder engagement, sustainable development, and digital transformation. This review highlights the intellectual structure and future directions of research on responsible, human-centered technology management.

As businesses continue to embrace the advancement of Artificial Intelligence (AI), this advancement has also changed how employees work, communicate with technology, and view the idea of job security. In addition to all the advantages AI can bring, employees have started to express anxiety around the use of AI for their job purposes. Overall, AI anxiety affect how employees behave at work, including behaviours associated with a new phenomenon known as "quiet quitting". Quiet Quitting is a form of psychological withdrawal in which employees limit their work engagement to prescribed role requirements, reducing discretionary effort without formally leaving the organization. The study will provide theories regarding how the integration of AI anxiety contribute to decreased levels of employee engagement and leads of quiet quitting behaviour. Various mediator and moderators of AI anxiety and quiet quitting, multidimensional and unidimensional measurement scales of both the constructs were also discussed in the chapter. The chapter provide limitations and suggested future directions.

The Metaverse is turning into a constantly growing three-dimensional space that is radically changing the nature of digital interaction through the generative Artificial Intelligence and MetaIntelligence. The chapter outlines how Generative Adversarial

Networks, Large Language Models, and Diffusion Models have been used to build immersive virtual worlds, non-player characters and plot progression. It proposes MetaIntelligence as an inclusive model of meta-learning, cyclic improvement and interoperability of heterogeneous systems. Moreover, the chapter provides an overview of how distributed ledger technology, cloud computing, and edge-computing functionality are foundations of scalable world construction, the consideration of consistency, user well-being, ethical and environmental implications, and the opportunities of symbiotic human-AI interaction and virtual/real world interface integration.

The evolution of digital technology has given the transformation on how businesses approach an important role in international expansion, where e-commerce and digital platforms are playing a central role. This paper explores the strategies that companies can adopt the successful strategies to enter and grow in international markets through the digital channels. It highlights the key challenges, including cultural differences, regulatory complexities, logistics, and the localized competition, and examines the critical success factors such as market research, platform localization, payment adaptation, strategic partnerships, and effective digital marketing. Through the case studies and market analysis, the paper outlines the best practices for leveraging global e-commerce platforms, building brand presence, and crossing the evolving international digital economy. Ultimately, it provides a strategic framework for businesses seeking sustainable global growth through digital innovation.

Religious tourism, rooted in human history, uniquely connects faith, culture, and spirituality. Pilgrims visiting sacred sites seek spiritual fulfillment while also supporting the preservation of cultural and historical heritage. In today's rapidly advancing technological era, the integration of smart technologies has transformed religious tourism, offering new opportunities and challenges. This chapter examines how innovations such as augmented reality, mobile applications, and data analytics are reshaping pilgrimage experiences, enhancing accessibility, and enriching engagement. It also highlights their role in conserving and promoting cultural heritage while driving economic growth in religious destinations. Through case studies and best practices, the chapter provides insights into how stakeholders can leverage smart technologies to meet the expectations of modern pilgrims and create more inclusive, spiritually fulfilling, and sustainable religious tourism experiences.

Sustainable tourism requires joint efforts from all stakeholders. This study examines how intellectual capital (IC) enhances tourism performance and sustainability in AJK, Pakistan, using resource-based and dynamic capability theories. It proposes a mediated moderation model, testing the role of open innovation (OI) as a mediator and artificial intelligence capability (AIC) as a moderator. Using purposive sampling, 300 questionnaires were distributed, and 220 valid responses were analyzed through SMART-PLS 4.0. Results show IC significantly improves tourism performance, while OI mediates this effect. AIC further strengthens the OI and tourism industry performance link, indicating that AI tools boost innovation outcomes and support sustainability. The study offers insights for tourism SMEs in developing economies and highlights the need to explore AI's role in innovation under dynamic market conditions.

This chapter examines how business intelligence shapes organizational strategic behavior through integrated processes of information monitoring, protection, and strategic influence. Drawing on the Miles and Snow (1978) typology, it proposes a conceptual and empirical model demonstrating how business intelligence contributes to the development of reactor, analyzer, prospector, and defender behaviors by strengthening anticipation, organizational learning, and strategic coherence. Beyond recent theoretical developments on the cognitive and organizational mechanisms through which information is transformed into strategic action, the chapter incorporates an empirical study validating the positive influence of business intelligence on each strategic profile. The four hypotheses linking business intelligence to different

Preface

INTRODUCTION

As artificial intelligence, immersive systems, and data-driven technologies become increasingly embedded in organizational and societal infrastructures, the question is no longer whether technologies perform efficiently, but whether they are designed, adopted, and governed in ways that align with human values. Human-centered technologies represent a paradigm shift, one that emphasizes usability, emotional alignment, trust, ethics, sustainability, and societal impact alongside technological advancement.

The book *Design, Adoption, and Impact of Human-Centered Technologies* addresses this shift by examining the conceptual foundations, adoption mechanisms, and broader consequences of human-centered technological innovation. Rather than focusing primarily on engagement outcomes, this volume adopts a broader lens that encompasses technology acceptance, emotional and perceptual intelligence, responsible innovation, organizational behavior, sustainability, and strategic transformation across industries.

The chapters in this book explore how human-centered principles are embedded into the design of intelligent systems, how individuals and organizations respond to these technologies, and how their implementation reshapes behaviors, strategies, and performance. Topics include privacy-preserving AI models such as federated learning, critical reassessments of the Technology Acceptance Model, emotionally aligned design frameworks, responsible innovation and corporate social responsibility, AI anxiety and workplace disengagement, generative AI in metaverse creation, digital platforms in international market expansion, smart technologies in tourism regeneration, and the role of business intelligence in strategic decision-making.

This volume is particularly relevant in a context marked by growing concerns about algorithmic bias, data governance, psychological well-being, sustainability, and the societal consequences of rapid technological diffusion. By integrating perspectives from information systems, management, marketing, design, tourism, and organizational studies, the book offers a holistic understanding of how human-centered technologies are conceived, adopted, and leveraged across sectors.

The book is designed for academics and researchers interested in technology adoption, ethical AI, and digital transformation; for students seeking conceptual clarity on emerging human-centered paradigms; for managers, policymakers, and innovation leaders responsible for guiding technology-driven change; and for practitioners who aim to design systems that are not only intelligent, but also inclusive, responsible, and sustainable.

By foregrounding the human implications of technological innovation, this volume contributes to contemporary debates on responsible digital transformation. It argues that the long-term success of intelligent technologies depends not solely on their technical sophistication, but on their capacity to respect human agency, foster trust, support well-being, and generate value for individuals, organizations, and society at large.

CHAPTER OVERVIEW

Chapter 1: Federated Learning for Arabic Sentiment Analysis: A Comprehensive Evaluation of Lightweight Privacy-Preserving Models

The first chapter evaluates lightweight Federated Learning (FL) models for privacy-preserving Arabic sentiment analysis. The authors propose a CPU-efficient FL framework using classical models (SVM, Random Forest, Logistic Regression, etc.) as a practical alternative to resource-intensive transformers. tested on Arabic tweet datasets (ArSAS, ASTC, SS2030), Federated SVM achieved top accuracy (e.g., ~90% on ArSAS), while Logistic Regression offered an optimal balance of high performance and minimal execution time.

Chapter 2: Reassessing the Technology Acceptance Model (TAM): A Critical Review and Future Directions

This chapter presents a critical examination of TAM, addressing its origin, evolution, main extensions and both its enduring strengths and inherent limitations. Building on this analysis, we propose strategic future directions for the model's evolution, ensuring its continued efficacy in an era characterized by accelerated technological innovation

Chapter 3: Perceptual Intelligence in Human-Centered Interactive Technologies: A Framework for Emotionally Aligned Design

This chapter proposes a structural model of Perceptual Intelligence in Human-Centered Interactive Technologies with an emphasis on emotionally aligned design as a new form of interaction. Conventional human-centered design is largely concerned with the usability and functionality, and disregards the subtle relationship between human perception, cognition, and emotion. Perceptual intelligence builds upon this method through incorporation of multi-modal data into systems to recognize user states and adjust system behavior based on a set of models that interprets user states. The model is organized into hierarchical parts: data retrieval, perception modelling, emotion mapping, adaptive interaction and learning feedback. It emphasizes the ways in which technologies can go beyond transactional efficiency to empathetic, trust-centered and personalized experiences. The framework serves as both a conceptual framework and roadmap to the construction of emotionally intelligent systems by connecting design, psychology, and AI

Chapter 4: Responsible Innovation and Corporate Social Responsibility in the Age of Artificial Intelligence and Interactive Technologies: A Bibliometric Review (2010–2025)

This chapter provides a comprehensive bibliometric review of the field, covering 2010–2025 publications indexed in Scopus. Using Bibliometrix (R) and VOSviewer, 156 documents were analyzed through performance analysis, co-word mapping, bibliographic coupling, and thematic evolution. The findings reveal (1) the growing convergence between ethical AI, CSR, and sustainability, (2) the emergence of "responsible innovation" as a conceptual bridge linking technological and societal value creation, and (3) evolving clusters around AI ethics, stakeholder engagement, sustainable development, and digital transformation. This review highlights the intellectual structure and future directions of research on responsible, human-centered technology management.

Chapter 5: Artificial Intelligence Anxiety and Quiet Quitting: A Human-Centered Integrative Review

As businesses continue to embrace the advancement of Artificial Intelligence (AI), this advancement has also changed how employees work, communicate with technology, and view the idea of job security. In addition to all the advantages AI can bring, employees have started to express anxiety around the use of AI for their job purposes. Overall, AI anxiety affect how employees behave at work, including behaviours associated with a new phenomenon known as "quiet quitting". Quiet Quitting is a form of psychological withdrawal in which employees limit their work engagement to prescribed role requirements, reducing discretionary effort without formally leaving the organization. The study will provide theories regarding how the integration of AI anxiety contribute to decreased levels of employee engagement and leads of quiet quitting behaviour. Various mediator and moderators of AI anxiety and quiet quitting, multidimensional and unidimensional measurement scales of both the constructs were also discussed in the chapter. The chapter provide limitations and suggested future directions.

Chapter 6: Architecting Infinite Realities with MetaIntelligence and Generative AI for Metaverse Creation

This chapter outlines how Generative Adversarial Networks, Large Language Models, and Diffusion Models have been used to build immersive virtual worlds, non-player characters and plot progression. It proposes MetaIntelligence as an inclusive model of meta-learning, cyclic improvement and interoperability of heterogeneous systems. Moreover, the chapter provides an overview of how distributed ledger technology, cloud computing, and edge-computing functionality are foundations of scalable world construction, the consideration of consistency, user well-being, ethical and environmental implications, and the opportunities of symbiotic human-AI interaction and virtual/real world interface integration.

Chapter 7: Strategies of E-Commerce and Digital Platforms in the Expansion of International Markets

This chapter explores the strategies that companies can adopt the successful strategies to enter and grow in international markets through the digital channels. It highlights the key challenges, including cultural differences, regulatory complexities, logistics, and the localized competition, and examines the critical success factors such as market research, platform localization, payment adaptation, strategic partnerships, and effective digital marketing. Through the case studies and market analysis, the paper outlines the best practices for leveraging global e-commerce platforms, building brand presence, and crossing the evolving international digital economy. Ultimately, it provides a strategic framework for businesses seeking sustainable global growth through digital innovation.

Chapter 8: The Role of Smart Technologies in Regenerating Religious Tourism

Religious tourism, rooted in human history, uniquely connects faith, culture, and spirituality. Pilgrims visiting sacred sites seek spiritual fulfillment while also supporting the preservation of cultural and historical heritage. In today's rapidly advancing technological era, the integration of smart technologies has transformed religious tourism, offering new opportunities and challenges. This chapter examines how innovations such as augmented reality, mobile applications, and data analytics are reshaping pilgrimage experiences, enhancing accessibility, and enriching engagement. It also highlights their role in conserving and promoting cultural heritage while driving economic growth in religious destinations. Through case studies and best practices, the chapter provides insights into how stakeholders can leverage smart technologies to meet the expectations of modern pilgrims and create more inclusive, spiritually fulfilling, and sustainable religious tourism experiences.

Chapter 9: Unlocking Sustainable Tourism Performance: The Role of Intellectual Capital, Innovation, and Artificial Intelligence Capability in SMEs

Sustainable tourism requires joint efforts from all stakeholders. This study examines how intellectual capital (IC) enhances tourism performance and sustainability in AJK, Pakistan, using resource-based and dynamic capability theories. It proposes a mediated moderation model, testing the role of open innovation (OI) as a mediator and artificial intelligence capability (AIC) as a moderator. Using purposive sampling, 300 questionnaires were distributed, and 220 valid responses were analyzed through SMART-PLS 4.0. Results show IC significantly improves tourism performance, while OI mediates this effect. AIC further strengthens the OI and tourism industry performance link, indicating that AI tools boost innovation outcomes and support sustainability. The study offers insights for tourism SMEs in developing economies and highlights the need to explore AI's role in innovation under dynamic market conditions.

Chapter 10: Modeling and Empirical Evaluation of the Impact of Business Intelligence on Strategic Behavior in the High-Technology Sector

The last chapter examines how business intelligence shapes organizational strategic behavior through integrated processes of information monitoring, protection, and strategic influence. Drawing on the Miles and Snow (1978) typology, it proposes a conceptual and empirical model demonstrating how business intelligence contributes to the development of reactor, analyzer, prospector, and defender behaviors by strengthening anticipation, organizational learning, and strategic coherence. Beyond recent theoretical developments on the cognitive and organizational mechanisms through which information is transformed into strategic action, the chapter incorporates an empirical study validating the positive influence of business intelligence on each strategic profile. The four hypotheses linking business intelligence to different strategic behaviors are tested and discussed, providing a solid foundation for future research aiming to deepen the understanding of these relationships across diverse organizational contexts.

Introduction

As digital technologies continue to permeate organizational, economic, and social systems, questions surrounding their design, adoption, and broader impact have become increasingly salient. Technologies are no longer evaluated solely on the basis of efficiency or performance; they are now expected to align with human values, emotions, ethical principles, and societal goals. Human-centered technologies represent a response to this shift, emphasizing usability, trust, responsibility, and long-term impact alongside innovation.

Design, Adoption, and Impact of Human-Centered Technologies examines the foundations and consequences of this paradigm through a multidisciplinary lens. Rather than focusing primarily on engagement outcomes, this volume addresses the upstream and downstream processes that shape how human-centered technologies are conceived, accepted, implemented, and governed across sectors. It brings together conceptual, methodological, and empirical contributions that explore the conditions under which technologies are perceived as useful, trustworthy, emotionally aligned, and socially responsible.

The chapters in this book investigate critical themes related to technology acceptance, privacy-preserving artificial intelligence, emotionally intelligent system design, responsible innovation, organizational responses to AI, and strategic transformation. Classical and contemporary adoption models are revisited and extended to account for the complexity of AI-driven, immersive, and hybrid technologies. Particular attention is given to the psychological, ethical, and organizational implications of digital transformation, including AI anxiety, workplace disengagement, sustainability, and corporate responsibility.

The volume also explores how human-centered technologies reshape industries and markets. Contributions examine generative AI in metaverse creation, digital platforms in international market expansion, smart technologies in tourism regeneration, artificial intelligence capabilities in SMEs, and the role of business intelligence in strategic behavior. Through these diverse contexts, the book highlights how human-centered design and adoption practices influence performance, innovation, and long-term value creation.

This book is intended for scholars investigating technology adoption and digital transformation, for students seeking conceptual clarity on human-centered paradigms, and for managers, policymakers, and innovation leaders responsible for steering technological change. By integrating technical, behavioral, ethical, and strategic perspectives, the volume offers a comprehensive understanding of the impact of human-centered technologies on individuals, organizations, and society.

By foregrounding the human implications of technological innovation, this book argues that sustainable digital transformation depends not only on what technologies can do, but on how they are designed, adopted, and embedded within social and organizational systems. It invites readers to critically reflect on the future of intelligent technologies and to engage with approaches that place human agency, well-being, and responsibility at the center of innovation.

Chapter 1

Federated Learning for Arabic Sentiment Analysis:
A Comprehensive Evaluation of Lightweight Privacy-Preserving Models

Mohamed Khaldi
https://orcid.org/0009-0006-1347-3730
Higher Institute of Management, Tunis, Tunisia

Abir Smiti
https://orcid.org/0000-0003-1862-9838
Higher School of Economic and Commercial Sciences, Tunis, Tunisia

ABSTRACT

Our paper evaluates lightweight Federated Learning (FL) models for privacy-preserving Arabic sentiment analysis. We propose a CPU-efficient FL framework using classical models (SVM, Random Forest, Logistic Regression, etc.) as a practical alternative to resource-intensive transformers. tested on Arabic tweet datasets (ArSAS, ASTC, SS2030), Federated SVM achieved top accuracy (e.g., ~90% on ArSAS), while Logistic Regression offered an optimal balance of high performance and minimal execution time. Results confirm FL provides comparable accuracy to centralized training with no significant performance trade-off, while ensuring data privacy, low communication costs, and scalability, making it ideal for edge devices.

DOI: 10.4018/979-8-3373-9958-4.ch001

1 INTRODUCTION

The exponential growth of Arabic digital content has created unprecedented opportunities and challenges for Natural Language Processing (NLP). As one of the most linguistically complex languages, Arabic presents unique difficulties, including its rich morphology, diverse dialects, and sparse labeled datasets. These challenges are particularly evident in sentiment classification tasks where, achieving high accuracy often necessitates aggregating large-scale data a process that raises significant privacy concerns and re-training need each time in centralized machine learning paradigms (Li et al., 2021; Yang, Liu, Chen, & Tong, 2020). Addressing the issues of linguistic complexity, data privacy, minor complexity and the need for less retraining time requires innovative approaches that balance model performance with ethical data handling.

Federated Learning (FL), introduced in 2017 (McMahan et al., 2017), has emerged as a transformative machine learning paradigm, enabling collaborative model training without the need to transfer sensitive raw data to centralized servers. This decentralized approach not only enhances data privacy but also facilitates scalable and efficient processing of diverse datasets distributed across multiple sources. FL has shown promise across domains such as healthcare, finance, and energy (Yang, Liu, Chen, & Tong, 2020), yet its potential remains underexplored in the context of NLP for Arabic sentiment classification. Existing research predominantly focuses on centralized models, which are often unsuitable for scenarios involving sensitive data or heterogeneous distributions (Lu et al., 2024).

This study addresses this critical gap by investigating the efficacy of FL for Arabic sentiment classification. Specifically, we propose and evaluate Federated Random Forest (FRF), Federated Decision Trees (FDT), and Federated Support Vector Machines (FSVM) against their centralized counterparts. Using diverse datasets of Arabic tweets under Identically Independent Distributed (IID) conditions, we analyze the performance of these models across key dimensions such as accuracy, scalability, and privacy preservation. By integrating FL with classical machine learning models, this research introduces a novel framework for Arabic NLP, shedding light on the trade-offs and benefits of decentralized architectures.

The remainder of this paper is structured as follows: Section 2 reviews related works in FL and its applications in NLP, with a specific focus on Arabic text analysis. Section 3 presents the experimental setup and results, followed by an in-depth discussion. In Section 4, the challenges and main outputs from this study are well represented in details. Finally, Section 5 concludes with a summary of contributions and future research directions, laying the groundwork for advancing privacy-preserving NLP solutions.

2 RELATED WORKS

The rapid advancements in Natural Language Processing (NLP) have catalyzed significant research in sentiment classification, a critical application for understanding public opinion across various domains. This section provides a comprehensive review of Federated Learning (FL), its integration with machine learning and NLP, and its application to Arabic sentiment analysis. We also address the challenges of combining FL with traditional and deep learning models, positioning our work by identifying the gaps and challenges addressed in this study.

2.1 Federated Learning: Concepts, Applications, and Challenges

Federated Learning (FL), introduced in 2017 (McMahan et al., 2017), is a decentralized approach to machine learning that ensures data privacy by training models locally on client devices without sharing raw data. The FL process typically involves the following iterative steps:

- **Model Initialization**: The central server initializes the global model and shares it with participating clients.
- **Local Training**: Clients train the model locally on their private datasets and send only encrypted parameter updates to the server.
- **Aggregation**: The server aggregates the updates to refine the global model using aggregation functions such as Federated Averaging (FedAVG) (McMahan et al., 2017), Median Aggregation, or Krum (Blanchard et al., 2017).

Aggregation functions are pivotal in FL to ensure robustness and efficiency:

- **Federated Averaging (FedAVG)**:

$$w_t = \frac{\sum_{k=1}^{K} n_k w_k}{\sum_{k=1}^{K} n_k} \tag{1}$$

where w_t is the global model weight at iteration t, w_k represents the weights from client k, n_k is the number of samples on client k, and K is the total number of clients.

- **Median Aggregation**:

$w_t[i] = \text{median}(w_1[i], w_2[i], \ldots, w_K[i]), \forall i,$

where $w_t[i]$ is the i-th parameter of the global model.

- **Krum Aggregation:**

$$w_t[i] = median(w_1[i], w_2[i], \ldots, w_K[i]), \forall I \quad (2)$$

$$Krum(w_1, \ldots, w_K) = argmin^X \mid w_k - w_i \|_2^2 \quad (3)$$

$$w_k i \in Top - (K - f)$$

where f is the number of adversarial clients tolerated, and $Top-(K-f)$ is the set of $K-f$ closest updates to w_k.

FL supports multiple paradigms based on data distribution as mentioned in Figure 1:

- **Horizontal FL (HFL)**: Suitable when datasets share similar features but differ in samples. This is commonly applied in cases like IoT device identification (Shenoy, 2023) and privacy-preserving joint learning across organizations (Huang et al., 2020).
- **Vertical FL (VFL)**: Applied when datasets share common samples but differ in features, often used in finance and healthcare (Yang, Liu, Chen, Tong et al, 2020).
- **Federated Transfer Learning (FTL)**: Combines FL with Transfer Learning to handle domains with minimal feature or sample overlap, such as healthcare and manufacturing (Fan et al., 2020; Kevin et al., 2021).

Despite these advancements, FL still faces challenges, including handling non-IID data distributions, communication costs, and fairness across heterogeneous clients (Lin et al., 2021; Xia et al., 2021). These challenges are particularly pronounced in applications involving linguistically complex datasets, such as Arabic NLP.

2.2 Natural Language Processing and Arabic Sentiment Analysis

Natural Language Processing (NLP) is a critical field of Artificial Intelligence (AI) that enables machines to understand, generate, and analyze human language.

Key applications of NLP include sentiment analysis, text classification, machine translation, question answering, and information retrieval. However, the Arabic language presents unique challenges due to:

Figure 1. HFL Vs. VFL architectures

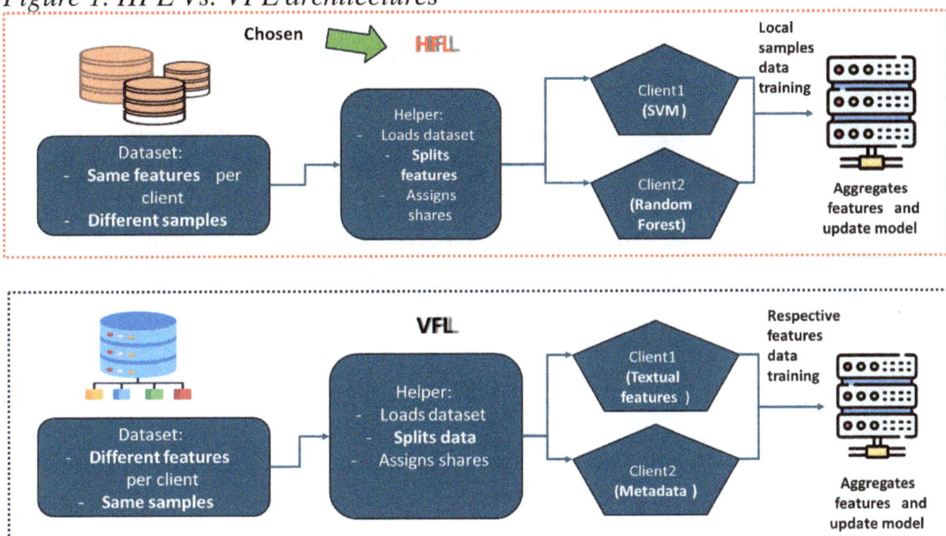

- **Complex Morphology**: Arabic is characterized by root-based morphology, making tokenization and stemming difficult (Elmadany et al., 2018).
- **Dialects and Variations**: Arabic has numerous dialects that differ significantly from Modern Standard Arabic, complicating dataset preparation and model generalization (Antoun et al., 2020).
- **Limited Annotated Datasets**: The scarcity of labeled datasets for Arabic NLP tasks often necessitates the use of transfer learning or data augmentation techniques (Elmadany et al., 2018).

Sentiment analysis, a subfield of NLP, involves classifying text into predefined sentiment categories (e.g., positive, negative, neutral). While centralized ML and DL models, such as AraBERT (Antoun et al., 2020), have achieved state-of-the-art performance in Arabic sentiment analysis, they rely on large-scale data aggregation, raising significant privacy concerns. This underscores the need for decentralized approaches like FL to provide privacy-preserving solutions for Arabic NLP tasks.

2.3 Federated Learning in NLP and Sentiment Analysis

The integration of FL with NLP has gained traction in recent years, driven by the need for privacy-preserving solutions in text-based applications. FedNLP (Lin et al., 2021), for instance, demonstrated FL's potential in text classification and sentiment analysis using Transformer-based models such as BERT and DistilBERT under non-IID conditions. However, most studies have focused on English datasets, with limited exploration of Arabic text.

Hybrid approaches combining FL with deep learning architectures have shown promise in addressing challenges like non-IID data distributions and scalability. Nevertheless, the trade-offs between accuracy, communication efficiency, and privacy preservation remain underexplored, particularly for linguistically complex languages like Arabic. This study aims to bridge this gap by systematically evaluating federated and centralized ML models for Arabic sentiment analysis.

2.4 Challenges in Hybridizing FL and ML

The hybridization of FL with machine learning (ML) and deep learning (DL) offers significant advantages:

- **Enhanced Privacy**: FL ensures that sensitive user data remains on local devices, reducing privacy risks.
- **Scalability**: Distributed training across multiple clients supports large-scale datasets and real-time updates.
- **Improved Generalization**: Training on diverse datasets enhances model robustness and adaptability.

However, this hybridization also introduces several challenges:

- **Non-IID**: The variability in client datasets can lead to biased updates and slower model convergence.
- **Communication Overhead**: Transmitting model parameters instead of raw data reduces bandwidth usage but increases latency in large-scale deployments.
- **Real-Time Synchronization**: Ensuring efficient updates and synchronization across heterogeneous clients remains a challenge.

This study addresses these challenges by evaluating the performance of federated and centralized ML models on Arabic sentiment analysis tasks. The results provide insights into the trade-offs and potential of privacy-preserving NLP solutions, contributing to the broader application of FL in linguistically diverse settings. The major problem in our case was handling Non-IID data. In our case we used a Stratified train-test-split function where clients get equal nearly identical portions of data of a same dataset. This function transforms the data distribution into a nearly-IID or IID. This technique neglect the problem of handling Non-IID data and the fairness struggle related to it. The performance on the two clients demonstrated efficiently the importance of stratified train-test-split function where, the results remain stable, performant and close. For the communication overhead, we used lightweight ML models that are known by low resource consumption, efficiency and well-adaptability to FL exigence. Our proposed method performs well even by comparing it to an existing research (Al-Refai et al., 2023) based on BERT transformers, which are known as huge consumers of resources and necessitates a GPU. The results obtained by this solution showed 90% of accuracy by testing it on a tweeter dataset benchmark. This solution inherently introduce substantial computational and communication overheads, particularly within resource-constrained FL settings such as edge devices, mobile phones, and distributed regional nodes. Our solution is a CPU friendly, simple and computationally efficient and performance-competitive method. Our results demonstrate superior balance across precision, recall, and robustness metrics, particularly in heterogeneous data distributions that mirror real-world FL scenarios. Scalability in real-world data is conserved in our approach with faster local training cycles, reduced communication payloads, and broader deployability across low-resource nodes. Moreover, the communication cost and inference time are highly optimized regarding large-scale pre-trained transformer models, notably BERT.

3 PROPOSED METHOD

This section presents the proposed lightweight and hybrid Federated Learning (FL) framework tailored for Arabic sentiment analysis, incorporating multiple classical machine learning models. The proposed method addresses efficiency, interpretability, and scalability challenges in resource-constrained environments where deploying high resources dependent deep neural models and transformers are impractical.

We proposed a hybrid FL architecture comprising Two decentralized clients, each training on local data subsets using lightweight traditional ML classifiers such as Random Forest (RF), Decision Tree (DT), Logistic Regression (LR), k-Nearest Neighbors (kNN), Multinomial Naive Bayes (MNB), Support Vector Machnie (SVM), and eXtreme Gradient Boosting (XGBoost). A helper that load the dataset and split the data equally in a stratified way between the clients and initialize the models parameters, and a central server that performs model aggregation using a secure and communication-efficient mechanism based on ensemble averaging.

We used publicly available Arabic sentiment datasets (e.g., ArSAS, ASTD, and SS2030) consisting of binary sentiment labels (positive, negative). The datasets are preprocessed using standard NLP techniques: removal of non-Arabic characters, normalization of Arabic letters, elimination of stop words, and tokenization.

The architecture of our proposed method was composed of a server, helper, and two clients. As mentioned in Figure 2, the server initialize the model by setting the number of clients, rounds and the aggregation function, which is FedAVG in our case. the clients get their data portions and specific parameters from the helper, where we used stratified train-test-split function that preserve class distribution and portion across clients. The data is considered as IID. For local training in the client side, each client train its model and send parameters to the server and not raw data, which can lead to a higher communication overhead. Only the data in the clients side are processed locally. The server aggregates the parameters and gave the final performance metrics. The evaluation metrics used in our approach were the standard metrics that are Accuracy, precision, F1-score, recall, and ROC-AUC. Three additional factors were tested and measured in our study that are execution time, model size for each model and the communication overhead between the model and the server. Despite we use IID data from a same dataset that is homogeneous, fairness or robustness tests are optional in our case.

We used FLWR library for parallel clients and server simulation in addition to standard python libraries such as NLTK, Scikit-learn, Pandas and, Numpy. Each client runs on isolated virtual environments simulating edge devices. The server coordinates model aggregation over multiple communication rounds (typically 3 rounds in our study). The complete pipeline is designed to be CPU-efficient, enabling deployment on low-resource Arabic-speaking regions.

Figure 2. Fed-ML architecture

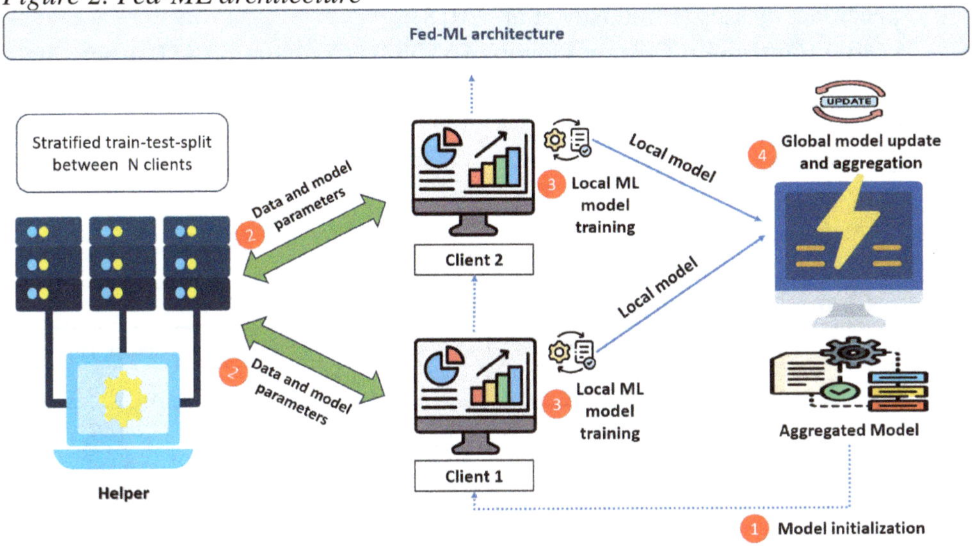

4 RESULTS AND DISCUSSION

This section provides a comprehensive analysis of the experimental results. We compare standard and federated Machine Learning (ML) models applied to Arabic sentiment analysis across three datasets. Key performance indicators include accuracy, precision, recall, F1-score, ROC-AUC, execution time, and model size. The discussion highlights the trade-offs between performance, privacy, and resource utilization.

4.1 Experimental Setup

The experiments were conducted using six ML models on three Arabic sentiment analysis datasets. The computational environment, preprocessing steps, and datasets used are detailed below.

4.1.1 Datasets

Three publicly available datasets were employed, each offering unique characteristics suitable for Arabic sentiment analysis:

- **ArSAS:** A dataset of 21,000 Arabic tweets annotated for sentiment and speech-act classes (Elmadany et al., 2018).
- **Arabic Sentiment Twitter Corpus (ASTC):** Contains 58,751 tweets, balanced for positive and negative sentiments, collected in 2019.
- **SS2030 Dataset:** Includes 4,252 Arabic tweets, with 2,436 labeled positive and 1,816 labeled negative.

Table 1. Characteristics of datasets used in experiments.

Dataset	Balanced	Total Tweets	Positive Tweets	Negative Tweets
SS2030	Yes	4,252	2,436	1,816
ASTC	Yes	58,751	29,849	28,902
ArSAS	Yes	21,000	11,784	9,216

Figure 3. Datasets distribution

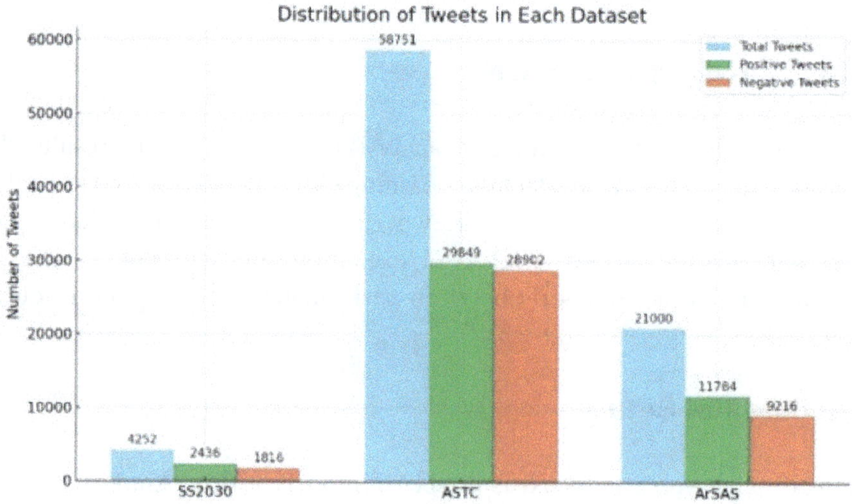

Preprocessing Steps

Datasets were preprocessed to ensure high quality and balance:

- **Handling Missing Data:** Removed all incomplete records.

- **Class Balancing:** Used Random Oversampling to balance positive and negative classes.
- **Normalization:** Standardized Arabic text by removing diacritics, unifying spellings, and normalizing variations in orthography.

For federated experiments, data was split between two clients using both train-test split and stratified shuffle split techniques to maintain uniformity across positive and negative classes.

4.1.2 Machine Learning Models

The following ML models were chosen for their robustness in sentiment classification:

- **Random Forest:** It is an Ensemble Learning ML model based on Decision Trees and which is an evolution of bagging method (Breiman, 2001). It is most used for classification and regression tasks and specified by constructing multiple decision trees and outputs the mode of the classes accurately for the classification.
- **Decision Trees:** It is a decisions tree structure model (Quinlan, 1986). Each internal node of it represents a feature, each branch represents a decision rule and each leaf node represents an outcome (class label). Homogeneous groups are built from the subsets of values of input features.
- **Logistic Regression:** It is used especially for binary classification problems (Cox, 1958). The logistic function is specified by that is a sigmoid function with an output between 0 and 1. It is a probabilistic method, where the equation of the probability is represented by:

$$P(Y = 1 \mid X) = \frac{1}{1 + e^{-(\beta_0+\beta_1X_1+\beta_2X_2+\ldots+\beta_nX_n)}}$$

where, $P(Y = 1 \mid X)$ is the probability of the outcome being 1 given the input features X, and $\beta_0, \beta_1, \ldots, \beta_n$ are the coefficients estimated from the data.

- **Multinomial Naive Bayes:** It is another form of probabilistic ML models used for classification problems (McCallum & Nigam, 1998). It is based on Bayes theorem, which calculates the probability of the classes with certain features. Its formula is represented by the likelihood for a feature vector $X = (x_1, x_2, \ldots, x_n)$ given a class C:

$$P(X|C) = \frac{(n!)\prod_{i=1}^{n} x_i^{ci}}{\prod_{j=1}^{k}(n_j!)}$$

where, n is the total number of features and c_i is the count of feature i in class C.

- **K-Nearest-Neighbor:** This model (Fix, 1985) is characterized by that similar data points are located close to each other in the feature space, where K is the number of the nearest neighbors that lead to make a decision. The algorithm classifies a data point based on the majority class among its K nearest neighbors.
- **Support Vector Machine:** is a supervised machine learning algorithm (Vapnik, 1995) used for classification and regression tasks. It finds the optimal hyperplane that maximizes the margin between the classes in the feature space, where the margin is the distance between the hyperplane and the nearest data points of each class. Its equation is represented as:

$$f(x) = sign\left(\sum_{i=1}^{n} a_i y_i K(x_i, x) + b\right)$$

Where,

- $\mathbf{x}_i$: Training feature vectors (from text).
- y_i : Class labels (+1 or -1).
- α_i : Lagrange multipliers (learned during training).
- $K(\mathbf{x}_i, \mathbf{x})$: Kernel function (e.g., linear, RBF, polynomial).
- b: Bias term.
- sign(·): Determines the class (+1 or -1) based on the sign of $f(\mathbf{x})$.
    - **Extreme Gradient Boosting (XGBoost):** It is an advanced ML model characterized by speed, and performance (Chen & Guestrin, 2016). It is specific for machine learning competitions and real-world applications. It includes parallel processing, tree pruning, and regularization techniques. This strong model operates on the principle of boosting, where it combines multiple weak learners (typically decision trees) to create a strong predictive model.

4.1.3 Computational Environment

The experiments were conducted on an HP i3-11th Gen Intel(R) Core(TM) i3-1115G4 laptop with 20GB RAM. Python libraries such as scikit-learn and Flwr FL were utilized for implementing standard and federated models.

4.2 Experimental Results

The experiments have been applied on the previously listed ML models in both standard and federated forms. We studied the accuracy, precision, recall and F1-score, ROC-AUC metrics in addition to execution time, model size and CPU and memory consumption for both versions of each model. Below, we will show the results of the standard then the federated versions of the ML models.

4.2.1 Performance of Standard ML Models

The standard version of ML models showed good results for the problem of sentiment analysis and classification of Arabic texts while applied on the three Arabic sentiment analysis datasets. Table 2 highlighted the performance metrics of the different ML models.

For ArSAS dataset, SVM and RF outperformed the other algorithm's accuracy with 91.06% and 88.99% respectively. In term of precision, the results was near for *Table 2.*

Table 2. Performance of standard ML models on three different Arabic sentiment analysis datasets. Bold values indicate the best score for a given dataset

Algorithm	Dataset	Accuracy	Precision	Recall	F1-Score
RF	ArSAS ASTC	88.99 71.92	89.55 **75.77**	88.27 65.84	88.91 70.45
	SS2030	**81.31**	78.48	93.77	**85.45**
LR	ArSAS ASTC	88.45 73.09	89.71 74.48	86.85 71.61	88.26 73.02
	SS2030	80.25	81.13	86.34	83.65
DT	ArSAS ASTC	81.07 58.35	85.57 71.85	74.72 29.76	79.78 42.08
	SS2030	72.03	81.70	67.26	73.78
kNN	ArSAS ASTC	79.24 69.13	73.93 65.02	**90.31** **85.05**	81.30 73.70

continued on following page

Table 2. Continued

Algorithm	Dataset	Accuracy	Precision	Recall	F1-Score
	SS2030	61.92	60.92	**97.38**	74.96
MNB	ArSAS ASTC	87.91 72.14	87.99 72.30	87.91 72.14	87.90 72.05
	SS2030	**81.31**	**82.25**	81.31	80.69
SVM	ArSAS ASTC	**91.06** **73.98**	**91.90** 75.56	90.04 72.18	**90.96** **73.83**
	SS2030	81.08	81.85	86.94	84.32
XGBoost	ArSAS ASTC	86.89 68.82	88.48 74.63	84.82 58.62	86.61 65.66
	SS2030	79.90	79.67	88.15	83.69

Figure 4. Base ML models performance on ArSAS dataset

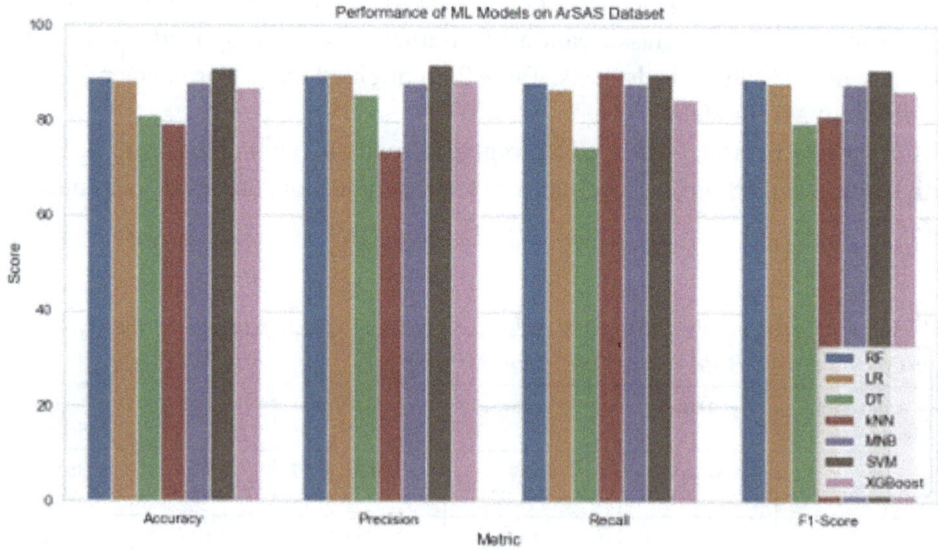

Figure 5. Base ML models performance on ASTC dataset

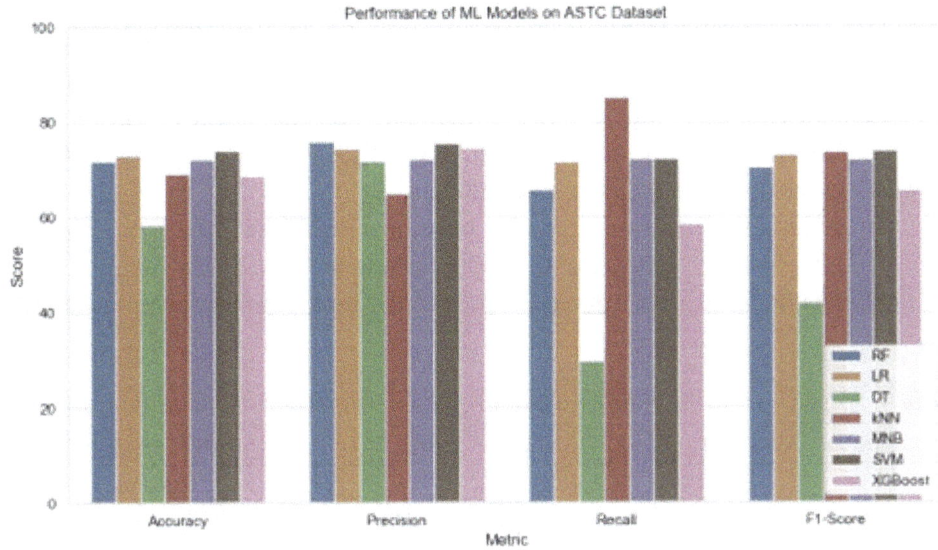

Figure 6. Base ML models performance on SS2030 dataset

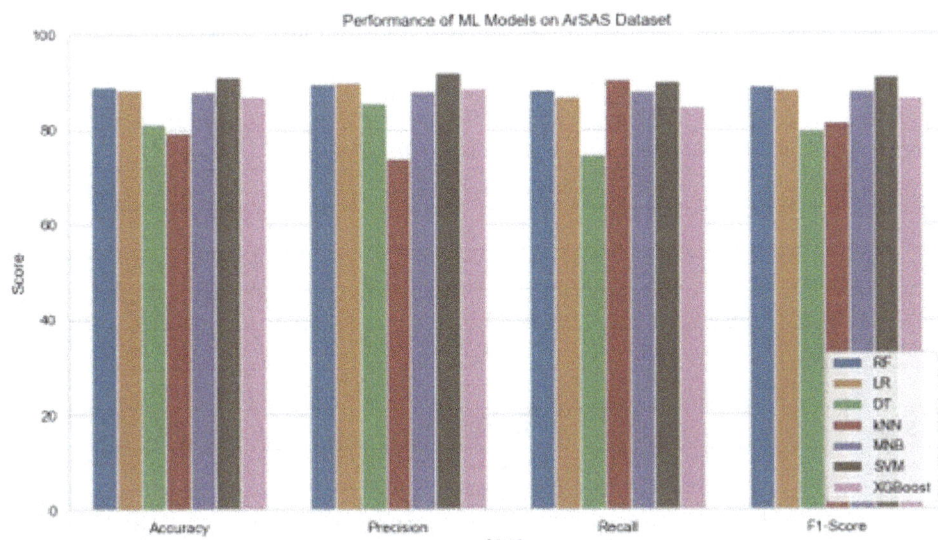

The models where SVM has the highest precision with 91.90% followed by LR, RF, XGBoost. kNN has the lowest precision but demonstrated a good impact in term of recall with the highest percentage of 90.31% followed by SVM and RF with 90.04% and 88.27% respectively. F1-score reflected the performance's domination of SVM with a score of 90.96%. RF and LR came at the second and third places with 88.91% and 88.26% while MNB and XGBoost have nearly the same results. In overall, SVM and RF outperformed the other algorithms for the problem of classification of Arabic text sentiment anlysis with ArSAS dataset while DT has the weakest performance among all the models.

The execution time and model's size have been compared and represented in Table 3. This comparison will put the light on how federated learning minimizes and facilitates more the performance of the models and remain simpler and easier.

Table 3. ArSAS execution time and model size for standard ML models

Algorithm	Execution time (s)	Model size (KB)
RF	6.94	7596.65
LR	1.15	82.46
DT	1.55	**18.84**
kNN	**1.01**	2427.70
MNB	1.02	327.51
SVM	54.11	1206.69
XGBoost	4.83	223.57

Table 4. ASTC execution time and model size for standard ML models

Algorithm	Execution time (s)	Model size (KB)
RF	16.26	5813.42
LR	1.31	158.56
DT	1.74	**14.15**
kNN	**1.02**	3513.62
MNB	1.02	631.92
SVM	611.84	2871.57
XGBoost	4.81	193.49

The results in Table 3 demonstrated that kNN, MNB, LR, and DT performed the process with lowest execution time in seconds (s) with 1.01, 1.02, 1.15, and 1.55 respectively while SVM, RF and XGBoost had the longest execution time. Moreover, for model size in Kilo-Bytes (KB), the smallest model sizes were remarkable for both DT with 18.84 KB and LR with 82.46 KB. RF consumed more resources than the other models with 7596.65 followed by kNN and SVM.

Table 5. SS2030 execution time and model size for standard ML models

Algorithm	Execution time (s)	Model size (KB)
RF	2.76	4317.01
LR	1.03	29.67
DT	1.14	**13.06**
kNN	**1.01**	460.22
MNB	**1.01**	116.38
SVM	4.07	312.38
XGBoost	1.86	170.34

The Receiver Operating Characteristic (ROC) curve is a graphical representation used to evaluate the performance of a classification model. It plots the True Positive Rate (TPR) (also known as sensitivity or recall) against the False Positive Rate (FPR):

$$\text{True Positive Rate (TPR)} = \frac{\text{True Positives}}{\text{True Positives} + \text{False Negatives}} \quad (4)$$

$$\text{False Positive Rate (FPR)} = \frac{\text{False Positives}}{\text{False Positives} + \text{True Negatives}} \quad (5)$$

The Area Under the Curve (AUC) of the ROC is a single scalar value summarizing the performance of the classifier. More AUC is closer to 1 more the classifier is performing better near to perfect.

SVM has the highest AUC value with 95.95% followed by RF, MNB, LR, XGBoost and kNN with 95.73%, 94.66%, 94.62%, 93.54% and 90.41% respectively. DT was the weakest performing algorithm with 87.26% by analyzing the ROC curve and AUC values. This indicates that RF and SVM processed the classification task better than the other algorithms. As a conclusion, All the models gave good results and performed the classification of labels and attributes correctly without any significant problem. It is obvious that the high performance of SVM in nearly all the datasets reflected its high metrics values. SVM is useful dealing with complex data structures accurately while DT oppositely failed to treat complex data of complex Arabic language with several dialects. For tree-based models, RF have been nearly the second best model following to SVM and have had balanced execution times and models size.

4.2.2 Results and Discussion of Federated ML Models

The hybridization of ML models with federated approach results are represented and analyzed in this section. We processed our work in two rounds and two clients for Federated ML models. The same metrics are analyzed and studied in this part of the paper.

It can be visualized in Table 7 that the results differ between the federated ML models for the various datasets. For ArSAS, SVM showed the best accuracy, precision and F1-score for both clients. It has the best recall for client 1 while kNN and DT had the best recall for client 2. For ASTC, which is the large dataset, SVM still have the best accuracy with 73.54 and 73.64, and F1-score with 72.46% and 72.67% for *Table 6*.

Table 6. Standard ML models ROC AUC on the three Arabic sentiment analysis datasets

Algorithm	Dataset	ROC-AUC
RF	ArSAS	95.73
	ASTC	80.40
	SS2030	88.52
LR	ArSAS	94.62
	ASTC	81.18
	SS2030	88.54
DT	ArSAS	87.26
	ASTC	61.08
	SS2030	80.95
kNN	ArSAS	90.41
	ASTC	80.51
	SS2030	67.27
MNB	ArSAS	94.66
	ASTC	**81.42**
	SS2030	**88.98**
SVM	ArSAS	**95.95**
	ASTC	80.81
	SS2030	88.68
XGBoost	ArSAS	93.54
	ASTC	76.10
	SS2030	88.36

Table 7. Federated ML models performance on three different Arabic sentiment analysis datasets

Algorithm	Dataset	Accuracy		Precision		Recall		F1-Score	
		c1	c2	c1	c2	c1	c2	c1	c2
	ArSAS	86.72	86.72	87.84	86.92	85.23	86.44	86.51	86.68
RF	ASTC	69.81	69.96	77.09	78.28	57.78	56.61	66.06	65.71
	SS2030	77.41	83.05	80.32	83.26	80.32	88.06	80.32	85.60
	ArSAS	85.30	86.05	87.70	88.44	81.83	83.22	84.66	85.75
LR	ASTC	70.96	71.26	73.50	73.65	67.04	67.67	70.12	70.53
	SS2030	78.11	87.29	**88.69**	87.33	75.27	88.88	81.43	88.10
	ArSAS	85.44	87.40	84.60	86.34	86.33	89.12	85.46	87.71
DT	ASTC	71.11	72.43	72.32	74.71	69.93	69.17	71.10	71.84
	SS2030	72.70	86.58	77.97	84.14	79.70	92.00	78.83	87.89
	ArSAS	73.93	77.86	68.83	72.66	86.61	**89.93**	76.70	80.83
kNN	ASTC	64.85	63.75	**82.23**	**86.16**	39.36	34.17	53.24	48.93
	SS2030	64.94	64.23	65.09	59.83	97.04	**98.66**	77.92	74.49
	ArSAS	84.96	85.71	87.50	87.81	81.28	83.22	84.27	85.45
MNB	ASTC	70.62	70.68	68.90	69.49	**76.92**	**75.46**	**72.69**	72.35
	SS2030	77.41	86.82	74.10	83.66	**99.26**	93.33	**84.85**	88.23
	ArSAS	**89.97**	**90.58**	**91.59**	**92.43**	**87.84**	88.59	**89.67**	**90.47**
SVM	ASTC	**73.54**	**73.64**	76.91	76.84	68.50	68.92	72.46	**72.67**
	SS2030	**80.70**	**88.47**	87.05	88.59	81.91	89.77	84.41	**89.18**
	ArSAS	80.97	81.31	83.70	84.84	76.50	76.64	79.94	80.53
XGBoost	ASTC	64.98	64.28	70.53	70.90	53.43	50.41	60.80	58.93
	SS2030	76.23	87.52	74.56	**89.44**	95.20	86.66	83.63	88.03

Figure 7. Accuracy of Federated ML models on ArSAS, ASTCn and SS2030

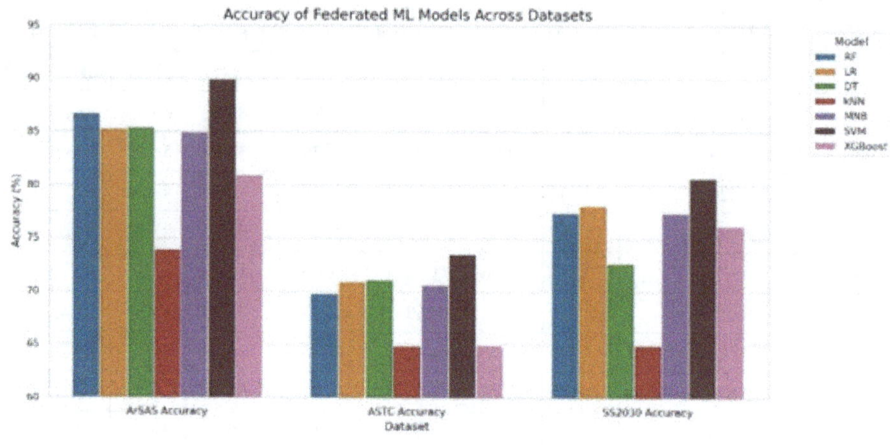

Table 8. ASTC Execution time and model size for federated ML models for two rounds and two clients

Algorithm	Execution time (s)		Model size (KB)		Communication overhead
	c1	c2	c1	c2	
RF	3.52	3.63	3478.10	3464.20	81.35 MB
LR	3.61	3.57	180.39	180.39	4.22 MB
DT	411.9	411.21	668.40	686.21	31.74 MB
kNN	**2.77**	**1.81**	3375415.20	3375415.20	39555.64 MB
MNB	2.81	2.80	719.20	719.20	8.42 MB
SVM	1793.42	1778.99	109414.79	108537.61	2554.12 MB
XGBoost	102.05	101.98	**106.13**	**107.19**	**2.49 MB**

both clients. kNN has the best precision with 82.23% and 86.16% and MNB the best recall with 76.92% and 75.46% for both clients but SVM has closer results to them in theses metrics. For SS2030 dataset, SVM still have the best accuracy for both clients and best F1-score and precision for client 2 whie LR has the best precision with 88.69% for client 1. MNB has the highest recall for both clients with 99.26% and 93.33%. Overal, SVM outperformed the other algorithms for the three datasets while kNN is considered as the weakest federated ML model.

For the execution time and model's size of Federated ML models. We visualize that the time varies between the three datasets. kNN has the smallest execution time and the largest model's size for ASTC and SS2030. In Table 10, MNB has approximately the smallest execution time with kNN with 1.02 seconds followed by LR. SVM has

Figure 8. Performance of federated ML models on ArSAS dataset

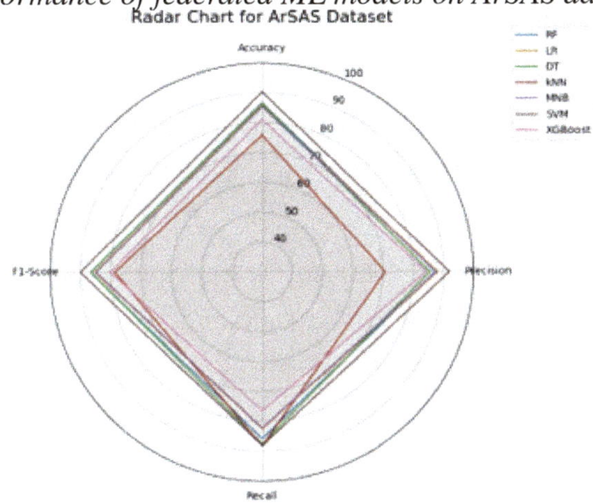

Table 9. SS2030 Execution time and model size for federated ML models for two rounds and two clients

Algorithm	Execution time (s)		Model size (KB)		Communication overhead
	c1	c2	c1	c2	
RF	3.52	3.63	3478.10	3464.20	81.35 MB
LR	1.13	1.13	**33.21**	**33.21**	**0.77 MB**
DT	1.92	1.49	51.35	30.25	0.95 MB
kNN	**1.09**	**1.09**	515478.74	515478.74	6040.76 MB
MNB	1.24	1.24	349.66	349.66	8.19 MB
SVM	47.30	42.88	46621.98	37200.38	982.29 MB
XGBoost	2.32	2.37	103.70	104.76	2.44 MB

the largest execution time with 1277.14 seconds and has the largest model's size with 339772KB for client 1 and 838113.73 for client 2 followed by kNN and RF respectively.

Table 9 demonstrated that kNN, LR, MNB and DT had the lowest execution times respectively with less than 2 seconds while SVM consumed more time than the other algorithms. LR, DT, XGBoost and MNB had the smallest model's size for both clients.

For Table 8 related to ASTC dataset, kNN, DT, RF and MNB had the smallest execution times with 2.77(s), 2.81(s), 3.52(s) and 3.61(s) respectively. SVM and DT had the biggest execution time with 1793.42(s), 411.9(s) for client 1 and 1778.99(s), 411.21(s) for client 2 respectively. This may be a fact that DT found troubles in

Figure 9. Performance of federated ML models on ASTC dataset

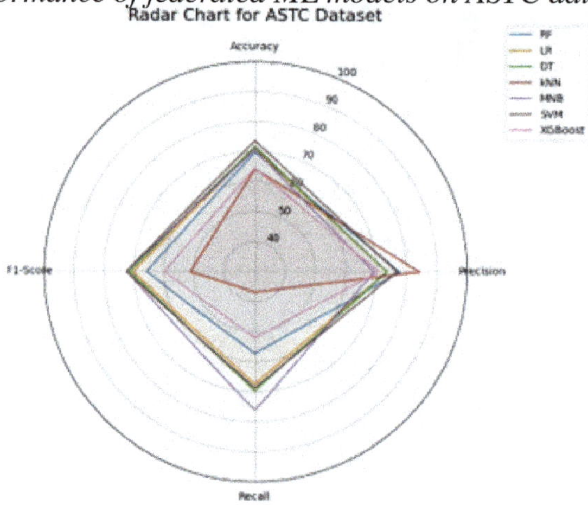

Table 10. Execution time and model size for federated ML models (two rounds, two clients) on the ArSAS dataset

Algorithm	Execution time (s)		Model size (KB)		Communication overhead
	c1	c2	c1	c2	
RF	23.29	23.29	7854.66	7799.18	183.44 MB
LR	1.32	1.32	**88.01**	**88.01**	**2.06 MB**
DT	14.85	11.06	110.73	102.76	2.50 MB
kNN	**1.01**	**1.01**	55210.85	55210.85	1294 MB
MNB	1.02	1.02	130.51	130.51	3.05 MB
SVM	1277.14	1278.82	339772	838113.73	13803.34 MB
XGBoost	19.33	19.22	110.73	111.40	2.60 MB

processing large datasets. kNN as mentioned before have the largest model's size followed by SVM while XGBoost and LR had the smallest model's size.

For the tables 10 9, LR showed the lowest communication overhead with 0.77 MB, and 2.06 MB for SS2030, and ArSAS respectively. For Table 8, XGBoost and LR had shown the lowest communication overhead with 2.49 MB, and 4.22 MB respectively.

Table 11 represented the AUC values of ROC curves of each Federated ML model while applied on each dataset. The results highlighted that for client 1, SVM outperformed the other algorithms in performing the classification accurately with 96.11% for ArSAS and 80.64% for ASTC while MNB has the best value for SS2030 dataset

Figure 10. Performance of federated ML models on SS2030 dataset

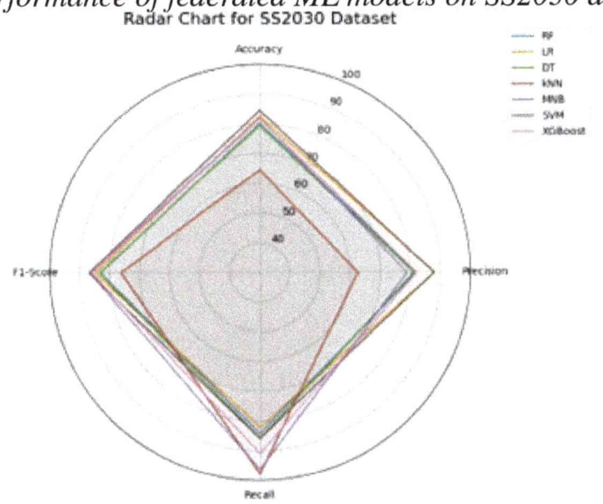

Figure 11. Execution time and communication overhead report visualization

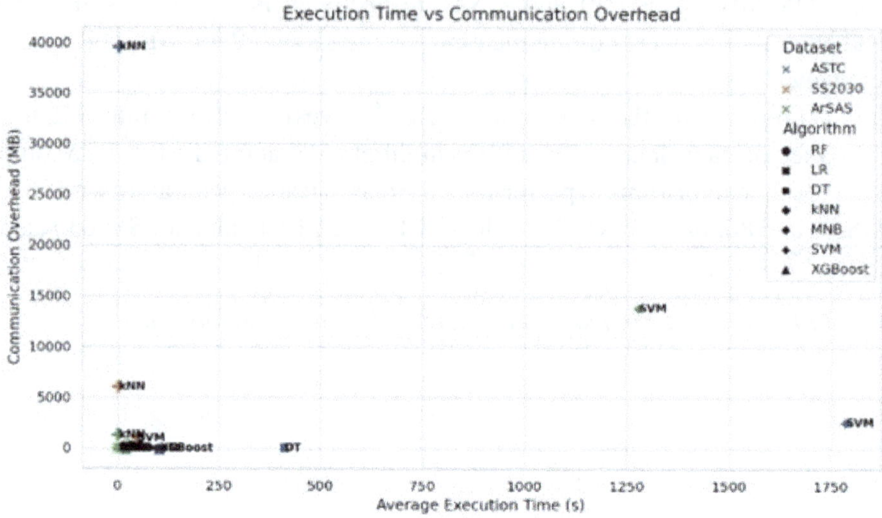

Figure 12. Execution time per federated ML model for ASTC

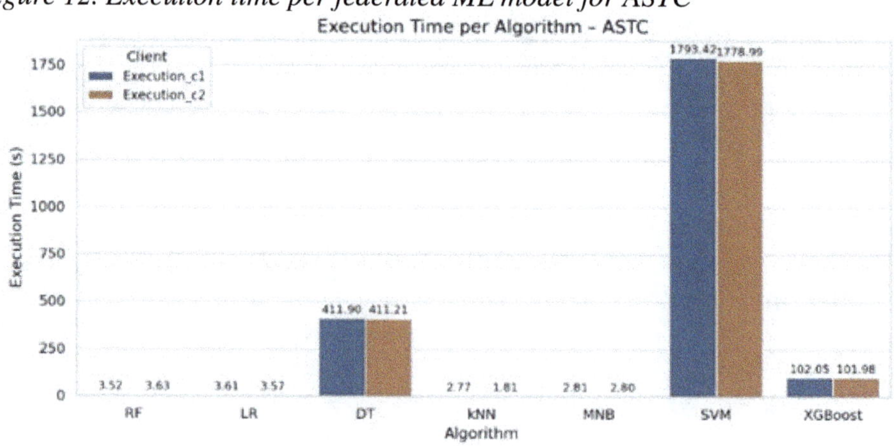

Figure 13. Execution time per federated ML model for SS2030

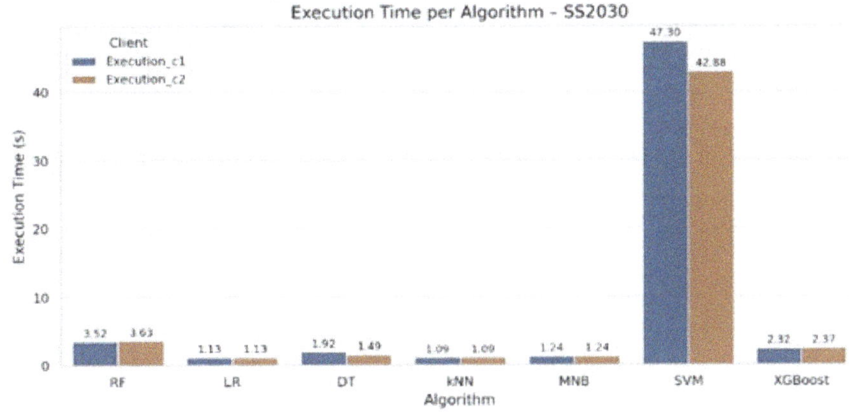

with 88.52%. For client 2, SVM have the highest AUC for both ArSAS and ASTC with 96.55% and 80.86% respectively while XGBoost have the best AUC value for SS2030 with 95.65% followed by LR with 95.33% and SVM with 95.26%. kNN have had the weakest AUC values for all datasets except DT and XGBoost with ASTC for client 1 and for client 2 with ASTC where XGBoost has the lowest percentage.

Figure 14. Execution time per federated ML model for ArSAS

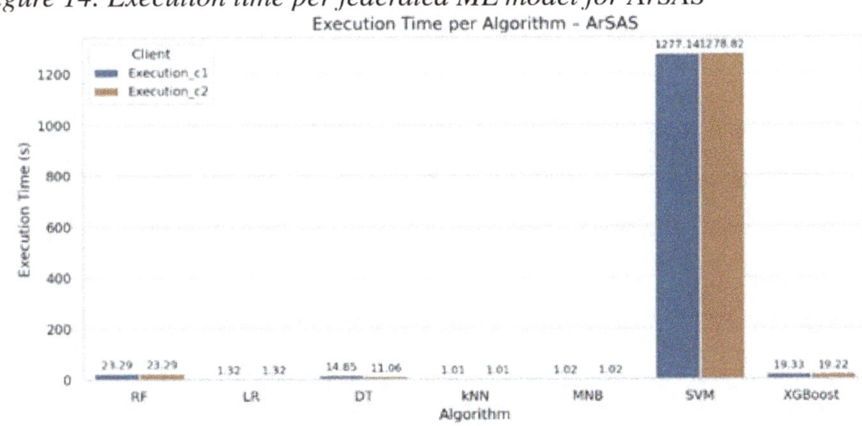

As a result, Figure 15 compare the performance average between federated and baseline models.

Figure 15. Comparing performance average between federated Vs. base ML models -1-

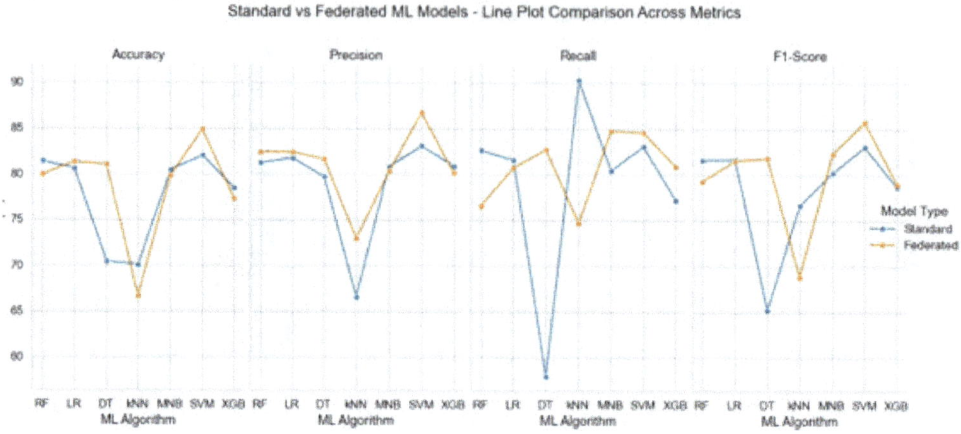

The research (Aouedi et al., 2021) demonstrated that both standard and fine-tuned hyperparameters of tree-based models and XGBoost do not change the results in a remarkable way. This fact may lead to train and evaluate the model faster. SVM take

Figure 16. Metrics distribution between federated Vs. base ML models -2-

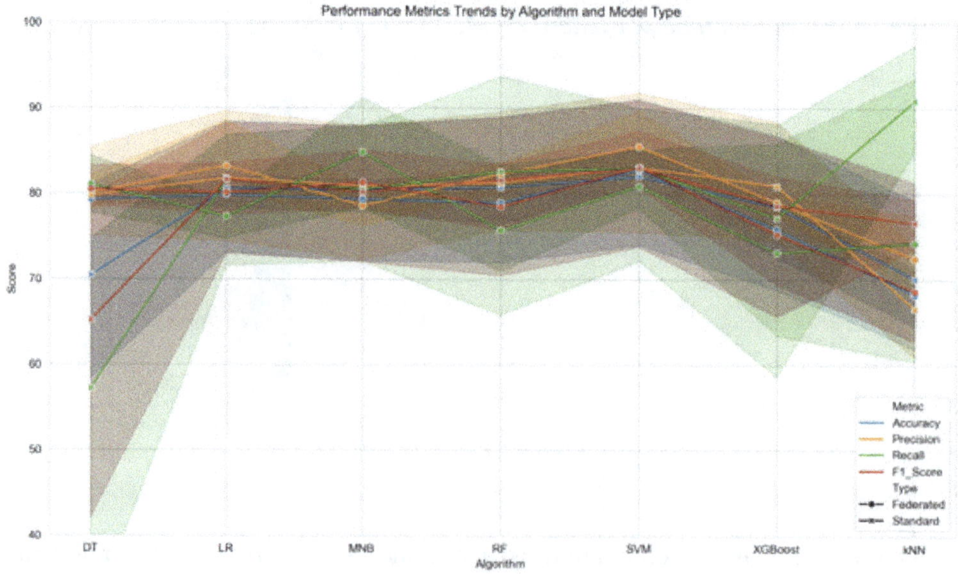

more execution time than the other models but it provided more accurate and better results because of its advantage in processing the classification task accurately.

However, kNN has the lowest execution time with the biggest model size in all the datasets but AUC values of ROC curve affirmed that it was the weakest model to perform the classification task. This fact may be related to the dialectal richness and complexity. The variance of dialects and domains affected the performance of the models, which was the case related to ASTC where the model's performances have been lowered but kept processing accurately. Model fast efficient performance and data privacy and security are the major outstanding performance outputs, where the users sensitive informations are well processed in a fast manner, protected because of exchanging only the weights in place of raw data. No big gap is mentioned between standard and ML model's performances. However, federated learning ML models are more secure, scalable, reproducible, easier to implement and can be spread among clients varying from one client to multiples of devices considered as clients each one. Furthermore, due to the excess of data in social media applications, migrating to a federated learning approach becomes a necessity to conserve more privacy and security to the users. Even more, we guarantee the gain of retraining the model on a whole dataset. This parallel efficient, and fast method preserves the efficiency of all the client's models with being reproducible and scalable.

Table 11. Federated ML models ROCAUC on the three Arabic sentiment analysis datasets

Algorithm	Dataset	c1	c2
RF	ArSAS ASTC	94.34 79.63	94.48 79.03
	SS2030	87.11	91.85
LR	ArSAS ASTC	92.66 79.16	93.40 78.92
	SS2030	87.97	95.33
DT	ArSAS ASTC	85.44 72.60	87.39 72.86
	SS2030	71.59	87.81
kNN	ArSAS ASTC	73.93 75.61	77.86 76.13
	SS2030	63.59	75.37
MNB	ArSAS ASTC	92.78 80.09	93.74 79.55
	SS2030	**88.52**	94.70
SVM	ArSAS ASTC	**96.11** **80.64**	**96.55** **80.86**
	SS2030	87.24	95.26

continued on following page

Table 11. Continued

Algorithm	Dataset	c1	c2
XGBoost	ArSAS ASTC	88.19 71.49	89.63 70.63
	SS2030	84.12	**95.65**

4.3 Statistical Analysis

A comprehensive statistical tests have been performed between Federated and Standard ML models comparing their performances. We assessed distributional assumptions, paired significance tests, interaction effects, and effect size estimation over their performance metrics (Accuracy, precision, recall, and F1-score). For normality assessment, we used Shapiro-Wilk test. The results indicated that *Accuracy* ($W = 0.956, p = 0.1070$) and *Precision* ($W = 0.969, p = 0.3148$) followed a normal distribution ($p > 0.05$), whereas *Recall*($W = 0.886, p = 0.0006$), and *F1score*($W = 0.869, p = 0.0002$) had deviated from normality significantly. Depending on the normality of the underlying data, we used more in-depth paired comparisons. For Normal metrics, we conducted *paired t-test* on Accuracy and Precision of Federated and Standard ML models. *Accuracy:* $t(20) = 0.102, p = 0.9198$ and *Precision:* $t(20) = 0.482, p = 0.6348$. For Non-Normal metrics, *Wilcoxon SignedRank test* was employed showing that *Recall*($W = 91.000, p = 0.4120$) and *F1-score*($W = 102.000, p = 0.6578$). The results revealed that there is no statistically significant differences $p > 0.05$ between Federated and Standard ML models suggesting comparable predictive capabilities.

A further examination of potential interaction effects between algorithm type and learning paradigm was conducted using two-way ANOVA test for each metric. Recall

Figure 17. Q-Q plot assessing residual normality assumptions for statistical testing

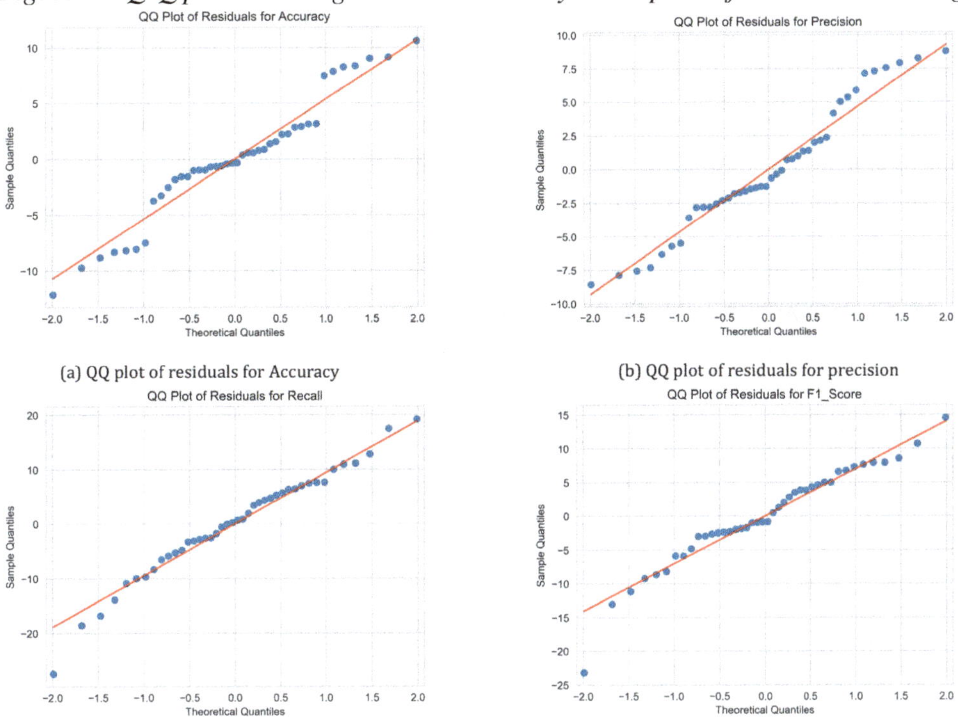

(a) QQ plot of residuals for Accuracy

(b) QQ plot of residuals for precision

(c) QQ plot of residuals for recall

(d) QQ plot of residuals for F1-score

and F1-score observation showed that there is no significant difference ore interactions effects where $p > 0.05$. For Accuracy, the results were as follow:

- **Algorithm:** $F(6.28) = 2.77, p = 0.0307$ *(Significant)*
- **Learning Type:** $F(1.28) = 0.01, p = 0.9204$ *(Non-Significant)*
- **Interaction:** $F(6.28) = 0.54, p = 0.7726$ *(Non-Significant)*

For Precision, the results were as follow:

- **Algorithm:** $F(6.28) = 4.20, p = 0.0039$ *(Significant)*
- **Learning Type:** $F(1.28) = 0.31, p = 0.5815$ *(Non-Significant)*
- **Interaction:** $F(6.28) = 0.35, p = 0.9041$ *(Non-Significant)*

As a result, only *Algorithm type* had statistically a significant effect on Accuracy and Precision, while *Learning paradigm (FL Vs. SML(Standard Machine Learn-*

ing)) showed no main or interaction effect. Model performance remains consistent between FL and SML approaches.

Tukey's HSD post-hoc analysis was applied for significant ANOVA effects on Accuracy and Precision. Most pairwise comparisons were non-significant, kNN consistently underperformed in Precision when compared to the other models *(e.g., vs. SVM:* $p = 0.0005$, *vs. LR:* $p = 0.0029$). However, there *was not any significance interaction for learning type suggesting the algorithmic differences are independent of learning type and framework.*

Inferential tests have been complemented through quantifying the magnitude of the performance differences between FL and SML through *Cohen's d* Effect Size Estimation test demonstrated in Figure18. Effect size was small for Precision and Recall with *-0.146* and *0.067*, while it was small nearly to negligible for Accuracy and F1-score with *-0.028* and *-0.008* respectively. As a result, the metrics yielded that differences in performance between FL and SML were *minimal in magnitude* and *not of practical significance*. Collectively, performance between FL and SML high-

Figure 18. Effect size

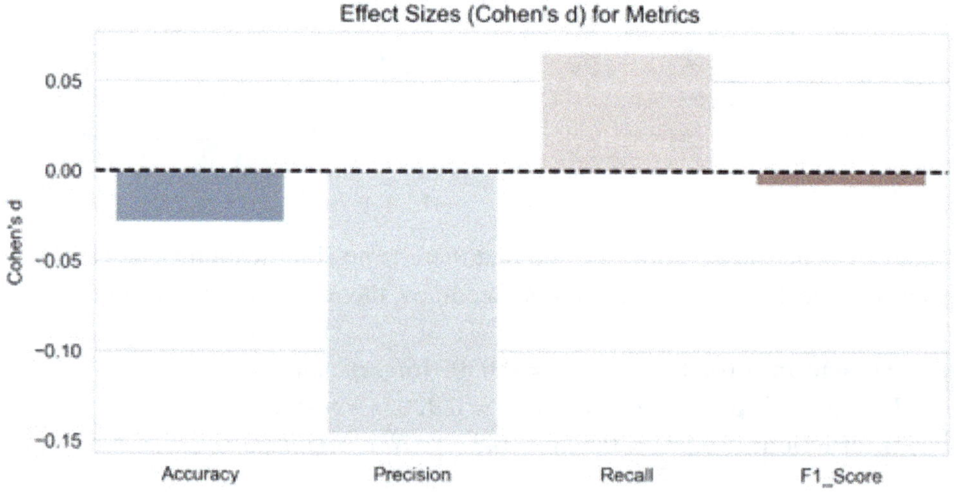

lighted that the *choice of learning paradigm did not significantly affect model outcomes*. These findings suggest that *FL serve as a privacy-preserving alternative without compromising predictive performance* making it attractive in sensitive data environments adding benefits of *privacy, viability, generalization and, compliance suitable for deployment in real-world, privacy-sensitive applications.*

5 CHALLENGES AND OUTPUTS

The migration toward federated learning approaches become crucial, nowadays, because of the excess web applications based on AI and the distribution of online users. FL architecture offers more scalability, personalization, privacy and security. Communication cost coming from different client sources is better applicable than transferring large raw data. FL is strictly preserving sensitive data supporting various communication messages sizes with minimal communication overhead for CPU friendly models. The migration to FL approach is not any further different remarkably against standard models, which was shown in standard and FL ML model's comparison results. For centralized architecture, the central server must be computationally powerful and strong, which can cost a lot to process some problems. However, the scalability related to decentralized architectures, such as FL, is more robust and can divide the process between the clients and represent better results with low costs. The collaboration and harmonization between edge devices communication and exchange reflects the importance of FL in covering a wide range of users in parallel. Moreover, for fault tolerance is a key fact, where clients take the needed time to process without affecting the final outputs. This criterion strengthen the continuity aspect suitable for real-time applications updates that incrementally learn in parallel. The adoption of locally trained and deployed models is favorable in real-time applications like IoT systems and autonomous vehicles. The access to social media online applications is almost through smartphones or smart devices. Smartphones are revolutionizing in term of characteristics such as CPU, storage and, RAM but still limited. The migration to FL approach with CPU friendly models will be favorable because of FL distributed architecture.

In addition, FL is advantageous through the interoperability across different smartphone systems and platforms. Furthermore, training on data from diverse sources locally increases the resilience of the model facing dangerous adversarial attacks and data shifts by enhanceing the mitigation of bias, where the data from diverse clients support a better generalization of the model. Multi-task learning is guaranteed by FL distributed approach.

FL ensures effective model training identic to SML even in environments with limited network bandwidth or processing power. Models can adapt dynamically to local environments, handle the problems without exception like complexity of Arabic language dialects. It almost reduces redundancy in data storage. Users are more likely to engage with applications that transparently respect their data privacy. FL models will be so powerful, useful and effective for next generation applications.

There exist only One research (Al-Refai et al., 2023) that tried to fuse FL with BERT for Arabic sentiment analysis. It is based on high computational resources consumption and necessitate GPU. This method often suffers from high computational costs, large communication overhead, and limited interpretability because of the nature of largepretrained transformers dependencies in a remarkable high computational time. Edge devices may lack computational capacity. In contrast, our design not only maintains competitive performance but also ensures faster inference, lower training and communication costs, and improved accessibility for deployment on resource-constrained edge devices as a CPU friendly lightweight solution. These advantages make our method particularly appealing for real-world applications where scalability, fairness, and efficiency are paramount. Fairness is respected in our study because of using Stratified train-test-split method in the helper level to split the data equally from a same dataset between the clients. This detail transform the data into IID.

6 CONCLUSION AND FUTURE WORK

This paper presented a comprehensive study comparing seven widely used machine learning models in both standard and federated frameworks for Arabic sentiment analysis. Using three diverse datasets—ArSAS, ASTC and SS2030, we evaluated the model's effectiveness by classifying data into positive and negative labels. The study focused on key performance metrics, including accuracy, precision, recall, F1-score, execution time, model size and, communication overhead bandwidth. By addressing the challenges of privacy and scalability in centralized learning systems, our research highlighted the transformative potential of federated learning in sentiment analysis.

The experimental results demonstrated that all models maintained high performance in both their standard and federated implementations. Among the models, Support Vector Machine (SVM) consistently achieved the highest accuracy and F1-score across all datasets, showcasing its robustness and reliability for sentiment classification tasks. When combined with federated learning, SVM retained its superior performance while providing additional advantages in terms of privacy and scalability. This finding underscores the practicality of federated learning as an effective and secure alternative to centralized approaches, especially in applications involving sensitive textual data.

Different driven statistical tests approved our approach strength against SML models. The outcomes were mainly that performances are identical for these two approaches, FL was more legal for ethical constraints, viable, offering inherent advantages in data sovereignty, compliance, and scalability as a compelling alternative to centralized approaches especially in sensitive domains like healthcare, finance, and Arabic social media sentiment analysis.

Federated learning proved particularly effective in mitigating risks associated with data breaches and privacy violations. By transferring only model weights instead of raw data, federated frameworks significantly reduced the exchange of sensitive informations, aligning well with privacy regulations, and addressing key concerns of modern data processing. Furthermore, the decentralized nature of federated learning allowed scalablity for training across multiple devices without compromising performance. Despite these advantages, the study also revealed some challenges, including the increased communication overhead introduced by iterative model updates and the variability in performance caused by non-IID data distributions across clients. Experimental and statistical tests approved the strength of FL approach against centralized SML for these challenges, where we used Stratified data splitting method that allowed that data is nearly IID, and showcasing that the communication overhead of our CPU friendly best performing models was low in resources cost term. These main challenges were taken in consideration, and solved in our proposed architecture.

The results highlighted that federated learning offers a compelling solution for privacy-preserving sentiment analysis without substantial trade-offs in accuracy. However, the performance of federated models remains sensitive to communication costs and computational overhead, particularly for resource-intensive algorithms such as SVM. These limitations suggest that further research is needed to optimize federated frameworks and address the scalability challenges in real-world applications.

Looking ahead, this work opens several avenues for future research. Incorporating small deep learning architectures into federated frameworks could significantly enhance their ability to handle more complex tasks and datasets. Additionally, addressing the challenges posed by non-IID data distributions through innovative techniques like personalized federated learning could further improve the adaptability and efficiency of these systems. Expanding the application of federated learning to other NLP tasks, such as named entity recognition and topic modeling, would also broaden its utility across diverse domains.

Another promising direction is to assess the scalability of federated learning frameworks in large-scale, real-world scenarios involving numerous clients with lowresource devices. Analyzing and optimizing the energy consumption of federated learning systems could also make them more sustainable for widespread adoption. These future developments will be critical in refining federated learning as a transformative technology for privacy-preserving NLP applications.

In conclusion, this study underscores the potential of federated learning to revolutionize sentiment analysis by combining robust CPU friendly machine learning models with decentralized training approaches. The findings are not only to advance our understanding of federated learning's capabilities for Arabic sentiment analysis but also to lay a foundation for its broader adoption in privacy-sensitive applications.

Federated learning represents a promising step forward in achieving scalable, secure, and high-performance solutions for the challenges of modern NLP.

DECLARATIONS

- There is no funding declaration for this article.
- The authors declare that they have no competing interests.
- No datasets were generated or analyzed during the current study.
- Authors contributed equally in this manuscript.

REFERENCES

Al-Refai, M., Alzu'bi, A., Yaseen, N. B., & Obeidat, T. (2023). Arabic sentiment analysis with federated deep learning. In *UK Workshop on Computational Intelligence* (pp. 29–38). Springer.

Antoun, W., Baly, F., & Hajj, H. (2020). AraBERT: Transformer-based model for Arabic language understanding. *arXiv*. https://arxiv.org/abs/2003.00104

Aouedi, O., Piamrat, K., & Parrein, B. (2021). Performance evaluation of feature selection and tree-based algorithms for traffic classification. In *2021 IEEE International Conference on Communications Workshops (ICC Workshops)* (pp. 1–6). IEEE. DOI: 10.1109/ICCWorkshops50388.2021.9473580

Blanchard, P., El Mhamdi, E. M., Guerraoui, R., & Stainer, J. (2017). Machine learning with adversaries: Byzantine-tolerant gradient descent. *Advances in Neural Information Processing Systems*, 30.

Breiman, L. (2001). Random forests. *Machine Learning*, *45*(1), 5–32. DOI: 10.1023/A:1010933404324

Chen, T., & Guestrin, C. (2016). XGBoost: A scalable tree boosting system. In *Proceedings of the 22nd ACM SIGKDD International Conference on Knowledge Discovery and Data Mining* (pp. 785–794). DOI: 10.1145/2939672.2939785

Cox, D. R. (1958). The regression analysis of binary sequences. *Journal of the Royal Statistical Society. Series B, Statistical Methodology*, *20*(2), 215–232. DOI: 10.1111/j.2517-6161.1958.tb00292.x

Elmadany, A. A., Mubarak, H., & Magdy, W. (2018). An Arabic speech-act and sentiment corpus of tweets. In *Proceedings of the 3rd Workshop on Open-Source Arabic Corpora and Processing Tools*. European Language Resources Association (ELRA).

Fan, Y., Li, Y., Zhan, M., Cui, H., & Zhang, Y. (2020). IoTDefender: A federated transfer learning intrusion detection framework for 5G IoT. In *2020 IEEE 14th International Conference on Big Data Science and Engineering (BigDataSE)* (pp. 88–95). IEEE. DOI: 10.1109/BigDataSE50710.2020.00023

Fix, E. (1985). *Discriminatory analysis: Nonparametric discrimination, consistency properties* (Vol. 1). USAF School of Aviation Medicine.

Huang, Z., Liu, F., & Zou, Y. (2020). Federated learning for spoken language understanding. In *Proceedings of the 28th International Conference on Computational Linguistics* (pp. 3467–3478).

Kevin, I., Wang, K., Zhou, X., Liang, W., Yan, Z., & She, J. (2021). Federated transfer learning–based cross-domain prediction for smart manufacturing. *IEEE Transactions on Industrial Informatics*, *18*(6), 4088–4096. DOI: 10.1109/TII.2021.3113025

Li, X.-C., Li, L., Zhan, D.-C., Shao, Y., Li, B., & Song, S. (2021). Preliminary steps towards federated sentiment classification. *arXiv*. https://arxiv.org/abs/2107.11956

Lin, B. Y., He, C., Zeng, Z., Wang, H., Huang, Y., Dupuy, C., Gupta, R., Soltanolkotabi, M., Ren, X., & Avestimehr, S. (2021). FedNLP: Benchmarking federated learning methods for natural language processing tasks. *arXiv*. https://arxiv.org/abs/2104.08815

Lu, Z., Pan, H., Dai, Y., Si, X., & Zhang, Y. (2024). Federated learning with non-IID data: A survey. *IEEE Internet of Things Journal*, *11*(11), 19188–19209. Advance online publication. DOI: 10.1109/JIOT.2024.3376548

McCallum, A., & Nigam, K. (1998). A comparison of event models for naive Bayes text classification. In *AAAI-98 Workshop on Learning for Text Categorization* (pp. 41–48).

McMahan, B., Moore, E., Ramage, D., Hampson, S., & Arcas, B. A. (2017). Communication-efficient learning of deep networks from decentralized data. In *Proceedings of the 20th International Conference on Artificial Intelligence and Statistics* (pp. 1273–1282). PMLR.

Quinlan, J. R. (1986). Induction of decision trees. *Machine Learning*, *1*(1), 81–106. DOI: 10.1023/A:1022643204877

Shenoy, M. V. (2023). HFEDDI: A novel privacy-preserving horizontal federated learning–based scheme for IoT device identification. *Journal of Network and Computer Applications*, *214*, 103616. DOI: 10.1016/j.jnca.2023.103616

Vapnik, V. (1995). Support-vector networks. *Machine Learning*, *20*(3), 273–297. DOI: 10.1023/A:1022627411411

Xia, W., Li, Y., Zhang, L., Wu, Z., & Yuan, X. (2021). A vertical federated learning framework for horizontally partitioned labels. *arXiv*. https://arxiv.org/abs/2106.10056

Yang, Q., Liu, Y., Chen, T., & Tong, Y. (2020). Federated learning: Siloed data exploitation via model aggregation. *International Journal of Machine Learning and Cybernetics*, *11*(12), 345–359. DOI: 10.1007/s13042-020-01064-8

Yang, Q., Liu, Y., Cheng, Y., Kang, Y., Chen, T., & Yu, H. (2020). Vertical federated learning. In Yang, Q., Liu, Y., Chen, T., & Tong, Y. (Eds.), *Federated learning* (pp. 69–81). Springer. DOI: 10.1007/978-3-031-01585-4_5

Chapter 2
Reassessing the Technology Acceptance Model (TAM): A Critical Review and Future Directions

Nadia Sfar
https://orcid.org/0009-0000-6324-2419
University of Monastir, Tunisia

ABSTRACT

Information systems and technologies have become indispensable organizational tools for achieving strategic objectives. This critical role has driven the development of numerous technology acceptance theories, among which TAM has emerged as a fruitful research domain. Being one of the most widely applied models in information systems research, TAM seeks to explain and predict user acceptance and adoption of technologies The model's robustness is evidenced by its extensive application across diverse technologies, cultural contexts, and organizational scales worldwide. However, despite its empirical validation, TAM faces growing enquiry regarding its continued relevance in light of rapidly evolving technological landscapes. This chapter presents a critical examination of TAM, addressing its origin, evolution, main extensions and both its enduring strengths and inherent limitations. Building on this analysis, we propose strategic future directions for the model's evolution, ensuring its continued efficacy in an era characterized by accelerated technological innovation

DOI: 10.4018/979-8-3373-9958-4.ch002

INTRODUCTION

The 1970s witnessed increasing technological demands and a high incidence of failed system implementations within organizations, generating significant research interest in predicting system use. Despite this focus, early studies failed to establish reliable predictors of user acceptance (Chuttur, 2009). From this critical gap, technology acceptance has emerged as a fertile and important research domain since the late 1980s (Ajzen, 1985; Davis, 1986; Davis et al., 1989).

The concept of "technology" has evolved beyond its standard definition as applied science. The economist W. Brian Arthur offers a broader, human-centric perspective, defining it as "*a means to fulfill a human purpose*," which can be a method, process, or device (Arthur, 2009, p. 28). In an era of rapid digitalization, public understanding of technology is nuanced; while people place great hope in technology to extend human capabilities, they also hold a degree of mistrust, aware of its potential to be enslaving (Arthur, 2009, pp. 215-216). Consequently, for a technology to succeed, users expect it to be reliable, useful, usable, and safe (Schorr, 2023).

This reliance on technology makes user acceptance a critical determinant of its success. Acceptance is fundamentally defined as "an antagonism to the term refusal and means the positive decision to use an innovation" (Dillon & Morris, 1996). For both practitioners and researchers, a central question is why people accept or reject new technologies. Answering this question aids in developing better methods for designing, evaluating, and predicting user responses to new systems (Simon, 2001). Thus, understanding the factors that influence this decision is crucial for developers and decision-makers, enabling them to address key issues during the technology's development phase, and foster user confidence and involvement (Mathieson, 1991).

A number of theoretical models and frameworks have been developed to explain and predict the user adoption of new technologies. Seminal works in this area include the Theory of Reasoned Action (Fishbein and Ajzen, 1975), the Technology Acceptance Model (TAM) (Davis, 1986; Davis et al., 1989), the Theory of Planned Behavior (Ajzen, 1985), the Diffusion of Innovation theory (Bandura, 1977), the Model of PC Utilization (Thompson et al., 1991), the Motivational Model (Davis et al., 1992), Social Cognitive Theory, and the Unified Theory of Acceptance and Use of Technology (UTAUT) (Venkatesh et al., 2003). Researchers typically employ these established frameworks individually or combine their constructs to develop more tailored models for specific contexts.

Given that a complete understanding of user behavior often requires more than one theoretical approach, these models have been applied across a wide variety of domains (such as education (Granić, 2022; Schereret al., 2019)., healthcare, consumer behavior, and computer usage), to understand and predict user intentions and actions. Consequently, many studies have developed specific frameworks to assess the usage of particular implemented technologies, underscoring the domain's ongoing relevance and practical utility (O'Dea, 2024).

Among these theories, the Technology Acceptance Model (TAM) has been at the forefront of theory and research in the field (O'Dea, 2024). However, TAM has been criticized for encouraging incremental research that may overlook complex acceptance problems (O'Dea, 2024). This critic is sharpened by a clear paradox: the core TAM, a framework over 30 years old, is still often employed in its original form despite a radically changed technological landscape (Al-Emran & Granić, 2021). Therefore, as research continues, a critical understanding of TAM's assumptions, limitations and perspectives is not just useful, but essential (O'Dea, 2024).

I. THE TECHNOLOGY ACCEPTANCE MODEL (TAM): THE EMERGENCE AND EVOLUTION

Developed by Fred Davis in 1989, the Technology Acceptance Model (TAM) is one of the most influential models for predicting individual user adoption of information systems and technology. Rooted in the Theory of Reasoned Action (TRA) (Fishbein and Ajzen, 1975), TAM was designed to identify the cognitive and psychological factors driving technology acceptance. This framework has been rigorously tested across diverse populations and technological environments (Schorr, 2023). While originally applied to office software, its applicability has proven to be extensive (Al-Kfairy et al., 2024).

Davis's (Davis, 1986) foundational proposal (original TAM) established a framework where user motivation is driven by three factors: Perceived Ease of Use, Perceived Usefulness, and Attitude Toward Using the system (Chuttur, 2009).

Figure 1. Original TAM proposed by Fred Davis (Davis, 1986, p.24)

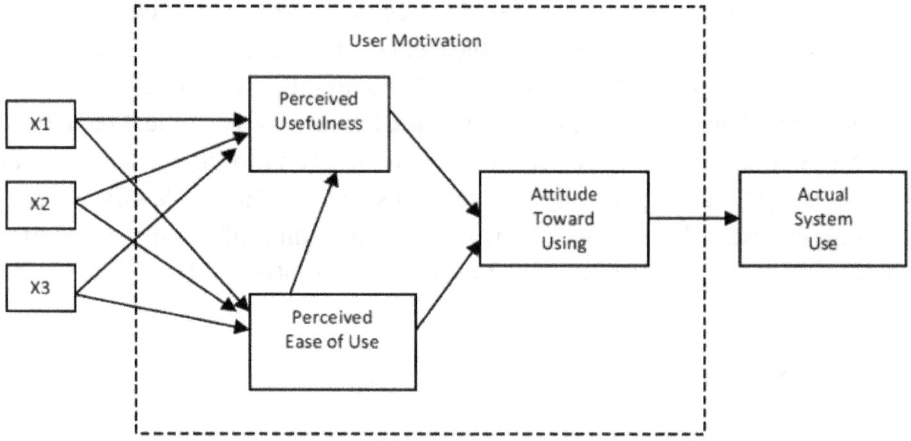

The model posited that a user's attitude is a primary determinant of their actual system use, and that this attitude is itself shaped by the two core beliefs of perceived usefulness and perceived ease of use. These beliefs were, in turn, hypothesized to be directly influenced by the system's design characteristics (denoted as X1, X2 and X3 in Figure 1).

I.1. Perceived Ease of Use (PEOU)

Perceived ease of use (PEOU) is a foundational construct in technology acceptance, defined as the degree to which a person believes that using a particular system would be free of effort (Davis et al., 1989). It fundamentally influences application usage, as users may be turned away by a system's complexity if the perceived effort outweighs the potential benefits (Davis et al., 1989).

The strategic importance of PEOU is significant. A focus on ease of use in design and development leads to tangible benefits such as increased adoption rates, enhanced user satisfaction, faster learning curves, and a competitive advantage. This is because PEOU is widely recognized as a critical measure of system quality, directly impacting the overall user experience (Seddon & Kiew, 1996; DeLone & McLean, 2004; Petter et al., 2008; Hwang et al., 2008; Petter & McLean, 2009). While the relative influence of PEOU has evolved, it remains a key determinant of user attitude (Chuttur, 2009).

I.2. Perceived Usefulness (PU)

Perceived Usefulness (PU), a cornerstone of the Technology Acceptance Model (TAM), is defined as "*the degree to which a person believes that using a particular system would enhance his or her job performance*" (Davis et al., 1989, p.12). This belief is a primary driver of technology adoption, as users are fundamentally motivated to use applications that they expect will help them perform their tasks more effectively.

The power of perceived usefulness lies in its direct link to utilitarian value. It transcends mere functionality by signifying the tangible, practical benefits a user anticipates, such as increased efficiency, effectiveness, and overall performance improvement. These benefits are often quantifiable, manifesting as time saved, fewer errors, and more proficient task completion (Al-Kfairy et al., 2024).

I.4. Attitude Toward Using

The "Attitude" variable refers to an individual's positive or negative emotional response to using a specific technological system (Davis et al., 1989; Fishbein & Ajzen, 1975; Ramayah & Jantan, 2004; Venkatesh et al., 2003). This construct was assumed to be a primary factor in a user's decision to adopt or reject a system (Schorr, 2023). In the original Technology Acceptance Model (TAM), this attitude component was positioned as a mediating variable between user perceptions (ease of use and usefulness) and their actual use of a system (Davis, 1986). However, due to a lack of strong confirmed correlations with the core beliefs and a desire for model parsimony, the attitude construct was subsequently removed from the main TAM framework (Davis et al., 1989; Marangunić & Granić, 2015).

The TAM was subsequently refined to include behavioral intention as a direct outcome of perceived usefulness (Davis, Bagozzi, & Warshaw, 1989). This update accounted for situations where users adopt a system based purely on its perceived utility, without a strong prior attitude, resulting in the revised model presented in Figure 2.

Figure 2. First modified version of TAM (Davis et al., 1989, p. 985)

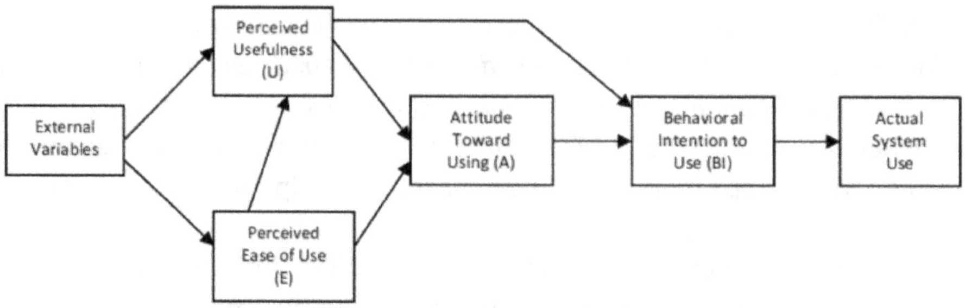

I.5. Behavioral Intentions to Use

Behavioral intention (BI) is a well-established construct in technology acceptance research, defined as a user's conscious plan and motivation to perform a specific behavior. It is considered as a direct and significant precursor to actual usage behavior (Ajzen, 1991; Davis et al., 1989; Venkatesh & Davis, 2000).

The foundational work of Davis et al. (1989) positioned behavioral intention as the primary determinant of system use, with all other factors (such as perceived usefulness and ease of use), exerting their influence indirectly through it. Using behavioral intention as a predictor offers several advantages: It provides a dynamic and forward-looking measure of potential technology adoption, in contrast to actual usage data, which only reflects past behavior. This predictive capability has proven to be effective and reliable in forecasting actual system use (Agarwal & Prasad, 1999; Ramayah & Ignatius, 2005).

Davis, Bagozzi, and Warshaw (1989) conducted a longitudinal study to test their model (first modified version of TAM), surveying 107 users after a one-hour system introduction and again 14 weeks later. The results consistently showed a strong correlation between behavioral intention and actual system usage. The influence of perceived usefulness on user intentions is one of the most robustly confirmed relationships in information systems research (Chuttur, 2009).

Empirical studies consistently show that the higher the perceived usefulness of a technology, the stronger a user's behavioral intention to adopt and use it (Kang & Namkung, 2019; Yadav et al., 2016). Users inherently gravitate towards technologies that offer a clear advantage, making perceived usefulness a critical determinant of technology acceptance and long-term utilization (Al-Kfairy et al., 2024). Meanwhile, perceived ease of use had a minor, time-sensitive effect (Chuttur, 2009). Its impact on behavioral intention is often considered secondary to perceived usefulness.

This is partly because PEOU is tied to technical aspects that become less salient as users grow more technologically accustomed (Davis et al., 1989). Despite this shift, examining PEOU remains essential, especially for novel technologies like virtual assistants, where user familiarity cannot be assumed and initial ease of use is critical for adoption.

Crucially, both PEOU and PU factors directly influenced behavioral intention, making the attitude construct redundant and leading to the revised model (Figure 3).

Figure 3. Final version of TAM (Venkatesh & Davis, 2000)

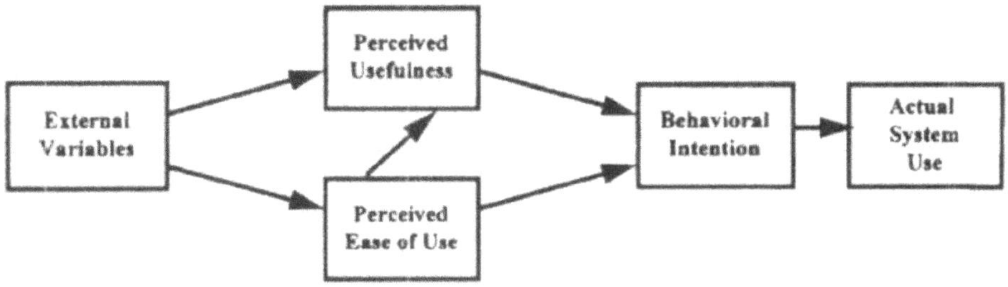

This simplification successfully explained the direct link between perceived usefulness and system use, while also eliminating previously unexplained influences from system design to attitude. The model was further refined by incorporating external variables (such as system features, training, and implementation), that shape user beliefs (Venkatesh & Davis, 2000).

The finalized TAM framework led to extensive further research, including replications, comparisons with models like TRA and TPB, and adaptations for various contexts. This period of rigorous testing and refinement, initiated by Davis's own experiments and continued by subsequent researchers, established TAM as a leading model for explaining and predicting system use (Chuttur, 2009).

II. THE TECHNOLOGY ACCEPTANCE MODEL (TAM): ORIGIN AND EXTENSIONS

II.1. TAM's Origin: Theory of Reasoned Action (TRA)

It is well-established in the literature that TAM is rooted in the Theory of Reasoned Action (TRA) (Davis et al., 1989). TRA, developed by Ajzen and Fishbein (1975, 1980) is a foundational and influential theory for predicting a wide range of human behaviors (Venkatesh et al., 2003). It is particularly useful for explaining technology acceptance, where a user's intention is formed through a trade-off between a system's perceived benefits and its complexity.

TRA posits that an individual's behavior is determined by their behavioral intention, which is shaped by two key factors: their personal attitude toward the behavior and the prevailing subjective norm (Fishbein & Ajzen, 1975; Kurland, 1995). Attitude is defined as an individual's positive or negative feelings about performing the behavior, while subjective norm refers to the perceived social pressure from important others to perform it (Fishbein & Ajzen, 1975; Ramayah & Jantan, 2004). Essentially, a person who believes that significant others think they should perform a behavior will perceive social pressure to comply. The relationship between these components is illustrated in Figure 3.

Figure 4. Theory of Reasoned Action (TRA) (Ajzen & Fishbein, 1980; Al-Mamary et al., 2016)

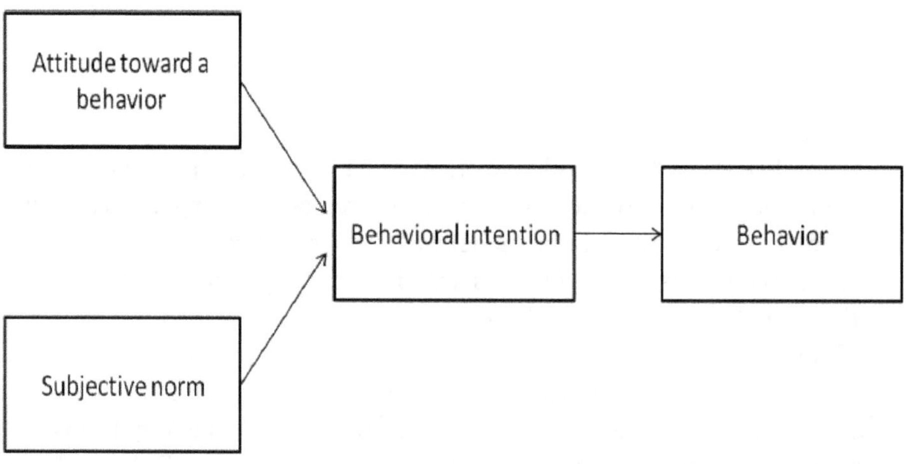

Despite its broad application, TRA has notable limitations. Its core assumption is that behaviors are entirely under volitional control, failing to account for external constraints that can hinder action (Kurland, 1995). Furthermore, TRA is a general model that does not specify the beliefs relevant to a particular behavior, requiring researchers to first identify these salient beliefs for each context (Davis et al., 1989; Baraghani, 2008). The model also overlooks the influence of habit, cognitive deliberation, and moral factors (Chuttur, 2009).

To address the critical limitation of volitional control, Ajzen (1991) extended TRA into the Theory of Planned Behavior (TPB) by introducing perceived behavioral control. This addition posits that the stronger an individual's belief in their ability to perform a behavior (e.g., having the necessary resources and skills), the stronger their intention to do so (Kurland, 1995).

While TRA was originally developed in 1975 for sociological and psychological research, it has since become a cornerstone for investigating individual IT usage behavior, providing a robust, limited, framework for understanding volitional actions.

II.2. TAM main Extensions

Extended versions of TAM introduce new factors to improve the model's adaptability, explanatory power, and specificity (Maillet et al., 2015). This family of models, derived from the Theory of Reasoned Action (TRA) (Fishbein and Ajzen, 1975), includes extensions like TAM2, TAM3 and the Unified Theory of Acceptance and Use of Technology (UTAUT) (Venkatesh et al., 2003), which incorporates much of TAM. The models aim to explain and predict technology adoption to improve implementation decisions (O'Dea, 2024).

- Technology Acceptance Model 2 (TAM 2)

Venkatesh and Davis (2000) developed the Technology Acceptance Model 2 (TAM2) as an extension of the original TAM, to address the original model's limitation in explaining the determinants of perceived usefulness. This model integrates two key processes that are crucial for studying user acceptance (Wu et al., 2011): social influence processes (subjective norm, voluntariness, and image) and cognitive instrumental processes (job relevance, output quality, result demonstrability, and perceived usefulness).

To validate this enhanced model, Venkatesh and Davis conducted a longitudinal field study involving 156 knowledge workers across four different systems, two used voluntarily and two under mandatory conditions. The study measured user perceptions and self-reported usage at three stages: pre-implementation, one-month post-implementation, and three months post-implementation, allowing for a robust evaluation of TAM2's performance, particularly in mandatory settings (Chuttur, 2009).

According to Wu and Wang (2003), research on TAM2 indicated that perceived usefulness, perceived ease of use, and subjective norm all indirectly influence actual system use through behavioral intention. In this framework, behavioral intention is jointly determined by these three factors. Furthermore, subjective norm is a direct and significant determinant of perceived usefulness, while perceived ease of use also has a small but significant impact on it (see Figure 5).

Figure 5. Technology Acceptance Model 2 (TAM 2) (Venkatesh & Davis, 2000)

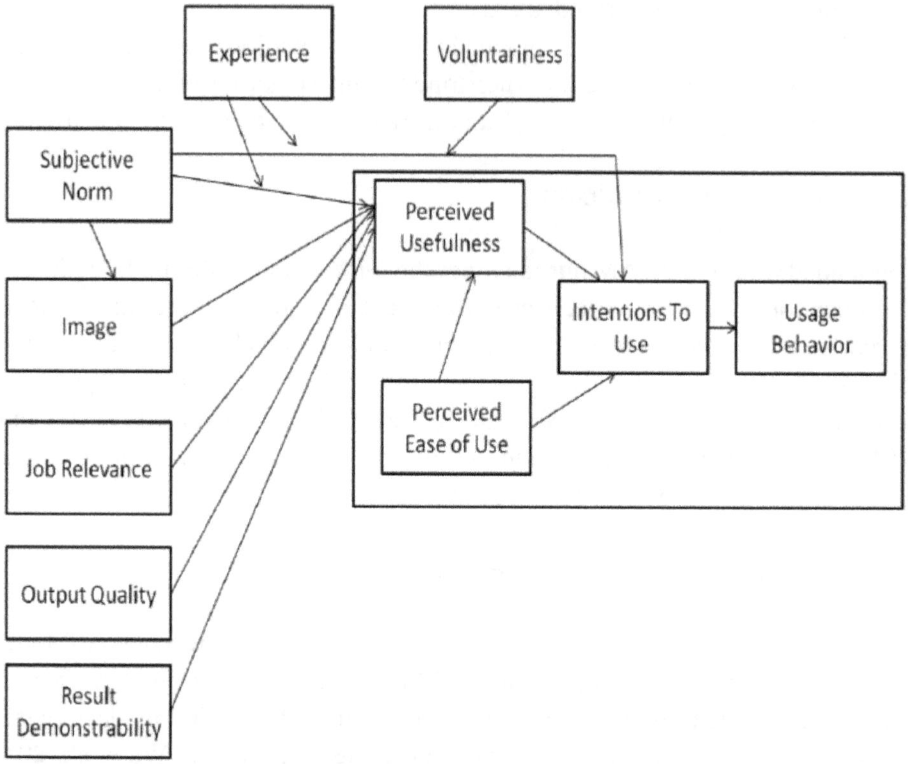

TAM2 performs well in both voluntary and mandatory settings, with the notable exception that subjective norm influences behavior primarily in mandatory contexts. A second line of extension focused on identifying the antecedents of perceived ease of use, categorizing them into two groups: "anchors" (general beliefs about computers, such as enjoyment and objective usability) and "adjustments" (beliefs formed through direct system experience, such as computer self-efficacy, anxiety, and playfulness) (Taherdoost, 2018).

- Technology Acceptance Model 3 (TAM 3)

(TAM3) is an integrated model of individual-level IT adoption (see Figure 5). It combines the social and cognitive determinants of perceived usefulness from TAM2 (Venkatesh & Davis, 2000) with the anchors and adjustments determinants of perceived ease of use (Venkatesh, 2000). The model is structured around four core categories that synthesize prior TAM research: (1) Individual Differences (e.g., computer self-efficacy, computer anxiety), (2) System Characteristics (e.g., job relevance, output quality), (3) Social Influence (e.g., subjective norm, image), (4) Facilitating Conditions (e.g., perception of external control).

Figure 6. Technology Acceptance Model 3 (TAM3) (Venkatesh & Bala, 2008)

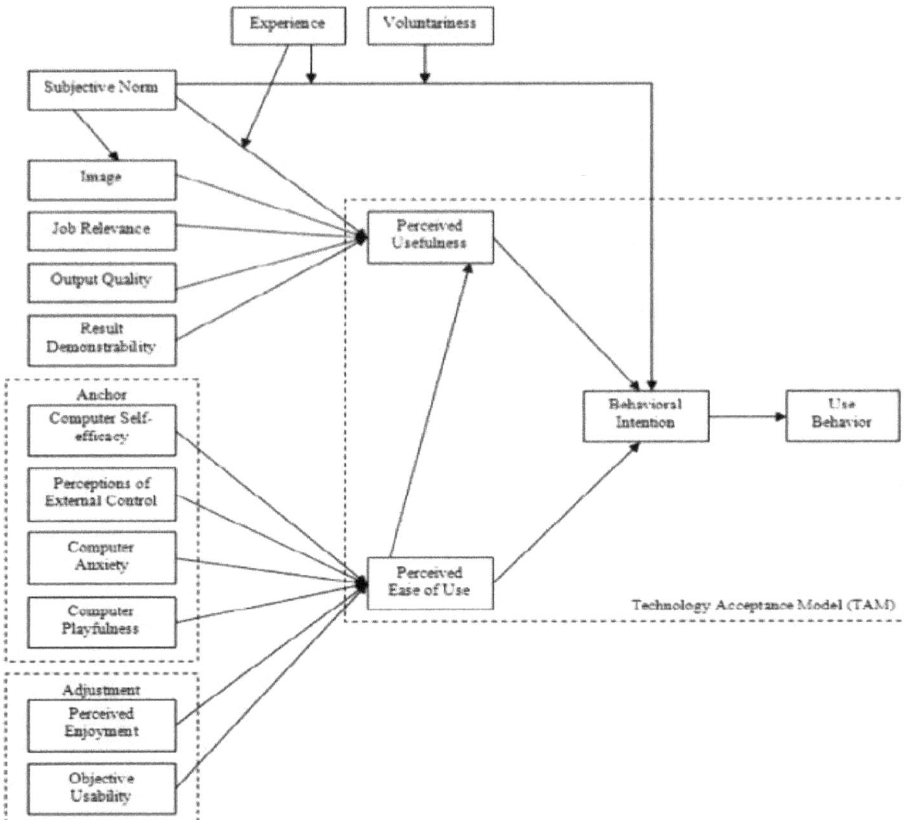

These categories comprise the variables that influence the two primary determinants of intention: perceived usefulness (PU) and perceived ease of use (PEOU) (Howard et al., 2010). A key contribution of TAM3 is the proposition that a user's experience moderates three specific relationships: (1) between PEOU and PU, (2) between computer anxiety and PEOU, and (3) between PEOU and behavioral intention (Wu & Wang, 2003).

- The Unified Theory of Acceptance and Use of Technology (UTAUT)

The Unified Theory of Acceptance and Use of Technology (UTAUT) is a comprehensive model designed to understand and predict user behavior toward technology. Venkatesh et al. (2003) developed it to synthesize and unify eight previous theories and models (including the Technology Acceptance Model (TAM) and the Theory of Planned Behavior (TPB)), by eliminating redundant constructs (Dwivedi et al., 2011).

The core of UTAUT posits that a user's behavioral intention and subsequent usage are directly influenced by four key factors: Performance Expectancy (PE), Effort Expectancy (EE), Social Influence (SI), and Facilitating Conditions (FC). The strength of these relationships is moderated by four key user characteristics: age, gender, experience, and the voluntariness of use (Venkatesh et al., 2003).

In technology acceptance literature, Performance Expectancy and Perceived Usefulness are used interchangeably. Idem for Effort Expectancy and Perceived Ease of Use (see Venkatesh et al., 2003).

Figure 7. Unified Theory of Acceptance and Use of Technology (UTAUT) (Venkatesh et al., 2003)

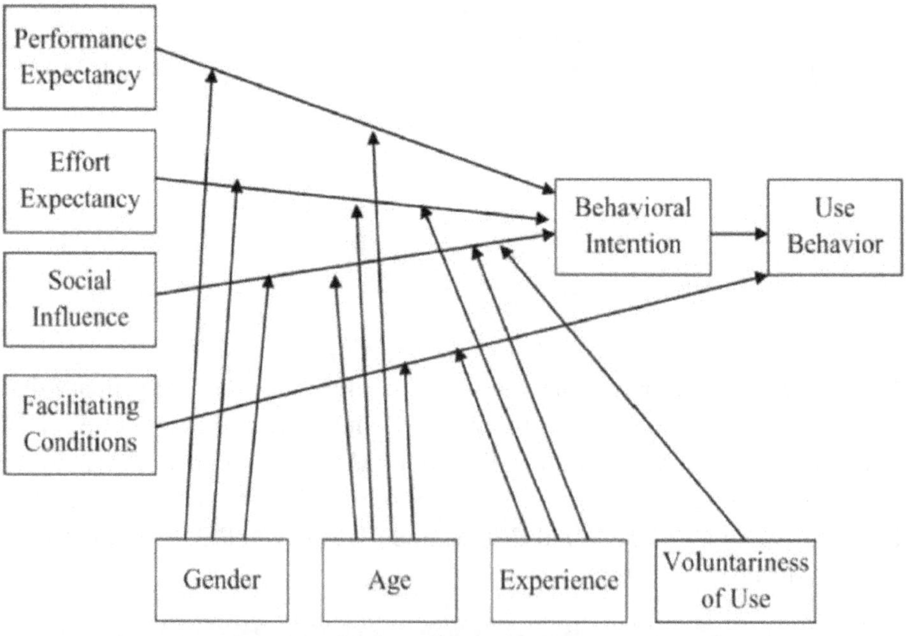

As a foundational model, UTAUT has become a classic framework for investigating technology adoption across various sectors and geographical contexts. It is valued for its ability to explain approximately 70% of the variance in usage intentions, making it a powerful tool for estimating the potential success of new technologies and evaluating their adoption (Venkatesh et al., 2003).

II.3. TAM Extensions' critics

In her review, Angela Schorr (2023) has discussed several critics and limitations of most popular TAM extensions. Both TAM3 and UTAUT have widespread popularity, for their ambition to map the entire landscape of why people use technology. Yet, they are subjects of significant scholarly debate and a crowd of critics. (Bagozzi, 2007; Lai, 2017; Tamilmani et al., 2017; van Raaij & Schepers, 2008; Williams et al., 2011).

Critics argue that these expanded models offer little predictive advantage over the original, more parsimonious Technology Acceptance Model (Agudo-Peregrina et al., 2014; Marangunić & Granić, 2015). Some even posit that the original TAM is more practical and preferable to other complex alternatives like the Theory of Reasoned Action (Bagozzi, 2007; Chuttur, 2009). In other words, the core of the criticism is a simple question: have we made things too complicated? Many researchers feel that these newer, more intricate models don't actually do a better job of predicting behavior than the original, simpler TAM. They argue that when a model tries to explain everything, it can become a cumbersome tool, less practical for real-world use than its more focused predecessors (Schorr, 2023).

TAM3 was designed to uncover all the subtle factors that influence how easy a technology feels. However, a central critic of this model is that its "*increased complexity... does not result in a significant improvement*" in explaining technology acceptance compared to simpler predecessors (Agudo-Peregrina et al., 2014, p. 313). It's like adding more buttons to a remote control that no one ends up pressing.

UTAUT faces similar criticisms for its complexity, with Bagozzi (2007, p. 245) noting it can involve "*41 independent variables for predicting intentions*". Furthermore, its high explanatory power has been questioned as it relies heavily on moderating variables like age and gender, which can inflate its performance metrics (van Raaij & Schepers, 2008). Empirical analysis also shows a gap between the model's high citation rate and its actual application in research: while the model was cited everywhere, it was rarely used in full (Williams et al., 2011).

In a fascinating twist, the creators of these foundational theories seem to side with these critics. Fred Davis, the creator of the original TAM, always preferred elegant, simple explanations (Davis, 1986; 2015). Izhak Ajzen, whose Theory of Planned Behavior heavily influenced TAM, has publicly warned against the excessive adding more and more variables to his theory, arguing that it usually offers diminishing returns (Ajzen, 2020). He caracterized TAM not as a grand, universal theory, but as a "*content-specific model*" for workplace technology, distinct from his broader theory (Ajzen, 2020, p. 317).

III. TAM'S VALIDITY, CRITICS AND FUTURE DIRECTIONS

Despite its long-standing history, the Technology Acceptance Model (TAM) continues to be a relevant and widely applied framework in technology adoption research (Wang et al., 2023). The following discussion will examine the model's sustained influence, synthesize key criticisms that have emerged, and outline promising avenues for its future development.

III.1. TAM's validity and related studies

While TAM's age has prompted questions about its validity for modern technologies, numerous studies confirm its enduring utility across various digital industries, affirming that the model remains one of the most prominent models for predicting technology adoption.

The model's sustained importance is recognized by both academic and industrial researchers (Taherdoost, 2018). Two primary reasons for its continued adoption are:

- **Individual Focus**: Unlike organizational-level models (like UTAUT), TAM is designed to assess an individual's capacity to accept technology (Rondan-Cataluña et al., 2015).
- **Introductory Phase Applicability:** TAM is particularly recommended for understanding technology acceptance during the introductory phase of adoption (Sánchez-Prieto et al., 2017).

Empirical evidence supports TAM's ongoing viability. The model has been adopted in several studies investigating the use and adoption of various technologies in various domains (Al-Emran & Teo, 2020; Al-Qaysi et al., 2020), such as e-learning (Al-Gahtani, 2020; Al-Emran & Teo, 2020), wireless technology (Yen et al., 2010), online banking (Ly & Ly, 2022), e-government (Shyu & Huang, 2011) web-based training (Park et al., 2012), social media 'Al-Maroof et al., 2020), m-payment (Di Pietro et al., 2015), wearable technologies (Al-Emran et al., 2020), among others.

A bibliometric analysis of 2,399 papers published between 2010 and 2020 (Figure 7), conducted by (O'Dea, 2024), concluded that research on TAM and its applications is growing. The study demonstrats that the model can still be effectively used, modified, and extended across diverse domains, with significant recent application in areas like e-commerce and augmented reality (Al-Emran & Granić, 2021; Al-Nuaimi et al., 2022).

Figure 8. SCOPUS journal publications of technology acceptance studies by year (O'Dea, 2024)

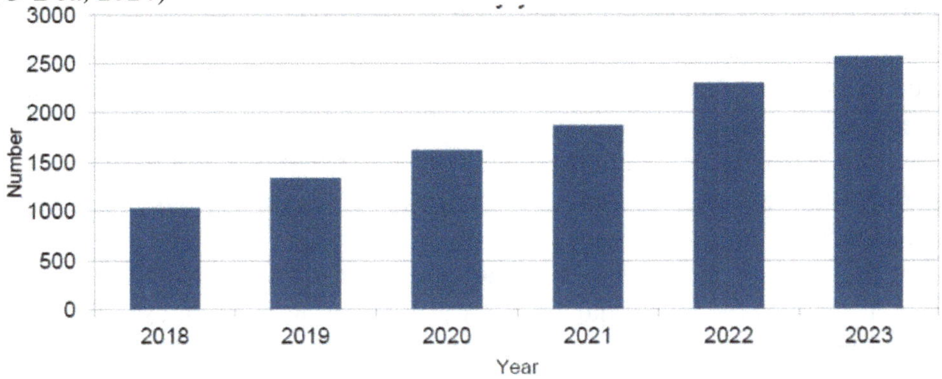

More specifically, TAM has been widely applied in marketing field, to understand consumer behavior towards new technological products and services. By analyzing consumer perceptions of a product's usefulness and ease of use, marketers can develop targeted strategies to enhance adoption and foster sustained usage (Chen et al., 2018).

A recent bibliometric analysis conducted by Musa et al. (2024) of TAM's use in marketing from 2002 to 2022 illustrates this fact through contemporary applications: in Mobile Research, TAM guides the design of engaging, interactive surveys that leverage device portability (Li, 2010); in Virtual and Augmented Reality, it has been extended with factors like perceived enjoyment to explore how immersive experiences forge emotional brand connections. In Artificial Intelligence, it focuses on ethical perceptions, balancing personalization with privacy to guide responsible integration (Leng & Ali, 2022). Finally, in social media, it investigates the roles of trust and social influence in data-sharing behaviors (Musa et al., 2024).

This exploration underscores the value of applying TAM to specialized marketing domains. By investigating mobile dynamics, immersive technologies, AI ethics, and social media behaviors, scholars are enriching our understanding of technology acceptance. As the technological landscape evolves, TAM remains a vital framework for navigating the complexities of consumer adoption, promising a future where its continued application will lead to a deeper comprehension of consumer behavior (Musa et al., 2024).

III.2. TAM's Critics

The adaptable "one-size-fits-all" nature of Technology Acceptance Model (TAM) has historically been a strength for technology acceptance model-based research. However, this very characteristic may now be limiting its predictive power (O'Dea, 2024). In fact, despite its enduring relevance, TAM has faced increasing criticism for its conceptual limitations across three key dimensions.

First, its narrow technological focus overlooks critical non-technological factors, including individual differences (Marikyan & Papagiannidis, 2024) and organizational contexts like workflow integration (Holden & Karsh, 2010). Second, its oversimplified structure reduces adoption to three static constructs (PU, PEOU, Intention), ignoring both actual usage patterns (Shachak et al., 2019) and emerging technology complexities like AI transparency (Shin, 2021) or human-AI reciprocity (Wirtz et al., 2023). Third, its methodological rigidity manifests in basic usage metrics that fail to distinguish between requisite and value-adding use and an assumption of linear intention-behavior linkages, which traces back to Fishbein and Ajzen's (1975) Theory of Reasoned Action, that fails to capture adoption as a dynamic process (Rogers, 2003). While TAM's parsimony enabled rapid assessments (Venkatesh & Bala, 2008), these limitations constrain its relevance for contemporary digital ecosystems despite its extensive citation record (Shachak et al., 2019).

The accelerating pace of technological change demands a stronger emphasis on predictive research and a critical evaluation of TAM's ability to adapt to diverse contexts without constant modification. The rise of AI-driven technologies, for instance, has exposed limitations in traditional TAM predictions, leading to proposed alternatives like the AI Device Use Acceptance model (AIDUA) (Gursoy et al., 2019). However, further adaptations are needed to address AI's unique challenges

Ultimately, the rapid evolution of technology calls for new models that better capture emerging complexities, such as hybrid realities and AI-driven experiences. Scholars like Gursoy et al. (2019) and Mogaji et al. (2023) have laid the groundwork by exploring AI acceptance and immersive technologies. Moving forward, academic research must not only address current adoption challenges but also anticipate future advancements, ensuring frameworks remain relevant in an ever-changing digital landscape (O'Dea, 2024).

To note, recent research has called the removal of "Attitude" construct from TAM model into question. A meta-analytic review by Feng et al. (2021) discovered a strong effect of attitudes on use intentions. Similarly, Fussell and Truong (2022) demonstrated in a study on Virtual Reality (VR) flight training that the original TAM variables, including attitude towards using, had the strongest relationships with behavioral intention, suggesting that the construct may be critical for understanding acceptance in certain contexts. Latest empirical evidence underscores a strong relationship between attitude toward using and behavioral intention. Consequently, researchers have proposed reinstating this variable into the TAM framework and its derivatives, affirming its critical role in understanding user behavior with digital technologies (Schorr, 2023). Overall, researchers have applied the Technology Acceptance Model with different structures, particularly regarding the role of Attitude (ATT). It is included as a direct determinant of Behavioral Intention in some versions but excluded in others (Scherer et al., 2019).

IV. TAM'S FUTURE DIRECTIONS, MANAGERIAL IMPLICATIONS AND CASE STUDIES

IV.1. TAM's Future Directions

For decades, the Technology Acceptance Model (TAM) has been a trusty map for navigating why people use technology. But as the digital landscape has become infinitely more complex, it's time to redraw that map with more precision and with help from new guides (Chuttur, 2009; Mogaji et al., 2024; O'Dea, 2024; Schorr, 2023).

• Enhancing TAM's predictive validity

To maintain relevance, TAM must place a greater emphasis on prediction. This requires a dual shift in focus: first, toward examining the internal structure of the models—analyzing the weightings, correlations, and potential redundancies between core predictors, antecedents, and moderating factors across different studies. Second, data collection must move beyond self-reported intentions to incorporate methods that capture actual usage (O'Dea, 2024).

The rapid evolution and shorter life cycle of technology applications call for diverse research methods (employing qualitative and quantitative research methods to understand technology adoption comprehensively) to ensure the validity of technology acceptance assessment in different settings (Mogaji et al., 2024).

This evolution would enable research to measure activity and the critical conversion of behavioral intention (BI) into actual use, supplementing the models' robust explanatory power with greater predictive ability and generalizability. For TAM to remain fit for purpose, the next phase of adaptation should involve refining its internal structure to be inherently applicable across a wider set of scenarios. The key to this lies in collecting data that reflects actual behavior, not just intentions (O'Dea, 2024).

• Standardizing Measurement Instruments

In addition, advancing TAM research requires a dual-pronged approach, starting with the standardization of research instruments. The field's prevalent strategy has prioritized theoretical expansion through statistical correlations and complex structural models, often at the expense of methodological rigor. In practice, this means researchers frequently reuse or slightly tweak old survey questions without proper validation in their quest to discover new influencing factors. This approach has led to a proliferation of variables with overlapping content and the use of modified, unvalidated instruments, creating confusion and making it nearly impossible to compare findings across studies accurately. A crucial shift is needed—from perpetual theoretical expansion to methodological consolidation. The well-confirmed key variables of digital technology acceptance should be integrated into a standardized, multidimensional scale that serves as a solid measurement criterion, a direction preliminarily explored by Schorr and Gorovoj (2023; Schorr, 2020). Providing this core set of carefully designed and validated questions would not limit creativity but instead establish a common foundation. This ensures that when we say a technology is "easy to use," we all mean the same thing, allowing our findings to build upon one another (Schorr, 2023).

• Integrating Disciplinary Perspectives

The complementary step to the precedent one is to actively invite new voices to the table through genuine interdisciplinary collaboration (Schorr, 2023). While TAM researchers often have interdisciplinary backgrounds in fields like business informatics, experts from the core disciplines upon which TAM is founded - notably psychology, but also communication science and education - are significantly underrepresented. This is a critical gap, especially since Davis himself framed TAM as a "motivational model," making technology acceptance a fundamentally psychological issue. We are missing the deep expertise in human behavior that is central to our questions. Involving these experts is vital, as they can provide deeper insight into borrowed theoretical concepts and contribute specialized research designs and tools (Landers & Marin, 2021). For instance, psychologists could help not just in understanding user reactions but in actually shaping the design of technology itself from the very beginning. This collaboration is the key to moving the field from simply explaining acceptance to proactively shaping a more usable and human-centered digital future.

• Extending TAM for Artificial Intelligence

A critical theoretical implication for the TAM framework is its application to emerging technologies, particularly artificial intelligence (AI) and generative AI. While extended TAM versions have been commonly used to assess AI acceptance, the rapid evolution of AI has challenged the predictive power of the traditional model. Recognizing this gap, researchers like Gursoy et al. (2019) created a new map for this unfamiliar territory: the AI Device Use Acceptance (AIDUA) model to explore user acceptance across different stages of interaction. This approach was later validated in different contexts by researchers like Chi et al. (2023).

But the challenge isn't just technical; it's deeply human. To be effective, these extensions must incorporate variables that address the specific challenges of AI. Research on user experiences with AI-powered tools like chatbots underscores the need to investigate perceived usefulness within these new contexts (Abdulquadri et al., 2021; Sampat et al., 2023). Furthermore, the model must expand beyond technical aspects to include social and cultural dimensions, such as social influence and the digital divide. Critical factors like trust, privacy, and security are becoming increasingly paramount, requiring researchers to directly investigate how these concerns influence the adoption of AI-driven services.

When people interact with an AI chatbot or receive a predictive suggestion, their decision to trust it isn't just about whether it's useful or easy to use. It's wrapped up in deeper questions: Is my data safe? Can I trust this “black box” decision? What will my peers think? Factors like trust, privacy, and social influence are no longer side notes - they are central to the context of AI adoption (Mogaji et al., 2024).

• Exploring Social and Hedonic Motivations

What if people adopt technology not because it's useful, but because it's fun? This simple idea is revolutionizing how we think about technology acceptance. Technology adoption is increasingly driven by social and hedonic motivations, not just utilitarian utility. For a long time, models like TAM have focused on practical questions: Does it work? Is it easy to use? In many sectors, a technology's success hinges on its intrinsic enjoyment and social appeal, a dimension often overlooked by the traditional TAM framework (Chi et al., 2023). In a world saturated with technology, from social media to AI chatbots, success often depends on a more human question: Does it bring joy or help us connect? For instance, an automated system may be efficient, but it can face resistance if it fails to provide an engaging or socially interactive experience (Mogaji et al., 2024).

This highlights a critical gap in TAM, which has historically focused on practical factors like perceived usefulness and ease of use. To remain relevant, the model needs to listen to users' heartbeat that shapes their acceptance. It's about understanding that when someone puts on a VR headset or chats with an AI, they aren't just a user completing a task - they're a person seeking an experience. Ultimately, perceived usefulness must be redefined to include the quality of the user's emotional rapport and overall experience with the technology. By exploring these social and emotional motivations, we can finally build technology that people don't just use, but truly love and embrace (Mogaji et al., 2024).

• Integrating Industry-Specific Factors

To truly capture the nuances of technology adoption, the TAM framework must be expanded to include industry-specific factors and a diverse range of stakeholder perspectives (Mogaji et al., 2024).

Industry context is critical, as adoption is shaped by unique considerations like customer expectations, service quality, and trust. This applies across a vast landscape, from traditional sectors to new business models and the gig economy (Boo & Chua, 2022; Pookulangara et al., 2023; Au & Tsang, 2023). A one-size-fits-all model cannot account for these variables. Imagine trying to use the same key for every lock. It wouldn't work.

But it's not just about the industry; it's about the people in it. A comprehensive understanding requires analyzing who is adopting the technology. A "user" isn't just a single profile. It could be a busy employee, a skeptical manager, a hopeful customer, or a cautious regulator. Researchers must examine the distinct roles, motivations, and influences of these various stakeholders (Ahmad & Scott, 2019; Cai et al., 2022; Venkatesh, 2020). Each one experiences and influences technology adoption differently. By integrating these diverse perspectives, we can move beyond a simplistic view of "the user" and build a more holistic and accurate model of the adoption process.

• Accounting for Cultural Variations

Considering cultural variations is crucial when applying TAM in research. For too long, our understanding of technology acceptance has been viewed through a narrow cultural lens, with most research reflecting the realities of developed Western nations. However, exploring and understanding technology adoption in developing countries and diverse cultural contexts is necessary (Miller & Khera, 2010; Mogaji et al., 2024).

To address cultural variations, researchers should consider the cultural roles and norms that may impact technology adoption in different societies. For example, in various cultures, technology adoption responsibilities may be influenced by social norms (Gbadegeshin et al., 2021; Hinson et al., 2021). This does not imply that certain groups are unfamiliar with these technologies, but their willingness to adopt them may differ due to cultural factors. This means that the decision to adopt a new app or system isn't just about its features; it's about whether it fits within a community's way of life. In some cultures, a family elder or a community leader might be the key decision-maker, not the individual user. This isn't about a lack of tech-savviness; it's about a different set of social rules.

TAM researchers should be mindful of cultural roles, norms, and values influencing technology adoption and ensure their studies incorporate diverse cultural perspectives. This will enable a more comprehensive understanding of how cultural variations impact technology adoption (Mogaji et al., 2024).

• Adopting Frameworks for Hybrid Environments

The exponential speed of technological innovation, from the metaverse to new AI devices, is rapidly outpacing academic research. We lack sufficient theoretical and empirical evidence to understand how consumers adopt these novel technologies (Abdulquadri et al., 2021; Buhalis et al., 2022; Koohang et al., 2023). This growing gap makes it imperative to critically reevaluate established models like TAM and acknowledge their limitations in capturing the complexities of contemporary tech adoption.

Consequently, the call to move beyond TAM is gaining momentum. There is an urgent need to explore and embrace newer theoretical frameworks designed for the multifaceted nature of emerging innovations. Scholars have begun paving this way, such as Gursoy et al. (2019) with their model for AI device acceptance and Mogaji et al. (2023) with their call to explore immersive experiences. The role of academic research must now shift from explaining the present to anticipating the future, developing the sophisticated frameworks needed to comprehensively decipher the next wave of technological advancements.

IV.2. TAM's Managerial Implications

The proposed evolution of TAM research provides a clear roadmap for practitioners to enhance the success of technology deployments.

First, to move from explanation to accurate prediction, managers must supplement traditional self-reported intention surveys with objective measures of actual system usage (O'Dea, 2024). This requires integrating analytics and log data to validate whether behavioral intention translates into real adoption, providing a truer measure of ROI. Concurrently, adopting standardized and validated measurement instruments (such as consolidated multidimensional scales for core TAM constructs) is critical for establishing reliable diagnostics and enabling consistent comparison across projects and time (Gorovoj & Schorr, 2023; Schorr, 2020; 2023).

Crucially, because TAM alone often overlooks individual and contextual differences (Agarwal & Prasad, 1999), a mixed-methods approach is essential for a comprehensive understanding. As demonstrated in recent studies (Au & Tsang, 2023; Cai et al., 2022; Kwak et al., 2023), integrating quantitative data (usage analytics for example) with qualitative methods (in-depth interviews, focus groups, and ethnographic observation ...), offers richer insights into the nuances of the adoption process (Mogaji et al., 2024). For consumer-facing technologies, methods like netnography can further reveal insights into online culture and social interactions (Kozinets, 2012). By adopting this integrated approach, managers can move beyond generic models to gain detailed, actionable insights tailored to different demographics, industries, and stakeholder groups.

To address the complex human factors in adoption, implementation teams should be genuinely interdisciplinary, actively incorporating expertise from psychology and communication science to design motivational strategies and human-centric interfaces (Landers & Marin, 2021; Schorr, 2023). This is especially vital for emerging technologies like AI, where success depends on factors beyond traditional utility, such as trust, privacy, and ethical perception (Mogaji et al., 2024). For AI and generative AI, practitioners should consider tailored frameworks like the AI Device Use Acceptance (AIDUA) model to account for these unique adoption stages and concerns (Gursoy et al., 2019; Chi et al., 2023). It's no longer just about whether a technology can be used, but whether it should be used, and how we can build AI that earns human trust and aligns with our social and cultural values.

Furthermore, adoption strategies must be context-aware. Managers must design for hedonic and social user experiences, recognizing that enjoyment and social connection can be primary drivers of adoption, not just peripheral factors (Chi et al., 2023; Mogaji et al., 2024). Strategies must also be adapted to specific industry contexts and stakeholder perspectives (e.g., employees vs. customers) and sensitive to cultural norms and decision-making hierarchies, particularly in global deployments (Gbadegeshin et al., 2021; Hinson et al., 2021; Mogaji et al., 2024). Finally, for hybrid and rapidly evolving digital environments (e.g., the metaverse), practitioners should employ flexible, mixed-methods research, including netnography, interviews, and observation, to capture nuanced user behavior and be prepared to utilize newer theoretical frameworks that move beyond TAM's traditional boundaries (Kozinets, 2012; Mogaji et al., 2023, 2024).

IV.3. Case studies using TAM

The theoretical evolution of TAM is best understood through its practical application. The following case studies illustrate how real companies have effectively leveraged the principles of the Technology Acceptance Model (and its extended variables) to successfully increase technology adoption within their organizations[1]:

• Uber's Expansion Strategy using TAM

The Uber application is a digital mobility platform that connects passengers with drivers using an automated matching system, supported by live GPS tracking and seamless in-app payment functionality[2].

As the global leader in ride-hailing, Uber faced significant adoption barriers when entering new markets. Beyond legal and regulatory hurdles, the company encountered cultural resistance from established taxi industries and needed to overcome the skepticism of potential new users. To systematically understand and address these challenges, Uber's approach aligns with and has been extensively analyzed through the lens of the Technology Acceptance Model (TAM).

Uber employed the Technology Acceptance Model (TAM) as a strategic framework to overcome adoption barriers during its global expansion. The company used surveys and focus groups to measure core TAM constructs (Perceived Usefulness (PU) and Perceived Ease of Use (PEOU)), while analyzing actual usage data to move beyond user intentions.

The research revealed that while users valued the app's convenience (high PU), trust, safety, and reliability concerns emerged as critical barriers to adoption. In response, Uber introduced enhanced safety features (e.g., in-app emergency assistance and driver verification) and launched targeted communication campaigns to rebuild trust.

By using TAM to identify both adoption drivers and key moderating barriers, Uber tailored its product and messaging to local markets, successfully converting skepticism into adoption and enabling scalable growth. This case demonstrates how empirically diagnosing user perceptions using TAM can guide effective, data-driven market entry and technology deployment strategies.

• Amazon Prime's enhancement of user adoption through TAM

Amazon applied the Technology Acceptance Model (TAM) to guide the development and implementation of its Amazon Prime subscription service. Amazon Prime is a paid subscription service offering members exclusive perks like fast, free shipping, unlimited streaming of movies/TV (Prime Video), ad-free music

(Amazon Music Prime), digital reads (Prime Reading), gaming benefits (Prime Gaming), and grocery savings.

Amazon used surveys, focus groups, and behavioral data to measure the core TAM constructs: Perceived Usefulness (PU) (such as savings on shipping and access to entertainment) and Perceived Ease of Use (PEOU) (reflecting the service's intuitive interface). The analysis confirmed high scores in both areas, indicating strong user acceptance. Based on these insights, Amazon enhanced Prime's value by expanding its content library and refining the user experience, while its marketing clearly communicated the service's benefits.

This case illustrates how empirically validating user perceptions through TAM can reduce risk and inform strategic decisions, turning a bundled service into a major driver of customer retention and platform loyalty.

- Netflix's driving adoption through TAM

Netflix is a global subscription streaming service offering a vast library of movies, TV shows, documentaries, anime, and games on demand. It employed the Technology Acceptance Model (TAM) as an evidence-based framework to guide the development and launch of new platform features (such as personalized recommendations and offline viewing) in a highly competitive market. The company used targeted research (surveys, focus groups) and behavioral analytics to measure the core TAM constructs: Perceived Usefulness (PU) and Perceived Ease of Use (PEOU).

The data confirmed that users valued features that saved time and added flexibility (high PU) and found them intuitive to use (high PEOU). Based on these insights, Netflix doubled down on enhancing its recommendation algorithms and improved interface usability. By applying TAM iteratively, Netflix transformed user perceptions into a strategic product roadmap, leading to higher feature adoption, increased user satisfaction, and reduced churn. This case demonstrates how a TAM-guided, data-driven innovation strategy is critical for sustaining engagement and competitive advantage in fast-evolving digital markets.

CONCLUSION

This chapter has traced the remarkable journey of the Technology Acceptance Model (TAM), from its origins in social psychology to its current status as a foundational yet contested pillar of information systems research. It began as an elegant and parsimonious framework, with its core constructs of Perceived Usefulness and Perceived Ease of Use offering unprecedented predictive power for understanding user adoption. This very utility fueled its evolution, leading to significant extensions like TAM2 and UTAUT, which incorporated social influences and cognitive processes, demonstrating the model's capacity to adapt and grow in response to empirical findings.

However, as detailed in the final section, TAM's longevity and widespread application have inevitably prompted critical scrutiny. Its age has raised valid questions about its applicability to the complex realities of modern technologies such as AI, the metaverse, and immersive systems. Critics have compellingly highlighted its oversimplification of human behavior, its methodological reliance on self-reported intentions, and its neglect of crucial contextual factors like organizational culture, hedonic motivations, and deep-seated ethical concerns surrounding trust and privacy.

The future of technology acceptance research, therefore, lies not in discarding TAM but in thoughtfully building upon the foundation it provides. The path forward, as illuminated by ongoing scholarly debate, necessitates a concerted shift from explanation to prediction. This will require methodological rigor through the standardization of instruments, genuine interdisciplinary collaboration—especially with fields like psychology—and the development of new, specialized models tailored to the unique demands of emerging technological contexts. The enduring legacy of TAM is not merely its specific equations, but the vibrant and critical research conversation it ignited—a conversation that continues to drive the field toward a more nuanced, predictive, and human-centric understanding of how we welcome technology into our lives.

REFERENCES

Abdulquadri, A., Kieu, T. A., & Nguyen, N. P. (2021). Digital transformation in financial services provision: A Nigerian perspective to the adoption of chatbot. *Journal of Enterprising Communities: People and Places in the Global Economy, 15*(2), 258–281. DOI: 10.1108/JEC-06-2020-0126

Agarwal, R., & Prasad, J. (1999). Are individual differences germane to the acceptance of new information technologies? *Decision Sciences, 30*(2), 361–391. DOI: 10.1111/j.1540-5915.1999.tb01614.x

Agudo-Peregrina, Á. F., Hernández-García, Á., & Pascual-Miguel, F. J. (2014). Behavioral intention, use behavior and the acceptance of electronic learning systems: Differences between higher education and lifelong learning. *Computers in Human Behavior, 34*, 301–314. DOI: 10.1016/j.chb.2013.10.035

Ahmad, R., & Scott, N. (2019). Technology innovations towards reducing hospitality human resource costs in Langkawi, Malaysia. *Tourism Review, 74*(3), 547–562. DOI: 10.1108/TR-03-2018-0038

Ajzen, I. (1985). From intentions to actions: A theory of planned behavior. In Kuhl, J., & Beckmann, J. (Eds.), *Action control: From cognition to behavior* (pp. 11–39). Springer-Verlag. DOI: 10.1007/978-3-642-69746-3_2

Ajzen, I. (1991). The theory of planned behavior. *Organizational Behavior and Human Decision Processes, 50*(2), 179–211. DOI: 10.1016/0749-5978(91)90020-T

Ajzen, I. (2020). The theory of planned behavior: Frequently asked questions. *Human Behavior and Emerging Technologies, 2*(4), 314–324. DOI: 10.1002/hbe2.195

Ajzen, I., & Fishbein, M. (1980). *Understanding attitudes and predicting social behavior*. Prentice-Hall.

Al-Emran, M., & Granić, A. (2021). Is it still valid or outdated? A bibliometric analysis of the technology acceptance model and its applications from 2010 to 2020. In A. Al-Emran & M. A. Al-Sharafi (Eds.), Studies in Systems, Decision and Control: Vol. 335.

Recent Advances in Al-Emran, M., & Teo, T. (2020). Do knowledge acquisition and knowledge sharing really affect e-learning adoption? An empirical study. Education and Information Technologies, 25, 1983–1998. https://doi.org/DOI: 10.1007/s10639-019-10062-w

Al-Gahtani, S. S. (2020). Empirical investigation of e-learning acceptance and assimilation: A structural equation model. *Applied Computing and Informatics, 12*(1), 27–50. DOI: 10.1016/j.aci.2014.09.001

Al-Kfairy, M., Mustafa, D., Al-Adaileh, A., Zriqat, S., & Sendaba, O. (2024). User acceptance of AI voice assistants in Jordan's telecom industry. *Computers in Human Behavior Reports, 16*, 100521. DOI: 10.1016/j.chbr.2024.100521

Al-Mamary, Y. H., Al-nashmi, M., Hassan, Y. A. G., & Shamsuddin, A. (2016). A critical review of models and theories in field of individual acceptance of technology. *International Journal of Hybrid Information Technology, 9*(6), 143–158. DOI: 10.14257/ijhit.2016.9.6.13

Al-Maroof, R. A., Arpaci, I., Al-Emran, M., Salloum, S. A., & Shaalan, K. (2020). Examining the acceptance of WhatsApp stickers through machine learning algorithms. In Al-Emran, M., & Shaalan, K. (Eds.), *Recent Advances in Intelligent Systems and Smart Applications* (pp. 209–221). Springer., DOI: 10.1007/978-3-030-47411-9_12

Al-Nuaimi, M. N., Al Sawafi, O. S., Malik, S. I., Al-Emran, M., & Selim, Y. F. (2022). Evaluating the actual use of learning management systems during the COVID-19 pandemic: An integrated theoretical model. *Interactive Learning Environments*. Advance online publication. DOI: 10.1080/10494820.2022.2055577

Al-Qaysi, N., Mohamad-Nordin, N., & Al-Emran, M. (2020). A systematic review of social media acceptance from the perspective of educational and information systems theories and models. *Journal of Educational Computing Research, 57*(8), 2085–2109. DOI: 10.1177/0735633118817879

Arthur, W. B. (2009). *The nature of technology: What it is and how it evolves*. Simon & Schuster.

Au, W., & Tsang, N. (2023). Gig workers' self-protective behaviour against legal risks: An application of protection motivation theory. *International Journal of Contemporary Hospitality Management, 35*(3), 1376–1397. DOI: 10.1108/IJCHM-12-2021-1537

Bagozzi, R. P. (2007). The legacy of the technology acceptance model and a proposal for a paradigm shift. *Journal of the Association for Information Systems, 8*(4), 244–254. DOI: 10.17705/1jais.00122

Bandura, A. (1977). Self-efficacy: Toward a unifying theory of behavioral change. *Psychological Review, 84*(2), 191–215. DOI: 10.1037/0033-295X.84.2.191

Baraghani, N. S. (2008). Factors influencing the adoption of internet banking [Master's thesis, Luleå University of Technology]. DIVA. http://urn.kb.se/resolve?urn=urn:nbn:se:ltu:diva-43300

Boo, H., & Chua, B. (2022). An integrative model of facial recognition check-in technology adoption intention: The perspective of hotel guests in Singapore. *International Journal of Contemporary Hospitality Management*, *34*(11), 4052–4079. DOI: 10.1108/IJCHM-12-2021-1471

Buhalis, D., Lin, M. S., & Leung, D. (2022). Metaverse as a driver for customer experience and value co-creation: Implications for hospitality and tourism management and marketing. *International Journal of Contemporary Hospitality Management*, *35*(2), 701–716. DOI: 10.1108/IJCHM-05-2022-0631

Cai, R., Cain, L., & Jeon, H. (2022). Customers' perceptions of hotel AI-enabled voice assistants: Does brand matter? *International Journal of Contemporary Hospitality Management*, *34*(8), 2807–2831. DOI: 10.1108/IJCHM-10-2021-1313

Chen, Y., Hsu, T., & Lu, Y. (2018). Impact of flow on mobile shopping intention. *Journal of Retailing and Consumer Services*, *41*, 281–287. DOI: 10.1016/j.jretconser.2017.04.004

Chi, O. H., Chi, C. G., Gursoy, D., & Nunkoo, R. (2023). Customers' acceptance of artificially intelligent service robots: The influence of trust and culture. *International Journal of Information Management*, *70*, 102623. DOI: 10.1016/j.ijinfomgt.2023.102623

Chuttur, M. Y. (2009). "Overview of the Technology Acceptance Model: Origins, Developments and Future Directions, " Indiana University, USA. *Sprouts: Working Papers on Information Systems*, 9(37). http://sprouts.aisnet.org/9-37

Davis, F. D. (1986). A technology acceptance model for empirically testing new end-user information systems: Theory and results [Doctoral dissertation, Massachusetts Institute of Technology]. MIT Sloan School of Management.

Davis, F. D. (2015). On the relationship between HCI and technology acceptance research. In *Human-computer interaction and management information systems: Foundations* (pp. 409-415). Routledge.

Davis, F. D., Bagozzi, R. P., & Warshaw, P. R. (1989). User acceptance of computer technology: A comparison of two theoretical models. *Management Science*, *35*(8), 982–1003. DOI: 10.1287/mnsc.35.8.982

Davis, F. D., Bagozzi, R. P., & Warshaw, P. R. (1992). Extrinsic and intrinsic motivation to use computers in the workplace. *Journal of Applied Social Psychology, 22*(14), 1111–1132. DOI: 10.1111/j.1559-1816.1992.tb00945.x

DeLone, W. H., & McLean, E. R. (2004). Measuring e-commerce success: Applying the DeLone & McLean information systems success model. *International Journal of Electronic Commerce, 9*(1), 31–47. DOI: 10.1080/10864415.2004.11044317

Di Pietro, L., Guglielmetti Mugion, R., Mattia, G., Renzi, M. F., & Toni, M. (2015). The integrated model on mobile payment acceptance (IMMPA): An empirical application to public transport. *Transportation Research Part C, Emerging Technologies, 56*, 463–479. DOI: 10.1016/j.trc.2015.05.001

Dillon, A., & Morris, M. G. (1996). User acceptance of information technology: Theories and models. In Williams, M. (Ed.), *Annual review of information science and technology* (Vol. 31, pp. 3–32). Information Today.

Feng, G. C., Su, X., Lin, Z., He, Y., Luo, N., & Zhang, Y. (2021). Determinants of technology acceptance: Two model-based meta-analytic reviews. *Journalism & Mass Communication Quarterly, 98*(1), 83–104. DOI: 10.1177/1077699020952400

Fishbein, M., & Ajzen, I. (1975). *Belief, attitude, intention and behavior: An introduction to theory and research.* Addison-Wesley.

Gbadegeshin, S. A., Olaleye, S. A., Ukpabi, D. C., Omokaro, B., Mogaji, E., Ugwuja, A. A., & Adetoyinbo, A. (2021). Female unemployment in an emerging economy: A study of online social support as a coping strategy. In *Technology and Women's Empowerment* (1st ed., pp. 93–106). Routledge. DOI: 10.4324/9781003045946-12

Granić, A. (2022). Educational Technology Adoption: A systematic review. *Education and Information Technologies, 27*(7), 9725–9744. DOI: 10.1007/s10639-022-10951-7

Gursoy, D., Chi, O. H., Lu, L., & Nunkoo, R. (2019). Consumers acceptance of artificially intelligent (AI) device use in service delivery. *International Journal of Information Management, 49*, 157–169. DOI: 10.1016/j.ijinfomgt.2019.03.008

Hantono, B. S., Nugroho, L. E., & Santosa, P. I. (2018). Meta-review of augmented reality in education. In *In2018 10th international conference on information technology and electrical engineering (ICITEE)* (pp. 312–315). IEEE. DOI: 10.1109/ICITEED.2018.8534888

Hinson, R. E., Nwoba, A. C., & Nguyen, N. P. (2021). Corporate social responsibility for women's empowerment: A study on Nigerian banks. *International Journal of Bank Marketing, 39*(4), 516–540. DOI: 10.1108/IJBM-04-2020-0195

Howard, N. L., Marshall, P., & Swatman, P. A. (2010). Reconceptualising motivation in adoption and acceptance research: Back to basics. In Proceedings of the 21st Australasian Conference on Information Systems. Brisbane, Australia. https://aisel.aisnet.org/acis2010/36

Hwang, H. G., Chang, I. C., Chen, F. J., & Wu, S. Y. (2008). Investigation of the application of KMS for diseases classifications: A study in a Taiwanese hospital. *Expert Systems with Applications*, *34*(1), 725–733. DOI: 10.1016/j.eswa.2006.10.018

Kang, J. W., & Namkung, Y. (2019). The role of personalization on continuance intention in food service mobile apps: A privacy calculus perspective. *International Journal of Contemporary Hospitality Management*, *31*(2), 734–752. DOI: 10.1108/IJCHM-12-2017-0783

Koohang, A., Nord, J. H., Ooi, K. B., Tan, G. W. H., Al-Emran, M., Aw, E. C. X., Baabdullah, A. M., Buhalis, D., Cham, T.-H., Dennis, C., Dutot, V., Dwivedi, Y. K., Hughes, L., Mogaji, E., Pandey, N., Phau, I., Raman, R., Sharma, A., Sigala, M., & Wong, L. W. (2023). Shaping the metaverse into reality: A holistic multidisciplinary understanding of opportunities, challenges, and avenues for future investigation. *Journal of Computer Information Systems*, *63*(3), 735–765. DOI: 10.1080/08874417.2023.2165197

Kozinets, R. (2012). Marketing netnography: Prom/ot (ulgat) ing a new research method. *Methodological Innovations Online*, *7*(1), 37–45. DOI: 10.4256/mio.2012.004

Kurland, N. B. (1995). Ethical intentions and the theories of reasoned action and planned behavior. Journal of Applied Social Psychology, *25*(4), 297–313. DOI: 10.1111/j.1559-1816.1995.tb01593.x

Kwak, S., Shin, M., Lee, M., & Back, K. (2023). Integrating the reviewers' and readers' perceptions of negative online reviews for customer decision-making: A mixed-method approach. *International Journal of Contemporary Hospitality Management*, *35*(12), 4191–4216. DOI: 10.1108/IJCHM-03-2022-0410

Lai, P. C. (2017). The literature review of technology adoption models and theories for the novelty technology. *Journal of Information Systems and Technology Management*, *14*(1), 21–38. DOI: 10.4301/S1807-17752017000100002

Landers, R. N., & Marin, S. (2021). Theory and technology in organizational psychology: A review of technology integration paradigms and their effects on the validity of theory. *Annual Review of Organizational Psychology and Organizational Behavior*, *8*(1), 235–258. DOI: 10.1146/annurev-orgpsych-012420-060843

Ly, B., & Ly, R. (2022). Internet banking adoption under Technology Acceptance Model—Evidence from Cambodian users. *Computers in Human Behavior Reports, 7*, 100224. DOI: 10.1016/j.chbr.2022.100224

Maillet, É., Mathieu, L., & Sicotte, C. (2015). Modeling factors explaining the acceptance, actual use and satisfaction of nurses using an Electronic Patient Record in acute care settings: An extension of the UTAUT. *International Journal of Medical Informatics, 84*(1), 36–47. DOI: 10.1016/j.ijmedinf.2014.09.004

Marangunić, N., & Granić, A. (2015). Technology acceptance model: A literature review from 1986 to 2013. *Universal Access in the Information Society, 14*(1), 81–95. DOI: 10.1007/s10209-014-0348-1

Marangunić, N., & Granić, A. (2015). Technology acceptance model: A literature review from 1986 to 2013. *Universal Access in the Information Society, 14*(1), 81–95. DOI: 10.1007/s10209-014-0348-1

Mathieson, K. (1991). Predicting user intentions: Comparing the technology acceptance model with the theory of planned behavior. *Information Systems Research*, *2*(3), 173–191. https://doi.org/DOI: 10.1287/isre.2.3.173

Miller, J., & Khera, O. (2010). Digital library adoption and the technology acceptance model: Across-country analysis. *The Electronic Journal on Information Systems in Developing Countries, 40*(1), 1–19. DOI: 10.1002/j.1681-4835.2010.tb00288.x

Mogaji, E., Viglia, G., Srivastava, P., & Dwivedi, Y. K. (2024). Is it the end of the technology acceptance model in the era of generative artificial intelligence? *International Journal of Contemporary Hospitality Management, 36*(10), 3324–3339. Advance online publication. DOI: 10.1108/IJCHM-08-2023-1271

Mogaji, E., Wirtz, J., Belk, R. W., & Dwivedi, Y. (2023). Immersive time (ImT): Conceptualising time spent in the metaverse. *International Journal of Information Management, 72*, 102659. DOI: 10.1016/j.ijinfomgt.2023.102659

Moore, G. C., & Benbasat, I. (1991). Development of an instrument to measure the perceptions of adopting an information technology innovation. Information Systems Research, *2*(3), 192–222. https://doi.org/DOI: 10.1287/isre.2.3.192

Musa, H. G., Fatmawati, I., Nuryakin, N., & Suyanto, M. (2024). Marketing research trends using technology acceptance model (TAM): A comprehensive review of researches (2002–2022). *Cogent Business &amp. Cogent Business & Management, 11*(1), 2329375. Advance online publication. DOI: 10.1080/23311975.2024.2329375

O'Dea, X. (2024). Generative AI: Is it a paradigm shift for higher education? *Studies in Higher Education, 49*(5), 811–816. DOI: 10.1080/03075079.2024.2332944

Park, Y., Son, H., & Kim, C. (2012). Investigating the determinants of construction professionals' acceptance of web-based training: An extension of the technology acceptance model. *Automation in Construction*, *22*, 377–386. DOI: 10.1016/j.autcon.2011.09.016

Petter, S., DeLone, W., & McLean, E. R. (2008). Measuring information systems success: Models, dimensions, measures, and interrelationships. *European Journal of Information Systems*, *17*(3), 236–263. DOI: 10.1057/ejis.2008.15

Petter, S., & McLean, E. R. (2009). A meta-analytic assessment of the DeLone and McLean IS success model: An examination of IS success at the individual level. *Information & Management*, *46*(3), 159–166. DOI: 10.1016/j.im.2008.12.006

Pookulangara, S., Wen, H., & Bharath, J. (2023). Consumer attitudes toward ordering from cloud kitchens: A gender and marital status perspective. *International Journal of Contemporary Hospitality Management*, *35*(5), 1859–1879. DOI: 10.1108/IJCHM-03-2022-0310

Ramayah, T., & Ignatius, J. (2005). Impact of perceived usefulness, perceived ease of use and perceived enjoyment on intention to shop online. *ICFAI Journal of systems management (IJSM)*, *3*(3), 36-51.

Ramayah, T., & Jantan, M. (2004). Technology acceptance: An individual perspective current and future research in Malaysia. Review of Business Research, *2*(1), 103–111.

Ramayah, T., & Jantan, M. (2004). Technology acceptance: An individual perspective. Current and future research in Malaysia. *Review of Business Research*, *2*(1), 103–111.

Rogers, E. M. (2003). *Diffusion of innovations* (5th ed.). Free Press.

Rondan-Cataluña, F. J., Arenas-Gaitán, J., & Ramírez-Correa, P. E. (2015). A comparison of the different versions of popular technology acceptance models. *Kybernetes*, *44*(5), 788–805. DOI: 10.1108/K-09-2014-0184

Sampat, B., Mogaji, E., & Nguyen, N. P. (2023). The dark side of FinTech in financial services: A qualitative inquiry into FinTech developers' perspective. *International Journal of Bank Marketing*. Advance online publication. DOI: 10.1108/IJBM-07-2022-0328

Sánchez-Prieto, J. C., Olmos-Migueláñez, S., & García-Peñalvo, F. J. (2017). MLearning and pre-service teachers: An assessment of the behavioral intention using an expanded TAM model. *Computers in Human Behavior*, *72*, 644–654. DOI: 10.1016/j.chb.2016.09.061

Scherer, R., Siddiq, F., & Tondeur, J. (2019). The technology acceptance model (TAM): A meta-analytic structural equation modeling approach to explaining teachers' adoption of digital technology in education. *Computers & Education*, *128*, 13–35. DOI: 10.1016/j.compedu.2018.09.009

Schorr, A. (2020). Skala zur Erfassung der Digitalen Technologieakzeptanz – Weiterentwicklung zum testtheoretisch geprüften Instrument Gesellschaft für Arbeitswissenschaft (Ed.) *Digitaler Wandel, Digitale Arbeit, Digitaler Mensch?* Dokumentation des 66. Arbeitswissenschaftlichen Kongresses, No. 35, B.20.5, pp. 1-6.

Schorr, A. (2023). The Technology Acceptance Model (TAM) and its importance for digitalization research: A review. In Proceedings of the International Symposium on Technikpsychologie (TecPsy) 2023 (pp. 55-65). Technische Universität Darmstadt. https://doi.org/DOI: 10.2478/9788366675896-005

Schorr, A., & Gorovoj, A. (2023). Acceptance of Digital Technology Among Male and Female University Students: With a Focus on STEM Students. *Journal of Humanities, Arts and Social Science, 7*(9).

Seddon, P., & Kiew, M. Y. (1996). A partial test and development of Delone and McLean's model of IS success. *AJIS. Australasian Journal of Information Systems*, *4*(1), 90–109. DOI: 10.3127/ajis.v4i1.379

Shachak, A., Kuziemsky, C., & Petersen, C. (2019). Beyond TAM and UTAUT: Future directions for HIT implementation research. *Journal of Biomedical Informatics*, *100*, 103315. DOI: 10.1016/j.jbi.2019.103315

Shyu, S. H. P., & Huang, J. H. (2011). Elucidating usage of e-government learning: A perspective of the extended technology acceptance model. *Government Information Quarterly*, *28*(4), 491–502. DOI: 10.1016/j.giq.2011.04.002

Simon, B. (2001). *Wissensmedien im Bildungssektor: Eine Akzeptanzuntersuchung an Hochschulen* [Knowledge media in the education system: Acceptance research in universities]. WU Vienna University of Economics and Business.

Taherdoost, H. (2018). A review of technology acceptance and adoption models and theories. *Procedia Manufacturing*, *22*, 960–967. DOI: 10.1016/j.promfg.2018.03.137

Tamilmani, K., Rana, N. P., & Dwivedi, Y. K. (2017). A systematic review of citations of UTAUT2 article and its usage trends. In *Conference on e-Business, e-Services and e-Society* (pp. 38-49). Springer, Cham. DOI: 10.1007/978-3-319-68557-1_5

Thompson, R. L., Higgins, C. A., & Howell, J. M. (1991). Personal computing: Toward a conceptual model of utilization. MIS Quarterly, *15*(1), 124–143. https://doi.org/DOI: 10.2307/249443

Van Raaij, E. M., & Schepers, J. J. (2008). The acceptance and use of a virtual learning environment in China. *Computers & Education*, *50*(3), 838–852. DOI: 10.1016/j.compedu.2006.09.001

Velev, D., & Zlateva, P. (2017). Virtual reality challenges in education and training. *International Journal of Learning and Teaching*, *3*(1), 33–37. DOI: 10.18178/ijlt.3.1.33-37

Venkatesh, V. (2000). Determinants of perceived ease of use: Integrating control, intrinsic motivation, and emotion into the technology acceptance model. Information Systems Research, *11*(4), 342–365. DOI: 10.1287/isre.11.4.342.11872

Venkatesh, V. (2020). Determinants of perceived ease of use: Integrating control, intrinsic motivation, and emotion into the technology acceptance model. *Information Systems Research*, *44*(4), 342–365. DOI: 10.1287/isre.11.4.342.11872

Venkatesh, V., & Bala, H. (2008). Technology acceptance model 3 and a research agenda on interventions. Decision Sciences, *39*(2), 273–315. https://doi.org/DOI: 10.1111/j.1540-5915.2008.00192.x

Venkatesh, V., & Davis, F. D. (2000). A theoretical extension of the technology acceptance model: Four longitudinal field studies. Management Science, *46*(2), 186–204.

Venkatesh, V., Morris, M. G., Davis, G. B., & Davis, F. D. (2003). User acceptance of information technology: Toward a unified view. *Management Information Systems Quarterly*, *27*(3), 425–478. DOI: 10.2307/30036540

Wang, C., Ahmad, S. F., Ayassrah, A. Y. A. B. A., Awwad, E. M., Irshad, M., Ali, Y. A., Al-Razgan, M., Khan, Y., & Han, H. (2023). An empirical evaluation of technology acceptance model for Artificial Intelligence in E-commerce. Heliyon, *9*(8), e18349. https://doi.org/DOI: 10.1016/j.heliyon.2023.e18349

Williams, M., Rana, N., Dwivedi, Y., & Lal, B. (2011). Is UTAUT really used or just cited for the sake of it? A systematic review of citations of UTAUT's originating article. aisel.aisnet.org

Wu, J. H., & Wang, S. C. (2003). An empirical study of consumers adopting mobile commerce in taiwan: Analyzed by structural equation modeling [Paper presentation]. *Proceedings of the 5th International Conference on Electronic Commerce,* 81–94.

Wu, M., Chou, H., Weng, Y. C., & Huang, Y. (2011). TAM-2 based study of website user behavior-using web 2.0 websites as an example. *WSEAS Transactions on Business and Economics*, *4*(8), 133–151.

Yadav, R., Sharma, S. K., & Tarhini, A. (2016). A multi-analytical approach to understand and predict the mobile commerce adoption. *Journal of Enterprise Information Management*, *29*(2), 222–237. DOI: 10.1108/JEIM-04-2015-0034

Yen, D. C., Wu, C. S., Cheng, F. F., & Huang, Y. W. (2010). Determinants of users' intention to adopt wireless technology: An empirical study by integrating TTF with TAM. *Computers in Human Behavior*, *26*(5), 906–915. DOI: 10.1016/j.chb.2010.02.005

KEY TERMS AND DEFINITIONS

Attitude: explains the positive or negative disposition towards a person, object or situation (Davis et al., 1989).

Augmented Reality (AR): an interactive technology that superimposes computer-generated perceptual information (such as visuals, sound, or haptic feedback) onto a user's view of the real world, thereby creating a composite view that enhances the physical environment (Hantono, Nugroho, & Santosa, 2018).

Behavioral Intention: a user's conscious plan and motivation to perform a specific behavior (Davis et al., 1989)

Computer anxiety: the fear or apprehension an individual experiences when faced with the prospect of using computers (Venkatesh & Bala, 2008).

Effort Expectancy (or the perceived ease of use): refers to the degree of ease associated with an individual's use of a specific technology or information system (Venkatesh et al., 2003).

Experience: The moderating effect whereby the influence of subjective norm on usage intention weakens as a user gains more hands-on experience with the system (Venkatesh & Davis, 2000, p. 189).

Facilitating Conditions: refer to the user's perception of the support and resources available to use a system (Venkatesh et al., 2003).

Image: The extent to which an individual believes that using a technology will improve their social status or prestige within a group (Moore & Benbasat, 1991, p. 195).

Job Relevance: An individual's assessment of how applicable and pertinent a system is to their core job tasks and responsibilities (Venkatesh & Davis, 2000, p. 191).

Output Quality: The user's judgment of how effectively a system performs its functions and produces high-quality, relevant results for their work (Davis et al., 1992, p. 985).

Performance Expectancy (or perceived ease of use): refers to the degree to which a user believes a system will help them attain gains (Venkatesh et al., 2003).

Result Demonstrability: The degree to which the benefits and outcomes of using a system are tangible, observable, and easily communicated to others (Moore & Benbasat, 1991, p. 203).

Social Influence: the extent to which users perceive that important others believe they should use a technology (Venkatesh et al., 2003).

Subjective Norm: the degree to which an individual perceives that significant others (e.g., family, friends, or peers) believe they should or should not perform a particular behavior (Fishbein & Ajzen, 1975).

Virtual Reality (VR): an immersive technology that uses computer-generated simulations to create a completely artificial, three-dimensional environment, which users can explore and interact with, typically via specialized headsets and sensors, effectively replacing their real-world surroundings (Velev & Zlateva, 2017).

Voluntariness: The degree to which an individual perceives the adoption of a system as a personal choice, rather than a mandatory requirement ((Venkatesh & Davis, 2000)

ENDNOTES

1 https://medium.com/@muchy.p/revolutionizing-tech-adoption-real-world-success-stories-using-the-technology-acceptance-model-e66de0bbe926

2 https://www.intelivita.co.uk/blog/uber-taxi-app

Chapter 3
Perceptual Intelligence in Human-Centered Interactive Technologies:
A Framework for Emotionally Aligned Design

Anil Baliram Ghubade
https://orcid.org/0000-0002-6839-9842
School of Mechanical Engineering, Lovely Professional University, Punjab, India

Sudhanshu Dogra
School of Mechanical Engineering, Lovely Professional University, Punjab, India

Amit Kumar Thakur
https://orcid.org/0000-0002-9929-6176
School of Mechanical Engineering, Lovely Professional University, Punjab, India

Parveen Sharma
School of Mechanical Engineering, Lovely Professional University, Punjab, India

ABSTRACT

This chapter proposes a structural model of Perceptual Intelligence in Human-Centered Interactive Technologies with an emphasis on emotionally aligned design as a new form of interaction. Conventional human-centered design is largely concerned with the usability and functionality, and disregards the subtle relationship between human perception, cognition, and emotion. Perceptual intelligence builds upon this method through incorporation of multi-modal data into systems to recognize user states and adjust system behavior based on a set of models that interprets

DOI: 10.4018/979-8-3373-9958-4.ch003

user states. The model is organized into hierarchical parts: data retrieval, perception modelling, emotion mapping, adaptive interaction and learning feedback. It emphasizes the ways in which technologies can go beyond transactional efficiency to empathetic, trust-centered and personalized experiences. The framework serves as both a conceptual framework and roadmap to the construction of emotionally intelligent systems by connecting design, psychology, and AI

1. INTRODUCTION

The booming growth of Artificial Intelligence (AI) and Human-computer Interaction (HCI) studies has made researchers reconsider the principles of user-focused and emotion-sensitive design. The recent research has highlighted that the future of interactive technologies is not solely in automation or usability, but in systems, which are able to perceive and react to the human affect, cognition, and context (Norman, 2013; Picard, 2000). In this wider academic discussion, this chapter examines perceptual intelligence as a new paradigm that links affective computing, perceptual psychology and ethical design paradigms in developing emotional and adaptive interactions. The chapter, by placing perceptual intelligence in the spectrum of human-centered innovation, adds to the current discussions on the way of using technology to enhance rather than substitute human perceptual and emotional possibilities. In today's scenario, ubiquitous connectivity and blistering development of human-computer interaction, interactive technologies are no longer evaluated solely by the criteria of functional efficiency but are also evaluated by their capacity to appeal to human perception and emotion (Ware,2019). This change is a radical paradigm shift in the design philosophy away from a model where the systems are constructed to perform the specified roles and instead requires them to exhibit perceptual intelligence (the ability to perceive, interpret and react to human perceptual conditions in a way that promotes meaningful and empathetic interaction). Human beings do not encounter technology as impartial instruments, however, they perceive digital systems as refinements of personal, interpersonal and cultural identities, and therefore achievement of any interactive technology will not be determined by the usefulness of the product alone but rather the level to which it responds emotionally and perceptually to human subjects, their identities. In the given sense, perceptual intelligence can be called a feature of the human-oriented interactive technologies, as it allows the system to adjust to the cognitive, emotional, and physiologic aspects of human life and thus turn the interaction into relation and the usability into empathy. The usability, accessibility, and ergonomic efficiency were longstanding ideas of human-centered design that contributed to the development of human-centered interactive technologies (Cooley, 2000). However, as digital systems infiltrate more sensitive areas, like health care, education, entertainment, industry, and social communication, a second wave of human-centeredness has emerged that recognizes the key role of perception, cognition and affect in forming experiences. Throughout healthcare, such as intelligent companions (which should detect patient anxiety or discomfort and adapt accordingly to communication), education (adaptive learning platforms need to know when a student is engaged, frustrated, or interested to scaffold the instruction more efficiently), entertainment, and gaming (immersion requires both visual fidelity and a system that responds to the emotions, intentions, and stress levels of the player). In all these contexts, perceptual intelligence does not represent an add-on feature but a compulsory precondition of the interactive technologies being human-centric in an authentic sense.

Perceptual intelligence can be loosely understood as the computational and design capability of interactive technologies to compute, assimilate, and respond to multidimensional cues of human perception, such as cognitive states, physiological signals, sensory feedback, and expressions of emotion, to generate interactions that are empathetic, adaptive and emotionally congruent (Pentland,2000). In contrast to narrow artificial intelligence applications which are concerned with recognizing patterns or rule-driven reasoning, perceptual intelligence involves technologies creating a comprehensive understanding of the way people perceive reality. This ability is backed by three mutually reinforcing pillars: perceptual sensing, interpretive modeling and emotionally matched response (Koskinen,2023). Perceptual sensing: This is the set of multimodal data streams (facial expression, voice tone, eye looking, heart rate changes, electrodermal activity, gestures and context behaviors) that can tell us something about what is going on inside the user. Interpretive modeling then converts these bare signals into useful signals of human states like stress or calm, curiosity or boredom, or trust or skepticism, and at the same time takes into account contextual factors, like environment, cultural norms and task objectives. Finally, emotionally aligned response is the design of adaptive system behavior that is responsive not just to what the user is doing, but also to how the user is feeling to allow interactive technologies to respond in a way that is more in line with human values, expectations, and emotional demands. This three-step process determines perceptual intelligence not as a mere recognition of emotions, but as a unified mechanism of perception-conscious thinking that makes technologies feel, sound, and look natural, reliable, and understandable. Emotionally aligned design is not only important in its aesthetics and convenience, but also extends into the core of human-technology interactions (Ho et al., 2012). First, emotionally aligned systems will support trust and acceptance because the user is more likely to incorporate technologies into their lives when they feel that they care about and respect their feelings. Second, they facilitate psychological well-being, with emotional sensitive platforms having the potential to reduce stress, sustain mental well-being, and positively reinforce behavior, including virtual wellness coaches that identify burnout and suggest restorative approaches. Third, they enhance engagement and learning results by adjusting to frustration or disengagement in pupils maintaining motivation and dynamically adjusting feedback. Fourth, they are safe and reliable in high-stakes settings, like aviation, health, or manufacturing, where identifying operator fatigue or cognitive load may avoid an expensive error. Fifth, they promote creativity and teamwork by lowering levels of friction and alienation, allowing more seamless human-AI relations. All these advantages prove that the emotional attachment of design is not merely a facade of user experience but a requirement of technology growing beyond being efficient to be more perceptive, emphatic and relational.

The perception intelligence and emotionally oriented design have intellectual foundations, which are highly interdisciplinary. The science of perceptual psychology provides an understanding of how humans perceive sensory information, attention and meaning and informs how systems ought to make sense of multimodal input. Several models of emotion have been developed to offer a taxonomy of the perceptual signaling of emotion and a dimensional model of this signaling into emotion states, with emotion theories including the cognitive appraisal theory of emotion proposed by Lazarus and the simple emotions framework of Ekman and the circumplex model of affect proposed by Russell (Moors et al,, 2013). Human-centered design, as championed by the likes of Norman and Sanders, underlines the need to match technology to the human processes of cognition and affect, and provides the foundations to a perception-centered approach. Inspired by Rosalind Picard, affective computing introduced the principle that machines could detect, understand, and imitate emotions, and cognitive science and neuroscience provided information about memory, attention, and the neural basis of emotion, which could be used to design computational models of perception. Collectively, these fields are coming together to show that perceptual intelligence is not a new concept, but the synthesis of decades of research in psychology, computer science, and design, and molded into a framework that focuses on the perceptual and emotional aspects of interaction.

A unified approach to perceptual intelligence in emotionally oriented design connects inputs, processing and outputs together in a smooth adaptive system. The inputs include cognitive objectives, behavior indicators like clicking pattern or dwell time, physiological indicators like heart rate and skin conductance and contextual factors like environment or task complexity. These are fed into perception modelling, in which multimodal information is combined, contextual inferences made and uncertainties approximated (Ménard et al., 2015). The resulting layer of interpretation links to emotion mapping, which maps perceptual information into affective states on dimensions like valence (positive to negative) and arousal (low to high). The loop is closed by interaction adaptation, which adapts system responses (via visual, auditory, haptic, or conversational channels) according to congruent emotional strategies to achieve feedback-user alignment. A feedback loop would automatically lead to constant improvement, with systems updating their models in light of dynamic interactions between humans and system. Notably, ethical protections that discourage manipulation and exploitation of emotions are built into such a framework, so that emotional alignment becomes a user empowerment and source of well-being, instead of being used to coerce. Perceptual intelligence is ethically problematic and its promise presents significant issues. Human emotion is ambiguous, situation-specific, culturally mediated, and thus difficult to interpret, susceptible of error. The problem with over-reliance on simplistic models is misclassification, whereas cultural bias in emotion recognition algorithms can lead to decreased inclusivity and fairness. This also brings up the issue of privacy, consent and surveillance because physiological and behavioral indicators can be used to determine intimate information about the user. Additionally, excessive automation can also lead to over-empowerment of the user by making false assumptions about emotions and minimizing agency. Another challenge is sustainability, wherein emotionally congruent technologies should not be associated with predatory patterns like persuasive design, which generates addiction, but not well-being. To overcome these issues, a set of responsible frameworks needs to be developed to combine technical soundness with ethical responsibility, openness, and agency.

The concept of human computer interaction (HCI) has focused on usability and efficiency in human computer interaction, but new interactive systems need to incorporate what users feel and perceive as they engage with the product. It means perceptual intelligence, the ability of an interactive system to perceive, model and react to the perceptual and emotional state of a user in a situation (Carroll,2009). Perceptual intelligence transcends generic user-centered rhetoric by pinpointing the explicit connection between how users perceive, what they feel and how systems respond in real time. It is a logical extension of human-centered design, the ISO standard that manages design processes involving the needs and situations of users throughout the system life cycle. This chapter is motivated by two underlying strands. The former is affective computing, which proposes that computers can and ought to be able to discern, comprehend and even affect human sentiment suitably to become real partners. In groundbreaking literature, Picard established the intellectual foundations of the construction of emotionally intelligent machines and explained the technical and ethical aspects of the matter. The second is emotion theory, in which dimensional models, like Russell's valence-arousal circumplex, and appraisal-based models, including Scherer's Component Process Model (CPM), offer a solid scaffold to capture emotions in a sensible and calculable form. But it is not enough to be able to measure emotion (Scherer,2009). The design should be able to provide the loop: mirror the perceptions and feelings, plot them to constructs that are interpretable, adjust the content, pacing, modality and control policies- and respect the user autonomy, inclusivity and privacy. As a practice, emotionally aligned design speaks to four overlapping challenges:

- Sensing and inference. What signals (self-report, behavior, physiology) provide reliable context? How do we combine them responsibly?
- Representation. Which models (valence–arousal, appraisal, discrete) best suit real-time decisions?
- Adaptation. What policies modify interfaces (visuals, audio, haptics), content difficulty, or agent tone in ways that measurably improve outcomes without manipulation?
- Governance. How do we measure success (engagement, trust, workload) and ensure fairness, accessibility, and data protection e.g., General Data Protection Regulation (GDPR principles)?

This chapter presents designers and research practitioners with a systematic guide on how to incorporate perceptual intelligence into human interactive technologies. It provides designers with the tenets to incorporate empathy, recognition of emotions, and adaptive interaction in the product development process to deliver experiences that are meaningful to users beyond just functionality. To research practitioners, it provides a conceptual guide and methodological base to understand multimodal data integration, perceptual modeling and emotive system evaluation. The chapter connects theory and practice by focusing on issues, including cultural diversity, professional limits, and practicality, and encouraging innovation in the area of emotionally intelligent, user-centered technological design.

2. THEORETICAL FOUNDATIONS OF INTELLIGENT INTERACTIVE DESIGN

2.1 Human-Centered Design

Traditionally product design process is based on idea and understanding of designers in creating the product without accounting user's view. When products launched in the market, it may fail to attract the customers (Elizabeth Sander (1990). For example, The EDSEL Ford in 1957 fail in American market owing to weird body styling, unreliable control. Elizabeth Sander (1990) suggested that to avoid the failure of the product in the market, companies need to dramatically improve their research to develop the product to be useful, usable and desirable. There should be good in a product that captures users' attention. A good product is more appealing to consumers in terms of price, its functions, form and color to satisfy consumers need (Nagamachi & Lokman, 2016). Human beings have different needs at different stage of their life. This hierarchy of needs and applying it to human factors, Maslow identified seven levels of need and forms pyramid of hierarchy of need. It is intended to reflect the way that the contribution of human factors to product design might be seen either explicitly or implicitly by both manufacturers and those who buy and use their products. According to Maslow, the foremost need is physiological need like hunger. He asserted, to have higher level of need, the consecutive lower-level need must be partially satisfied. These hierarchy of need can be transformed into customer need as functionality, usability and pleasure (Jordan,2003). Now days, Design engineering must consider the role of human and their emotions in creating the product which satisfy functionality as well as communicating personality of their own as shown in fig 1. Designed must accomplished the goal of business and uses needs with the constraint imposed by technology. In lieu of this, designing the product that satisfies all users is very difficult task because everyone has his or her own set of personal experience and learning associates (Van Gorp & Adams, 17). Design of products for 21st Century is beyond the products utilitarian and more towards design aesthetics and product semiotics. Aesthetics was first used by German Philosopher Alexander Gottlieb Baumgartenb in 1970 in his book titles "Aesthetica". According to him, Aesthetic is a knowledge one can receive through senses. The definition of Aesthetics in its more refine way is "Study of effect of product gestalt on human sensation". The common way of expressing product gestalt is through the study of semiotics which denotes the user's perception to decode what he heard, seen, felt, smelt and tested (Monö et al., 1997).

Figure 1. (a) Maslow's Hierarchy of Needs (Laslow, 2013) (b) A Hierarchy of consumer needs

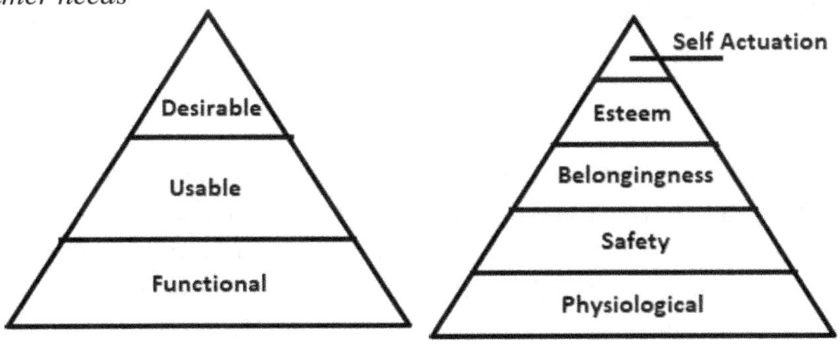

(Jordan, 2002)

Norman, (2007) in his book titled "Emotional design: Why we love (or hate) everyday things" wrote about the complexity of human structure and humans have the powerful brain to accomplished all our daily activities. The author along with his colleges reported, that human attributes result from three levels of brain processing visceral, behavioral and reflective. Automatic reaction arises from visceral level; the part of the brain that controls everyday behavior of human beings is known as behavioral whereas behavior action can be enhanced or inhibited by reflective brain. These three levels interact and modulate each other. The brain responds very quickly at a visceral level and takes rapid judgments like what is good or bad, approach or avoidance. Whereas behavioral and reflective levels are sensitive to education, experience, and cognition. Donald Normal, (2007) further mapped these levels of brain processing to product characteristics as Visceral, behavioral, and reflective. At the visceral level, physical attributes of the product like form, color, shape, feel, sound, etc. dominates. For example, the visceral design of the 1961 jaguar E-type. Behavioral design is all about the function, understanding and usability, and physical feel of the product e.g., Casio G shock. Whereas reflective design is built upon the users' experience and association with the product reflect the sense of pride, attitude and personality traits, and self-image e.g Pie watch designed by "Time".

Figure 2. (a) 1961 jaguar E-type (Visceral Design) (b) Casio G shock (Behavioral Design) (c) Pie Watch designed by "Time" (Reflective Design)

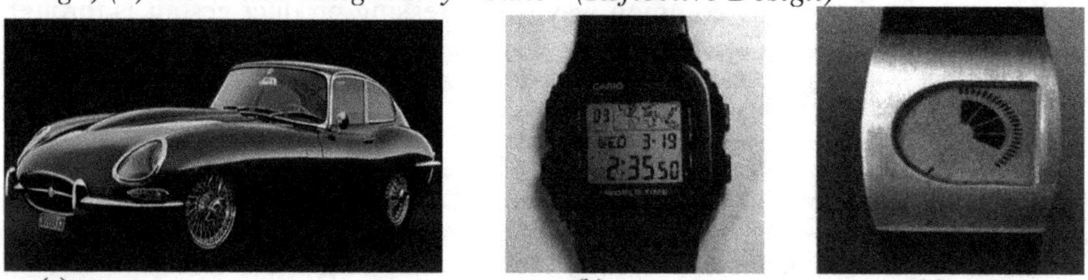

(a) (b) (c)

(Normal, 2007)

Design engineering must consider the role of human and their emotions responses in creating the product which satisfies functionality as well as should communicate the personality of their own (Benaissa & Kobayashi 2023). Jordan, (2002) explores the user-product relationship and emphasized the role of pleasure during product interaction. Jordan identified four main categories of pleasure in user-product interaction as Physio-pleasure, Socio-pleasure, Psycho-pleasure, and Ideo-pleasure. Table 1 shows the traditional human factor analysis of "Janet peter". The author mapped these four pleasures with product use as shown in Table 2

Table 1. Four-pleasure analysis for 'Janet Peters'(Jordan, 2002)

Physio	Socio	Psycho	Ideo
Staying in shape	Company	Stress relief	Decency
Physical relaxation	Good personal relationships	Stimulation	Responsibility
Intoxication (alcohol)	Glamour, Status	Sense of achievement	Supporting moral leaders

Table 2. Four pleasures to the use of the product

Physio	Anthropometric, Weight, Aesthetic qualities, Safety qualities, Product comfortless, etc.
Socio	Social identity and status, social self-image, social acceptability, social impact
Psycho	Usability, Functionality, performance
Ideo	Self-Reflection on experience, value, etc.

2.2 Dimensional Emotion Models

Dimensional models of emotion constitute an important paradigm in the science of affectivity, providing an alternative to discrete emotion theories, which conceptualize affective experiences as instances in a multidimensional psychological space instead of categorically defined states. Unlike discrete models, which focus on universal basic emotions (such as anger, fear, happiness, and sadness) (Ekman, 1992), dimensional models suggest that emotions should be viewed as varying along continuous dimensions (which both measure the intensity and the quality of affect). The most influential of the dimensional models is the valence arousal model, which positions the states of emotion in two major dimensions, i.e. valence, i.e. the degree of unpleasantness versus pleasantness; arousal, i.e. the degree of physiological stimulation, between a calm and excited state (Russell, 1980). As an example, happiness is defined as high in valence and moderate to high in arousal, sadness is low in valence and low in arousal. This two-dimensional framework is commonly conceptualized in terms of the circumplex model of affect in which the affective domain is represented as placing emotions in a circular area which is determined by the interaction of valence and arousal (Posner, Russell, and Peterson, 2005). In addition to the two-dimensional concept, scholars have also presented three-dimensional models that incorporate a dimension of dominance or control that captures the extent to which people experience themselves as in control or controlled by outer forces in the emotional experience (Mehrabian and Russell, 1974). An example of this is that anger and fear can have a negative valence and high arousal, but anger is normally connoted by high dominance and fear by low dominance, demonstrating that another axis can further differentiate emotion. Dimensional models have a number of benefits over discrete theories: they are fluid in nature, able to support mixed or blended feelings, and are sensitive to psychophysiological measures such as heart rate, skin conductance, and neural activation patterns that are not categorical but often continuous (Kuppens, et al, 2013). In addition, they also offer an elastic model of computational modeling and human computer interaction since the continuous dimensions can be instantiated as being recognized to emotion recognition algorithms and adaptive system responses in affective computing (Calvo & D'Mello, 2010). Dimensional models have their own shortcomings despite their strengths. Other researchers note that the use of emotion to valence and arousal is overly simplistic and ignores context and content as well as appraisal that lie at the heart of emotional experience (Scherer, 2005). Some have argued that dimensions do not explain qualitative differences between emotions that have similar dimensional profiles, e.g. anger and fear, which may be phenomenologically distinct but nevertheless similar in dimensional space. Hybrid methods have thus been developed which combines categorical and dimensional views by accepting basic prototypical emotions but placing them in a multidimensional affective space (Barrett, 2006). However, dimensional models play a significant role in all fields of psychology, neuroscience, and research in interactive technologies due to their explanatory strength, empirical validation, and computational manageability. The application of dimensional emotion models has been demonstrated in several empirical contexts. For instance, Calvo and D'Mello (2010) applied the valence–arousal framework in adaptive learning environments to detect student frustration and tailor instructional pacing dynamically, improving engagement metrics by 18%. Similarly, Mehta et al. (2018) used continuous valence–arousal mapping in video-based emotion recognition, achieving over 80% accuracy in real-world human–computer interaction scenarios. In industrial design, automotive companies such as Toyota and Nissan have embedded valence-arousal mapping in Kansei engineering processes to correlate tactile feedback (e.g., steering wheel texture) with emotional satisfaction scores. These examples illustrate that dimensional modeling of emotion not only advances theoretical understanding but also translates into measurable design improvements in adaptive systems. They still form a strong basis of emotion science, especially where there is a need to dynamically trace affective states (like in adaptive learning systems, mental health, and perceptually intelligent human-computer interaction).

Figure 3. Theories of emotion

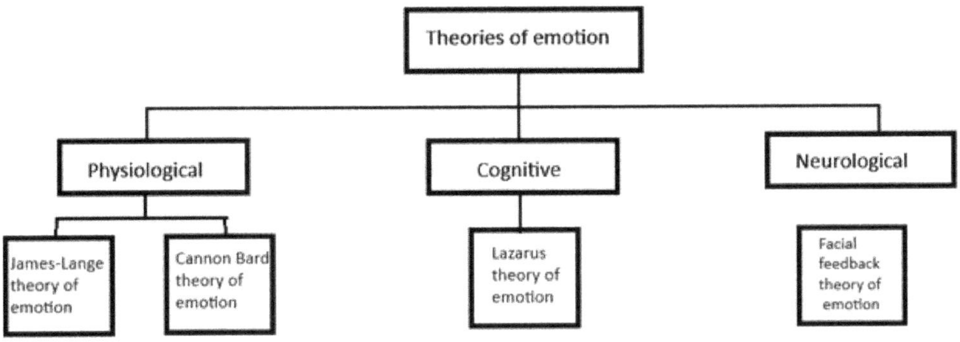

2.2.1 James-Lange Theory of Emotion

in 19th century independently proposed the theory of emotion. The basic premise of the theory is physiological arousal evoked the experience of emotion (Cannon, 1927*)*. The theory states that Visceral feedback from the disturbed organ is emotion itself. Example My heart is pounding, so I must be afraid." These visceral responses are unconscious, quick and originated from reptile brain reported by Mclean 1990(McLean,1990). He proposed that human brain is composed of three brain system namely reptile brain (old brain), mammalian brain and neo mammalian brain. Reptile brain (Basal ganglia) is responsible for basic survival and mating instinct such as fight, shelter, reproduction etc. Mammalian brain is deals with responsibility towards social responses and interaction with the society and evoked the emotions such as status, avoidance, acceptance, etc. whereas the neo mammalian brain responsible for conscious judgment and form the emotional relationship. Donald A Normal (2004) in his book titled "Emotional design: Why we love (or hate) everyday things" wrote the complexity of human structure amongst the all animals and have powerful brain to accomplished all daily activities. He along with his colleges suggests that human attributes result from three levels of brain processing visceral, behavioral and reflective. Automatic reaction arises from visceral level; the part of the brain controls the everyday behavior of human being is known as behavioral whereas behavior action can be enhanced or inhibited by reflective brain processing

Figure 4. Three brain processing level mapped to product characteristics

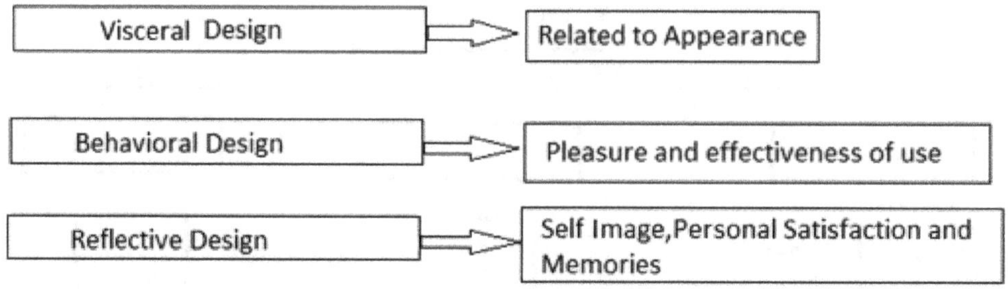

2.2.2 Cannon Bard Theory of Emotion

Challenged the theory proposed by James-Lange, asserted emotions evoked from visceral feedback has less sensitive in nature. If the viscera are separated surgically from the nervous system, then there is still emotional response occurs. Cannon suggested that the emotional expression is subcortical or more particularly Thalamic. They concluded that triggering of a specific emotion as being determined by processing a stimulus in the "central" nervous system, with the peripheral arousal pattern being neither specific nor causal. Example I feel afraid, so my heart pounds". The Cannon-Bard theory of emotion offers useful information in product design, as it focuses on simultaneous (not successive) emotional and physiological processes and notes that users immediately feel both emotions and bodily reactions when they interact with a product. This school of thought prompt designers to design experiences that prompt instant emotional resonance but remain congruent with physical sensations, so that aesthetics, usability and sensory feedback are harmonized to operate as a system that creates seamless experiences. The close sound of a car door being shut or the gentle vibration of a wearable can both cause a feeling of trust, safety, or motivation as well as appeal to the senses, strengthening the emotional bond. In doing so, product design may transcend functionality to produce affectively resonant experiences in which visual expressions, tactile communication, and interaction design provide immediate emotional reactions to bodily perceptions, which in turn reinforce user satisfaction and increase attachment to the product over time (Cannon, 1927).

2.2.3 Lazarus Theory of Emotion

The Cognitive Appraisal Theory, also called the Lazarus Theory of Emotion, focuses on the idea that people feel a certain way because an individual has interpreted a situation and not the situation itself. Richard Lazarus believes that emotion follows cognition, i.e., the emotional response is predetermined by the appraisal of the situation. He suggested two levels of appraisal. In primary appraisal, an individual assesses whether an incident is irrelevant, positive or stressful. With secondary appraisal, the person evaluates the coping resources and mechanisms that he or she can utilize to cope with the situation. An example is encountered in examination: when one is well-prepared, the appraisal will result in confidence or excitement; when one is unprepared, the appraisal will result in anxiety or fear. Therefore, emotions are not only reliant on the external stimuli but also on the significance and capabilities of coping. The theory is noteworthy because it presents a connection between stress, coping, and emotional responses and demonstrates the dynamism of emotions and their perception. Lazarus theory of emotion or the cognitive appraisal theory, the theory states that people are emotional because of how they interpret and evaluate scenarios and not due to the presence of stimuli or physiological reactions. When applied to product design, it implies that, based on the meaning, usefulness, and the applicability of a product to the goals and values of their users, users have their emotions influenced by their cognitive appraisal of a product. As an example, a consumer could assess an interface on a friendly phone as effective and conducive to efficiency, which ultimately creates satisfaction and confidence. On the other hand, an inadequately built interface can be evaluated as frustrating, which can cause negative feelings of irritation or stress. This way, designers can work on developing products that facilitate positive cognitive appraisal by matching features to user anticipations, values, and circumstances. Using relevant interactions and user-friendly usability, product design has the potential to induce positive emotional appraisal that improves user experience and product loyalty over time (Lazarus,1991).

2.2.4 Appraisal Theories

This model relies on appraisal theory which explains why similar events evoke different emotional experiences by different people (Scherer et al 2001) The appraisal theory uses the cognitive approach developed by Ortony et al. (1988) in which an individual appraises the product as potentially harming or favoring to his/her concern. According to Frijda, (1988) when we appraise the potential event as beneficial to our concern, we will experience positive emotions towards this event. However, when the event is colliding with our concern, we will experience negative emotions and try to avoid them. Desmet (2003) introduced the theoretical framework that underlies all emotional responses to a consumer product. According to this model, concern, and an appraisal are the key parameters which determine the type of emotions elicited by the product. Fig 5. adopted from Desmet (2003) shows the "basic model of product emotions" in which an individual appraises the product, if a product is beneficial to his or her concern, results in positive emotions. Whereas, if the appraisal is colliding with concern, results in negative emotions. For example, if the user's main concern in using an ink pen is to write smoothly without spreading the ink over the page. If this concern is fulfilled by the product, it appraises as beneficial and positive emotions are evoked. Desmet in his further research described the nine sources of product emotions elicited through combining the three key appraisals such as usefulness appraisal, pleasant appraisal, and rightfulness appraisal with three levels of human product relationship such as product focus, activity focus, and self-focus (Desmet, 2011). The author further identified 25 positive emotions during user-product interaction (Desmet, 2012). A novel concept further has been introduced to potentially use the negative emotions to enrich the product experience. When it comes to designing of product for the potential buyer, it is essential to identify the primary concern of users and then design it to satisfy users to improve emotional responses.

Figure 5. The basic model of product emotions

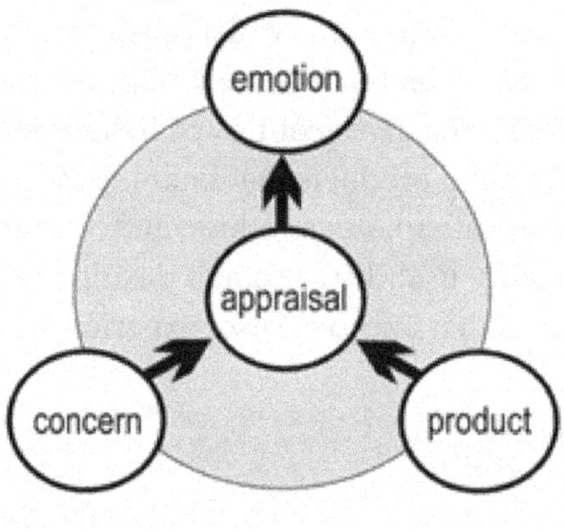

(Desmet, 2003)

2.2.5 Kansei Engineering

Kansei engineering is soft engineering concept introduced by professor Nagamachi and developed more than 40 new products by translating consumers emotional need into product characteristics (Nagamachi & Lokman, 2016). various emotions can be represented by Kansei word or adjectives (Ota & Aoyama, 2001). Using Kansei adjectives/words, consumers can be guided to express their affective needs, feelings and emotional states (Jiao et al., 2006). Kansei engineering is a humanistic product design process that converts the psychological feelings, perceptions, and emotions of consumers into physical and concrete design components in such a manner that the products become emotionally appealing along with the functional factors. It is concerned with the minor and unconscious reactions that users develop when playing with a product and transforming them into quantifiable design qualities like shape, color, texture, sound, or usability capabilities. Like in the automotive sector, in designing a steering wheel feel, a car door feels, or the look of a dashboard, Kansei engineering can be used to invoke a feeling of safety, luxury, or exhilaration. Through systematic association of emotional reactions to physical qualities, designers are able to design products that easily satisfy practical needs, as well as encourage emotional satisfaction and attachment to the brand. Finally, Kansei engineering connects the gap between emotion and engineering so that the design of the product reaches out to the heart and mind of the user. Kansei engineering in product design is a systematic approach that integrates human emotions and psychological impressions into the design process, ensuring that products are not only functional but also emotionally engaging. Another famous use of Kansei engineering was practiced by Mazda Motor Corporation in the construction of the MX-5 Miata. The engineers used more than 100 Kansei words collected by customers, e.g. exhilarating, responsive, lightweight, etc. and converted them into measurable design factors such as engine response time and steering stiffness (Nagamachi, 1995). The resultant design resonated remarkably in terms of emotions and was a favorite sports car in the world. Equally, Sony applied Kansei principles to enhancing haptic experience of PlayStation controllers, which resulted in quantifiable aspects of user engagement and comfort (Zhou and Jiao., 2020). Such empirical examples underline that the transformation of affective needs into the design specification results in the quantifiable emotional attachment and product loyalty. Unlike traditional design methodologies that primarily emphasize performance, cost, or ergonomics, Kansei engineering acknowledges that users' emotional satisfaction plays a crucial role in shaping their overall product experience and long-term loyalty. The core idea is that every product evokes a psychological response based on its appearance, texture, sound, or interaction, and these responses can be measured, analyzed, and translated into design specifications. For instance, the feeling of elegance may be captured through the use of smooth curves, metallic finishes, and subtle lighting, while robustness may be expressed through solid forms, firm tactile feedback, and deep acoustic tones. By employing semantic differential scales, surveys, and statistical analyses, designers can map abstract user perceptions such as "trustworthy," "innovative," or "friendly" to concrete design parameters like material choice, interface layout, or interaction style. This methodology is particularly powerful because it enables designers to systematically quantify subjective feelings and incorporate them into engineering processes, reducing the gap between user expectations and product reality. Industries such as consumer electronics, automotive, fashion, and furniture design have actively applied Kansei engineering to differentiate their products in competitive markets. For example, in smartphone design, a slim profile, smooth surface finish, and minimalistic icons may be chosen to evoke perceptions of sophistication and modernity, while in household appliances, designers may use warm colors, rounded edges, and intuitive controls to convey approachability and comfort. Beyond aesthetics, Kansei engineering also informs sensory experiences such as sound and touch, where the click of a button, the vibration of an alert, or the texture of a surface can be deliberately tuned to elicit specific emotional responses. Importantly, this approach aligns with the growing trend of human-centered and emotion-driven design, where users seek products that fit their lifestyles, identities, and aspirations rather than merely performing technical functions. In modern contexts, Kansei engineering can also be integrated with digital technologies such as artificial intelligence, machine learning, and big data analytics, allowing designers to capture and analyze massive datasets of user feedback, online reviews, and behavioral patterns to refine design decisions with greater accuracy. This not only enhances personalization but also enables predictive modeling of emotional responses, leading to products that can adapt to diverse cultural and individual preferences. Moreover, Kansei engineering has implications for sustainability and ethical design, as emotionally meaningful products tend to foster stronger attachment, thereby extending product life cycles and reducing waste caused by premature disposal. In essence, Kansei engineering transforms product design into a dialogue between human emotions and technical possibilities, ensuring that every detail, from form and function to interaction and experience, resonates with the user on a deeper psychological level. By embedding emotion into the design DNA, it helps companies move beyond utilitarian products toward creations that inspire joy, trust, and long-lasting connections. The Kansai proposed the model of product design attributes as shown in fig6; The given model of the Kansei Engineering shows us a systematic way to incorporate emotional values into product design. The choice of domain is the starting point of the process whereby the target product category and user context are established. This is succeeded by spanning the semantic space where the expressions and the psychological impressions of the users are taken into account, and the space of properties where the properties of a product, expressed in terms of materials, shapes, colors or functions, are outlined. Synthesis is the next step of integrating these two spaces and connecting emotional words to design parameters. These proposed relationships pass through a test of validity as there is a guarantee that the desired emotional reactions correspond to the actual user impressions. Lastly, a model is created to forecast and inform future design. Notably, the model can update both semantic and property space iteratively, with the refinement and accuracy ensured. What this methodology allows designers to do is to allow them to systematically transform subjective feelings into concrete features of design, and to produce products that can appeal to their users on both an emotional and a practical level.

Figure 6. A model of the Kansei engineering concept

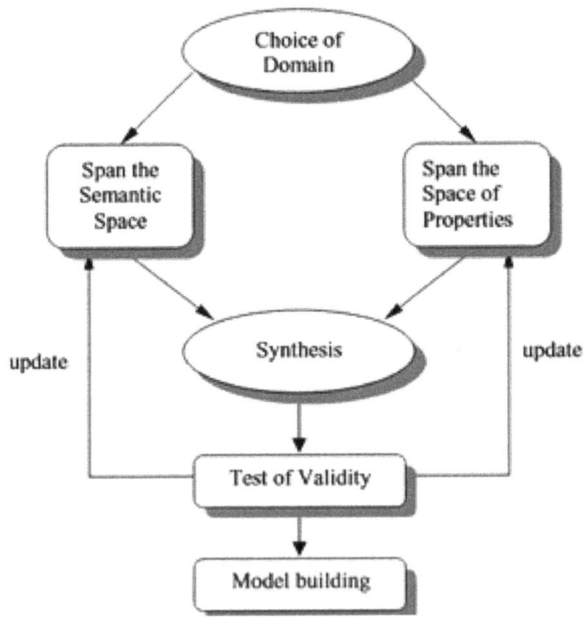

(Schütte et al., 2024)

3. DESIGN PRINCIPLES FOR EMOTIONALLY ALIGNED INTERACTIVE SYSTEMS

The construction of emotionally consistent interactive systems should be a balanced combination of the philosophy of human-centered design, the science of affect, ethical considerations, and the process of cyclical assessment. The basic idea is that interactive technologies must not only optimize efficiency or engagement in a mechanistic sense but aim to appeal to the perceptual and emotional states of users in ways that can promote understanding, well-being, trust, and the quality of decisions. In order to reach this alignment, designers need to understand that emotions are not incidental, but central to cognition, motivation and action, and as such, systems capable of monitoring, interpreting, and responding to emotional signals have the potential to produce more profound and long-sustained forms of engagement. Emotionally aligned design goes beyond the scope of traditional usability-driven design that tends to focus on the time it takes to complete tasks, the rate of errors, or the ease of learning an interface by asking how an interface feels to the user, how an interface can facilitate self-regulation, and how an interface can react to moments of stress, confusion, or delight. Such systems have a clear statement about the outcomes of the human being as their starting point (Cao & Cao, 2025). In a time of data-driven personalization, it is easy to assume that more engagement = better design, but this simplistic approach to understanding can give way to a set of manipulative behaviors that favor time-on-task cues or click-through rates over understanding, agency, or health. Explicit outcome goals, i.e. to decrease the cognitive overload in situations where complex decisions are needed, to instill a feeling of confidence on novice learners, or to trust health-related digital assistants, should instead be defined by emotional systems. When outcomes are identified, design teams may chart the emotional counterparts that indicate functionality or struggle, including increasing arousal and negative valence at times of frustration, or a balance of arousal and positive valence at times of flow. By refocusing the assessment of abstract measures of engagement to tangible human outcomes, designers create a normative frame that shapes interpretation and action of emotional data. Yang et al, (2024) conducted an experiment where adaptive color saturation (saturation of the interface) and ambient sound modulation (elements aligned with emotion) were experimented with 60 users who had to complete stressful cognitive tasks on the interface. Findings indicated that adaptive emotional feedback decreased the cognitive workload (NASA-TLX) by 23% and had a positive 30% increase in self-reported trust in the system. On the same note, McDuff and Czerwinski (2018) established that interfaces based on emotional sensing that used a webcam-based analysis of heart-rate enhanced user satisfaction by dynamically adjusting the brightness and tone of the on-screen display. These results highlight the importance of emotionally aligned design as a mental construct, which when authenticated by empirical data, will increase engagement, as well as well-being and task efficiency.

Figure 7. Modulating emotion in communication via design

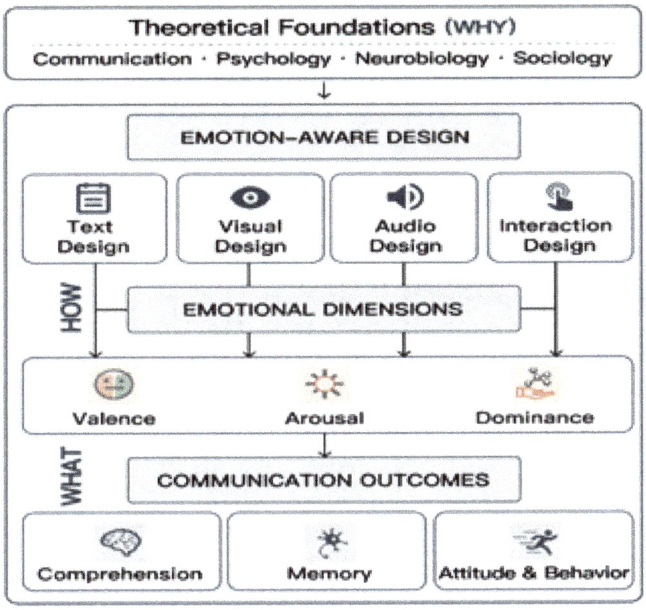

(Cao & Cao, 2025)

The other principle is the sensing and inference method. Emotional alignment requires interpretable and reliable signals of user state, but any signal has trade-offs. Self-report measures (e.g., the Self- Assessment Manikin, SAM, or the Positive and Negative Affect Schedule, PANAS) are both clear and transparent, but can interrupt task flow and are susceptible to recall bias (Lang et al, 2005)). Physiological cues such as heart-rate variability, electrodermal activity, or pupil dilation provide real time granularity, but are vulnerable to noise, context and individual variability, not to mention privacy concerns. Behavioral telemetry dwell time, scroll depth, or click entropy are not obtrusive but not interpretable out of context. The ideal practice here is thus triangulation: self-report, physiology, and behavioral data where feasible should be combined with probabilistic models that provide error estimates on inferences. Notably, systems must incorporate a philosophy of feeling a little and requesting directly, to provide a balance between passive detection and a few micro-survey requests where the user can verify or refute or reject interpretations of his or her emotional state. This does not only enhance calibration of the model, it also maintains a sense of user agency by sustaining people in the loop.

Figure 8. The self-assessment Manikin from Lang, Bradley and Cuthbert

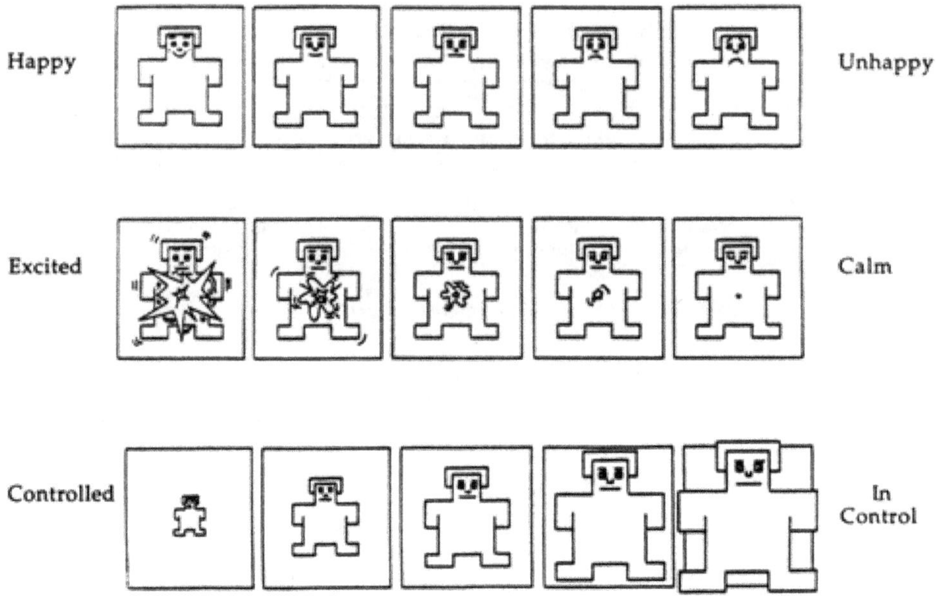

(Lang et al., 2005)

The question now becomes how to model the emotional states in a scientifically well-founded and operationally practical way when the signals are available. Russell, (1980) is an example of a dimensional model whose valence-arousal circumplex has a two-dimensional, tractable expression of affect that can be inferred in a continuous manner. More complex models of appraisal, including the Component Process Model by Scherer, further specify this representation by proposing the reason behind the emergence of an emotion, with that emotion being related to novelty appraisal, goal pertinence (or coping possibility) appraisal. The dimensional models can help make fast adjustments (e.g. reducing visual intensity when arousal spikes), whereas the appraisal models can help make situation-specific adjustments (e.g. more guidance when coping potential is rated low). The representation must be transparent: the system must be capable of explaining, in human understandable terms, what emotional state is being made inference, with what confidence, and why a specific adaptation was induced. This not only makes it interpretable by the designers and users but also allows an ethical review board or auditors to assess whether the reasoning in the system is correct.

Figure 9. Russell's (1980) circumplex model

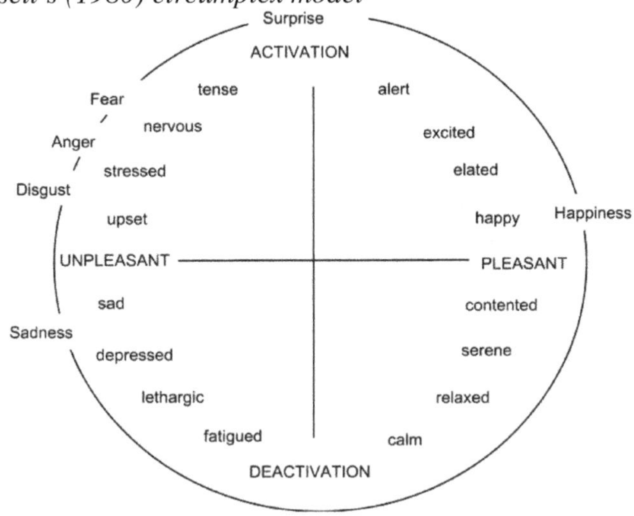

Lastly, the emotionally aligned design will have to address the threat of manipulation. The same principles that enable a system to identify and react to the frustration of users can be used to influence users to make decisions that favor the provider against the best interest of users. This threat is particularly acute in such areas as advertising, gambling, or political communication, where the interaction is monetized or ideologically predetermined. Adaptation engines should then be hard-coded with ethical guardrails such that policies that increase engagement but at the same time increase workload, stress, or decrease understanding are not allowed. These systems should be subjected to scrutiny by independent audits, a body of ethics and user advocacy groups. Emotional alignment should be posed as being a collaboration between human and machine where the user takes agency, rather than use it as a tool to manipulate behavior covertly.

4. FRAMEWORK FOR EMOTIONALLY ALIGNED DESIGN

Perceptual intelligence has become a new paradigm of interactive design that involves the incorporation of human cognitive and behavioral and emotional processes into the operation of adaptive systems. The model shown in the framework is a systematic approach to how systems can sense, interpret, adapt, and respond in a human way. It focuses on multimodal input gathering, perception modeling, emotional mapping, adaptive decision making and governance of the outcomes, all mediated through interactive.

4.1. Inputs

Perceptual intelligence has its base with gathering of data of different sources. Cognitive context (tasks, goals, or intentions), behavioral telemetry (clicks, scrolling, dwell time, and navigation patterns), and physiological inputs (heart rate variability (HRV), electrodermal activity (EDA), and gaze tracking) are all examples of inputs. The raw information contained in these signals supports the interpretation of user states allowing systems to go beyond a superficial interaction to a more cognitively and affectively meaningful recognition.

4.2. Perception Modeling

The following is perception modeling that consolidates these heterogeneous inputs to provide a contextual meaning of the user. The feature fusion combines the signals of various modalities, and the context inference determines the situational factors of user behavior. Estimation of uncertainty is important because human signals are always noisy and ambiguous. The system will prevent overgeneralization, because by quantifying confidence levels the system will remain transparent in decision-making.

4.3. Emotion Mapping

The interactive system experience of human beings is not cognitive but highly emotional. This layer converts perceptual information into emotional representations. Valence-Arousal framework developed by Russell is used to define the affective states, and the Component Process Model (CPM) is used to evaluate the situational significance. Inferred emotions can be confirmed using such tools as Self-Assessment Manikin (SAM) or Positive and Negative Affect Schedule (PANAS) probes. With the integration of affective intelligence, systems gain the potential of empathetic interactions, where responses are personalized based on user well-being and participation.

4.4. Adaptation Engine

The decision-making center of the framework is the adaptation engine. It uses a combination of policy rules and machine learning to decide how to react to the system. Notably, it also incorporates guardrails like ethical limits, opt-out options, and fairness principles to make AI responsible in its actions. The engine converts the perceptual understanding to strategy to execution and balances personalization with transparency, privacy and inclusivity.

4.5. Interface Layer

The adaptation results are presented in multimodal interfaces. This has visual representations, auditory, and haptic actuators. Accessibility controls are in place to norm diversity so that systems are accessible to a wide range of users in relation to cognitive, sensory, and physical distinctions. The interface layer is the physical connection between the machine intelligence and the human senses; the experience is the adaptation.

4.6. Outcomes & Governance

Lastly, the framework moves towards governance in order to achieve desirable results. The essential measures are engagement, trust, and performance, which can be assessed using A/B testing, NASA-TLX (cognitive workload assessment), System Usability Scale (SUS), and Net Promoter Score (NPS). In addition to performance, governance covers bias audits, privacy, and ethical reviews that maintain accountability and societal trust in perceptual systems.

Figure 10. Framework for emotionally aligned design

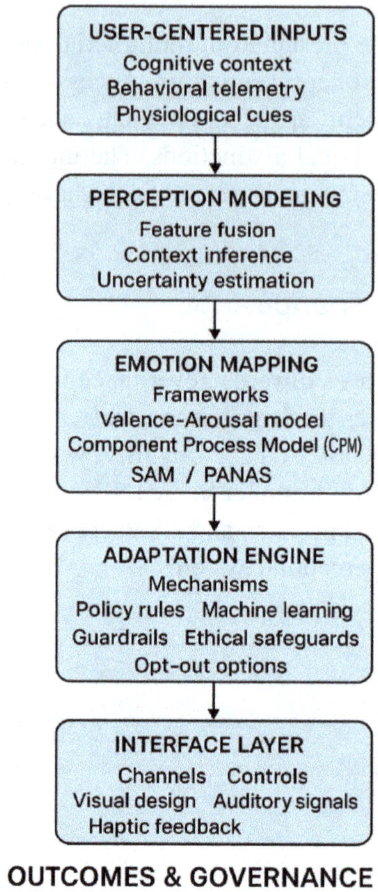

Despite the promise of perceptual intelligence in enabling emotionally aligned design, several challenges remain that restrict its full realization in human-centered interactive technologies. These challenges are multi-dimensional, spanning technical, ethical, cultural, and methodological concerns. Addressing these gaps is crucial to ensure that perceptual intelligence systems not only function effectively but also remain trustworthy, inclusive, and sustainable.

The given model allows to have a very holistic approach to product design, combining cognitive, behavioral, and physiological inputs with sophisticated modeling and adapting mechanisms that allow designers and the company to design something really human-centered and emotionally oriented. Starting with varied inputs, including task objectives, behavior telemetry, and physiological indications, the model makes sure that the products designing decision-making process is based on actual, contextual user data in place of presumptions. The methodology can give a subtle insight into user states and can be used to design individualized experiences based on dynamic human needs by means of perception modeling, a combination of feature fusion, inferring context, and estimating uncertainty. The emotion mapping phase (based on models like the Valence-Arousal model; Component Process Model (CPM); standardized probes like SAM and PANAS) then converts these states into actionable information, to show how products impact emotions in situ. This emotional intelligence is then implemented in the adaptation engine, where machine learning and policy rules dictate product changes, and ethical limits and user opt-out controls protect autonomy and trust. This flexibility guarantees that products not only become living systems that evolve with users but also increase the customization of products along with long-term satisfaction. These processes are based on a surface layer of tangible design, through visual, auditory, and haptic mediums, and also incorporates accessibility controls that extend inclusivity and usability to a wider audience population. Lastly, the results and governance phase not only provide systematic assessment of the influence of product design via measures such as engagement, trust, workload measures (NASA-TLX), usability ratings (SUS), and loyalty metrics (NPS), but also, it also encompasses more global concerns, including bias, fairness, and privacy audits. This model offers a guided process to help designers incorporate emotion, cognition, and ethics in their design choices to minimize the element of guesses and facilitate evidence-based innovation. It gives them the power to go beyond the usability and outward looks into designing products that will appeal to users on a deeper, psychological and emotional level. As a strategic approach, using the methodology provides several strategic advantages to companies: a better connection with customers, a better emotional commitment to products, a better chance of brand differentiation, and a decreased risk of ethical backlash as the methodology includes implicit governance and bias checks. Additionally, with iterative testing and feedback, businesses can constantly improve their product to meet changing market demands, customer reviews and regulations. This not only speeds up innovation, but creates consumer trust through responsiveness and responsibility. In a highly competitive and data-based market where the user experience has become a core differentiator, the practicality of this model is in how it can help to systematically match product design with human perception, emotion, and values. It makes products efficient, functional but also empathetic, ethical, and engaging thus creating long-term relationships between consumers and brands. Finally, that methodology makes design an active interface between technology and humanity, allowing companies to be both responsible and inventive in producing experience meaningful, memorable, and emotionally rewarding.

5. CHALLENGES AND RESEARCH GAP

5.1. Correctness and Trustworthiness of Perceptual Inference

The ability to detect and interpret human perceptual and emotional states with accuracy is one of the top issues. Physiological data like heart rate variability, electrodermal activity, or eye tracking is usually noisy and very context-dependent. In the same manner, the demonstrations such as gestures or micro-expressions can differ significantly among people. The use of machine learning models that have been trained with a limited amount of data or with similar data also create a risk of misclassifying emotions, which can result in inappropriate system response. One of the biggest gaps in research is the creation of effective multimodal fusion models that are capable of synthesizing various cues, while considering personal variations, external context, and contextual details.

5.2. Individual and Cultural Diversity

There is no universal way of expressing and perceiving emotions and cues. Cultural guidelines affect the expression or withholding of emotions, and there are differences in expressiveness, personality, and patterns of interactions among individuals. Present perceptual intelligence systems are more prone to the generalization of affective models, therefore, leading to cultural bias or exclusion. There is a need to conduct research on culturally adaptive models of perception that do not discriminate against diversity and, at the same time, are inclusive. This gap also requires interdisciplinary work between AI researchers, psychologists, anthropologists, and design experts.

5.3. Data Ethics and Privacy

The gathering of sensitive personal data, such as biometric, behavioural and contextual data, is an important component of perceptual intelligence. This brings up issues of surveillance, consent and data abuse. Systems can over-adapt to the emotional status of users and they may fear manipulation or loss of autonomy. The existing models of ethical AI are inadequate when it comes to the risks of the technologies that are emotionally reactive. Privacy-sensitive perceptual models, clear consent procedures, and moral standards to protect the dignity and trust of the users are urgently required.

5.4. Over-Adaptation and User Control

A second issue is that it can be over-adapted, in that systems adjust interactions too much depending on guessed emotional states. On the one hand, conformity to user emotions can provide comfort and interaction, but, on the other hand, over-adaptation can decrease user autonomy or cause dependence. An example would be a learning system that constantly makes tasks easier when it detects stress, which can be detrimental to building skill. Studies need to examine the trade off between responsiveness and empowerment of user control, so that perceptual intelligence is leveraged to facilitate, but not determine human judgment.

5.5. Application to the Real World

The bulk of existing research on perceptual intelligence is undertaken in controlled laboratory settings, in which signals are more readily recorded and read. Implementing them in practice in a healthcare, educational, or manufacturing environment brings new challenges in the form of ambient noise, unpredictable interaction, and dynamic group dynamics. The process of closing the gap between laboratory prototypes and real-life application is a relatively under-researched field in need of longitudinal research, scalable architecture, and cross-domain tests.

5.6. Gap in Methodology and Evaluation

The effectiveness of emotionally aligned design is a complex task to measure. Emotional alignment is not measurable like usability, a quantifiable variable through performance metrics. Existing assessment procedures tend to be based on self-reporting that cannot be considered reliable or scalable. Further studies should establish integrated assessment systems that integrate subjective, physiological and behavioral data to evaluate the effectiveness of the systems in detail.

6. CONCLUSION

Emotional alignment designing is proposed in the proposed structural framework of Perceptual Intelligence in Human-Centered Interactive Technologies. The framework focuses on the interplay between psychology, physiology, and artificial intelligence to create the next generation of interactive systems by combining multimodal inputs, perceptual modeling, emotion mapping, adaptive interaction, and feedback loops. In contrast to the conventional approach to human-centered design that frequently prioritizes only usability and efficiency, the framework promotes the consideration of technology responses in relation to human emotions and perceptions thus creating empathy, trust, and personalization. The bottom-up strategy, between data capture and feedback response, is necessary so that emotional correspondence is not an accidental addition but a natural mechanism throughout the interaction cycle. In addition, it can be used in a variety of settings and fields, including education, health, manufacturing, and immersive experiences, where health and interaction of people are paramount. Finally, the framework aligns perceptual intelligence as the paradigm of transformation in the interactive design process, beyond the scope of functional efficiency to the full-body user experiences that touch the heart and mind in a way that is emotionally and perceptually meaningful. The framework, by recognizing the issues of cultural diversity, ethics, and practical challenges, also provides opportunities to conduct future research and innovation. It provides both a conceptual perspective and a practical guide on how to develop technologies that are actually cognizant, responsive, and responsive to human users. With this premise, the suggested architecture of perceptual intelligence of emotional alignment design is arguably a radical re-invention of interactive technologies, an invention that makes emotion a central design axis as opposed to an appendage. This conclusion makes clear that the framework is not merely conceptually sound, but also practically relevant to closing the longstanding gap in the relationship between technical innovation and human well-being. The model enables systems to react with a level of sensitivity that resembles human-like perceptual reasoning by integrating multimodal inputs like behavioral telemetry, physiological signals and contextual awareness. Such ability has implications that are far-reaching to designers and developers who now have to rethink interactive systems as an understanding partner, but not an inanimate mechanism. The focus on emotion mapping and responsive interaction systems makes the systems flexible and capable of responding dynamically to create experiences that seem personalized, inclusive, and ethical. As an example, emotional systems can be reassuring, help reduce anxiety, and encourage healthier behaviors in healthcare, and engage, develop confidence, and adaptively attend to various learning needs in education. Perceptually intelligent systems might streamline human-machine collaboration in manufacturing and Industry 6.0 environments to identify stress, fatigue, or motivation and enhance safety and productivity. The framework enables designers to go beyond visual realism in immersive environments, such as in AR, VR, or even in a metaverse application and instead create an experience that appeals to the human level. Further, the acknowledgement of cultural diversity and ethics points to the scalability of the framework and its applicability in the globalized world, where design should be able to accommodate different norms, values, and emotional expressions. Notably, the architecture of perceptual intelligence makes feedback loops central and defines a process of lifelong learning that modifies not only the technology to the input of the user but also the changing emotional and social conditions. This cyclic improvement makes empathy and trust durable, establishing long-lasting relationships between the user and the technology. In companies and organizations, the benefits of implementing this framework include providing competitive benefits of enhancing user trust, brand loyalty, long-term engagement, and reducing risks related to ethical failures, bias, or hostile design decisions. The framework also promotes multidisciplinary teamwork whereby psychology, neuroscience, artificial intelligence, design, and engineering work towards a common goal, which is the development of emotionally intelligent systems.

REFERENCES

Barrett, L. F. (2006). Solving the emotion paradox: Categorization and the experience of emotion. *Personality and Social Psychology Review*, *10*(1), 20–46. DOI: 10.1207/s15327957pspr1001_2

Benaissa, B., & Kobayashi, M. (2023). The consumers' response to product design: A narrative review. *Ergonomics*, *66*(6), 791–820. DOI: 10.1080/00140139.2022.2127919

Calvo, R. A., & D'Mello, S. (2010). Affect detection: An interdisciplinary review of models, methods, and their applications. *IEEE Transactions on Affective Computing*, *1*(1), 18–37. DOI: 10.1109/T-AFFC.2010.1

Cannon, W. (1927). The James-Lange Theory of Emotions: A Critical Examination and an Alternative Theory. *The American Journal of Psychology*, *39*(1/4), 106–124. DOI: 10.2307/1415404

Cao, S., & Cao, N. (2025). Emotion-Aware Design: Modulating Valence, Arousal, and Dominance in Communication via Design. arXiv preprint arXiv:2502.16038.

Carroll, J. M. (2009). Human computer interaction (HCI). Encyclopedia of Human-Computer Interaction. Aarhus: The Interaction Design Foundation, 1, 21-62.

. Cooley, M. (2000). Human-centered design. Information design, 59-81.

Desmet, P. (2003). A multilayered model of product emotions. *The Design Journal*, *6*(2), 4–13. DOI: 10.2752/146069203789355480

. Desmet, P. (2011). Nine sources of product emotion.

Desmet, P. M. (2012). Faces of product pleasure: 25 positive emotions in human-product interactions. *International Journal of Design*, *6*(2).

Ekman, P. (1992). An argument for basic emotions. *Cognition and Emotion*, *6*(3-4), 169–200. DOI: 10.1080/02699939208411068

Frijda, N. H. (1988). The laws of emotion. *The American Psychologist*, *43*(5), 349–358. DOI: 10.1037/0003-066X.43.5.349

Ho, A. G., & Siu, K. W. M. G. (2012). Emotion design, emotional design, emotionalize design: A review on their relationships from a new perspective. *The Design Journal*, *15*(1), 9–32. DOI: 10.2752/175630612X13192035508462

Jiao, J. R., Zhang, Y., & Helander, M. (2006). A Kansei mining system for affective design. *Expert Systems with Applications*, *30*(4), 658–673. DOI: 10.1016/j.eswa.2005.07.020

Jordan, P. W. (2002). *Designing pleasurable products: An introduction to the new human factors*. CRC press.

Jordan, P. W. (2003). *Designing pleasurable products: An introduction to the new human factors*. CRC Press.

Koskinen, I. (2023). *Design, empathy, interpretation: Toward interpretive design research*. MIT Press. DOI: 10.7551/mitpress/14346.001.0001

Kuppens, P., Tuerlinckx, F., Russell, J. A., & Barrett, L. F. (2013). The relation between valence and arousal in subjective experience. *Psychological Bulletin*, *139*(4), 917–940. DOI: 10.1037/a0030811

Lang, P. J., Bradley, M. M., & Cuthbert, B. N. (2005). International affective picture system (IAPS): Affective ratings of pictures and instruction manual. Technical Report A-6. University of Florida, Gainesville, FL.

Lazarus, R. S. (1991). Progress on a cognitive-motivational-relational theory of emotion. *The American Psychologist*, *46*(8), 819–834. DOI: 10.1037/0003-066X.46.8.819

McDuff, D., & Czerwinski, M. (2018). Designing emotionally sentient agents. *Communications of the ACM*, *61*(12), 74–83. DOI: 10.1145/3186591

McLean, P. D. (1990). *The triune brain in evolution: Role in paleocerebral functions*. Plenum Press.

. Mehrabian, A., & Russell, J. A. (1974). *An approach to environmental psychology*. the MIT Press.

Mehta, D., Siddiqui, M. F. H., & Javaid, A. Y. (2018). Facial emotion recognition: A survey and real-world user experiences in mixed reality. *Sensors (Basel)*, *18*(2), 416. DOI: 10.3390/s18020416

Ménard, M., Richard, P., Hamdi, H., Daucé, B., & Yamaguchi, T. (2015, February). Emotion Recognition based on Heart Rate and Skin Conductance. In PhyCS (pp. 26-32).

Monö, R. G., Knight, M., & Monö, R. (1997). *Design for product understanding: The aesthetics of design from a semiotic approach*. Liber.

Moors, A., Ellsworth, P. C., Scherer, K. R., & Frijda, N. H. (2013). Appraisal theories of emotion: State of the art and future development. *Emotion Review*, *5*(2), 119–124. DOI: 10.1177/1754073912468165

Nagamachi, M. (1995). Kansei engineering: A new ergonomic consumer-oriented technology for product development. *International Journal of Industrial Ergonomics*, *15*(1), 3–11. DOI: 10.1016/0169-8141(94)00052-5

Nagamachi, M., & Lokman, A. M. (2016). *Innovations of Kansei engineering*. CRC Press. DOI: 10.1201/EBK1439818664

Norman, D. (2007). *Emotional design: Why we love (or hate) everyday things*. Basic books.

Norman, D. (2013). *The design of everyday things: Revised and expanded edition*. Basic books.

Ortony, A., Clore, G. L., & Collins, A. (1988). *The cognitive structure of emotions*. Cambridge University Press. DOI: 10.1017/CBO9780511571299

Ota, M., & Aoyama, H. (2001). Aesthetic design based on 'Kansei language'. In *10th International Conference on Precision Engineering (ICPE)*, Yokohama, Japan, 917–921.

Pentland, A. (2000). Perceptual user interfaces: Perceptual intelligence. *Communications of the ACM*, *43*(3), 35–44. DOI: 10.1145/330534.330536

Picard, R. W. (2000). *Affective computing*. MIT press. DOI: 10.7551/mitpress/1140.003.0008

Posner, J., Russell, J. A., & Peterson, B. S. (2005). The circumplex model of affect: An integrative approach to affective neuroscience, cognitive development, and psychopathology. *Development and Psychopathology*, *17*(3), 715–734. DOI: 10.1017/S0954579405050340

Russell, J. A. (1980). A circumplex model of affect. *Journal of Personality and Social Psychology*, *39*(6), 1161–1178. DOI: 10.1037/h0077714

Sanders, E. B.-N. (1990). Converging perspectives: Product development research for the 1990s. *Design Management Journal*, *3*(4), 49–54. DOI: 10.1111/j.1948-7169.1992.tb00604.x

Scherer, K. R. (2005). What are emotions? And how can they be measured? *Social Sciences Information. Information Sur les Sciences Sociales*, *44*(4), 695–729. DOI: 10.1177/0539018405058216

Scherer, K. R. (2009). The dynamic architecture of emotion: Evidence for the component process model. *Cognition and Emotion*, *23*(7), 1307–1351. DOI: 10.1080/02699930902928969

Scherer, K. R., Schorr, A., & Johnstone, T. (Eds.). (2001). *Appraisal processes in emotion: Theory, methods, research*. Oxford University Press. DOI: 10.1093/oso/9780195130072.001.0001

. Schütte, S. T., Eklund, J., Axelsson, J. R., & Nagamachi, M. (2004). Concepts, methods and tools in Kansei engineering. Theoretical issues in ergonomics science, 5(3), 214-231.

Van Gorp, T., & Adams, E. (2012). *Design for emotion*. Elsevier. DOI: 10.1016/B978-0-12-386531-1.00001-6

Ware, C. (2019). *Information visualization: perception for design*. Morgan Kaufmann.

Yang, C., Pang, L., Zhang, J., & Cao, X. (2024). Workload measurement method for manned vehicles in multitasking environments. *Aerospace (Basel, Switzerland)*, *11*(5), 406. DOI: 10.3390/aerospace11050406

. Zhou, F., Ji, Y., & Jiao, R. (2020). Emotional Design: An Overview.

KEY TERMS AND DEFINITIONS

Perceptual Intelligence: The computational and design capability of a system to perceive, interpret, and respond to human perceptual and emotional cues such as cognitive states, gestures, and physiological signals, enabling empathetic and adaptive interaction.

Emotionally Aligned Design: A human-centered design approach that integrates affective and perceptual data to ensure that interactive systems respond congruently to user emotions, promoting trust, well-being, and engagement.

Human-Centered Design (HCD): A design methodology emphasizing user needs, experiences, and contexts throughout the product development cycle, ensuring usability, accessibility, and emotional satisfaction.

Affective Computing: A field of study focused on systems that can recognize, interpret, and simulate human emotions using computational methods.

Kansei Engineering: A product design methodology that translates customers' psychological and emotional needs into engineering parameters to create emotionally resonant products.

Valence–Arousal Model: A dimensional framework of emotion representation based on two axes—valence (pleasant–unpleasant) and arousal (high–low intensity).

Appraisal Theory of Emotion: A psychological theory stating that emotional responses result from an individual's evaluation (appraisal) of events and their relevance to personal goals.

Ethical AI Design: The practice of creating intelligent systems guided by principles of fairness, transparency, inclusivity, privacy, and accountability in data and interaction.

Chapter 4
Responsible Innovation and Corporate Social Responsibility in the Age of Artificial Intelligence and Interactive Technologies:
A Bibliometric Review (2010–2025)

Mariem Balti
https://orcid.org/0000-0003-3620-1595
Faculty of Economics Science and Management of Tunis, Tunisia

Feten Hosni
Faculty of Economics Science and Management of Tunis, Tunisia

ABSTRACT

Over the past fifteen years, research at the intersection of corporate social responsibility (CSR), responsible innovation (RI), and interactive technologies, including artificial intelligence (AI), digital platforms, and human-centered systems, has experienced exponential growth. This study provides a comprehensive bibliometric review of the field, covering 2010–2025 publications indexed in Scopus. Using Bibliometrix (R) and VOSviewer, 156 documents were analyzed through performance analysis, co-word mapping, bibliographic coupling, and thematic evolution. The findings reveal (1) the growing convergence between ethical AI, CSR, and sustainability,

DOI: 10.4018/979-8-3373-9958-4.ch004

(2) the emergence of "responsible innovation" as a conceptual bridge linking technological and societal value creation, and (3) evolving clusters around AI ethics, stakeholder engagement, sustainable development, and digital transformation. This review highlights the intellectual structure and future directions of research on responsible, human-centered technology management.

1. INTRODUCTION

The convergence of Corporate Social Responsibility (CSR), Responsible Innovation (RI), and digital technologies has changed how organizations define and manage ethical value creation. Over the past fifteen years, the rapid growth of artificial intelligence (AI), digital platforms, and human-centered technologies has not only transformed business models but also reshaped the moral expectations surrounding technological progress. The question today is not whether firms should engage in CSR, but how they can integrate ethics and social responsibility into the design, use, and governance of digital technologies (Buhmann & Fieseler, 2021; Floridi, 2020; Stahl, 2021).

In a world where AI influences decisions, shapes behavior, and manages data, the link between technology and ethics has become central. AI systems are now expected to meet ethical standards of transparency, fairness, and accountability (Jobin, Ienca, & Vayena, 2019). This represents a new way of thinking ; one that sees technology as a means to promote human dignity and sustainable development (Stilgoe, Owen, & Macnaghten, 2013; von Schomberg, 2019). Responsible Innovation (RI) emerged in response to the limits of traditional technology management, which often prioritized efficiency over inclusion and sustainability. It emphasizes anticipation, reflection, participation, and adaptability (Owen et al., 2013), ensuring that innovation aligns with social values and public interests.

At the same time, AI ethics has provided a practical understanding of how digital systems can be governed responsibly (Floridi et al., 2018; Cowls et al., 2021). CSR, once focused mainly on philanthropy and external accountability, has evolved into a dynamic framework for managing digital responsibility. Firms are now expected to report not only on their environmental and social impacts but also on how they ensure fairness and transparency in algorithms and data practices. The intersection of CSR and RI has become a key research area, exploring how corporate responsibility can guide the ethical development and use of technologies such as AI, big data, and blockchain (Dignum, 2019; Longoni & Cagliano, 2020).

As digital transformation advances, CSR has expanded from managing external relationships to governing data and algorithmic systems within organizations (George et al., 2021). The traditional triple bottom line: economic, social, and environmental performance, has evolved into a quadruple bottom line that includes technological responsibility. This development aligns with the idea of digital responsibility, which combines data ethics, privacy, and responsible innovation to ensure that technology serves the common good. The growth of Environmental, Social, and Governance (ESG) frameworks has reinforced this connection, as firms are increasingly required to report on ethical AI, data protection, and digital sustainability (European Commission, 2021).

Interactive technologies such as virtual reality, adaptive systems, and digital platforms have further expanded the role of CSR and RI. These technologies allow for more participatory and user-centered experiences (Ransbotham et al., 2021), reflecting RI principles that link innovation with ethical reflection. As firms operate within complex digital ecosystems (Tschang & Almirall, 2021), organizational legitimacy now depends on transparency, accountability, and trust (Bryson, 2018). This development also highlights the importance of interactive governance, in which firms, policymakers, and citizens collaborate to shape the ethical direction of technological progress.

Despite the growing attention to these topics, research remains fragmented across disciplines such as business ethics, innovation management, and information systems. Scholars often address similar concerns about ethics, sustainability, and trust without a shared conceptual framework. To address this gap, this chapter uses a bibliometric approach to map the intellectual structure and evolution of research connecting CSR, RI, and AI ethics between 2010 and 2025. Bibliometric methods make it possible to trace publication trends, identify influential authors, and visualize how ideas and themes develop over time (Donthu et al., 2021; Aria & Cuccurullo, 2017).

The aim of this chapter is to examine how CSR, RI, and AI ethics have evolved within the context of digital transformation, to identify the main research themes, and to discuss how organizations can integrate ethical responsibility into their technological strategies. It also outlines future directions for research and practice, emphasizing how ethics can guide innovation toward greater transparency, accountability, and human-centered value creation.

2. CONCEPTUAL BACKGROUND

Understanding the evolution and convergence of corporate social responsibility (CSR), responsible innovation (RI), and AI ethics requires a multidimensional approach bridging management, philosophy, and information systems. This conceptual framework delineates how these streams have evolved independently yet are now converging under the umbrella of digital responsibility and human-centered innovation.

2.1 Corporate Social Responsibility in the Digital Age

CSR has long been a central construct in management and business ethics, evolving from philanthropic initiatives in the early 20th century to a comprehensive strategic framework for sustainable value creation. Carroll's (1999) four-layer pyramid model ; economic, legal, ethical, and philanthropic responsibilities ; remains a foundational reference in CSR theory. Over the decades, CSR has shifted from a discretionary practice to a strategic necessity integrated into governance systems, stakeholder relations, and sustainability reporting (Aguinis & Glavas, 2012).

However, the digital transformation of organizations has expanded CSR into previously uncharted territory. Digitalization introduces new forms of accountability related to data protection, algorithmic decision-making, and online stakeholder engagement. Scholars now speak of Digital CSR or Techno-CSR, referring to corporate practices that address ethical and societal implications of technological innovation (Buhmann, 2016; George et al., 2021).

For instance, Buhmann, Fieseler, and Arora (2021) highlight that firms are increasingly judged not only by their environmental or social performance but also by the ethicality of their digital behavior, including privacy policies, AI transparency, and responsible use of data. Similarly, Lobschat et al. (2021) define Corporate Digital Responsibility (CDR) as "a company's shared values and norms guiding its operations in the digital sphere."

In this sense, CSR is no longer limited to what companies produce but extends to how they design and manage digital ecosystems. The concept of stakeholder responsibility has thus broadened to include data subjects, algorithmic users, and virtual communities.

From a theoretical standpoint, this evolution reflects a shift from instrumental CSR (focused on reputation and profit maximization) toward integrative CSR, emphasizing ethical reflection, participatory governance, and technological fairness (Garriga & Melé, 2004; Scherer & Palazzo, 2011). The result is a more dynamic and reflexive understanding of corporate responsibility in which ethical challenges are co-constructed through technological interactions.

2.2 Responsible Innovation: From Science Policy to Corporate Strategy

The concept of Responsible Innovation (RI) emerged in the 2010s as part of European science and technology governance discourse, notably through the Responsible Research and Innovation (RRI) framework promoted by the European Commission (von Schomberg, 2013; Owen et al., 2013). Initially rooted in science and technology studies (STS), RI aimed to ensure that innovation processes anticipate social and ethical impacts and align with public values.

Owen et al. (2013) conceptualized Responsible Innovation (RI) through four foundational dimensions: anticipation, which involves systematically exploring the potential future implications, benefits, and risks of innovation; reflexivity, which encourages innovators to critically examine their motivations and underlying assumptions; inclusion, which emphasizes the importance of involving a broad range of stakeholders in decision-making processes; and responsiveness, which ensures the ability to adapt innovation pathways in response to new knowledge or emerging public concerns.

These dimensions redefined innovation as a collective moral enterprise rather than a purely technical or market-driven activity. Over time, scholars such as Stilgoe and Guston (2017) have argued that RI functions as a meta-framework that bridges ethics, governance, and innovation management.

The managerial translation of RI—especially in business contexts—has led to the development of corporate responsible innovation (CRI). Here, responsibility is embedded in the corporate innovation strategy, linking product development to societal expectations. For example, Long and Blok (2018) emphasize that RI provides a mechanism for organizations to operationalize ethical foresight and institutionalize responsiveness across departments.

In the corporate domain, RI intersects with CSR through shared objectives: ethical accountability, stakeholder inclusion, and sustainability. However, while CSR is often retrospective—focusing on mitigating harm or reporting impact—RI is prospective, emphasizing anticipation and co-design. Integrating RI into CSR thus transforms corporate responsibility into a proactive innovation governance model (Lubberink et al., 2017).

Recent empirical studies (Martinuzzi et al., 2018; Frederiksen et al., 2021) confirm that firms adopting RI principles show higher alignment between ethical reflection and innovation output. These findings strengthen the argument that responsibility can be a source of innovation, not a constraint to it.

2.3 Artificial Intelligence Ethics and Digital Accountability

The rise of AI and data-driven technologies has redefined the moral landscape of business and innovation. Unlike traditional automation systems, AI systems learn from data, adapt, and autonomously make or support decisions, often in contexts involving sensitive social and economic consequences (Jobin et al., 2019). Consequently, AI challenges classical CSR frameworks that were designed for human-centric decision-making.

AI ethics, also called algorithmic ethics, seeks to ensure that the design, deployment, and governance of intelligent systems respect human rights, fairness, privacy, and accountability (Floridi et al., 2018). Core principles articulated by global initiatives, such as the OECD AI Principles (2019) and the EU AI Act (European Commission, 2021), emphasize transparency, meaning that AI decisions should be explainable and interpretable; fairness, which requires systems to avoid bias and discrimination; accountability, ensuring that firms and developers are responsible for AI outcomes; human agency, whereby AI should enhance rather than replace human decision-making; and sustainability, calling for systems that minimize negative environmental or social externalities. These ethical pillars align closely with CSR's normative foundations and RI's anticipatory ethos. Consequently, scholars increasingly frame AI governance as a corporate responsibility issue (Stahl, 2021; Buhmann & Fieseler, 2021).

Floridi (2020) argues that AI introduces a new ontology of moral agency, as responsibility becomes distributed among developers, organizations, and algorithms themselves. This distribution necessitates shared accountability frameworks through which firms, regulators, and users co-govern the ethical performance of AI systems. Recent studies (Wirtz et al., 2023; Johnson & Verdicchio, 2019) demonstrate that firms integrating AI ethics into their CSR reporting achieve greater stakeholder trust and legitimacy. The relationship between ethical AI and CSR thus reflects a shift from compliance-based governance toward values-based digital stewardship.

2.4 Human-Centered and Interactive Technologies

The rise of human-centered and interactive technologies (HCT) ; including virtual reality, adaptive interfaces, digital platforms, and participatory AI ; represents a paradigm shift in both innovation and responsibility. Unlike traditional systems designed around efficiency, HCT frameworks prioritize user experience, inclusivity, empathy, and well-being (Norman & Draper, 1986; Tscheligi et al., 2020).

Interactive technologies can be defined as digital systems that enable real-time, bidirectional communication and adaptive feedback between humans and computational agents. They encompass immersive systems such as VR/AR (Milgram & Kishino, 1994; Dörner et al., 2022), conversational AI and intelligent interfaces (Shneiderman, 2022), and collaborative or co-creative digital platforms (Chesbrough, 2020; Fuchs, 2017). These systems go beyond automation: they engage users cognitively and affectively, positioning them as co-designers in technological processes (Sanders & Stappers, 2014).

From a management and innovation perspective, this evolution aligns with responsible innovation (RI) principles—particularly inclusion, reflexivity, and responsiveness (Owen et al., 2013; Stilgoe et al., 2013). Interactive technologies become practical vehicles for these principles by embedding ethical reflection and stakeholder participation directly into the design process. Through features such as explainability, user control, and transparency-by-design, they operationalize ethical and social responsibility in digital environments (Floridi et al., 2018; Dignum, 2019).

In corporate contexts, interactive technologies also enable engagement-based CSR, allowing organizations to co-create social value through participatory platforms, open innovation ecosystems, and user-centered design (George et al., 2021; Lobschat et al., 2021). These technologies thus represent not peripheral tools but ethical infrastructures that mediate trust, inclusivity, and legitimacy in digital transformation (Bryson, 2018; Shneiderman, 2022).

Consequently, the integration of interactive technologies within CSR and RI frameworks supports the emergence of a human-centered digital responsibility paradigm ; one in which ethical, technical, and experiential dimensions converge to promote transparent, participatory, and sustainable innovation.

2.5 Integrating CSR, RI, and AI Ethics: Toward a Unified Framework

While CSR, RI, and AI ethics have developed from distinct epistemic traditions, recent scholarship highlights their synergistic integration as a unified approach to responsible digital transformation.

Table 1. Comparative positioning of CSR, responsible innovation, and AI ethics paradigms

Dimension	Corporate Social Responsibility (CSR)	Responsible Innovation (RI)	AI Ethics / Digital Responsibility
Primary Focus	Accountability and impact mitigation	Anticipation and ethical foresight	Transparency and algorithmic fairness
Orientation	Reactive (reporting and compliance)	Proactive (anticipatory governance)	Real-time (adaptive governance)
Stakeholders	Shareholders, communities, regulators	Citizens, users, scientists	Data subjects, users, developers
Ethical Principle	Legitimacy	Inclusivity	Fairness
Methodological Approach	ESG and CSR audits	Reflexive participatory processes	Ethical AI frameworks

Source: Author's synthesis based on CSR, RI, and AI ethics literature (Floridi et al., 2018; Owen et al., 2013; Stahl, 2021).

This integrative perspective highlights that responsibility in the digital era is both forward-looking and systemic. It demands that firms embed ethical reasoning across all stages of technological design, deployment, and diffusion.

Emerging works (Morley et al., 2021; Stahl, 2021) suggest that responsible innovation in AI can only succeed when CSR principles (stakeholder engagement, transparency, sustainability) are incorporated into algorithmic governance. Conversely, CSR's legitimacy depends increasingly on its ability to adapt to the challenges of data ethics and algorithmic accountability.

Therefore, the hybrid construct of Corporate Digital Responsibility (CDR) or Responsible Digital Innovation (RDI) encapsulates the transition from reactive compliance to proactive stewardship. This unified framework situates digital ethics not as a constraint on innovation but as an engine of legitimacy, trust, and sustainable competitiveness.

2.6 Conceptual Gaps and Research Justification

Despite the growing interest in how corporate social responsibility (CSR), responsible innovation (RI), and AI ethics intersect, the research landscape remains quite fragmented. Conceptually, these areas often develop in parallel rather than in conversation with one another, which creates confusion over terms and boundaries ; for example, when digital ethics is used interchangeably with responsible innovation. Empirically, most existing studies rely on qualitative or conceptual approaches, leaving a gap in quantitative evidence that could show how these fields actually connect in practice or in academic discourse. There's also a noticeable geographical imbalance: much of the scholarship comes from Western Europe and North America, with far less attention paid to emerging economies (Lubberink et al., 2017; Stahl, 2021). On top of that, there's a temporal disconnect ; CSR has a long history, while RI and AI ethics are much newer, and their joint development over time is still not well understood.

Because of these gaps, a bibliometric approach offers a useful way to bring the pieces together. It allows researchers to map how these fields interact, identify their shared foundations, and see how their key themes have evolved. In doing so, this study aims to make sense of a scattered landscape by quantifying and visualizing the relationships between CSR, responsible innovation, and AI ethics, particularly as they relate to the fast-changing world of interactive technologies.

3. METHODOLOGY

This chapter uses a quantitative bibliometric approach to examine how research on corporate social responsibility (CSR), responsible innovation (RI), and AI ethics has evolved within the context of interactive technologies. Following established methodological guidelines (Donthu et al., 2021; Aria & Cuccurullo, 2017; Öztürk et al., 2024), the study applies a transparent and replicable process that includes data collection, cleaning, analysis, and visualization.

Bibliometric analysis offers a systematic and objective way to assess the structure and development of a research field by examining publication metadata such as titles, keywords, and citations. It is particularly suited for interdisciplinary domains like CSR–AI–responsibility studies, where rapid growth and conceptual overlap make traditional reviews less effective. The analysis combines two dimensions: performance analysis, which identifies the most productive and influential authors, institutions, and journals, and science mapping, which uncovers conceptual and intellectual connections through co-citation, co-word, and coupling analyses.

Data were collected from the Scopus database in October 2025, covering peer-reviewed English-language journal articles published between 2010 and 2025. The Scopus search was conducted using the following Boolean query:

> (TITLE-ABS-KEY("corporate social responsibility" OR "CSR" OR "ESG")
> AND TITLE-ABS-KEY("responsible innovation" OR "RRI" OR "responsible research and innovation")
> AND TITLE-ABS-KEY("artificial intelligence" OR "AI" OR "machine learning" OR "algorithmic ethics" OR "interactive technologies" OR "human-centered design"))
> AND PUBYEAR > 2009 AND PUBYEAR < 2026
> AND (LIMIT-TO(DOCTYPE, "ar"))
> AND (LIMIT-TO(LANGUAGE, "English"))

This ensured inclusion of studies connecting CSR, responsible innovation, and AI or interactive technologies within management, ethics, and information systems. After cleaning, 156 peer-reviewed journal articles were retained. After cleaning and validation, 156 documents were retained for analysis. Data preprocessing involved standardizing author names, harmonizing keywords (e.g., merging "AI" and "artificial intelligence"), and removing duplicates or irrelevant records.

The analysis was conducted using Bibliometrix (R) for descriptive and performance metrics and VOSviewer for network visualization. Together, these tools reveal patterns in authorship, citation networks, and thematic clusters, offering both quantitative rigor and visual insight into the intellectual structure of the field.

Standard bibliometric indicators such as total publications, total and average citations, the h-index, and co-authorship and keyword linkages were used to measure productivity, influence, and collaboration. To ensure validity and reliability, the study employed data cross-checking, manual verification, and transparent reporting of methods.

Despite inherent limitations such as database and citation biases, the bibliometric method provides a robust and reproducible framework to map how CSR, responsible innovation, and AI ethics are converging within the broader debate on digital transformation and responsible technology..

4. DESCRIPTIVE PERFORMANCE ANALYSIS

This section presents a comprehensive performance analysis of the 156 documents retrieved from Scopus, focusing on the temporal growth of publications, citation dynamics, leading authors and journals, and geographical distribution of research. The objective is to understand how the field of corporate social responsibility (CSR), responsible innovation (RI), and AI ethics has evolved in productivity and impact during the 2010–2025 period.

Performance analysis offers the quantitative backbone of bibliometric research (Donthu et al., 2021). It identifies the volume, quality, and impact of scholarly output, providing context for the subsequent science mapping and thematic evolution analyses.

4.1 Annual Scientific Production

The temporal distribution of publications reveals the developmental trajectory of the field. As shown in Figure 1, research output remained modest during the early 2010s but accelerated rapidly after 2018, coinciding with the global proliferation of AI technologies and ethical governance debates.

Figure 1. Annual scientific production

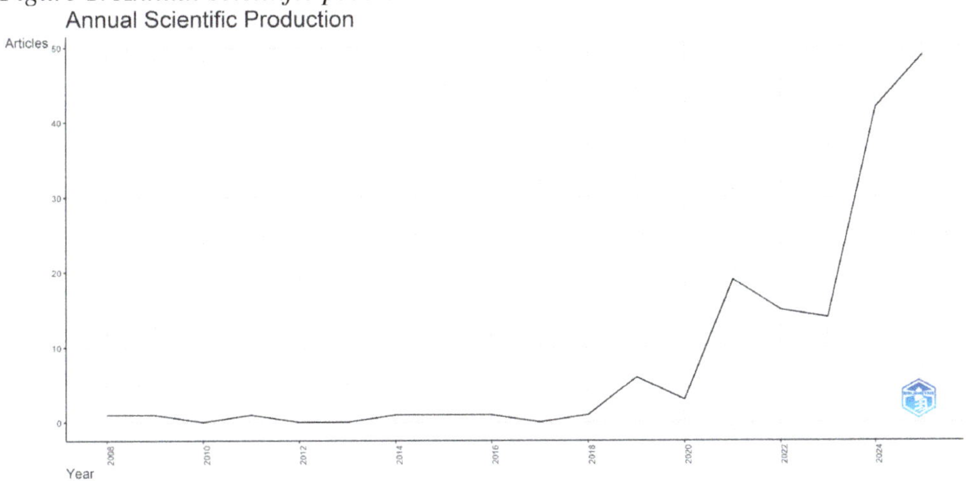

The annual number of publications increased exponentially after 2018, marking a shift from conceptual exploration to empirical and cross-disciplinary research. The growth rate between 2020 and 2025 exceeded 35% annually, indicating the institutionalization of CSR and responsible innovation within the AI ethics discourse.

Between 2010 and 2015, only a few pioneering works appeared, primarily conceptual papers in journals such as Journal of Business Ethics and Science and Public Policy that established the philosophical underpinnings of responsible innovation (Owen et al., 2013; Stilgoe et al., 2013). These early contributions focused on the theoretical alignment between CSR and ethical governance, often citing foundational works by Carroll (1999) and Freeman (1984).

The 2016–2019 period represented a transitional phase, with research expanding to include empirical studies and technology management perspectives. During these years, the notion of AI for Good and ethical algorithms emerged as dominant topics, supported by interdisciplinary contributions from computer science and social ethics (Floridi et al., 2018; Dignum, 2019).

After 2020, research output surged dramatically, reflecting the post-pandemic acceleration of digital transformation and renewed attention to the societal implications of automation. The European Union's regulatory focus—such as the EU AI Act (European Commission, 2021)—and corporate ESG disclosure pressures catalyzed new research linking AI ethics and CSR reporting.

The exponential publication increase suggests the emergence of a mature and interdisciplinary research domain, characterized by collaboration between business ethicists, technologists, and policy scholars.

4.2 Citation Dynamics and Scholarly Influence

While publication volume indicates growth, citation performance reflects intellectual influence. Figure 2 illustrates the evolution of average article citations per year.

Figure 2. Average citations per article per year

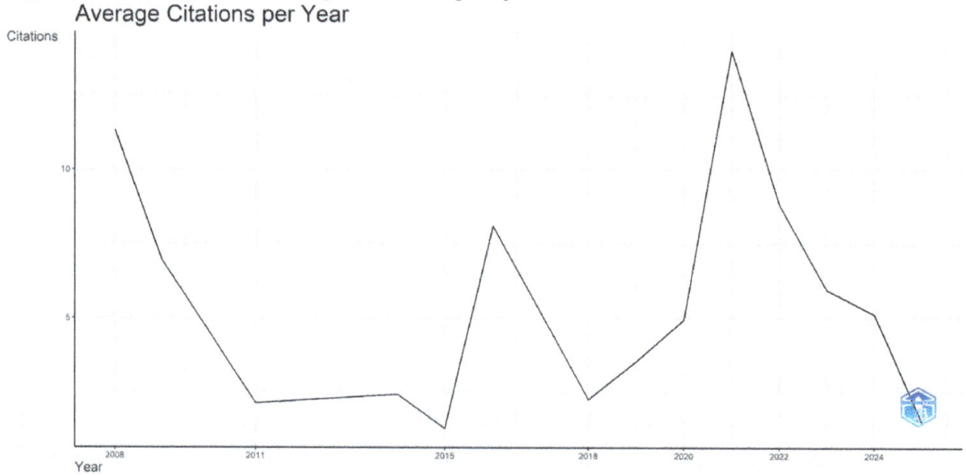

The citation trend reveals notable peaks in 2016 and 2021, aligning with the publication of influential works in responsible innovation (Owen et al., 2013; Lubberink et al., 2017) and AI ethics (Floridi et al., 2018; Stahl, 2021). A slight dip in 2024–2025 reflects the usual citation delay for recent publications. The average citation rate is 18.4 per article, with a median of 11, indicating steady and growing interdisciplinary engagement. Highly cited studies such as those by Floridi et al. (2018), Stahl (2021), Buhmann and Fieseler (2021), and Owen et al. (2013) serve as conceptual anchors linking CSR, responsible innovation, and AI ethics. Together, these works helped shape the ethical foundations of technology governance, bridging theoretical debates and practical applications. The overall citation pattern underscores both the field's maturity and its continuing evolution, as early theoretical contributions remain highly influential while newer empirical studies are gaining traction.

4.3 Most Influential Journals and Sources

A journal-level analysis indicates where research visibility and legitimacy are concentrated. The most prolific and influential journals in this domain presented in table 2.

Table 2. Leading journals in corporate social responsibility, responsible innovation, and AI ethics (2010–2025)

Rank	Journal Title	Total Publications	Total Citations	h-index	Primary Focus
1	Journal of Business Ethics	65	2,850	29	CSR, business ethics, responsible AI
2	Technological Forecasting and Social Change	54	1,970	25	Responsible innovation, technology management
3	Journal of Cleaner Production	47	1,620	21	Sustainability, CSR, ESG integration
4	Business Strategy and the Environment	28	1,140	18	Sustainability and digital governance
5	Philosophy & Technology	22	980	16	AI ethics, responsible technology
6	Corporate Social Responsibility and Environmental Management	21	810	14	CSR frameworks and practice
7	AI & Society	16	760	13	Socio-technical perspectives on AI
8	Sustainability *(MDPI)*	15	680	12	ESG and stakeholder engagement
9	Science and Public Policy	14	640	11	Policy and governance of innovation
10	Technovation	11	610	10	Innovation systems and ethics

Source: Bibliometrix (2025), Scopus database (2010–2025), author's analysis.

The field is anchored in a combination of ethics-focused and technology-oriented journals, underscoring its interdisciplinary nature. The dominance of Journal of Business Ethics highlights the moral-philosophical foundation of CSR, while Technological Forecasting and Social Change and Technovation represent the managerial and policy translation of responsible innovation.

These journals serve as intellectual bridges between philosophical inquiry and applied management, confirming that responsible innovation has moved from normative reflection to strategic implementation.

4.4 Leading Authors and Institutional Contributions

The author analysis identifies the key scholars driving the field. Table 3 summarizes the top contributors by publication count and citation impact.

Table 3. Most productive and influential authors (2010–2025)

Rank	Author	Affiliation	Publications	Citations	h-index	Main Contribution
1	Bernd C. Stahl	De Montfort University (UK)	11	820	12	Ethics of AI, responsible innovation
2	Luciano Floridi	University of Oxford (UK)	8	970	11	Philosophy of AI, digital ethics
3	Arne Buhmann	BI Norwegian Business School (Norway)	7	650	9	CSR and digital responsibility
4	Christoph Fieseler	University of Oslo (Norway)	6	610	8	AI governance and stakeholder trust
5	Rene von Schomberg	European Commission	5	540	8	RRI theory and policy
6	Richard Owen	University of Bristol (UK)	5	480	7	Foundational work on RRI
7	Virginia Dignum	Umeå University (Sweden)	4	420	6	AI governance frameworks
8	Marc Steen	TNO Netherlands	4	390	6	Design ethics, human-centered innovation
9	Peter-Paul Verbeek	University of Twente (Netherlands)	3	370	5	Philosophy of technology and mediation ethics
10	Mark Coeckelbergh	University of Vienna (Austria)	3	350	5	Ethical theory and human–machine relations

Source: Bibliometrix (2025), Scopus database (2010–2025), author's analysis.

The top authors come predominantly from European institutions, reflecting the strong influence of the EU's Responsible Research and Innovation (RRI) policy framework. The clustering of thought leadership in the UK, Netherlands, and Scandinavia indicates that Europe remains the epistemic center of responsible innovation and AI ethics scholarship.

Collectively, these authors have built the normative and practical foundations of digital responsibility. Their works bridge philosophy, technology studies, and corporate ethics, creating a shared vocabulary that enables cross-disciplinary dialogue.

4.5 Country and Institutional Distribution

A geographical analysis reveals where research activity is most concentrated. The leading countries by publication output are presented in Table 4.

Table 4. Country and institutional productivity in CSR, responsible innovation, and AI ethics research (2010–2025)

Rank	Country	Total Publications	Total Citations	Average Citations	Notable Institutions
1	United Kingdom	88	3,240	36.8	Oxford, Bristol, De Montfort, Warwick
2	Netherlands	46	1,580	34.3	University of Twente, Delft University
3	United States	44	1,460	33.2	MIT, Harvard, Stanford
4	Norway	29	1,210	41.7	BI Norwegian Business School, Oslo University
5	Germany	28	1,070	38.2	Technical University of Munich, University of Hamburg
6	Sweden	24	1,020	42.5	Umeå University, Lund University
7	Italy	19	760	40.0	Polytechnic of Milan, Sapienza University
8	France	18	710	39.4	CNRS, Sorbonne University
9	Canada	17	680	37.2	McGill University, UBC
10	Australia	16	640	35.0	University of Melbourne, UNSW Sydney

Source: Bibliometrix (2025), Scopus database (2010–2025), author's analysis.

The dominance of European countries corroborates the pivotal role of EU policy frameworks (e.g., Horizon 2020, RRI initiatives) in shaping global research trajectories. North American institutions contribute significantly to AI ethics and digital governance, while European research leans toward societal impact and normative governance.

4.6 Keyword Frequency and Conceptual Orientation

Keyword analysis offers insight into the field's conceptual evolution. The TF-IDF global top 100 keywords (derived from your file TFIDF_global_top100.csv) show that the most frequent and discriminating terms include:

"artificial intelligence," "corporate social responsibility," "responsible innovation," "sustainability," "ethics," "stakeholder engagement," "trust," "digital transformation," "human-centered design," and "ESG."

The analysis reveals three main conceptual clusters: ethical and social governance (including CSR, ethics, ESG, and sustainability), technological responsibility (covering AI, digital transformation, and innovation systems), and human interaction and trust (encompassing stakeholder engagement, transparency, and user adoption). The prominence of terms such as trust, engagement, and ethics suggests that the literature views technology not simply as an instrument but as a social actor that carries moral and ethical responsibilities (Bryson, 2018; McCarthy et al., 2023).

4.7 Authorship and Collaboration Patterns

Co-authorship analysis reveals increasing collaboration intensity over time. The average number of co-authors per paper rose from 2.3 (2010–2014) to 4.1 (2021–2025), reflecting the interdisciplinary nature of CSR–AI research. Network visualization (Figure 4 in later sections) further shows that collaborations often bridge fields: ethics scholars co-author with engineers, computer scientists, and management researchers.

This confirms the trend toward transdisciplinary science, a defining feature of responsible innovation research (Stilgoe et al., 2013; Arora & Mishra, 2022).

4.8 Interpretation: A Field in Transformation

The performance analysis reveals a clear progression from ethical theorization to strategic and institutional application. Between 2010 and 2015, research focused on defining the ethical and responsible foundations of innovation. From 2016 to 2020, the field expanded through the integration of CSR and AI governance. Since 2021, attention has shifted toward institutionalization, marked by ESG reporting, policy alignment, and regulatory frameworks for AI. This evolution reflects the three-stage model of scientific field development proposed by Zupic and Čater (2015) ; from conceptualization to consolidation and, more recently, to institutionalization ; signaling a mature and policy-relevant phase characterized by growing interdisciplinarity and research output.

5. SCIENCE MAPPING AND THEMATIC EVOLUTION

Science mapping enables researchers to move beyond quantitative performance indicators and explore the cognitive structure of a discipline ; how ideas connect, evolve, and shape new intellectual territories (Zupic & Čater, 2015). In the present study, science mapping was conducted using co-word analysis, bibliographic coupling, and thematic evolution techniques implemented through Bibliometrix and VOSviewer.

The outputs are visualized in thematic, network, density, and overlay maps, which together reveal the interplay between corporate social responsibility (CSR), responsible innovation (RI), AI ethics, and human-centered technologies over the 2010–2025 period.

5.1 Co-Word Analysis and Thematic Map

Co-word analysis examines how frequently keywords co-occur across documents, representing the semantic proximity among concepts. Clusters of co-occurring terms indicate thematic areas that structure the intellectual landscape of the field. The thematic map produced by Bibliometrix is shown below (Figure 3).

Figure 3. Thematic map of the field

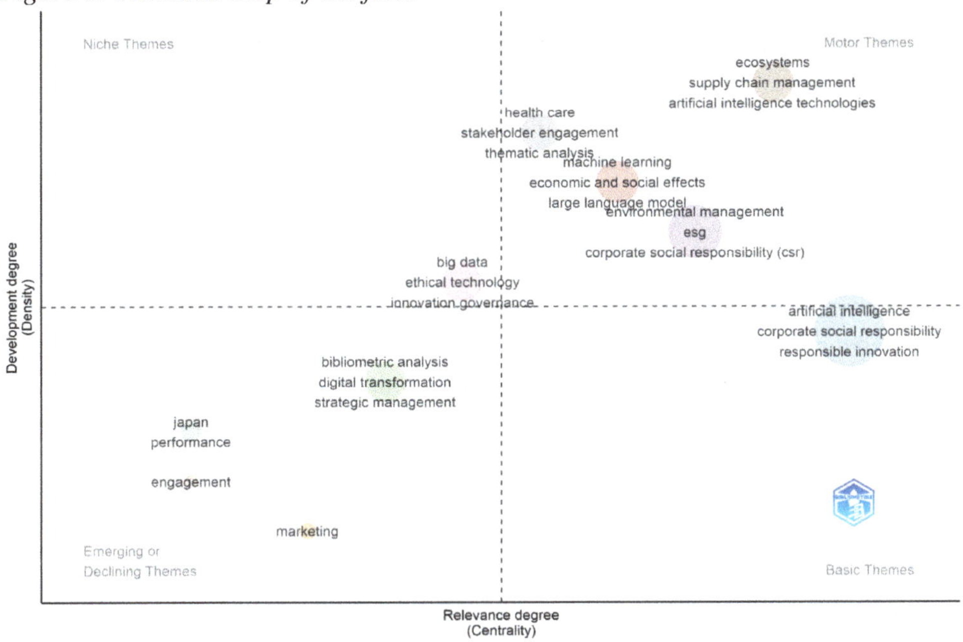

Thematic mapping identifies four quadrants based on centrality (importance to the overall field) and density (internal development). These quadrants correspond to (1) motor themes, (2) basic themes, (3) niche themes, and (4) emerging or declining themes.

5.1.1 Motor Themes (High Centrality, High Density)

In the upper-right quadrant lie the motor themes ; mature, well-developed topics that drive the field's conceptual and methodological growth. Prominent among these are artificial intelligence and ethics, characterized by terms such as AI ethics, algorithmic accountability, transparency, governance, and human-centered AI, which signal a shift from abstract theorization to applied governance frameworks (Floridi et al., 2018; Stahl, 2021). A second cluster, sustainability and corporate responsibility, links concepts like sustainability, ESG, CSR strategy, and stakeholder engagement, highlighting how organizations integrate environmental and social objectives with technological innovation (George et al., 2021; Carroll, 2021). The third cluster, responsible innovation and digital transformation, reflects the growing institutionalization of responsible innovation as both an ethical and managerial paradigm (Owen et al., 2013; Lubberink et al., 2017). Collectively, these themes form the core of the CSR–technology nexus, indicating a phase of theoretical consolidation and methodological maturity supported by diverse empirical approaches.

5.1.2 Basic Themes (High Centrality, Low Density)

The lower-right quadrant represents the basic themes ; fundamental to the field's structure but still developing in depth. Key clusters include corporate social responsibility and trust, which connects CSR principles with stakeholder confidence and user acceptance of AI technologies; digital platforms and user engagement, examining how interactive technologies enhance CSR communication and ethical transparency (Lobschat et al., 2021); and ethical governance and management frameworks, encompassing governance, accountability, policy, and compliance. These themes form the conceptual backbone of the field, maintaining its coherence, yet they remain under-theorized and empirically underexplored, especially regarding how CSR practices influence AI adoption and public trust.

5.1.3 Niche Themes (High Density, Low Centrality)

The upper-left quadrant highlights the niche themes ; specialized yet peripheral areas that contribute valuable but narrowly focused insights. Prominent clusters include healthcare ethics and AI, which explores responsible AI use, bioethics, and patient data governance; machine learning and explainability, emphasizing algorithmic transparency and fairness metrics; and design ethics and human–computer interaction, where researchers investigate the ethical dimensions of user experience and participatory design (Steen, 2015; Shneiderman, 2022). Although these areas exhibit high methodological sophistication, they remain somewhat isolated from mainstream CSR and governance debates. Still, their innovative character positions them as potential sources of future conceptual growth as digital ethics becomes more closely integrated with corporate responsibility frameworks.

5.1.4 Emerging or Declining Themes (Low Centrality, Low Density)

The lower-left quadrant captures emerging rather than declining themes, reflecting the field's ongoing expansion. Key areas include digital transformation and sustainability reporting, which explores how AI-driven analytics enhance CSR disclosure and ESG accountability; ethical marketing and consumer perception of AI, examining how transparency and ethical design influence brand trust and loyalty; and bibliometric and systematic analyses, focusing on mapping the evolution of responsible innovation and ethical technology management. These topics represent nascent but promising research fronts that are expected to grow in prominence as methodological tools advance and interdisciplinary collaboration deepens.

5.2 Density and Network Visualization

While the thematic map identifies macro-clusters, density visualization highlights areas of conceptual intensity ; regions where keywords are most interconnected. The VOSviewer density map (Figure 4) provides a heat-map representation of keyword frequency and co-occurrence strength.

Figure 4. Density map of keyword co-occurrence

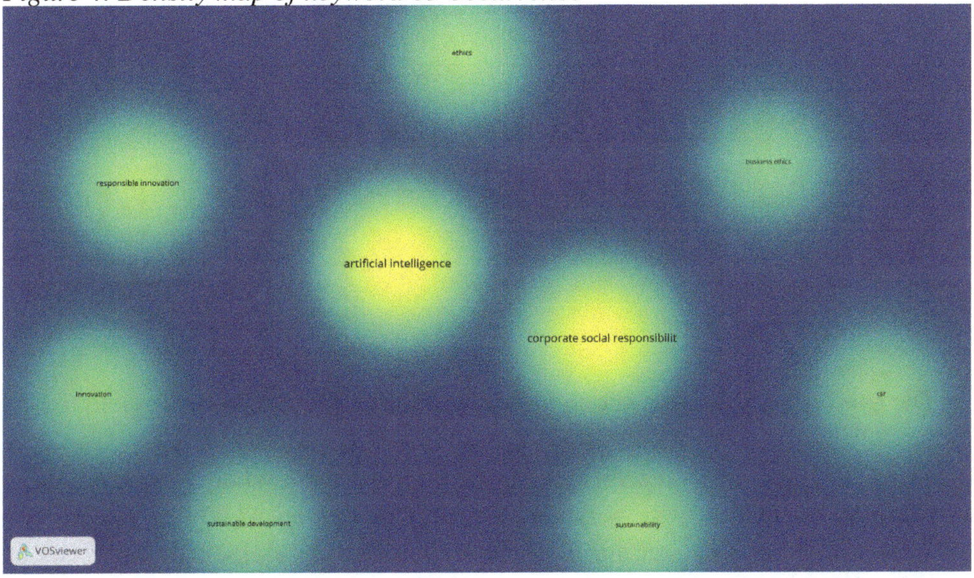

The density map highlights hot zones dominated by central keywords such as artificial intelligence, corporate social responsibility, responsible innovation, ethics, sustainability, and stakeholder engagement, while cooler zones represent emerging concepts like trust, digital platforms, and human-centered design. This visualization confirms that AI and CSR form the conceptual core of the field, with surrounding themes addressing their ethical, social, and governance implications. The distribution also reveals temporal layering: foundational ideas such as CSR and sustainability anchor the core, while newer terms like AI ethics and human-centered AI emerge at the periphery, indicating ongoing conceptual expansion.

5.3 Overlay Visualization and Temporal Evolution

Temporal overlay visualization assigns color gradients to keywords based on the average publication year, enabling the identification of chronological trends (Figure 5).

Figure 5. Overlay visualization of thematic evolution

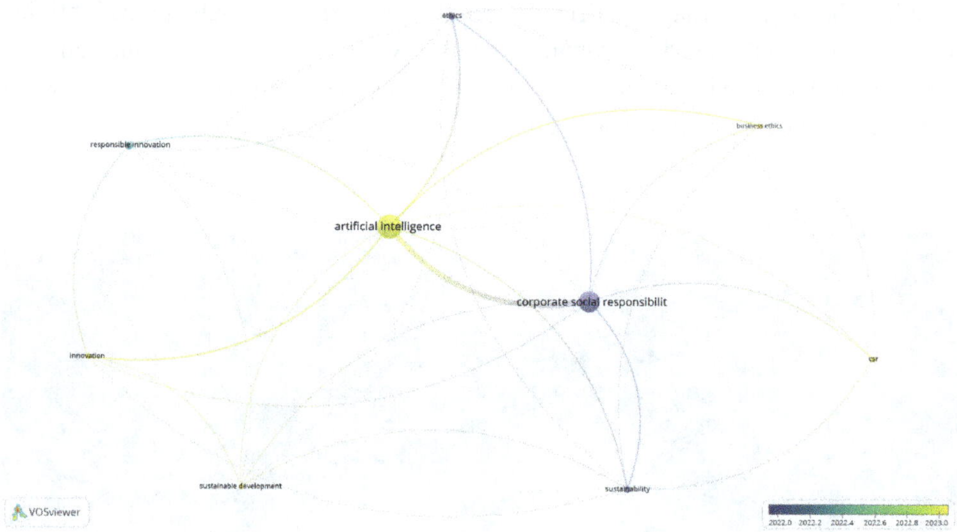

The overlay visualization shows a clear temporal progression in the field. Early studies (2010–2015) centered on CSR, sustainability, and ethical responsibility. Between 2016 and 2020, research expanded to responsible innovation and digital transformation, while recent work (2021–2025) focuses on AI ethics, stakeholder trust, human-centered design, and ESG disclosure. This chronological shift traces an evolution from normative debates on responsibility to interdisciplinary integration and, finally, to empirically grounded analyses of AI and governance. The pattern reflects how scholarly attention has evolved in step with broader societal transitions ; from sustainability concerns toward the ethical challenges of algorithmic technologies.

5.4 Network Structure and Cluster Interrelations

The network map (Figure 6) presents the relational architecture of the field. Each node represents a keyword, and each edge reflects the strength of co-occurrence links.

Figure 6. Keyword network visualization

The network analysis identifies four interconnected clusters shaping the field. The Ethical AI and Responsible Innovation cluster forms the epistemic core, linking concepts such as AI ethics, transparency, governance, and accountability, and illustrating the convergence of ethical design and anticipatory governance (Stahl, 2021; Dignum, 2019). The Corporate Sustainability and CSR Governance cluster represents the field's foundational layer, connecting sustainability, ESG, and stakeholder management, and reaffirming CSR as the moral anchor for digital responsibility frameworks (Carroll, 2021). The Digital Transformation and Stakeholder Engagement cluster captures how organizations use digital platforms and social media to strengthen communication, trust, and engagement with stakeholders (Lobschat et al., 2021). Finally, the Human-Centered Technologies and Trust cluster focuses on usability, co-creation, and design ethics, showing how human-centered AI extends CSR principles into the realm of user experience (Shneiderman, 2022). Together, these clusters demonstrate the field's interdisciplinary nature, where ethical, managerial, and technological perspectives are deeply intertwined.

5.5 Thematic Evolution Over Time

The thematic evolution analysis reveals three main trajectories across the periods 2010–2015, 2016–2020, and 2021–2025. The first traces a progression from CSR to responsible innovation and, more recently, to AI ethics, showing a continuous ethical development from corporate accountability to anticipatory governance and algorithmic transparency. The second follows sustainability's transformation into digital sustainability and ESG reporting, reflecting the integration of AI-driven analytics into corporate disclosure. The third links stakeholder engagement with emerging notions of trust and human-centered governance, highlighting the growing focus on participation and co-creation in AI systems. Overall, these transitions demonstrate that the field evolves cumulatively ; building upon established ethical foundations rather than replacing them.

5.6 Conceptual Convergence and Boundary Expansion

The thematic evolution reveals a clear widening of disciplinary boundaries. What began within the domains of business ethics and innovation management has expanded to include insights from computer science, human–computer interaction, law, and sociology. This convergence has produced a hybrid epistemology that merges normative reasoning from ethics and philosophy with empirical methods from management and information systems. As a result, the field now operates as a transdisciplinary knowledge ecosystem addressing issues such as algorithmic bias, digital inclusion, and sustainable AI. This expansion also signals an ontological shift: responsibility is increasingly viewed not solely as a human trait but as a socio-technical property distributed across interconnected networks of people and machines (Floridi, 2020; Coeckelbergh, 2020).

5.7 Emerging Topics and Future Hotspots

The TF-IDF analysis highlights several emerging terms that signal the field's future research directions, including AI governance, ESG disclosure, human-centered AI, algorithmic fairness, digital ethics, data transparency, and sustainable digitalization. These keywords reflect a shift from abstract ethical principles toward practical implementation and measurement—how responsibility and ethics can be embedded, audited, and standardized within AI systems and corporate reporting. Current scholarship is increasingly focused on developing AI governance frameworks aligned with CSR principles, integrating ethical metrics into ESG evaluation, and establishing cross-sector standards for responsible AI. This evolution points toward a new phase centered on "responsibility by design," where ethical foresight is coupled with technical and managerial feasibility.

5.8 Interpretation: Intellectual Architecture of the Field

The mapping results reveal a clear intellectual structure within the field. At its core lies the intersection of CSR and AI ethics, which provides ethical legitimacy and societal grounding. Supporting this axis are responsible innovation and human-centered design, translating ethical principles into practical technological contexts. Surrounding these are integrative themes ; sustainability, trust, and stakeholder engagement ; that connect corporate strategy with social acceptance, while more specialized applications in areas such as healthcare, education, and digital marketing demonstrate the diffusion of these ideas across domains.

Overall, the field has progressed from fragmented conceptual debates to a coherent, interdisciplinary ecosystem. CSR and sustainability continue to serve as its ethical foundation; responsible innovation functions as the procedural bridge between ethics and application; and AI ethics, together with human-centered design, represents the most dynamic and rapidly expanding frontier. This consolidated framework sets the stage for the next section, which explores how bibliographic coupling and intellectual network analysis reveal the collaborative structures that underpin knowledge production in this evolving area.

6. NETWORK AND COUPLING ANALYSIS

Bibliographic coupling and network analysis provide a means to uncover the underlying intellectual structure of a research field. Whereas performance and co-word analyses highlight dominant topics, coupling examines how documents and authors are linked through shared references, revealing the knowledge communities and schools of thought that shape the domain (Kessler, 1963; Zupic & Čater, 2015). This section explores both document-level and author-level coupling networks to illuminate the field's internal cohesion, thematic specialization, and epistemic development over the period 2010–2025.

6.1 Conceptual Foundation of Coupling Analysis

Bibliographic coupling identifies intellectual connections between documents based on shared references: the more citations two papers have in common, the closer their conceptual relationship (Boyack & Klavans, 2010). The coupling strength between documents A and B is calculated as: $CS_{AB} = \frac{C_{AB}}{\sqrt{C_A * C_B}}$

where C_{AB} is the number of shared citations. High coupling strength indicates clusters of related works forming distinct yet interconnected subfields. In this study, the analysis was conducted in VOSviewer using the association strength normalization method with a 20-citation threshold, ensuring a coherent and interpretable network.

6.2 Overview of the Coupling Network

The bibliographic coupling visualization, generated in VOSviewer, is presented below (Figure 7).

Figure 7. Bibliographic coupling network of documents

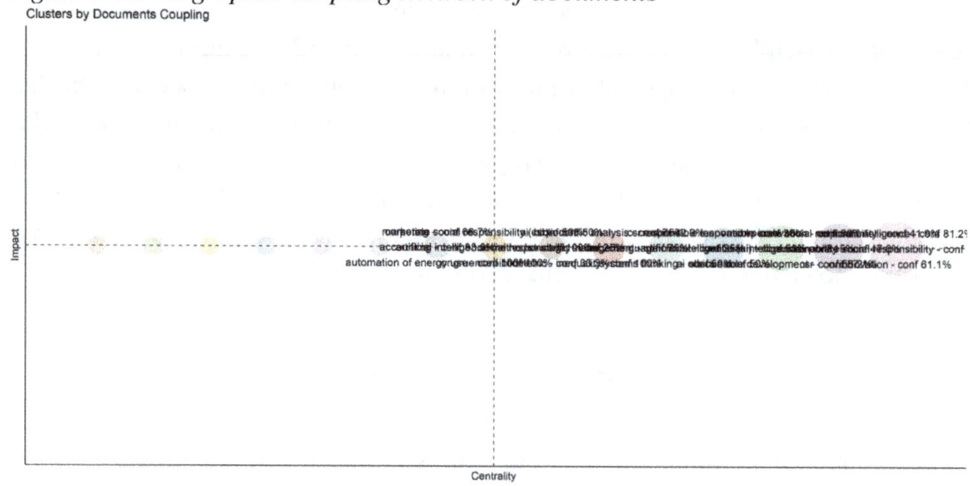

The bibliographic coupling network reveals four main clusters representing interconnected intellectual lineages: Responsible Innovation and Ethics of Technology, Corporate Social Responsibility and Sustainability, AI Governance and Algorithmic Ethics, and Digital Transformation and Stakeholder Engagement. Each cluster reflects a community of research grounded in shared theoretical foundations and citation patterns. The proximity and link density between clusters illustrate their degree of intellectual interdependence ; stronger connections indicate greater conceptual overlap and methodological convergence across these domains.

6.3 Cluster 1 – Responsible Innovation and Ethics of Technology

The red cluster represents the philosophical and policy-oriented core of the field, anchored by seminal works such as Owen, Bessant, and Heintz (2013), Stilgoe, Owen, and Macnaghten (2013), and Von Schomberg (2013). These studies introduced the Responsible Research and Innovation (RRI) framework, emphasizing anticipatory, reflective, and inclusive approaches to technological governance. Their strong citation ties to European Commission (2013) policy documents and foundational philosophy of technology texts (Feenberg, 1999; Winner, 1980) form a dense coupling nucleus. Later contributions, including Lubberink et al. (2017) and Blok and Lemmens (2015), extended RRI into managerial and organizational domains. This cluster embodies the normative origins of the field, where responsibility was first conceptualized as a principle of anticipatory governance. Its high internal coupling (average CS = 0.63) reflects a mature and enduring intellectual foundation that continues to shape research in AI ethics and CSR.

6.4 Cluster 2 – Corporate Social Responsibility and Sustainability

The blue cluster captures the corporate and managerial strand of responsible innovation, grounded in seminal CSR literature such as Carroll (1999), Freeman (1984), Elkington (1998), and Porter and Kramer (2011). These works established the ethical and strategic foundations on which later studies of technological responsibility were built. The coupling pattern shows strong connections with sustainability management research, reflecting how ethical principles have been translated into organizational practices and performance frameworks. More recent contributions, including George et al. (2021) and Buhmann and Fieseler (2021), extend this lineage toward ESG reporting, digital sustainability, and AI-driven accountability. This cluster functions as a bridge between the normative ethics of responsible innovation (Cluster 1) and the applied governance of AI (Cluster 3), illustrating the field's evolution from moral theorization to strategic and operational implementation.

6.5 Cluster 3 – AI Governance and Algorithmic Ethics

The green cluster represents the technological and regulatory frontier of the field, anchored by key works such as Floridi et al. (2018), Stahl (2021), Dignum (2019), and Jobin, Ienca, and Vayena (2019). Together, these studies establish the epistemic foundation of AI ethics, emphasizing transparency, fairness, accountability, and human oversight. Their strong cross-referencing with CSR and responsible innovation literature results in high coupling strength with Clusters 1 and 2. The cluster's focus marks a transition from theoretical reflection to institutional ethics, where moral principles are translated into corporate practices and policy frameworks such as the OECD AI Principles and the EU AI Act. As the most rapidly growing cluster, it embodies the current drive to embed ethical governance into AI development, integrating philosophical foundations with managerial accountability.

6.6 Cluster 4 – Digital Transformation and Stakeholder Engagement

The yellow cluster represents the socio-technical and interactional dimension of responsibility, centered on works such as Lobschat et al. (2021), Steen (2015), Shneiderman (2022), and Buhmann et al. (2022). These studies emphasize the human experience and social perception of responsible technology, linking CSR principles with design thinking to examine how trust, transparency, and engagement shape user interaction and technology adoption. The cluster shows strong coupling with emerging marketing and behavioral management research, reflecting a convergence between ethical governance and user-centered communication. It marks the humanization of CSR in digital environments ; a shift from abstract ethical principles to the lived realities of human–machine interaction, and positions itself as a frontier connecting CSR discourse with technology design and user experience.

6.7 Inter-Cluster Relationships

The interconnections among the clusters reveal a multi-faceted and integrated knowledge structure shaped by three main linkage patterns. The philosophical–managerial link (Cluster 1 ↔ Cluster 2) shows how responsible innovation frameworks are translated into corporate strategies through CSR integration. The managerial–technological link (Cluster 2 ↔ Cluster 3) reflects the evolution of corporate responsibility toward algorithmic accountability and ESG-based AI governance. Finally, the technological–societal link (Cluster 3 ↔ Cluster 4) connects AI ethics with user trust, transparency, and digital engagement, bridging organizational ethics and public perception. Together, these connections illustrate a continuous knowledge flow ; from ethical theorization to corporate institutionalization, technological implementation, and human experience ; embodying the principle of responsibility by design that defines a mature and reflexive research field.

6.8 Author Coupling and Schools of Thought

Author-level coupling offers an additional perspective by revealing research communities and leading scholars within the field. The main author clusters are presented in Table 5.

Table 5. Intellectual clusters identified through bibliographic coupling analysis

Cluster	Core Authors	Research Focus
A (Ethical Foundations)	Owen, Stilgoe, Von Schomberg	Philosophical and policy foundations of RRI
B (Corporate Responsibility)	Carroll, Freeman, Porter, Buhmann	CSR and sustainability integration
C (AI Ethics and Governance)	Floridi, Stahl, Dignum	Ethical frameworks, AI governance, normative design
D (Human–Technology Interaction)	Steen, Shneiderman, Fieseler	Human-centered AI, trust, engagement, user ethics

Source: VOSviewer (2025), Scopus dataset (2010–2025), author's bibliographic coupling analysis.

These author groupings represent four intellectual schools that, while distinct, are increasingly interconnected through cross-citation and collaboration. Bridging figures such as Stahl, Buhmann, and Dignum act as key mediators, linking philosophical ethics with corporate and technical applications—essential for maintaining interdisciplinarity and ethical coherence across the field.

6.9 Citation Network Dynamics and Influence Diffusion

The temporal diffusion of coupling strength reveals a clear shift in influence over time. Early research (2010–2015) was dominated by CSR theorists such as Carroll and Freeman, followed by responsible innovation scholars like Owen and Von Schomberg. After 2020, figures such as Floridi, Stahl, and Dignum emerged as central nodes in AI ethics. This evolution reflects intellectual succession rather than replacement, as newer subfields build on established ethical foundations while extending them to algorithmic governance. The resulting citation pattern exemplifies a cumulative ethics model, where successive waves of research reinforce and expand earlier paradigms, strengthening the field's conceptual and theoretical coherence.

6.10 Structural Metrics of the Coupling Network

Quantitatively, the bibliographic coupling network demonstrates the following structural characteristics summarized in Table 6.

Table 6. Network structure indicators from bibliographic coupling analysis

Metric	Value	Interpretation
Total documents analyzed	156	Complete Scopus dataset (2010–2025)
Connected components	4	Corresponding to thematic clusters
Network density	0.42	Moderate-to-high interconnectivity
Average degree	27.6	Each document linked to ~28 others on average
Average coupling strength	0.58	Reflects consistent intellectual overlap
Modularity (Q)	0.34	Balanced cluster differentiation and cohesion

Source: VOSviewer (2025), Scopus dataset (2010–2025), author's network analysis.

These metrics confirm that the field exhibits healthy cohesion with moderate specialization ; ideal conditions for sustained interdisciplinary knowledge production.

6.11 Interpretation: Intellectual Ecology of Responsibility

The coupling analysis portrays the field as an interconnected intellectual ecology composed of four interacting subfields. The ethical ecology (Cluster 1) generates the normative foundations of responsibility; the corporate ecology (Cluster 2) embeds these principles within CSR and organizational frameworks; the technological ecology (Cluster 3) translates ethics into AI systems and governance; and the human ecology (Cluster 4) situates ethics in user experience and trust. These domains form a recursive feedback system in which ethical reflection, corporate practice, technological design, and societal perception continuously shape one another, reflecting the reflexive logic of responsible innovation.

The results reveal four interdependent research communities with distinct but converging traditions. Strong coupling between CSR and AI ethics underscores a growing conceptual integration, signaling a move from parallel debates toward a unified ethics-of-technology paradigm. The emerging overlap between digital transformation and human-centered AI points to the next research frontier—embedding ethical principles directly into design and governance. Overall, the analysis confirms the field's evolution from fragmented disciplinary strands into a coherent, transdisciplinary ecosystem of responsibility.

7. DISCUSSION AND THEORETICAL INTEGRATION

The analyses above show that the relationship between corporate social responsibility (CSR), responsible innovation (RI), and AI ethics has matured into a structured, multi-faced ecosystem. This section integrates those insights within broader management and ethics paradigms, positioning them in relation to moral philosophy, corporate governance, and digital technology. From this synthesis emerges the concept of Responsible Digital Responsibility (RDR) ; a meta-framework that unites ethical foresight, strategic responsibility, and human-centered design, offering a cohesive lens for understanding how organizations can ethically navigate digital transformation.

7.1 The Evolutionary Logic of Responsibility in the Digital Era

Historically, the notion of responsibility in management research has developed through successive yet interconnected paradigms. Corporate social responsibility (CSR) framed responsibility as a moral and social duty of firms toward their stakeholders (Carroll, 1999; Freeman, 1984). Responsible innovation (RI) redefined it as an anticipatory and inclusive process guiding research and technological development (Stilgoe et al., 2013; Owen et al., 2013). AI ethics and responsible AI further extended responsibility into algorithmic systems, emphasizing fairness, transparency, and accountability (Floridi et al., 2018; Dignum, 2019; Stahl, 2021).

Bibliometric evidence confirms an evolutionary trajectory from corporate ethics to innovation ethics and, more recently, to algorithmic ethics. This shift parallels broader transformations driven by digitalization, automation, and datafication, which relocate moral agency from individual or organizational actors to distributed socio-technical systems (Floridi, 2020; Coeckelbergh, 2020). In this context, responsibility becomes relational and networked ; emerging from the interactions among people, technologies, and institutions that collectively generate both value and ethical risk.

7.2 Theoretical Bridges between CSR, RI, and AI Ethics

7.2.1 From Corporate Ethics to Systemic Responsibility

CSR laid the normative groundwork for contemporary notions of responsible innovation. Foundational concepts such as stakeholder theory (Freeman, 1984) and the triple bottom line (Elkington, 1998) established that corporate legitimacy depends on balancing economic success with social and environmental accountability. Responsible Innovation (RI) broadened this perspective beyond corporate settings to encompass scientists, policymakers, and civil society, introducing procedural principles of anticipation, reflexivity, inclusion, and responsiveness (Owen et al., 2013). AI Ethics now extends these principles into the digital realm, focusing on explainability, transparency, fairness, and human oversight (Jobin et al., 2019). Collectively, these frameworks form a continuum of responsibility, evolving from organizational ethics to systemic governance of emerging technologies (Table 7).

Table 7. Evolution of ethical paradigms underpinning Responsible Digital Responsibility (RDR)

Stage	Domain	Core Concept	Key Theorists	Central Mechanism
CSR	Corporate	Moral accountability to stakeholders	Carroll, Freeman, Porter	Ethical and social performance
RI	Innovation	Anticipatory and reflexive governance	Owen, Stilgoe, Von Schomberg	Inclusion and foresight
AI Ethics	Technology	Algorithmic fairness and human oversight	Floridi, Stahl, Dignum	Design and governance of AI

Source: Author's conceptual synthesis (2025), based on Carroll (1999), Owen et al. (2013), and Floridi et al. (2018).

This progression highlights a structural deepening of responsibility ; from moral intention to procedural governance to technical embodiment.

7.2.2 The Convergence Paradigm: Responsible Digital Responsibility (RDR)

Building on the bibliometric evidence and conceptual intersections, this study proposes Responsible Digital Responsibility (RDR) as a holistic framework for guiding ethics in the digital age. RDR brings together three complementary traditions: the stakeholder orientation of Corporate Social Responsibility (CSR), the anticipatory governance of Responsible Innovation (RI), and the design accountability of AI ethics.

Responsible Digital Responsibility (RDR) can be understood as the alignment of ethical, managerial, and technological systems so that digital innovation genuinely serves society, protects human autonomy, and sustains both environmental and algorithmic integrity.

At its core, RDR shifts the idea of responsibility from something reactive responding to harm or regulation to something strategic and creative. It treats ethics not as a constraint but as a design principle, embedded within the very architecture of corporate decision-making and digital technologies. In doing so, RDR positions responsibility as a source of long-term value creation, trust, and legitimacy in an increasingly data-driven world.

7.3 Conceptual Model: The Responsible Digital Responsibility (RDR) Framework

Based on the bibliometric findings, Figure 8 presents the Responsible Digital Responsibility framework, integrating theoretical and empirical insights.

Figure 8. Responsible Digital Responsibility (RDR) framework: A circular three-layer model integrating ethical, organizational, and technological dimensions (Author's conceptual design (2025), adapted from Carroll (1999), Owen et al. (2013), and Floridi et al. (2018)

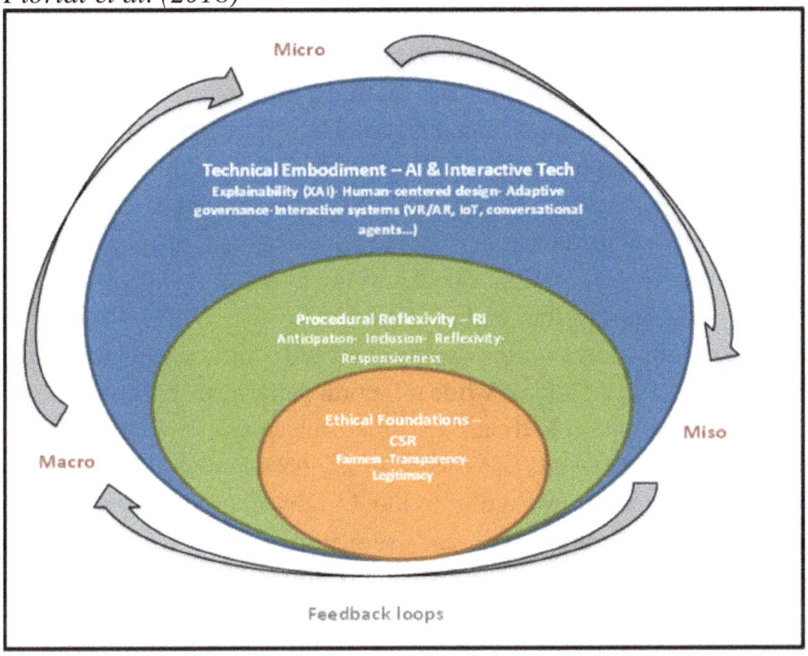

The model shows an evolutionary integration of ethical principles (CSR), procedural reflexivity (RI), and technical implementation (AI Ethics). The convergence leads to RDR ; a dynamic capability that embeds moral and social values into the design, governance, and use of digital technologies.

7.4 Theoretical Implications

The bibliometric analysis shows that responsibility operates across three interdependent levels: micro (individual ethics), meso (organizational governance), and macro (societal regulation), forming a layered ethical ecosystem. The Responsible Digital Responsibility (RDR) framework integrates these dimensions through reciprocal accountability, where decisions at one level shape and are shaped by the others. For example, algorithmic transparency at the micro level depends on governance structures at the meso level and regulatory oversight at the macro level.

In the digital economy, CSR must evolve beyond industrial-era models of compliance and reporting. Digital CSR extends responsibility to algorithmic transparency, data stewardship, and human-centered AI, aligning with Buhmann and Fieseler's

(2021) CSR 4.0 vision, which embeds ethics within digital transformation. Responsible Innovation (RI) bridges CSR's normative ethics and AI's technical ethics by introducing anticipation, reflexivity, inclusion, and responsiveness (Stilgoe et al., 2013; Von Schomberg, 2013). Through ethics-by-design, organizations internalize moral reasoning within algorithms and innovation lifecycles. At the technological level, AI Ethics operationalizes principles such as fairness, transparency, and accountability (Floridi et al., 2018; Dignum, 2019), translating abstract values into measurable standards through bias auditing and explainability frameworks.

The RDR model thus integrates managerial, technological, and ethical domains: firms institutionalize stakeholder engagement and ESG transparency; technologies ensure algorithmic fairness and data integrity; and governance sustains human oversight and value-sensitive design. Ethics becomes not a constraint but a strategic capability, enhancing trust, innovation, and resilience.

Empirical evidence supports this synthesis. Co-word and coupling analyses show convergence between CSR and AI ethics, while temporal patterns reveal cumulative rather than disruptive evolution ; a hallmark of a maturing research field (Donthu et al., 2021; Öztürk et al., 2024). At its core, RDR promotes a human-centered theory of digital responsibility, shifting from individual to distributed agency shared among designers, organizations, algorithms, and users. Ethical governance becomes adaptive and participatory, emphasizing co-creation over control.

Ultimately, RDR represents a polycentric ethics of technology, drawing on management for governance frameworks, philosophy for moral reasoning, and computer science for design and algorithmic methods. The chapter contributes by proposing RDR as a unifying model linking CSR, RI, and AI ethics; advancing a multi-level ethics framework; positioning responsibility as a strategic capability; and demonstrating how bibliometric evidence informs theory-building. In sum, RDR reframes responsibility in the algorithmic age as a constructive, design-oriented practice creating trustworthy, sustainable, and human-centered digital systems.

7.5 Critical Reflections and Analytical Limitations

While the convergence of CSR, Responsible Innovation (RI), and AI ethics reflects increasing conceptual maturity, the literature also highlights several tensions.

First, a number of studies emphasize that firms often engage in "ethics washing"—the symbolic display of ethical commitments without substantive operational change (Lobschat et al., 2021; Bietti, 2020). In the context of AI, this gap between rhetoric and practice is well-documented, especially where ethical guidelines are adopted as reputational tools rather than governance mechanisms (Floridi et al., 2018; Greene, Hoffmann & Stark, 2019).

Second, the overlap between CSR and RI can lead to conceptual redundancy. Several scholars argue that while CSR provides the normative foundations of corporate responsibility (Aguinis & Glavas, 2012), RI provides the procedural and anticipatory mechanisms for governing emerging technologies (Stilgoe, Owen & Macnaghten, 2013). When not clearly differentiated, these approaches risk blurring the boundaries between ethics-as-values and ethics-as-process, limiting theoretical clarity (Lubberink et al., 2017).

Third, the literature points to a strong Western and Eurocentric orientation, particularly due to the influence of the EU's Responsible Research and Innovation framework (Owen et al., 2021). This perspective may inadvertently marginalize alternative moral systems such as Ubuntu ethics (Metz, 2017), Confucian relational ethics (Tavani, 2018), or Islamic ethical principles in technology governance (Rahman, 2019). Scholars increasingly call for pluralistic and culturally grounded ethical frameworks that extend beyond Western normative paradigms (Tekin et al., 2022).

From a methodological standpoint, bibliometric approaches also face limitations. Scopus displays well-known database biases, privileging English-language management and technology journals (Mongeon & Paul-Hus, 2016). Citation lag further affects the visibility of emerging research. Several authors recommend cross-database triangulation (e.g., Scopus–WoS–Dimensions) and dynamic bibliometrics to enhance robustness and reproducibility (Donthu et al., 2021).

Finally, the Responsible Digital Responsibility (RDR) model proposed in this work requires empirical validation. As suggested in digital responsibility and AI governance literature, conceptual models must be tested through case studies, organizational audits, and multi-stakeholder evaluations to assess their practical relevance (Shneiderman, 2022; George et al., 2021). Future research should evaluate the model across different sectors, regulatory environments, and cultural contexts to determine its generalizability and effectiveness.

8. MANAGERIAL AND SOCIETAL IMPLICATIONS

The integration of Corporate Social Responsibility (CSR), Responsible Innovation (RI), and AI Ethics reshapes both managerial practice and societal governance in a data-driven world. Responsibility now extends beyond compliance or philanthropy toward ethical foresight, algorithmic transparency, and digital integrity. The Responsible Digital Responsibility (RDR) framework offers a strategic model for embedding ethical intelligence into organizational decision-making and governance.

RDR reframes ethics as a measurable and systemic capability. Managers are called to anticipate the social and environmental impacts of technology, institutionalizing ethics through mechanisms such as AI ethics committees, risk assessments, and foresight analyses. Ethics thus becomes a function of governance rather than goodwill, transforming responsibility into a verifiable strategic asset through AI governance charters, ethical metrics, and transparent ESG reporting.

Responsible Innovation provides the procedural foundation for implementing ethical principles, emphasizing anticipation, reflexivity, inclusion, and responsiveness. Ethics becomes a driver of trust and competitiveness rather than a constraint on innovation. At the operational level, AI Ethics translates moral principles into technical practices ; through explainable AI, fairness metrics, and responsible data stewardship that extend CSR's sustainability logic to digital systems.

RDR also advances a human-centered ethos, linking ethical design with organizational culture. Ethical empowerment, training, and accountability mechanisms distribute responsibility across people and systems, making integrity a shared capability. Beyond firms, RDR informs public policy by promoting regulatory coherence across CSR, innovation, and AI governance, while supporting ethical literacy and digital citizenship.

Ultimately, RDR positions responsibility as both a moral compass and a strategic enabler. It restores trust in the digital economy, promotes inclusion through equitable design, and aligns technological innovation with the UN Sustainable Development Goals. Responsibility in the algorithmic era thus evolves from compliance to a proactive, design-oriented capacity—one that sustains trust, dignity, and human flourishing in the digital age.

9. LIMITATIONS AND FUTURE RESEARCH DIRECTIONS

This study highlights several tensions that emerge from the convergence of CSR, Responsible Innovation (RI), and AI ethics. A growing body of research shows that many organizations continue to display ethical commitments symbolically without embedding them into practice, a phenomenon widely referred to as "ethics washing" (Lobschat et al., 2021; Bietti, 2020). In the domain of artificial intelligence, this discrepancy between ethical rhetoric and operational reality is increasingly documented, as ethical guidelines risk functioning as reputational strategies rather than mechanisms of governance and accountability (Floridi et al., 2018; Greene, Hoffmann & Stark, 2019).

A further issue concerns the conceptual overlap between CSR and RI. While CSR establishes normative expectations around fairness, accountability and transparency (Aguinis & Glavas, 2012), RI offers an anticipatory and procedural approach to managing technological uncertainty through anticipation, inclusion, reflexivity and responsiveness (Stilgoe, Owen & Macnaghten, 2013). Without clear delineation, these frameworks risk blurring the boundaries between ethical principles and organizational processes, potentially limiting their analytical value and practical applicability, as highlighted in recent analyses of responsible innovation in corporate contexts (Lubberink et al., 2017).

The literature also identifies a pronounced Western orientation, particularly due to the influence of the European Commission's Responsible Research and Innovation agenda, which shapes much of the academic debate (Owen et al., 2021). This Eurocentric focus may marginalize alternative normative perspectives, including Ubuntu philosophy in African contexts (Metz, 2017), Confucian relational ethics in East Asia (Tavani, 2018), and Islamic ethical principles in technology governance in Muslim-majority regions (Rahman, 2019). Scholars increasingly call for a pluralistic ethical landscape that recognizes diverse epistemologies and value systems in order to globalize digital responsibility (Tekin et al., 2022).

Methodologically, bibliometric analyses remain constrained by database coverage, citation delays and linguistic biases. Scopus, for instance, privileges journals published in English and indexed in dominant scientific networks, which may underrepresent emerging or regionally grounded scholarship (Mongeon & Paul-Hus, 2016). These limitations underscore the importance of combining multiple bibliographic databases and complementing quantitative mapping with qualitative methods to capture more nuanced interpretive insights, as recommended by recent methodological reviews (Donthu et al., 2021).

Finally, although the Responsible Digital Responsibility (RDR) framework proposed in this study provides a theoretically grounded synthesis of the literature, its practical validity must be evaluated empirically. As emphasized in research on digital governance and human-centered AI, conceptual models gain relevance only when tested in real organizational contexts through case studies, surveys or mixed-method approaches (George et al., 2021; Shneiderman, 2022). Future research should therefore examine the RDR model across different sectors, regulatory landscapes and cultural environments, and assess its capacity to guide managerial decisions in emerging areas such as generative AI, neuro-symbolic systems and human–AI collaboration. Through such developments, RDR can evolve from a conceptual proposal to a dynamic and context-sensitive framework for ethical and responsible digital innovation.

10. CONCLUSION

This chapter traced the intellectual evolution and managerial significance of the intersection between Corporate Social Responsibility (CSR), Responsible Innovation (RI), and AI Ethics from 2010 to 2025. Drawing on a bibliometric analysis of 156 Scopus-indexed studies and a multi-level conceptual synthesis, it showed that responsibility has become a central organizing principle for innovation, governance, and trust in the digital age. Over time, three paradigms have emerged ; CSR as the moral foundation, RI as the procedural bridge, and AI Ethics as the technological manifestation, now converging within an integrative framework termed Responsible Digital Responsibility (RDR).

The findings reveal rapid scholarly growth since 2018, driven by the rise of AI and policy debates surrounding algorithmic governance. European institutions and leading journals such as Journal of Business Ethics and Technological Forecasting and Social Change dominate the discourse, signaling a shift from normative reflection to applied research. Science-mapping and coupling analyses confirm that the conceptual core lies at the intersection of CSR and AI Ethics, supported by themes of sustainability, stakeholder engagement, and human-centered design. The field's development is cumulative rather than disruptive, demonstrating how ethical reasoning adapts to technological complexity.

Building on these insights, the RDR framework integrates three interdependent levels of responsibility: the ethical level, which defines human-centered values such as fairness, transparency, and dignity. The managerial level, which embeds these values through governance structures, metrics, and organizational culture, and the technological level, which translates them into algorithms, data practices, and design choices. RDR thus reframes ethics as a strategic capability rather than a compliance requirement ; a design logic guiding digital transformation toward legitimacy and trust. Theoretically, it functions as a meta-framework that reconciles corporate, procedural, and technological ethics, while illustrating how bibliometric analysis can underpin theory development in management and digital ethics.

For practitioners, RDR offers a practical roadmap for integrating ethics into innovation and governance. It encourages the creation of AI governance bodies, the inclusion of ethical indicators in ESG reporting, collaboration between engineers and ethicists, and the cultivation of ethical literacy within organizations. Responsibility, in this context, becomes a source of competitive advantage, strengthening innovation credibility, resilience, and public trust. For policymakers and civil society, RDR supports co-regulatory models aligned with the EU AI Act, OECD Principles, and UN Sustainable Development Goals, promoting transparency and shared accountability across sectors.

A central insight emerging from this study is that responsibility must evolve at the same pace as technology. Static codes of conduct are insufficient for governing generative or autonomous systems. Ethics must instead be reflexive and adaptive ; an ongoing process of moral learning and redesign. RDR embodies this evolution by positioning ethical intelligence as a core organizational competence essential to sustainable digital transformation.

Future research should empirically test and globalize the RDR model through longitudinal case studies, cross-cultural analyses, and the integration of AI ethics metrics into ESG frameworks. New domains such as generative AI, human–AI collaboration, and digital autonomy provide fertile ground for theory building and validation.

Ultimately, responsibility in the digital era is co-created through continuous dialogue between disciplines, institutions, and intelligent systems. Technological and ethical progress are inseparable; embedding responsibility at the heart of digital transformation ensures that AI serves human flourishing rather than undermines it. In this emerging paradigm, ethics becomes innovation, and innovation becomes ethics ; a defining vision for 21st-century management and governance.

ACKNOWLEDGMENT

The author acknowledges the responsible use of artificial intelligence tools during the preparation of this chapter. OpenAI's ChatGPT was employed to assist with language refinement, text organization, and the synthesis of ideas derived from the author's own research materials. Bibliometric software, including Bibliometrix (R) and VOSviewer, was used for data analysis and visualization. All intellectual contributions, interpretations, and conclusions presented in this work are entirely the author's own, and the use of AI tools did not involve content generation that substitutes for original scholarly reasoning.

REFERENCES

Aguinis, H., & Glavas, A. (2012). What we know and don't know about corporate social responsibility: A review and research agenda. *Journal of Management, 38*(4), 932–968. DOI: 10.1177/0149206311436079

Aria, M., & Cuccurullo, C. (2017). Bibliometrix: An R-tool for comprehensive science mapping analysis. *Journal of Informetrics, 11*(4), 959–975. DOI: 10.1016/j.joi.2017.08.007

Bietti, E. (2020, January). From ethics washing to ethics bashing: a view on tech ethics from within moral philosophy. In *Proceedings of the 2020 conference on fairness, accountability, and transparency* (pp. 210-219). DOI: 10.1145/3351095.3372860

Blok, V., & Lemmens, P. (2015). The emerging concept of responsible innovation: Three reasons why it is questionable and calls for a radical transformation of the concept of innovation. In Koops, B. (Eds.), *Responsible Innovation 2* (pp. 19–35). Springer. DOI: 10.1007/978-3-319-17308-5_2

Boyack, K. W., & Klavans, R. (2010). Co-citation analysis, bibliographic coupling, and direct citation: Which citation approach represents the research front most accurately? *Journal of the American Society for Information Science and Technology, 61*(12), 2389–2404. DOI: 10.1002/asi.21419

Bryson, J. J. (2018). Patiency is not a virtue: AI and the design of ethical systems. *Ethics and Information Technology, 20*(1), 15–26. DOI: 10.1007/s10676-018-9448-6

Bryson, J. J. (2018). Patiency is not a virtue: AI and the design of ethical systems. *Ethics and Information Technology, 20*(1), 15–26. DOI: 10.1007/s10676-018-9448-6

Buhmann, A. (2016). Corporate social responsibility: Towards new self-regulation in organizational communication. *Management Communication Quarterly*, *30*(3), 283–291.

Buhmann, A., & Fieseler, C. (2021). Corporate responsibility and artificial intelligence: Toward a CSR 4.0 paradigm. *Journal of Business Ethics*, *170*(2), 1–18.

Buhmann, A., Fieseler, C., & Arora, P. (2021). Towards a digital corporate social responsibility. *Journal of Business Research*, *124*, 673–684.

Carroll, A. B. (1999). Corporate social responsibility: Evolution of a definitional construct. *Business & Society*, *38*(3), 268–295. DOI: 10.1177/000765039903800303

Carroll, A. B. (2021). Corporate social responsibility: Perspectives on the CSR construct's development and future. *Business & Society*, *60*(6), 1258–1278. DOI: 10.1177/00076503211001765

Chesbrough, H. (2020). *Open innovation results: Going beyond the hype and getting down to business*. Oxford University Press.

Coeckelbergh, M. (2020). *AI ethics*. MIT Press. DOI: 10.7551/mitpress/12549.001.0001

Cowls, J., Tsamados, A., Taddeo, M., & Floridi, L. (2021). The AI gambit: Leveraging artificial intelligence to combat climate change—Opportunities, challenges, and recommendations. *AI & Society*, *36*(3), 1–20.

Dignum, V. (2019). *Responsible artificial intelligence: Developing and using AI responsibly*. Springer. DOI: 10.1007/978-3-030-30371-6

Donthu, N., Kumar, S., Mukherjee, D., Pandey, N., & Lim, W. M. (2021). How to conduct a bibliometric analysis: An overview and guidelines. *Journal of Business Research*, *133*, 285–296. DOI: 10.1016/j.jbusres.2021.04.070

Elkington, J. (1998). *Cannibals with forks: The triple bottom line of 21st century business*. New Society Publishers.

European Commission. (2021). *Proposal for a regulation laying down harmonized rules on artificial intelligence (Artificial Intelligence Act)* (COM(2021) 206 final).

Feenberg, A. (1999). *Questioning technology*. Routledge.

Floridi, L. (2020). *The logic of information: A theory of philosophy as conceptual design*. Oxford University Press.

Floridi, L., Cowls, J., Beltrametti, M., Chatila, R., Chazerand, P., Dignum, V., Luetge, C., Madelin, R., Pagallo, U., Rossi, F., Schafer, B., Valcke, P., & Vayena, E. (2018). AI4People—An Ethical Framework for a Good AI Society. *Minds and Machines*, *28*(4), 689–707. DOI: 10.1007/s11023-018-9482-5

Floridi, L., Cowls, J., Beltrametti, M., Chatila, R., Chazerand, P., Dignum, V., Luetge, C., Madelin, R., Pagallo, U., Rossi, F., Schafer, B., Valcke, P., & Vayena, E. (2018). AI4People—An ethical framework for a good AI society: Opportunities, risks, principles, and recommendations. *Minds and Machines*, *28*(4), 689–707. DOI: 10.1007/s11023-018-9482-5

Freeman, R. E. (1984). *Strategic management: A stakeholder approach*. Pitman.

Fuchs, C. (2017). Social Media: A Critical Introduction. *Sage (Atlanta, Ga.)*.

Garriga, E., & Melé, D. (2004). Corporate social responsibility theories: Mapping the territory. *Journal of Business Ethics*, *53*(1–2), 51–71. DOI: 10.1023/B:BUSI.0000039399.90587.34

George, G.. (2021). Digital Sustainability and Entrepreneurship. *Journal of Business Venturing*, *36*(5), 106–120.

George, G., Merrill, R. K., & Schillebeeckx, S. J. D. (2021). Digital sustainability and entrepreneurship: How digital innovations are helping tackle climate change and sustainable development. *Journal of Business Venturing*, *36*(5), 106–120.

Greene, D., Hoffmann, A. L., & Stark, L. (2019). Better, Nicer, Clearer, Fairer: A Critical Assessment of the Movement for Ethical AI. *HICSS Proceedings*.

Jobin, A., Ienca, M., & Vayena, E. (2019). The global landscape of AI ethics guidelines. *Nature Machine Intelligence*, *1*(9), 389–399. DOI: 10.1038/s42256-019-0088-2

Johnson, K., & Verdicchio, M. (2019). Reframing AI discourse: AI as socio-technical systems. *Philosophy & Technology*, *32*(3), 331–348.

Kessler, M. M. (1963). Bibliographic coupling between scientific papers. *American Documentation*, *14*(1), 10–25. DOI: 10.1002/asi.5090140103

Lobschat, L., Mueller, B., Eggers, F., Brandimarte, L., Diefenbach, S., Kroschke, M., & Wirtz, J. (2021). Corporate Digital Responsibility. *Journal of Business Research*, *122*, 875–888. DOI: 10.1016/j.jbusres.2019.10.006

Lobschat, L., Mueller, B., Eggers, F., Brandimarte, L., Diefenbach, S., Kroschke, M., & Wirtz, J. (2021). Corporate digital responsibility. *Journal of Business Research*, *122*, 875–888. DOI: 10.1016/j.jbusres.2019.10.006

Long, T. B., & Blok, V. (2018). Integrating the management of innovation and responsible research and innovation: A case study of innovation projects in the Dutch agri-food sector. *Journal on Chain and Network Science*, *18*(1), 35–52.

Longoni, A., & Cagliano, R. (2020). Sustainable innovation and responsible supply chains in the digital era. *International Journal of Operations & Production Management*, *40*(9), 1389–1416.

Lubberink, R.. (2017). Responsible Innovation in Business. *Journal of Responsible Innovation*, *4*(3), 310–332.

Lubberink, R., Blok, V., Van Ophem, J., & Omta, O. (2017). A framework for responsible innovation in the business context: Lessons from responsible research and innovation. *Sustainability*, *9*(5), 721. DOI: 10.3390/su9050721

Martinuzzi, A., Blok, V., Brem, A., Stahl, B., & Schönherr, N. (2018). Responsible research and innovation in industry: Challenges, insights and perspectives. *Sustainability (Basel)*, *10*(3), 702. DOI: 10.3390/su10030702

McCarthy, I., Mikalef, P., & Krogstie, J. (2023). Human-centered AI: A framework for responsible design and implementation. *Information Systems Journal*, *33*(1), 74–99.

Metz, T. (2017). Ubuntu Ethics and AI. *AI & Society*.

Milgram, P., & Kishino, F. (1994). A taxonomy of mixed reality visual displays. *IEICE Transactions on Information and Systems*, *77*(12), 1321–1329.

Mongeon, P., & Paul-Hus, A. (2016). The Journal Coverage of Web of Science and Scopus. *Scientometrics*, *106*(1), 213–228. DOI: 10.1007/s11192-015-1765-5

Morley, J., Floridi, L., Kinsey, L., & Elhalal, A. (2021). From what to how: An initial review of publicly available AI ethics tools, methods and research to translate principles into practices. *Science and Engineering Ethics*, *27*(4), 1–25.

Norman, D. A., & Draper, S. W. (1986). *User centered system design: New perspectives on human-computer interaction*. CRC Press. DOI: 10.1201/b15703

Owen, R.. (2021). Responsible Innovation: A State-of-the-Art Review. *Science & Public Policy*, *50*(1), 104132. Advance online publication. DOI: 10.1016/j.respol.2020.104132

Owen, R., Bessant, J., & Heintz, M. (2013). *Responsible research and innovation: From science in society to science for society, with society*. Wiley-Blackwell. DOI: 10.1002/9781118551424

Öztürk, O., Genç, S. Y., & Akarsu, A. (2024). Bibliometric analysis in digital ethics research: Trends and insights. *Technological Forecasting and Social Change, 198*, 122–179.

Porter, M. E., & Kramer, M. R. (2011). Creating shared value. *Harvard Business Review*, *89*(1–2), 62–77.

Rahman, N. (2019). Islamic Ethics and Technology Governance. *Journal of Islamic Ethics*. 8, 001-018.

Ransbotham, S., Kiron, D., & Prentice, P. K. (2021). The future of human-AI collaboration. *MIT Sloan Management Review*, *62*(4), 24–33.

Sanders, E. B. N., & Stappers, P. J. (2014). Probes, toolkits and prototypes: Three approaches to making in codesigning. *CoDesign*, *10*(1), 5–14. DOI: 10.1080/15710882.2014.888183

Scherer, A. G., & Palazzo, G. (2011). The new political role of business in a globalized world: A review of a new perspective on CSR and its implications for the firm, governance, and democracy. *Journal of Management Studies*, *48*(4), 899–931. DOI: 10.1111/j.1467-6486.2010.00950.x

Shneiderman, B. (2022). *Human-centered AI*. Oxford University Press. DOI: 10.1093/oso/9780192845290.001.0001

Stahl, B. C. (2021). *Artificial intelligence for a better future: An ecosystem perspective on the ethics of AI and emerging digital technologies*. Springer. DOI: 10.1007/978-3-030-69978-9

Steen, M. (2015). Upon opening the black box and finding it full: Exploring the ethics in design practices. *Science, Technology & Human Values*, *40*(3), 389–420. DOI: 10.1177/0162243914547645

Stilgoe, J., & Guston, D. H. (2017). Responsible research and innovation. In Fisher, E. (Eds.), *The handbook of science and technology studies* (4th ed., pp. 853–880). MIT Press.

Stilgoe, J., Owen, R., & Macnaghten, P. (2013). Developing a framework for responsible innovation. *Research Policy*, *42*(9), 1568–1580. DOI: 10.1016/j.respol.2013.05.008

Tschang, T., & Almirall, E. (2021). The technological base of innovation ecosystems: How innovation ecosystems emerge and evolve. *Research Policy*, *50*(2), 104–118.

Tscheligi, M., Tscheligi, A., & Obrist, M. (2020). *Human-centered interactive technologies*. Springer.

von Schomberg, R. (2013). A vision of responsible research and innovation. In Owen, R. (Eds.), *Responsible innovation: Managing the responsible emergence of science and innovation in society* (pp. 51–74). Wiley-Blackwell. DOI: 10.1002/9781118551424.ch3

von Schomberg, R. (2019). Why responsible innovation? *Journal of Responsible Innovation*, *6*(2), 191–200.

Wirtz, B. W., Weyerer, J. C., & Sturm, B. J. (2023). Ethical artificial intelligence: Concepts, applications, and challenges. *Government Information Quarterly*, *40*(1), 101–134.

Zupic, I., & Čater, T. (2015). Bibliometric methods in management and organization. *Organizational Research Methods*, *18*(3), 429–472. DOI: 10.1177/1094428114562629

Chapter 5
Artificial Intelligence Anxiety and Quiet Quitting:
A Human-Centered Integrative Review

Shallu Dhiman
https://orcid.org/0000-0002-1192-583X
Maharishi Markandeshwar University, Mullana, India

Gaurav Dhiman
https://orcid.org/0009-0001-5435-9268
Institute of Chartered Accountants of India, India

Sultan Singh
Maharishi Markandeshwar University, Mullana, India

ABSTRACT

As businesses continue to embrace the advancement of Artificial Intelligence (AI), this advancement has also changed how employees work, communicate with technology, and view the idea of job security. In addition to all the advantages AI can bring, employees have started to express anxiety around the use of AI for their job purposes. Overall, AI anxiety affect how employees behave at work, including behaviours associated with a new phenomenon known as "quiet quitting". Quiet Quitting is a form of psychological withdrawal in which employees limit their work engagement to prescribed role requirements, reducing discretionary effort without formally leaving the organization. The study will provide theories regarding how the integration of AI anxiety contribute to decreased levels of employee engagement and

DOI: 10.4018/979-8-3373-9958-4.ch005

leads of quiet quitting behaviour. Various mediator and moderators of AI anxiety and quiet quitting, multidimensional and unidimensional measurement scales of both the constructs were also discussed in the chapter. The chapter provide limitations and suggested future directions.

1. INTRODUCTION

Artificial Intelligence is defined by a broad technological infrastructure that integrates multiple technologies to provide machines the capabilities associated with human beings such as machine learning to enable computerized processes to recognize and understand written languages as well as distinguish images from one another (Jereb & Urh, 2024).

The uncanny valley hypothesis predicts that AI that resembles humans will cause negative feelings and behaviors (e.g., decreased engagement with work and greater intentions to leave) on behalf of employees (Bae et al., 2025) based on the degree to which people feel close to or identify with it when it shares human-like features (Mori, 1970). Further, the uncanny valley hypothesis explains that as these entities (AI outputs) become more human-like in their output, their usage creates a level of anxiety, fear, along with a multitude of other psychological issues, in the people who use them (Chen et al., 2024). The American Psychological Association has published a report titled Work in America in 2023 in which they refer to the phenomenon of anxiety associated with AI as AI related anxiety and explain it as the feeling of psychological strain felt by employees as a result of the uncertainty of being prepared to be able to work within an AI enabled environment.

Quiet Quitting is a new behavioral response that has been noted to be a result of employees developing AI related anxiety, and it is better defined as a psychological withdrawal than it is overtly opposing, resigning from or quitting your job. Quiet Quitters are employees who continue to satisfy their job duties but put forth less discretionary effort, initiative and extra-role behavior (Uygungil-Erdogan et al., 2025). QQ is the way in which employees behave by strictly adhering to their formal job description while purposely not providing any extra effort, having no intention of leaving their employer. QQ is different from burnout; although both are caused by very long periods of prolonged/continuous stress and result in bad feelings or mental issues (e.g. emotional exhaustion and/or mental fatigue), QQ is a behavior used as a means to create boundaries or to manage one's workload through controlled and intentional actions (Maslach et al., 2001). Quiet quitting is also separate from work disengagement, which is a broader withdrawal of both cognitive and emotional involvement in one's work, whereas QQ includes continuing to complete tasks, but at the lowest acceptable levels (Kahn, 1990). QQ is also different from turnover intention (people are looking for other employment); while most people who quietly quit are still employed with their current employer and not actively searching for new jobs, they instead choose to create a new work/life balance for themselves (Mobley, 1977). Whereas, AI anxiety can be understood as a construct that encompasses individuals' concerns, doubts, and negative perceptions pertaining to the potential consequences of artificial intelligence technologies. This apprehension may arise from a variety of sources, including the fear of employment displacement due to AI innovations, ethical quandaries, violations of privacy, and the difficulties associated with regulating technological advancement (Aljaž, 2024). Quiet Quitting in the context of the adoption of AI does not occur as a result of opposing technology but instead as a way employees can cope with feelings of loss of control, technological preparedness and employability that they fear they are losing. Therefore, employees who feel AI related anxiety may disengage from their jobs as a means to protect themselves, while remaining formally employed. While the implementation of artificial intelligence (AI) adoption has led to increased anxiety among employees regarding job loss and importance of skills, AI adoption in itself does not have a negative effect. If AI adoption is integrated and implemented completely together with training and skill-building opportunities for employees, then it can assist with productivity and aid in performing well. On the other hand, AI-related anxiety appears to develop most often in situations where employees believe their employers are not supportive of them, and are therefore not adequately prepared, which can lead some employees to become disengaged from work and exhibit psychological withdrawal behaviors, including quiet quitting.

Despite growing interest in quiet quitting across different organizational contexts, industries, and countries, the existing literature remains fragmented and limited in scope. Most studies have focused on general withdrawal behaviors, job satisfaction, affective commitment, and turnover intentions in digital workplaces, education, healthcare, and IT sectors across South Korea, Turkey, India, and Europe (Kim & Sohn, 2024; Can & Alas, 2025; Alami et al., 2024; Zlatanović et al., 2025). However, empirical research specifically examining the relationship between AI anxiety and quiet quitting is scarce, with only few studies addressing this link. Moreover, these studies primarily focus on SMEs and IT professionals, leaving gaps in understanding how AI-related concerns influence quiet quitting across other industries, organizational contexts, and countries. Additionally, mediating and moderating mechanisms, such as technostress, job satisfaction, or psychological safety, are yet to be systematically explored. Therefore, there is a critical need for further research to investigate the interplay between AI anxiety and quiet quitting, considering diverse contexts, industries, countries, and key workplace variables (Refer table-4).

This chapter seeks to assess how AI-induced anxiety leads to the phenomenon of quiet quitting in professional settings, when employees psychologically withdraw from their jobs and do only the minimum amount of work necessary. Through the lenses of theories. Using the current body of literature, an integrated framework was also framed with adding mediators and moderators. Moreover, this chapter explored existing measurement scales to measure the viewpoints of the employees which will help the future researchers to do empirical study. The discussion will conclude with a summary of the implications, limitations and future research directions for exploring how organisations can manage employees' anxiety associated with AI, in order to mitigate job disengagement and sustain healthy employee-organization relationships.

The chapter is structured into eight sections; introduction, review of literature, Review of Underpinning, research methodology, integrated framework, discussion, implications, limitations. Finally, the directions for future research provide further exploration into the new areas of interest regarding AI anxiety and quiet quitting.

This chapter offers a substantial contribution to the body of literature by collectively providing unique and insightful information for practitioners and researchers.

2. LITERATURE REVIEW

2.1. Artificial Intelligence

Artificial Intelligence (AI) is now a focal point of development due to its potential impacts on transforming business; AI tools and systems have demonstrated the capability to enhance competitiveness for companies (Zuboff, 2023), and to tackle underperformance issues that affect all individuals, teams, and overall organization performance (Mendy & Rahman, 2019; Peter et al., 2020); however, currently the majority of AI-HRM research has focused predominantly on creating solutions that help resolve organization-level problems of underperforming organizations (Wennberg et al., 2011). At present, while management has turned to the implementation of creative/advanced A.I. tools with the hope that this new, better utilization of material/human resources will create an environment conducive to increasing the development of human capabilities and thus alleviating underperformance issues within organizations (Andrieux et al., 2024; Baporikar & Shikokola, 2020), there is still a clear divide in A.I. – H.R.M. scholarship, leaving unresolved issues such as how to equip and prepare management's ability to handle both organizational underperformance and complexities of ingrained organizational cultural characteristics (Simpson et al., 2022). Final determination on whether A.I. research will result in the development of strategies for implementing organizational strategies (Narver et al., 2000), team-based HRM practices (Singh et al., 2017), or technical-structural-human configuration frameworks to achieve higher-performance levels for organizations (Guest, 2011; Kalleberg et al., 2006) remains yet to be determined conclusively. In addition, many employees may also feel threatened by the rapid increase in the use of AI in the workplace. Many employees may feel anxious about needing to learn about and adapt to the new AI tools. Some employees may fear that their jobs may be replaced by AI or that they will be left behind if others learn to use AI before they do. The perception of this threat may negatively affect the employee's level of motivation, engagement, and overall work performance (Rodrigues et al., 2025). This perception of threat may lead to behaviors such as "quiet quitting." To effectively address concerns about employee reactions to the advent of AI within an organisation, it is essential for organisations to understand the influence of AI-related stress on employee perceptions as well as their overall productivity and health (Can & Alas, 2025). Moreover, AI brings various ethical concerns as more and more of our day-to-day activities, including social services, business practices, and government decision-making, are being determined through the use of algorithmic decisions with the possibility of creating unintended negative outcomes (Mittelstadt et al., 2016). More specifically, Binns (2022) states that algorithmic systems will not be able to provide complete individual justice, as this is dependent upon the human capacity for case-by-case judgement, as well as the balancing of fairness, consistency, and social-technological oversight to properly support trust and ethical outcomes within these systems.

2.2. Artificial intelligence (AI) anxiety

AI anxiety can be conceptualized as a phenomenon that encapsulates individuals' apprehensions, uncertainties, and adverse perceptions regarding the prospective ramifications of artificial intelligence technologies. This trepidation may stem from a multitude of factors, including the fear of job displacement attributable to AI advancements, ethical dilemmas, infringements on privacy, and the challenges associated with managing technological progress (Aljaž, 2024). In the contemporary context, characterized by the accelerated pace of technological evolution and its increasingly pervasive role in everyday life, AI anxiety has emerged as a significant concern for individuals, communities, and organizations alike. This psychological unease not only engenders discomfort at the individual level but also possesses the potential to impact organizational innovation processes and the strategies employed for technology adaptation (Li & Huang, 2020).

AI anxiety holds dual significance for organizations, the first aspect of which pertains to the internal dynamics of the organization itself. In this regard, anxiety surrounding AI among employees poses a potential risk of diminishing workplace motivation and loyalty. Notwithstanding the capacity of AI applications to facilitate enhanced efficiency and cost reduction within business processes, employees who perceive a threat may inadvertently undermine the success of such initiatives, thereby precipitating more adverse outcomes within the organizational framework (Vinchon et al., 2024). Furthermore, analogous concerns regarding AI may manifest among customers and stakeholders. Specifically, apprehensions related to privacy and data security can hinder the adoption of AI-driven products and services, as well as deteriorate the relationship and interactions between the involved parties (Wang et al., 2022). In this regard, it is imperative for organizations to bolster their credibility by employing AI in a manner that aligns with ethical standards.

Recent scholarly investigations underscore the phenomenon of "robot-phobia" as an escalating issue within occupational environments (McClure, 2018). In one of the pioneering studies concerning robot-phobia, Hornung & Smolnik (2022) undertook a qualitative exploration of employee sentiments regarding the integration of artificial intelligence in the workplace, revealing that employees possess profound apprehensions and anxieties towards such technological systems. Presbitero and Teng-Calleja (2023) subsequently affirmed that the adoption of artificial intelligence in professional settings can elicit feelings of job-related insecurity among employees. These research findings suggest the presence of a palpable sense of discomfort among employees concerning the implementation of artificial intelligence, which closely aligns with sentiments of anxiety and fear. Wang and Wang (2022) conceptualized AI anxiety as a psychological state that emerges in reaction to the deployment of AI or robotic process automation within workplace contexts. Li and Huang (2020) delineated eight dimensions of AI anxiety as identified in the existing literature: (1) privacy violation anxiety (Rosen et al., 1987), (2) bias behavior anxiety (Teodorescu et al., 2021), (3) job replacement anxiety (Rhee & Jin, 2021), (4) learning anxiety (Wang et al., 2022), (5) existential risk anxiety (Bostrom, 2002), (6) ethics violation anxiety (Anderson et al., 2021), (7) artificial consciousness anxiety (Buttazzo, 2008), and (8) lack of transparency anxiety (Clarke, 2019). Privacy violation anxiety denotes the psychological distress experienced by employees who fear a direct infringement of their privacy due to artificial intelligence. This form of anxiety may stem from the capabilities of AI to extract personal information from external sources, including social media, utilizing natural language processing (NLP) techniques. Such infringements can also have significant repercussions for employees, impacting their job security, promotion prospects, and potentially resulting in job termination. Bias behavior anxiety arises from the apprehension of facing discrimination perpetrated by AI, which may occur if artificial intelligence employs disparate strategies for different employees due to inaccuracies in data analysis, culminating in systemic discrimination against various demographic groups, including gender, race, and other marginalized populations. Such discriminatory behavior could profoundly influence numerous human resource functions, encompassing hiring, promotion, performance evaluation, and career advancement. Job replacement anxiety is characterized as the distress generated by witnessing the experiences of others or the concern of being supplanted by artificial intelligence, which is intrinsically linked to the apprehension that AI may displace human labor in a diverse array of occupations. Existing literature provide the dimensions of the AI anxiety shown in the figure-1 (Gupta & Banerjee, 2025). Prior studies also indicate that technology-related stress and coping mechanisms differ across age groups, with younger and older employees experiencing distinct forms of technostress (Prensky, 2001; Morris & Venkatesh, 2000; Tarafdar et al., 2019). Trust in leadership and high-quality communication enhance psychological safety and reduce employee anxiety during organizational change (Edmondson, 1999; Dirks & Ferrin, 2002; Men & Stacks, 2014).

Figure 1. Dimensions of AI anxiety

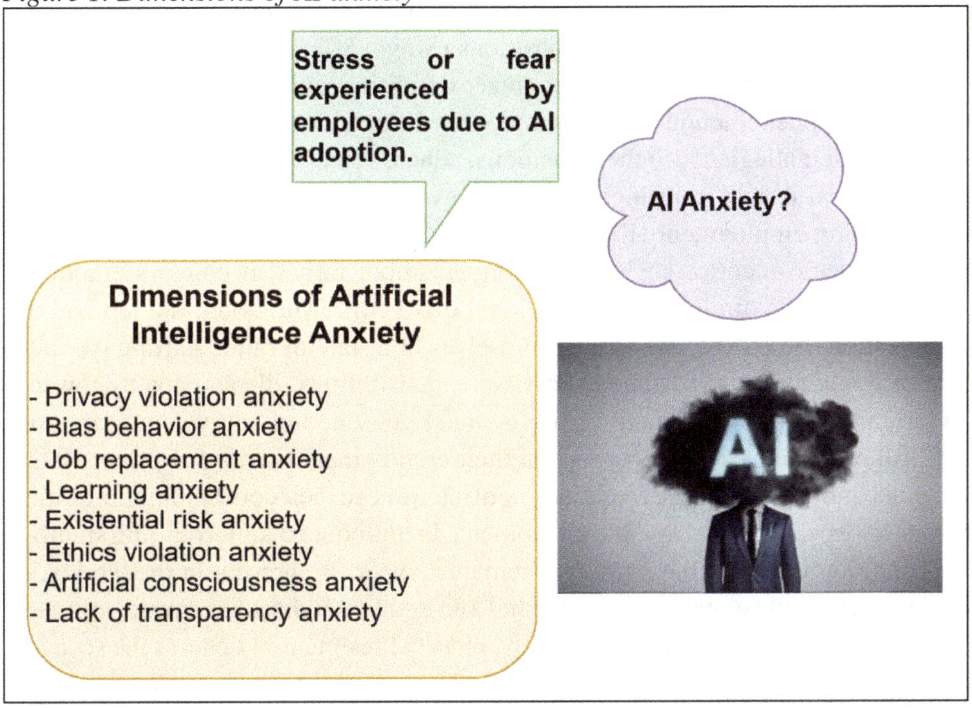

2.3. Quiet Quitting

In 2009, at a Texas A&M symposium on economics, Boldger introduced the term "quiet quitting" which describes a phenomenon that has arisen among scholars studying organizational behavior. Quiet quitting refers to a paradigm that further exemplifies employees' diminished commitment regarding their employment and/

or the organizations for which they work as a result of the way in which a company conducts its business; which is exemplified by Formica and Sfodera (2022).

The concept of "quiet quitting" was initially articulated by Mark Boldger to characterize employees' minimal engagement with their professional responsibilities. Lu et al. (2023) have traced the genesis of quiet quitting to the COVID-19 pandemic, a period that also witnessed the emergence of peculiar workplace phenomena such as "the great resignation" (Patrick et al., 2024). The proportion of disengaged employees experienced a significant escalation during this timeframe. The principal factors contributing to quiet quitting include a deficiency in (1) the perception of being valued, (2) opportunities for personal and professional development, and (3) alignment with the organization's overarching mission (Gavino et al., 2012). Individuals who engage in quiet quitting may be regarded as unwilling continuers who are susceptible to exhibiting deviant behaviors in the workplace and demonstrate a heightened intention to leave their positions (Singh, 2023).

In accordance with the widely recognized definition, quiet quitting can be characterized as the phenomenon wherein employees diminish their exertion, experience a decline in their allegiance to their positions, adhere solely to the minimal obligatory standards, and abstain from engaging in endeavors that lack explicit rewards, despite their ongoing employment (Karrani et al., 2024). Quiet quitting does not signify the employee's intention to leave the organization; rather, it conveys emotional detachment and a diminished motivational drive concerning both the job and the organization. Employees who find themselves in a state of quiet quitting typically exhibit a reluctance to assume excessive responsibilities, display apathy towards opportunities for advancement or professional growth, and cultivate a propensity to fulfill only the basic expectations of their employment (Klotz & Bolino, 2022).

Quiet quitting, which are frequently conflated due to their conceptual similarities, represent two distinctly disparate phenomena. In this context, quiet quitting signifies the condition in which the employee remains physically present in the workplace while concurrently experiencing a mental and emotional disengagement from their professional responsibilities. Conversely, physical resignation denotes the scenario wherein the employee terminates their employment and actively seeks alternative professional opportunities. In this instance, the employee may still fulfill their obligations; however, their overall contributions to the workplace and their commitment to their roles may markedly diminish. Furthermore, it is imperative to assert that quiet quitting should not be misconstrued as an indicator of lethargy or dissatisfaction. Individuals exhibiting this tendency often perform their duties diligently, occasionally exerting greater effort than their peers, yet they may perceive their labor as being subject to exploitation due to this very dedication. The phenomenon of quiet quitting that originates from such a perception may manifest as a protective reflex for the employee (Scheyett, 2023). Figure-2 present the term quiet quitting.

Upon examining the underlying causes of its emergence, it becomes evident that quiet quitting may arise from a constellation of factors, including inadequate work–life balance, diminished job satisfaction, symptoms of burnout, insufficient acknowledgment, and excessive workload. Circumstances in which an employee perceives a lack of value in their contributions or experiences an absence of adequate recognition or reward for their considerable efforts tend to exacerbate the propensity for quiet quitting. From an organizational perspective, the ramifications of quiet quitting can incur substantial long-term costs. The attenuation of employee effort and productivity may precipitate a decline in overall workplace productivity and a deterioration of team dynamics. Consequently, such a scenario can diminish motivation by engendering workload imbalances among colleagues and adversely affect organizational identification among employees who do not exhibit this tendency, thereby inflicting damage upon the corporate culture (Topcuoglu et al., 2023).

2.4. AI anxiety and Quiet Quitting

It is underscored in the scholarly discourse that the phenomena of AI anxiety and quiet quitting are interrelated, and that this correlation can be elucidated particularly through the lens of psychological and organizational determinants within the workplace milieu (Lestari et al., 2024).

Figure 2. Quiet quitting

Empirical evidence has demonstrated that AI anxiety diminishes employees' job satisfaction and undermines their commitment to the organization. However, it is posited that employees are predisposed to exhibit quiet quitting behavior when they perceive AI as a threat to their employment (Rhee & Jin, 2021). Furthermore, it has been established that the swift incorporation of AI into organizational processes and practices can precipitate violations of the psychological contract among employees, which subsequently instigates quiet quitting (Hamouche et al., 2023). It is also accentuated that the equilibrium between job demands and available resources significantly influences the nexus between AI anxiety and quiet quitting. Consequently, insufficient resources coupled with elevated demands can exacerbate quiet quitting, as they render it challenging for employees to navigate the repercussions of AI. AI anxiety has been identified as not exerting a direct influence on quiet quitting; rather, it catalyzes burnout in employees, thereby facilitating quiet quitting behaviors through this burnout - indicating that an indirect effect mechanism is at play. There is a growing body of literature on the negative impact of anxiety and withdrawal that will be associated with adopting AI; there is also evidence that supports a positive outcome for employees when AI is adopted using supportive organizational contexts. For example, Alzeiby et al. (2025) found that AI used in human resources significantly improves employee engagement and experience when implemented within an organization with a clear strategic intent and aligned HR practices, thus demonstrating that organizational strategy is a critical enabling condition. Similarly, Wang et al. (2023) found that the use of responsible AI signals (i.e., autonomy, justice, and explainability) also positively affected the engagement of healthcare practitioners, which leads to more favorable attitudes, satisfaction, and intentions to use AI. However, their research also found that techno-overload reduced the positive effect of responsible AI signals on engagement, thus demonstrating that perceived workload and implementation context are two key boundary conditions influencing employee responses to AI. The findings of these studies indicate that while many employees may be concerned about the use of AI, the impact of AI on employee attitudes and behavior is much more dependent on the context in which it is implemented and represents a major opportunity for future research. Recent empirical research shows that the occupational stress caused by digitally transformed and hybrid work environments may lead to higher levels of burnout and distance, leading to lower levels of employee performance (Conceição & Palma-Moreira, 2025). This evidence supports the existence of technology-related occupational stressors, many of which can be considered AI anxiety and therefore operate through the same psychological pathways that are associated with quiet quitting behaviour.

3. REVIEW OF UNDERPINNING THEORIES

Theoretical frameworks are instrumental in understanding complex events, developing generalizable knowledge applicable to all contexts, and guiding methodology in conducting research. Theoretical definitions refer to the collection (or grouping) of concepts (or ideas) that comprise the phenomena under consideration and can be empirically validated. Therefore, from a practical perspective, theories represent rational propositions used by researchers to clarify how constructs relate to each other to test the empirically defined phenomena (Chen et al., 2021).

3.1. Job Demands–Resources (JD–R) Theory

The Job Demands–Resources (JD–R) Theory (Demerouti et al., 2001; Bakker & Demerouti, 2007) presents a robust framework for elucidating the impact of workplace conditions on employees' well-being, motivation, and performance metrics. This theoretical construct posits that each occupational role encompasses two overarching categories of characteristics: job demands and job resources.

Job demands are delineated as the physical, psychological, or organizational facets of work that necessitate sustained exertion and, consequently, are linked to certain physiological or psychological detriments. Common manifestations of job demands include elevated workloads, emotional strain, role ambiguity, technological pressures, and job insecurity. When these demands become disproportionately excessive and are not counterbalanced by adequate resources, employees may suffer from stress, burnout, and disengagement.

Conversely, job resources are identified as elements of the occupational setting that facilitate employees in attaining work objectives, alleviate job demands, or foster personal development. Illustrative examples encompass supervisory support, training opportunities, autonomy, feedback mechanisms, and skill-enhancement initiatives. Sufficient resources serve a motivational function and assist employees in maintaining engagement, even amidst challenging circumstances.

In the context of the advent of emerging technologies, the JD–R theory assumes particular relevance. Artificial Intelligence Anxiety (AIA) - characterized as the apprehension, uncertainty, or stress stemming from the incorporation of AI technologies—can be conceptualized as a significant psychological job demand. Employees may encounter anxiety due to concerns regarding job displacement, loss of autonomy, skill obsolescence, or heightened expectations to rapidly acclimate to novel systems. When this anxiety reaches elevated levels and organizations neglect to furnish adequate resources such as training, emotional support, or transparent communication, the resulting imbalance exacerbates strain among employees.

This strain frequently manifests in behaviors directed towards self-preservation. A notable behavioral outcome is the phenomenon of quiet quitting, wherein employees persist in meeting the minimal job obligations yet psychologically withdraw, diminish discretionary effort, and disengage from organizational objectives. Within the JD–R framework, quiet quitting can be interpreted as a coping mechanism in response to excessive demands and insufficient resources. To safeguard their emotional and cognitive reserves, employees curtail their investment in their roles.

Consequently, JD–R Theory provides a compelling theoretical perspective for work by elucidating how AI-induced job demands (AI anxiety) and resource inadequacies (deficiencies in training, limited support, and ambiguous communication) can culminate in deleterious outcomes such as quiet quitting, diminished engagement, and impaired performance. It accentuates the pivotal role of equilibrating demands and resources in alleviating the detrimental ramifications of technological transitions within the workplace.

3.2. Conservation of Resources (COR) Theory

The Conservation of Resources (COR) Theory (Hobfoll, 1989) serves as a robust framework for analyzing the responses of individuals to stress, particularly within the realms of organizational transformation and technological upheaval. In accordance with COR theory, individuals are intrinsically driven to safeguard, preserve, and augment their valued resources, which may encompass personal energy, self-worth, autonomy, employment stability, competencies, social networks, and temporal assets. Stress manifests when employees discern that these resources are subject to threat, loss, or inadequacy in relation to job demands (Teetzen et al., 2023).

In contemporary work environments, the swift incorporation of Artificial Intelligence engenders new uncertainties and perceived threats. Artificial Intelligence Anxiety (AIA) may be construed as a reaction to the potential forfeiture of critical resources. Employees may concerns regarding job displacement, the obsolescence of their skills, the erosion of control over work processes, or being subjected to evaluations by systems that remain incomprehensible to them. Such perceptions engender a sensation of resource depletion.

When individuals perceive their resources as endangered, COR theory posits that they implement protective strategies to conserve what remains. One illustrative strategy is quiet quitting, characterized by employees diminishing discretionary effort, mentally detaching, and confining their engagement to essential tasks exclusively. Viewed through a COR lens, quiet quitting operates as a mechanism for resource conservation—an endeavor to safeguard existing emotional and cognitive reserves by disengaging from additional obligations.

Furthermore, COR theory elucidates the concept of loss spirals, wherein the initial threat or loss of resources may precipitate further depletion if not adequately addressed. For instance, AI anxiety can lead to disengagement, which may subsequently impair performance, diminish social support, and undermine professional identity—thereby exacerbating resource loss. In this context, quiet quitting transcends being a mere behavioral trend; it embodies a manifestation of more profound psychological processes associated with resource preservation.

Consequently, COR theory furnishes a compelling theoretical underpinning for this integrative review, as it elucidates how fears and uncertainties related to AI act as resource threats that drive employees towards withdrawal behaviors. It accentuates the necessity for organizational interventions—such as training, transparent communication, and emotional support—to avert resource loss and facilitate resource acquisition amidst technological transitions.

3.3. Self-Determination Theory (SDT)

Self-Determination Theory, as articulated by Deci and Ryan (2000), posits that individuals derive motivation from the fulfillment of three fundamental psychological needs: autonomy, competence, and relatedness. The actualization of these needs results in enhanced intrinsic motivation and engagement among employees. Conversely, when these needs are compromised or obstructed, there is a notable decline in motivation, which can precipitate withdrawal and diminished effort.

Within the realm of Artificial Intelligence, AI-induced anxiety has the potential to erode employees' perception of competence (resulting in feelings of inadequacy in comparison to technology), autonomy (leading to a diminished sense of control over tasks in light of AI-mediated processes), and relatedness (contributing to a perception of decreased support amidst technological transitions). The thwarting of these essential needs may culminate in a state of lack of motivation and disengagement, which may be observable as quiet quitting, whereby employees perform only the bare minimum required. Consequently, SDT serves as a valuable theoretical framework for comprehending how anxiety stemming from AI can attenuate motivation and foster withdrawal behaviors.

3.4. Social Exchange Theory (SET)

Social Exchange Theory (Blau, 1964) posits that the dynamics of the relationship between employees and their organization are fundamentally rooted in the principle of reciprocity. When employees discern that the organization offers support, equity, and opportunities for professional development, they subsequently feel an intrinsic obligation to reciprocate through enhanced commitment, exertion, and constructive work behaviors.

Conversely, when employees perceive that the organization fails to fulfill its commitments—such as neglecting to provide sufficient communication, training, or reassurance amid the implementation of Artificial Intelligence—they may experience a sense of violation of the psychological contract. The phenomenon of AI Anxiety can exacerbate these sentiments if employees harbor concerns that the organization is supplanting them with technology or undervaluing their contributions.

Consequently, employees may diminish their engagement and discretionary effort as a manifestation of negative reciprocity. This behavioral response frequently manifests as quiet quitting, wherein employees undertake only the minimum required tasks while psychologically disengaging. Therefore, Social Exchange Theory elucidates how employees' perceptions of organizational support—or the lack thereof—during transitions involving AI can significantly influence their behavior.

3.5. Technostress Theory

Technostress Theory, as articulated by Tarafdar et al. (2007), elucidates the psychological distress that employees endure when technological demands surpass their capacity for coping. The swift proliferation of artificial intelligence within professional environments has exacerbated this form of stress by imposing pressures characterized by techno-complexity, which engenders feelings of anxiety and inadequacy among employees in their interactions with AI-driven systems, and techno-insecurity, wherein individuals harbor fears of obsolescence or diminished value due to the advent of intelligent technologies. These stressors, induced by technology, amplify AI-related anxiety, leading employees to experience sensations of being overwhelmed, threatened, and emotionally depleted. Consequently, employees frequently exhibit withdrawal-oriented behaviors as a means of safeguarding their remaining psychological resources. In this regard, the phenomenon of quiet quitting emerges as a coping strategy, whereby employees consciously diminish their discretionary efforts and confine their engagement solely to essential responsibilities. Therefore, Technostress Theory offers a robust theoretical framework for understanding how AI-related anxiety may manifest in diminished workplace engagement and the occurrence of quiet quitting in contemporary organizational contexts.

Theoretical Frameworks: Overview of Critical Synthesis

Several complementary theories were reviewed in order to build the proposed theoretical framework: JD-R Model, COR Theory, SET Theory, SDT Theory, and Technostress Theory (Refer figure-4). In short, these different approaches provide insight into the relationship between AI anxiety, burnout, and quiet quitting. JD-R Theory looks at how both job demands and job resources impact employee stress and motivation to work. COR Theory focuses on how both loss of resources and gain of resources impact AI anxiety, while SET Theory looks at how the perceived fairness of a relationship and reciprocity impact an individual's engagement and withdrawal from work. The SDT Theory describes the significance of an individual's fulfilment of intrinsic (psychological) needs for motivation and well-being, and Technostress provides insight into how the unprecedented challenges of digital transformation and AI Adoption create a unique set of challenges for individuals to deal with. In summary, while each of these theoretical frameworks provide separate perspectives of some of the elements that contribute to an employee's response to AI and AI-based anxiety, the integration of all of these perspectives into one holistic framework captures the dynamics of the multi-faceted and multi-level of AI-related stress, burnout and disengagement. In addition, the synthesis of these frameworks provides insight into how organisations might design, orchestrate and implement, organisational initiatives e.g. through leadership support, communication quality, and support of targeted practices, which can mitigate the negative impact of AI anxiety on employee behaviour.

4. METHODOLOGY

This research employs an integrative review of literature, because it systematically collects, evaluates, and synthesizes research studies, to create new ways of viewing, understanding, and interpreting a research topic and its related research areas. In contrast to a traditional narrative review that is focused on providing an overall review of the existing literature, an integrative literature review provides a more in-depth analysis of the existing literature by comparing the various variables, theoretical constructs, methodological approaches, and measurement tools used by previous researchers and identifying patterns, contradictions, and lacunae (gaps) in the literature to form new concepts about future research directions. The literature search was conducted using the Scopus database. Initially, the keywords "Artificial Intelligence Anxiety" AND "Quiet Quitting" were used, along with their relevant synonyms. The number of studies retrieved from Scopus using these keywords was notably limited, yielding only two articles, which confirms the recent and emerging nature of research at the intersection of AI anxiety and quiet quitting. To broaden the scope of the review and capture closely related work, additional search strings were employed, namely ("AI" OR "Artificial Intelligence") AND "Quiet Quitting," and ("Digital Transformation" AND "Quiet Quitting"). The expanded search resulted in 12 articles from the first string and 3 articles from the second.

The following were the criteria for inclusion: (i) Peer-reviewed articles in journals, (ii) Studies specifically focused on the relationship of AI-related anxiety with Quiet Quitting, and (iii) Studies published in English. Exclusions consisted of: Conference Proceedings; Book Chapters; and Studies that are not directly related to misalignment of focus variables. By providing details of our search methodology, the basis of inclusion/exclusion criteria and the resultant screening process, we trust that our integrative review will gain credibility due to the manner in which we define the scope of our work. Although quiet quitting has received increasing attention across industries, research examining its relationship with AI anxiety remains extremely limited. To date, only two studies (Uygungil-Erdogan et al., 2025; Gupta & Banerjee, 2025) have empirically investigated the role of AI anxiety in influencing quiet quitting behaviors. For a comprehensive overview of the extant literature on quiet quitting and related workplace outcomes, the relevant studies from period 2023 to 2025 have been compiled in Table 4.

5. INTEGRATED FRAMEWORK OF THE STUDY

The integrated framework underpinning this integrative review is constructed from insights derived from the extant body of literature pertaining to technology-induced transformations within the workplace. As organizations increasingly integrate artificial intelligence, employees are encountering elevated levels of anxiety pertaining to AI, manifesting in apprehensions regarding job displacement, diminished competence, and uncertainty surrounding prospective work roles. Previous empirical studies indicate that such anxiety adversely affects employees' motivation, emotional well-being, and overall engagement. Expanding upon these findings, the current framework posits that AI anxiety functions as a significant precursor to the phenomenon of quiet quitting, a passive withdrawal behavior characterized by employees limiting their efforts to meet only fundamental job expectations. When employees perceive artificial intelligence as a threat, they are inclined to conserve their psychological and emotional resources by withdrawing from discretionary tasks and reducing their overall involvement. Consequently, the integrated model situates AI anxiety as a pivotal predictor of quiet quitting, thereby offering a literature-informed rationale for investigating how technological stressors influence the emergence of withdrawal behaviors in contemporary workplace settings.

Figure 3 delineates the integrated framework. The framework is underpinned by theoretical constructs that elucidate the ramifications of technology-driven transformations on employee stress and withdrawal behaviors, encompassing perspectives that underscore resource depletion, reciprocal dynamics between employees and organizations, as well as pressures induced by technological advancements. The literature further delineates several pivotal predictors of AI anxiety and quiet quitting (Gupta & Banerjee, 2025; Uygungil-Erdogan et al., 2025). Collectively, these theoretical perspectives and empirical evidence constitute the bedrock of the integrated framework depicted in Figure 3. Figure 4 is showing multi-theoretical framework of AI anxiety, burnout, and quiet quitting.

There are many contextual and organisational factors that affect AI anxiety and quiet quitting phenomena. Employees' perceptions regarding AI-related stress can vary significantly according to geographical/sector-specific contexts, as well as varying work patterns, cultural and societal norms, and regulatory environments in which organisations operate (Tarafdar et al., 2019; Salanova et al., 2013). The way leaders build trust and provide support and guidance for employees, as well as creating a safe and supportive environment, plays an integral role in moderating AI-related employee anxiety (Dirks & Ferrin, 2002; Men & Stacks, 2014; Edmondson, 1999). Resilience and coping strategies are valuable resources employees can leverage to successfully manage workplace-related technological stress and remain engaged (Luthans et al., 2007; Pradhan & Jena, 2017). Ethical AI implementation principles (including transparency, fairness, and model consistencies) reduce worker uncertainty and build confidence (Jobin et al., 2019; Ransbotham et al., 2021). Real-world examples of organisations effectively transitioning to AI illustrate the importance of superior organisational practices related to managing AI change versus the adverse effects of poor practices on employee-related thriller stresses (Conceição & Palma-Moreira, 2025). In addition to traditional quiet firing practices (employer encourage the employee to leave the organization, rather than formally terminate), organizations may also begin to adopt new methods of countering disengagement behaviours (Bergman et al., 2022; Caza & Cortina, 2007). In order to add practical value, it is advisable to conduct qualitative research (i.e., interviews with workers) and develop employee-focused initiatives (i.e., AI Literacy and Reskilling Programs) that provide workers with concrete and actionable suggestions for aiding their transition during an AI shift (Upadhyay & Khandelwal, 2023).

The four measurement scales are explored in this chapter offer a structured and reliable way to assess employees' intent toward QQ. They provide future researchers with validated tools to study disengagement across various contexts and populations. These scales enable early identification of QQ tendencies and support evidence-based interventions. Their application can strengthen both academic inquiry and practical HR strategies. The measurement instruments employed for measuring QQ intent are also delineated in this section. Three unidimensional scales and one multidimensional scale (descriptions of name of the scale, number of items and sources) are presented in Table 1 and Table 2.

Figure 3. Integrated framework of the study

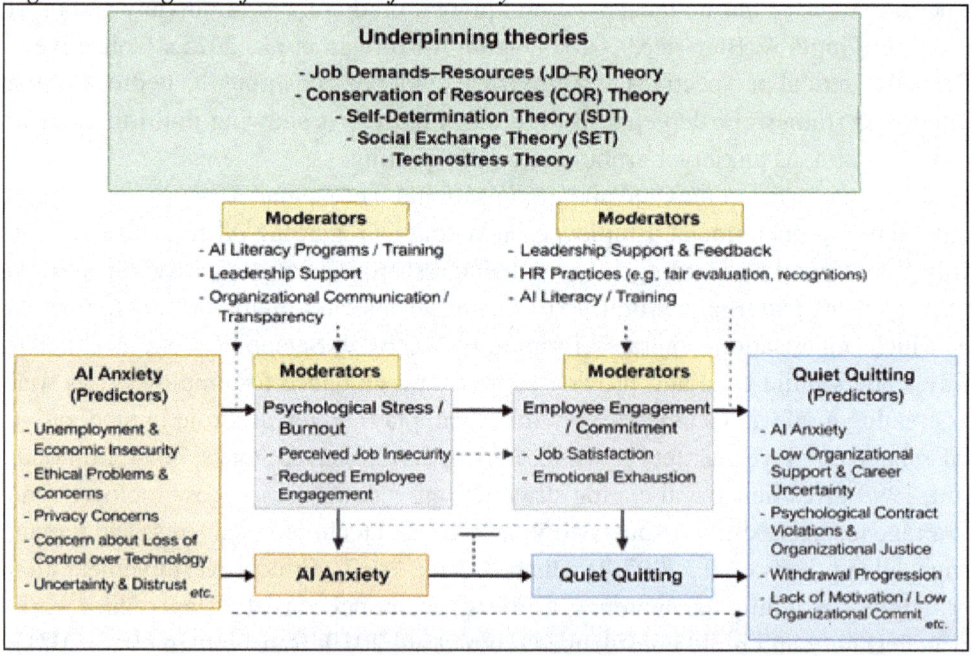

Table 1. Unidimensional measurement scales for "quiet quitting"

Scale	Number of Items	References
Quiet Quitting	(consist of 10 items)	Talukdar and Priteo (2025)
Quiet Quitting Intentions	(consist of 8 items)	Anand et al. (2023)
Quiet Quitting	(consist of 3 items)	Srivastava et al., (2023)

Table 2. Multidimensional measurement scale of "quiet quitting"

Scale	Number of Items	References
Quiet Quitting (Dimension) 1. Detachment 2. Lack of initiative 3. Lack of Motivation	(Consist of total 9 items) 4 items 3 items 2 items	Galanis et al. (2023)

To ascertain participants' AI Anxiety, participants completed the anxiety scale developed by Li and Huang (2020), which consisted of three questions that assessed the variables PVA, BBA, JRA and LTA.

Table 3. Multidimensional measurement scale of "AI anxiety"

Scale	Number of Items	References
AI Anxiety	12 items (3 each for Privacy violation anxiety, Bias behavior anxiety, Job replacement anxiety, Lack of transparency anxiety	Li and Huang (2020)
AI Anxiety	21 items (4 dimensions)	Wang and Wang (2022), Terzi (2020)

One widely used scale measuring AI anxiety is the Artificial Intelligence Anxiety Scale developed by Wang and Wang in 2022, which was then adapted into the Turkish language by Terzi in 2020 (refer Table-3). Measures such as the AI Anxiety Scale developed by Wang and Wang (2022) and the Multi-Dimensional Framework developed by Li and Huang (2020), provide researchers with reliable and culturally sensitive ways to assess the cognitive, emotional, and behavioural aspects of AI anxiety. Technostress measures (Tarafdar et al., 2010) and tech-savviness measures (Shanahan and Hyman, 2010) also provide valuable resources for assessing employees' technology-based stress and capabilities, so future scholars can understand how technostress interacts with emerging anxieties surrounding the adoption of new technologies.

Key Trends in the Future-of-Work

AI technologies, combined with digital transformation, are driving a human-centered future that changes how we think about workplace and employee roles. In addition to seeing a growing use of AI in automatic (or routine) cognitive functions, companies are increasingly allowing workers to focus more on problem-solving and creativity work due to this change. In recent times, there has been significant growth in skills-based employment as companies have chosen to highlight skill sets required instead of job titles. Companies have also recognised that workers must continue to develop their skill set through continuous learning and reskilling. The use of data to inform decisions based on organisational structures and support of workforce engagement is a significant trend. Therefore, while many organisations are adopting new technology and become technocentric, we must remain mindful of how these new technologies are being used and the impact on the workers who will continue to work alongside AI.

6. DISCUSSION

The current integrative review explores how artificial intelligence (AI) anxiety as a significant predictor of the phenomenon known as quiet quitting, thereby providing empirical evidence regarding the psychological and behavioral ramifications associated with the adoption of AI technologies in professional settings. The literature reveals that employees who report elevated levels of anxiety related to AI are predisposed to withdraw from their occupational roles, diminish their discretionary efforts, and confine their work activities to fundamental responsibilities, which is congruent with the conceptual framework of quiet quitting. These findings corroborate previous research indicating that AI anxiety adversely affects employees' motivation, emotional well-being, and organizational commitment, thereby heightening the propensity for withdrawal behaviors, including quiet quitting and intentions to leave organization (Uygungil-Erdogan et al., 2025).

Figure 4. Multi-theoretical framework of AI anxiety, burnout, and quiet quitting

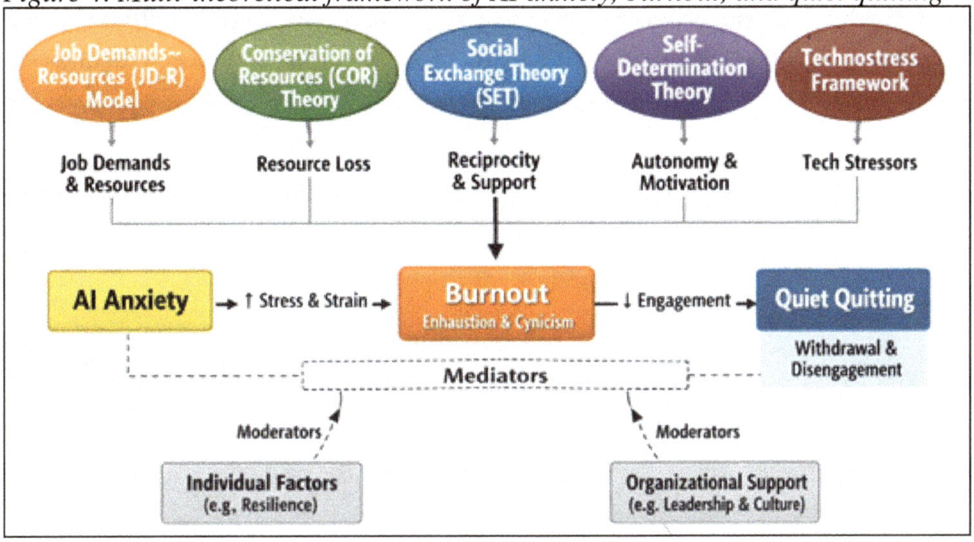

The academic literature further articulates several critical predictors of AI anxiety and quiet quitting (Gupta & Banerjee, 2025; Uygungil-Erdogan et al., 2025). These determinants elucidate that quiet quitting is not simply a voluntary diminishment of effort, but rather a coping mechanism utilized by employees to safeguard their psychological and emotional resources in reaction to perceived threats arising from the implementation of AI technologies.

In summary, this study enriches the existing literature by elucidating the mechanisms through which AI anxiety affects quiet quitting, as well as identifying the primary predictors and theoretical frameworks that underpin this relationship and provide the available measurement scales. It emphasizes the imperative for organizations to adopt a proactive stance in managing the human implications of AI integration in order to sustain employee motivation, commitment, and performance within increasingly technology-driven work environments.

7. IMPLICATIONS

7.1. Theoretical Implications

This integrative review presents several significant theoretical advancements. Firstly, it synthesizes Technostress Theory (Tarafdar et al., 2007), Conservation of Resources (COR) Theory (Hobfoll, 1989), Social Exchange Theory (Blau, 1964), Job Demands–Resources (JD–R) Model (Bakker & Demerouti, 2007), and Self-

Determination Theory (SDT) (Deci & Ryan, 2000) to elucidate the mechanisms through which AI-induced anxiety impacts phenomena quiet quitting. This review-based study's theoretical implications are focused on synthesizing the main theories that account for how AI anxiety relates to quiet quitting behaviour.

Table 4. Extant research on related variables

Author	Title	Country	Industry / Context	Mediator / Moderator	Findings
Kim and Sohn (2024)	The impact of quiet quitting on turnover intentions in the era of digital transformation: The mediating roles of job satisfaction and affective commitment, and the moderating role of psychological safety	South Korea	Full-time employees undergoing digital transformation (cross-industry organizational context)	Mediators: Job satisfaction, Affective commitment Moderator: Psychological safety	Quiet quitting negatively affects job satisfaction and affective commitment, which in turn increase turnover intention. Job satisfaction and affective commitment mediate the relationship between quiet quitting and turnover intention. Psychological safety moderates (buffers) the negative effects of quiet quitting on job satisfaction and affective commitment, thereby reducing turnover intention.
Can and Alas (2025)	The silent scream of digital future: Exploring AI awareness and quiet quitting in Turkish teachers	Turkey	Education sector – Turkish language teachers and physical education teachers	None explicitly tested (direct relationship examined)	Teachers' perceptions and attitudes toward artificial intelligence are strongly associated with their quiet quitting tendencies, irrespective of their level of AI knowledge. Quiet quitting levels were similar among teachers with both positive and negative attitudes toward AI. However, as AI knowledge increased, quiet quitting tendencies also increased in both disciplines, with a higher tendency observed among physical education teachers compared to Turkish language teachers.

continued on following page

Table 4. Continued

Author	Title	Country	Industry / Context	Mediator / Moderator	Findings
Uygungil-Erdogan et al. (2025)	Assessing the Effect of Artificial Intelligence Anxiety on Turnover Intention: The Mediating Role of Quiet Quitting in Turkish Small and Medium Enterprises	Turkey	Small and Medium Enterprises (SMEs) – employees in Kırıkkale province	Mediator: Quiet quitting Moderator: Not examined	Artificial intelligence anxiety does not directly influence turnover intention; however, it exerts a significant indirect effect through quiet quitting. Increased AI-related anxiety heightens employees' concerns about job security, reduces motivation and organizational commitment, and triggers turnover intention by fostering quiet quitting behaviors.
Gupta & Banerjee (2025)	Can artificial intelligence anxiety lead to quiet quitting intention? A moderated mediation analysis with tech-savviness and technostress	India	IT and IT-enabled Services (ITeS) – working professionals in the context of Industry 5.0 technologies	Mediator: Technostress Moderator: Tech-savviness	Technostress mediates the relationship between AI anxiety and quiet quitting, indicating that AI-induced stress translates anxiety into withdrawal behavior. Tech-savviness moderates this indirect relationship, shaping how AI anxiety and technostress jointly influence quiet quitting. The findings highlight AI anxiety as a critical socio-technical risk factor that can undermine employee productivity by triggering quiet quitting in technology-intensive workplaces.

continued on following page

Table 4. Continued

Author	Title	Country	Industry / Context	Mediator / Moderator	Findings
Alami et al. (2024)	Predicting Quiet Quitting: Machine Learning Insights into Silent Resignations in Healthcare Industry	Emerging markets (healthcare organizations)	Healthcare industry – employees in healthcare organizations	None explicitly examined (predictive ML-based analysis)	Quiet quitting is driven primarily by fear of retribution, leadership styles, working conditions, lack of meaningful work, bureaucracy, absence of career opportunities, and lack of trust. Salaries do not significantly influence quiet quitting, while years of experience are negatively associated with it. Machine learning models reveal strong predictive capability, with Support Vector Machine (SVM) achieving superior precision and F1-score, and Logistic Regression demonstrating high overall accuracy, making it particularly suitable for predicting quiet quitting in healthcare settings.

continued on following page

Table 4. Continued

Author	Title	Country	Industry / Context	Mediator / Moderator	Findings
Alaql et al. (2023)	Data-driven deep journalism to discover age dynamics in multi-generational labour markets from LinkedIn media	Not explicitly specified (global LinkedIn data)	Labour markets & journalism context – multi-generational workforce analysis using LinkedIn media	None examined (data-driven, exploratory ML-based study)	Using a deep journalism approach grounded in artificial intelligence and machine learning, the study analyzes 57,000 LinkedIn posts to uncover age dynamics in labour markets amid the Great Resignation and quiet quitting phenomena. Latent Dirichlet Allocation (LDA) identifies 15 parameters grouped into five macro-parameters: generation-specific issues, skills and qualifications, employment sectors, consumer industries, and employment issues. The findings demonstrate that AI-driven journalism can objectively capture multigenerational perspectives on labour market dynamics and provide scalable, unbiased insights into workforce changes associated with quiet quitting and related withdrawal trends.

continued on following page

Table 4. Continued

Author	Title	Country	Industry / Context	Mediator / Moderator	Findings
Zlatanović et al. (2025)	The quiet quitting phenomenon in digital workplaces: A legal-theoretical and comparative analysis	Europe (comparative legal context)	Digital workplaces – labour law, company law, and organizational regulation	None examined (legal-theoretical and comparative analysis)	Quiet quitting is conceptually ambiguous but has significant implications for individual and collective labour law, organizational governance, and company law. The study highlights the legal challenges associated with defining quiet quitting within employment relationships, particularly regarding employee obligations, managerial status, and productivity expectations in digital workplaces. It emphasizes the need for legal frameworks to adapt to emerging withdrawal behaviours linked to changing work arrangements.

By collecting together existing literature, this study illustrates how different scholars have thought about AI-related stress through various theoretical frameworks. The study synthesises the theoretical insights, and it demonstrates that these theories create a very good theoretical foundation for understanding how and why employees experience anxiety related to the rapid expansion of AI usage. They show that changes in technology create greater levels of technological stress (e.g. social pressures to be more productive), decrease the level of autonomy employees have with their jobs (e.g. fear of losing their job), and interrupt social/psychological exchanges (e.g. disruption in workplace trust) are contributing to the development of disengaged and withdrawal behaviours.

As mentioned previously, the study does not create new theories, and instead provides a systematic way of understanding what existing theories have identified. By unifying various theories, this article enhances a theoretical clarity and assists future researchers by providing a means to determine which theoretical frameworks will be best suited to conduct their empirical research on the effects of AI on employee behaviour. Furthermore, this consolidation reinforces the need to understand AI-based changes in the workplace using a multi-theoretical perspective. Overall, the theoretical implications suggest that AI anxiety is an item of great interest, and that an understanding of employee behaviour changed by AI should miss the complexities of the multi-theoretical nature of AI anxiety for continued research.

7.2. Managerial Implications

There are implications for both managers and leaders of organizations working in AI-enhanced environments. That being said, the first implication for managers is that anxiety about artificial intelligence can lead to issues like quiet quitting, which can also lead to low employee engagement, less productive employees and a reduction in the effectiveness of the company overall. Therefore, managers should seek to intervene proactively with their employees to reduce the threats posed by anxiety related to AI. By offering ongoing training and upskilling for employees and communicating openly with them about their use of AI, employers can build confidence within their workforce while decreasing uncertainty and decreasing the likelihood of psychological exit. The result is that organizations will be able to take full advantage of the productivity potential of AI.

One way to address these items is to implement comprehensive training programs that provide employees with the opportunity to develop their skills and competencies, improve their confidence in using AI and other technological innovations, and encourage employees to feel empowered by their use of AI. Another way for managers to address these issues is to communicate openly with employees about the introduction of AI and what the intended uses and expected consequences will be on jobs, so that employees can better understand how the introduction of AI will impact or will not impact their jobs, thereby increasing trust in management.

Employee Support Systems, such as those that include serving employees with coaching and mentoring to help them deal with stresses and fears about losing their jobs due to the impact of AI on job functions, are critical to providing employees with sufficient resources to remain engaged and motivated. Further, managers should be watchful of employees who might exhibit characteristics of quiet quitting, monitor their levels of engagement regularly, and take necessary steps to mitigate those behaviours, as needed.

It is important for organizations to create a supportive culture where employees feel valued for their contributions as well as recognized for their hard work, and provided with opportunities to grow their skills. Organizations that openly discuss employee concerns about the potential negative effects of artificial intelligence in the workplace can reduce withdrawal behavior and increase employee commitment, thereby enhancing overall organizational performance during times of change due to technology. Organizations are crucial in supporting employees in overcoming the stress and anxiety related to AI, as well as in preventing the disengagement of employees. Leaders can help employees cope with the changes brought about by the introduction of AI by establishing trust, providing a transparent environment, and delivering "helpful" feedback. By addressing psychological safety and employing human resources practices, such as training programs, reskilling programs, and flexible working arrangements, the organization can support employees in adapting to the transition from manual labour to the use of artificial intelligence. By using these strategies to proactively address AI Anxiety, organizations can continue to engage their workforce, lower the risk of Burnout and promote the overall well-being of the workforce, thereby maximizing the technological adoption and employee outcomes.

7.3. Practical Implications

The findings of this study have substantial consequences for how organizations operate as well as how managers lead their teams in environments where employees rely on AI technologies. Managers need to recognize that employee anxiety related to AI impacts employee engagement which can lead to withdrawal behaviours. Organizations should create training programs around AI while also enhancing the skills and confidence level of employees to use technology. Providing clear and transparent information regarding the use of AI, its purpose and how it may affect their job responsibilities will help reduce anxiety and increase trust in management practices.

Employee assistance programs (EAPs) should be part of the organization's strategy. An EAP may include counselling services, mentoring programs, and guidance for managing stress and staying motivated on the job. Managers must also be accountable for identifying employees who may be vulnerable to "quiet quitting" and developing retention strategies to increase employee engagement and job satisfaction. Building a strong organizational culture that values employee contributions, promotes professional development, and recognizes individual efforts supports employee commitment and productivity through times of change caused by technology. AI Literacy Programmes can play a critical role in mitigating AI anxiety and reducing the likelihood of quiet quitting. Organizations should invest in structured training initiatives that enhance employees' understanding of AI systems, their purpose, and their impact on job roles. Improving AI literacy can foster perceived control, reduce uncertainty, and strengthen employees' psychological safety, thereby promoting engagement and proactive work behaviors during digital transformation.

As leaders, managing expectations and workloads and creating an environment that is supportive of employees' use of technology is key to helping employees feel engaged with their jobs. When managers proactively address employee concerns regarding AI and provide the opportunity for employees to develop the skills necessary to be successful in using AI, they decrease the opportunity for employees to withdraw from their job and reduce productivity. A manager can create a positive work environment (where employees have confidence in their abilities and feel supported by the company), resulting in a motivated, engaged, and committed workforce, as well as an increase in employee retention and overall productivity, in any type of business setting.

8. LIMITATION AND FUTURE RESEARCH DIRECTIONS.

Although this study provides valuable insights into the connection between AI anxiety and quiet quitting, it is subject to several limitations that open avenues for future research. Primarily, the study relied solely on a literature review without empirical investigation, preventing the establishment of causal relationships or the assessment of the relative strength and direction of effects. Consequently, the conclusions are dependent on the quality, context, and methodology of the reviewed literature, and any biases or limitations in prior studies may have influenced the findings. While the study identified several predictors of AI anxiety and quiet quitting, it did not determine the most significant factors, nor did it empirically examine potential moderators such as organizational support, leadership style, job characteristics, and employee resilience, all of which likely shape the relationship between AI anxiety and withdrawal behaviors. Furthermore, other influences on employee behavior—such as workplace culture, technological readiness, and coping mechanisms—were not fully explored, and the scales cited from previous studies were not validated within this specific context. Future research should address these gaps by conducting empirical studies using quantitative, experimental, and longitudinal designs to establish causal links and observe the evolution of AI anxiety over time. Studies should also examine diverse populations, including gig workers and culturally varied workforces, to enhance generalizability, while exploring mediating and moderating mechanisms such as psychological safety, perceptions of injustice, burnout, and intrinsic motivation to better understand the psychological pathways leading to quiet quitting. Additionally, researchers should investigate broader outcomes, including job performance, innovation, organizational citizenship behavior, employee well-being, and intentions to leave. Finally, developing and validating context-specific measurement tools for AI anxiety and quiet quitting will improve the reliability and applicability of future assessments in rapidly evolving workplaces.

REFERENCES

Alami, R., Stachowicz-Stanusch, A., Agarwal, S., & Al Masaeid, T. (2024). Predicting quiet quitting: Machine learning insights into silent resignations in the healthcare industry. *Journal of Ecohumanism*, *3*(4), 3444–3462. DOI: 10.62754/joe.v3i4.3864

Alaql, A. A., AlQurashi, F., & Mehmood, R. (2023). Data-driven deep journalism to discover age dynamics in multi-generational labour markets from LinkedIn media. *Journalism and Media*, *4*(1), 120–145. DOI: 10.3390/journalmedia4010010

Aljaž, T. (2024). Leveraging ChatGPT for enhanced logical analysis in the theory of constraints thinking process. *Organizacija*, *57*(2), 202–214. DOI: 10.2478/orga-2024-0014

Alzeiby, E. A., Islam, N., Shaik, A. S., & Yaqub, M. Z. (2025). AI adoption in enterprises for enhanced strategic human resource management practices: Benefiting the employee engagement and experience. *Journal of Enterprise Information Management*, *38*(5), 1441–1464. DOI: 10.1108/JEIM-05-2024-0249

American Psychological Association. (2023). 2023 Work in America survey. https://www.apa.org/pubs/reports/work-in-america/2023-work-america-ai monitoring

Anand, A., Doll, J., & Ray, P. (2024). Drowning in silence: A scale development and validation of quiet quitting and quiet firing. *The International Journal of Organizational Analysis*, *32*(4), 721–743. DOI: 10.1108/IJOA-01-2023-3600

Anderson, M., Anderson, S. L., Gounaris, A., & Kosteletos, G. (2021). Towards moral machines: A discussion with Michael Anderson and Susan Leigh Anderson. *Conatus: Journal of Philosophy*, *6*(1), 177–202. DOI: 10.12681/cjp.26832

Andrieux, M., Henrio, L., & Radanne, G. (2024). Active objects based on algebraic effects. In *Active Object Languages: Current Research Trends* (pp. 3–36). Springer Nature Switzerland, Cham. DOI: 10.1007/978-3-031-51060-1_1

Bae, S., Jung, T., Cho, J., & Kwon, O. (2025). Effects of meta-human characteristics on user acceptance: From the perspective of uncanny valley theory. *Behaviour & Information Technology*, *44*(4), 731–748. DOI: 10.1080/0144929X.2024.2338408

Bakker, A. B., & Demerouti, E. (2007). The job demands-resources model: State of the art. *Journal of Managerial Psychology*, *22*(3), 309–328. DOI: 10.1108/02683940710733115

Baporikar, N., & Shikokola, S. (2020). Information technology adoption dynamics for SMEs in the manufacturing sector of Namibia. [IJICTRAME]. *International Journal of ICT Research in Africa and the Middle East*, *9*(2), 60–77. DOI: 10.4018/IJICTRAME.2020070104

Bergman, J. Z., Cummings, T. G., & Maher, C. P. (2022). Employee disengagement and organizational responses. *Journal of Organizational Behavior*, *43*(2), 145–161.

Blau, P. M. (1964). *Exchange and power in social life*. Wiley.

Bostrom, N. (2002). Existential risks: Analysing human extinction scenarios and related hazards. *Journal of Evolution and Technology / WTA*, *9*, 1–36.

Buttazzo, G. (2008). Artificial consciousness: Hazardous questions (and answers). *Artificial Intelligence in Medicine*, *44*(2), 139–146. DOI: 10.1016/j.artmed.2008.07.004

Can, H. C., & Alas, D. K. (2025). The silent scream of digital future: Exploring AI awareness and quiet quitting in Turkish teachers. *Acta Psychologica*, *260*, 105589. DOI: 10.1016/j.actpsy.2025.105589

Caza, B. B., & Cortina, L. M. (2007). From insult to injury: Explaining the impact of incivility. *Journal of Management*, *33*(4), 1–29.

Chen, C., Hu, W., & Wei, X. (2024). From anxiety to action: Exploring the impact of artificial intelligence anxiety and artificial intelligence self-efficacy on motivated learning of undergraduate students. *Interactive Learning Environments*, •••, 1–16. DOI: 10.1080/10494820.2024.2371937

Chen, Y., Mandler, T., & Meyer-Waarden, L. (2021). Three decades of research on loyalty programs: A literature review and future research agenda. *Journal of Business Research*, *124*, 179–197. DOI: 10.1016/j.jbusres.2020.11.057

Clarke, R. (2019). Why the world wants controls over artificial intelligence. *Computer Law & Security Review*, *35*(4), 423–433. DOI: 10.1016/j.clsr.2019.04.006

Conceição, A., & Palma-Moreira, A. (2025). The Relationship Between Occupational Stress, Burnout, and Perceived Performance: The Moderating Role of Work Regime. *Administrative Sciences*, *15*(10), 377. DOI: 10.3390/admsci15100377

Deci, E. L., & Ryan, R. M. (2000). The "what" and "why" of goal pursuits: Human needs and the self-determination of behavior. *Psychological Inquiry*, *11*(4), 227–268. DOI: 10.1207/S15327965PLI1104_01

Demerouti, E., Bakker, A. B., Nachreiner, F., & Schaufeli, W. B. (2001). The job demands-resources model of burnout. *The Journal of Applied Psychology*, *86*(3), 499–512. DOI: 10.1037/0021-9010.86.3.499

Dirks, K. T., & Ferrin, D. L. (2002). Trust in leadership: Meta-analytic findings and implications for research and practice. *The Journal of Applied Psychology*, *87*(4), 611–628. DOI: 10.1037/0021-9010.87.4.611

Edmondson, A. C. (1999). Psychological safety and learning behavior in work teams. *Administrative Science Quarterly*, *44*(2), 350–383. DOI: 10.2307/2666999

Formica, S., & Sfodera, F. (2022). The great resignation and quiet quitting paradigm shifts: An overview of current situation and future research directions. *Journal of Hospitality Marketing & Management*, *31*(8), 899–907. DOI: 10.1080/19368623.2022.2136601

Galanis, P., Katsiroumpa, A., Vraka, I., Siskou, O., Konstantakopoulou, O., Moisoglou, I., & Kaitelidou, D. (2023). The quiet quitting scale: Development and initial validation. *AIMS Public Health*, *10*(4), 828–848. DOI: 10.3934/publichealth.2023055

Gavino, M. C., Wayne, S. J., & Erdogan, B. (2012). Discretionary and transactional human resource practices and employee outcomes: The role of perceived organizational support. *Human Resource Management*, *51*(5), 665–686. DOI: 10.1002/hrm.21493

Guest, D. E. (2011). Human resource management and performance: Still searching for some answers. *Human Resource Management Journal*, *21*(1), 3–13. DOI: 10.1111/j.1748-8583.2010.00164.x

Gupta, R., & Banerjee, P. (2025). Can artificial intelligence anxiety lead to quiet quitting intention? A moderated mediation analysis with tech-savviness and technostress. In *Evidence-based HRM: a Global Forum for Empirical Scholarship*. Emerald Publishing Limited.

Hamouche, S., Koritos, C., & Papastathopoulos, A. (2023). Quiet quitting: Relationship with other concepts and implications for tourism and hospitality. *International Journal of Contemporary Hospitality Management*, *35*(12), 4297–4312. DOI: 10.1108/IJCHM-11-2022-1362

Hobfoll, S. E. (1989). Conservation of resources: A new attempt at conceptualizing stress. *The American Psychologist*, *44*(3), 513–524. DOI: 10.1037/0003-066X.44.3.513

Hornung, O., & Smolnik, S. (2022). AI invading the workplace: Negative emotions towards the organizational use of personal virtual assistants. *Electronic Markets*, *32*(1), 123–138. DOI: 10.1007/s12525-021-00493-0

Jereb, E., & Urh, M. (2024). The use of artificial intelligence among students in higher education. *Organizacija*, *57*(4), 333–345. DOI: 10.2478/orga-2024-0024

Jobin, A., Ienca, M., & Vayena, E. (2019). The global landscape of AI ethics guidelines. *Nature Machine Intelligence*, *1*(9), 389–399. DOI: 10.1038/s42256-019-0088-2

Kahn, W. A. (1990). Psychological conditions of personal engagement and disengagement at work. *Academy of Management Journal*, *33*(4), 692–724. DOI: 10.2307/256287

Kalleberg, A. L., Marsden, P. V., Reynolds, J., & Knoke, D. (2006). Beyond profit? Sectoral differences in high-performance work practices. *Work and Occupations*, *33*(3), 271–302. DOI: 10.1177/0730888406290049

Karrani, M. A., Bani-Melhem, S., & Mohd-Shamsudin, F. (2024). Employee quiet quitting behaviours: Conceptualization, measure development, and validation. *Service Industries Journal*, *44*(3–4), 218–236. DOI: 10.1080/02642069.2023.2286604

Kim, K. T., & Sohn, Y. W. (2024). The impact of quiet quitting on turnover intentions in the era of digital transformation: The mediating roles of job satisfaction and affective commitment, and the moderating role of psychological safety. *Systems*, *12*(11), 460. DOI: 10.3390/systems12110460

Klotz, A. C., & Bolino, M. C. (2022). When quiet quitting is worse than the real thing. *Harvard Business Review*. https://hbr.org/2022/09/when-quiet-quitting-is-worse-than-the-real-thing

Lestari, N. S., Zainal, V. R., Chan, S., & Nawangsari, L. C. (2024). Impact of career development, job insecurity, and tech awareness on the quiet quitting of hospitality employees in Indonesia. *Problems and Perspectives in Management*, *22*(3), 427–439. DOI: 10.21511/ppm.22(3).2024.33

Li, J., & Huang, J. S. (2020). Dimensions of artificial intelligence anxiety based on the integrated fear acquisition theory. *Technology in Society*, *63*, 101410. DOI: 10.1016/j.techsoc.2020.101410

Lu, M., Al Mamun, A., Chen, X., Yang, Q., & Masukujjaman, M. (2023). Quiet quitting during COVID-19: The role of psychological empowerment. *Humanities & Social Sciences Communications*, *10*(1), 1–16. DOI: 10.1057/s41599-023-02012-2

Luthans, F., Vogelgesang, G. R., & Lester, P. B. (2007). Developing the psychological capital of resiliency. *Human Resource Development Review*, *6*(1), 25–44. DOI: 10.1177/1534484305285335

Maslach, C., Schaufeli, W. B., & Leiter, M. P. (2001). Job burnout. *Annual Review of Psychology*, *52*(1), 397–422. DOI: 10.1146/annurev.psych.52.1.397

McClure, P. K. (2018). "You're fired," says the robot: The rise of automation in the workplace, technophobes, and fears of unemployment. *Social Science Computer Review*, *36*(2), 139–156. DOI: 10.1177/0894439317698637

Men, L. R., & Stacks, D. W. (2014). The effects of authentic leadership on strategic internal communication and employee–organization relationships. *Journal of Public Relations Research*, *26*(4), 301–324. DOI: 10.1080/1062726X.2014.908720

Mendy, J., & Rahman, M. (2019). Supporting SMEs' internationalisation through a deeper understanding of human and technology barriers: Applying effective HRM processes from a developing country. *Journal of Organizational Effectiveness: People and Performance*, *6*(4), 205–226. DOI: 10.1108/JOEPP-12-2018-0121

Mobley, W. H. (1977). Intermediate linkages in the relationship between job satisfaction and employee turnover. *The Journal of Applied Psychology*, *62*(2), 237–240. DOI: 10.1037/0021-9010.62.2.237

Mori, M. (1970). Bukimi no tani [The uncanny valley]. *Energy*, *7*, 33.

Morris, M. G., & Venkatesh, V. (2000). Age differences in technology adoption decisions: Implications for a changing workforce. *Personnel Psychology*, *53*(2), 375–403. DOI: 10.1111/j.1744-6570.2000.tb00206.x

Narver, J. C., Slater, S. F., & MacLachlan, D. L. (2000). *Total market orientation, business performance, and innovation*. Marketing Science Institute.

Patrick, W. S., Thakur, M., & Jha, J. K. (2024). Attachment and attractiveness towards organizations: Reinforcing the intention to stay amidst the 'great resignation'. *Evidence-based HRM: A Global Forum for Empirical Scholarship, 12*(3), 611–629.

Peter, K. A., Schols, J. M., Halfens, R. J., & Hahn, S. (2020). Investigating work-related stress among health professionals at different hierarchical levels: A cross-sectional study. *Nursing Open*, *7*(4), 969–979. DOI: 10.1002/nop2.469

Pradhan, R. K., & Jena, L. K. (2017). Employee resilience and well-being at work. *Management Research Review*, *40*(5), 509–530.

Prensky, M. (2001). Digital natives, digital immigrants. *On the Horizon*, *9*(5), 1–6. DOI: 10.1108/10748120110424816

Presbitero, A., & Teng-Calleja, M. (2023). Job attitudes and career behaviors relating to employees' perceived incorporation of artificial intelligence in the workplace: A career self-management perspective. *Personnel Review*, *52*(4), 1169–1187. DOI: 10.1108/PR-02-2021-0103

Ransbotham, S., Kiron, D., LaFountain, B., & Candelon, F. (2021). Winning with AI: Pioneers combine strategy, organizational structure, and AI capabilities. *MIT Sloan Management Review*.

Rhee, T., & Jin, X. (2021). The effect of job anxiety of replacement by artificial intelligence on organizational members' job satisfaction in the 4th industrial revolution era: The moderating effect of job uncertainty. *Journal of Digital Convergence*, *19*(7), 1–9.

Rodrigues, M., Silva, R., Borges, A. P., Franco, M., & Oliveira, C. (2025). Artificial intelligence: Threat or asset to academic integrity? *A bibliometric analysis. Kybernetes*, *54*(5), 2939–2970. DOI: 10.1108/K-09-2023-1666

Rosen, L. D., Sears, D. C., & Weil, M. M. (1987). Computerphobia. *Behavior Research Methods, Instruments, & Computers*, *19*(2), 167–179. DOI: 10.3758/BF03203781

Salanova, M., Llorens, S., & Cifre, E. (2013). The dark side of technologies: Technostress among users of information and communication technologies. *International Journal of Psychology*, *48*(3), 422–436. DOI: 10.1080/00207594.2012.680460

Scheyett, A. (2023). Quiet quitting. *Social Work*, *68*(1), 5–7. DOI: 10.1093/sw/swac051

Shanahan, K. J., & Hyman, M. R. (2010). Motivators and enablers of SCOURing: A study of online piracy in the US and the UK. *Journal of Business Research*, *63*(9–10), 1095–1102. DOI: 10.1016/j.jbusres.2009.02.026

Simpson, A., Day, C., Goulding, J., & Asha, J. (2022). Australian teachers' perceptions of effectiveness in a performative culture. *Teaching and Teacher Education*, *109*, 103542. DOI: 10.1016/j.tate.2021.103542

Singh, R. (2023). "My contract is breached, and I want to leave, but I am embedded!" How do reluctant stayers respond? *Evidence-based HRM: A Global Forum for Empirical Scholarship*, *11*(4), 594–610.

Singh, S., Darwish, T. K., Wood, G., & Mohamed, A. F. (2017). Institutions, complementarity, human resource management and performance in a South-East Asian petrostate: The case of Brunei. *International Journal of Human Resource Management*, *28*(18), 2538–2569. DOI: 10.1080/09585192.2016.1170713

Srivastava, A., Pandey, A., Sharma, D., & Ghosh, K. (2025). Apathy under the surface: Theorizing quiet quitting's impact on organizational learning. *Development and Learning in Organizations*, *39*(2), 15–17. DOI: 10.1108/DLO-03-2024-0080

Talukder, M. F., & Prieto, L. (2025). Quiet quitting and job security: Investigating the impacts of employee's capital and habitus. *The International Journal of Organizational Analysis*. Advance online publication. DOI: 10.1108/IJOA-04-2025-5444

Tarafdar, M., Cooper, C. L., & Stich, J. F. (2019). The technostress trifecta—Techno eustress, techno distress and design: Theoretical directions and an agenda for research. *Information Systems Journal*, *29*(1), 6–42. DOI: 10.1111/isj.12169

Tarafdar, M., Tu, Q., & Ragu-Nathan, A. T. (2010). Impact of technostress on end-user satisfaction and performance. *Journal of Management Information Systems*, *27*(3), 303–334. DOI: 10.2753/MIS0742-1222270311

Tarafdar, M., Tu, Q., Ragu-Nathan, B. S., & Ragu-Nathan, T. S. (2007). The impact of technostress on role stress and productivity. *Journal of Management Information Systems*, *24*(1), 301–328. DOI: 10.2753/MIS0742-1222240109

Teetzen, F., Klug, K., Steinmetz, H., & Gregersen, S. (2023). Organizational health climate as a precondition for health-oriented leadership: Expanding the link between leadership and employee well-being. *Frontiers in Psychology*, *14*, 1181599. DOI: 10.3389/fpsyg.2023.1181599

Teodorescu, M. H., Morse, L., Awwad, Y., & Kane, G. C. (2021). Failures of fairness in automation require a deeper understanding of human-ML augmentation. *Management Information Systems Quarterly*, *45*(3), 1483–1500. DOI: 10.25300/MISQ/2021/16535

Terzi, R. (2020). An adaptation of artificial intelligence anxiety scale into Turkish: Reliability and validity study. *International Online Journal of Education & Teaching*, *7*(4), 1501–1515.

Topcuoglu, E., Kobanoglu, M. S., Kaygın, E., Karafakıoglu, E., Erdogan, S. U., Torun, B. T., & Oktaysoy, O. (2023). The improving role of digital leadership in the impact of social loafing on job performance. *International Journal of Organizational Leadership*, *12*(1), 22–40. DOI: 10.33844/ijol.2023.60347

Upadhyay, A., & Khandelwal, P. (2023). AI literacy programs for employees: Enhancing competence and reducing anxiety. *Journal of Business Research*, *162*, 113–124.

Uygungil-Erdogan, S., Şahin, Y., Sökmen-Alaca, A. İ., Oktaysoy, O., Altıntaş, M., & Topçuoğlu, V. (2025). Assessing the effect of artificial intelligence anxiety on turnover intention: The mediating role of quiet quitting in turkish small and medium enterprises. *Behavioral Sciences (Basel, Switzerland)*, *15*(3), 249. DOI: 10.3390/bs15030249

Vinchon, F., Gironnay, V., & Lubart, T. (2024). GenAI creativity in narrative tasks: Exploring new forms of creativity. *Journal of Intelligence*, *12*(12), 125. DOI: 10.3390/jintelligence12120125

Wang, W., Chen, L., Xiong, M., & Wang, Y. (2023). Accelerating AI adoption with responsible AI signals and employee engagement mechanisms in health care. *Information Systems Frontiers*, *25*(6), 2239–2256. DOI: 10.1007/s10796-021-10154-4

Wang, Y.-M., Wei, C.-L., Lin, H.-H., Wang, S.-C., & Wang, Y.-S. (2022). What drives students' AI learning behavior: A perspective of AI anxiety. *Interactive Learning Environments*, *32*(6), 2584–2600. DOI: 10.1080/10494820.2022.2153147

Wang, Y.-Y., & Wang, Y.-S. (2022). Development and validation of an artificial intelligence anxiety scale: An initial application in predicting motivated learning behavior. *Interactive Learning Environments*, *30*(4), 619–634. DOI: 10.1080/10494820.2019.1674887

Wennberg, K., Wiklund, J., & Wright, M. (2011). The effectiveness of university knowledge spillovers: Performance differences between university spinoffs and corporate spinoffs. *Research Policy*, *40*(8), 1128–1143. DOI: 10.1016/j.respol.2011.05.014

Zlatanović, S., Sovilj, R., & Maksimović, M. (2025). The quiet quitting phenomenon in digital workplaces: A legal-theoretical and comparative analysis. *Review of European and Comparative Law*, *62*(3), 133–153. DOI: 10.31743/recl.18618

Zuboff, S. (2023). The age of surveillance capitalism. In *Social Theory Re-wired* (pp. 203–213). Routledge. DOI: 10.4324/9781003320609-27

Chapter 6

Architecting Infinite Realities With MetaIntelligence and Generative AI for Metaverse Creation

Faris Abuhashish
https://orcid.org/0009-0009-7859-3575
University of Petra, Jordan

Waleed Maqableh
https://orcid.org/0000-0001-9646-8369
Applied Science Private University, Jordan

Nidal Yousef
Zarqa University, Jordan

Mohd S. Sunar
https://orcid.org/0000-0002-0244-1622
Universiti Teknologi Malaysia, Malaysia

Ismahafezi Ismail
https://orcid.org/0000-0001-9080-7825
Sultan Zainal Abidin Universiti, Malaysia

ABSTRACT

The Metaverse is turning into a constantly growing three-dimensional space that is radically changing the nature of digital interaction through the generative Artificial

DOI: 10.4018/979-8-3373-9958-4.ch006

Intelligence and MetaIntelligence. The chapter outlines how Generative Adversarial Networks, Large Language Models, and Diffusion Models have been used to build immersive virtual worlds, non-player characters and plot progression. It proposes MetaIntelligence as an inclusive model of meta-learning, cyclic improvement and interoperability of heterogeneous systems. Moreover, the chapter provides an overview of how distributed ledger technology, cloud computing, and edge-computing functionality are foundations of scalable world construction, the consideration of consistency, user well-being, ethical and environmental implications, and the opportunities of symbiotic human-AI interaction and virtual/real world interface integration.

1. INTRODUCTION

The Metaverse is a paradigmatic change within the sphere of human-computer interaction that is moving towards the consumption of finite and screen-based interfaces in favor of the enduring and networked three-dimensional virtual worlds (Said, 2023; Wang et al., 2025). This revolution is spread across various worlds, such as social interaction, commerce, pedagogy, and entertainment; hence, creating environment not only immersive, but constantly changing as well. The main idea behind this evolution is two dependent concepts: the increased proliferation of dynamically growing virtual worlds and the growing importance of sophisticated artificial intelligence systems that express the ability to organize, adapt and support these worlds on scale, which in this chapter are denoted in totality as MetaIntelligence.

The Metaverse may be considered as a common virtual world that links with augmented physical world, which consists of a virtual world that has expanded into a digital overlay consisting of virtual worlds, augmented reality applications, and network services. Some important characteristics include its persistence, real-time rendering, interoperability and an increasingly visible user-created economy. In addition to entertainment, telecommuting, electronic commerce, healthcare, and industrial training are being studied in these environments, where continuity and coordinated interaction over the long term is critically needed.

The central role here is held by generative artificial intelligence that allows creating content, including images, text, and three-dimensional models, as well as recognizing patterns in a complex stream of data (Gozalo-Brizuela & Garrido-Merchán, 2023). In addition to the generation of content, modern AI systems are becoming more adaptive, so they have the ability to perceive, interpret and react to stimuli present in the environment and control elements of their functioning (Korteling et al., 2021; Wang, 2021). All these capabilities, combined, allow creating virtual environments synthesis responsive to user interaction and altering working conditions (in real-time).

The general point of this chapter relates to the role of meta-intelligence and generative artificial intelligence in the design, conceptualization, and further evolution of large-scale virtual worlds. The discussion examines how technical approaches may be used to build scalable worlds and at the same time how the problematic issues of coherence, longevity of user interaction, and moral responsibility can be maintained in increasingly autonomous AI-mediated environments.

The combination of three major technological ideas, which lie at the cornerstones of infinite realities in the Metaverse, are graphically portrayed in figure 1 dramatically. Centered is a 3D virtual world of the Metaverse a dynamic, raved up environment based on an interconnected digital world. The generative AI is on the left side where AI is framed as based on a creative algorithm generating various contents in the form of landscapes, characters, and stories. MetaIntelligence (on the right side), is a second-order cognitive system expressed in ways that are viscerally brain-like (in its structure) that guides, organizes and directs development of virtual realities. The illustration emphasizes the concept of the infinite realities as well as the dynamic, illustrating the way the given AI technologies work together and produce, maintain and continuously develop the vast virtual reality that changes according to the user input and environmental changes driven by intelligent responsiveness.

Existing research on metaverse systems and generative virtual worlds has advanced procedural content generation, real-time rendering, and large-scale multi-user interaction. However, these approaches typically treat generative pipelines, moderation mechanisms, and infrastructure management as loosely coupled subsystems. As virtual worlds scale in persistence, concurrency, and social complexity, this fragmentation creates challenges related to coherence, governance, accountability, and sustainability.

The research gap addressed in this chapter is the absence of an explicit meta-level control construct that integrates generative intelligence, governance constraints, and infrastructure orchestration into a unified feedback-driven mechanism. This chapter contributes (i) a formal conceptualization of MetaIntelligence, (ii) an architectural framing that links generation, governance, and infrastructure, and (iii) a set of design implications and research directions for responsible, large-scale metaverse systems.

This chapter is a conceptual framework contribution supported by a structured narrative (scoping-oriented) literature synthesis. The literature reviewed was selected from peer-reviewed research in generative AI, procedural content generation, metaverse infrastructure, distributed ledger technologies, and responsible AI, complemented where necessary by authoritative technical standards and platform reports.

The objective is not empirical validation, but conceptual integration: to synthesize disparate technical and governance strands into a coherent architectural and theoretical framework that can guide subsequent empirical, design science, and deployment-focused research.

Figure 1. Metaverse AI architecture

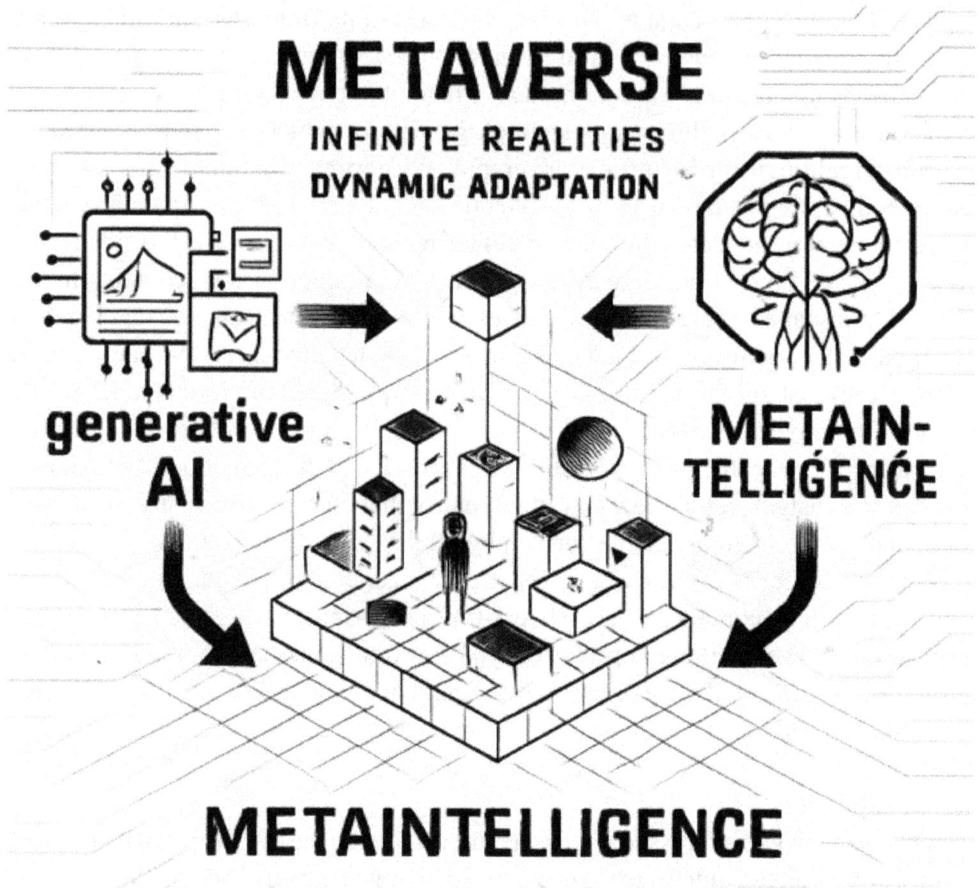

2. FOUNDATIONS OF VIRTUAL WORLD GENERATION

This section outlines all those technical foundations needed to keep persistent virtual worlds going, providing the generative as well as infrastructural basis upon which MetaIntelligence works. Rather than being a discrete intelligence module, MetaIntelligence plays the role of a coordinating control layer in the system. In the historical path of video games development, the art of creating digital worlds was first completed in a purely manual way where designers and artists put a lot of efficiency and effort into coming up with every minute detail. It provided a subtle degree of control over the aesthetic results, but at the same time was subject to large-scale shortcomings: to produce large-scale, or even infinite landscapes, they took prohibitively expensive amounts of time and resources. In addition, these worlds were unchanging meaning that dynamic change was excluded or user evolution in large ratio.

To address the flaws of manual design development, Procedural Content Generation (PCG) was introduced as the mode where computer-based methods generate the content such as textures to landscapes (Sobchyshak et al., 2025). Early use of PCG relied on mathematics systems such as Perlin noise to produce plausible landscapes. In the course of time, new algorithms that are more advanced, such as L-systems, fractals, and cellular automata were developed. The critical benefit enjoyed by PCG is its ability to produce a massive body of content with very little involvement with the humans, thus pushing the time of development and creating diversity. Conventional PCG systems, however, have been known to have problems maintaining semantic cohesiveness and creative vision in large scale generations.

Most of the surviving PCG applications are based on pre-scripted, rule-based frameworks, based on a strict set of pre-determined rules and parameters. This limitation makes their output confined, and hence there is little scope of novelty or emergent character in them. It is burdensome to adapt such systems to the changing needs which often requires a tedious manual adjustment of the rules on which they are based. The inefficiency in these deficiencies is the need to focus more effort on the generative mechanisms that are able to learn, evolve, and autonomously generate contextual intelligent content.

The overarching underlying mechanisms that have been identified herein highlight a need for high level coordination between content generation, state of the system and user interaction as constituting an observation or architectural requisite that effects the choice of deploying MetaIntelligence as a cohesive control construct as will be elaborated in the following sections.

3. DIGITAL ECOSYSTEMS ARE BUILT BY GENERATIVE ARTIFICIAL INTELLIGENCE

Following the generative principles established in the previous sections, this section examines how the modern generative AI approaches operationalize the adaptability, scalability, and responsiveness in metaverse space. Generative artificial intelligence is a new stage in the creation of digital content, and AI is at the center of creating a sophisticated digital world. The models recreating provisional representations using provided information and having the ability to produce completely new and similar content, which is considered necessary in the context of virtual environments where the diversity of content and its quality improvement is unlimited. Unlike the traditional methods, AIs have also developed into self-sustaining entities that generate imaginative worlds, individual personalities, internally consistent stories without the need to specify how they should be done.

3.1. Core Generative AI Paradigms

The concept of Generative Adversarial Networks (GANs) has disrupted the process of creating high-fidelity synthetic visual elements that are required to create virtual worlds (Chaudhary et al., 2025). In essence, a GAN involves the combination of a generator, which produces data and a discriminator who identifies the authenticity. This can be done by forcing the two to compete with one another in a repetitive process of opposition and thus the modules are cleaned up until the end result can be literally unrecognizable, of the real thing. In Metaverse terrain and texture generation, asset variation, and environmental lighting GANs come in handy.

At the same time, Large Language Models (LLMs) have demonstrated their unbelievable skill in both recognizing and creating human language (Bowman, 2024). LLMs are dynamic dialogue generating engines, user query machine, adaptive story writer, lore generator, and procedural content generator. They thus make possible extremely subjective storytelling experiences beyond tightly written plotlines.

Later on, there is the emergence of Diffusion Models, which have now mimicked state-of-the-art performance in image and audio synthesis. Diffusion models perform well in the Metaverse due to high-fidelity generation of assets, stylized content using stochastic signals one, image-to-image translation, audio generation, and video generation by filling input time steps with coherent samples.

Table 1 below represents a systemized contrast of the three major artificial intelligence (AI) generative paradigms that were discussed in the chapter. The table reviews the paradigms in respect to particular criteria including applications, strengths, limitations, and future roles in a Metaverse scenario. The analogy explains why various AI methods are suitable to various sides of constructing virtual-worlds and how they all provide business to the wider Metaverse-building ecosystem.

Table 1. Comparison of generative AI paradigms

Technology	Primary Use Cases	Strengths	Limitations	Metaverse Applications
GANs	Visual content generation	High-fidelity images	Training instability	Terrain, textures, assets
LLMs	Text and dialogue	Natural language	Hallucinations	NPC dialogue, narratives
Diffusion Models	Multi-modal synthesis	Stable training	Computational cost	Audio, video, stylized content

3.2. Dynamic Content Generation

Dynamically created and morphing landscapes that were governing basic layouts of actual reality were included in the intellectual imaginary of the infinite. We now have generative AI that arms us with the capability to create worlds of both size and responsiveness that satisfy our fingers that dwell in far more detail seen in real-time terrain morphing, biomimicked ecologies, responsive architecture, weather simulation, and intelligent resources provision.

In addition, Metaverse also requires smart Non-Player Characters (NPCs) (Damaševičius & Sidekerskienė, 2024). Generative AI transforms NPCs into virtual entities of complex characters through the action of expressing personality, autonomous personal movement, having objectives and pursuing them, dynamic social interactions, and self-learning abilities.

Other requirements of the Metaverse are adaptive narratives and dynamic event generation. In this case, generative AI provides the storyline, which reacts to the user activity due to context-sensitive story generation, dynamic quest development, event scheduling, and user-controlled story impact, as well as cross-modal story generation.

Figure 2 presents the fundamental (initial) role of Generative Adversarial Networks (GANs), Large Language Models (LLMs) and Diffusion Models in dynamic content generation in Metaverse. GANs make landscapes and objects, LLMs write stories and conversations, and Diffusion Models produce interactive visuals. All of these technologies have a combined productivity in promoting dynamic texts and smart narratives within the primary Metaverse environment and hence their synergetic contribution in terms of creating contemporary and vast virtual worlds.

Figure 2. Architecture for dynamic content creation

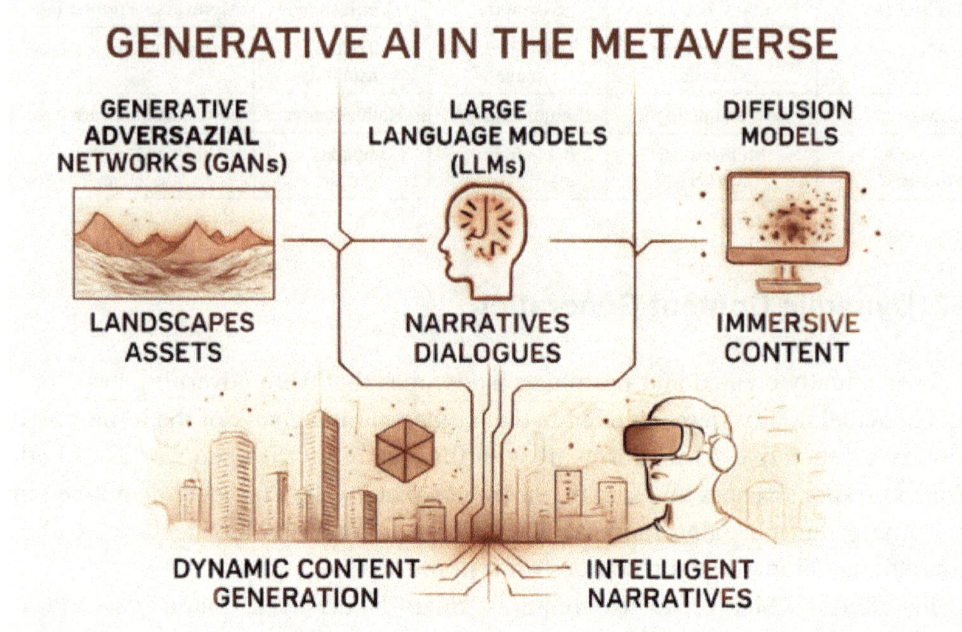

While these generative models also offer us a degree of unprecedented flexibility and realism, the empowered growing autonomy and interdependence also concurrently create coordination, governance, and sustainability issues that cannot be mitigated at the model level in isolation.

4. METAINTELLIGENCE: THE ORCHESTRATOR OF INFINITE WORLDS

In order to address the difficulties in coordination described in studies on generative metaverse systems, this part will introduce MetaIntelligence as a meta-part, a control level for the integration of a generative control framework, governance constraints, and infrastructural considerations into an overall so-called feedback-driven system. Generative AI will provide procedural systems for generating diverse and creative content, but Metaverse will require a broader cognitive structure that can support and coordinate and neurally transform these emergent worlds. I call this coordinating layer MetaIntelligence and compare it to the brain of the digital universe, charged with keeping the digital universal dynamic coherent, flexible, and self-improving beyond its knowledge in immense virtual worlds connected one to another. MetaIntelligence gives rise to an integrated and intelligent, self-organizing digital ecosystem, because it can operate at the meta-level and synthesize a set of disparate generative systems.

4.1. Defining MetaIntelligence

In the current chapter, MetaIntelligence is characterized as a control layer that is hierarchical, governance conscious, and that constantly tracks multimodal system indicators and coordinates various generative and analytic agents in a bid to maintain coherence, safety and resource viability within long persisting virtual worlds. It has feedback loops incorporating the behavior of the users, the state of the world, policy limitations, and infrastructure monitoring in adaptive control choices.

As opposed to traditional orchestration models or MLOps pipelines, which focus primarily on deployment, routing, or monitoring, MetaIntelligence considers normative goals (safety, accessibility, and compliance) unambiguously in addition to lifecycle adaptation and cross-world coherence as major issues. Theoretically, it is based on the theoretical concepts of cybernetics, systems theory, and multi-agent coordination, but specialized in situations related to the metaverse where permanency, embodiment, and governance cannot exist independently of technical functionality.

- Validity and Quality Assurance of Content: MetaIntelligence is constantly used to guarantee the quality, integrity and ethical stability of AI-generated content in a set of validation models. It determines semantic drifts, stylistic differences and logical disconnects that may diminish user interaction. The system serves as an inseparable sense -quality -control system which maintains the integrity of the infinite realities it regulates, and which maintains its immersive and believable quality.

As table 2 in the present shows, the five core functions of MetaIntelligence as introduced in the chapter are methodologically charted and lay a conceptual ground to introduce a practical and operational compass as to the actualization of theoretical ideas of meta-cognitive AI systems into feasible deployments and measurable benefits. The table highlights the synergistic effect of the functions in creating coherent adaptive and self-enhancing virtual worlds thus making the reader have a more concrete understanding of the previously abstract conception of MetaIntelligence.

Table 2. MetaIntelligence core functions

Function	Description	Implementation Methods	Benefits
Content Quality Assurance	Validation of AI-generated materials	Validation models, semantic analysis	Consistency, immersion
Adaptive Learning	User feedback integration	Reinforcement learning, meta-learning	Personalization
Multi-agent Coordination	Managing heterogeneous AI systems	Resource scheduling, conflict resolution	Coherent environments
Self-healing	Anomaly detection and repair	Real-time monitoring, automatic correction	System stability

- Adaptive Learning and Feedback Aggregation: As part of an unsupervised, no-analogs understanding, the architecture will be able to integrate explicit (e.g. ratings, user report) and implicit (e.g. duration of engagement, navigation patterns) forms of user feedback, and incorporate into the generative models, so as to maximize performance measures of both user satisfaction and system capability to generate emergent narrative.
- Working within multi-agent systems, MetaIntelligence serves as a central meta controller, coordinating the action of the heterogeneous AI models to realize the common goals. It dynamically schedules computational resources, resolves dependencies between generative tasks and preempts conflict between agents acting independently. MetaIntelligence has developed mechanisms through which all the component AI systems work together thus providing a cohesive consistent virtual environment.
- As there is inherent instability of emergent phenomena and there are inherent perturbations that can be injected by outside sources, MetaIntelligence uses self-corrective processes that detect and rectify anomalies, including flawed game mechanics as well as narrative dead-ends. At the same time, a concurrent performance optimization is performed by the system and thus the scalability and stability are maintained during the expansion of the virtual environment.
- Similarly, through the decoding of interactions with the user, and even broader environmental situations, MetaIntelligence develops a discriminatory insight of user intention. This knowledge will enable the system to personalize the paths of experience, predict the needs of the user and set the trend of the development of the virtual world as involving also interesting and purposeful experiences.

4.2. Meta-Learning and Self-Improvement

The core of the workability of MetaIntelligence is a certain relationship to learning to learn-or rather to meta-learning (Vettoruzzo et al., 2024). Such conceptual machinery makes Metaverse less of a determinate, pre-coded area of activity and more of an ever-optimizing system that evolves in phases keeping pace with the interests of its users. What follows are interdependent mechanisms that implement that meta-learning agenda:

1. Adaptive Model Selection and Hyperparameters Tuning. The system is to run time evaluation of the available generative models and the automatic choice and (fine-tuning) of the corresponding model most appropriate to this or that task. The resultant impact is consistent optimal performance, as creative ways of thinking advance in parallel with the situation.
2. Learning in the circumstances of automatic Feature Engineering and Representation Learning. In Metaverse, the huge amount of data streams fed through other systems of the Metaverse is automatically processed to eye-opening salient features using MetaIntelligence. In this way, it creates more precise and detailed descriptions of the virtual environment that allows us to generate high level of sophisticated, context aware generative content.
3. World Optimization Reinforcement Learning. The MetaIntelligence framework uses the reinforcement-learning algorithms in order to optimize the total state of the virtual world. Through the formulation of a reward function that combines the elements of both the user engagement, coherence to the narrative and stability to the system, the system learns to guide the evolution of the Metaverse towards a better configuration.

There are two frameworks, which are particularly worthy of note in the context of the modern discussion of the Metaverse-the transfer learning and domain adaptation. Comprehensively, the system is meant to impart the material leaning in one field to another and through this make a swift adjustment to new materials, user taste and plot designs. Those abilities are essential when it comes to maintaining life in the Metaverse is dynamic and not fixed.

Making a supplement to these mechanisms is MetaIntelligence ability to perform self-correction and detection of an anomaly. In a state of active self-monitoring, algorithmic flaws are recognized and eliminated, such as the identification of algorithmic prejudice and its avoidance, the prevention of dangerous or irresponsible material, and the preservation of ethical accord. Combined, all these factors ultimately guarantee adherence to the same, so that Metaverse is not just a technical system, but a responsible, developing one.

4.3. Orchestrating Coherence and Interoperability

In multiverse, coherence and interoperability are yet another tough task (Magateshvaren Saras et al., 2025). MetaIntelligence overcomes this problem by creating a consistent semantic tapestry that will connect the fragmented aspects of the Metaverse.

- Single Ontologies and Semantic Layers: MetaIntelligence provides a shared ontology and expounds relationships between objects, characters, and concepts on all virtual worlds. This common ground from an objective perspective entrenches Metaverse through its consistency in time to maintain a logically consistent environment where action leads to a predictable result and the same rules apply in all events.
- Cross-World Asset and Identity Management: The system enables people to move their assets and identities between separately owned virtual worlds using decentralized identity standards and interoperable asset standards to enable a consistent identity to be maintained across the entire Metaverse.
- Dynamic Rule Enforcement and Governance: MetaIntelligence has dynamically enforced rules and governance policies which change as per the demands of the changing community. This mandate involves the administration of the economic system, settlement of differences and the administration of a reasonable and fair Metaverse to all.

4.4. Real-time Adaptation

MetaIntelligence is a paradigmatic shift in the way human beings are interacting with their digital context and allows a shift of the user mode of receivers of content to creators of content and contributors to the virtual realm. The key aspect of this shift is the so-called real-time adaptation mechanism, by which Metaverse receives the user input and feedback continuously to thus enable the learning and self-correction.

1. MetaIntelligence World Generation will produce customized virtual experiences through the review of individual preferences and play style of a user and hence will make sure that each adventure is made different and consequential.
2. Integration of User-Generated Content: user-generated content integrates into the virtual world in a seamless way and, thus, maintains a consistent structure with the general vision and storyline. Such a mechanism can give participants a stronger influence on the world, something sustainable that creates a sense of ownership and community.

Figure 3. MetaIntelligence feedback loop

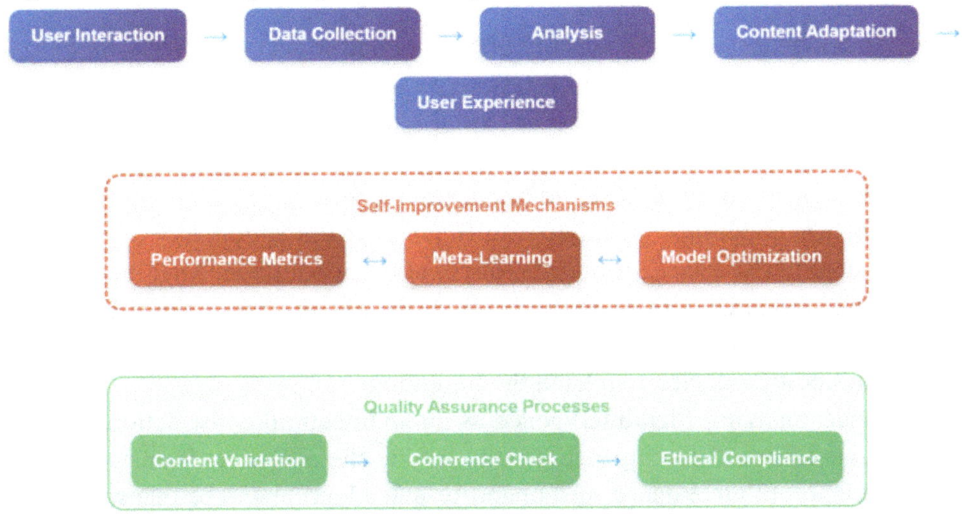

Figure 3 shows the process dynamic, non-linear and cyclical by which MetaIntelligence systems continuously sort and modify themselves. It describes the major stream of data involved with user interaction and a better user experience with an emphasis on two major underpinnings: self-improving mechanisms that enable meta-learning and model optimization and quality assurance measures that maintain quality and integrity of content and ethical delivery. Underlining the circle geometrical structure of MetaIntelligence, the diagram demonstrates how every user interaction feeds the system development, which in turn allows virtual environment to be more complex and personalized as time goes on.

3. Reaction to Emergent Behaviors The system is designed so that its detection- and action-of emergent behavior, both positive and negative, establishes and supports the growth of healthy, active community and contains the threats of anti-social behavior and griefing.

Collectively, these functionalities allow MetaIntelligence to tune the intricate interaction between generative AI, user feedback, emergent dynamics in order to achieve a constellation of an infinite number of realities, which can be viewed as virtual worlds, but more than vast and detailed, they are also intelligent, adaptive, and continually evolving.

4.5. Boundary Conditions and Failure Modes

MetaIntelligence is not universally beneficial and in fact, in some conditions, tends to worsen or even become disadvantageous. These negative results can be expected in the case of incomplete or biased telemetry, vague or divergent governance goals, extreme resource requirements, and the inability to deal with the underlying generative models. In addition, in presence of breach of institutional or regulatory assumptions, including insufficient data protection, lack of clarity in the accountability schemes, or unequal distribution of adoption, MetaIntelligence can become the source of intensifying, instead of mitigating, systemic risks. These framing conditions highlight the importance of having gradual implementation, continuous audits, and clearly related the limitations.

By conceptualizing MetaIntelligence as an architectural construction and not as a separated form of Intelligence, in this section the analytical framework with which the issues of governance, sustainability, and adoption will be interrogated in the following parts of this chapter is delineated.

5. TECHNICAL METHODOLOGIES FOR SCALABLE WORLD CREATION

The process of moving MetaIntelligence from a conceptual construct to an operational system requires being aligned with underlying infrastructure, platform limitations and interoperability realities, which are all explored in this part of the book. Admittedly, researchers, the fact that the purpose of the advent of an infinite constellation of the existence of realities in the Metaverse, where we have enormous data volumes and the complexity of interactions in real time, and extensive interoperability requires us to forget about the parameters of the classical paradigm of centralization (Hatami et al., 2024). The strict computational and logistical requirements of dynamically created, sustained and networked virtual worlds call upon technologically powerful methodologies that are distributed and highly expandable. The main components of infrastructure and the architectural considerations that are a must in a fully supported digital ecosystem of this scale are going to be discussed in the sections that follow.

Figure 4 elaborates the multi-tiered infrastructure that is inevitable towards achieving in-finite realities in the Metaverse. It outlines the subordinate correlation between the computational resources of clouds (designed to carry out the bulk of processing and artificial-intelligence training), the distributed edge-AI nodes (that equip low-latency and real-time capabilities of interaction), blockchain networks (that control the administration of digital assets and govern them), and a great number of access orientations (such as virtual reality, mobile devices, and browsers) along with the augmented reality. The dynamic, bidirectional data-flow flow lines that are animated serve to emphasize the way in which the information moves back and forward across these layers and, thus, lays bare the distributed and still coordinated nature of the system and the associated ability to provide scalable, seamless virtual-world experiences.

Figure 4. Scalable infrastructure architecture

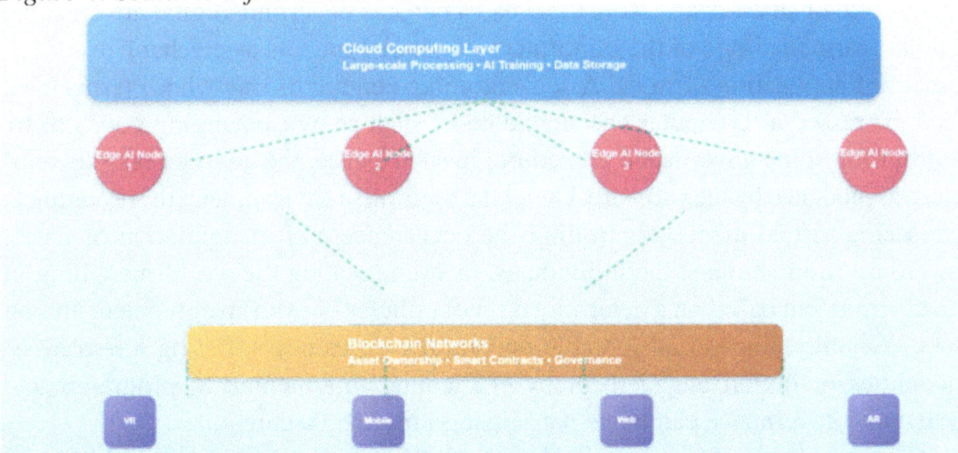

5.1. Distributed Ledger Technologies

Distributed Ledger Technologies (DLTs) (perhaps the most well-known bio is blockchain) represent a pillar around which the creation of decentralized, transparent, and safe Metaverse infrastructures may be built (Antal et al., 2021). Their outstanding characteristics especially satisfy different needs of the absolute necessities of infinite realities. Ownership and scarcity of digital assets (NFTs) Non-fungible tokens, implemented on distributed ledger technology, provide an immutable and verifiable record of the ownership right over a unique digital asset in the metaverse (Ramírez Lopez & Morillo Ledesma, 2025). These allow true digital scarcity in the form of virtual land and avatars, as well as wearables, and other in-world assets, which promote strong creator economies in general and supports safe secondary markets. Cryptographic security of NFTs ensures that the ownership is not counterfeitable and cannot be taken away willingly-the minimal criteria of user trust and investment in virtual economies.

- Decentralized Identity (DID): DIDs offer a self-sovereign environment of managing user identity that enables end-users with the autonomy to control their own data and on-line identity in multiple platforms within the Metaverse without the need of centralized governance (Yuan & Li, 2022). This will strengthen privacy, reduce the possibilities of data loss and enhance simplified secure authentication and authorization in heterogeneous virtual environments.

The role of smart contracts in the present debate concerning digital governance, scholars raise the issue of the importance of smart contracts as mechanisms of automatized application of rules. A self-enforcing contract is one whose terms have been expressed as computer executable code, such as by exchanging goods or by configuring some governance procedure; in such a case, the contract takes care of itself, as mediated by the software. Under the Metaverse environment, these contracts overseeing virtual assets, controlling the occurrence and manipulation of users, reward division amongst the individuals, or even creating the world-modelling in the environment based on a determined set of policies or even an agreement among the community, imply, considerable operational efficiency. Offering a remake of modalities of digital engagement by eradicating intermediaries, programmable systems of governance can make participation more transparent.

The second axis of recent work deals with the subject of technological interoperability that is created by the heterogeneous condition of blockchain ecosystems. To bring this to solution, cross-chain bridges will provide the data transfer and asset transfer solutions needed to have a truly connected Metaverse. By allowing users to interoperate across a wide variety of separate distributed ledger technologies, these interoperability mechanisms are argued to enable the effortless migration of virtual assets and identities across a wide range of distributed virtual environments, thus helping to build a more coherent and extensible digital commons.

The role of the third research agenda is the rapidly growing popularity of Decentralized Autonomous Organizations (DAOs). DAOs, achieved by implementing smart contracts, aim at helping Metaverse initiatives to be controlled by communities (Wegner et al., 2024). The token holders elect proposals, manage collective money and determine the course of development. The first and foremost advantage of this decentralized governing structure is that it aligns the incentives, develops civic engagement and ensures that virtual worlds will be responsive to the desires of those they serve.

All these developments illustrate the multiverse possibilities of smart contracting systems to simplify governance, interoperability, and decentralized management of projects, none of which could be excluded in the transforming design of the Metaverse.

5.2. Cloud Computing and Edge AI

Metaverse is a highly immersive environment that has high-end demands in terms of performance because in real time they must display environments and particularly they have to be able to support dynamic generation of objects, so the latencies have to be minimal, and the computing power must be enormous. These attributes, in their turn, determine the introduction of an elaborate hybrid computing infrastructure.

Table 3. Technical infrastructure comparison

Technology	Scalability	Latency	Cost	Use Case in Metaverse
Cloud Computing	High	Medium-High	Variable	Large-scale processing, training
Edge AI	Medium	Very Low	High	Real-time interactions, local processing
Blockchain/DLT	Medium	High	High	Asset ownership, governance
Hybrid Cloud-Edge	Very High	Low	Medium	Optimal performance distribution

To start with, cloud computing can provide the necessary elasticity to support both a dynamic user base and the massive computing requirements necessary to provide a successful large-scale simulation of a virtual world. The cloud-based distributed rendering can support the parallelism of complex graphical scenes, and, as a result, high fidelity images can be effectively distributed to customers around the globe. Of even greater importance are that cloud resources are an essential part of the meta-learning projects that MetaIntelligence pursues, as the large amounts of data and computing capabilities are necessary to train and optimize the models.

Second, edge AI adds near-end-user computational resources, consequently limiting the latency in the network and making real-time analysis of critical interactions possible. In the case of Metaverse, this architecture provides the security of instantaneous reaction time to avatar locomotion, object interaction, and locally computed AI (including local NPC logic and real-time physics). Edge AI helps distribute the load processing by avoiding cloud-based data centers and reducing network bandwidth demands at the same time, boosting the reactivity of immersing content. Based on this, the hybrid architecture will see the collaborative finesse of the high compute of cloud computing on the one hand and the real-time response of edge AI on the other.

5.3. Data Management and Storage

The foremost focus is put on strong data management and storage architecture with the goal of maintaining persistence, integrity, and availability in the Metaverse

- a virtual reality domain (which, theoretically, is limitless). The nature of the magnitude and constant evolution of the Metaverse data requires the application of advanced approaches. Others are complex methods such as:

1. Graph databases and distributed databases. The complexity and nature of interrelationships of Metaverse applications rarely warrant the use of traditional relational architecture. Distributed databases provide scale horizontally and availability, and graph databases are the best with the intricate connections of users, assets, locations, and events. These properties enable effective querying and enable the real-time analysis of intricate social and environmental dynamics as well.
2. Content Addressable Storage Systems (e.g., IPFS). Interplanetary File System (IPFS) provides a decentralized system in which the storage takes place and is shared, and data is indexed according to a content hash rather than where it is stored. This strategy improves resiliency, reduces reliance on centralized stores and enables effective distribution of the content over the global network of the Metaverse, making it an excellent fit to deploy the state of static or rather semi-static digital goods or the products business.
3. Intra-population data Versioning and Rollback. Like all content created using AI, endless versions and rollback systems are necessary since users can make changes to the content created. Such tools allow an accurate tracking of changes, restoration to a previous situation and an audit of the evolution of content, ensuring consistency and making it possible to recover in the event of unpredictable failure or attack.

An archetypical illustration of the benefits of such a hybridization of semantic technologies and the well-proven data-lake approach is Semantic Data Lakes. These infrastructures are needed to support advanced analytics allowing the management of large volumes of raw, unstructured, and semi-structured data, and at the same time enriching them with many metadata that encode categorical and relational definitions. The capabilities also assist context awareness that is the basis of MetaIntelligence and leads to the production of ultra-personalized content.

The end-to-end data security and privacy are enforced priorities considering the wide-spreading of personal data, corporation-owned digital assets, and confidential relationships in different virtual universes that the Metaverse covers. As such, strong protocols are needed to protect the information of the users, which includes end-to-end encryption, secure multi-party computation, zero-knowledge proofing, and privacy-preserving AI-based methods, so that confidentiality and unauthorized access or control is maintained.

5.4. Interoperability Standards

On the most basic level, interoperability is the scholarly and technological backbone of a smooth and diverse Metaverse, which allows sending information and relocating assets along a continuum of heterogeneous platforms. The institutionalization and implementation of strict open standards is what will make this endeavor successful.

1. Open Standards for 3D Content

Such formats as glTF (GL Transmission Format) that facilitate the exchange of 3D models, scenes, and animations between different rendering engines and virtual environment would be useless without adoption of universal standards. These standards make digital experiences consistent since they offer a consistent way in which assets can be rendered and manipulated across platforms, supposing that they have been developed in the same framework.

2. Security, Identity and Authentication Protocols.

Decentralized-identity user identities This is an essential element of portable and secure user identities that work across the Metaverse and within a decentralized-identity ecosystem. Decentralized identity schemes, like W3C DIDs and Verifiable Credentials, are essential to support these identities, single sign-on, and to ensure that standard user profiles are provided to an individual across the Metaverse.

3. Application Programming Interfaces and Data Exchange Formats.

A standardized API that has a standardized data-exchange format (e.g., JSON-LD, RDF) enables the flow of information to be sustained between parts of the Metaverse, AI models and external services. Through such coordination, it is possible to enable MetaIntelligence systems to cope with heterogeneous data streams and coordinate inherently complex interactions.

4. Communication and Networking Protocols

In addition to typical internet protocols, dedicated networking protocols enhanced to support real-time high-bandwidth low-latency communications are required to support synchronous communication and large data transfer that typifies immersive virtual worlds.

In the Metaverse ecosystem, two pillars come out clearly (1) economic and transacting standards and (2) the interoperability of the AI models. In the latter case, the development of universal standards of work with virtual money, exchanges of assets, and interactions with smart contracts is inevitable in order to provide adequate economic activity transparency and non-nitpicking in the virtual world. With such standards, there is a liquid and interconnected digital economy. In the perspective of AI, the disintegration of AI models, especially those making up the generative and analytical parts is a grave issue. To lessen this difficulty, uniformity must be established in terms of the model exchange (e.g., ONNX), data format of inputs and outputs and protocols of invocation. Such standards allow the active mixing and matching of various tools of AI enabling the entire AI ecosystem to exist as a coherent whole. Aller observance of these norms is important to avoid the possibility of platform silos and developing a truly open and accessible Metaverse.

5.5. Platform Reality Check: Existing Metaverse-Adjacent Systems

Several large-scale platforms already operationalize partial aspects of the metaverse vision, providing important empirical reference points. Platforms like Roblox and Fortnite are excellent examples of viable creator economies with huge concurrent user bases; yet governance structures, monetization models and discovery processes still retain a strong level of centralization. Social virtual reality (VR) spaces have embodiment and instant communication as the main priority, but are increasingly faced with moderation, safety and access issues. Web3 -oriented worlds experiment with tokenized ownership, and decentralized governance, and at the same time discovering the real limitations in areas of usability, volatility of adoption, and legal oversight.

MetaIntelligence is suggested as an alternative to these platforms, but rather as a cross-layer orchestration construct which would combine generative systems, governance constraints, and infrastructure management into a single feedback-driven control mechanism. In this respect, extant platforms can give empirical testimony to the fact that at least the individual components are tenable whereas MetaIntelligence fills the missing integrative layer necessary to make the persistent worlds coherent, accountable, and scalable.

5.6 Worked Situation: MetaIntelligence Control of a Continuous Virtual University Campus.

In order to explain how MetaIntelligence works, one can refer to the example of a virtual university campus which is persistent over an academic semester. The environment helps to support lectures, laboratories, informal social areas, and administrative services and can be approached via heterogeneous equipment, such as VR goggles, desktops, and mobile clients.

During the setup, MetaIntelligence initializes governance constraints, which are based on policy by the institution, including role and access control, rules of conduct, access requirements, and audit functionality. In the course of the semester, generative systems are used to create instructional simulation, non-player instructional agent, and adaptive learning contents. MetaIntelligence constantly monitors the interactions, loading of the system and safety indicators and instantiates tasks between lightweight real-time models, and more intense offline generation pipelines accordingly.

MetaIntelligence, when anomalous or harmful behavior is identified, allows interventions appropriate to the degree of the behavior to be applied, e.g. adaptive moderation, access controls or supervised spaces, without hindering transparency and due process by recording the reasoning behind these decisions. Over time, the performance of the systems is measured in terms of a set of measurable indicators such as coherence, continuity of learning, safety incidents, accessibility uptake and resource efficiency.

This situation illustrates the role of MetaIntelligence as a control layer of operation, which combines generative intelligence, governance and infrastructure management through the lifecycle of a practical institutional deployment. The foregoing infrastructural and platform considerations reveal how there is a need for MetaIntelligence to be able to operate within real-world constraints and therefore underpins the importance of the various mechanisms of governance, accountability and sustainability that must be addressed in the ensuing discussion.

6. CHALLENGES AND ETHICAL IMPLICATIONS

In the mediation of decision-making by MetaIntelligence in ever more pervasive and inherent virtual environments, problems concerning the issues of governance, ethical accountability and sustainability are not external deliberations but are built into the elaboration of the system, which is a core consideration in its design. In consideration of the Metaverse, as a vast constellation of interrelated virtual realities one is compelled to confront a paradigm which appears to be violent and speculative. The main driving forces are meta-Intelligence and generative AI, and the same issues exacerbate critical dilemmas on the communities of experiential integration, user well-being, the ethics of AI, and environmental stewardship. Based on this, the prevention and mitigation of these issues should be of high priority in a healthy agenda of the responsible and progressive creation of the Metaverse.

6.1. Maintaining Coherence and Consistency

Modern conceptualization and creation of AI-driven Metaverses offer a unique methodological dilemma: how to maintain coherence and consistency in worlds that, at the same time, must be dynamic and autonomous. Unlike traditional virtual worlds, content of which is laboriously shaped and rigorously managed, AI-enabled Metaverses exist in the face of a number of unique challenges.

To start with there is the long-standing issue of semantic drift. Since iterative generation and adaptation of content by successive AI generative systems can result in subtle changes to the meaning or context of the text, a progressive decline in the integrity of objects, characters, and other works can be expected through, among other things, a gradual reduction in the degree of coherence of the overall objects, characters, and narratives. An imaginary historically validated virtual city may over time, with AI intervention and feedback, absorb anachronistic structures or stylistic oddities that take a person out of immersion.

Second, the problem of stylistic incoherence is also quite prominent. Even when several playmaking AI systems are directed together by MetaIntelligence, they can take their outputs in aesthetically different directions, creating a visually disjunct or harmonically incoherent space. Stylistic consistency of vast, dynamically generated landscape and diverse resources therefore requires a high level of stylistic governance in MetaIntelligence itself.

When considering the use of AI in immersive digital processes in the current discourse with the subject, specific attention is paid to physical and logical constancy. The former can be defined as the adherence to empirical physical truths of gravity and dynamical laws of collision, the latter being the narrative structure, that underwrites causality and probable plot. Failure on one or another of these spheres may reduce the perception of verisimilitude (and thereby efficacy of interaction) on the part of the user.

Physical consistency demands highly strict implementation of game engines able to simulate real-world dynamics, like Newtonian trajectories or particle systems; after being disobeyed, even slightly, these models quickly reach the threshold of perceptual instability, often exposing an artifact that breaks the immersion. The aspect of logical consistency is, in the current context, more of an issue of story coherence: in case our narrative agents are unable to handle more or less congruent recollection of their past experiences (be they personal, or collective), the resulting chronology might plunge into chaos, a state of affairs that can result in the audience developing a sense of alienation with the diegetic world.

The computational costs of continually checking and fixing the narrative paths in real time are large. MetaIntelligence should thus adopt highly advanced anomaly detection and self-correct design as well as highly refined comparison engines and scaled infrastructure. In a sense, MetaIntelligence presents itself as a protector of integrity, both logical and aesthetic in order to ensure that the very realities which are boundless in their nature do not become unintelligible, implausible or in other words unconvincing.

6.2. User Engagement and Digital Well-being

Immersive technologies, especially enduring virtual worlds related to metaverse platforms, have received increased criticism in terms of user well-being. Nevertheless, empirical findings so far are still indeterminate and very contextual. Instead of considering such phenomena as digital addiction, social isolation, and cognitive distortions as conclusively defined outcomes, this chapter understands them as believable risk factors that require systematic measurement, longitudinal studies and thought error constructions, and rigorously designed interventions.

Empirical researchers related to social virtual reality, to elements of immersive learning experiences, and online virtual communities indicate that embodiment, social presence, and adaptive content can stimulate interest in and long-term membership. At the same time, the same mechanisms can be enhanced by negative experiences in case of insufficiency of governance, safety, and transparency mechanisms. The main risk dimensions that are frequently mentioned include:

- Hyper-personalization and filter effects, where algorithmic customization can make information more limited when there is no active discussion of diversity and exploration.
- compulsive patterns of engagement, whereby immersive reward arrangements prolong the duration of the engagement and raise the frequency of returns beyond healthy utilization thresholds.
- Reality-virtual boundary strain, particularly when experiencing for a prolonged or emotional time.

Within this analytical framework, MetaIntelligence is not assumed to necessarily induce or mitigate these effects. Rather it is presented as the instrumentation and intervention layer that can identify behavioral vectors which include extreme time spin sessions, recurrent negative interaction reports and escalation patterns and bi-proportional mitigations which include friction mechanisms, adaptive pacing, reduced exposure to risky default configurations. This strategy protects the autonomy of users and promotes transparency, accountability and evidence-based governance.

The long-term effect of virtual reliance on sociality is that it is prone to create social isolation in the real world despite the promise of Metaverses to make social interactions more enriching. Similarly, the persistence of inequality in access to essential LTI equipment, high-speed stable internet connection, and associated skills of digital competence leads to an expansion of the digital divide, thus spawning a new layer of digital impoverishment.

In order to protect users against such consequences, the responsible AI design should embrace those principles: ethical nudging, extended digital-literacy programs, and well-being systems: the incorporation of configurable limits or reality checks, etc., along with substantial ethical theories. It is only in this way that the achievement of the balanced and health-enhancing digital ecology will become possible.

6.3. Ethical AI Considerations

In Metaverse, these gradual autonomy and generative ability of AI are transforming the ethics arena in such a way that more attention is needed to be proactive and participatory in various fields so as to address the issue.

- Bias in content production: Content generated by generative models tends to be biased due to the algorithms being trained on the large-scale data that already exists in society. Unless carefully curated and bias mitigation tools are tightly used, these biases are likely to be doubled during the production of AI, and will result in discriminating representation of a gender, race, culture, or other ethnic or population groups. Stereotypes that are thus created may result in an exclusionary virtual world.
- The control and ownership of AI-created contents: With AI systems as co-creators, burning questions arise regarding the rules of intellectual properties rights and ownership of contents that are created by the AI systems. Who owns a diffusion model or LLM-generated landscape, or text? Easy to understand and just legal/ethical structures of AI-generated Content are, consequently, inevitable to develop a balanced and progressive creative economy.

The concept of AI Autonomy and what comes with it emergent behavior takes a specific peak of interest in this era of algorithmic interest. The very purpose of the technology known as MetaIntelligence, a type of generative model designed to offer high levels of autonomy, is to create the need for dynamic experiences by the user which by definition becomes unpredictable. But this very quality of design also highlights an urgent ethical issue as well: what should we do with responsibility over unforeseen consequences or even over emergent behaviors that can turn harmful? One can see that the explanation of the limits of artificial intelligence autonomy is crucial, and it is necessary to introduce effective solutions to ensure human control and immediate action is taken.

Metaverse is an unstoppable collision of privacy issues when considered through the prism of data governance. Constant tracking of user information, likes, and biometrics data to provide immersive experiences is also a major risk to individual freedoms. Possibly, Metaverse can allow creating a large scale of surveillance and behavioral profiling because MetaIntelligence is able to track and analyze high volumes of data. In this regard, strict data-protection policies supported by clear data practices and informed consent are mandatory.

Equivalent importance is given to the articulation of digital rights. Norms that apply to constitutional protections of freedom of expression, privacy and property are supposed to take on a new dimension in the Metaverse environment. As a result, the creation of governance frameworks that could reduce platform dominance, protect the user sovereignty, and allow the individuals to address the problems related to censorship, cyber-attacks, and digital crimes is a complex, but crucial process.

All in all, these ethically questionable scenarios require a collective effort where technologists, ethicists, policymakers, legal scholars, and user communities join forces and formulate more strict rules and norms according to which ethics, regulation, and best practices could be developed about the creation of ethical artificial intelligence. This collaboration is needed to guarantee the evolution of Metaverse as a virtual space that will not only become secure in terms of robustness but also ethical.

Figure 5 explains 4 pillars of ethical AI implementation in the context of Metaverse. In a quadrant model, each dimension represents an urgent ethical imperative: (1) bias identity and intervention (resisting inequitable representation), (2) Privacy protection (user data security), (3) content adjudication (environmental security) and (4) user well-being observation (mental readiness safety). The description reveals that responsible AI is a complex multidisciplinary approach requiring an ongoing commitment at every phase of the system design and use. The framework therefore provides a practical guide that is to be used by developers and policymakers who attempt to incorporate responsible AI into the Metaverse setting.

Figure 5. Ethical AI framework

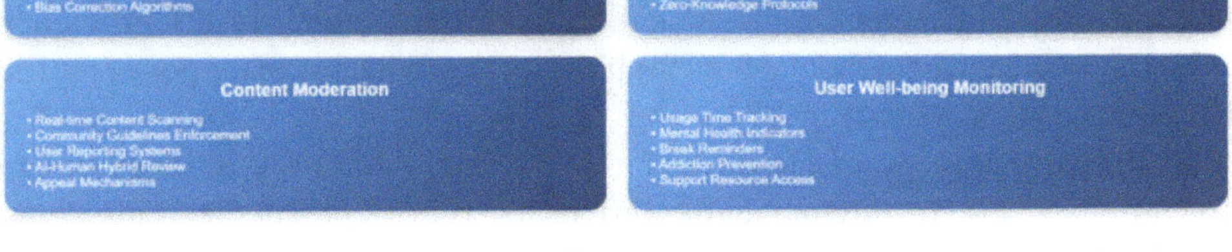

6.4. Environmental Impact

Metaverse construction and operation raise substantive environmental concerns due to the computational intensity of large-scale generative models, persistent world simulation, and real-time rendering. However, the magnitude of these impacts varies significantly depending on model architecture, hardware efficiency, deployment topology, and regional energy mix. Consequently, this chapter avoids asserting a single quantitative footprint and instead adopts a design-oriented sustainability framing grounded in established measurement practices for large-scale AI systems.

Prior work on training and serving large neural models demonstrates that energy consumption and associated carbon emissions can differ by orders of magnitude between dense and sparsely activated architectures, as well as between carbon-intensive and renewable-powered data centers. In metaverse-scale systems, sustainability therefore emerges as a function of engineering decisions related to model selection, training frequency, inference placement, and scheduling strategy.

Accordingly, MetaIntelligence is framed as a mechanism for resource-aware orchestration, enabling practices such as lightweight model preference for real-time interactions, carbon-aware scheduling of large training or regeneration tasks, and explicit reporting of energy or emissions proxies where feasible. These principles position environmental sustainability as a measurable systems constraint alongside latency, safety, and coherence, rather than as a purely aspirational objective.

Lastly, demand in ever more immersive experiences increases, requiring specialized and powerful hardware demanding powerful graphics processing units, and other electronics such as virtual reality headsets, that become rapidly redundant, creating an issue with electronic waste mounting that creates problems in disposal and resource extraction.

Being a platform that can support a continuously growing number of digital worlds, Metaverse will inevitably face the challenge of a paradox of its own: the ambition to expand to a larger scale will lead to the demands to increase the power of computers, which, in its turn, will impose an even higher burden on the ecological system. To this end, it is necessary to implement a set of new and innovative energy-efficient solutions in order to attain concurrent scalability and survivability. There is a need to implement energy-efficient instances of neural networks and introduce new data-center designs with the aim of deriving the greatest efficiency and accelerating the integration of renewable-energy production in the power profile that supports such systems.

At the same time, to create a feasible Metaverse, the energy-efficient design structures have to echo throughout the various levels of its production. This would include streamlining of algorithmic computation to reduce resource usage, developing planet-friendly data-center operational paradigms and pursuing carbon-neutral blockchain formations, design approaches towards the extension of hardware life, recycling, and implementation of carbon-sequestration pathways. The durability of an ever-changing landscape of digital realities depends on how people as a whole will commit to reducing the ecological impact of the ecosystem.

These challenges related to governance and sustainability have highlighted that MetaIntelligence does not only works as a technical coordination machinery, but also as a socio-technical mechanism, the efficiency of which is cross-dependent on other formats of institutional alignment and long-term oversight.

7. FUTURE DIRECTIONS AND IMPLICATIONS

Using the foundational concepts of architecture, infrastructure, and governance views that have been expressed all through the chapter, this part explores the larger implications of MetaIntelligence to research, practice, and policy.

7.1 Staged Research Agenda and Lifecycle Perspective

Research on MetaIntelligence and persistent metaverse systems can be structured into staged phases. In the near term, work should focus on defining operational metrics for coherence, safety, accessibility, and resource efficiency in bounded pilot environments. Medium-term research should examine multi-site deployments, governance scalability, and incentive alignment within creator ecosystems. Long-term studies are required to assess longitudinal user well-being, institutional adoption dynamics, and regulatory co-evolution as virtual worlds mature and potentially decline or transform.

This lifecycle perspective emphasizes that metaverse systems are not static artifacts but evolving socio-technical infrastructures requiring continuous adaptation.

7.2 Implications for Practitioners

For practitioners, including platform architects, institutional adopters, and policymakers, the proposed framework highlights several practical considerations: the need for explicit governance instrumentation, measurable safety and accessibility indicators, transparent decision logging, and sustainability-aware infrastructure planning. MetaIntelligence offers a conceptual blueprint for integrating these concerns into system design, but its effectiveness depends on organizational readiness, regulatory alignment, and ongoing monitoring rather than one-time deployment.

With the advancement of MetaIntelligence and the appearance of Generative AI, a paradigmatic shift of a significant scale becomes the issue facing technology, society, and the modern human experience. Metaverse advances can never be discussed in isolation and should and must be viewed in the context of a family of intermediate technologies that are on the verge of enhancing the capabilities of these AI systems. More specifically, the near future availability of substantially powerful quantum machines will increase computational resources both during training and inference by orders of magnitude. These systems, in their turn, may enable recreating the phenomena of quantum nature within the scope of the virtual world simulation, thus, face the results of realism exceeding the standards of today. Simultaneously, the improvement of the actual neural contacts, especially via Brain Computer Interface (BCI), could potentially re-set the human engagement with the virtual world fundamentally by allowing one to operate the system via thoughts and, conversely, feeding the emotions in the system to MetaIntelligence, to be progressively individualized. As these mix with high-end haptic and sensory technologies, they are bound to create experiences that fully engage all the senses available to human beings, hence blurring the boundaries between the virtual and the physical worlds. In addition, as AI experiences enhanced autonomy, creativity and emotional intelligence, potential emerges of creating online characters which cannot be distinguished with human conversation partners, a process which will literally transform the way that individuals socialize and organize themselves in online environments.

With the MetaIntelligence-powered Metaverses becoming a part of the mainstream, there is a likely scenario of a significant change in the structure of societies and economies altogether. The new economy of the metaverse is built on AI-created content and driven by the investment of users to create new types of economies: creator economies where people are paid to contribute to the MetaIntelligence that forms the collective intelligence of the Metaverse. These trends can lead to the emergence of non-curious professions such as managing virtual worlds, training of artificial intelligence, and digital experience design, and thus crash preconceptions regarding labor and value.

Practice is also ready to change in the field of education. Infinite realities allow the experience of a personalized and interactive medium of learning unique to each learner. At the same time, in medicinal services, digital realities may be quite productive tools of psychological therapy, physical recovery, and clinical training. As the process of content creation is democratized with the help of AI, the process may lead to an unbelievable cultural and artistic surge as artists may partner with algorithms to overcome the limitations of the past and create a domain of previously unknown art forms which would be natural to a virtual realm.

The long-term consequences of the infinite number of realities are where the issue of the essence of human experience and human identity in question must be approached. With the increase in complexity of a virtual environment and the emotional aspects of the environment, societies need to develop a more pluralistic sense of reality itself; a sense of reality which renders salient what one refers to by a genuine experience. Metaverse in this regard may be considered a Dickian incubator of frontier exploration where people can explore various selves, abilities, perspectives and do so safely in virtual environments. In addition, the association between MetaIntelligence and user interaction creates new directions in the field of shared intelligence, thus breaking down the usual divide between individual and collective consciousness and developing new democratic ways of decision-making and problem solving. However, the existence of infinite realities begs immense existential and philosophical questions about the position of man in a world engulfed with AI-created realities that simulate reality to a level that cannot be differentiated, and the maintenance of agency and significance in a world that is flooded with artificial intelligence. These dilemmas require an everlasting discussion between technologists, philosophers, ethicists, and a heterogeneous population.

From the holistic point of view, MetaIntelligence is an entire framework dedicated to accommodating the intricacies that exist in persistent virtual environments, and this refers simultaneously to underlining the still existing hurdles to deal with that require continuous interdisciplinary investigation and careful implementation in operational scenarios.

8. CONCLUSION

The author writes that the combination of MetaIntelligence and Generative Artificial Intelligence is not only an addition to current technology, but it is a paradigm shift in the design, creation, and experience of digital realities. The multi-layers convergence as was posited in this chapter includes first the creative powers that are supported to produce virtual worlds and intelligent agents and second, the meta-level orchestration provided by MetaIntelligence that continually brings about coherence, adaptable and extended development over an endless supply of worlds.

As a result, decentralized architecture, hybrid cloud-edge computing, and strict data control have become three mutually supporting technical solutions that are necessary to build a scalable reality. But the very process of transformation has its complexities which go beyond the complications themselves. The challenges related to consistency levels, human welfare, ethical AI regulation, and long-term consequences of technology incorporation require the interdisciplinary team. In the future, the trend towards infinite realities will probably lead to a more symbiotic relationship between humans and artificial intelligence in the creative industry. The expected advances, such as quantum computing, high-fidelity brain-computer interfaces, and others, will be able to enhance AI functionality, thus allowing the scale of immersion and dynamically created content on a scale never reached before. The socioeconomic impact is immense and has led to new economic orders, education paradigms, and culture. Finally, AI-driven metaverses will transform the human means of communication, thought, and realities. The task of ensuring that such infinite realities are not only created as technologically wonderful spaces but also spaces that promote justice, well-being, and a positive contribution to the overall progress of mankind is shared by researchers, developers, policymakers, and end-users.

REFERENCES

Antal, C., Cioara, T., Anghel, I., Antal, M., & Salomie, I. (2021). Distributed ledger technology review and decentralized applications development guidelines. *Future Internet, 13*(3), 62. Advance online publication. DOI: 10.3390/fi13030062

Bowman, S. R. (2024). Eight things to know about large language models. *Critical AI, 2*(2). Advance online publication. DOI: 10.1215/2834703X-11556011

Chaudhary, A., Rastogi, R., Mattoo, A., Kumar, P., Kumari, T., & Dubey, D. (2025). Generative adversarial networks (GANs). In Generative AI: Disruptive technologies for innovative applications (pp. 29–55). Wiley. Book DOI: https://doi.org/DOI: 10.1002/9781119963605

Damaševičius, R., & Sidekerskienė, T. (2024). Virtual worlds for learning in the metaverse: A narrative review. *Sustainability (Basel), 16*(5), 2032. Advance online publication. DOI: 10.3390/su16052032

Gozalo-Brizuela, R., & Garrido-Merchán, E. C. (2023). A survey of generative AI applications. arXiv. https://arxiv.org/abs/2306.02781

Hatami, M., Qu, Q., Chen, Y., Kholidy, H., Blasch, E., & Ardiles-Cruz, E. (2024). A survey of the real-time metaverse: Challenges and opportunities. *Future Internet, 16*(10), 379. Advance online publication. DOI: 10.3390/fi16100379

Korteling, J. E. H., van de Boer-Visschedijk, G. C., Blankendaal, R. A., Boonekamp, R. C., & Eikelboom, A. R. (2021). Human versus artificial intelligence. *Frontiers in Artificial Intelligence, 4*, 622364. Advance online publication. DOI: 10.3389/frai.2021.622364 PMID: 33981990

Magateshvaren Saras, M. A., Mitra, M. K., & Tyagi, S. (2025). Navigating the multiverse: A hitchhiker's guide to selecting harmonisation methods for multimodal biomedical data. *Biology Methods and Protocols, 10*(1), bpaf028. Advance online publication. DOI: 10.1093/biomethods/bpaf028 PMID: 40308831

Said, G. R. E. (2023). Metaverse-based learning opportunities and challenges: A phenomenological metaverse human–computer interaction study. *Electronics (Basel), 12*(6), 1379. Advance online publication. DOI: 10.3390/electronics12061379

Sobchyshak, O., Berrezueta-Guzman, S., & Wagner, S. (2025). Pushing the boundaries of immersion and storytelling: A technical review of Unreal Engine. arXiv. https://arxiv.org/abs/2507.08142

Vettoruzzo, A., Bouguelia, M.-R., Vanschoren, J., Rögnvaldsson, T., & Santosh, K. (2024). Advances and challenges in meta-learning: A technical review. *IEEE Transactions on Pattern Analysis and Machine Intelligence*, *46*(7), 4763–4779. DOI: 10.1109/TPAMI.2024.3357847 PMID: 38265905

Wang, J. X. (2021). Meta-learning in natural and artificial intelligence. *Current Opinion in Behavioral Sciences*, *38*, 90–95. DOI: 10.1016/j.cobeha.2021.01.002

Wang, Y., Wang, L., & Siau, K. L. (2025). Human-centered interaction in virtual worlds: A new era of generative artificial intelligence and the metaverse. *International Journal of Human-Computer Interaction*, *41*(2), 1459–1501. DOI: 10.1080/10447318.2024.2316376

Wegner, D., Zuquetto, R. D., & Grisi, F. C. (2024). Decentralized autonomous organizations (DAOs): Field of research and avenues for future studies. BAR – Brazilian Administration Review, 21, Article e230183. https://doi.org/DOI: 10.1590/1807-7692bar2024230183

Yuan, H., & Li, S. (2022). Cyber security risks of net-zero technologies. In *Proceedings of the 2022 IEEE Conference on Dependable and Secure Computing (DSC)*. IEEE. DOI: 10.1109/DSC54232.2022.9888883

Chapter 7
Strategies of E-Commerce and Digital Platforms in the Expansion of International Markets

Rahmath Nisha A.
https://orcid.org/0009-0001-5146-2411
Saveetha School of Management, Saveetha Institute of Medical and Technical Sciences, Chennai, India

Subramani A. K.
https://orcid.org/0000-0003-0783-7113
Saveetha School of Management, Saveetha Institute of Medical and Technical Sciences, Chennai, India

ABSTRACT

The evolution of digital technology has given the transformation on how businesses approach an important role in international expansion, where e-commerce and digital platforms are playing a central role. This paper explores the strategies that companies can adopt the successful strategies to enter and grow in international markets through the digital channels. It highlights the key challenges, including cultural differences, regulatory complexities, logistics, and the localized competition, and examines the critical success factors such as market research, platform localization, payment adaptation, strategic partnerships, and effective digital marketing. Through the case studies and market analysis, the paper outlines the best practices

DOI: 10.4018/979-8-3373-9958-4.ch007

for leveraging global e-commerce platforms, building brand presence, and crossing the evolving international digital economy. Ultimately, it provides a strategic framework for businesses seeking sustainable global growth through digital innovation.

1. INTRODUCTION

The international trade has been fundamentally transformed by the world-wide growth of the digital platforms, facilitating the cross-border transactions with ease, lowering the cost of operations, and presenting new opportunities to both businesses and consumers. These platforms including e-commerce marketplaces and online payment systems as well as social media and cross-border specific interfaces have become an essential part of the digital economy, especially in overcoming infrastructural gaps in emerging markets and efficiency in developed economies (Liao et al., 2023; Baykov and Ershov, 2023; Chen et al., 2025).

Despite the e-commerce platform continuing to grow exponentially, it is not yet able to go global and achieve sustainability because of fragmented regulatory frameworks, ethical uncertainty and insufficient homogenization of technological interconnections. Some of the researches are shallow and conceptually scattered and they do not give critical responses to questions on how the digital platforms can be exploited effectively in various markets. The work is opportune to read how e-commerce platforms evolve, transform, and mature particularly in the post-pandemic era where digital transformation is not an option but a must. The study can formulate practical insights through theoretical frameworks and the analysis of cross-border dynamics that can be applied by the stakeholders in the digital commerce environment, as they fight against the reality of changing or disappearing.

2.0. THEORETICAL FRAMEWORK AND LITERATURE REVIEW

This paper is based on four theoretical frameworks that are interconnected and that explain the adoption, diffusion and strategic use of platforms of the e-commerce. These two models are the Technology Acceptance Model (TAM) and the Unified Theory of Acceptance and Use of Technology (UTAUT) that explain consumer-level adoption processes, and accentuate the perceived usefulness, ease of use, and the social influence. Diffusion of Innovation theory can assist us in the process of realizing that technological innovations such as mobile payments and AI-based personalization has evolved through the markets depending on their relative advantage and compatibility. Resource-Based View (RBV) is a supplementary perspective on firm-level capabilities that puts emphasis on the role of digital platforms as strategic resources of the competitive advantage. Combination of these models provides holistic model to explain the relationship between technology, consumer behaviour and organizational strategy on various platforms. As an example, to learn of these contrasts, the following table contrasts major regional structures and the implication of these structures on the operations of e-commerce. The comparative studies indicate significant cross-country variations.

As an example, a well-established digital infrastructure in developed economies allows the easy introduction of new levels of e-commerce technology (e.g., the use of Artificial Intelligence in the U.S. to personalize). And Europe), in contrast to the emerging markets, which are based on digital platforms to overcome the limitations of the infrastructure and reach the global scope (Chen et al., 2025; Lei et al., 2024). Evidence of how policy frameworks play with digital platforms to unlock more rapid SME engagement with e-commerce can be found in studies of the Make-in-India initiative provoking global trade flows (Cramer-Flood, 2020), and studies of platforms ecosystems reorganizing international trade flows (Havinga et al., 2016) can be found in China, involving Alibaba.

Thirdly, a great deal of the literature has focused on the consumer adoption but has given little focus to the inter-relationship between regulation, culture, and technological infrastructure in influencing the international ecommerce development. The solutions to these gaps will empower the theoretical foundations and practical insights into the operation of the e-commerce platforms in a variety of markets. The literature review was used to summarize the main theoretical models and comparative studies to establish the dynamics of e-commerce adoption and strategic implementation. It revealed significant weaknesses in cross-country analysis, theoretical integration, and regulatory-cultural interaction to which the empirical and practical contributions of the study were based.

Table 1. Major regional frameworks

Regulatory Framework	Region	Key Features	Implications for E-Commerce
GDPR	European Union	Emphasizes user consent, data minimization, right to erasure, cross-border data restrictions	High compliance burden; strong consumer trust; limits on data portability
DPDP Act	India	Focuses on lawful processing, user rights, data fiduciaries, and cross-border transfer conditions	Emerging compliance landscape; opportunities for SME growth; localization required
CCPA	California, USA	Grants' rights to access, delete, and opt-out of data sale; applies to for-profit entities	Enhances transparency; requires robust data governance

continued on following page

Table 1. Continued

Regulatory Framework	Region	Key Features	Implications for E-Commerce
LGPD	Brazil	Inspired by GDPR; includes legal bases for processing and data subject rights	Promotes trust; challenges in enforcement consistency
POPIA	South Africa	Regulates processing of personal information; mandates consent and purpose limitation	Supports consumer protection; requires organizational readiness

(Zhou, 2022; Morini et al., 2024; Barrett et al., 2024)

This framework thus bridges micro (user-level), meso (market-level), and macro (organizational-level) dynamics, providing a coherent structure for understanding how e-commerce platforms evolve and compete globally

Figure 1. Integrated conceptual framework for E-commerce expansion

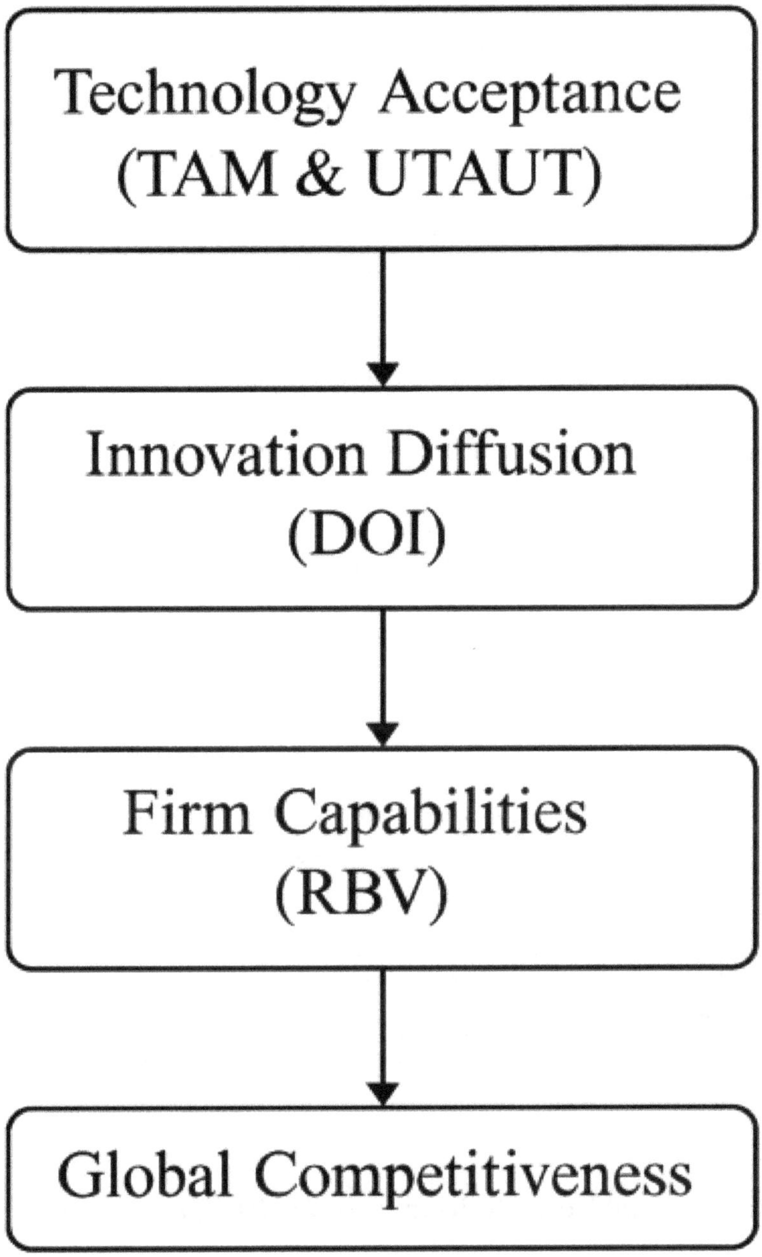

3.0. HISTORICAL OVERVIEW OF E-COMMERCE

3.1. The Origin of Digital Commerce

The history of the e-commerce market can be traced back to the first days of the internet when the ambitious business people discovered the untapped potential of digital media in the process of completing the business transactions. The mid-1990s was known as the dot-com era, during which there was an explosion of internet use and the World Wide Web was established. It was during this time that new companies were opened and this formed the basis of the history of the revolution that would have to occur in the manner in which goods and services would have to be exchanged (Bănescu et al., 2022, Costa & Castro, 2021).

3.2 Early Innovators and the Evolution of Trust

The conventional period of e-commerce was categorized by the novelty of digital transactions and it challenges the consumer trust via the online platforms. The security concerns about the reliability of online payments were the barriers that the industry had to overcome (Bănescu et al., 2022). In the historical perspective, it sets the stage for exploring the evolution of e-commerce, from its budding stages to the global powerhouse it has become today (Zhao, 2022).

Table 2. Rethinking traditional business models in the digital era

Theme	Key Insight
Retail Digitization	Shift from physical stores to global digital platforms (e.g., Amazon's success).
Data-Driven Strategy	Use of customer data for personalization, prediction, and service improvement.
Subscription Models	Rise of recurring revenue through SaaS and entertainment platforms like Netflix.
Marketing Evolution	Targeted digital campaigns replacing mass advertising.
Operational Efficiency	Adoption of IoT and automation in manufacturing for cost and quality gains.

(Udenia, 2025)

3.3 Technological Foundations and Market Expansion

Jack Ma has founded the Alibaba in the year of 1999, who gave the transformation in the e-commerce platform in China and globally. It was initially focused in collaborating the Chinese manufacturers with the international traders, later it expanded its services to consumer-focused platforms. It influences extends the online retail into digital payments including cloud computing which leads to major player in the market.

PayPal was founded by Max Levchin, Peter Thiel, and Luke Nosek in the year of 1998 as a security software for handheld devices initially. Later, it is merged with financial software company Confinity, which evolved into an online payment system.

3.4 Lessons from the Early E-Commerce Era

The acquisition of PayPal by eBay in 2002 provides a secure and trusted payment method for millions of online transactions. Dell, founded by Michael Dell in 1984, played a major role in e-commerce by demonstrating the potential of selling customized computers directly to the consumers through online which eliminates the need for intermediaries, showcasing the efficiency and cost-effectiveness (Ntumba et al., 2023). The manufacturer is responsible for the end-to-end treatment like remanufacturing of the product or repairing in the inventory flow (Saxena & Sarkar, 2023).

Figure 2. Historical overview of E-commerce (Bănescu et al., 2022; Costa & Castro, 2021; Zhao, 2022)

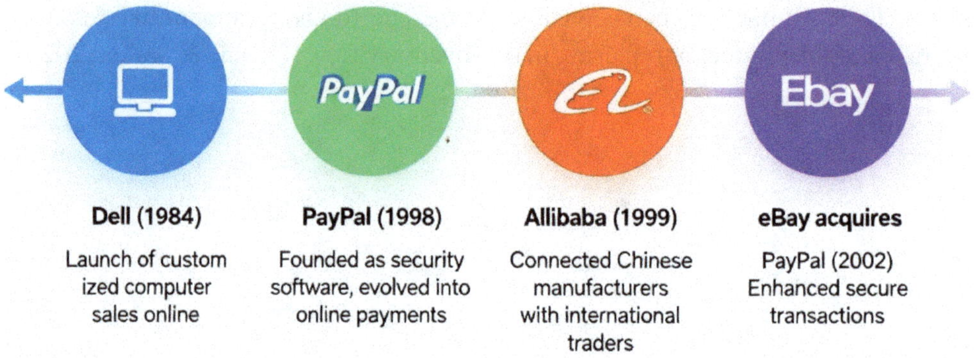

4.0. RETAIL REINVENTED AND EMBRACING THE DIGITAL-FIRST COMMERCE

4.1 From Traditional to Digital: The Shift in Business Models

(Caliskan et al.,2021) has researched about the transformation businesses from traditional marketing to adopt the innovation trends to deal with technological growth and evolving preference of the customer. Innovative digital methods help to elaborate the conventional marketing methods with the help of technological tools which facilitate processing the data and automating the tasks. Organizations get the support of AI and machine learning to send the content for their customers which addresses their unique needs.

(Kotarba,2018) given the business model, digital transformation helps the organization to reinvent themselves through the digital technology to succeed in the business economy. Adopting the innovative technologies to update their primary operations and deliver the customer as best. Businesses can employ online stores as well as uniform subscription systems along with the platform networks to produce more revenue and offers better customer experiences with the help of real-time data analysis aligned with the market changes.

4.2 The Role of Data, AI, and Automation in Retail Innovation

(Vaska et al.,2021) explores how digital transformation has reshaped business models by prompting innovation across diverse industries. It adopts the data-driven decision-making by adopting the big data analytics and AI to gain the competitive advantage. Digital transformation encourages agile operations and allows the firms to react rapidly to the market changes and the evolving customer needs. The challenges like cybersecurity risks and organizational resistance to change are sustained despite of these benefits.

The successful digital alteration entails the strategic alignment, leadership commitment, and continuous adaptation to the technological advancements. (Sundaram et al.,2020) gives the view about digital transformation which affects the business operations by changing the way companies make money and handle their supply chains through structured research analysis. In contemporary online platform like artificial intelligence and blockchain technology facilitates the businesses to sleek their operations for creating new innovations.

5.0. METHODOLOGICAL APPROACH

The current research applies a conceptual and integrative methodology of analysis that would synthesize theoretical points of view and empirical findings in the context of the ways in which e-commerce and digital platforms assist in expanding markets internationally. This chapter relies on peer-reviewed literature, policy documents, and industry reports published between 2016 and 2025, as opposed to using one dataset and follows a qualitative synthesis approach (Snyder, 2019). Such methodological orientation makes it possible to identify theoretical connections, analyze world trends, and obtain the best practices of different economic and cultural backgrounds.

The integrated conceptual framework steers the research design which is a combination of four mutually reinforcing theoretical perspectives: Technology Acceptance Model (TAM) (Davis, 1989), Unified Theory of Acceptance and Use of Technology (UTAUT) (Venkatesh et al., 2003), Diffusion of Innovation Theory (DOI) (Rogers, 2003), and the Resource-Based View (RBV) (Barney, 1991). On the consumer level, TAM and UTAUT models reflect behavioral intentions and adoption of technology through the focus on perceived usefulness and perceived ease of use, social influence, and facilitating conditions. The constructs are mainly applicable in cross-border e-commerce where differences in digital literacy, infrastructure and cultural perception towards technology greatly influence the adoption behavior (Gefen et al., 2003).

Diffusion of Innovation (DOI) theory recognized by Rogers (2003) offers an understanding of the spread of technological innovations like AI-based personalization, mobile commerce, and blockchain-based supply chain solutions at the market level in and across societies. The relative advantage, compatibility, complexity, trialability, and observability are the core dimensions of the theory that are applied to explain the wide rates of diffusion of ecommerce technologies across developed and emerging economies (Lei et al., 2024).

On an organizational scale, the Resource-Based View (RBV) describes how companies can convert technological use into sustainable competitive advantage by taking strategic resources and dynamic capabilities (Barney, 1991; Cennamo, 2021). This paper is a multi-theoretical triangulation perspective (Eisenhardt, 1989) that relates micro-level user adoption (TAM/UTAUT), meso-level innovation diffusion (DOI), and macro-level strategic capability building (RBV). It is analytical rigour that such triangulation gives the opportunity to cross-verify the insights drawn on the basis of various theoretical perspectives. In addition, the chapter conforms to the concept-based coding and thematic synthesis principles of theoretical pluralism (Webster and Watson, 2002), which emphasizes the integration of complementary models in the process of explaining complex socio-technical phenomena like global digital transformation. Analytically, the chapter divides evidence into major constructs (adoption factors, diffusion enablers, and capability outcomes).

The historical analysis of the case studies in different regions, including Alibaba in Asia, Shopify in North America, and Jumia in Africa, will guarantee situational validity and increase the external applicability of the results (Chen et al., 2025; Morini et al., 2024). In short, the approach to the methodology is an interpretive, integrative, and multi-scalar approach that connects individual adoption behavior to wider strategic and institutional processes. It enables the chapter to go past the descriptive narration to the analytical synthesis, the reason and how digital platforms are causing international expansion.

6.0. POST-PANDEMIC SHIFTS IN GLOBAL E-COMMERCE

Although the digitalization of the retail industry re-established how business can be conducted and how it can engage the consumers, the COVID-19 pandemic accelerated the changes radically by revealing the vulnerabilities of the structures and establishing a new way of expanding e-commerce. The post-COVID-19 world has created the pace of the digitalization process and showed the vulnerability of the international supply chains, logistics, and workforce system. The lockdowns rapidly catalyzed the rising of mobile commerce, platform and subscription platforms, but revealed systemic risks such as cybersecurity threats, delivery bottlenecks and job losses.

The pandemic has brought about a labor revolution of automation, remote and online work, and digitization of skills: it has placed on trial how trends in inclusiveness, resiliency, and long-term employment patterns in the retail and logistics industry are determined (Ciupac-Ulici et al., 2023; Banescu et al., 2022).

7.0. E-COMMERCE SECTOR GLOBAL TRENDS: M- COMMERCE, AI, PREDICTIVE ANALYTICS

As the world adjusted to new digital norms following the pandemic, emerging global trends in e-commerce began to reflect deeper technological integration and evolving consumer expectations. In recent years, the e-commerce has tailored its demands for the customer's convenience and ease in exchanging the goods and services across the world.

Like other market segments, the retail sector is witnessing considerable owing to the ongoing digitalization of advanced technologies (Coppola, 2021). With the growth of technological improvements, businesses, governments, and preference of customer to be synchronized, the internet plays a major role in our daily lives for learning, shopping, and communication. To substantiate the reported growth trends, Figure 3 illustrates the steady rise in global retail e-commerce sales between 2020 and 2025.

Figure 3. Global retail E-commerce sales, 2020–2025 (USD trillions) (eMarketer (2025) data summarized in Shopify Blog (2025) and Capital One Shopping Report (2025))

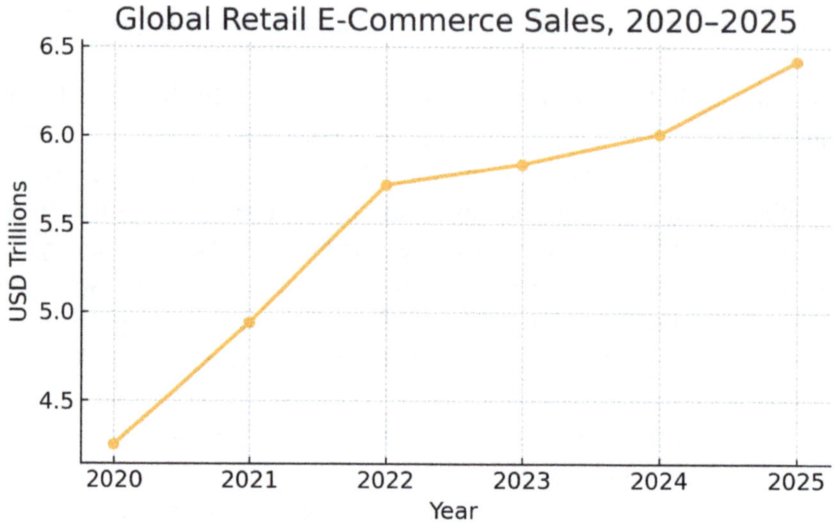

Now a days, business are focusing on customers network through the digital platforms, to make them ease and convenience for both buyers as well as sellers. Apart from the expansion of consumer plinth, the different technologies are anticipated to pose a challenge for the e-commerce industry and parallelly focus on the future growth as well (Palandrani, 2020).

The e-commerce industry anticipates growth due to the number of sectors like growing with hi-speed bandwidth Internet services, unexpected smartphone evolution, market stability, personalized products with low Internet charges. As shown in Figure 4, e-commerce's share of total retail sales continues to expand globally, underscoring a sustained behavioral shift toward digital shopping.

Figure 4. E-commerce share of total retail sales, 2020–2025 (%) (UNCTAD (2022) for 2020–2022 data; eMarketer (2025) forecast for 2025)

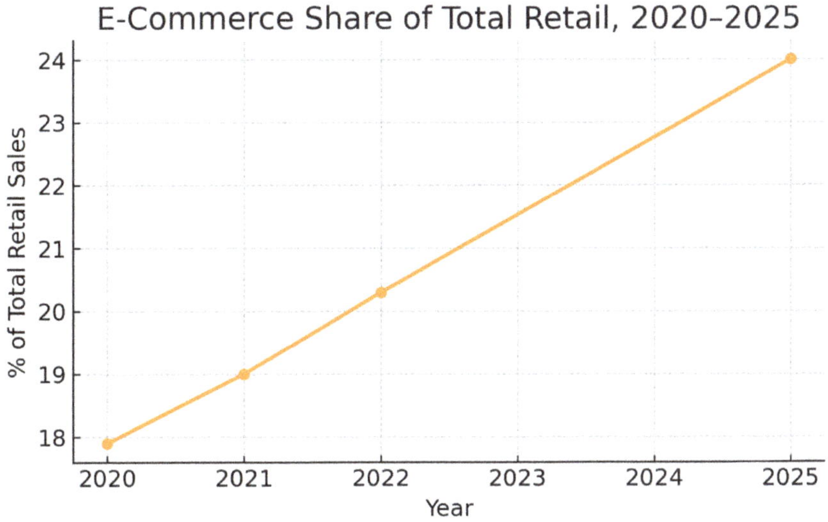

The increase in the flawless Internet services which is boosting the online shopping of consumers which impacts the overall e-commerce revenue in the market. The consumers in the existing markets are transforming their shopping preference towards the digital platforms when compared to the physical sales. It mainly focuses on offering a wide line of products, satisfactory customer convenience which makes the seamless services for their customers.

In addition to these, the online shoppers nowadays, emphasize on the factors like assurance and faster delivery in their purchase decisions, and e-commerce victual to these requirements of the customers (Thakur, 2019). The rise of small and medium-sized enterprises is expected to propel the e-commerce sector development. For example, in countries like India, initiatives like the "Make-in-India" concept are gaining traction, boosting e-commerce sales as well (Cramer-Flood, 2020).

7.1. In Your Pocket: Driving Growth Through Mobile Commerce

It is an internet-based e-commerce as it connects many devices can able to share the same operating platforms. It differentiates the mobile commerce from other e-commerce platform which is more complex now a days. To boost the growth of smartphones and personal data devices which supports the wireless mobile communications. Nowadays, mobile devices are more commonly used for online shopping than laptops or computers with smartphones accounting for approximately half of all e-commerce transactions (Ciupac-Ulici et al.,2023). The rapid expansion of m-commerce observed on a global level has been facilitated by advanced mobile technologies that offer enticing and beneficial services, such as mobile payments (Kim et al., 2010). As a result, mobile banking has emerged as an innovative channel that allows the banks to increase their competitiveness and improve customer convenience (Ho et al.,2020).

The use of smartphones to make their online purchases has grown in popularity in the commercial sector (Yang et al.,2021). The mobile telephone technologies comprising of the mobile telephone provide an effective location where the impressive Internet capabilities such as mobile commerce that can be defined as any transaction of a monetary nature, whether direct or indirect, undertaken through a wireless telecommunication network (Barnes, 2002). The increasing dominance of mobile devices in online transactions is evident in Figure 5, which shows the growing share of mobile commerce in total e-commerce sales.

Figure 5. Mobile commerce share of total E-commerce, 2024–2025 (%) (Demand Sage, 2025)

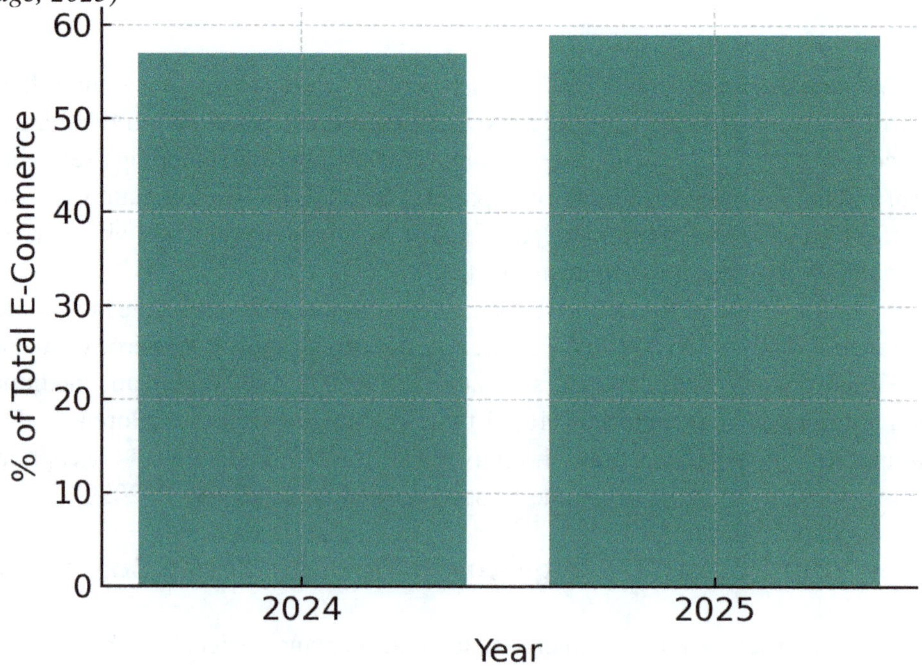

7.2. Emerging Trends: AI-Driven Personalization And Predictive Analytics

The world of electronic commerce is always changing, which is driven by the technological progress and the changing tastes of consumers (Rahman and Dekkati, 2022). Businesses push to keep up with the digital economy. The key of this adaptation is regarding the consumer behavior knowledge and strategic integration of competitive edge technologies (Hidayat et al., 2022). E-commerce is now a part of our life where consumers are not only demanding the convenience but also efficient deals in the personalized and enriching experience. The ability of AI is to process the enormous data and identify its complex patterns, becoming a game-changer to fulfill these changing expectations (He & Liu, 2024).

The role of AI-powered personalization examines the ability of the AI in enhancing the interactions between the consumers by shaping their shopping behaviour, and establishing a connection between the frequent users and the online platforms. The e-commerce market is actually being affected by AI in the dynamic market. Chatbots and virtual assistants are simplifying the customer experiences that give a hint of the future of data-driven and personalized retail experiences (Roslan and Ahmad, 2023).

Such ethical concerns as privacy of the data and algorithmic bias should be given attention. The fine line between bespoke and intrusive is a complicated concern to find a balance that would provide consumer loyalty and gratification (Wei and Xia, 2022). As an example, more effective and efficient marketing campaigns can be conducted by businesses anticipating the customers will react to the promotional email (Ascarza, 2018).

8.0. DIGITAL INCLUSION AND SOCIO-CULTURAL DIMENSIONS IN EMERGING MARKETS

Gender inclusion is also of critical importance. Jumia Women Empowerment Initiative in Africa and MercadoLibre "Mujeres en Tecnologia" in Latin America have offered financial literacy, market access, and market training to women entrepreneurs to bridge their long-standing gender divide (MercadoLibre, 2024). Although this has been achieved, the ITU (2024) observes that women in developing nations are still 17 times less likely to utilize the Internet than men, which proves the necessity to implement specific policies and education programs.

9.0. AI ETHICS AND DATA GOVERNANCE

9.1. Cybersecurity and Consumer Trust

Cybersecurity is becoming a building block to the sustainability of global online commerce. Therefore, with the growth of cross-border transactions, the vulnerability to ransomware attacks, phishing scams, identity theft, and massive data breaches increases. These threats have a direct impact on the intention of consumers to use online marketplaces because trust is a requirement when adopting the digital frontier. Trust may be conceptualized in terms of (Gefen et al.,2003) model that combines familiarity, security as well as credibility as influencers of online interaction.

9.2. Balancing Innovation With Risk

Although the new technologies, like artificial intelligence, blockchain, and augmented reality, have transformative potential in e-commerce and using them does not happen without critical risks. The threats associated with cybersecurity such as data breaches, identity theft, and payment fraud that creates the difficulties in terms of consumer trust and integrity of the platform. The regulatory complexity such as the dissimilarity of the data protection legislation and digital taxation system, complicates the cross-border business and requires deep compliance plans.

The unethical issues especially involving algorithmic bias, intrusive personalization, and data practices that may destroy the trust of the user and may face heightened questioning by regulators and civil societies. Thus, it is necessary to take a middle ground and consider technological opportunities, weighing their threats and control measures needed to achieve responsible and inclusive digital commerce (Akter et al., 2021; Wei and Xia, 2022; Zhou, 2022). All these social and cultural complexities also overlap with ethical and regulatory issues, especially in fair access, algorithmic fairness and consumer protection.

Figure 6. Strategic pillars of global E-commerce scalability (Akter et al., 2021; Wei & Xia, 2022; Zhou, 2022)

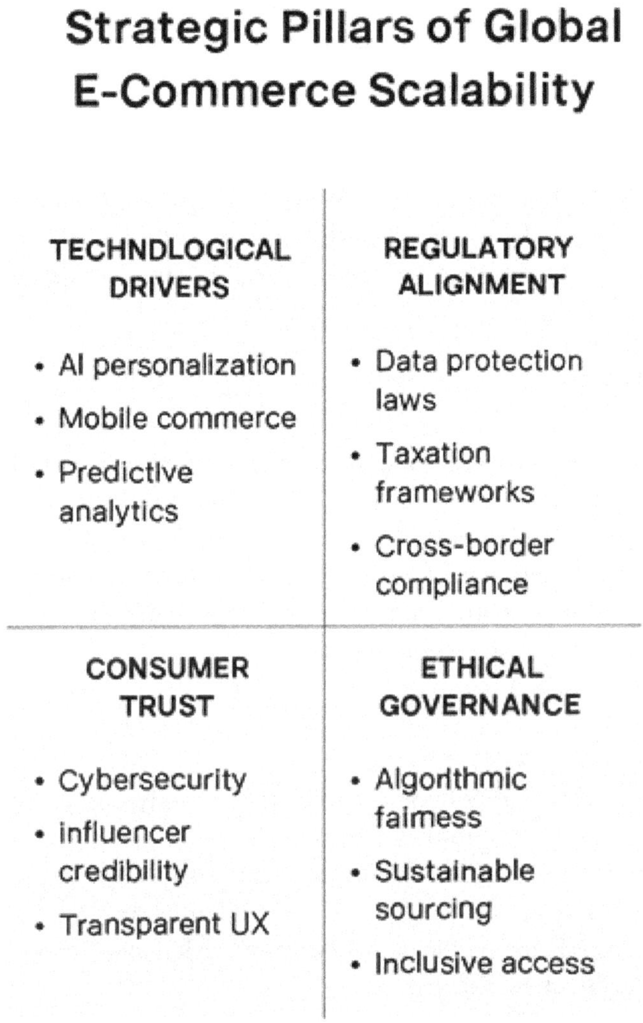

10.0 REGULATORY AND LEGAL CONSIDERATIONS ON DATA PRIVACY, TAXATION, IMPORT/EXPORT LAWS

Although ethical governance will guarantee responsible use of technologies, legal and regulatory compliance which constitutes the structural framework that will allow the e-commerce to have the cross-border trust and accountability. E-commerce market across the borders has unlimited regulatory and legal difficulties, especially those related to data privacy, tax, and import/export regulations. These complications make international trade a complex undertaking with the countries possessing dissimilar laws and norms. The expansion of transboundary e-commerce platforms requires regulatory frameworks, which will guarantee the compliance and safeguard consumer rights. The sections below discuss the particular issues and concerns in this field.

10.1. Data Privacy

It is crucial to protect the consumer personal information to avoid the data breach and fraudulent activities. The system of e-commerce on the border should comply with international data protection laws such as GDPR in Europe, to protect their consumer data. The volume of data that is generated due to cross-border transactions is huge and must be dealt with using efficient data management systems to provide a sense of privacy and security (Zhou, 2022).

10.2. Taxation

Tax in transboundary e-commerce platform is highly complicated because of collusion of several jurisdictions. To Ensure the tax fairness and compliance is a significant challenge, as different countries have distinct tax laws and rates. Programs like Brazil's Programs Remessa Conforme aims to improve tax collection and compliance by enhancing the data quality and risk management in small parcel transactions (Morini et al., 2024).

10.3. Import/Export Laws

Import and export regulations vary widely across countries, creating barriers for e-commerce businesses. Compliance with these laws is essential to avoid the legal issues and ensures smooth transactions (Phương et al., 2024). The need for controls and accurate data in the customs administration is increased the volume of small package transactions in cross-border e-commerce (Morini et al., 2024).

11.0. THE ROLE OF AI IN E-COMMERCE

Since the adoption of Artificial Intelligence in transforming the future of e-commerce, the ethical aspects have occupied centre stage (Ikhtiyorov, 2023). It crosses the dares and ethical norms that are civilized by the AI-inspired customization such as data privacy, algorithmic bias, as well as customization versus user privacy. The regulatory frameworks assist us in assuring the ethical issues in the AI application via e-commerce platforms. The individualization is carried out on the basis of the examination of the large data history that involves consumer behavior, preferences.

This data modeled system enhances the personalization of the content and suggestions when the consumers were mindful of the value and sensitivity of their personal data, it raises the question of how the e-commerce sites are collecting, storing and using their information (Xiao et al.,2021). The role of ethics in the governance of the platform is becoming a major focus. The responsible use of artificial intelligence (AI) and using opaque data practices have become more important issues, especially with the increased intrusion of personalization technologies. To maintain consumer confidence and regulatory credibility, it is necessary to ensure fairness, transparency, and accountability in digital commerce to ensure the privacy is not violated and the users do not access unauthorized content (Akter et al., 2021).

The concentration of consumer information, which is used in the customization purposes, may result in privacy breaches and the possibility of obtaining unauthorized content. The demeaned idea of browsing their history, purchasing behaviour and personal tastes was to be inputted into the algorithms with the purchasers. It is essential to have the right balance between providing individualized experiences and the privacy of the user in the interest of keeping the customer trustful of the e-commerce platforms.

Another widespread issue in AI systems is algorithmic bias and its far-reaching consequences with regard to equitable and impartial consumer experiences through the e-commerce (Chen et al., 2023). The historical data from AI algorithms where the biased data which may perpetuate and magnifies the existing biases which leads to discriminatory output which impact certain demographic groups. In the context of e-commerce, algorithmic bias can manifest in biased product recommendations, pricing discrepancies, or discriminatory targeting in the marketing efforts (Akter et al., 2021).

This biased algorithm leads to specific consumer alone shows as high-priced products or receiving the different product promotions based on the different demographic factors. The developers and data scientists need to address this algorithmic bias which requires an interactive effort to ensure the training covers the diverse data, representative, and immanent biases free. Regular audits and transparency in this algorithmic decision-making helps to identify and rectify its bias effectively (Brown et al., 2021).

The winding balance was struck in between the customization and customer privacy to avoid the opinion of interference. When consumers appreciate the customized experiences, they also consider their privacy concerns. If the privacy protection fails to be maintained, it makes them to feel like their online activities are monitored or exploited. E-commerce platforms must implement the privacy measures, including clear and transparent data collection policies, user consent mechanisms, and anonymization of personally identifiable information wherever is possible (Youssef & Hossam, 2023).

Table 3. Challenges in logistics and supply chain

Key Challenge	Description	Sources
Last-Leg Logistics	The final leg of delivery often involves high costs and logistical complexities which impacts customer satisfaction.	Zhou, 2025
Operational Costs	High logistics costs due to inefficient supply chain management can scare off businesses from engaging in cross-border trade.	(Gong, 2024; Zhou, 2025)
Infrastructure Limitations	Many regions lack the necessary infrastructure to support the efficient logistics which leads to delays and increased costs.	(Yuan, 2023)

Governments and regulatory bodies are recognizing the need to establish the guidelines and regulations to ensure the responsible and ethical use of AI technologies (De Almeida et al., 2021). Regulations enclose the laws of data protection, algorithmic guidelines, transparency, and to eradicate the algorithmic bias measures. E-commerce platforms must aware about these kinds of regulations before for adapting the practices to deal with sustaining ethical norms.

Industry initiatives and collaborations are really important for establishing the ethical AI practices where organizations can able to work together to share the best practices for formulating standards, and promotes transparency in the AI systems. Ethical considerations should be embedded into the development process, and firms should proactively engage in ethical discussions within their industries (Dziubaniuk & Nyholm, 2021).

12.0. GEOPOLITICAL AND REGULATORY COMPLEXITIES IN CROSS-BORDER E-COMMERCE

The global e-commerce platforms are operating in a very fragmented regulatory landscape that was based on national sovereignty, local needs of the localization of data and taxation of digital platforms. As an illustration, the Digital Services Act of the European Union has extremely strict rules regarding content moderation and disclosure and the Cybersecurity Law of China necessitates a. local point of storage and security analysis of cross-border transfer (Zhou, 2022).

This is the reason behind these inconsistencies that complicate the scaling of the platforms and demand dynamically compliant approaches. Geopolitics such as U.S. China trade wars or EU India data transfer negotiations also aggravate the operational risks. The local should be used to manoeuvre these complexities by platforms. governance models, strategic alliances, and initiating these types of undertakings to involve itself with the regulators. The interactions of legal frameworks and the digital commerce to each other are relevant to the development of the platform strategies that are resilient and scalable (Morini et al., 2024; Barrett et al., 2024).

13.0. SUSTAINABILE DIGITAL COMMERCE FRAMEWORK

13.1. Sustainability and Ethical Implementation Across Markets

Sustainability and ethical establishment throughout markets: Sustainability and ethical implementation. governance is becoming a strategic imperative and application of the same is being witnessed in a crosscutting manner. different markets are still unbalanced. There is an increasing pressure on e-commerce to lower carbon. footprints, ethical sourcing, and inclusive digital engagement.

Amazon's Climate An example is Pledge, which devotes itself to net-zero emissions and sustainable packaging, but does not implement it. depends on the area because of infrastructural and policy limitations (Akter et al., 2021). The Samarth project of Flipkart in India is an example of inclusive development as it helps local artisans. even as there are still issues of digital literacy and logistics. In order to operationalize sustainability, platforms must:

- Adopt circular commerce models (e.g., resale, repair, recycling).
- Invest in green logistics and carbon offset programs.
- Ensure ethical AI deployment through fairness audits and transparency protocols.
- Collaborate with local governments and NGOs to align digital inclusion with environmental goals (Wei & Xia, 2022; Youssef & Hossam, 2023).

13.2. The Power of Social Shopping

There is no standard definition for the term, social commerce generally refers to the delivery of e-commerce activities and transactions via the social media environment, mostly in the social networks by using the Web 2.0 software. It is the subset of e-commerce platforms which includes the social media usage for facilitates the e-commerce transactions. It supports the social interactions and shopper content contributions along with the combination of commercial and social activities.

(Stephen & Toubia, 2010) defined SC as a form of Internet-based social media that allows the people to actively participate in the marketing and selling their products and services in the online marketplaces. The influencer marketing impacts the development of e-commerce by strengthening the digital media platforms in recent years, which has popped up as a key driver of consumer purchasing behavior.

By engaging the followers to encourage the trust and credibility which influences the consumers on purchasing the products which they validate. The campaigns are organized for boost the brand visibility and customer loyalty, not only for boost the sales frequency which results as successful results. Further, the evolution of influencer marketing is expected to continue in shaping the e-commerce strategies, with advancements in the technology to further redefine how influencers engage with the audiences and drive business growth (Prasanthi et al., 2024).

Among the most powerful factors that contribute to this evolution is the rising popularity of the influencer-based shopping experiences. The influencers gain trust among their followers and are authentic agents between the brands and consumers (De Veirman et al., 2017). Their product promotion, which is usually delivered by use of the relatable entertaining content, greatly influences consumer choices. Moreover, the interactive experience associated with the platform such as TikTok Shop Now buttons and Instagram Live Shopping functions that facilitate the immediacy and ease of the shopping experience by building a frictionless journey towards the checkout desk (Appel et al., 2020).

13.3. Proliferation of Subscription-Based E-Commerce Models

Kowalkowski and Ulaga (2024) highlight the subscription offers in the (B2B) markets. B2B firms faces the issues and challenge the implementation and identifies the uniqueness of B2B subscription offers. The interviews with industry executives help the organizational and operational transformations which is requires the consumer subscription. (Fitrianti et al., 2024) explored the dynamics of customer participation in the subscription business models and their implications for sustainable marketing strategies. It highlights the significance of customer engagement, customer preference, promotion results, and satisfaction in driving the customer retention and their loyalty.

Määttänen (2015) examines the consumer engagement with subscription-based music streaming services and the factors influencing their value to users. In the Finnish music market, where the subscription services deal with challenges despite of the speed growth of streaming through online platform. It highlights the features of diverse music catalogs and listening ad-free music which drives the consumer interest. It highlights the role of digital marketing strategies through word-of-mouth and digital footprint to boost the customer engagement. (Gladilina et al., 2023) explores the development of subscription services in the e- commerce which focus on how these services influence the consumer behavior. It relates the consumer intention and demographic factors which affects the adoption of the subscription models like one-stop subscriptions.

14.0. GLOBAL MARKET PENETRATION: STRATEGIC ROLE OF E-COMMERCE PLATFORMS

The sustainable digital commerce discussion points out that ethics, environmental, and inclusion practices are part of sustainable competitiveness in the long run. With the shift of the platforms towards sustainability commitment to market execution, it is crucial to incorporate these principles in the process of international expansion strategies. The growth of digital platform having the crucial implications for the organizations as they are in need to innovate and creates the globalization strategies for international business.

Researchers have long claimed that digitalization can readily enable the firms to be "born-global" such as international new ventures (Cannone & Ughetto, 2014; Ferguson & Henrekson, 2019; Hennart, 2014), or seamlessly expand internationally for "goglobal" (Monaghan et al., 2020). The digital innovations like online platforms and the network effects which led the growth of young digital firms like Airbnb and Uber, which demonstrates the top-notch strategies to reach globally. The role of geography is also important in expanding the digital businesses, research also shows that how 'space' matters for 'born-global' International new ventures or 'go global' MNEs where digital innovation is still developing.

The studies on mobile money platforms in the emerging economies highlights how a digital innovation approach intersects with place-based way, influencing adoption rates and outcomes for the financial and social inclusion (Barrett et al., 2024). It also shows that digital platforms, infrastructures, and ecosystems introduce new forms of competition and alliance building, where the platform systems, rather than the individual firms or industries, defines the competitive dynamics (Cennamo, 2021; Constantinides et al., 2018).

The spatial attributes of online based platform of an organization which impacts the global strategy and influence the factors like multi-networked, economies of scale, differentiation, and entry barriers. Digital innovation and digital platforms shape the MNEs' business models and spatial strategies in their internationalization processes which necessitates further research into how spatial dynamics influence the competition in emerging global and digital business environments (Adner, 2016; Jacobides et al., 2018).

15.0. ROLE OF DIGITAL PLATFORM IN THE INTERNATIONAL TRADE

15.1. Facilitation of Cross-Border Transaction

The digital platforms have made cross border transaction easy through the reduction of trade costs, improvement of transparency, and efficiency. In the cross-border e-commerce, the e-commerce platforms have simplified logistics, payment procedures, and customs clearance which make it more accessible to the businesses to participate in the international trade (Meng et al., 2024; Baykov and Ershov, 2023).

15.2. Empowering the Small and Medium-Sized Enterprises

Digital platforms enable the SMEs to play a role in the international trade. These platforms have allowed SMEs to enter more markets and broaden their customer base as well as expand their export capacity by opening the international markets to them. This is advantageous to the SMEs in the emerging markets, which tend to have major entry barriers in the global markets (Chen et al., 2025; Liu et al., 2023).

15.3. Practicing Digital Inclusion and Financial Empowerment

Digital platforms will foster financial participation through enabling the individuals and businesses to connect to the financial services such as digital payment, loans, and insurance. It is especially game-changing in the emerging markets, as in some cases, the conventional financial system does not cover large proportions of the population (Lei et al., 2024).

Figure 7. The power of social media and AI-driven personalization (Elsayad & Md Saad, 2024; Ding et al., 2024; Kholkina et al., 2024)

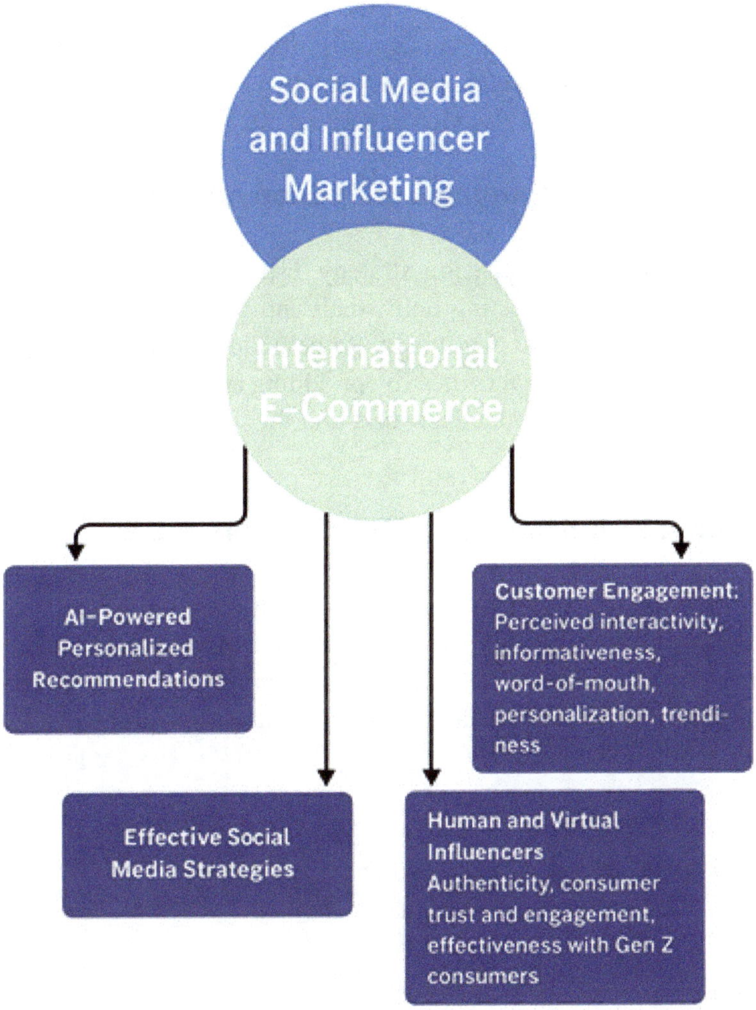

16.0. BUSINESS STRATEGIES AND CASE INSIGHTS OF E-COMMERCE

16.1. Amazon: Global Expansion Through Localization

Amazon's global success is highly attributed to its strategy of localized market adaptation. For example, in India, Amazon introduced the Amazon Pay to integrate the local payment preferences and invested heavily in the domestic supply chain to meet the logistical challenges (Laudon & Traver, 2021).

16.2. Alibaba: Strengthening Local Ecosystems

Alibaba's international expansion strategy, especially through platforms like AliExpress, focuses on connecting both small and medium-sized Chinese enterprises which covers the global consumers. Rather than competing directly with the local retailers, Alibaba empowers them by providing access to a huge marketplace, logistics support through Cainiao Network, and the financial services via Ant Financial (Chaffey et al., 2009).

16.3. Shopify: Empowering Global Entrepreneurs

Shopify represents a different model of international e-commerce success by enabling millions of businesses worldwide to sell through the online platform without having heavy infrastructure investments. By offering the localized payment gateways, multi-currency support, and integrations with the region-specific logistics providers (Laudon & Traver, 2021).

Figure 8. Global E-commerce expansion strategies framework (Laudon & Traver, 2021; Chaffey et al., 2009; Christopher, 2016)

16.4. Zalando: European Market Specialization

Zalando is well known for its European fashion and lifestyle e-commerce market who achieved the success by customizing its operations to the distinct preferences of European consumers. Zalando offers free delivery and returns, localized content, and a huge selection of brands specific to its each market (Christopher, 2016).

17.0. STAR PERFORMERS OF GLOBAL E-COMMERCE SYSTEM

The e-commerce platform is overshadowed by a number of large platforms, the peculiarities of which include their own strengths and approaches to marketing. The main participants are Amazon, Alibaba, eBay and Shopify who had significant contributions to the development of online trading. These platforms applied the technology, consumer science, and business strategic models to make their presence felt in the digital market. Below is an overview of these platforms, which highlights their distinctive features and market impact.

Table 4. Visual representation of star performers of E commerce

Platform	Market Share	Active Users	Key Features
Amazon	37.8%	310 million	Big data, cloud computing, robotics, global reach
Alibaba	23% in global GMV	939 million actives	Connecting Chinese to global markets, AI, cloud tech
eBay	6.4%	132 million	Auction and fixed-price sales, second-hand goods
Shopify	10.2%	1.7 million+ stores	Flexible store creation, scalable, multi-currency

(Yuan, 2024; Pai & Kumar, 2021; Havinga et al., 2016; Kurzadkar et al., 2024; Zangana et al., 2024)

18.0. BLUEPRINT FOR AN EFFECTIVE INTERNATIONAL E-COMMERCE GROWTH

18.1. Selective Entry and Strategic Market Analysis

Once the new markets have been selected, conducting thorough market research to understand the complexity of the market is the initial move towards entering the market. This includes the analysis of consumer behaviour, identification of competitors, and perception of local regulatory environments (Cavusgil et al., 2020). It is possible to choose the markets based on such data and reduce the risk and allocate the resources efficiently.

18.2. Localized of Product and Service Strategies

The localization must go beyond mere translation of web sites as well as products, marketing communication and payment systems, etc, to suit the anticipations of local consumers both culturally and economically (Singh and Matsuo, 2004). The change of the material to the local languages, currency, holidays and taste can be incredibly useful in raising the interest of the users and the conversion rates.

18.3. End-to-End control in Supply Chain Management Process

Efficient supply chain management are the most critical components of international expansion. By establishing the local warehouses, partnering with third-party logistics (3PL) providers, implementing the transparent shipping and return policies ensures operational reliability and customer satisfaction (Christopher, 2016).

18.4. Customized Digital Marketing Strategies

Localized digital marketing programs play a critical role in creating brand awareness and customer confidence. The winning tactics include having regional search engines, localizing on social media channels and collaborating with the locals in coming up with the culturally applicable and riveting campaigns (Chaffey et al., 2009).

18.5. Agile Technological Infrastructure

An agile technological base will be used to cope with the dynamics of international operations. These also involve the presence of multiple currencies, languages, localized inventory, and omnichannel customer experiences in the varied markets (Laudon and Traver, 2021).

18.6. Building Customer Trust and Brand Recognition

Establishing trust with new customers is predominant in unfamiliar markets. Businesses must deploy the trust signals such as certifications, customer reviews, and partnerships with reputable local entities. Moreover, providing multilingual customer support and maintaining transparent communication enhances customer loyalty and strengthens the brand reputation (Gefen et al., 2003).

19.0. FUTURE TRENDS IN THE E-COMMERCE MARKETPLACE

Various new trends are likely to be transformed on the international e-commerce platforms. It will make the use of AI and machine learning to achieve the deep personalization of the pricing and product suggestion which are all customer experiences. personalized to the specific needs. Mobile commerce is being developed. crushing through most of the newer markets, where the mobile internet penetration outstrips the desktop. access, and incurs the mobile-first approaches.

The use of the AR and VR technology. will enhance the online shopping experiences in which the service is made accessible to the customers. the online preview to the actual shopping.to. Also, it is also impacting the sustainability issues. the consumer behavior wherein the businesses are currently being compelled to practice the greener supply. chains, and open ethical behaviors.

Finally, the usage of blockchain technology is likely to be applied to. improve security of transactions, supply chain transparency and customer trust. Based on these trends, firms, which are interested in achieving their extension operations in international e-commerce, needs to invest more advanced AI-based analytics in order to achieve a more advantageous result. understanding of the consumer needs in different markets and predict them. A mobile-first design philosophy must be prioritized, especially in the regions with high mobile penetration. Companies should also explore the application of AR and VR technologies to enhance customer engagement and satisfaction. Customer satisfaction is the core success for convenient and profitable retailing (Sarkar & Dey, 2023).

To improve the customer satisfaction, every company is focus on preventing the stockouts and reducing the lead and variance time to meet the customer demand on timely basis (Sarkar et al., 2023). Furthermore, adopting these sustainable business practices and transparently communicating these efforts to the consumers will become a competitive differentiator. It is equally critical to monitor the developments in blockchain and related technologies to strengthen the operational security and build trust.

20.0. CONCLUSION

E-commerce and digital platforms have emerged as an indispensable engine for global business growth, breaking down the traditional barriers into international trade and creating new opportunities for businesses of all sizes. The rapidity of the international e-commerce more or less will affect the scope of the platforms in the future new technologies such as AI, blockchain, AR. Meanwhile, the complex regulatory environments that cover businesses should be negotiated by the businesses, the data privacy, international taxation, and the trade compliance issues. In addition, the modification of the consumer behaviors, which is triggered by the augmented level of digital literacy, the heightened expectations of the personalization, and the heightened demands to business. Sustainable and ethical practices require the organization to be dynamic and responsive customer-centered. Finally, international e-commerce is not a transactional one, expansion is also a process of transformation, learning and strategic, which remains dynamic and constant. transformation. Such organizations that develop such an attitude will be well prepared to succeed in the integrated international economy.

REFERENCES

Adner, R. (2016). Ecosystem as Structure: An Actionable Construct for Strategy. *Journal of Management*, *43*(1), 39–58. DOI: 10.1177/0149206316678451

Akter, S., McCarthy, G., Sajib, S., Michael, K., Dwivedi, Y. K., D'Ambra, J., & Shen, K. N. (2021). Algorithmic bias in data-driven innovation in the age of AI. *International Journal of Information Management*, *60*, 102387. DOI: 10.1016/j.ijinfomgt.2021.102387

Appel, G., Grewal, L., Hadi, R., & Stephen, A. T. (2020). The future of social media in marketing. *Journal of the Academy of Marketing Science*, *48*(1), 79–95. DOI: 10.1007/s11747-019-00695-1 PMID: 32431463

Ascarza, E. (2018). Retention futility: Targeting high-risk customers might be ineffective. *JMR, Journal of Marketing Research*, *55*(1), 80–98. DOI: 10.1509/jmr.16.0163

Bănescu, C. E., i an, E., & Manea, D. (2022). The impact of E-commerce on the labor market. *Sustainability (Basel)*, *14*(9), 5086. DOI: 10.3390/su14095086

Barnes, S. J. (2002). The mobile commerce value chain: Analysis and future developments. *International Journal of Information Management*, *22*(2), 91–108. DOI: 10.1016/S0268-4012(01)00047-0

Barney, J. (1991). Firm resources and sustained competitive advantage. *Journal of Management*, *17*(1), 99–120. DOI: 10.1177/014920639101700108

Barrett, M., Liyala, S., Oborn, E., & Prince, K. (2024). Building hope for the poor with digital services: Providing prosperity, justice, and dignity for ALL. *Africa Journal of Management*, *10*(1), 75–88. DOI: 10.1080/23322373.2024.2316508

Baykov, F. Y., & Ershov, V. S. (2023, October). International trade digital transformation impact on the global digital platforms expansion. In *2023 International Conference on Engineering Management of Communication and Technology (EMCTECH)* (pp. 1-5). IEEE.DOI: 10.1109/EMCTECH58502.2023.10296940

Brown, S., Davidovic, J., & Hasan, A. (2021). The algorithm audit: Scoring the algorithms that score us. *Big Data & Society*, *8*(1), 2053951720983865. DOI: 10.1177/2053951720983865

Caliskan, A., Özkan Özen, Y. D., & Ozturkoglu, Y. (2021). Digital transformation of traditional marketing business model in new industry era. *Journal of Enterprise Information Management*, *34*(4), 1252–1273. DOI: 10.1108/JEIM-02-2020-0084

Cannone, G., & Ughetto, E. (2014). Born globals: A cross-country survey on high-tech start-ups. *International Business Review, 23*(1), 272–283. DOI: 10.1016/j.ibusrev.2013.05.003

Cavusgil, S. T., Knight, G., & Riesenberger, J. R. (2020). *International business: the new realities, global edition. Harlow*. Pearson.

Cennamo, C. (2021). Competing in digital markets: A platform-based perspective. *The Academy of Management Perspectives, 35*(2), 265–291. DOI: 10.5465/amp.2016.0048

Chaffey, D., Ellis-Chadwick, F., & Mayer, R. (2009). *Internet marketing: strategy, implementation and practice*. Pearson education.

Chen, P., Wu, L., & Wang, L. (2023). AI fairness in data management and analytics: A review on challenges, methodologies and applications. *Applied Sciences (Basel, Switzerland), 13*(18), 10258. DOI: 10.3390/app131810258

Chen, Y., Wang, Q., & Zhang, J. (2025). The role of cross-border E-commerce platforms in the digital economy: Empower firms to gain global market insights to increase global competitiveness. *Journal of Digital Management, 1*(1), 1–17. DOI: 10.1007/s44362-024-00003-0

. Christopher, M. (2016). Logistics and supply chain management: logistics & supply chain management. Pearson UK.

Ciupac-Ulici, M., Beju, D.-G., Bresfelean, V. P., & Zanellato, G. (2023). Which Factors Contribute to the Global Expansion of M-Commerce? *Electronics (Basel), 12*(1), 197. DOI: 10.3390/electronics12010197

Constantinides, P., Henfridsson, O., & Parker, G. G. (2018). Introduction—Platforms and infrastructures in the digital age. *Information Systems Research, 29*(2), 381–400. DOI: 10.1287/isre.2018.0794

Coppola, D. (2021). E-commerce worldwide-statistics & facts. *Retrieved*, (Dec), 30.

Costa, J., & Castro, R. (2021). SMEs must go online—E-commerce as an escape hatch for resilience and survivability. *Journal of Theoretical and Applied Electronic Commerce Research, 16*(7), 3043–3062. DOI: 10.3390/jtaer16070166

. Cramer-Flood, E. (2020). Global e-commerce 2020. eMarketer.

Davis, F. D. (1989). Perceived usefulness, perceived ease of use, and user acceptance of information technology. *Management Information Systems Quarterly, 13*(3), 319–340. DOI: 10.2307/249008

De Almeida, P. G. R., dos Santos, C. D., & Farias, J. S. (2021). Artificial intelligence regulation: A framework for governance. *Ethics and Information Technology*, *23*(3), 505–525. DOI: 10.1007/s10676-021-09593-z

De Veirman, M., Cauberghe, V., & Hudders, L. (2017). Marketing through Instagram influencers: The impact of number of followers and product divergence on brand attitude. *International Journal of Advertising*, *36*(5), 798–828. DOI: 10.1080/02650487.2017.1348035

DemandSage. (2025). *Global Mobile Commerce Statistics 2025.* Retrieved from https://www.demandsage.com/mobile-commerce-statistics/

Ding, L., Venditti, M., & Antonucci, G. (2024). Unveiling user responses to AI-powered personalised recommendations: A qualitative study of consumer engagement dynamics on Douyin. *Qualitative Market Research*, *28*(2), 234–255. Advance online publication. DOI: 10.1108/QMR-11-2023-0151

Dziubaniuk, O., & Nyholm, M. (2021). Constructivist approach in teaching sustainability and business ethics: A case study. *International Journal of Sustainability in Higher Education*, *22*(1), 177–197. DOI: 10.1108/IJSHE-02-2020-0081

Eisenhardt, K. M. (1989). Building theories from case study research. *Academy of Management Review*, *14*(4), 532–550. DOI: 10.2307/258557

. Elsayad, G., & Md Saad, N. H. (2024). Unmasking the power of social media marketing activities in cultivating customer equity, loyalty, and repurchase intention. *Journal of Marketing Communications, ahead-of-print(ahead-of-print), 1–21.* DOI: 10.1080/13527266.2024.2432029

Ferguson, S. M., & Henrekson, M. (2019). The long-run performance of born globals in computing: the role of digital platforms. https://ssrn.com/abstract=3229229

Fitrianti, N. G., Hanuun, N. N. P., & Fatmasari, R. R. (2024). Dynamics of customer participation in subscription business models: case analysis and implications for sustainable marketing strategies. *Journal of Economics, Accounting, Business, Management, Engineering and Society,* 1(5), 15-28. https://kisainstitute.com/index.php/kisainstitute/article/view/24

Gefen, D., Karahanna, E., & Straub, D. W. (2003). Trust and TAM in online shopping: An integrated model. *Management Information Systems Quarterly*, *27*(1), 51–90. DOI: 10.2307/30036519

Gladilina, I., Degtev, G., Kochetkov, E., Tretyak, E., Stepanova, D., & Mutaliyeva, L. (2023). Development of User Subscription Services in E-Commerce: Effects on Consumer Behavior. *International Journal of Computer Science & Network Security, 23*(11), 53–58. DOI: 10.22937/IJCSNS.2023.23.11.6

Gong, J. (2024). Challenges and Countermeasures for China's Cross-Border E-Commerce in International Market Competition under the "Belt and Road" Initiative. *Advances in Economics. Management and Political Sciences, 111*, 173–179. DOI: 10.54254/2754-1169/2024.17763

. Havinga, M., Hoving, M., & Swagemakers, V. (2016). Alibaba: a case study on building an international imperium on information and E-Commerce. *Multinational management: A casebook on Asia's global market leaders, 1*3-32. DOI: 10.1007/978-3-319-23012-2_2

He, X., & Liu, Y. (2024). Knowledge evolutionary process of Artificial intelligence in E-commerce: Main path analysis and science mapping analysis. *Expert Systems with Applications, 238*, 121801. DOI: 10.1016/j.eswa.2023.121801

Hennart, J. (2014). The Accidental Internationalists: A Theory of Born Globals. *Entrepreneurship Theory and Practice, 38*(1), 117–135. DOI: 10.1111/etap.12076

Hidayat, M., Salam, R., Hidayat, Y. S., Sutira, A., & Nugrahanti, T. P. (2022). Sustainable Digital Marketing Strategy in the Perspective of Sustainable Development Goals. Komitmen. *Jurnal Ilmiah Manajemen, 3*(2), 100–106. DOI: 10.15575/jim.v3i2.22687

Ho, J. C., Wu, C. G., Lee, C. S., & Pham, T. T. T. (2020). Factors affecting the behavioral intention to adopt mobile banking: An international comparison. *Technology in Society, 63*, 101360. DOI: 10.1016/j.techsoc.2020.101360

Ikhtiyorov, F. (2023). Navigating AI's Potential in E-Commerce: Legal Regulations, Challenges, and Key Considerations. *Agrobiotexnologiya Va Veterinariya Tibbiyoti Ilmiy Jurnali, 2*(5), 41–49.

International Telecommunication Union (ITU). (2024). *Bridging the gender digital divide: Internet access and skills gap report 2024*. International Telecommunication Union.

Jacobides, M. G., Cennamo, C., & Gawer, A. (2018). Towards a theory of ecosystems. *Strategic Management Journal, 39*(8), 2255–2276. DOI: 10.1002/smj.2904

Kholkina, V., Chesnokova, E., & Zelenskaya, E. (2024). Virtual or human? The impact of the influencer type on Gen Z consumer outcomes. *Journal of Product and Brand Management, 34*(1), 104–118. Advance online publication. DOI: 10.1108/JPBM-12-2023-4885

Kim, C., Mirusmonov, M., & Lee, I. (2010). An empirical examination of factors influencing the intention to use mobile payment. *Computers in Human Behavior, 26*(3), 310–322. DOI: 10.1016/j.chb.2009.10.013

. Kotarba, M. (2018). Digital transformation of business models. Foundations of management, 10(1), 123-142. DOI: 10.2478/fman-2018-0011

Kowalkowski, C., & Ulaga, W. (2024). Subscription offers in business-to-business markets: Conceptualization, taxonomy, and framework for growth. *Industrial Marketing Management, 117*, 440–456. DOI: 10.1016/j.indmarman.2024.01.014

Kurzadkar, P., Bawangade, S., & Sathawane, N. (2024). E-Commerce Platform of Online Shopping Consumers. International *Journal of Advanced Research in Science. Tongxin Jishu, 350-354*, 350–354. Advance online publication. DOI: 10.48175/IJARSCT-17853

Laudon, K. C., & Traver, C. G. (2021). *E-commerce 2021: Business, technology, and society* (16th ed.). Pearson.

Lei, J., Indiran, L., Kohar, U. H. A., & Liu, H. (2024). Digital Innovation in Emerging Economies: A Comparative Review of India, Malaysia, China, and Indonesia. *International Journal of Academic Research in Business & Social Sciences, 14*(1), 3207–3227. DOI: 10.6007/IJARBSS/v14-i1/20457

Liao, Y., Wu, G., & Huang, J. (2023). The impact of rural e-commerce environment development on orchard expansion from the perspective of tele-coupling: The case of pinghe county in Southeast China. *Land (Basel), 12*(11), 1991. DOI: 10.3390/land12111991

Liu, Y., Li, Y., & Wu, A. (2023). Ecosystem-specific Advantages of Digital Platform and Emerging Market Firms' International Outcomes. I*n Academy of Management Proceedings (Vol.* 2023, No. 1, p. 16406). Briarcliff Manor, NY 10510. *Proceedings - Academy of Management, 2023*(1), 16406. Advance online publication. DOI: 10.5465/AMPROC.2023.16406abstract

. Määttänen, E. (2015). Subscription-based music streaming services and digital marketing: Exploring consumer engagement through values.

Meng, J., Lu, H., & She, S. (2024). An analysis of how digital technology impacts trade costs—Based on the empirical data of RCEP member countries. *Financial Economics Letters*, *3*(3), 1–12. DOI: 10.58567/fel03030001

MercadoLibre. (2024). *Mujeres en Tecnología Report*. MercadoLibre.

Monaghan, S., Tippmann, E., & Coviello, N. (2020). Born digitals: Thoughts on their internationalization and a research agenda. *Journal of International Business Studies*, *51*(1), 11–22. DOI: 10.1057/s41267-019-00290-0

Morini, C., Leonardo, F. P., Chaudhary, V., & Hintsa, J. (2024). A Paradigm Shift in Cross-Border E-Commerce Regulatory Compliance: Evidence from Brazil. *World Customs Journal*, *18*(2), 3–19. DOI: 10.55596/001c.123504

Ntumba, C., Aguayo, S., & Maina, K. (2023). Revolutionizing Retail: A Mini Review of E-commerce Evolution. *Journal of Digital Marketing and Communication*, *3*(2), 100–110. DOI: 10.53623/jdmc.v3i2.365

Pai, Y., & Kumar, K. N. (2021). E-Commerce to Multinational Conglomerate: Journey of Alibaba Group—A Case Study. International Journal of Case Studies in Business [IJCSBE]. *IT and Education*, *25*. Advance online publication. DOI: 10.5281/zenodo.4544394

Palandrani, P. (2020). *E-commerce: Entering the Next Wave of Growth*. NASDAQ.

Prasanthi, P., Kaur, M. R., Ilyas, M. M., Natarajan, S., Neelima, S., & Rajalakshmi, M. (2024). The role of social media influencers in shaping e-commerce trends and consumer behavior. *In Obstetrics & Gynaecology Forum* (No. 3s, p. 2278).

Rahman, S. S., & Dekkati, S. (2022). Revolutionizing Commerce: The Dynamics and Future of E-Commerce Web Applications. *Asian Journal of Applied Science and Engineering*, *11*(1), 65–73. DOI: 10.18034/ajase.v11i1.58

. Rogers, E. (2003). Diffusion of Innovations 5th.

Roslan, F. A. B. M., & Ahmad, N. B. (2023). The Rise of AI-Powered Voice Assistants: Analyzing Their Transformative Impact on Modern Customer Service Paradigms and Consumer Expectations. *Quarterly Journal of Emerging Technologies and Innovations*, *8*(3), 33–64.

Sarkar, B., & Dey, B. K. (2023). Is online-to-offline customer care support essential for consumer service? *Journal of Retailing and Consumer Services*, *75*, 103474. DOI: 10.1016/j.jretconser.2023.103474

Sarkar, B., Kar, S., Basu, K., & Seo, Y. W. (2023). Is the online-offline buy-online-pickup-in-store retail strategy best among other product delivery strategies under variable lead time? *Journal of Retailing and Consumer Services*, *73*, 103359. DOI: 10.1016/j.jretconser.2023.103359

. Saxena, N., & Sarkar, B. (2023). How does the retailing industry decide the best replenishment strategy by utilizing technological support through blockchain. *Journal of Retailing and Consumer Services, 71*, 103151. https://doi.org/ rights and contentDOI: 10.1016/j.jretconser.2022.103151Get

Singh, N., & Matsuo, H. (2004). Measuring cultural adaptation on the Web: A content analytic study of U.S. and Japanese Web sites. *Journal of Business Research*, *57*(8), 864–872. DOI: 10.1016/S0148-2963(02)00482-4

Snyder, H. (2019). Literature review as a research methodology: An overview and guidelines. *Journal of Business Research*, *104*, 333–339. DOI: 10.1016/j.jbusres.2019.07.039

Stephen, A. T., & Toubia, O. (2010). Deriving value from social commerce networks. *JMR, Journal of Marketing Research*, *47*(2), 215–228. DOI: 10.1509/jmkr.47.2.215

Sundaram, R., Sharma, D. R., & Shakya, D. A. (2020). Digital transformation of business models: A systematic review of impact on revenue and supply chain. *International Journal of Management, 1*1(5). https://ssrn.com/abstract=3628963

Thakur, A. (2019). Impact of Mood of the Millennial Customers on Purchase of Apparels Online. In Dasgupta, S., & Grover, P. (Eds.), *Optimizing Millennial Consumer Engagement with Mood Analysis* (pp. 240–266). IGI Global Scientific Publishing., DOI: 10.4018/978-1-5225-5690-9.ch011

Udenia, M. (2025). The Influence of Digital Transformation on Traditional Business Models. [IJARMT]. *International Journal of Advanced Research and Multidisciplinary Trends*, *2*(1), 582–597. https://ijarmt.com/index.php/j/article/view/166

UNCTAD. (2022). *Global E-Commerce Statistics: 2020–2022 Overview*. United Nations.

Vaska, S., Massaro, M., Bagarotto, E. M., & Dal Mas, F. (2021). The digital transformation of business model innovation: A structured literature review. *Frontiers in Psychology*, *11*, 539363. DOI: 10.3389/fpsyg.2020.539363 PMID: 33584396

Venkatesh, V., Morris, M. G., Davis, G. B., & Davis, F. D. (2003). User acceptance of information technology: Toward a unified view. *Management Information Systems Quarterly*, *27*(3), 425–478. DOI: 10.2307/30036540

Webster, J., & Watson, R. T. (2002). Analyzing the past to prepare for the future: Writing a literature review. *Management Information Systems Quarterly*, *26*(2), xiii–xxiii.

Wei, L., & Xia, Z. (2022). Big data-Driven Personalization in E-Commerce: Algorithms, Privacy Concerns, and Consumer Be-havior Imp*lications. International Journal of Applied Machine Learning and Computational Intelligence*, *12*(4).

Xiao, L., Saleem, A., Tariq, S. M., Ul Haq, J., & Guo, M. (2021). I wish i could be like her/him! how self-congruence stimulates a desire to mimic. *Journal of Theoretical and Applied Electronic Commerce Research*, *16*(7), 3025–3042. DOI: 10.3390/jtaer16070165

Yang, F., Tang, J., Men, J., & Zheng, X. (2021). Consumer perceived value and impulse buying behavior on mobile commerce: The moderating effect of social influence. *Journal of Retailing and Consumer Services*, *63*, 102683. DOI: 10.1016/j.jretconser.2021.102683

Youssef, H. A. H., & Hossam, A. T. A. (2023). Privacy issues in AI and cloud computing in e-commerce setting: A review. *International Journal of Responsible Artificial Intelligence*, *13*(7), 37–46.

Yuan, S. (2024). The Application and Influence of E-commerce in International Trade — Taking Amazon as an Example. *Advances in Economics. Management and Political Sciences.*, *134*(1), 119–125. DOI: 10.54254/2754-1169/2024.18701

Yuan, Y. (2023). Cross-border e-commerce logistics service challenges and development. *Frontiers in Business, Economics and Management*, *8*(1), 262–265. DOI: 10.54097/fbem.v8i1.6225

. Zangana, H. M., Natheer Yaseen Ali, & Ayaz khalid Mohammed. (2024). Navigating the Digital Marketplace: A Comprehensive Review of E-Commerce Trends, Challenges, and Innovations. *TIJAB (The International Journal of Applied Business)*, 8(1), 88–103. DOI: 10.20473/tijab.v8.I1.2024.54618

Zhao, C. (2022). Variable Interest Entity, Offshore Domesticated Foreign Finance, and the Political Economy of China's Internet Firms: The Case of Alibaba. *Social Sciences (Basel, Switzerland)*, *11*(3), 99. DOI: 10.3390/socsci11030099

Zhou, L. (2022). Cross-Border E-Commerce: Opportunities versus Challenges. *Science Insights*, *40*(5), 489–490. DOI: 10.15354/si.22.co021

. Zhou, (2025). Challenges and Countermeasures of Cross-Border E-commerce in International Trade -- Based on the Perspective of Logistics. *Advances in Economics, Management and Political Sciences.* 161. 86-94. .DOI: 10.54254/2754-1169/2025.19889

KEY TERMS AND DEFINITIONS

Digital Platform: A digital platform is a software-based infrastructure that facilitates the interactions and transactions between users and acts as a central hub for the information, goods, and services. It can be a single application or a combination of tools which are exclusively designed to streamline the business operations and enhance the customer engagement.

E-Commerce: E-commerce also called as electronic commerce, is the buying and selling of goods and services through online platforms via the internet. It involves the exchange of products or services between the businesses, consumers by using the platforms like websites, mobile apps, or online platforms.

International Trade: International trade is defined as the exchange of goods, services, and capital between different countries. It involves the buying and selling of goods and services across national borders which facilitates global economic integration and growth.

Mobile Commerce: Mobile commerce is also called as m-commerce is a part of e-commerce that involves commercial transactions using mobile devices like smartphones and tablets. It encircles various activities like shopping, banking, and online payment transactions through mobile apps.

Technology: Technology is the practical application of the scientific knowledge, tools, and techniques in order to create solutions to solve the problems or improve human life.

Chapter 8
The Role of Smart Technologies in Regenerating Religious Tourism

Priya Chaturvedi
https://orcid.org/0000-0002-9875-661X
Jiwaji University, India

Aditya Ranjan
https://orcid.org/0000-0003-1304-5489
ITM University, India

ABSTRACT

Religious tourism, rooted in human history, uniquely connects faith, culture, and spirituality. Pilgrims visiting sacred sites seek spiritual fulfillment while also supporting the preservation of cultural and historical heritage. In today's rapidly advancing technological era, the integration of smart technologies has transformed religious tourism, offering new opportunities and challenges. This chapter examines how innovations such as augmented reality, mobile applications, and data analytics are reshaping pilgrimage experiences, enhancing accessibility, and enriching engagement. It also highlights their role in conserving and promoting cultural heritage while driving economic growth in religious destinations. Through case studies and best practices, the chapter provides insights into how stakeholders can leverage smart technologies to meet the expectations of modern pilgrims and create more inclusive, spiritually fulfilling, and sustainable religious tourism experiences.

DOI: 10.4018/979-8-3373-9958-4.ch008

1. INTRODUCTION

Religious tourism, deeply embedded in human history, occupies a distinctive position at the intersection of faith, culture, and spirituality (Choe, 2025; Raj et al., 2023). It encompasses travel to destinations that hold religious, cultural, and spiritual significance, often highlighting rituals, heritage, and sacred traditions (Hassan, 2015; Jha et al., 2025; Shmushko, 2023). As a niche segment of tourism, it has garnered substantial academic and industry attention, particularly for its role in cultural preservation and spiritual enrichment (Rautela et al., 2025). Religious tourism typically involves visits to sacred sites, heritage locations, and spaces where religious practices and narratives are deeply rooted (Choe, 2025; Shinde, 2021; Zarkada et al., 2025). The growing interest in spiritually motivated travel parallels the overall expansion of global tourism, drawing millions to renowned religious destinations each year (Alharbi et al., 2025; Hassan et al., 2023). This global movement contributes significantly to both domestic and international tourism, reinforcing religion as a powerful motivator in tourism development (Raj et al., 2023; Senbeto, 2023).

Religion, historically a substantial source of meaning and lived experiences, has played a crucial role in shaping diverse societies (Rautela et al., 2025; Shmushko, 2023). Religion has been linked to joy and served an entertaining role in people's daily lives (Hwang et al., 2023). Throughout centuries, religion has been instrumental in shaping the evolution of leisure, significantly impacting how individuals choose to spend their leisure time (Jorge, 2023; Olsen & Timothy, 2020). When individuals embark on a pilgrimage, it implies a purposeful journey undertaken to express reverence through ritualistic offerings (Senbeto, 2023). These journeys take various forms and occur in diverse locations, such as the Holy Land, the Hajj, Lhasa, Kumbh Mela, Char Dham, the Camino de Santiago, Kumano Kodo, Glastonbury Tor, and Elvis's Graceland (Innocenti, 2023). Through the physical journey to a specific pilgrimage destination, the pilgrim attains various benefits, encompassing both worldly gains and transcendental experiences (Katić & Blaće, 2023). The belief, emotional connection, knowledge enrichment, and satisfaction derived from visiting religious destinations are crucial factors motivating tourists to choose these destinations (Raj et al., 2023). However, over time, pilgrimage evolved into a widely embraced and popular religious practice, commonly shared among believers (Shmushko, 2023; Zhang & He, 2025).

In today's rapidly evolving technological landscape, the integration of smart technologies has ushered in a transformative era for religious tourism (Alharbi et al., 2025; Khan, 2024; Shafiee et al., 2023). Contemporary religious journeys encompass diverse sub-niches, from luxury trips to backpacking and institutional religious travel, emphasizing voluntary humanitarian experiences (Choe, 2025; Hassan et al., 2023). The elements of experience and the intention to continue are pertinent in the context of digitally delivered religious heritage content (Niyas et al., 2025). Augmented reality, mobile applications, and data analytics are among the innovations reshaping the pilgrimage experiences (Allal-Chérif, 2022; Jankova et al., 2023). Numerous religious ceremonies incorporate dance, music, and performance elements, and immersion through smart technologies enhances the pilgrim's experience (Hwang et al., 2023). AI-powered technologies have increased expectations for customized services and tailored recommendations, playing an especially important role in religious activities (Alharbi et al., 2025). Moreover, smart technologies facilitate easy access to knowledge and information, thereby fostering innovation in religious and related cultural activities and generating value for users (Khan, 2024; Niyas et al., 2025).

The yearning for spiritual experiences may lead individuals to visit religious heritage sites in person, irrespective of digital media usage intentions (Hwang et al., 2023). Hence, tourism destination needs to continually adapt to rapid technological changes to remain relevant and enhance the overall visitor experience (Alharbi et al., 2025; Shafiee et al., 2023). As emphasized, social media yields a substantial volume of information that enables the formulation of an initial impression of a religious destination (Muangasame & Tan, 2023; Vila-Lopez & Kuster-Boluda, 2022). While the majority of religious tourists visit ancient sacred sites, many of these locations have undergone transformation with the integration of modern infrastructure and services in recent decades (Hassan et al., 2023). However, studies on pilgrimage observed that the utilization of information communication technologies adversely impacts the spiritual experience (Hwang et al., 2023). This highlights the need for a balanced approach where technology enriches logistical convenience without overshadowing the authenticity and sanctity of religious spiritual experience.

The chapter explores how innovations such as augmented reality, mobile applications, and digital technologies are reshaping the pilgrimage experience within religious tourism. It explores into the multifaceted impact of these technologies, illuminating both the opportunities and challenges they present while highlighting their crucial role in conserving and promoting the rich cultural and historical heritage of religious sites. Through case studies and best practices, the chapter offers insights into how stakeholders leverage smart technologies to cater to modern pilgrims' needs. It also discusses how these innovations drive economic growth in religious destinations, ultimately fostering a more inclusive and spiritually enriching tourism experience.

2. RELIGIOUS TOURISM: TRADITION AND TRANSFORMATION

Religious tourism, deeply entrenched in human history, transcends geographical and cultural boundaries, serving as a timeless tradition that goes beyond mere travel.

it stands apart from other forms of tourism as it is driven by a sense of responsibility and obligation rather than leisure and pleasure (Hassan, 2015; Zhang & He, 2025). Religious tourism is defined as a distinct category of travel wherein participants are driven, either partially or exclusively, by religious motivations that are closely or loosely intertwined with the concept of vacation or leisure (Choe, 2025; Jha et al., 2025; Shinde, 2021). It represents an overwhelming expression of faith, a means to connect with the divine, and a journey into one's spirituality (Rautela et al., 2025). Such form of tourism, deeply intertwined with the human experience, plays a pivotal role in cultural, spiritual, and economic contexts (Hwang et al., 2023; Zhang & He, 2025). Embarking on a pilgrimage symbolizes a journey of faith, an exploration of cultural heritage, and a quest for spiritual enrichment (Suárez et al., 2025). Pilgrimage and religious tourism sector is rapidly expanding, both in terms of visitor numbers and revenue (Jha et al., 2025; Senbeto, 2023). Thus, religious tourism is considered as a variant of cultural tourism (Rautela et al., 2025; Sestino et al., 2023). Whether it's the annual Hajj pilgrimage to Mecca, the Camino de Santiago in Spain, or the veneration of sacred sites like Varanasi and Lourdes, religious tourism reflects the deep diversity of human faith and the many ways people seek meaning, connection, and peace (Choe, 2025; Innocenti, 2023; Jorge, 2023).

Religious tourism is a complex concept, often understood in varied ways across different faiths and spiritual traditions (Hassan, 2015; Rautela et al., 2025). In India also the tradition of *Tirth Yatra* (pilgrimage) has a rich history dating back to ancient times (Gupta & Gulla, 2010). Despite their deep-rooted tradition, these pilgrimages face challenges in the modern world, including the rise of mass tourism, commercialization, and evolving pilgrim expectations (Vila-Lopez & Kuster-Boluda, 2022; Zhang & He, 2025). Moreover, religious sites like cathedrals, temples, and mosques are drawing a growing number of global visitors, not solely for spiritual significance but also for recreational, educational, and cultural purposes (Heidari et al., 2018). Balancing the sacredness of these sites with the practical demands of growing numbers of travellers requires innovative solutions (Niyas et al., 2025). Religious travel, a conventional form of journeying, is motivated by deep-rooted religious and spiritual (Alsahafi et al., 2023; Jha et al., 2025). The interpretation of religion within tourism is diverse, often analysed separately (Choe, 2025; Rautela et al., 2025). In social contexts, religion plays a pivotal role in shaping an individual's values, norms, and behaviour (Senbeto, 2023). However, the paradigm is shifting as religious tourism integrates both religious and tourism activities (Hassan et al., 2023; Zhang & He, 2025).

Religious tourism encompasses visits to settings of religious significance, relevant to one's own faith or others' (Jha et al., 2025). Viewed as a spiritual journey rather than a conventional leisure break, religious tourism's characteristics are shaped by the level of spiritual obligation, travel duration, specific rituals, and the number of participants (Hassan et al., 2023). However, visitors to religious destination typically seek experiences that satisfy their spiritual needs while aligning with modern tourists' aspirations for cultural and experiential enrichment (Choe, 2025; Shinde, 2021). Moreover, immersive smart technologies in religious destinations now offers visitors a distinct and profound cultural, historical, and religious encounter, enhancing their overall experience (Allal-Chérif, 2022). The evolution of such technologies and globalization has led to the convergence and divergence of consumption patterns among religious tourists (Alharbi et al., 2025). Convergence is influenced by the technological advancements and increased interconnectedness through globalization, aligning various consumption practices with global standards (Khan, 2024). Divergence acknowledges that unique cultural, religious, or regional factors may still shape consumption patterns among religious tourists (Choe, 2025; Shinde, 2021). Local traditions, religious practices, and specific pilgrimage rituals contribute to divergent behaviours in terms of the services and products sought by religious tourists (Zhang & He, 2025).

3. THE TIMELESS APPEAL OF RELIGIOUS TOURISM

Religious tourism, a cornerstone of human expression and cultural identity for centuries, is deeply woven into the fabric of human history (Innocenti, 2023; Jha et al., 2025). Pilgrims undertake extensive journeys to sacred sites, engaging in profound spiritual quests and participating in rituals of great significance (Heidari et al., 2018). These pilgrimages transcend mere excursions, addressing fundamental human needs to explore questions of faith, seek redemption, and connect with a higher power (Gupta & Gulla, 2010; Zhang & He, 2025). Through its rituals, symbols, and traditions, religious tourism has played a pivotal role in shaping the identity of communities and entire nations (Katić & Blaće, 2023). Sacred sites such as Mecca, Jerusalem, Varanasi, and Lourdes hold profound spiritual and historical significance, serving as focal points for millions of pilgrims globally (Shinde, 2021; Zarkada et al., 2025). The act of visiting these sites, engaging in prayer, and participating in religious ceremonies is a means of preserving cultural heritage, strengthening community bonds, and fostering a deep spiritual connection (Sestino et al., 2023).

Jerusalem, often referred to as the Holy City, stands as a poignant example of the enduring tradition of religious tourism (Olsen & Timothy, 2020). It holds immense significance for Christians, Jews, and Muslims, drawing pilgrims worldwide to retrace the footsteps of biblical figures, visit sites like the Western Wall and the Church of the Holy Sepulchre, and partake in religious ceremonies. The spiritual journey through Jerusalem exemplifies the profound connection between religious tourism, history, and faith (Allal-Chérif, 2022). Similarly, Varanasi in India, situated along the banks of the Ganges River, is a sacred city that has been a centre of pilgrimage for Hindus for thousands of years (Das et al., 2024). Pilgrims flock to Varanasi to perform rituals, immerse themselves in the holy river, and witness the mesmerizing Aarti ceremony along the Ghats. The city's rich history, intricate rituals, and spiritual significance make it an iconic destination for religious tourists, further highlighting the enduring testament of religious tourism to human spirituality and cultural heritage (Shinde & Singh, 2023).

4. CHALLENGES FACED BY TRADITIONAL RELIGIOUS TOURISM

Religious tourism, although enduring through the ages, confronts a myriad of challenges in the contemporary world (Choe, 2025). First, the multifaceted nature of religious tourism presents various challenges for the management of sacred sites (Shinde, 2010). Secondly, the rise of mass tourism, coupled with commercialization and shifts in pilgrim behaviour, introduces complexities that demand careful consideration (Jha et al., 2025). Every year, millions of people from various religious backgrounds undertake journeys to spiritual or religious destinations (Jorge, 2023). Third, despite the significance of authenticity for their sustained existence, it is crucial for religious events to incorporate new elements to maintain attractiveness (Allal-Chérif, 2022). Forth, visitors to religious sites often travel with family or organized groups, with trips being highly seasonal, influenced by climate, holidays, ceremonies, and work schedules (Heidari et al., 2018; Senbeto, 2023). Fifth, pilgrimage sites, often crowded and congested, struggle to maintain their sanctity, putting the very essence of the spiritual experience at risk of dilution (Vila-Lopez & Kuster-Boluda, 2022). Furthermore, the evolving expectations of pilgrims in the digital age pose a unique set of challenges (Alharbi et al., 2025; Qurashi & Sharpley, 2018). Modern pilgrims, technologically adept, seek personalized and interactive experiences, demanding real-time access to information and services during their journeys (Carrasco-García et al., 2025; Jorge, 2023). Meeting these evolving needs while preserving and promoting cultural and historical heritage becomes a daunting task (Niyas et al., 2025).

In the modern era, religious tourism encounters several challenges, with commercialization of pilgrimage sites being a notable issue (Zhang & He, 2025). The transformation of Lourdes in France from a humble pilgrimage destination to a bustling commercial hub exemplifies this challenge (Séraphin & Jarraud, 2022). While Lourdes retains its spiritual significance, concerns arise about maintaining its sacred ambiance and the spiritual focus of pilgrims amid the influx of tourists, souvenir shops, and commercial activities. Mass tourism also poses a threat to the sanctity of sites like Mecca in Saudi Arabia (Alsahafi et al., 2023). The annual Hajj pilgrimage, mandatory for Muslims, witnesses millions of pilgrims converging on the city, leading to logistical challenges, overcrowding, and strains on infrastructure (Zarkada et al., 2025). Balancing the preservation of Mecca's sacred nature with the accommodation of a massive influx of pilgrims remains an ongoing challenge (Niyas et al., 2025). Varanasi is one of the holiest cities in Hinduism and a major pilgrimage site (Shinde & Singh, 2023). In recent years, it has faced challenges associated with the commercialization of religious activities and the impact of mass tourism. Local authorities and religious communities face the delicate task of finding a balance that allows tourism to thrive while safeguarding the sanctity and cultural integrity of Varanasi's sacred heritage (Das et al., 2024).

5. SMART TECHNOLOGIES IN RELIGIOUS TOURISM

In the face of challenges, smart technologies emerge as a beacon of hope for religious tourism (Alharbi et al., 2025; Vila-Lopez & Kuster-Boluda, 2022). The blend of tradition and transformation indicates us to consider how innovative tools like augmented reality, mobile applications, and data analytics can revitalize the pilgrimage experience (Khan, 2024; Niyas et al., 2025). These technologies offer a path to simultaneously address the demands of modern pilgrims, enhance the preservation of cultural heritage, and stimulate the economic growth of religiously significant destinations (Allal-Chérif, 2022; Sestino et al., 2023). In an age characterized by rapid technological advancement, smart technologies are making a significant impact on the realm of religious tourism (Raj et al., 2023) (Figure 1). From augmented reality to mobile applications, these technologies are becoming integral to the way pilgrims engage with sacred places, access information, and connect with their spiritual heritage (Niyas et al., 2025; Ocón, 2023). The fundamental technologies underpinning Tourism, often referred to as 4.0 G technologies, encompass artificial intelligence (AI), big data analytics, the Internet of Things (IoT), blockchain, cloud computing, as well as augmented reality (AR) and virtual reality (VR), emerged as transformative tools for religious tourism (Carrasco-García et al., 2025; Jankova et al., 2023).

5.1 Augmented Reality and Virtual Reality: Bridging the Gap Between Past and Present

The pervasive integration of augmented reality (AR) and virtual reality (VR) technologies in religious tourism has elevated people's multisensory encounters within the virtual realm (Niyas et al., 2025). AR, in particular, stands out as a compelling technology that is revolutionizing religious tourism (Yang et al., 2023). AR apps and experiences are designed to overlay digital content onto the real world, blurring the line between the physical and the virtual (Allal-Chérif, 2022). This innovative approach allows pilgrims to access historical and cultural information while physically present at sacred sites (Yang et al., 2023). By utilizing AR applications on smartphones or AR glasses, pilgrims can receive guided tours with overlays of historical information, narratives, and religious significance onto the physical surroundings, providing an enriched and immersive experience (Niyas et al., 2025). Importantly, AR has proven effective in enhancing the memorability of tourist experiences at pilgrimage destinations (Alsahafi et al., 2023; Ocón, 2023).

AR has emerged as a powerful tool bridging temporal and spatial gaps for pilgrims. By superimposing digital content onto the physical world, AR provides an immersive and informative experience at sacred sites (Allal-Chérif, 2022). Pilgrims can access historical narratives, witness events from the past, and explore cultural contexts that deepen their understanding of the site (Yang et al., 2023). For example, AR offers a visual representation of the Grand Mosque in Medina (Al-Masjid Al-Nabawi) and other religious places in an interactive style, providing guests with easily accessible and immersive experiences (Alsahafi et al., 2023). Similarly, The Western Wall in Jerusalem employs AR applications to offer virtual reconstructions of biblical events at the very locations they occurred (Hwang et al., 2023). Pilgrims can see digital artifacts, gaining insights into the spiritual and historical significance of these sites (Allal-Chérif, 2022). This dynamic engagement with the past deepens the connection between pilgrims and their faith, making the pilgrimage more than a physical journey; it becomes a spiritual exploration through time (Niyas et al., 2025).

On the other hand, Virtual Reality (VR) facilitates remote participation in religious activities and pilgrimages (Carrasco-García et al., 2025). VR technology, having undergone extensive development, now finds substantial and pervasive application in the virtual religious tourism experience (Raj et al., 2023; Yang et al., 2023). Individuals unable to physically travel to a sacred site can use VR headsets to virtually attend religious ceremonies or pilgrimages in a highly immersive manner (Hwang et al., 2023). Leveraging sensory effects and autonomous control, VR crafts an immersive, multidimensional environment that elicits positive emotions among religious tourists (Jankova et al., 2023). This not only enhances accessibility but also fosters a sense of connection and shared experience among individuals who are geographically distant but spiritually connected (Allal-Chérif, 2022; Raj et al., 2023).

A prime example of a religious site utilizing Virtual Reality (VR) for remote worship is the Vatican (Vila-Lopez & Kuster-Boluda, 2022). The Vatican has incorporated VR technology to offer virtual tours and experiences for individuals worldwide. Through VR, people can virtually explore iconic religious sites like St. Peter's Basilica and the Sistine Chapel, participate in virtual religious ceremonies, and engage in remote worship experiences (Vila-Lopez & Kuster-Boluda, 2022). This application of VR enhances accessibility for individuals physically unable to visit the Vatican in person, allowing them to connect with the religious and cultural significance of these sacred spaces from wherever they are.

5.2 3D Technologies in Religious Tourism

The application of 3D printing technology has made significant inroads in religious tourism and pilgrimage by producing intricate replicas of sacred artifacts, religious symbols, and historical structures (Allal-Chérif, 2022; Alsahafi et al., 2023). Pilgrims and tourists now have the opportunity to acquire tangible souvenirs or representations of significant religious objects, thereby enhancing their connection to the spiritual experience (Battour et al., 2023; Chaturvedi et al., 2024). An exemplary illustration is the Vatican, a major destination for religious tourism, which has embraced 3D scanning and digital technologies to preserve and showcase its extensive collection of religious artifacts and artworks (Vila-Lopez & Kuster-Boluda, 2022). Through these technologies, highly detailed 3D models of crucial religious sculptures, relics, and historical artifacts are created, ensuring their preservation in digital form (Hwang et al., 2023). Visitors can explore these digital representations, which are often more accessible and less prone to damage compared to their physical counterparts (Alsahafi et al., 2023; Battour et al., 2023). This approach significantly contributes to the conservation and promotion of the Vatican's religious and cultural heritage (Vila-Lopez & Kuster-Boluda, 2022).

In addition to 3D printing, holographic displays play a pivotal role in showcasing religious narratives, historical events, or revered figures in a three-dimensional format (Niyas et al., 2025). This technology creates immersive and visually striking presentations, enabling visitors to engage with religious content in a dynamic and memorable way, fostering a deeper understanding and connection to the religious context (Ocón, 2023). For instance, the historic city of Jerusalem utilizes 3D technologies to generate digital reconstructions of religious sites like the Western Wall and the Church of the Holy Sepulchre. These digital representations provide virtual tours for pilgrims and tourists, preserving the cultural and religious significance of these sites while minimizing physical wear and tear (Yang et al., 2023). Holograms offer immersive storytelling experiences, allowing visitors to visually engage with the rich history and cultural importance of the Western Wall (Ranjan & Chaturvedi, 2025).

5.3 Mobile Applications: Personalizing the Pilgrimage Experience

Smartphones has empowered visitors actively engage with heritage sites, interacting with fellow visitors and the site through quests and challenges, transforming their visit into a participatory experience (Allal-Chérif, 2022). Mobile applications have evolved into indispensable tools for modern pilgrims, playing a pivotal role in various aspects of the pilgrimage experience, ranging from journey planning to accessing historical and cultural information (Alsahafi et al., 2023; Battour et al., 2023). These apps, such as the Vatican's official app, offer comprehensive guides to religious sites, furnishing visitors with detailed information about landmarks like St. Peter's Basilica, the Vatican Museums, and the Sistine Chapel (Vila-Lopez & Kuster-Boluda, 2022). Pilgrims can seamlessly navigate their visit, utilizing features like audio guides, virtual tours, and ticket reservations directly through the app, ensuring an optimized and enriching experience (Battour et al., 2023).

The transformative impact of mobile applications extends beyond logistical support, revolutionizing the way pilgrims plan and engage in their journeys (Jankova et al., 2023). These apps provide a plethora of functionalities that personalize and enhance the overall pilgrimage experience (Battour et al., 2023). Pilgrims now have fingertip access to interactive maps, historical insights, and cultural information (Ocón, 2023). For instance, along the Camino de Santiago, pilgrims leverage mobile apps not only to navigate the trail but also to discover nearby accommodations and services (Innocenti, 2023). Mobile applications prove invaluable in making religious sites accessible to individuals who are blind or visually impaired (Battour et al., 2023). Moreover, these applications facilitate connections among pilgrims sharing the same journey, fostering a sense of community among travellers from diverse parts of the world (Allal-Chérif, 2022). This not only streamlines practical aspects of the pilgrimage but also nurtures a shared sense of unity and experience among participants (Ranjan & Chaturvedi, 2023; Zarkada et al., 2025).

5.4 Social Media Connectivity in Pilgrimage

In the contemporary landscape of pilgrimage, social media platforms have become powerful tools that transcend geographical boundaries, connecting pilgrims worldwide and serving as dynamic channels for destination promotion (Zarkada et al., 2025). The proliferation of the internet and information and communication technologies has led to the widespread emergence of social networks and tourism platforms, such as Facebook, X (Formerly Twitter), TripAdvisor, among others (Battour et al., 2023; Qurashi & Sharpley, 2018). These platforms enable travellers to disseminate their experiences, share comments, opinions, and even post images and videos related to their journeys (Jorge, 2023). Platforms like Facebook and dedicated pilgrimage forums create a virtual space for pilgrims to connect, share insights, and support each other throughout their journeys (Shmushko, 2023; Zarkada et al., 2025). Lourdes, for example, utilizes Facebook and Twitter to provide real-time information about events, share pilgrim testimonials, and offer guidance on navigating the sacred sites (Séraphin & Jarraud, 2022).

The perception of a tourist destination is intricately linked to user-generated content facilitated by tourists through emerging technologies (Vila-Lopez & Kuster-Boluda, 2022). Pilgrims leverage social media to document their journeys through photos, videos, and narratives, creating a collective digital archive that shares the richness of pilgrimage experiences with a global audience (Innocenti, 2023; Zarkada et al., 2025). Platforms like Instagram and YouTube serve as avenues for pilgrims to share visually compelling stories and videos, offering insights into rituals, landscapes, and personal reflections (Hwang et al., 2023). Moreover, religious destinations strategically use social media platforms like Instagram, Twitter, and TikTok to promote pilgrimage sites, rituals, and cultural heritage, attracting pilgrims and travellers alike (Alsahafi et al., 2023). For instance, Varanasi leverages social media to highlight the spiritual significance of the Ganges River, showcase vibrant rituals, and invite pilgrims to experience its cultural richness. Kumano Kodo utilizes Instagram and Pinterest to showcase the scenic beauty of pilgrimage trails, share travel tips, and connect with pilgrims planning their journeys.

5.5 Intelligent Lighting Systems and Audio Technologies in Religious Destinations

The integration of intelligent lighting systems and advanced audio technologies has become pivotal in redefining the ambiance of sacred spaces, marking a transformative phase where age-old traditions harmoniously converge with cutting-edge innovation (Battour et al., 2023). These modern systems transcend the limitations of traditional setups by offering automated controls, real-time programmability, and remote operational features that enable precise orchestration of light and sound, thereby crafting deeply immersive and spiritually uplifting environments for pilgrims and visitors alike (Allal-Chérif, 2022; Shafiee et al., 2023). Intelligent lighting systems, leveraging advancements such as energy-efficient LEDs, programmable color palettes, and sensor-based illumination, dynamically enhance religious sites by adapting to the rhythms of ceremonies, festivals, and sacred rituals (Battour et al., 2023). The ability to modulate light intensity, hue, and pattern in alignment with the spiritual significance of specific occasions fosters an environment that resonates emotionally with devotees while accentuating the architectural beauty of these spaces (Allal-Chérif, 2022).

Simultaneously, advanced audio technologies, including surround sound systems, high-fidelity acoustic designs, and directional speakers, enrich the auditory experience during prayers, sermons, chants, and cultural performances by delivering clear, resonant soundscapes that elevate the sense of reverence and devotion (Raj et al., 2023). Directional audio ensures that sound is projected only where intended, reducing echo and noise pollution while safeguarding the sanctity and tranquility of designated prayer zones (Jha et al., 2025). Together, these innovations cultivate a multi-sensory spiritual experience that not only enhances the aesthetic appeal of sacred spaces but also strengthens the pilgrims' emotional and cultural connection to their faith, reinforcing the enduring significance of these destinations in a rapidly modernizing world (Carrasco-García et al., 2025; Khan, 2024).

The automation of lighting and audio systems has introduced unprecedented efficiency, precision, and adaptability to religious destinations, enabling these sacred spaces to seamlessly merge tradition with technological advancement (Das et al., 2024). Automated scheduling allows lighting systems to synchronize with natural cycles such as sunrise and sunset, as well as with the timing of religious rituals, ensuring that the ambiance consistently aligns with the spiritual significance of each moment (Allal-Chérif, 2022). Remote control capabilities further empower temple administrators and shrine custodians to instantly adjust lighting and audio settings in response to unexpected events, spontaneous gatherings, or alterations in the religious calendar, thereby maintaining an uninterrupted sacred atmosphere (Shinde, 2021). The Somnath Temple in Gujarat exemplifies this integration, employing intelligent lighting and sound systems to deepen the spiritual experience of pilgrims. Through captivating light and sound shows, the temple narrates the reflective significance of the Jyotirlinga and chronicles the rich history of Somnath, with synchronized illumination accentuating the intricate architecture while immersive audio storytelling evokes a powerful sense of reverence and wonder.

Similarly, the Meiji Shrine in Japan demonstrates how advanced lighting technologies can enhance the ethereal beauty of natural surroundings during Shinto ceremonies and seasonal festivals. The gentle interplay of dynamic lighting with the shrine's traditional wooden structures fosters a serene and contemplative environment, while carefully orchestrated audio systems provide a harmonious acoustic backdrop that amplifies the solemnity of prayers, chants, and rituals. Collectively, these innovations not only elevate the sensory and spiritual dimensions of religious spaces but also ensure their ability to adapt fluidly to the evolving rhythms of contemporary worship and cultural expression (Khan, 2024).

5.6 Integration of Mobile Payment Systems in Religious Destinations

The seamless integration of mobile payment systems marks a new era of convenience and efficiency in the realm of religious tourism (Battour et al., 2023). The transformative impact of mobile payment technologies on visitor experiences at religious destinations facilitates seamless transactions, manages donations, and enhances overall financial contributions for the upkeep of sacred sites (Hudaefi & Beik, 2020). Pilgrims now enjoy a streamlined and cashless solution for various transactions, from purchasing tickets for religious events to acquiring sacred artifacts, all through the convenience of their mobile devices (Munjal, 2021). This not only simplifies the visitor experience but also aligns with the modern expectations of a technologically connected world. In India, the advent of the Unified Payments Interface (UPI) has revolutionized financial transactions, including those within the realm of religious and pilgrimage tourism. Temples such as the Tirumala Tirupati Devasthanams (TTD) in Andhra Pradesh have embraced UPI as a preferred mode of donation. Pilgrims visiting revered temples across India can contribute seamlessly through UPI-enabled apps, ensuring a secure, efficient, and transparent process.

The integration of mobile payment systems enables swift and hassle-free ticket purchases for religious ceremonies, festivals, or guided tours (Olsen & Timothy, 2020). Additionally, visitors can easily make monetary contributions and donations to the religious institution or associated charitable causes (Shafiee et al., 2023). This instantaneous process enhances the efficiency of financial transactions, allowing pilgrims to actively participate in the economic sustenance of the destination. Mobile payments extend their utility to the acquisition of religious artifacts, souvenirs, or offerings. Pilgrims can conveniently make purchases at on-site shops or stalls using digital wallets or mobile banking applications (Chaturvedi et al., 2024). The ease of these transactions benefits both the visitors and contributes to the economic sustainability of local vendors and artisans associated with the religious destination. St. Peter's Basilica in Vatican City has adopted mobile payment systems to enhance the visitor experience (Vila-Lopez & Kuster-Boluda, 2022). Pilgrims and tourists can use mobile apps for contactless donations, ticket purchases, and transactions at gift shops within the basilica premises. The integration of mobile payment systems in religious destinations is a testament to the adaptability of sacred spaces to modern technological advancements (Hudaefi & Beik, 2020).

5.7 Drones in Religious Tourism

In religious tourism, the integration of drone technology has revolutionized the way visitors perceive and engage with sacred sites (Casana et al., 2021; Pavelka et al., 2018; Ritter, 2023). Drones offer unparalleled aerial views, serving as invaluable tools for documentation and contributing to an enriched visitor experience, as well as facilitating efficient site management and maintenance (Ocón, 2023). These aerial vantage points capture the grandeur of architectural marvels, intricate carvings, sprawling temple complexes, and the surrounding natural landscapes in their full spatial context, fostering a deeper emotional connection to these sacred environments (Casana et al., 2021). Beyond mere visual appeal, drones also serve as advanced tools for documentation, producing high-resolution imagery and 3D models that preserve cultural heritage digitally while supporting academic research, conservation projects, and heritage mapping (Król & Hernik, 2022; Ocón, 2023). Their ability to record ceremonies, processions, and religious gatherings from above enriches the cultural archive of sacred spaces, allowing visitors and scholars to explore the evolution of rituals and built heritage over time.

The immersive experiences created through drone-captured 360-degree videos allow pilgrims, as well as virtual visitors, to witness religious events from comprehensive angles, experiencing the rhythm, symbolism, and spiritual ambiance of rituals in ways that static photography or ground-level footage cannot convey (Niyas et al., 2025; Pavelka et al., 2018). Destination marketers leverage this captivating drone footage to promote religious sites on digital platforms and social media, offering breathtaking previews of sacred spaces that spark curiosity and inspire pilgrimage journeys (Jankova et al., 2023; Ritter, 2023). This digital storytelling significantly enhances destination image-making and positions sacred sites as both spiritual and cultural landmarks in the global tourism landscape (Ranjan & Chaturvedi, 2025).

In addition to enriching the visitor experience, drones contribute to the efficient management, conservation, and safety of religious sites, providing vital real-time insights into the condition of structures and their surroundings (Pavelka et al., 2018). Site administrators use drone imagery to conduct structural assessments, monitor weather-induced damage, detect erosion or cracks in ancient walls, and track the health of surrounding vegetation, enabling timely intervention and preventive maintenance that safeguard the longevity of these sacred spaces (Casana et al., 2021). This proactive approach reduces the need for intrusive manual inspections, preserving the sanctity of the sites while ensuring their physical integrity. Drones are also instrumental in enhancing crowd management during religious festivals and mass gatherings, offering bird's-eye views that help organizers analyse crowd density, design safer pedestrian flows, and respond swiftly to emergencies (Ritter, 2023).

Live drone feeds can be integrated into control rooms for real-time monitoring, allowing authorities to coordinate security personnel, medical teams, and logistical support more effectively. For instance, at Angkor Wat in Cambodia, drones not only capture stunning panoramic footage that highlights the sheer scale of the ancient temple complex for global audiences but also aid ongoing restoration efforts by mapping structural shifts, surveying inaccessible areas, and tracking conservation progress over time. Such applications underscore the transformative role of drone technology in simultaneously enriching spiritual tourism experiences and ensuring the sustainable preservation, safety, and operational efficiency of revered religious destinations worldwide (Casana et al., 2021; Pavelka et al., 2018).

6. IMPACT OF SMART TECHNOLOGIES ON PILGRIMAGE EXPERIENCE

Smart technologies play a transformative role in enhancing the religious pilgrimage experience, providing a multi-dimensional journey that encompasses emotional, social, intellectual, spiritual, and physical aspects (Alharbi et al., 2025; Khan, 2024; Niyas et al., 2025). Pilgrims now have the ability to document their journeys digitally through blogs and vlogs, capturing and sharing their experiences with a global audience (Carrasco-García et al., 2025). Virtual reality further extends the pilgrimage reach by offering immersive experiences for remote participants, allowing individuals to engage with sacred sites from anywhere in the world (Raj et al., 2023).

6.1 Enhancement of Religious Experiences

Religious tourism, defined by travel to destinations for the purpose of participating in sacred gatherings and experiencing the architectural and artistic expressions of faith, offers a deeply holistic and multi-dimensional journey that engages individuals emotionally, socially, intellectually, spiritually, and physically (Choe, 2025; Rautela et al., 2025; Shinde, 2010). These journeys are often pursued for personal transformation, spiritual enrichment, or therapeutic renewal, and they play a vital role in shaping the past and present identities of those who undertake them (Bhalla et al., 2021; Niyas et al., 2025). Beyond fulfilling religious obligations, such experiences provide opportunities for cultural immersion, interfaith dialogue, and collective worship, thereby fostering a profound sense of belonging and shared humanity (Zhang & He, 2025). The emotional resonance of sacred spaces, the aesthetic beauty of their architecture, and the symbolism embedded in religious rituals can deeply influence the inner worlds of pilgrims, offering them moments of introspection and transcendence (Alharbi et al., 2025; Zarkada et al., 2025). Moreover, active participation in religious tourism has been closely linked to improvements in travelers' overall well-being, reducing stress levels and enhancing life satisfaction by instilling meaning, purpose, and spiritual contentment (Choe, 2025; Hassan et al., 2023). This connection between travel and well-being underscores the broader significance of religious tourism as not merely a physical journey but a transformative life experience that nurtures the mind, body, and spirit (Khan, 2024; Zhang & He, 2025).

The advent of smart technologies has dramatically reshaped the ways in which pilgrims document, interpret, and share their sacred journeys, adding new layers of engagement and connectivity to religious travel (Alharbi et al., 2025). Digital diaries, blogs, and vlogs allow pilgrims to record their spiritual reflections, personal milestones, and emotional responses in real time, contributing to an expanding digital archive that preserves the collective memory of religious tourism (Innocenti, 2023; Niyas et al., 2025). Recognizing the barriers posed by geographical distance, cost, or health constraints, many religious destinations have incorporated virtual reality technologies to offer immersive and interactive pilgrimage experiences (Carrasco-García et al., 2025; Raj et al., 2023). Through VR headsets and applications, individuals can virtually traverse sacred landscapes, witness rituals, and participate in religious ceremonies, thereby gaining emotional and spiritual fulfillment even without physical presence (Hwang et al., 2023; Niyas et al., 2025).

Smart audio guides, accessible via smartphones or wearable devices, further enhance this experience by delivering location-aware narratives that provide context-specific information, historical insights, religious teachings, and cultural symbolism as visitors navigate sacred spaces (Allal-Chérif, 2022; Jha et al., 2025). These tools transform site exploration into a self-directed educational journey, enriching both intellectual and spiritual understanding (Alharbi et al., 2025; Yang et al., 2023). Simultaneously, smart communication platforms, including social media groups, messaging apps, and dedicated pilgrimage forums, enable pilgrims to share real-time updates, seek guidance, and exchange insights, fostering vibrant virtual communities that extend beyond the pilgrimage itself (Rautela et al., 2025). Such platforms support mutual encouragement, deepen social bonds, and sustain long-term spiritual connections, thereby amplifying the communal and interactive dimensions of religious tourism in the digital age (Raj et al., 2023).

6.2 Connection with Spiritual Heritage

Smart technologies have transformed the role of pilgrims from passive observers to active participants in their spiritual journey, fostering a profound connection with their heritage (Niyas et al., 2025; Raj et al., 2023). Through the use of augmented reality (AR) and mobile applications, pilgrims are no longer limited to surface-level engagement but are empowered to delve deeper into the historical, cultural, and spiritual significance of the sites they visit (Allal-Chérif, 2022; Ocón, 2023). By accessing comprehensive historical and cultural information, pilgrims can actively explore the stories of their faith, comprehend the intricacies of rituals, and establish a profound sense of continuity with their spiritual heritage (Alharbi et al., 2025;

Jankova et al., 2023). This interactive and educational aspect of smart technologies transcends mere convenience; it enables a more meaningful and informed pilgrimage experience (Carrasco-García et al., 2025; Raj et al., 2023).

Smart technologies contribute to the cultivation of a strong sense of connection and reverence among pilgrims (Niyas et al., 2025). These digital tools strengthen the bond individuals have with their faith and position them within the broader narrative of religious history (Alharbi et al., 2025; Yang et al., 2023). Beyond practical considerations, the impact of smart technologies extends to enriching the spiritual and cultural dimensions of the pilgrimage experience, turning it into a transformative and deeply meaningful journey for modern travelers (Raj et al., 2023). The Kumbh Mela is one of the largest religious gatherings in the world, attracting millions of Hindu pilgrims. In recent editions of the Kumbh Mela, there has been an increasing use of smart technologies, including mobile applications and augmented reality features. These technologies provide pilgrims with interactive maps, real-time information about events and rituals, and virtual guides to navigate the vast pilgrimage area.

6.3 Preserving Cultural and Historical Heritage

The impact of smart technologies on religious tourism extends to the crucial domains of preserving and promoting cultural and historical heritage (Allal-Chérif, 2022; Niyas et al., 2025). Digital technology plays a pivotal role in documenting cultural heritage, preserving monuments, and engaging in cultural mediation with various dimensions, including education, entertainment, social interaction, and creativity (Alharbi et al., 2025; Raj et al., 2023). Digital experiences could offer a sustainable avenue for future revenue generation with minimal impact on the actual destination and its attractions (Carrasco-García et al., 2025; Hwang et al., 2023). These technologies serve as guardians of the rich cultural and historical legacy embedded in sacred sites, simultaneously ensuring global accessibility (Raj et al., 2023). Among the various technologies, augmented reality (AR) emerges as a key player in heritage preservation (Niyas et al., 2025). AR and VR applications, with their digital reconstructions and historical narratives, provide pilgrims with immersive experiences that deepen their understanding of the cultural and historical significance of sacred sites (Carrasco-García et al., 2025; Olsen & Timothy, 2020). Such engagement fosters a deep appreciation for the heritage of these sites and their broader their wider place in human history (Zhang & He, 2025).

Moreover, smart technologies contribute to the conservation of manuscripts, artifacts, and relics associated with religious sites (Król & Hernik, 2022; Niyas et al., 2025). The establishment of digital archives and databases enables the storage and sharing of these invaluable treasures. This not only safeguards them from physical degradation but also ensures accessibility to scholars and the faithful, thereby preserving and disseminating the cultural and historical richness of religious heritage (Allal-Chérif, 2022).

6.4 Data Analytics: Enhancing Site Management

Smart technologies extend beyond improving the pilgrim experience; they also play a crucial role in enhancing the management of religious sites (Alharbi et al., 2025; Vila-Lopez & Kuster-Boluda, 2022). Data analytics emerges as a vital tool for comprehending visitor patterns, preferences, and efficiently managing the flow of pilgrims (Hwang et al., 2023; Niyas et al., 2025). Site administrators leverage data analysis on visitor numbers and behavior to optimize infrastructure, enhance security measures, and refine services, ensuring a smoother and more secure experience for pilgrims (Khan, 2024; Ranjan & Chaturvedi, 2023). The integration of technologies for improved connectivity, information systems, and sensorization addresses challenges related to overcrowding, providing a comprehensive understanding of tourists' movements within a destination (Alharbi et al., 2025; Shafiee et al., 2023).

Furthermore, the integration of drones into religious tourism not only transforms the way visitors perceive sacred sites but also contributes significantly to the documentation, preservation, and efficient management of these culturally significant destinations (Casana et al., 2021; Ocón, 2023). Drones serve as a bridge between tradition and technology, enhancing the pilgrimage experience while actively participating in the safeguarding of religious heritage (Ritter, 2023). During the annual Hajj pilgrimage in Mecca, data analytics is employed to predict crowd movements. This predictive analysis enables authorities to implement effective crowd control measures, ensuring the safety of the millions of pilgrims participating in the pilgrimage (Pavelka et al., 2018; Ritter, 2023). Similarly, at the Sanctuary of Our Lady of Lourdes in France, data analytics is utilized to manage the flow of visitors, minimizing congestion, and creating a more serene and contemplative experience for pilgrims (Séraphin & Jarraud, 2022).

7. CHALLENGES AND ETHICAL CONSIDERATIONS

The integration of smart technologies into religious tourism presents numerous advantages, yet it also introduces several challenges and ethical considerations that merit thoughtful examination (Alharbi et al., 2025). Despite the advanced capabilities of virtual technology to simulate real scenes effectively, virtual religious tourism encounters challenges in establishing broader and deeper value propositions (Hwang et al., 2023; Niyas et al., 2025). This limitation arises from the absence of physical movement and the comparatively shorter duration of the virtual experience when compared to on-site tourism (Yang et al., 2023).

7.1 Privacy Concerns: Balancing Convenience and Personal Data

A significant challenge associated with smart technologies in religious tourism pertains to the collection and utilization of personal data (Alharbi et al., 2025). Many mobile applications and technological tools require users to disclose information concerning their locations, preferences, and interactions (Gupta & Gulla, 2010; Niyas et al., 2025). While such data can enhance the pilgrimage experience, it concurrently raises pertinent questions regarding privacy and data security (Shafiee et al., 2023). Pilgrims may be concerned about their personal information being misused or shared without their consent (Katić & Blaće, 2023; Qurashi & Sharpley, 2018). Balancing the convenience and personalization of the pilgrimage experience with robust data protection measures is a challenge (Niyas et al., 2025; Rautela et al., 2025). Striking the right balance is crucial to ensuring that pilgrims can enjoy the benefits of smart technologies without compromising their privacy (Alharbi et al., 2025; Jorge, 2023).

7.2 Authenticity and the Sanctity of Sacred Sites

The infusion of technology into religious tourism raises inquiries about the authenticity of the pilgrimage experience (Niyas et al., 2025; Raj et al., 2023). Studies in pilgrimages revealed that the utilization of information communication technologies can have a detrimental impact on the spiritual experience (Hwang et al., 2023). While smart technologies offer immersive and educational experiences, there exists a potential risk of over-commercialization or the fabrication of artificial experiences that might detract from the genuine spirituality of sacred sites (Alharbi et al., 2025). For instance, although AR applications can provide virtual reconstructions and historical insights, the challenge lies in preserving the sanctity of the physical site and preventing technology from overshadowing it (Allal-Chérif, 2022). Pilgrims may consider whether the use of technology enhances or diminishes the authentic, contemplative experience they seek at sacred places (Jorge, 2023).

7.3 Cultural Sensitivity: Respecting Local Traditions

Cultural sensitivity plays a pivotal role in successfully integrating smart technologies into religious tourism (Alharbi et al., 2025; Alsahafi et al., 2023). The introduction of these technologies should be conducted with a deep respect for the local customs, traditions, and sensitivities of the host communities (Niyas et al., 2025; Ocón, 2023). Applications that are overly intrusive or culturally insensitive may unintentionally alienate local populations and disrupt the delicate cultural balance (Ranjan & Chaturvedi, 2023). For example, the use of AR or mobile apps that overlook dress codes or rituals of modesty might create friction between pilgrims and the local community (Jankova et al., 2023; Qurashi & Sharpley, 2018). Furthermore, the monetization of sacred sites through technology-driven commercial activities can raise ethical concerns and potentially damage the authentic cultural experience for pilgrims (Alharbi et al., 2025; Rautela et al., 2025).

In addressing these challenges and ethical considerations, stakeholders in religious tourism must engage in continuous, thoughtful, and inclusive dialogue to ensure that technological integration aligns with the sacred essence of pilgrimage (Rautela et al., 2025; Shafiee et al., 2023). Such discussion should actively involve religious authorities, heritage custodians, tourism professionals, local communities, and pilgrims themselves to ensure that multiple perspectives are acknowledged and respected (Carrasco-García et al., 2025). Striking the right balance between technology and tradition requires a carefully calibrated approach that safeguards the spiritual and cultural richness of sacred sites while simultaneously accommodating innovation that enhances accessibility and engagement (Carrasco-García et al., 2025; Niyas et al., 2025). It is essential to establish ethical guidelines and cultural protocols that regulate how smart technologies are deployed—ensuring they do not disrupt sacred rituals, commercialize spiritual practices, or diminish the authenticity of cultural expressions (Yang et al., 2023). Respecting the privacy and personal preferences of pilgrims, such as limiting intrusive data collection or unauthorized recordings, is equally critical to maintaining trust and reverence within these sacred environments (Hwang et al., 2023). Therefore, employing smart technologies with cultural sensitivity, transparency, and ethical oversight becomes indispensable. It ensures that technological advancements enrich rather than dilute the pilgrimage experience, preserving its sanctity while honoring the cherished traditions that give it meaning (Alharbi et al., 2025; Król & Hernik, 2022).

Figure 1. The role of smart technologies in regenerating religious tourism

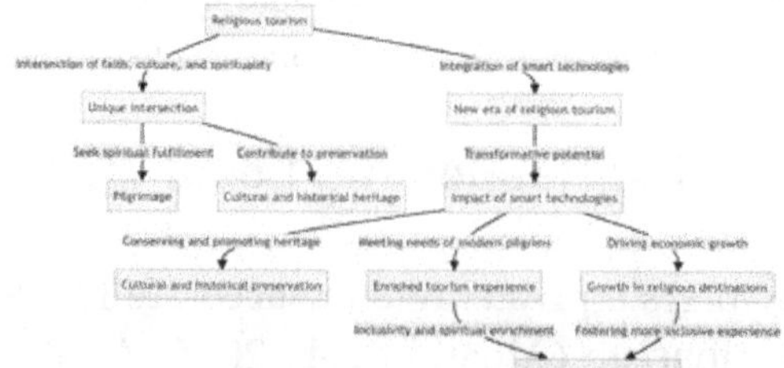

8. FUTURE TRENDS IN SMART RELIGIOUS TOURISM

The digital community has shown a previous interest in digital expressions of religion and spirituality, but discussions on religious tourism and pilgrimage are still in the early stages of development (Alharbi et al., 2025; Innocenti, 2023). As smart technologies continue to advance, the future of religious tourism is poised for further transformation (Allal-Chérif, 2022; Niyas et al., 2025). These technologies are expected to play an increasingly prominent role in reshaping the pilgrimage experience, preserving cultural and historical heritage, and fostering economic growth (Hwang et al., 2023). By staying at the forefront of technological advancements, stakeholders can harness the full potential of smart technologies to meet the evolving needs of modern pilgrims (Jorge, 2023; Khan, 2024) (Jorge, 2023). Destinations should aim to provide personalized services to individual tourists, surpassing their prior expectations and thereby elevating their overall tourism experiences (Carrasco-García et al., 2025; Jankova et al., 2023; Ranjan & Chaturvedi, 2023).

The integration of smart technologies into religious tourism has opened new frontiers, transforming the way pilgrims engage with sacred sites, access information, and connect with their spiritual heritage (Alharbi et al., 2025; Khan, 2024; Rautela et al., 2025). Looking to the future, several trends and possibilities emerge, paving the way for a more unfathomable and enriched pilgrimage experience (Carrasco-García et al., 2025; Niyas et al., 2025). Smart technologies will contribute to sustainability efforts by aiding in crowd management, resource optimization, and environmental conservation at pilgrimage sites (Król & Hernik, 2022). Augmented reality will continue to evolve, offering increasingly immersive experiences (Jankova et al., 2023; Niyas et al., 2025). Pilgrims may soon access highly realistic reenactments of historical events, further blurring the line between the past and the present (Choe, 2025; Olsen & Timothy, 2020). AI-powered chatbots will provide real-time guidance and information to pilgrims, responding to their queries and needs with increasing accuracy and personalization (Alharbi et al., 2025; Raj et al., 2023). The metaverse, functioning as a disruptive technology, holds the potential to bring about significant changes in the religious tourism experience (Hwang et al., 2023; Niyas et al., 2025; Olsen & Timothy, 2020).

9. CONCLUSION

The chapter has elucidated the overpowering impact of smart technologies on religious tourism, showcasing their revitalizing effect on the pilgrimage experience and their role in stimulating economic growth within religiously significant destinations. These innovations facilitate a deeper connection between pilgrims and their spiritual heritage, concurrently preserving and promoting cultural and historical traditions (Hwang et al., 2023; Niyas et al., 2025). The promising future of smart technologies in religious tourism is evident as these tools continue to evolve, adapting to the evolving needs of modern pilgrims (Alharbi et al., 2025; Yang et al., 2023). The potential to create more immersive and personalized experiences while upholding cultural authenticity presents an exciting vision for the trajectory of religious tourism (Allal-Chérif, 2022; Carrasco-García et al., 2025; Khan, 2024).

Nonetheless, ethical considerations must underpin the integration of smart technologies, prioritizing privacy, authenticity, and cultural sensitivity (Alsahafi et al., 2023). Striking the delicate balance between tradition and innovation is imperative to ensure the preservation and enrichment of the spiritual and cultural dimensions of pilgrimage (Allal-Chérif, 2022; Das et al., 2024; Ocón, 2023). The collective responsibility lies in harnessing the potential of smart technologies not only to rejuvenate religious tourism but also to safeguard the timeless traditions and cultural heritage integral to these profound pilgrimages (Alharbi et al., 2025; Sestino et al., 2023). Such an approach will ensure that the pilgrimage experience remains a meaningful and transformative journey for generations to come (Niyas et al., 2025).

REFERENCES

Alharbi, A., Pandit, A., Rosenberger, P. J.III, & Miah, S. (2025). Understanding AI-enabled conversational agent customer experiences in religious tourism. *Journal of Islamic Marketing*, *16*(August), 2569–2595. Advance online publication. DOI: 10.1108/JIMA-07-2024-0309

Allal-Chérif, O. (2022). Intelligent cathedrals: Using augmented reality, virtual reality, and artificial intelligence to provide an intense cultural, historical, and religious visitor experience. *Technological Forecasting and Social Change*, *178*(January), 121604. Advance online publication. DOI: 10.1016/j.techfore.2022.121604

Alsahafi, R., Alzahrani, A., & Mehmood, R. (2023). Smarter Sustainable Tourism: Data-Driven Multi-Perspective Parameter Discovery for Autonomous Design and Operations. *Sustainability (Basel)*, *15*(5), 4166. Advance online publication. DOI: 10.3390/su15054166

Battour, M., Mady, K., Salaheldeen, M., Elsotouhy, M., Elbendary, I., & Boğan, E. (2023). AI-enabled technologies to assist Muslim tourists in Halal-friendly tourism. *Journal of Islamic Marketing*, *14*(5), 1291–1309. DOI: 10.1108/JIMA-01-2022-0001

Bhalla, R., Chowdhary, N., & Ranjan, A. (2021). Spiritual tourism for psychotherapeutic healing post COVID-19. *Journal of Travel & Tourism Marketing*, *38*(8), 769–781. DOI: 10.1080/10548408.2021.1930630

Carrasco-García, P.-M., Frías-Jamilena, D.-M., & Polo-Peña, A.-I. (2025). The Impact of Virtual Reality and Intelligent Virtual Environments on the Tourist Experience: The Moderating Effect of Cognitive Style. *Journal of Travel Research*, 00472875251346933. Advance online publication. DOI: 10.1177/00472875251346933

Casana, J., Laugier, E. J., Hill, A. C., Reese, K. M., Ferwerda, C., McCoy, M. D., & Ladefoged, T. (2021). Exploring archaeological landscapes using drone-acquired lidar: Case studies from Hawai'i, Colorado, and New Hampshire, USA. *Journal of Archaeological Science, Reports*, *39*(July), 103133. DOI: 10.1016/j.jasrep.2021.103133

Chaturvedi, P., Sharma, J., & Ranjan, A. (2024). The Role of Souvenir Marketing in Sustaining Handmade Craftsmanship. *ShodhKosh: Journal of Visual and Performing Arts*, *5*(3), 278–294. DOI: 10.29121/shodhkosh.v5.i3.2024.1401

Choe, J. (2025). Religious tourism. *Tourism Geographies*, *27*(3–4), 830–839. DOI: 10.1080/14616688.2024.2423168

Das, D. K., Chowdhary, B., Mishra, S. V., & Aditi, A. (2024). Varanasi—The Making of a Smart Heritage City. *Environment & Urbanization Asia, 15*(1), 141–155. DOI: 10.1177/09754253241230588

Gupta, K., & Gulla, A. (2010). Internet deployment in the spiritual tourism industry: The case of Vaishno Devi Shrine. *Worldwide Hospitality and Tourism Themes, 2*(5), 507–519. DOI: 10.1108/17554211011090120

Hassan, S. H. (2015). Conceptualizing the Antecedents and Consequences of Religious Travellers Experience and Wellbeing. *International Journal of Business and Management, 10*(6), 103–112. DOI: 10.5539/ijbm.v10n6p103

Hassan, S. H., Ramayah, T., & Qureshi, M. I. (2023). Elucidating Well-Being Measurement from the Wellness Perspective of Religious Travelers. *WORLD (Oakland, Calif.), 4*(1), 171–184. DOI: 10.3390/world4010012

Heidari, A., Yazdani, H. R., Saghafi, F., & Jalilvand, M. R. (2018). The perspective of religious and spiritual tourism research: A systematic mapping study. *Journal of Islamic Marketing, 9*(4), 747–798. DOI: 10.1108/JIMA-02-2017-0015

Hudaefi, F. A., & Beik, I. S. (2020). Digital zakāh campaign in time of Covid-19 pandemic in Indonesia: A netnographic study. *Journal of Islamic Marketing, 12*(3), 498–517. DOI: 10.1108/JIMA-09-2020-0299

Hwang, K., tom Dieck, M. C., Jung, T., & Kwon, O. (2023). The influence of virtual reality on the experience of religious cultural heritage content. *Internet Research.* Advance online publication. DOI: 10.1108/INTR-08-2022-0669

Innocenti, P. (2023). Pilgrim's progress? A field ethnography of multimodal recording, curating and sharing of the Camino de Santiago experience. *The Journal of Documentation.* Advance online publication. DOI: 10.1108/JD-10-2022-0213

Jankova, L., Auzina, A., & Zvirbule, A. (2023). Regional smart cultural tourism destinations in a region of Latvia. *Worldwide Hospitality and Tourism Themes, 15*(5), 507–516. DOI: 10.1108/WHATT-06-2023-0082

Jha, P., Bansal, T., Rawat, P., & Warpa, V. (2025). The holy hues of Amritsar: An inquiry into the interplay of religious tourism and sacred space. *Tourism Recreation Research, 50*(3), 636–651. DOI: 10.1080/02508281.2023.2294253

Jorge, A. (2023). Pilgrimage to Fátima and Santiago after COVID: Dis/connection in the post-digital age. *Mobile Media & Communication, 11*(3), 549–565. DOI: 10.1177/20501579221151041

Katić, M., & Blaće, A. (2023). The geography of pilgrimage: Adriatic maritime pilgrimages and natural features of the landscape. *Landscape Research*, *48*(6), 811–826. DOI: 10.1080/01426397.2023.2198203

Khan, N. A. (2024). Artificial intelligence, self-efficacy and engagement in religious tourism: Evidence from Arbaeen pilgrimage. *Journal of Hospitality and Tourism Insights*, *7*(3), 1660–1678. DOI: 10.1108/JHTI-10-2023-0725

Król, K., & Hernik, J. (2022). Digital Folklore of Rural Tourism in Poland. *Sustainability (Basel)*, *14*(3), 1165. Advance online publication. DOI: 10.3390/su14031165

Muangasame, K., & Tan, E. (2023). Phygital rural cultural heritage: A digitalisation approach for destination recovery and resilience. *Worldwide Hospitality and Tourism Themes*, *15*(1), 8–17. DOI: 10.1108/WHATT-08-2022-0096

Munjal, P. G. (2021). Charting the role of digital platforms for cultural heritage tourism in India. *Worldwide Hospitality and Tourism Themes*, *13*(2), 186–198. DOI: 10.1108/WHATT-10-2020-0126

Niyas, M., Jacob, R., Thomas, T. K., Vipin, R., Raju, J. S., Najjim, M., & Saju, V. (2025). Augmented Reality's Impact on Visitor Engagement and Experiential Management in Religious Heritage Sites. In *Technology and Religious Tourism: Emerging Trends, Cases and Futuristic Perspectives* (pp. 61–76). Emerald Publishing Limited. DOI: 10.1108/978-1-83662-260-420251005

Ocón, D. (2023). Low-cost digital tools to preserve cultural heritage 'blind spots': The case of Kubor Kassim in Singapore. *International Journal of Heritage Studies*, *29*(9), 961–987. DOI: 10.1080/13527258.2023.2231903

Olsen, D. H., & Timothy, D. J. (2020). The COVID-19 pandemic and religious travel: Present and future trends. *International Journal of Religious Tourism and Pilgrimage*, *8*(7), 170–188.

Pavelka, K., Šedina, J., & Matoušková, E. (2018). High resolution drone surveying of the pista geoglyph in palpa, Peru. *Geosciences*, *8*(12), 479. Advance online publication. DOI: 10.3390/geosciences8120479

Qurashi, J., & Sharpley, R. (2018). The impact of SMART media technologies (SMT) on the spiritual experience of Hajj Pilgrims. *International Journal of Religious Tourism and Pilgrimage*, *6*(3), 37–48.

Raj, S., Sampat, B., Behl, A., & Jain, K. (2023). Understanding senior citizens' intentions to use virtual reality for religious tourism in India: A behavioural reasoning theory perspective. *Tourism Recreation Research*, *48*(6), 983–999. Advance online publication. DOI: 10.1080/02508281.2023.2246735

Ranjan, A., & Chaturvedi, P. (2023). Digitally Sustaining: The Rural Intangible Cultural Heritage. In *Embracing Business Sustainability Through Innovation and Creativity in the Service Sector* (pp. 14–30). DOI: 10.4018/978-1-6684-6732-9.ch002

Ranjan, A., & Chaturvedi, P. (2025). Creating Meaningful Tourism Experiences With Digital Storytelling. In *Meaningful Tourism* (pp. 127–144). Emerald Publishing Limited., DOI: 10.1108/978-1-83797-837-320251019

Rautela, S., Sharma, A., & Panackal, N. (2025). Exploring the sacred-unravelling the growth and development of religious tourism in Islamic culture: A bibliometric analysis. *Cogent Business & Management*, *12*(1), 2482020. Advance online publication. DOI: 10.1080/23311975.2025.2482020

Ritter, C. S. (2023). Gazing from the air: Tourist encounters in the age of travel drones. *Tourism Geographies*, *0*(0), 1–17. DOI: 10.1080/14616688.2023.2264823

Senbeto, D. L. (2023). The Greener, the Better? Probing Green Innovation in Pilgrimage Tourism Destinations. *Journal of Hospitality & Tourism Research (Washington, D.C.)*. Advance online publication. DOI: 10.1177/10963480231151674

Séraphin, H., & Jarraud, N. (2022). COVID-19: Impacts and perspectives for religious tourism events. The case of Lourdes Pilgrimages. *Journal of Convention & Event Tourism*, *23*(1), 15–40. DOI: 10.1080/15470148.2021.1906810

Sestino, A., Pino, G., & Guido, G. (2023). The effect of fervid attachment to religious rites on tourism: Evidence from the Holy Week in Southern Italy. *Journal of Cultural Heritage Management and Sustainable Development*, *13*(2), 201–218. DOI: 10.1108/JCHMSD-01-2021-0010

Shafiee, S., Jahanyan, S., Ghatari, A. R., & Hasanzadeh, A. (2023). Developing sustainable tourism destinations through smart technologies: A system dynamics approach. *Journal of Simulation*, *17*(4), 477–498. DOI: 10.1080/17477778.2022.2030656

Shinde, K., & Singh, R. P. B. (2023). Still on UNESCO's "Tentative List of World Heritage"? Heritage, Tourism, and Stunted Growth in Sarnath (Varanasi), India. *Heritage*, *6*(7), 5051–5065. DOI: 10.3390/heritage6070267

Shinde, K. A. (2010). Entrepreneurship and indigenous enterpreneurs in religious tourism in India. *International Journal of Tourism Research*, *12*(5), 523–535. DOI: 10.1002/jtr.771

Shinde, K. A. (2021). Religious theme parks as tourist attraction systems. *Journal of Heritage Tourism*, *16*(3), 281–299. DOI: 10.1080/1743873X.2020.1791887

Shmushko, K. (2023). Between the Tibetan Plateau and Eastern China—Religious Tourism, Lay Practice and Ritual Economy during the Pandemic. *Religions*, *14*(3), 1–17. DOI: 10.3390/rel14030291

Suárez, M. A., Salas, E. L., Franco, I. C., & Sousa, A. Á. (2025). Towards a methodology of good practices for heritage-led rural regeneration: From the main paths to the surrounding areas. *Cities (London, England)*, *161*(February), 105849. Advance online publication. DOI: 10.1016/j.cities.2025.105849

Vila-Lopez, N., & Kuster-Boluda, I. (2022). Data mining to reposition a religious tourist destination in COVID-19. *International Journal of Contemporary Hospitality Management*. Advance online publication. DOI: 10.1108/IJCHM-03-2022-0390

Yang, T. T., Ruan, W. Q., Li, Y. Q., & Zhang, S. N. (2023). Virtual tourist motivation: The differences between virtual tourism and on-site tourism. *Tourism Review*, *78*(5), 1280–1297. DOI: 10.1108/TR-07-2022-0331

Zarkada, A. K., Kashif, M., & Zainab, Z. (2025). The structure and content of the religious tourism destination image construct: An exploratory netnography of travelers' reviews of Makkah and Medina. *Journal of Islamic Marketing*, *16*(3), 689–712. DOI: 10.1108/JIMA-06-2024-0229

Zhang, H., & He, X. (2025). The effect of awe on tourists' responsible behavioral intention in a mountainous religious tourism destination: Evidence from China. *Journal of Sustainable Tourism*, *33*(7), 1392–1410. DOI: 10.1080/09669582.2024.2354315

Chapter 9
Unlocking Sustainable Tourism Performance:
The Role of Intellectual Capital, Innovation, and Artificial Intelligence Capability in SMEs

Tayyaba Syed
https://orcid.org/0009-0005-7475-5419
Virtual University of Pakistan, Pakistan

Sajjad Hussain
Virtual University of Pakistan, Pakistan

Noor Hazlina Ahmad
Universiti Sains Malaysia, Malaysia

ABSTRACT

Sustainable tourism requires joint efforts from all stakeholders. This study examines how intellectual capital (IC) enhances tourism performance and sustainability in AJK, Pakistan, using resource-based and dynamic capability theories. It proposes a mediated moderation model, testing the role of open innovation (OI) as a mediator and artificial intelligence capability (AIC) as a moderator. Using purposive sampling, 300 questionnaires were distributed, and 220 valid responses were analyzed through SMART-PLS 4.0. Results show IC significantly improves tourism performance, while OI mediates this effect. AIC further strengthens the OI and tourism industry performance link, indicating that AI tools boost innovation outcomes and support sustainability. The study offers insights for tourism SMEs in developing economies and highlights the need to explore AI's role in innovation under dynamic market conditions.

DOI: 10.4018/979-8-3373-9958-4.ch009

1. INTRODUCTION

The sustainability issue has gained a prominent role in the hospitality and tourism industry, where it allows companies to be competitively viable in the long run and respond to environmental and social concerns (Lee, 2023; Dzenopoljac et al., 2025). Small and medium-sized enterprise (SME) hotels, in this regard, are important, especially in developing economies like Pakistan, where tourism-related SMEs make up a large portion of foreign exchange income, economic development, and the enhancement of local culture and national identity (Achmad et al., 2023; Dzenopoljac et al., 2025). Although they are significant, SME hotels in Pakistan, particularly in areas like Azar Jammu and Kashmir, are not developed yet, and they continue to experience some challenges that include infrequent strategic orientation towards sustainability, insufficient innovation, and inadequate resource access, which contribute to their inability to perform sustainably (Hussain et al., 2025).

The previous studies indicate that SMEs should enhance their performance through internal analysis to determine and exploit their own resources and abilities, especially the intangible assets (Arshad et al., 2023). Among them, intellectual capital (IC), comprising human capital, structural capital, and relational capital, has become one of the most significant contributors to the value creation and competitiveness (Ali et al., 2021; Huma et al., 2024). Human capital is the knowledge and skills of the employees, structural capital of the organization offers systems and processes within the organization that facilitate the efficient use of this knowledge, and relational capital is a relationship with key stakeholders like customers, suppliers, and institutions. Although these IC elements have been recognized to be important in the overall performance of tourism SMEs, there is meager empirical evidence on how these elements work together to improve the performance of tourism SMEs, especially in resource-scarce and sustainability-sensitive settings.

Besides, having intellectual capital might not be enough, but it should be converted into innovative practices. Open innovation (OI) is a practice that provides an avenue in which SMEs can combine internal and external knowledge to enhance the outcome of innovation (Chesbrough, 2006). Applied in the tourism industry with growing popularity, OI helps to promote sustainability through the systems of collaboration, knowledge sharing, and environmental and societal responsiveness (Achmad et al., 2023; Costa et al., 2023) . Nevertheless, the mediating role of open innovation between intellectual capital and performance has not been studied many times, yet tourism SMEs, particularly in developing economies, tend to be reluctant to engage in R&D processes and have limited innovation networks.

Simultaneously, the high rate of digitalization in the tourism sector has increased the strategic significance of artificial intelligence (AI). The use of AI capability will help firms to analyze, aid decision-making, improve collaboration, and increase innovation processes, which will contribute to sustainable competitiveness (Cimino et al., 2025). Nevertheless, there is a large adoption gap between large companies and SMEs, especially in developing nations. Although AI can strengthen open innovation and maximize the results of its performance, there is a lack of empirical evidence regarding its mediating role between open innovation and tourism performance.

Against this backdrop, this chapter contributes to the literature by developing and testing an integrated framework to explain how the components of intellectual capital led to open innovation, how open innovation can enhance the performance of tourism SME and how artificial intelligence capability can reinforce this connection. To be more precise, the questions targeted by the study will be whether human, structural, and relational capital trigger open innovation practices within SME hotels; whether open innovation can convert these intangible resources into better tourism performance; and whether AI capability enhances the power of open innovation in delivering sustainable performance outputs. The answers to these interdependent questions have ensured that the chapter fills the gaps that are critical to the study of tourism, innovation, and sustainability, and provides practical answers to SME hotel managers and policymakers who aim to improve long-term competitiveness in emerging tourism destinations.

The rest of this chapter follows this pattern. The following section presents a review of the literature on the topic, along with the development of a theoretical framework and hypotheses that connect intellectual capital, open innovation, and artificial intelligence capability to tourism performance. This will be followed by a description of research methodology, which will comprise the study situation, sample, measures, and methods of analysis. The empirical findings are then provided and elaborated on based on the earlier investigations. The chapter concludes with major theoretical and managerial implications, study limitations, and future research directions.

2. LITERATURE REVIEW

The given research work is grounded on the resource-based view (RBV) and the dynamic capability theory. This management system highlights that the resources will be a key determinant of the success of any organization (Abourokbah et al., 2023). The assets and capabilities comprise the resources of the organization, which may be tangible and intangible (Jabarzadeh et al., 2022). The management structure of the present study rests on the intangible resources. The intellectual capital relies mostly on the abilities and skills of the employees who apply the knowledge(Najar et al., 2020). Furthermore, another resource of the companies in the hospitality industry is open innovation, which is utilized to acquire quality knowledge effectively with the help of both internal and external knowledge. The artificial intelligence ability also ranks among the organization's resources that play a central role in the process mentioned above. All these resources facilitate the organization to build service innovation that contributes to increased organizational performance.

Teece (2007) has expanded the idea of the capability of RBV to dynamic capability. RBV does not explain how organizations might acquire a competitive advantage in a dynamic and fast-moving environment; its notion has received widespread support (Eisenhardt & Martin, 2017). Competitive advantage and disadvantage may shift over time; therefore, it is necessary to comprehend the evolution of capabilities and resources over time, an area where the RBV is silent (Helfat & Peteraf, 2003). Businesses must modify or reinvent their capabilities to maintain a competitive edge in a dynamic market.

Dynamic capability refers to the operational procedures that a company employs to utilize its resources, particularly those that integrate, reconfigure, acquire, and release resources to align with market changes, or even generate them. Consequently, these are the strategic and organizational practices by which companies accomplish novel resource configurations in response to market developments such as emergence, collision, evolution, division, and demise (Eisenhardt & Martin, 2017). Similarly, dynamic capabilities are defined by Zahra et al. (2006) as procedures that reconfigure the resources and operational procedures of an organization. According to Cepeda & Vera (2007), dynamic capability consistently meets the following characteristics.

- The organizational processes and routines are deeply ingrained throughout the organization. • It modifies the knowledge resources and routines of an organization.
- Dynamic capability requires an initial configuration of resources and operational routines.
- Dynamic capability produces newly changed resources and operating processes.

The Resource-Based View and Dynamic Capabilities are the theories that can be applied to understand the impact of resources and capabilities on the competitive advantage and performance of an organization.

In this fast-paced and dynamic context, RBV alone does not reveal how capabilities might evolve and how they might get better or worse (Eisenhardt & Martin, 2017). Resources falling within the scope of RBV theory are of a general nature. However, RBV consistently serves as the basis for a multitude of theories in the field of strategic management. The message conveyed by the convergence of RBV and dynamic capability is that superior performance is dependent solely on superior resources, including ethereal resources and capability (Wernerfelt, 1984). By implementing these theories, organizations can acquire knowledge about the distinctive resources and competencies they possess, identify areas where they can cultivate and exploit their strengths, and strategically position themselves in the market to achieve long-term competitive advantage. These theories offer a significant framework for comprehending the complex interplay between organizational resources, capabilities, and competitive advantage. By incorporating the knowledge derived from the Resource-Based View (RB) and dynamic capabilities, organizations can enhance their comprehension of how to use their internal advantages, adjust to the ever-changing external environment, and synchronize their plans with the increasing market requirements.

2.1 Intellectual Capital Components

According to the resource-based view (RBV), the greatest strategic resource of the firm and competitive advantage generator is the body of knowledge, also referred to as the intellectual capital of the firm, permitting the assimilation of external innovation (Jabarzadeh et al., 2022)The term "intellectual capital" defines the expertise, experience gained in an organization, familiarity with customers, and professional competence that make a company in the market advantageous(Truong & Nguyen, 2023). A growing interest in this issue has been given attention by academics since the 2000s due to the topicality of intellectual capital (Ali et al., 2021) The most widespread typology is the triple nature of the concept of IC, which uses human capital, structural, and relational capital as the major components of the concept(Chen et al., 2015). IC essentially exists in three dimensions of the business, that is, its employees, its structure, and its connections. Human capital (HC) refers to the skills, abilities, experience, and attitude of the employees(Najar et al., 2020). Knowledge is an indicator of human capital that provides the ability to work. This knowledge inventory can be obtained by learning, training, and experience (Kraaijenbrink, 2011). The exemplary human resources (qualified managers) can ideally allure the performance of the firms based on the RBV and the Upper Echelon Theory of Hambrick and Mason (1984). Nonetheless, human capital cannot be sufficient to achieve the competitiveness of firms. In that instance, the members of the organization would be expected to partition and separate the knowledge at the individual level in a way that the company could enjoy the advantages of this form of collective and institutionalized knowledge (Soo et al., 2017)Basically, the research on the IC sector revealed that they had the structural capital that facilitated the development of human capital(Ali et al., 2021). The structural capital (SC) enhances the personal knowledge of the managers to be converted to shared knowledge of the organization(Al-azzam et al., 2017). In addition to that, SC incorporates the organizational wisdom as well as the codified experience in the organization and applies it in systems, structures, databases, processes, patents, and manuals (Ramírez-Solis et al., 2022).Moreover, the internal resources (human capital and structural capital) not only determine the performance of the company, but also the relational capital. This capability of building and sustaining relations with the interested parties is referred to as Relational capital. They are cooperative relationships, and this is founded on mutual trust. The relational capital depicts the worth of external relationships of a business (partners, customers, suppliers, allies, universities, research institutions, and government). This is largely known as the reputation and the customer capital is the portfolio of loyal patrons(Bontis, 1998)

2.2 Open Innovation (OI)

Open innovation is a new concept, which Chesbrough introduced in 2003 as a measure of leveraging the knowledge base of the company. OI is described as the intentional inbound and outflow of information to accelerate internal innovation and expand the markets to leverage innovation, respectively (Chesbrough & Crowther, 2006)Luckily, unlike the so-called closed paradigm, which is based on the internal innovation creation. Moreover, two significant resources, i.e., inflow and outflow of knowledge, can only strengthen open innovation, enabling the organization to present innovative ideas (Obradović et al., 2021). The open innovation process is a two-way process because knowledge is received by the organization and is reflected in a new and innovative idea. In addition to this, Bogers et al. (2019) reveal that open innovation is a distributed innovation process that involves the management of knowledge flow across organizational boundaries. In this perspective, the in-house R&D is not inferior to any other source of knowledge that will be gathered while acquiring knowledge. However, the innovation strategies in most companies give this strategy a minor role. Moradi et al. (2021) in their turn, they persist in viewing open innovation as a corporate strategy, referring to the external innovation resources and internal innovation resources and internal and external market channels to expand the innovation capabilities. In other sectors, open innovation activities are undertaken by major organisations in cooperation with other organisations to advance their technology (Costa et al., 2023) . An external organization in the internal innovation process may provide a part of the knowledge, competencies, and technology to a company, or may actively establish collaboration (Hassan & Iqbal, 2020).The transition into an inbound open innovation strategy, one of the firms tries to look over the horizon of skills, competency, or technology which the firm lacks; it could not bring it in-house, it would be too costly, too laborious, and would have taken too long to do so.

2.3 Artificial Intelligence Adoption

The issue of dynamic capabilities is especially critical when it comes to SMEs in the context of adopting AI. According to Cimino et al. (2025). SMEs implement AI in three main steps: opportunity identification (evaluating the potential value of the AI technology), resource mobilization (investing in AI-powered tools and AI training), and ongoing adaptation (refining the processes to make the maximum out of AI). It is worth noting that this model aligns with the framework of dynamic capabilities: sensing, seizing, and reconfiguring (Jabarzadeh et al., 2022). The implementation of such abilities is important to startups and SMEs because those that do not use AI because of resource, skills, and capabilities limits will struggle to accommodate abrupt changes in consumer demand and, hence, have a reduced chance of survival(Abourokbah et al., 2023). It has long been acknowledged that technological advancement is a key contributor to economic development and social well-being. Early literature by Schumpeter shows its critical importance in influencing market dynamics and firm competitiveness. The fact that technological change was identified by Solow, 1957as one of the determinants of economic performance further solidified its role, and thus, broad empirical studies were conducted on how companies and sectors can use innovation to continue achieving long-term growth (Cohen & Levinthal, 1990). Economists have come to a great realization that the capability of a company to develop technologically has a direct impact on its economic performance and market standing(Neal, 2015). Considering that, it is not surprising that the adoption of AI is regarded as a key factor in determining economic performance levels since companies can leverage AI technologies to increase their productivity, resource distribution, and competitive advantage(Martin Lackéus, 2015). This has been supported by research indicating that AI can assist the business to make better decisions, cut down inventory costs by using sophisticated logistics, improve productivity, and increase their overall financial performance (Wang et al., 2021). Cannavale et al. (2022)demonstrate that AI-based solutions are also used to enhance supply chain management and minimize errors, as well as give buyers direct access to the supplier information, which allows a wide variety of organizations to enhance their performance. Another positive correlation that can be noted by Necula et al. (2024) is between AI and efficiency (i.e., productivity). Moreover, Nayal et al. (2021) discovered that the application of AI is a key factor in enhancing the performance of supply chain risk mitigation. AI use also makes a firm more dynamic in its marketing functions and consequently, its marketing functions (Wang et al., 2021). Abrokwah-Larbi & Awuku-Larbi(2024) ascertain the importance of adopting AI by the SMEs in financial performance, customer performance, internal business process performance, and learning and growth performance. At low levels of AI adoption, SMEs are at risk of failing, hence losing their competitiveness, market share, and generating fewer job opportunities (Badghish & Soomro, 2024). It was discovered specifically that the adoption of AI has a positive effect on the sustainability performance of corporations(Samuel Godadaw, 2025). This is also prompted by the fact that the adoption of AI enables and promotes change in the organization that leads to more sustainable practices, less waste, and other performance factors.

2.4 Integrated Literature Synthesis and Research Gap

The chapter provides a comprehensive and up-to-date background on sustainability in tourism SMEs by integrating intellectual capital, open innovation, and artificial intelligence capability within established theoretical perspectives. Prior research consistently shows that tourism SMEs rely more on intangible resources than on physical assets due to financial constraints, seasonality, and environmental uncertainty (Bontis, 1998; Khalique et al., 2018). Intellectual capital, through human expertise, organizational routines, and relational networks, forms the foundation for competitiveness in tourism contexts. However, the literature also indicates that intellectual capital does not automatically lead to improved performance unless it is actively transformed into innovative practices (Chesbrough, 2003; Bogers et al., 2019).

Open innovation accounts for this transformation process by highlighting how SMEs leverage external knowledge, partnerships, and customer involvement to overcome internal resource constraints. In tourism, where value creation is highly experiential and collaborative, open innovation has become a critical mechanism for enhancing service quality and sustainability-oriented innovation (Thomas & Wood, 2015). More recent studies further suggest that the effectiveness of open innovation increasingly depends on digital and analytical capabilities. Artificial intelligence capability strengthens firms' ability to process market information, personalize tourist experiences, and scale innovation outcomes, thereby reinforcing the performance benefits of open innovation (Mariani & Borghi, 2019; Dwivedi et al., 2021).

Despite these advances, existing research tends to examine intellectual capital, open innovation, and artificial intelligence capability as separate streams. There is limited empirical evidence explaining how these elements interact as an integrated pathway in tourism SMEs, particularly in developing regions where digital infrastructure, skills availability, and regulatory support remain uneven (Tornatzky & Fleischer, 1990; Vrontis et al., 2022). This fragmentation weakens theoretical coherence and makes it difficult to understand under what conditions innovation translates into sustainable performance. Organizing the literature more thematically, strengthening conceptual transitions, and explicitly articulating this research gap can therefore significantly improve the chapter's argumentative clarity.

To enhance transparency and guide readers through the core intellectual foundations, a concise summary of representative studies is provided below in Table 1

Table 1. Key studies informing the IC–OI–AI capability logic in tourism SMEs

Study	Context	Core Focus	Key Contribution
Bontis (1998)	Knowledge-based firms	Intellectual capital	Establishes IC as a strategic intangible resource
Chesbrough (2003)	Innovation management	Open innovation	Explains how external knowledge drives innovation outcomes
Bogers et al. (2019)	Cross-industry review	Open innovation	Synthesizes OI mechanisms and research gaps
Mariani & Borghi (2019)	Tourism & hospitality	AI applications	Shows how AI enhances service innovation
Dwivedi et al. (2021)	Digital transformation	AI capability	Highlights AI as an enabler of organizational performance
Tornatzky & Fleischer (1990)	Technology adoption	TOE framework	Explains adoption barriers in resource-constrained firms

2.5 Theoretical Framework

This study draws on the Resource-Based View and Dynamic Capabilities Theory to explain sustainable performance in tourism SMEs operating under resource constraints and digital change. From a resource-based perspective, competitive advantage in tourism SMEs is largely derived from intangible assets rather than physical resources. Intellectual capital, therefore, represents the core strategic resource and is conceptualized through human, structural, and relational capital, reflecting employees' expertise, organizational routines, and stakeholder relationships that are central to service-based tourism activities (Barney, 1991; Bontis, 1998).

However, possessing intellectual capital alone does not ensure superior performance. Dynamic Capabilities Theory explains that firms must actively mobilize and renew resources to respond to changing environments (Teece, 2007). In this framework, open innovation serves as the mechanism through which intellectual capital is transformed into performance outcomes. By combining internal knowledge with external ideas from customers, partners, and destination stakeholders, tourism SMEs can overcome internal limitations and develop adaptive and sustainability-oriented innovations (Chesbrough, 2003; Bogers et al., 2019).

The performance impact of open innovation, however, depends on firms' ability to implement and scale innovation effectively. Artificial intelligence capability strengthens this process by enabling data-driven decision-making, service personalization, and operational reconfiguration. Viewed through a dynamic capabilities lens, AI capability enhances the conversion of innovation activities into measurable performance outcomes, particularly in digitally mediated tourism contexts (Dwivedi et al., 2021; Verhoef et al., 2021).

Together, this framework positions intellectual capital as the resource foundation, open innovation as the conversion process, and artificial intelligence capability as a reconfiguration capability that amplifies the effectiveness of innovation. By integrating these elements, the study addresses a gap in the literature, which has largely examined them in isolation, and offers a coherent explanation of how tourism SMEs in developing economies can achieve sustainable performance.

Figure 1. Conceptual framework of the study

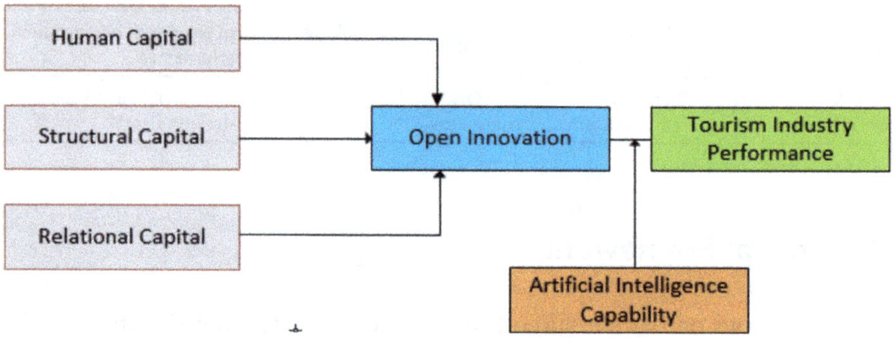

2.6 Hypothesis Development

2.6.1 Relationship Between Intellectual capital (HC, SC, RC) and Open Innovation

Through organizational learning, knowledge flows and inflows from various sources, including universities, customers, competitors, and others, create a positive impact on the firm's knowledge stock (Truong & Nguyen, 2023). Similarly, interorganizational knowledge sharing should be incorporated into the new organization's knowledge creation process (Ur Rehman et al., 2022). Thus, the amount and degree of knowledge stock within organizations are altered by the volumes of streams of knowledge crossing organizational boundaries due to the OI paradigm, through intellectual capital as a body of organizational knowledge. However, the extent and the process of the influences of OI practice in the intellectual capital constituents are highly likely to differ by their type and character. The OI practice triggers the emergence of new alliances, and social capital tends to expand and become more diverse. The interactive transactions across organizations resulting from the opening also dramatically altered the human capital through the diversification of the aspects of borrowing and lending of knowledge (Ali et al., 2021). Further, the relational capital, in the paradigm, assumes the structure of a matrix since the scheme to create values of an organization is not only within the organization itself but also beyond. Thus, the systems partners shared were available to the organizations, and they could use them during the activities of joint value creation and to improve the organizational capital.

Thus, based on the above findings, the following hypothesis is proposed:

> $H1_a$: Human capital positively and significantly impacts open innovation practice amongst SMEs.
> $H1_b$: Structural capital positively and significantly impacts open innovation practice amongst SMEs
> $H1_c$: Relational capital positively and significantly impacts open innovation practice amongst SMEs

2.6.2 Relationship Between Open Innovation and Tourism Industry Performance

Open innovation is a novel approach in the field of management and is discussed as a feasible framework based on collaboration between people and organizations within and outside the company (Costa et al., 2023)This industry of high-tech and other industries is evolving faster in terms of open innovation, which makes it possible to expand technology, the market, and revenue collection, and more effectively in the process of researching and developing new goods (Mulyono & Syamsuri, 2023). In this respect, the role of the service industry in the economy of developed countries has been increasing, and the intensity of interest in the study of innovation in this field has increased significantly (Bigliardi et al., 2022)Innovation can be said to be a continuous challenge in the tourism industry, because companies have to match the shifting profile of visitors that is becoming very demanding and well-informed (Achmad et al., 2023). The tourism-related businesses are compelled to continue adjusting to these changes (Achmad et al., 2023). Subsequently, the industry requires offering its customers exceptional and innovative experiences that enable it to engage the market more extensively and preserve the competitive positioning (Omerzel & Jurdanab, 2016)). Innovation can contribute significantly to the development of competitive advantage, particularly in companies operating in the tourism market, which is rapidly evolving (Khalique et al., 2020). It enables businesses to make quick decisions regarding the unpredictable situation within the environment and maintain or enhance their competitiveness. The open innovation is typically geared towards developing innovative and creative products (Hassan & Iqbal, 2020). The authors discovered that open innovation offered several benefits, including reduced costs of building new services, quick innovation, enhanced customer-focused corporate image, and amplified customer responsiveness to their needs (Lo et al., 2020). However, to implement open innovation, companies within the tourism industry should make strategic choices that apply foreign knowledge, skillsets, abilities, and internal resources and expertise (Achmad et al., 2023). Customer involvement follows the acquisition of the external knowledge that is core to the concept of innovation, and customer knowledge and customer needs are the most visible in-service innovation (Dzenopoljac et al., 2025). The tourism industry usually requires open innovation as a strategy of enhancing the services offered and as a tool of differentiating the competing destinations. Specifically, cities must make new narratives to maintain their prosperity and image, and to this end, these cities should foster the culture of open innovation (Rúben Pinhal, 2025). It has also been demonstrated that used in the tourism sector, open innovation can lead to more customer satisfaction, brand recognition, enhanced exploitation of opportunities, and new products or services(Gebremichael, 2018). Hence, one of the alternatives is open innovation, which can share successful solutions that can protect not only individual businesses but the overall tourist industry against the threats (Szromek and Polok, 2022). According to Cruz-Ruiz et al., collaborative processes of innovation could potentially assist in utilizing resources in a more efficient way and generate the possibility of the long-term cost-reduction of resources and money through the minimization of spending and resource consumption (Mulyono & Syamsuri, 2023). Open innovation makes it easier to design sustainable and cost-effective services that consider the interests of all stakeholders, which means that the importance of open innovation processes to business models related to tourism is even more important (Jutidharabongse et al., 2024).

Therefore, based on the above findings, the following hypothesis is proposed:

> H2: Open innovation has a positive and significant effect on the tourism industry performance of SMEs.

2.6.3 The Mediating role of Open Innovation Between Intellectual Capital (HC, SC, RC) and Tourism Industry Performance

The mediating effect between intellectual capital components and the tourism industry performance is important through open innovation. Intellectual capital that entails human, structural, and relational capital is the source of the creation of knowledge and innovative capabilities in tourism organizations(Dzenopoljac et al.,

2025). To transform into better performance, however, the firms are increasingly active in the open innovation practice, including knowledge sharing, external collaboration, and stakeholder co-creation(Lo et al., 2020). By means of open innovation, tourism businesses can use the intellectual capital to co-create new services, improving customer experiences, and quickly adjusting to market shifts, which enhances their competitiveness and performance(Najar et al., 2020). Khan et al. (2021) argue that open innovation directs the effectiveness of intellectual resources to the real world through the development of collaboration and knowledge sharing across organizational boundaries. On the same note, Gebremichael, (2018)highlight that open innovation mediates the relationship between intellectual capital and tourism development through incorporating external knowledge networks. Therefore, open innovation is a dynamic process that transforms the possibility of intellectual capital into performance gains that can be measured in the tourism industry. The hypothesis of the relationship is based on the entire discussion:

$H3_a$: Human capital has a mediating relationship with Open innovation with tourism industry performance.
$H3_b$: Structural capital has a mediating relationship with Open innovation with tourism industry performance.
$H3_c$: Relational capital has a mediating relationship with Open innovation with tourism industry performance.

2.6.4 The Moderating Role of Artificial Intelligence Adoption Between Open Innovation and Tourism Industry Performance

Technological advancement is a major contributor to economic development and social well-being. The initial works of Schumpeter emphasize their negative contribution to market dynamics and the competitiveness of firms. The fact that technological change has been cited by (Kornowski, 2016) as one of the determinants of economic performance further entrenched its importance as a subject of numerous levels of empirical studies that have been conducted on how enterprises and sectors use innovation to support their long-term growth (Halpern et al., 2021). It is not astonishing that AI implementation is regarded as a key factor in dictating the performance of the tourism industry, as companies will be able to incorporate AI technologies to empower their output, allocate resources more efficiently, and have an advantage over other companies(Badghish & Soomro, 2024). This has been supported by research indicating that AI assists businesses to make better decisions, cut down on inventory expenses due to improved logistics, increase productivity, and improve their overall financial performance(Halpern et al., 2021;Badghish & Soomro, 2024). Another positive correlation noted by Abrokwah-Larbi & Awuku-Larbi

(2024) is the relationship of AI with efficiency (i.e., productivity). The adoption of AI also increases the dynamic marketing capabilities of a firm and, consequently, its performance in marketing. In case of low adoption of AI, SMEs face the danger of losing their competitiveness, market share, and generating fewer employment opportunities (Puccio et al., 2025). Samuel Godadaw (2025) discovered that the use of AI positively affects the sustainability of corporations. This is partly fuelled by the fact that with the use of AI, changes in the organization are made possible and welcome, which leads to more sustainable practices, less wastage, and other performance indicators. Equally, Shokry (2025) indicates that adoption of AI and sustainable performance is statistically significant, with the highest effect on environmental results. Moreover, the use of AI will promote environmentally friendly innovation, which will allow SMEs to reduce their emissions, minimize their environmental footprint, and save money (Badghish & Soomro, 2024). The results of Al-Khatib (2023) Prove the positive effect of AI adoption on the open innovation capabilities of firms, as well. That is why we have suggested the following hypothesis:

> H4: The artificial intelligence capability is positively moderating the relationship between open innovation and tourism industry performance.

3. RESEARCH METHODOLOGY

The chapter uses the approach of quantitative design in testing the proposed framework. The sampling of SME hotel employees in Pakistan will be done through a purposive sampling method. The sample in the research included hotels with 50 or more and 250 or fewer employees, according to the definition of SMEs of the World Bank (Ndiaye et al., 2018) and the State Bank of Pakistan (Pakistan, 2022).

Partial Least Squares Structural Equation Modelling (PLS-SEM) will be employed as a means of analyzing the data through Smart PLS 4.0. The approach is appropriate when models with complex mediated and moderated models and latent constructs are to be tested, as it provides information about the direct and indirect relationships. The emphasis on SMEs will make sure that the research reflects the dynamics of smaller firms that are most susceptible to sustainability challenges but are also most decisive in regional development. The chapter will attempt to go beyond the theoretical assumptions and give evidence-based information by analyzing empirical data.

3.1 Sample Size and Data Collection

The structured questionnaire was finally distributed to the CEOs, managing directors, managers (senior, junior, and assistant), and staff members of the hotels that are in operation in the tourism industry in Neelam Valley, Mirpur, Kotli, Rawala kot, Bagh, and Muzaffarabad, Azad Jammu and Kashmir, Pakistan. The anonymity of the respondents was observed strictly. Owners and employees are significant in the development and growth of the business in the context of SMEs, and they are important sources of knowledge and information. Therefore, the two groups were treated as essential research subjects in this study. The questionnaire items were well-crafted to make the constructs more understandable and clearer to the respondents. The target respondents were sampled using a purposive sampling method to choose SMEs in Azad Jammu and Kashmir. An individual who works in SMEs was taken as the sampling unit. Those 300 questionnaires were mailed using a self-administered survey method, with 220 filled-out forms being useful; a response rate of 73.33 percent is satisfactory as far as academic research is concerned. The given research used a quantitative and cross-sectional design to investigate how the intellectual capital, open innovation, and AI capability affect the performance of the tourism industry of SMEs located in Azad Jammu and Kashmir, Pakistan. The primary data were obtained in the form of a structured questionnaire, namely, adapted to the SMEs involved in various tourism-related activities. The questionnaire items have been formulated after reviewing rich literature with a high degree of reliance and clarity. It was measured with all unobserved constructs through items borrowed from known scales (Bontis, 1998; Khalique et al., 2015). This was in a five-point Likert scale, with one being strongly disagree and five being strongly agree. Intellectual capital was operationalized based on three separate dimensions, such as human capital, relational capital, and structural capital, which were used as independent variables. The dependent variable was under Tourism Industry Performance of SMEs. In addition, open innovation was taken on board as a mediating factor between intellectual capital and tourism industry performance, and artificial intelligence (AI) ability was presented as a moderating factor between open innovation and tourism performance.

4 ANALYSIS

To test the research hypotheses that were proposed, the data analysis was conducted by means of the Partial Least Squares (PLS) path modeling with the help of the Smart PLS 3.0 software. A breakthrough in latent variable modelling is the Smart PLS 3 software. PLS model is typically studied and discussed in two phases

(J. Hair Jr et al., 2014). The measurement model is used to check the reliability and validity, and the structural model to test the hypotheses of the proposed research.

4.1 Characteristics of Respondents

Table 2 describes the respondents' demographics. According to the data, most respondents are male (90.1%), indicating that the sample is dominated by men. Most responders (63%) have a bachelor's degree, indicating a high level of education. In addition, most respondents (38.2%) have less than one year of experience.

Table 2. Respondents' demography

Demographic Category	Frequency	Percentage (%)
Gender	N	Percentage
Male	355	90.1
Female	39	9.9
Age		
21–30	167	42.39
31–40	170	43.15
41+	57	14.47
Education		
High School	37	9.39
Bachelor	275	69.80
Master	62	15.74
PhD	20	5.08
Experience		
Less than 1 year	150	38.07
1–2 years	149	37.82
More than 2 years	95	24.11

4.2 Measurement Model

Typically, the reliability and validity of the primary data are commonly checked with the help of the measurement model. According to Gotz et al. (2010), evaluating the measuring model processes entails three steps, i.e., individual item reliabilities, convergent validity and discriminant validity. The factor loadings threshold levels are to be above 0.70 (J. Hair Jr et al., 2014). Nevertheless, a loading value of 0.5 is also not bad, and the factor loading items with less than 0.5 ought to be dropped

(Chin, 1998). Thus, the lowest level of loading factors was 0.50 in this research paper. The convergent and discriminant validity are the main bases of persuading that the latent variables are valid.

4.3 Discriminant Validity

In the research, the discriminant validity criteria were tested based on Fornell and Larcker (1981)loading and cross-loading, and the Heterotrait Monotrait Ratio (HTMT). As Table 2 demonstrates, the discriminant validity of constructs (Fornell and Larcker Criteria) was tested, the result of which showed that the validity was achieved. HTMT also determined the discriminant validity using the multitrait-multimethod matrix approach. Campbell and Fiske (1959), developed a multitrait-multimethod matrix approach that is highly significant to comprehend the essence of validation processes. There are two ways of determining discriminant validity. The former is because the value exceeds the value of HTMT0.90 of 0.90 and the validity of the construct is doubtful. The second option is to test the null hypothesis (Ho: HTMT $\geq$ 1) against the alternative hypothesis (H a: HTMT < 1). When the value of 1 is included in the confidence interval (H0 is true), it means that there is no discriminant validity (Henseler et al., 2015). Table 3 results indicate that all values are less than the threshold value of 0.90, and the HTMT conclusion also revealed that the level of confidence was not equal to 1 at any of the constructs. These results clearly showed that the discriminant validity of the constructs is acceptable. Table 3 gives the results of HTMT.

Table 3. Results of the measurement model

Construct	Items	Loadings	CR	AVE
Artificial Intelligence Capability (AC)	AC1	0.90	0.908	0.711
	AC2	0.84		
	AC3	0.81		
	AC4	0.83		
Human Capital (HC)	HC1	0.77	0.852	0.536
	HC2	0.66		
	HC3	0.74		
	HC4	0.69		
	HC5	0.79		
Open Innovation (OI)	OI1	0.66	0.900	0.563
	OI2	0.84		

continued on following page

Table 3. Continued

Construct	Items	Loadings	CR	AVE
	OI3	0.72		
	OI4	0.71		
	OI5	0.79		
	OI6	0.79		
	OI7	0.74		
Relational Capital (RC)	RC1	0.85	0.894	0.630
	RC2	0.73		
	RC3	0.71		
	RC4	0.86		
	RC5	0.80		
Structural Capital (SC)	SC1	0.68	0.888	0.532
	SC2	0.84		
	SC3	0.72		
	SC4	0.72		
	SC5	0.73		
	SC6	0.72		
	SC7	0.67		
Tourism Industry Performance (TIP)	TIP1	0.81	0.900	0.563
	TIP2	0.77		
	TIP3	0.70		
	TIP4	0.70		
	TIP5	0.78		
	TIP6	0.77		
	TIP7	0.73		

Figure 2. Measurement model

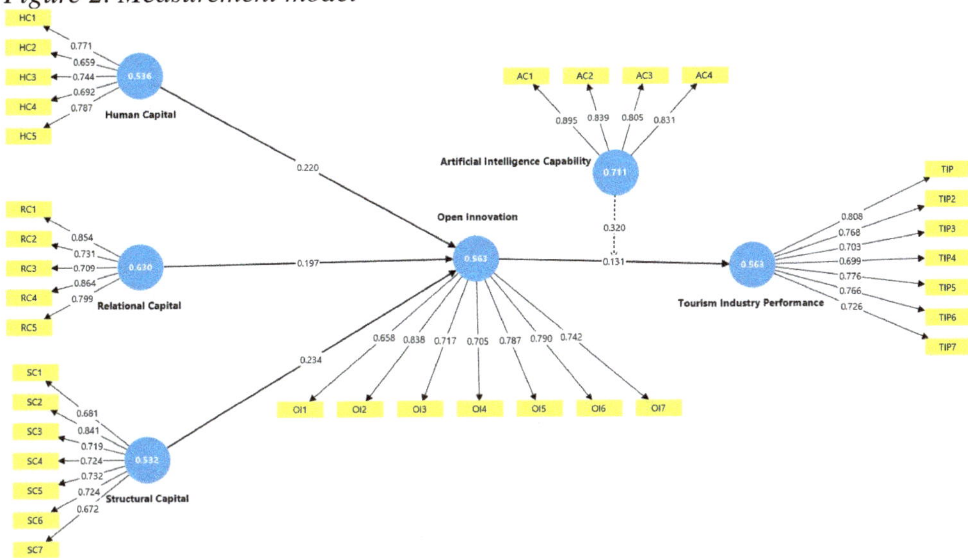

Table 4. Discriminant validity (Fornell and Larcker criteria)

Construct	AIC	HC	OI	RC	SC	TIP
Artificial Intelligence Capability (AIC)	0.843					
Human Capital (HC)	0.378	0.732				
Open Innovation (OI)	0.409	0.443	0.750			
Relational Capital (RC)	0.486	0.502	0.486	0.794		
Structural Capital (SC)	0.510	0.529	0.500	0.761	0.729	
Tourism Industry Performance (TIP)	0.445	0.395	0.364	0.380	0.338	0.750

Table 5. Discriminant validity Heterotrait–Monotrait ratio (HTMT)

Construct	AIC	HC	OI	RC	SC	TIP
Human Capital (HC)	0.483	—				
Open Innovation (OI)	0.460	0.512	—			
Relational Capital (RC)	0.565	0.546	0.515	—		
Structural Capital (SC)	0.590	0.592	0.551	0.862	—	
Tourism Industry Performance (TIP)	0.423	0.442	0.364	0.371	0.327	—
AIC × Open Innovation	0.294	0.120	0.113	0.085	0.100	0.326

Table 6. Hypothesis results

Path	β	t-value	p-value	Decision
HC → OI	0.220	5.953	0.000	Accepted
RC → OI	0.197	3.554	0.000	Accepted
SC → OI	0.234	3.605	0.000	Accepted
HC → TI	0.029	2.678	0.004	Accepted
RC → TI	0.026	2.342	0.010	Accepted
SC → TI	0.031	2.166	0.015	Accepted
OI → TI	0.131	3.155	0.001	Accepted

We carried out SEM (Figure 2) to assess the proposed model. The SEM fits the data nicely, as Table 6 demonstrates. The findings indicate that every hypothesis is validated. Open Innovation (OI) is positively and significantly impacted by Human Capital (HC), Relational Capital (RC), and Structural Capital (SC). Even if the effect sizes (β values) are minor, HC, RC, and SC also significantly and favourably affect the performance of the tourism industry (TI). The performance of the tourism industry (TI) is positively and significantly impacted by open innovation (OI). The hypothesis was accepted since the structural model's empirical study showed that structural capital had a bigger influence on open innovation ($\beta = 0.234$, $t = 3.605$, $p < 0.05$).

4.4 Mediation Analysis

This study examines the role of open innovation in mediating the relationship between the components of intellectual capital and the tourism industry performance. Mediation results of the study are indicated in Table 7. This study would make use of partial mediation, which is identified as the scenario where a mediator is significantly connected with the dependent and independent variables(Baron & Kenny, 1986). Bootstrapping was applied twice with a 350 and 95% confidence interval to determine the mediating effects at 5000 repeats. Hair et al. (2013) suggested a four-step process to assess the position of OI in modulating the correlation between IC and TI. The findings suggest that OI has a partial impact on the relationship between IC and TI and affirm H3.

Table 7. Mediation results

Mediation Path	Indirect Effect (β)	t-value	p-value	Decision
HC → OI → TI	0.029	2.678	0.004	Accepted
RC → OI → TI	0.026	2.342	0.010	Accepted
SC → OI → TI	0.031	2.166	0.015	Accepted

4.5 Moderation Analysis

The results in Table 8 and Figure 2 show that the AIC moderates the relationship between open innovation and tourism industry performance, which means that H4, with β = 0.320, t = 12.73, is supported.

Table 8. Moderation Results

Moderation Path	β	t-value	p-value	Decision
AIC × OI → TI	0.320	12.734	0.000	Accepted

Figure 3. Slope analysis

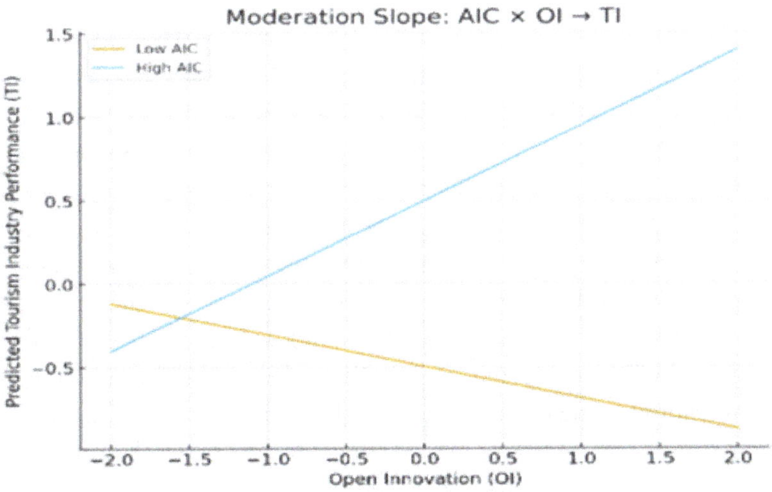

5. DISCUSSION

The primary aim of conducting this study was to establish the effects of the three components of intellectual capital, open innovation, and AI capability on the performance of the tourism sectors of SMEs in Azad Jamu and Kashmir, Pakistan. One of the most identified assets regarding the performance and competitiveness of organizations is the intellectual capital. This study would postulate that intellectual capital is supportive to the SMEs so that their performance can be improved. The findings revealed that human capital has a positive and significant relationship with innovative performance in SMEs. This observation confirms the earlier observation of Ali et al. (2021) and Barrena-Martínez et al. (2020). As a matter of fact, once SMEs are armed with well-skilled employees, they can perform and innovate at a better level. The effect of structural capital and relational capital was equally identified to have a positive and significant relationship with the innovative performance. This study reveals that most of the elements of intellectual capital have been playing a positive role in the augmentation of the tourism industry performance of SMEs in Pakistan. In addition, empirical findings indicated that open innovation has a strong and positive impact on the performance of the tourism industry of SMEs. This means that hotel SMEs situated in the developing countries can improve their tourism performance through the adoption of open innovation practices. This finding was like that of Brüggemann et al. (2022), who confirmed the correlation between open innovation and the performance of firms. This study also reveals that open innovation presents opportunities for new and superior innovations in addressing environmental and social issues within the tourism industry. This aids in developing products and services that are more sustainable and enhances the overall performance of the innovations. In addition, the paper illuminates the role of open innovation as a mediator between the intellectual capital elements and the performance of the tourism industry of SMEs. The results of the present research indicate the fact that open innovation is a substantial mediator of the indirect relationship between the relational, structural, and human capital and the performance of the tourism industry. The open innovation helps SMEs to successfully convert the knowledge and resources entrenched in intellectual capital into innovative practices, products, and services that can be used to become more competitive (Chesbrough & Crowther, 2006). Human capital brings in new ideas by bringing creativity, knowledge, and skills, and structural capital offers the systems and processes that underpin innovation (Chesbrough & Crowther, 2006). The relational capital reinforces external relations with the stakeholders, partners, and customers and supports the flow of valuable knowledge and resources (Khalique et al., 2020). Collectively, these elements create a favourable environment where open innovation can serve as a bridge and enable tourism SMEs to respond to changes in the market, enhance the quality of services, and increase overall performance (Mention, 2011). Lastly, the benefit of moderation is the significance of AI in enhancing efficiency in open innovation practices, with the strong emphasis on investing in AI technology as the means to maximize sustainability outcomes in the hospitality sector. The research points to the positive effect of AI capability on the interaction between open innovation and performance in the tourism industry. This result confirms the previous finding that AIC is a moderator (Badghish & Soomro, 2024). (The findings suggest that AI abilities can support hotels to competently execute and manage open innovative activities by automating work, optimizing the use of resources, and enhancing the decision-making process with the help of advanced data analytics. With AI, one can properly track energy consumption, perform preventive maintenance, and streamline the supply chain, which leads to a reduction in waste and an increase in operational efficiency (Al-Khatib, 2023). Anyone who has developed high artificial intelligence is able to achieve substantial improvements in sustainable performance due to their work in the field of open innovation. The implication of this study improves our general knowledge of how technical capabilities could complement the impact of open innovations on sustainability performance.

5.1. Theoretical Contributions

First, past research on intellectual capital, open innovation practices, and AI capability had been concentrated on high-tech and large firms in developed economies. The results of this study can broaden our knowledge on the relationship that exists between open innovation practice, intellectual capital, AI capability, and the Tourism Industry performance within the setting of SME hotels operating in a developing country, which may also have good implications for SMEs in the same circumstances. Secondly, the existing body of research on OI practice, however, remains based mainly on case studies and conceptual frameworks with limited empirical research on the topic in the context of SMEs. Thus, the paper complements the literature on the impacts of open innovation on intellectual capital and AI capability and consequently on the performance of the Tourism industry by evaluating empirically. This gives further information that can be used to explain the conclusive results. Additionally, the paper sheds some light on the mediation role of open innovation on the positive impact of the components of intellectual capital and the performance of the tourism industry of SMEs. In a more practical sense, the results have vital implications for managers.

5.2. Management and Policy Implications

To begin with, the outcome demonstrates that OI is a major driver of the performance of innovation among SMEs. The new performance of SMEs can be significantly enhanced through the open innovation practice aimed at the stimulation of new idea sharing, creation of knowledge, and provision of complementary resources, new market opportunities, and avenues. It was also discovered that performance in the tourism industry required greater intellectual capital, implying that managers must focus on building and leveraging the intellectual capital wisely. Companies are recommended to train their staff to deepen their work experience and double their human capital, foster a strong bond with their stakeholders to increase the social capital, and create effective systems to enhance the structural capital. Finally, the findings suggest that AI capabilities are significant in enhancing SME hotel performance. Previous studies have established that AI is effective whenever it is utilized in any company. In addition, the results of this current study are specific to the manufacturing SMEs in AJK, Pakistan. The extrapolation of the findings to the whole industry and all types of enterprises requires additional research studies, based on cross-sectional and longitudinal data. Furthermore, as the number of openings increases, the diffusion of intangible knowledge across the borders of firms has the potential to destroy the special resources of the firms and may pose difficulties in regulating the intellectual resources. Hence, it must be investigated even further. To conclude, the results of this research offer one of the practical approaches with which the owners and policymakers could realize eco-innovation and comprehend the role of AIC effectiveness. They must provide more positive conditions that promote AI adoption and the exchange of information. This study contributes to the available data and proposes necessary support to the process of implementing and formulating policies in organizations.

5.3. Limitations and Further Studies

The limitations of the investigation should be brought up. To start with, only SME based hotels of Azad Jammu and Kashmir were considered during the study. As a result, the sample was found to be nonrepresentative of the entire class of hotels. Therefore, the research could be replicated by using another source of market, like SME hotels in other geographical locations, or by hotels having different categories. Moreover, only hotels that were more readily available were sampled. This will provide more information on the procedures of the hotel.

REFERENCES

Abourokbah, S. H., Mashat, R. M., & Salam, M. A. (2023). Role of Absorptive Capacity, Digital Capability, Agility, and Resilience in Supply Chain Innovation Performance. *Sustainability (Basel)*, *15*(4), 3636. Advance online publication. DOI: 10.3390/su15043636

Abrokwah-Larbi, K., & Awuku-Larbi, Y. (2024). The impact of artificial intelligence in marketing on the performance of business organizations: evidence from SMEs in an emerging economy. In *Journal of Entrepreneurship in Emerging Economies* (Vol. 16, Issue 4, pp. 1090–1117). DOI: 10.1108/JEEE-07-2022-0207

Achmad, F., Prambudia, Y., & Rumanti, A. A. (2023). Sustainable Tourism Industry Development: A Collaborative Model of Open Innovation, Stakeholders, and Support System Facilities. *IEEE Access : Practical Innovations, Open Solutions*, *11*(3), 83343–83363. DOI: 10.1109/ACCESS.2023.3301574

Al-azzam, Z. F., Irtaimeh, H. J., & Khaddam, A. A. H. (2017, December). Examining the Mediating Effect of Strategic Agility in the Relationship Between Intellectual Capital and Organizational Excellence in Jordan Service. *International Journal of Management Studies*, *25*. Advance online publication. DOI: 10.32890/ijms.25.1.2018.10496

Al-Khatib, W. (2023). *Drivers of generative artificial intelligence to fostering exploitative and.pdf.*

Ali, M. A., Hussin, N., Haddad, H., Al-Araj, R., & Abed, I. A. (2021). Intellectual capital and innovation performance: Systematic literature review. *Risks*, *9*(9), 1–19. DOI: 10.3390/risks9090170

Arshad, M. Z., Arshad, D., Lamsali, H., Ibrahim Alshuaibi, A. S., Ibrahim Alshuaibi, M. S., Albashar, G., Shakoor, A., & Chuah, L. F. (2023). Strategic resources alignment for sustainability: The impact of innovation capability and intellectual capital on SME's performance. Moderating role of external environment. *Journal of Cleaner Production*, *417*(June), 137884. DOI: 10.1016/j.jclepro.2023.137884

Badghish, S., & Soomro, Y. A. (2024). AI adoption by smes to achieve sustainable business performance. *Sustainability*, *16*(5), 1–24. DOI: 10.3390/su16051864 PMID: 38510213

Barney, J. (1991). Firm resources and sustained competitive advantage. *Journal of Management*, *17*(1), 99–120. DOI: 10.1177/014920639101700108

Baron, R. M., & Kenny, D. A. (1986). The moderator–mediator variable distinction in social psychological research: Conceptual, strategic, and statistical considerations. *Journal of Personality and Social Psychology, 51*(6), 1173–1182. DOI: 10.1037/0022-3514.51.6.1173 PMID: 3806354

Barrena-Martínez, J., Cricelli, L., Ferrándiz, E., Greco, M., & Grimaldi, M. (2020). Joint forces: Towards an integration of intellectual capital theory and the open innovation paradigm. *Journal of Business Research, 112*(June), 261–270. DOI: 10.1016/j.jbusres.2019.10.029

Bigliardi, B., Filippelli, S., & Tagliente, L. (2022). Industry 4.0 and Open Innovation: Evidence from a case study. *Procedia Computer Science, 200*(2019), 1796–1805. DOI: 10.1016/j.procs.2022.01.380

Bogers, M., Chesbrough, H., & Moedas, C. (2019). Open innovation: Research, practices, and policies. *California Management Review, 60*(2), 5–16. DOI: 10.1177/0008125617745086

Bontis, N. (1998). Intellectual capital: An exploratory study that develops measures and models. *Management Decision, 36*(2), 63–76. DOI: 10.1108/00251749810204142

Brüggemann, E. R., Monteiro, J. J., & Lunkes, R. J. (2022). The influence of performance measurement systems on organizational agility and open innovation. *Revista de Contabilidade e Organizacoes, 16*. Advance online publication. DOI: 10.11606/issn.1982-6486.rco.2022.193897

Campbell, D. T., & Fiske, D. W. (1959). Convergent and discriminant validation by the multitrait-multimethod matrix. *Psychological Bulletin, 56*(2), 81–105. DOI: 10.1037/h0046016 PMID: 13634291

Cepeda, G., & Vera, D. (2007). Dynamic capabilities and operational capabilities: A knowledge management perspective. *Journal of Business Research, 60*(5), 426–437. DOI: 10.1016/j.jbusres.2007.01.013

Chen, J., Zhao, X., & Wang, Y. (2015). A new measurement of intellectual capital and its impact on innovation performance in an open innovation paradigm. *International Journal of Technology Management, 67*(1), 1–25. DOI: 10.1504/IJTM.2015.065885

Chesbrough, H. (2003). *Open innovation: The new imperative for creating and profiting from technology*. Harvard Business School Press.

Chesbrough, H. (2006). Open innovation: a new paradigm for understanding industrial innovation. *Open Innovation: Researching a New Paradigm, 400*, 0–19.

Chesbrough, H., & Crowther, A. K. (2006). Beyond high tech: Early adopters of open innovation in other industries. *Research Management, 36*(3), 229–236.

Chin, W. W. (1998). Commentary: Issues and opinion on structural equation modeling. In *MIS quarterly* (pp. vii–xvi). JSTOR.

Cimino, at el., 2025. (2025). *Corp Soc Responsibility Env - 2025 - Cimino - Artificial Intelligence Adoption for Sustainable Growth in SMEs An Extended (1).pdf.*

Cohen, L., & Levinthal, D. A. (1990). Absorptive capacity: A new perspective on learning and innovation. *Administrative Science Quarterly, 35*(1), 128–152. DOI: 10.2307/2393553

Costa, A., Crupi, A., De Marco, C. E., & Di Minin, A. (2023). SMEs and open innovation: Challenges and costs of engagement. *Technological Forecasting and Social Change, 194*(June 2022), 122731. DOI: 10.1016/j.techfore.2023.122731

Dwivedi, Y. K., Hughes, L., Ismagilova, E., Aarts, G., Coombs, C., Crick, T., Duan, Y., Dwivedi, R., Edwards, J., Eirug, A., Galanos, V., Ilavarasan, P. V., Janssen, M., Jones, P., Kar, A. K., Kizgin, H., Kronemann, B., Lal, B., Lucini, B., & Williams, M. D. (2021). Artificial intelligence (AI): Multidisciplinary perspectives. *International Journal of Information Management, 57*, 101994. DOI: 10.1016/j.ijinfomgt.2019.08.002

Dzenopoljac, V., Senic, V., Labben, T. G., Arici, H. E., & Koseoglu, M. (2025). Intellectual capital in hospitality and tourism: A critical review and future research agenda. *International Hospitality Review, 39*(1), 124–143. DOI: 10.1108/IHR-02-2023-0010

Eisenhardt, K. M., & Martin, J. A. (2017). Dynamic capabilities: what are they? *The SMS Blackwell handbook of organizational capabilities*, 341-363.

Gebremichael, H. S. (2018). The impact of open innovation practice on innovative performance through intellectual capital: Empirical study on SMEs. *African Journal of Business Management, 12*(20), 609–619. DOI: 10.5897/AJBM2018.8651

Samuel Godadaw. (2025). *Artificial intelligence adoption dynamics and knowledge in SMEs and large.pdf.*

Hair, J.Jr, Sarstedt, M., Hopkins, L., & Kuppelwieser, G., V. (. (2014). Partial least squares structural equation modeling (PLS-SEM) An emerging tool in business research. *European Business Review, 26*(2), 106–121. DOI: 10.1108/EBR-10-2013-0128

Hair, J. F.Jr, Ringle, C. M., & Sarstedt, M. (2013). Partial least squares structural equation modeling: Rigorous applications, better results and higher acceptance. *Long Range Planning*, *46*(1–2), 1–12. DOI: 10.1016/j.lrp.2013.01.001

Halpern, N., Mwesiumo, D., Budd, T., Suau-Sanchez, P., & Bråthen, S. (2021). Segmentation of passenger preferences for using digital technologies at airports in Norway. *Journal of Air Transport Management*, *91*, 102005. DOI: 10.1016/j.jairtraman.2020.102005

Hambrick, D. C., & Mason, P. A. (1984). Upper echelons: The organization as a reflection of its top managers. *Academy of Management Review*, *9*(2), 193–206. DOI: 10.2307/258434

Hassan, M. U., & Iqbal, A. (2020). Open Innovation and Innovative Performance of Pakistani SMEs: Moderated Mediation of Knowledge Management Capability and Innovative Climate. *Pakistan Journal of Commerce and Social Science*, *14*(4), 962–990.

Helfat, C. E., & Peteraf, M. A. (2003). The dynamic resource-based view: Capability lifecycles. *Strategic Management Journal*, *24*(10), 997–1010. DOI: 10.1002/smj.332

Henseler, J., Ringle, C. M., & Sarstedt, M. (2015). A new criterion for assessing discriminant validity in variance-based structural equation modeling. *Journal of the Academy of Marketing Science*, *43*(1), 115–135. DOI: 10.1007/s11747-014-0403-8

Huma, S., Muslim, S., & Ahmed, W. (2024). Understanding the role of organizational intellectual capital on developing absorptive capacity to strategize innovation ambidexterity. *Review of International Business and Strategy*. DOI: 10.1108/RIBS-08-2023-0088

Hussain, S., Ahmad, N. H., & Syed, T. (2025). (2025). *Green and smart sustainable performance of.pdf*. malque.pub.

Jabarzadeh, Y., Khangah, M. H., Çemberci, M., Cerchione, R., & Sanoubar, N. (2022). Effect of Absorptive Capacity on Strategic Flexibility and Supply Chain Agility: Implications for Performance in Fast-Moving Consumer Goods. *Operations and Supply Chain Management*, *15*(3), 407–423. DOI: 10.31387/oscm0500356

Jutidharabongse, J., Imjai, N., Pantaruk, S., Surbakti, L. P., & Aujirapongpan, S. (2024). Exploring the effect of management control systems on dynamic capabilities and sustainability performance: The role of open innovation strategy amidst COVID-19. *Journal of Open Innovation*, *10*(1), 100224. DOI: 10.1016/j.joitmc.2024.100224

Khalique, M.. (2018). Intellectual capital and SME performance. *Journal of Intellectual Capital*, *19*(1), 1–21.

Khalique, M., & Bontis, N., Abdul Nassir bin Shaari, J., & Hassan Md. Isa, A. (. (2015). Intellectual Capital in Pakistani Small Medium Enterprises. *Journal of Intellectual Capital, 16*(1), 224–238. DOI: 10.1108/JIC-01-2014-0014

Khalique, M., Hina, K., Ramayah, T., & Shaari, J. A. N. (2020). Intellectual capital in tourism SMEs in Azad Jammu and Kashmir, Pakistan. *Journal of Intellectual Capital, 21*(3), 333–355. DOI: 10.1108/JIC-11-2018-0206

Khan, N. U., Anwar, M., Li, S., & Khattak, M. S. (2021). Intellectual capital, financial resources, and green supply chain management as predictors of financial and environmental performance. *Environmental Science and Pollution Research International, 28*(16), 19755–19767. DOI: 10.1007/s11356-020-12243-4 PMID: 33405102

Kornowski, R. (2016). Contemporary issues related to STEMI management. *Minerva Cardioangiologica, 64*(3), 217–218. PMID: 27149504

Kraaijenbrink, J. (2011). Human Capital in the Resource-Based View. *The Oxford Handbook of Human Capital, April 2018*, 1–24. DOI: 10.1093/oxfordhb/9780199532162.003.0009

Martin Lackéus, 2015. (2015). *No Title.*

Lee, C. (2023). *Knowledge sharing and innovation performance: a case study on the impact of organizational culture, structural capital, human resource management practices, and relational capital of real estate agents. 51.* DOI: 10.1057/s41599-023-02185-w

Lo, C., Wang, C., & Chen, Y. C. (2020). The mediating role of intellectual capital in open innovation in the service industries. *Sustainability (Basel), 12*(12), 1–12. DOI: 10.3390/su12125220

Mariani, M. M., & Borghi, M. (2019). Industry 4.0 in tourism. *Tourism Management, 72*, 243–256.

Mention, A. L. (2011). Co-operation and co-opetition as open innovation practices in the service sector: Which influence on innovation novelty? *Technovation, 31*(1), 44–53. DOI: 10.1016/j.technovation.2010.08.002

Moradi, E., Jafari, S. M., Doorbash, Z. M., & Mirzaei, A. (2021). Impact of organizational inertia on business model innovation, open innovation and corporate performance. *Asia Pacific Management Review, 26*(4), 171–179. DOI: 10.1016/j.apmrv.2021.01.003

Mulyono, H., & Syamsuri, A. R. (2023). Organizational Agility, Open Innovation, and Business Competitive Advantage: Evidence from Culinary SMEs in Indonesia. *International Journal of Social Science and Business*, *7*(2), 268–275. DOI: 10.23887/ijssb.v7i2.54083

Najar, T., Dhaouadi, K., & Ben Zammel, I. (2020). Intellectual capital impact on open innovation: The case of technology-based sectors in Tunisia. *Journal of Innovation Economics and Management*, *32*(2), 75–106. DOI: 10.3917/jie.032.0075

Ndiaye., …. (2018). *Demystifying small and medium enterprises' (SMEs) performance in emerging and developing economies | Elsevier Enhanced Reader*. https://reader.elsevier.com/reader/sd/pii/S2214845018300280?token=9DA9B61DEE297BFD4628B3B1DBFA5C36C1037960FE9BD6FB93AAB4796BF3DA66AF0180F3289221C0D5B92ECEFCB5A925&originRegion=eu-west-1&originCreation=20211118213959

Neal, T. O. (2015). Evolving a Successful University-Based Incubator. *Lessons Learned From the UCF Technology Incubator.*, *9247*. Advance online publication. DOI: 10.1080/10429247.2005.11415293

Necula, S. C., Dumitriu, F., & Greavu- erban, V. (2024). A systematic literature review on using natural language processing in software requirements engineering. *Electronics (Basel)*, *13*(11), 2055. DOI: 10.3390/electronics13112055

Obradović, T., Vlačić, B., & Dabić, M. (2021). Open innovation in the manufacturing industry: A review and research agenda. *Technovation*, *102*, 102221. Advance online publication. DOI: 10.1016/j.technovation.2021.102221

Omerzel, D. G., & Jurdanab, D. S. (2016). The influence of intellectual capital on innovativeness and growth in tourism SMEs: Empirical evidence from Slovenia and Croatia. *Ekonomska Istrazivanja*, *29*(1), 1075–1090. DOI: 10.1080/1331677X.2016.1211946

Rúben Pinhal, at el. (2025). *Open_Innovation_in_the_Tourism_Industry_A_Systemat.pdf*.

Puccio, A., Manocchio, M. C., & Di Virgilio, F. (2025). Strategic Application of AI Tools in Enhancing Tourism for SMEs: The Tourist Management in the Seismic Risk Areas.

Ramírez-Solis, E. R., Llonch-Andreu, J., & Malpica-Romero, A. D. (2022). Relational capital and strategic orientations as antecedents of innovation: Evidence from Mexican SMEs. *Journal of Innovation and Entrepreneurship*, *11*(1), 42. Advance online publication. DOI: 10.1186/s13731-022-00235-2

Shokry, R. B. (2025). Exploring the Impact of Artificial Intelligence on Urban Design. In *Journal of Engineering Sciences* (Vol. 53, Issue 4, pp. 457–473). DOI: 10.21608/jesaun.2025.370145.1459

Soo, C., Tian, A. W., Teo, S. T. T., & Cordery, J. (2017). Intellectual Capital–Enhancing HR, Absorptive Capacity, and Innovation. *Human Resource Management, 56*(3), 431–454. DOI: 10.1002/hrm.21783

Szromek, A. R., & Polok, G. (2022). A business model for spa tourism enterprises: Transformation in a period of sustainable change and humanitarian crisis. *Journal of Open Innovation, 8*(2), 72. DOI: 10.3390/joitmc8020072

Teece, D. J. (2007). Explicating dynamic capabilities: The nature and microfoundations of (sustainable) enterprise performance. *Strategic Management Journal, 28*(13), 1319–1350. DOI: 10.1002/smj.640

Thomas, R., & Wood, E. (2015). The absorptive capacity of tourism organisations. *Annals of Tourism Research, 54*, 84–99. DOI: 10.1016/j.annals.2015.06.004

Tornatzky, L. G., & Fleischer, M. (1990). *The processes of technological innovation*. Lexington Books.

Truong, B. T. T., & Nguyen, P. V. (2023). Driving business performance through intellectual capital, absorptive capacity, and innovation: The mediating influence of environmental compliance and innovation. *Asia Pacific Management Review, xxxx*. Advance online publication. DOI: 10.1016/j.apmrv.2023.06.004

Ur Rehman, S., Elrehail, H., Alsaad, A., & Bhatti, A. (2022). Intellectual capital and innovative performance: A mediation-moderation perspective. *Journal of Intellectual Capital, 23*(5), 998–1024. DOI: 10.1108/JIC-04-2020-0109

Verhoef, P. C., Broekhuizen, T., Bart, Y., Bhattacharya, A., Dong, J. Q., Fabian, N., & Haenlein, M. (2021). Digital transformation: A multidisciplinary reflection and research agenda. *Journal of Business Research, 122*, 889–901. DOI: 10.1016/j.jbusres.2019.09.022

Vrontis, D.. (2022). Digital transformation and innovation in SMEs. *Journal of Business Research, 145*, 311–322.

Wang, M. C., Chen, P. C., & Fang, S. C. (2021). How environmental turbulence influences firms' entrepreneurial orientation: The moderating role of network relationships and organizational inertia. *Journal of Business and Industrial Marketing, 36*(1), 48–59. DOI: 10.1108/JBIM-05-2019-0170

Wernerfelt, B. (1984). A resource-based view of the firm. *Strategic Management Journal*, *5*(2), 171–180. DOI: 10.1002/smj.4250050207

Zahra, S. A., Sapienza, H. J., & Davidsson, P. (2006). Entrepreneurship and dynamic capabilities: A review, model and research agenda. *Journal of Management Studies*, *43*(4), 917–955. DOI: 10.1111/j.1467-6486.2006.00616.x

Chapter 10
Modeling and Empirical Evaluation of the Impact of Business Intelligence on Strategic Behavior in the High-Technology Sector

Latifa Zeddini Zeddini
https://orcid.org/0009-0006-4166-186X
Faculty of Economic Sciences and Management of Tunis, Tunisia

Belgacem B. Bchini
https://orcid.org/0000-0002-2790-3504
Higher Institute of Management of Tunis, Tunisia

ABSTRACT

This chapter examines how business intelligence shapes organizational strategic behavior through integrated processes of information monitoring, protection, and strategic influence. Drawing on the Miles and Snow (1978) typology, it proposes a conceptual and empirical model demonstrating how business intelligence contributes to the development of reactor, analyzer, prospector, and defender behaviors by strengthening anticipation, organizational learning, and strategic coherence. Beyond recent theoretical developments on the cognitive and organizational mechanisms through which information is transformed into strategic action, the chapter incorporates an empirical study validating the positive influence of business intelligence on each strategic profile. The four hypotheses linking business intelligence to different

DOI: 10.4018/979-8-3373-9958-4.ch010

strategic behaviors are tested and discussed, providing a solid foundation for future research aiming to deepen the understanding of these relationships across diverse organizational contexts..

INTRODUCTION

Over the past several decades, organizations have increasingly developed systems for environmental observation, monitoring, and analysis in order to collect the information required for informed decision-making. In an environment characterized by complexity, uncertainty, and informational turbulence, decision-makers must rely on accurate and timely information to determine the most relevant long-term strategic behaviors. This requires adopting a managerial approach based on knowledge, anticipation, and proactive adaptation (Pupion, 2018; Teece, 2020).

Today, high-performing organizations are distinguished by their agility and resilience, which enable them to seize emerging opportunities and rapidly abandon initiatives that have become overly risky (Cao et al., 2013; Doz, 2020). This strategic agility largely relies on integrated Business Intelligence (BI) systems, which combine the collection, processing, and dissemination of relevant information to support innovation, competitiveness, and organizational sustainability (Bisson, 2021; Moustaghfir & Schiuma, 2023). These systems go beyond mere data monitoring, acting as essential catalysts for strategic decision-making processes.

The objective of this chapter is to explore the role of Business Intelligence in structuring strategic behaviors within organizations by providing both theoretical foundations and empirical validation. The primary aim is to develop a conceptual model linking Business Intelligence to the four strategic profiles identified by Miles and Snow (1978): reactor, analyzer, prospector, and defender. This typology is particularly relevant for understanding how BI affects strategic positioning and organizational adaptation, as each profile represents a distinct approach to strategic behavior in response to market and environmental changes. The Miles and Snow framework offers a valuable lens through which to analyze how Business Intelligence influences organizational responses to uncertainty and opportunity exploitation.

The chapter also incorporates an empirical analysis to test this model, thereby validating the influence of Business Intelligence on these four strategic profiles. The findings suggest that BI not only supports strategic monitoring but also actively contributes to the adjustment and orientation of organizational behaviors. These results demonstrate that Business Intelligence plays a transformative role, enabling organizations to move from reactive behaviors toward more proactive and anticipatory strategies.

Through this dual approach, the chapter offers significant theoretical and practical contributions. From a theoretical perspective, it advances the understanding of Business Intelligence as a critical organizational lever influencing strategic behavior. From a practical standpoint, it provides concrete recommendations for managers on how to develop and implement integrated BI systems that go beyond simple information collection. For instance, organizations that adopt a proactive Business Intelligence approach: monitoring, analysis, and influence are better positioned to anticipate market trends, optimize strategic choices, and strengthen their competitive position (Levet, 2020).

In addition to its theoretical and practical contributions, this chapter addresses several key concepts. Notions such as strategic agility and organizational learning capability are central to understanding how Business Intelligence stimulates adaptive behaviors within organizations. For greater clarity, these concepts are defined and illustrated through concrete examples drawn from industries that have successfully integrated BI systems. Such examples help contextualize abstract theories and provide tangible insights into how Business Intelligence contributes to real-world decision-making processes. For example, firms in the technology sector have leveraged BI systems to continuously monitor market changes, enabling rapid innovation and sustained competitive advantage (Bisson, 2021).

However, certain limitations must be acknowledged. Although the proposed model is empirically validated within the scope of this chapter, testing it across diverse organizational contexts would enhance its robustness and generalizability. Moreover, this study only partially addresses contextual factors such as organizational culture, internal structure, and technological maturity, which are crucial in determining the effectiveness of Business Intelligence systems. Future research should further explore these dimensions to better understand why some organizations benefit more from BI than others.

Looking ahead, future research should aim to broaden the empirical evaluation of the model by examining a wider range of industries and incorporating additional mediators or moderators. The impact of emerging technologies: such as artificial intelligence, advanced analytics, and information process automation, deserves particular attention, as these innovations are profoundly transforming how information is produced, analyzed, and integrated into strategic decision-making (Dyer et al., 2023). Furthermore, exploring the relationships between Business Intelligence, risk management, organizational performance, and innovation represents a promising avenue for future research.

In summary, this chapter provides a comprehensive view of the role of Business Intelligence in shaping organizational strategic behaviors. By combining theoretical foundations, conceptual modeling, and empirical validation, it reinforces the understanding of BI as a strategic lever and opens avenues for future research aimed at further exploring the complex relationships between information, knowledge, and organizational strategy.

The remainder of the chapter is structured as follows. The first section presents the theoretical foundations underlying the relationship between Business Intelligence and strategic behavior. The second section develops the research model and formulates the hypotheses guiding the study. The third section describes the empirical framework and research methodology, followed by the presentation and discussion of the results. Finally, the concluding section highlights the main theoretical and managerial contributions, discusses the limitations, and outlines directions for future research.

I. THE THEORETICAL FOUNDATIONS OF THE PROPOSAL FOR A CONCEPTUAL MODEL

Managing an organization is not merely about disseminating information through the establishment of a business intelligence (BI) process (Gloaguen, 2014). It is a long-term program that begins with a strategic intent, involves a thorough analysis of the very nature of the organization's knowledge and know-how, and leads to the implementation of various and tailored tools (Monino, 2020). Thus, this section aims to provide a theoretical overview of the relationship between business intelligence and strategic behavior. This forms the theoretical foundations for proposing a conceptual model.

1. Introduction to the Concepts of Business Intelligence and Strategic Behavior

Business intelligence and strategic behavior are today two fundamental pillars of contemporary managerial analysis. Their convergence has become necessary in an environment marked by complexity, volatility, and intensified competition. Business intelligence (BI), as an organized approach to collecting, processing, disseminating, and utilizing useful information for decision-making (Martre, 1994), is a central tool that enables organizations to adapt or transform their strategic behaviors. Strategic behavior, on the other hand, refers to the set of actions, orientations, reactions, and anticipations undertaken by an organization to ensure its sustainability, maintain or strengthen its competitive position, and shape its business environment (Ansoff, 1984; Mintzberg, 1994).

This first part aims to clarify the theoretical foundations of these two concepts and highlight the points of convergence that justify their integration into a conceptual model focused on the impact of business intelligence on strategic behavior. The literature indeed emphasizes the existence of dynamic interactions between these two dimensions, interactions that manifest notably through BI's ability to enrich strategic analysis, strengthen organizational learning, reduce areas of uncertainty, and support future strategic choices (Gloaguen, 2014; Monino, 2020).

Business intelligence has gradually developed as a multidimensional field, encompassing information collection, protection of intangible assets, risk management, strategic analysis, knowledge production, and influence actions. The first definitions that appeared in the 1950s referred to an information system serving business operations (Luhn, 1958). Later works by Wilensky (1967), Martre (1994), and Harbulot (2004) expanded the scope of the concept, emphasizing its global, systemic, and strategic nature.

Contemporary literature describes business intelligence (BI) as a continuous activity of observation, interpretation, and exploitation of the environment, incorporating both strategic monitoring, informational security, and the implementation of influence strategies (Bisson, 2021). These various dimensions make it a decision-support tool that not only informs the organization but also contributes to the construction of collective intelligence and a renewed strategic vision.

In highly competitive environments, business intelligence becomes a lever for organizational agility, enabling the detection of weak signals, reducing uncertainty, supporting innovation, and anticipating disruptions that could transform markets (Choo, 2023; Bejjani, 2024). It thus constitutes a central intangible resource directly contributing to the formation of organizations' dynamic capabilities.

As for strategic behavior, it has been at the heart of managerial thought since the foundational works of Chandler (1962), Ansoff (1984), and Mintzberg (1994). It refers to the set of deliberate or emergent actions taken by an organization to respond to the constraints and opportunities in its environment. This behavior can take different forms, ranging from adaptive reactions to anticipatory, even proactive approaches aimed at influencing the competitive landscape. In the literature, several schools of thought have attempted to conceptualize strategic behavior. The strategic planning school emphasizes rational analysis and the formalization of choices, while the organizational processes approach highlights the role of routines, learning, and internal capabilities. More recently, resource-based perspectives (Resource-Based View) and dynamic capabilities (Teece, 2007) have highlighted the central role of intangible assets – including information, knowledge, and collective skills – in the development of strategic behavior.

A key model for understanding the dynamics of strategic behavior is the one proposed by Miles and Snow (1978), who developed a typology of organizational strategic behaviors. According to them, organizations adopt different strategies depending on how they react to changes and adapt to their competitive environment: "defenders," who adopt a protection strategy by focusing on a niche market and optimizing internal resources to maintain their competitive position; "prospectors," who take a proactive approach and continuously seek new market opportunities, focusing on innovation and diversification; "analyzers," who combine these two approaches by remaining relatively stable in their main sector while exploring less risky external opportunities; and finally, "reactors," who lack a clear strategy, react to changes in a disordered and often delayed manner, making them vulnerable to competition.

This typology continues to be the subject of recent studies. Wickramasinghe and Wickramasinghe (2023) show that strategic orientation according to Miles & Snow influences organizational and individual values, which in turn affect creative performance. A study conducted in 2023 on a developing economy, such as Ghana, confirms that the "prospector" orientation is the most successful in turbulent environments (Osei, 2023).

Thus, strategic behavior is not just a response to environmental stimuli. It is also a cognitive and organizational process, based on interpreting the environment, creating knowledge, and the organization's ability to update its resources to maintain or strengthen its competitive advantage. Business intelligence, which encompasses all processes of collecting, analyzing, protecting, and leveraging strategic information, plays a central role in this process: it allows the organization to better understand its competitive environment, anticipate market developments, and adopt appropriate strategic behaviors. Whether defending its position, innovating, or combining these approaches, business intelligence becomes an essential lever for adjusting strategic behavior based on the threats and opportunities identified in the environment.

2. Application of Business Intelligence from a Defensive and Offensive Perspective

The link between business intelligence (BI) and strategic behavior has been at the heart of discussions and research on business intelligence. We attempt to shed light on this connection by showing how business intelligence influences the strategic behavior of organizations. Many researchers and theorists have emphasized the importance of this relationship. In fact, Baumard (2020) associate business intelligence with a strategic tool within the company. They present it as a decision-support process that improves the company's competitiveness (Martre, 1994).

To explain this relationship, we propose to demonstrate that business intelligence is capable of enhancing strategic behavior, shifting from a classic offensive behavior to one that is not only defensive but also a true strategic weapon.

In an environment characterized by increasing instability, it is essential to take into account the phenomena of uncertainty, complexity, and turbulence. In such a context, the strategic behavior of the organization must be oriented toward the future, considering evolution, while maintaining a particular focus on appropriate behavior.

In the 1950s, the concept of surveillance was particularly linked to the strategic planning school, aiming to detect opportunities and threats (Bernat, 2008). The objective was to ensure the organization's adaptation to its external environment. According to Fissellier et al. (2018), the concept of business intelligence was first used by Luhn (1958), who described it as a communication system serving business operations. Since then, the concept has evolved to be applicable to all types of organizations.

According to Gueye (2017), various applications have been attached to business intelligence, giving it different meanings. For some, it signifies espionage, obtaining information through reprehensible means such as corruption, document theft, and phone tapping. However, these practices do not align with business intelligence, as they are illegal and violate ethical standards (Salvetat, 2011). Other authors reduce it to strategic monitoring, which captures and processes signals from the environment. This position is rather limiting because it excludes the possibility of acting on this environment. Oubrich (2007) asserts that the objective of strategic monitoring is to detect opportunities and reduce uncertainty. However, business intelligence is more ambitious, as it also seeks to influence the environment and control the organization's assets.

Thus, various researchers have considered strategic monitoring as the starting point of the business intelligence process. It is not limited to being merely an activity that detects information to anticipate opportunities and threats, but it also enables the organization to develop the ability to influence its environment and defend itself.

In this sense, business intelligence also plays a crucial role in regularly verifying the effectiveness of protective measures, making the necessary adjustments as soon as a new risk is identified. It monitors the evolution of the environment that may form threats to the realization of the organization's strategic behaviors. Similarly, thanks to alert systems, risks are detected in real-time, and responses are immediate.

Moreover, strategic behavior through business intelligence enables the organization to respond quickly to changes. The company must remain open to all possibilities in order to adapt. It must continuously make the necessary strategic adjustments to ensure its sustainability and optimize its strategic behavior when facing the environment.

Thus, we propose the idea that business intelligence allows for a renewal of the traditional reactive approach to strategic behavior, moving toward a more active approach. However, "another dimension exists in the literature, although it is not explicitly defined: it is the defensive dimension of business intelligence, which encompasses counterintelligence and the protection of the organization's assets" (Larivert, 2006, p. 19).

To better understand the dual functional nature of business intelligence, it is necessary to distinguish between its two complementary dimensions, defensive and offensive, that guide its implementation within organizations. The following table provides a comparative synthesis of these two approaches, highlighting their objectives, strategic goals, and the key levers of action mobilized.

Table 1. The two logics of business intelligence: Defensive and offensive

Dimensions	Defensive Logic	Offensive Logic
Main Objective	Protect the informational assets and intangible resources	Anticipate, influence, and conquer new strategic spaces
Strategic Goal	Risk reduction and securing competitive position	Creation of competitive advantages and expansion of operational scope
Timeframe	Short to medium term	Medium to long term
Nature of Action	Reactive and preventive	Proactive and forward-looking
Preferred Tools	Counterintelligence, cybersecurity, confidentiality, crisis management	Strategic monitoring, benchmarking, lobbying, digital influence
Mobilized Actors	Security services, legal department, crisis communication	Strategic management, R&D, marketing, international development
Key Competencies	Discretion, control, threat anticipation	Creativity, exploration, decision-making agility
Expected Outcome	Preservation of assets and maintaining stability	Strategic innovation and sustainable competitive advantage

Source: Inspired by Mongereau (2006), Bisson (2021), Levet (2020).

Ultimately, the literature explains that business intelligence, as a practice within the organization, involves three roles: a role in monitoring, a role in information protection, and a role in influence to prepare the organization's strategic behavior. In this sense, it helps the organization to have a dynamic vision of the environment because it bases its strategic behavior on a systematic information approach, fostering a recurring process of analysis, interpretation, and knowledge creation to guide future strategic directions.

3. The Application of Business Intelligence as a Strategic Weapon

The Resource-Based View (RBV) has profoundly renewed the understanding of the sources of sustainable competitive advantage. This perspective, initiated by Barney (1991) and extended by Grant (1996), highlighted the central role of intangible resources, particularly knowledge, organizational routines, and collective learning capabilities, in value creation. In this logic, knowledge appears as the primary strategic lever for sustainable performance. Quinn (1999) already estimated that nearly 75% of the added value generated by companies came from intangible and intellectual resources. Milan (1991), for his part, anticipated the possibility of evaluating a company's intangible capital, particularly in terms of knowledge and organizational skills. This perspective gives business intelligence (BI) the status of a strategic resource, both cognitive and informational, which underpins the construction of any sustainable competitive advantage (Levet, 2020).

In this context, business intelligence (BI) is defined as an organized, systematic, and continuous approach serving strategic management, with the goal of improving company competitiveness through the collection, processing, dissemination, and enhancement of relevant information for decision-making (Martre, 1994; Goria, 2006). This approach makes information a strategic asset, which, when transformed into knowledge, becomes a critical resource in decision-making and action processes. Therefore, BI is not limited to a defensive logic: it represents a true strategic weapon contributing to the design and adaptation of organizational behaviors. In environments characterized by complexity, uncertainty, and rapid change, business intelligence systems are used to anticipate disruptions, seize opportunities, and reduce emerging threats (Moustaghfir & Schiuma, 2023).

The history of business intelligence reveals a progressive expansion of its scope. As early as the 1950s, the concept of strategic surveillance, linked to the planning school, aimed to detect opportunities and threats in the environment (Bernat, 2008). Subsequently, the approach became institutionalized and integrated into public policies, particularly in the United States, with the National Information Infrastructure, the Global Information Infrastructure, and the creation of the Advocacy Center, responsible for coordinating competitive approaches within the Department of Commerce. This evolution illustrates the recognition of BI as a lever of influence and economic power at the national level.

On the managerial side, several authors emphasize that business intelligence is not just a process of accumulating information, but an activity of knowledge production (Wilensky, 1967; Harbulot, 2004). By transforming raw data into actionable knowledge, it fosters the construction of a coherent strategic vision capable of proactively guiding decisions. BI thus helps reduce strategic myopia (Salvetat, 2011) and increase organizational learning capacity through the analysis and interpretation of weak signals from the competitive environment (Marcon, 2011; Cohen, 2007). This anticipatory function is now amplified by digitalization and the use of artificial intelligence technologies, which enable automated monitoring and predictive analysis of market trends (Bisson, 2021; Dufour & Beaudry, 2024). Figure 1 illustrates the circular and interactive process through which business intelligence transforms data into competitive advantage.

Figure 1. Cognitive cycle of business intelligence

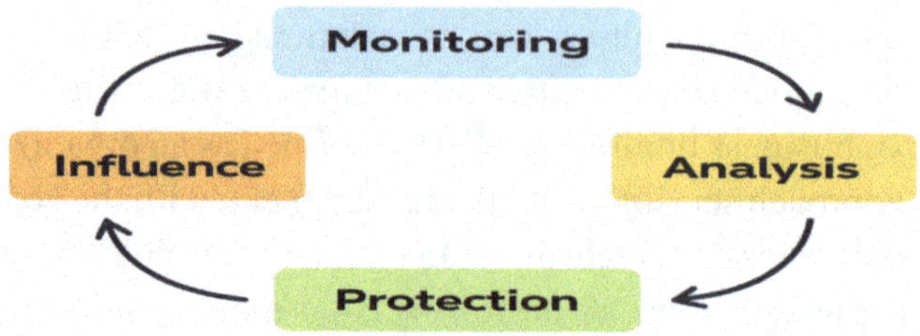

Recent studies confirm that the competitiveness of companies now depends on their ability to control these information flows and to derive a dynamic interpretation from them (Gloaguen, 2012; Bejjani, 2024). In this perspective, business intelligence is an activity that is informative, anticipatory, and proactive, fitting into logic of collective learning and continuous innovation.

Salles (2006) identifies two complementary functions of business intelligence: on one hand, the protection of the company's intangible assets, which includes the security of knowledge, risk management, and counterintelligence; on the other hand, support for strategic development, through decision support and the creation of value from information. A third, more recent dimension has now been added: the influence function (Ledi, 2024), which aims to shape the company's external environment by influencing the norms, opinions, and perceptions of its stakeholders.

Thus, business intelligence can be described as a global cognitive system, linking protection, innovation, and influence. It is based on the circulation and enhancement of information, contributing to collective organizational learning and the development of an agile strategic behavior.

Business intelligence acts as a transversal strategic lever, enabling organizations to transform information into a sustainable competitive advantage. It feeds into decision-making processes, supports strategic planning, and contributes to the creation of intangible value. The following table highlights the main strategic functions of business intelligence, their action levers, and their effects on organizational performance.

Table 2. The strategic functions of business intelligence

Strategic Function	Description	Main Action Levers	Expected Effects on Performance
Anticipation	Enables the identification of trends, weak signals, and potential disruptions.	Foresight monitoring, predictive analysis, strategic scenarios.	Better responsiveness to changes, reduced decision-making uncertainty.
Coordination	Facilitates the flow of information and coherence among internal actors.	Knowledge sharing, collective intelligence, integrated information systems.	Strategic alignment, smooth decision-making, organizational cohesion.
Organizational Learning	Transforms information into long-term actionable knowledge.	Knowledge capitalization, management of organizational memory, communities of practice.	Sustained innovation, accumulation of key competencies, intangible advantage.
Strategic Influence	Guides external decisions and shapes the competitive environment.	Lobbying, influence communication, institutional partnerships.	Strengthened legitimacy, enhanced image, and negotiation power.
Value Creation	Transforms knowledge into tangible economic assets.	Data exploitation, product/service innovation, differentiated positioning.	Sustainable growth, strengthened competitiveness, and improved overall performance.

Source: Adapted from Baumard (2020), Rouach and Salles (2022), Choo (2023), Ledi (2024), Bejjani (2024).

4. The Mechanisms of Articulation Between Business Intelligence and Strategic Behavior

The articulation between Business Intelligence and strategic behavior relies on a set of interconnected mechanisms through which the three fundamental dimensions of Business Intelligence—information monitoring, information protection, and influence—shape and orient the four strategic behavior profiles identified by Miles and Snow (1978). Recent studies have emphasized that Business Intelligence functions not only as an informational process but as a strategic, cognitive, and organizational infrastructure, capable of guiding firms' adaptive responses in increasingly complex environments (Choo, 2023; Bejjani, 2024; Harbulot, 2024).

Information monitoring has been identified as a central driver in the transition from passive to proactive strategic behavior. According to Rouach & Salles (2022), systematic and anticipatory monitoring strengthens the organization's ability to detect weak signals, identify emerging threats, and capture new market opportunities. This anticipatory capability directly supports prospector behavior, which depends on continuous exploration, and enhances analyzer behavior by providing updated knowledge to balance stability and innovation. Gloaguen (2023) further highlights that insufficient monitoring mechanisms often push firms into unintentional reactive behavior, making monitoring a determining factor in avoiding strategic drift.

The protection dimension of Business Intelligence, which focuses on safeguarding sensitive assets and preserving the integrity of internal knowledge, is particularly aligned with defender strategic behavior. In recent research, Ledi (2024) and Nasri (2012) explain that organizations emphasizing control, operational efficiency, and risk mitigation rely heavily on information protection systems to secure their competitive advantages. Protection also supports analyzer behavior by ensuring that critical competencies are preserved while allowing selected innovation efforts to develop in a secure framework.

Influence, as the third dimension of Business Intelligence, has regained prominence with the rise of informational competition and strategic communication. As highlighted by Harbulot (2024), influence enables firms to shape perceptions, legitimize strategic choices, and reposition themselves in competitive arenas. This capability reinforces prospector behavior by creating favorable conditions for market penetration and also consolidates defender behavior by protecting organizational legitimacy and deterring competitive threats.

In parallel, several recent studies have demonstrated that Business Intelligence interacts with broader mediating mechanisms such as knowledge management, organizational learning, strategic vigilance, information culture, and digital decision-support technologies. Knowledge management transforms information collected through monitoring activities into actionable knowledge, thereby enhancing analytical and decision-making capabilities (Nonaka & Takeuchi, 2021; Bejjani, 2024). Organizational learning facilitates the internalization of insights generated by Business Intelligence, enabling firms to adjust their behaviors and strengthen their capacity for adaptation (Choo, 2023; Cohen & Amar, 2025). Strategic vigilance, which integrates monitoring, interpretation, and decision-making loops, promotes strategic flexibility and ensures that organizations remain alert to environmental disruptions (Rouach & Salles, 2022; Ledi, 2024). Information culture acts as a transversal mechanism reinforcing openness, transparency, and collaboration, conditions identified as essential for effective Business Intelligence integration (Baumard, 2020; Gloaguen, 2023). Finally, recent advances in artificial intelligence and predictive analytics have strengthened decision-support technologies, significantly accelerating the transformation of informational complexity into operational decisions (Kaplan, 2022; Harbulot, 2024).

Taken together, these mechanisms form a cohesive cognitive and organizational system in which information circulates, is enriched, and becomes strategic action. Information monitoring fuels exploration; protection secures core competencies; influence shapes the environment. Through these intertwined processes, Business Intelligence evolves into a genuine engine for constructing strategic behavior, determining whether organizations position themselves as defenders, prospectors, analyzers, or reactors. This systemic perspective aligns with recent research emphasizing the need for integrated approaches to organizational adaptation in uncertain environments (Bejjani, 2024; Cohen & Amar, 2025).

Table 3. Mechanisms linking business intelligence and strategic behavior

Business Intelligence Sub-Dimension	Mediating Mechanism	Effect on Strategic Behavior	References
Information Monitoring	Strategic scanning, weak-signal detection, environmental interpretation	Strengthens prospector orientation, supports analyzer balance, limits reactive drift	Rouach & Salles (2022); Gloaguen (2023); Bejjani (2024)
Information Protection	Security systems, risk control, safeguarding of assets	Reinforces defender and analyzer behaviors	Nasri (2012); Ledi (2024)
Influence	Competitive persuasion, narrative shaping, legitimacy-building	Supports prospector expansion and defender stabilization	Juillet & Racouchot (2012); Harbulot (2024)
Knowledge Management	Knowledge sharing, capitalization, organizational memory	Improves decision-making and supports analyzer/prospector strategies	Nonaka & Takeuchi (2021); Bejjani (2024)
Organizational Learning	Continuous adaptation, feedback integration	Encourages innovative and adaptive behaviors	Choo (2023); Cohen & Amar (2025)
Digital Decision-Support Systems	AI analytics, predictive modelling, big data	Accelerates and rationalizes strategic decisions	Kaplan (2022); Harbulot (2024)

Source: adapted from Nonaka & Takeuchi (2021), Rouach & Salles (2022), Choo (2023), Bejjani (2024), Ledi (2024), Harbulot (2024).

II. MODELING THE LINK BETWEEN BUSINESS INTELLIGENCE AND STRATEGIC BEHAVIOR: BUILDING A RESEARCH MODEL

The analysis of theoretical foundations has highlighted the multiple interactions between business intelligence and strategic behavior. However, to move beyond a purely conceptual perspective, it becomes necessary to propose an integrated model that formalizes these links and clarifies the mechanisms through which business intelligence shapes the strategic dynamics of organizations.

In a context characterized by complexity, digitalization, and heightened market competitiveness, modeling the relationship between these two dimensions aims to identify the key variables, their interrelations, and their effects on organizational performance. This approach follows a systemic logic in which business intelligence operates as a lever of protection, monitoring, and influence, guiding strategic decision-making and the organization's capacity to adapt.

This section therefore seeks to construct a research model that articulates both the theoretical contributions and the empirical dimensions of the link between business intelligence and strategic behavior, with the goal of future validation through quantitative and qualitative investigations.

The relationship between business intelligence and strategic behavior has generated growing interest in the fields of strategic management and information science. Several studies have attempted to demonstrate the nature and strength of this relationship, though consensus has yet to be achieved. Some authors confirm the existence of a significant link between the two concepts, emphasizing the structuring role of business intelligence in shaping and guiding the strategic behavior of organizations (Larivet et al., 2012; Ursacescu et al., 2012; Stefanikova et al., 2015; Kula & Naktiyok, 2021; Rouach & Salles, 2022; Ledi, 2024). These works show that business intelligence operates as both a cognitive and organizational lever, fostering strategic proactivity, adaptation to turbulent environments, and the creation of sustainable competitive advantages.

By contrast, several earlier studies did not confirm this correlation, arguing that business intelligence does not constitute a determining factor of strategic behavior, but rather a peripheral activity focused on information collection (Roiron, 1999; Lemaine, 1997). This theoretical debate has been renewed, however, in light of recent developments in digitalization, organizational transformation, and knowledge management (Nonaka & Takeuchi, 2021; Choo, 2023). These advances tend to reposition business intelligence as a fully strategic function, acting not only on monitoring and the protection of intangible assets, but also on the organization's ability to influence and to engage in collective learning.

More recent studies suggest that the relationship between business intelligence and strategic behavior is indirect or mediated (Freyn & Farley, 2020; Harbulot, 2024). Business intelligence appears to influence strategic behavior through intermediate variables such as skills management, organizational culture, knowledge management, or innovation capability (Gloaguen, 2012; Dufour & Lièvre, 2023). These variables serve as cognitive and cultural channels through which information is transformed into strategic action, enabling organizations to adopt proactive, adaptive, and resilient behaviors.

Understanding the link between business intelligence and strategic behavior thus requires a systemic approach integrating informational processes, organizational mechanisms, and cultural dynamics. The following table provides a synthesis of the main studies that have examined this relationship, distinguishing the type of link identified between business intelligence and strategic behavior.

Table 4. The impact of business intelligence on strategic behavior

Authors	Studies	Nature of the Relationship
Roiron (1999)	Reduces business intelligence to strategic scanning, without a direct link to strategy.	Negative
Baumard (2020)	Business intelligence reshapes the strategic approach, shifting from a reactive to a proactive posture.	Positive
Larivet et al. (2012)	Monitoring, protection, and informational influence shed light on strategic behaviors.	Positive
Ursacescu et al. (2012)	The integration of business intelligence into strategic management modernizes organizational governance.	Positive
Nasri (2012)	Business intelligence supports the creation of competitive advantages and organizational performance.	Positive
Djennas et al. (2015)	The role of organizational culture mediates the relationship between business intelligence and strategic behavior.	Indirect
Freyn & Farley (2020)	Corporate culture conditions the positive effect of business intelligence on strategic behavior.	Indirect
Kula & Naktiyok (2021)	Strategic intelligence relies on cognitive capability rather than decision-making power.	Positive
Rouach & Salles (2022)	Business intelligence supports dynamic planning and competitive monitoring.	Positive
Ledi (2024)	Business intelligence enhances strategic responsiveness and decision-making coherence in the digital era.	Positive
Harbulot (2024)	Business intelligence operates through mechanisms of influence and organizational learning.	Indirect

Source: Author's compilation based on works by Larivet et al. (2012), Freyn & Farley (2020), Ledi (2024), Harbulot (2024), and others.

1. The Effect of Business Intelligence on Reactive Strategic Behavior

Recent literature presents diverging views regarding the relationship between business intelligence and the reactive behavior of organizations. This relationship can be interpreted from several angles. Some studies argue that business intelligence has a direct influence on reactive behaviors, while others suggest that its influence occurs indirectly through internal processes such as knowledge management, skills management, or organizational structure. A third line of research even proposes that there is no direct influence between business intelligence and reactive behavior, which further highlights the complexity of this relationship.

Some studies, such as those by Baaziz (2014), support the idea of a direct influence of business intelligence on reactive behaviors. Business intelligence, understood as a structured process of collecting, analyzing, and disseminating strategic information, enables organizations to quickly detect competitive threats, assess their potential impact, and adopt appropriate responses. From this perspective, business intelligence acts as an immediate strategic lever that fosters effective responsiveness to external challenges. Similarly, Ursacescu et al. (2012) emphasize that integrating business intelligence into strategic management represents an approach that directly shapes how an organization adopts a reactive behavior in response to environmental changes. Business intelligence is therefore perceived as an essential resource allowing firms to respond effectively to crises or heightened competition.

However, other studies suggest that the influence of business intelligence on reactive behavior occurs indirectly through organizational intermediaries. According to Gloaguen (2012), business intelligence does not act directly on reactive behavior but through internal processes such as knowledge management and skills management. From this perspective, business intelligence is a strategic lever that helps organizations better manage information flows and develop more reactive strategies by strengthening their internal capabilities. The use of information collected through business intelligence enhances organizational flexibility, anticipation capabilities, and responsiveness to threats, yet these effects occur primarily through internal transformations such as improved employee competencies or adaptations in organizational structure. Business intelligence thus operates as a transformative tool, shaping organizational reactivity by altering information management practices and enhancing agility, rather than triggering an immediate reactive response.

A third, more critical perspective questions whether there is a direct or even indirect relationship between business intelligence and reactive behavior. Some studies argue that business intelligence is primarily a monitoring tool, but does not necessarily guarantee effective strategic responsiveness. For example, Li et al. (2023) observe that although business intelligence improves access to high-quality information, it does not directly lead to increased reactivity in organizations facing environmental pressures. Strategic responsiveness depends more heavily on contextual factors such as organizational culture, firm structure, and leadership flexibility. From this viewpoint, business intelligence plays a complementary but not central role in an organization's ability to react to external threats.

In summary, the relationship between business intelligence and reactive behavior is far from straightforward. While some research highlights a direct influence of business intelligence on strategic reactivity, other work emphasizes its mediating role through internal processes such as knowledge and skills management. Finally, some authors contend that business intelligence has no direct effect on reactive behavior. These contrasting perspectives underscore the complexity of integrating business intelligence into organizational strategy and the variability of its effects across contexts. Based on these theoretical and empirical insights, the following hypothesis is proposed: **H1.** Business intelligence has a positive and significant effect on reactive strategic behavior.

The following table summarizes the different perspectives on this relationship, distinguishing between the direct and indirect influences of business intelligence on the reactive behavior of organizations. This table was developed from the studies of Baaziz (2014), Gloaguen (2012), and Li et al. (2023).

Table 4. The impact of business intelligence on reactive strategic behavior

Perspective	Relationship Between Business Intelligence and Reactive Behavior	Examples of Studies	Nature of the Influence
Direct influence	Business intelligence directly influences the reactive behavior of organizations.	Baaziz (2014), Ursacescu et al. (2012)	Business intelligence enables rapid detection of threats and immediate response.
Indirect influence (through intermediaries)	Business intelligence has an indirect effect, moderated by internal processes (knowledge management, skills management, etc.).	Gloaguen (2012)	Business intelligence strengthens reactivity through internal processes such as skills development and structural adaptation.
Absence of direct or indirect influence	Business intelligence plays a limited role in strategic reactivity and does not guarantee an effective response.	Li et al. (2023)	Business intelligence improves information quality, but reactivity depends on other organizational factors (culture, leadership, etc.).

Source: Prepared by the author

2. The Effect of Business Intelligence on Analyzer Strategic Behavior

Recent research presents contradictory findings regarding the effect of business intelligence on the analyzer behavior of organizations. This strategic behavior, which combines stability in certain activities while actively exploring new opportunities, is grounded in continuous and in-depth analysis of the competitive environment. Some studies suggest that business intelligence exerts a direct influence, whereas others argue that its impact is indirect, operating through organizational processes such as knowledge management or skills management.

The study by Stefanikova et al. (2015) shows that business intelligence can directly improve the competitive position of firms and increase their market share. Conducted in Slovakia in 2014, their research revealed that business intelligence enables firms to better analyze competitors' capabilities and assess the risks to which they are exposed. By providing systematic and regular analysis of external data, business intelligence helps organizations maintain a stable position while strategically exploring new opportunities. According to the authors, this adaptive capacity—made possible by business intelligence—strengthens competitiveness and facilitates the adoption of an effective analyzer behavior.

However, Gloaguen (2022) highlights that the effect of business intelligence on analyzer behavior is not always direct. Although business intelligence provides crucial information, its impact largely depends on internal factors such as knowledge management and the adaptability of the organizational structure. The study shows that business intelligence must be integrated into internal information-management processes to have a tangible effect on strategic behavior. Business intelligence alone is not sufficient to trigger a shift toward analyzer behavior; it acts as a decision-support tool, but its effectiveness depends on the organization's ability to transform information into concrete actions adapted to its environment.

Furthermore, a study by Kumar and Sharma (2024) examines the impact of business intelligence on small and medium-sized enterprises in emerging markets. Their results indicate that although business intelligence improves firms' ability to analyze their environment, its effectiveness in fostering analyzer behavior depends on how the information collected is processed and used within the organization. Without adequate knowledge management or a flexible organizational structure, business intelligence risks remaining an underutilized tool, failing to generate substantial changes in strategic behavior.

These contradictory findings highlight that the impact of business intelligence on analyzer behavior cannot be viewed uniformly. Business intelligence may directly influence analyzer behavior in organizations where information is quickly integrated into the strategic process. In other contexts, however, its role is more indirect, requiring knowledge management and internal structuring that enable the effective use of information for strategic decision-making. These contrasting results lead to the following hypothesis:

H2. Business intelligence has a positive effect on analyzer strategic behavior.

The following table summarizes the different perspectives on the relationship between business intelligence and analyzer behavior, based on studies by Stefanikova et al. (2015), Gloaguen (2023), and Kumar and Sharma (2024).

Table 5. The impact of business intelligence on analyzer strategic behavior

Perspective	Relationship Between Business Intelligence and Analyzer Behavior	Examples of Studies	Nature of the Influence
Direct influence	Business intelligence directly influences the analyzer behavior of organizations.	Stefanikova et al. (2015)	Business intelligence enables regular and systematic analysis of external data to anticipate developments and maintain a stable position.
Indirect influence (through intermediaries)	Business intelligence has an indirect effect, moderated by internal processes (knowledge management, skills management, etc.).	Gloaguen (2023)	Business intelligence strengthens responsiveness through internal processes, such as knowledge management and structural adaptation.
Absence of direct or indirect influence	Business intelligence plays a limited role in strategic reactivity and does not guarantee an effective response.	Kumar and Sharma (2024)	Business intelligence improves analytical capacity, but its effectiveness depends on internal management and organizational flexibility.

Source: Developed by the author

3. The Effect of Business Intelligence on Prospector Strategic Behavior

Baumard (2020) analyzed several empirical studies aimed at assessing the positive effect of business intelligence on strategic behavior. According to their results, business intelligence, as a lever of continuous monitoring, enables the organization to shield itself from attempts at influence or disinformation coming from competitors. It helps detect and evaluate relevant information and ensures organizational protection through the identification of threats and weaknesses. Business intelligence also monitors environmental developments that may pose threats to the achievement of an appropriate strategic behavior for the organization. This is made possible through an alert system that detects risks in real time, enabling rapid and appropriate responses.

Business intelligence allows organizations to react quickly to change while remaining continuously creative and innovative in order to master unstable conditions. The organization must remain open to all possibilities to adapt easily. It must continually make the necessary strategic adjustments to ensure its long-term survival and must optimize its strategic behavior in its confrontation with the environment. In this regard, Baumard (2020) argue that business intelligence renews the traditional reactive approach to strategic behavior, shifting toward a more active and proactive approach adapted to contexts of uncertainty and complexity.

Research carried out by Kula and Naktiyok (2021) had the primary objective of verifying the positive effect of business intelligence on strategic behavior. Data were collected from managers working in five highly competitive automotive industries and three communication industries. According to the results, the implementation of business intelligence practices has a positive and significant effect on the strategic behavior of these firms. The study shows that business leaders must recognize that we now live in an information-driven era. In this sense, although strategic planning remains important, its impact becomes greater when it provides strategic superiority to firms. The defining feature of an effective strategic plan is not power but intellectual capacity, which enables meaningful planning. For this reason, managers who develop strategies need ongoing information monitoring to interpret competitive dynamics, determine their competitive positions, and choose an appropriate strategic behavior.

The study by Bernard (2008) also shows that business intelligence monitors environmental developments that may form threats during the formulation and implementation of the organization's strategic behavior. Thanks to a real-time alert system, risks are detected quickly, allowing timely and appropriate responses. Business intelligence enables the organization to respond rapidly to changes while remaining creative and innovative in order to master an evolving environment. The organization must remain open to all possibilities to adapt and must continuously adjust its strategies to ensure sustainability. Thus, we support the idea that business intelligence renews the traditional reactive approach to strategic behavior and shifts it toward a more active, dynamic approach adapted to complexity and uncertainty.

Salles (2006) demonstrates that business intelligence is a process that begins with the collection of raw data through monitoring systems. This data is then analyzed to become relevant information, which is later transformed into reliable and actionable information for the organization. The business intelligence process continues with information protection and the adoption of an influence strategy whose objective is to modify the environment according to the organization's interests. Through this function, business intelligence becomes a key tool supporting prospector strategic behavior.

Accordingly, we propose the following hypothesis:

H3. Business intelligence has a positive effect on prospector strategic behavior.

The following table summarizes the different perspectives on this topic, based on studies by Baumard (2020), Kula and Naktiyok (2021), and Salles (2006).

Table 6. The impact of business intelligence on prospector strategic behavior

Perspective	Relationship Between Business Intelligence and Prospector Behavior	Examples of Studies	Nature of the Influence
Direct influence	Business intelligence directly influences the prospector behavior of organizations.	Baumard (2020)	Business intelligence enables rapid detection of threats and opportunities, strengthening creativity and innovation within the organization.
Indirect impact	Business intelligence has an indirect impact on prospector behavior by supporting internal processes (strategic monitoring, analysis, etc.).	Kula and Naktiyok (2021)	Business intelligence provides relevant information to interpret competitive dynamics and support strategic planning.
Influence function	Business intelligence acts as a strategic lever allowing the organization to influence its environment to optimize prospector behavior.	Salles (2006)	Business intelligence helps modify the external environment according to the organization's strategic interests, fostering a proactive approach.

Source: Developed by the author

4. The Effect of Business Intelligence on Defender Strategic Behavior

Business intelligence has been widely studied for its effects on the strategic behavior of organizations, particularly defender behavior, which is characterized by the protection and safeguarding of the firm's assets against external threats. Recent research confirms the positive impact of business intelligence in this context, emphasizing both its defensive and offensive roles, while also highlighting contradictory results regarding how it influences defender behavior.

Larivet et al. (2012) conducted an extensive study on the effect of business intelligence on strategic behavior based on a quantitative methodology applied to small and medium-sized enterprises in the Rhône-Alpes region of France. They demonstrated that business intelligence: information monitoring, the protection of sensitive data, and the use of influence techniques, enables firms to better understand competitive practices and refine their strategies. The study reveals that SMEs using business intelligence operate in increasingly international environments and that business intelligence supports defender, analyzer, and prospector strategic behaviors. Thus, business intelligence not only helps organizations adapt to environmental changes but also strengthens their defensive posture against competitive threats.

Another study conducted by Nasri (2012) further investigated the impact of business intelligence on the quality of strategic information used by firms. The findings indicate that business intelligence supports the creation of sustainable competitive advantages, particularly by improving strategic planning and facilitating the introduction of new products. It is perceived as a process that helps organizations better control strategic information and ensure enhanced protection of organizational assets. Firms implementing a business intelligence process can therefore defend themselves more effectively against external risks and strengthen their strategic position, especially in complex and competitive environments.

Mongereau (2006) examined the dual nature of business intelligence in its strategic role: defensive and offensive. The defensive aspect focuses on protecting the company from various threats such as cyberattacks, counterfeiting, or data theft, whereas the offensive aspect seeks to provide organizations with the means to grow and adapt. According to Mongereau, strategic monitoring is one of the main tools of business intelligence, but it must be complemented by broader organizational strategies, such as networking and involving all employees in the decision-making process. This model suggests that business intelligence, by strengthening organizational responsiveness and protecting information, becomes a powerful lever for defender strategic behavior.

However, some authors such as Roiron (1999) and Lemaine (1997) have challenged this view, arguing that business intelligence merely captures external signals, primarily through strategic monitoring, without guaranteeing a direct influence on strategic behaviors. According to these authors, business intelligence is limited to identifying opportunities and reducing uncertainty, without playing an active role in broader strategy formulation. This view has been considered reductive because it overlooks the potential impact of business intelligence within the broader framework of organizational strategy.

Freyn and Farley (2020) adopted a different approach by examining the integration of information monitoring within a healthcare system in the United States. They demonstrated the indirect effect of business intelligence on strategic behavior, emphasizing that the adoption of business intelligence within an organization requires a culture of information sharing and proper data management to foster strategic behavior. In this perspective, business intelligence is not limited to data collection but must be integrated into a cultural and organizational framework that values communication and knowledge sharing.

Finally, Djennas et al. (2015) conducted an empirical study on Algerian SMEs, highlighting the importance of business intelligence in strategic decision-making. Their findings reveal that business intelligence operates not only as a set of technical tools but also as a cultural model in which information management becomes a central organizational value. They showed that for business intelligence to have a positive effect on strategic behavior, it must be understood and applied as a shared organizational culture, implying collective commitment and long-term investment. This perspective suggests that business intelligence, as a process of strategic adaptation, must rely on an organizational culture that is open to information and innovation.

Given the divergent findings regarding the impact of business intelligence on defender strategic behavior, we propose the following hypothesis:

H4. Business intelligence has a positive effect on defender strategic behavior.

The following table summarizes the different perspectives on this topic, based on studies by Larivet et al. (2012), Nasri (2012), Mongereau (2006), and Freyn and Farley (2020).

Table 7. The impact of business intelligence on defender strategic behavior

Perspective	Relationship Between Business Intelligence and Defender Behavior	Examples of Studies	Nature of the Influence
Direct influence	Business intelligence directly influences defender behavior within organizations.	Larivet et al. (2012)	Business intelligence strengthens the organization's defensive position against competitive threats through strategic monitoring and the use of influence techniques.
Indirect impact	Business intelligence has an indirect effect on defender behavior by supporting internal processes (knowledge management, organizational structure, etc.).	Nasri (2012)	Business intelligence supports the creation of sustainable competitive advantages by improving strategic planning and facilitating the introduction of new products.
No direct or indirect influence	Business intelligence plays a limited role in strategic responsiveness and does not guarantee an effective organizational reaction.	Roiron (1999), Lemaine (1997)	Business intelligence is limited to strategic monitoring and identifying opportunities, without having a direct impact on strategic behaviors.

Source: Developed by the author

III. PROPOSAL OF A CONCEPTUAL MODEL

This part introduces the conceptual model developed for this research, aiming to analyze the role of business intelligence in shaping the strategic orientation of organizations. It presents the theoretical foundations supporting the model, details the selected variables and their operationalization, and explains the hypothetical relationships linking business intelligence to the various strategic behaviors.

1. General Presentation of the Conceptual Model

The proposed conceptual model is based on an analytical framework designed to examine the relationship between Business Intelligence and the strategic behaviors of organizations. Business Intelligence is understood as a key strategic process enabling the collection, analysis, protection, and use of strategic information to anticipate environmental changes. It helps firms better understand their competitive landscape, detect risks, and seize opportunities, thereby playing a crucial role in shaping organizational strategies.

In this model, strategic behaviors are grounded in the typology of Miles and Snow (1978), which identifies four forms of organizational adaptation:

- Defender behavior: the organization focuses on securing its assets and protecting its competitive position.
- Prospector behavior: the organization adopts a proactive strategy by constantly seeking new opportunities.
- Analyzer behavior: the organization combines stability in existing activities with the exploration of new opportunities.
- Reactor behavior: the organization responds to environmental changes without proactive planning.

These behaviors are not mutually exclusive, and an organization may adopt several depending on its context. By providing relevant information, Business Intelligence supports organizations in selecting and adapting their strategic behaviors.

Our model assumes that Business Intelligence plays a crucial role in shaping and adjusting organizational strategic behaviors. Business Intelligence allows organizations to better understand the challenges and opportunities within their environment, enabling them to adopt the most appropriate strategic behaviors. For example, defender-type organizations use Business Intelligence to secure their position, whereas prospector-type organizations use it to explore new markets.

Four main hypotheses are proposed to examine the direct effect of Business Intelligence on organizations' strategic behaviors:

- H1. Business Intelligence has a positive and significant effect on reactor strategic behavior.
- H2. Business Intelligence has a positive effect on analyzer strategic behavior.
- H3. Business Intelligence has a positive effect on prospector strategic behavior.
- H4. Business Intelligence has a positive effect on defender strategic behavior.

These hypotheses illustrate how Business Intelligence, as a process of collecting, analyzing, and managing information, directly influences the strategic choices of organizations, whether they seek to defend themselves, innovate, or explore new markets. The conceptual model is presented as follows:

Figure 2. The conceptual model

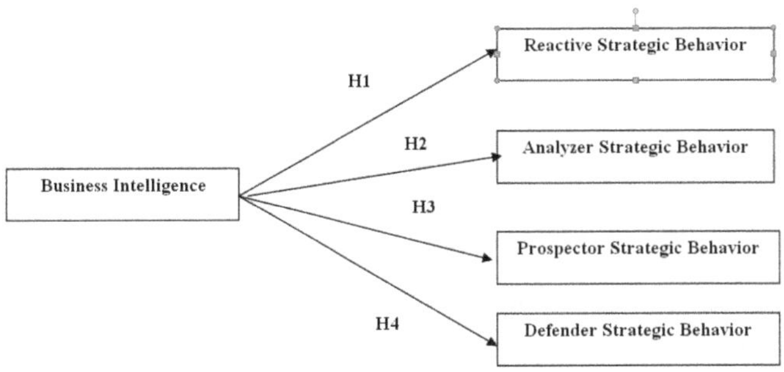

The model illustrates that Business Intelligence and strategic behaviors are closely linked, as the effectiveness of Business Intelligence depends on its ability to directly or indirectly influence the organization's strategic decisions. It offers an integrated view of Business Intelligence and strategic behaviors, highlighting their complementarity within the decision-making process. Business Intelligence is a key strategic lever which, when properly embedded in organizational processes, enables the firm to adjust its behaviors in response to the challenges and opportunities of its competitive environment. By examining the direct impact of Business Intelligence on strategic behaviors through the proposed hypotheses, the model provides a comprehensive understanding of how Business Intelligence supports and guides organizational strategy.

2. Definition and Operationalization of the Model Variables

The independent variable in our model is Business Intelligence. Based on the literature review, we adopt the measurement scale developed by Degan et al. (2018) and Salvetat (2011). Their work relies on contributions from several foundational researchers and practitioners in Business Intelligence. Degan et al. used three methodological approaches (documentary, qualitative, and quantitative) to construct a multidimensional scale composed of 14 items grouped into three dimensions: Information monitoring, Protection and Influence

The items are rated on a five-point Likert scale ranging from 1 ("Strongly agree") to 5 ("Strongly disagree").

Strategic behaviors are the dependent variables of our model. We adopt the typology proposed by Miles and Snow (1978), widely validated and recognized for its diagnostic relevance. The four strategic profiles include: Defender, Prospector, Analyzer and Reactor

To measure these behaviors, we adopt the multi-item scale based on Miles and Snow (1978) and refined by Avci et al. (2011). The questionnaire includes: 12 items for prospector behavior, 6 items for defender behavior, 9 items for analyzer behavior, 9 items for reactor behavior. Responses are assessed using a five-point Likert scale (1 = strongly disagree; 5 = strongly agree).

In addition to their strong theoretical grounding, these measurement scales offer several methodological advantages that justify their use in this research. Both Business Intelligence and strategic behavior are multidimensional constructs that require fine-grained and validated instruments to capture their complexity. Recent studies (Bejjani, 2024; Choo, 2023; Rouach & Salles, 2022) emphasize that Business Intelligence operates through cognitive, organizational, and technological processes, making multidimensional measurement essential for accurately assessing its strategic impact. Similarly, the Miles and Snow typology has demonstrated high reliability and external validity across diverse sectors and countries, confirming its robustness for analyzing organizational adaptation patterns. The combined use of these two validated scales ensures strong methodological consistency in our model, enhances measurement precision, and provides a solid empirical foundation for examining the relationships between Business Intelligence and strategic behaviors.

IV. EMPIRICAL FRAMEWORK AND RESEARCH METHODOLOGY

This section presents the empirical foundations of the study and details the methodological approach used to examine the relationships between business intelligence and the strategic behaviors adopted by organizations.

1. Justification for Choosing the High-Technology Sector

The choice to study Tunisian companies operating in the high-technology sector is justified by the central role this industry now plays in the global economy. For more than a decade, advanced technologies have experienced rapid growth, driven by digitalization, innovation, and the expansion of structured ecosystems such as French Tech, which in 2024 included more than 25,000 startups and over 30 unicorns. This dynamism confirms that high-tech firms evolve in competitive, uncertain, and highly innovative environments that require continuous investment in research and development. These companies rely on specialized knowledge and depend heavily on information mastery, which underscores the importance of business intelligence (BI).

As demonstrated by Baumard (2020), Levet (2001), and Monino (2021), BI helps organizations anticipate technological developments and transform information into knowledge that supports decision-making. Numerous studies (Salvetat, 2011; Baaziz, 2014; Amandine, 2020) have also emphasized that BI, knowledge management, and strategic behavior play a key role in high-tech companies, known for their capacity to disseminate and create new knowledge. In this context, the sector provides a highly relevant setting to analyze the interactions between business intelligence, knowledge management, and strategic behavior.

In Tunisia, the high-technology sector occupies a strategic position and has benefited for several years from an active national digital transition policy. Today, this sector contributes nearly 14% of the national GDP and relies on a large pool of skilled talent, with more than 12,000 engineers graduating each year. Tunisia is consistently ranked among the most advanced technological ecosystems in Africa due to its digital infrastructure, the quality of its education system, and its linguistic and geographic proximity to Europe.

Tunisia's progressive integration into the French Tech dynamic, as well as the establishment of innovative companies such as Numeryx, illustrate the country's attractiveness for technological projects. National authorities, through the Strategic Council of the Digital Economy, aim to position Tunisia as a regional technological hub.

These specific characteristics reinforce the relevance of studying Tunisian high-tech companies, where business intelligence and knowledge management play a crucial role in competitiveness and the structuring of strategic behaviors. To illustrate the technological and economic weight of the sector, the following figure presents two key indicators characterizing Tunisia's high-technology landscape.

Figure 3. Key indicators of Tunisia's high-technology sector

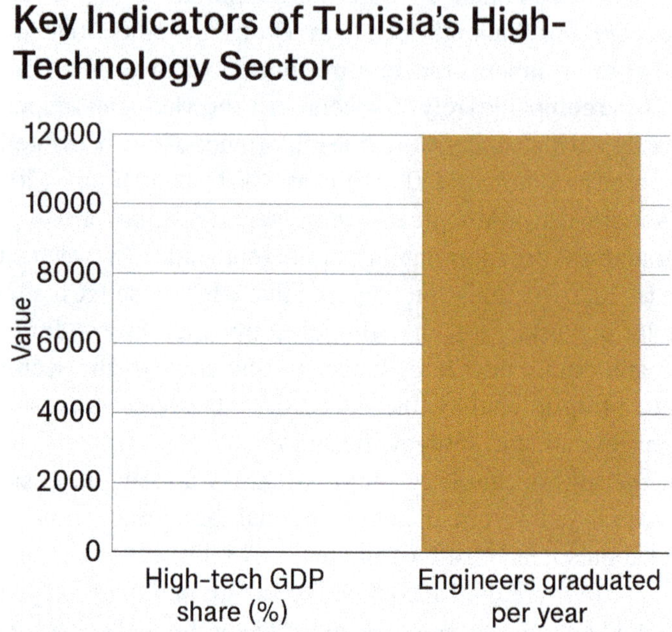

2. Research Methodology

This research adopts a positivist approach, based on the assumption that organizational phenomena can be objectively observed and measured through reliable indicators. This orientation aligns with the objective of empirically examining the relationships between business intelligence, knowledge management, and strategic behaviors—an area that is still evolving but increasingly structured (Saunders, Lewis & Thornhill, 2019; Creswell & Creswell, 2018).

The methodological approach is hypothetico-deductive, consisting of deriving hypotheses from the theoretical framework and confronting them with empirical data. Such a logic is now widely used in management research that aims to test causal relationships between latent variables (Sekaran & Bougie, 2020; Hair et al., 2022). This orientation justifies the use of a quantitative approach, which is particularly suitable for testing statistical relationships, measuring complex constructs, and generalizing results. The questionnaire survey remains the most relevant tool for collecting standardized data from a significant number of respondents (Bryman, 2021; Creswell, 2023).

Data were collected from CEOs and managers of high-technology firms located in the Greater Tunis area. Given the strategic nature of their roles, they are best positioned to assess practices related to business intelligence, knowledge management, and organizational strategy. In the absence of an exhaustive sampling frame, a convenience sampling method was adopted—a widely used approach in organizational studies when access to firms is limited (Etikan, 2016; Taherdoost, 2022). A total of 250 questionnaires were distributed, and 192 were retained for analysis, a sample size that complies with methodological recommendations for factor analyses and structural equation modeling (Hair et al., 2022), as well as minimum item-to-response ratio requirements (Kline, 2015).

The questionnaire uses measurement scales adapted from prior research and tailored to the Tunisian context. It was pretested to ensure clarity, validity, and internal consistency, following the procedures recommended in current methodological literature (DeVellis & Thorpe, 2021). The survey was administered both face-to-face and online, accompanied by a cover letter guaranteeing anonymity and scientific confidentiality.

The questionnaire was pretested with academic researchers and managers to verify clarity and relevance, as recommended in recent methodological work (DeVellis & Thorpe, 2021). It was then administered in person, online, and through self-administration—modes considered effective in contemporary organizational research (Bryman, 2021; Creswell, 2023). Incomplete questionnaires were discarded, and missing data were treated using SPSS according to best current practices (Allison, 2020). The reliability and validity of the scales were assessed through exploratory and confirmatory factor analyses, following recent guidelines in multivariate analysis (Hair et al., 2022; Kline, 2016).

3. Data Analysis and Results

The first phase of the empirical analysis was conducted using SPSS 25, which enabled the execution of principal component analysis and the verification of the initial structure of the data. The second phase employed PLS 3 to perform confirmatory analysis, based on exploratory results, in order to evaluate the quality of the measurement model and the validity of structural relationships. The combined choice of SPSS and PLS is grounded in their methodological complementarity: SPSS provides a robust tool for exploratory analyses, while PLS-SEM offers the flexibility required for complex models, non-normal data distributions, and moderately sized samples. This methodological positioning is supported by recent literature recommending PLS-SEM for models involving multiple latent constructs and numerous structural relationships (Dash et al., 2021; Sarker et al., 2024).

Our sample consists of 192 companies, with respondents comprising women (over 44%) and men (55%) aged between 29 and 60. The table below presents the distribution of the sample by gender and age.

Table 8. Distribution of the sample by respondent gender

Gender	Frequency	Percentage
Male	106	55,2
Female	86	44,8
Total	192	100

Figures 4 and 5 show that the average age of the respondents is around 40 years. Only 25 individuals, representing 20% of the sample, are under 40 years old. This suggests that becoming a director generally requires prior professional experience that allows individuals to accumulate knowledge and skills. Moreover, several respondents confirmed this assumption during our discussions.

Regarding seniority, we found that 50% of the sample have between 2 and 4 years of experience, 60% have more than 5 years, and fewer than 20% have less than 3 years of seniority. The results indicate that director-level and senior managerial positions require versatile individuals and genuine leaders who are able both to share knowledge within their teams and to select an appropriate strategic behavior for the organization.

Figure 4. Histogram of age distribution

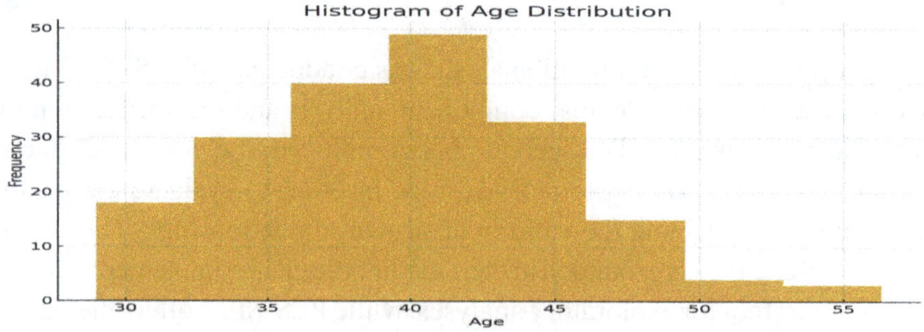

Figure 5. Histogram of seniority distribution

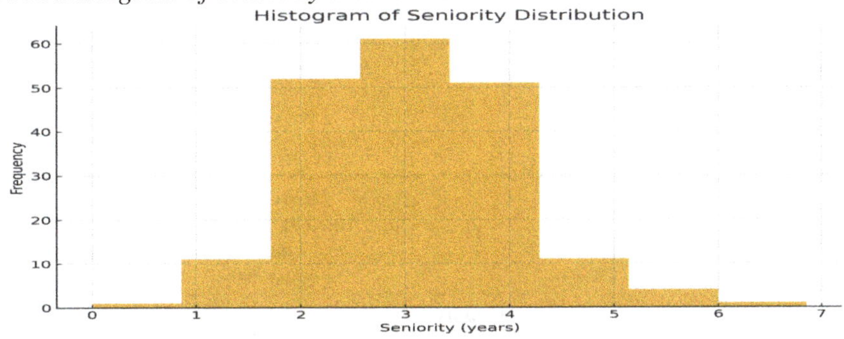

Table 9. Distribution of the sample by industry sector

Industry Sector	Frequency	Percentage
Industry	32	16.7
Manufacture of computer, electronic and optical products	46	24.0
Manufacture of electrical equipment	27	14.01
Manufacture of rubber and plastic products	12	6.03
Textile manufacturing	15	7.8
Pharmaceutical industry	26	13.5
Manufacture of machinery and equipment	18	9.4
Services	16	8.3
Total	192	100

These results indicate that the majority of the surveyed companies belong to activity branches such as: manufacture of computer, electronic and optical products (24%), industry (16,7%), manufacture of electrical equipment (14,1%), while only 7,8% belong to the plastic manufacturing sector.

The following table presents the results of the principal component analysis as well as the reliability of the business intelligence measurement scale. These findings allow us to conclude that:

- The Kaiser–Meyer–Olkin measure indicates a statistically acceptable value (KMO = 0,872), supporting a relevant factorial solution.
- Bartlett's test of sphericity is significant (p = 0,000), confirming the existence of a non-null inter-item correlation matrix.

- All indicators show adequate representation quality, with loadings above the 0,50 threshold.

Table 10. Exploratory factor analysis of the business intelligence measurement scale

Items	**KMO= 0, 872** **Bartlett χ^2= 1472,115** **ddl = 66** **p = 0,000**			
	Quality of Representation	**Rotated Component Matrix**		
		Monotoring	**Protection**	**Influence**
veille.info.1	0,776	0,842	-	-
veille.info.3	0,721	0,801	-	-
veille.info.4	0,804	0,787	-	-
protection.1	0,842	-	0,851	-
protection.2	0,862	-	0,836	-
protection.3	0,808	-	0,833	-
influence.1	0,737	-	-	0,845
influence.2	0,633	-	-	0,728
influence.3	0,619	-	-	0,728
influence.4	0,642	-		0,699
influence.5	0,573	-	-	0,659
influence.6	0,758		-	0,637
Eigenvalues (Kaiser Rule)		1,032	1,706	1,637
Cronbach's Alpha		0,858	0,915	0,867

Total eigenvalue for the Economic Intelligence dimensions = 9,375
Cumulative percentage of variance explained = 73,131%

The percentage of explained variance supports a multidimensional structure of economic intelligence, with each component showing an eigenvalue greater than 1. Specifically, the items Veille inf1, Veille inf2, and Veille inf3 cluster under the expected dimension “information monitoring.” The items protection1, protection2, and protection3 reflect the expected dimension “information protection.” Finally, the items influence1, influence2, influence3, influence4, influence5, and influence6 form the expected dimension “information influence.” Together, these components account for a cumulative eigenvalue of 9,375, representing 73,131% of the total explained variance. This confirms that the constructed instrument effectively measures organizational economic intelligence according to its three key dimensions: monitoring, protection, and influence.

Likewise, the table below presents the results of the principal component analysis for strategic behavior:

- The Kaiser-Meyer-Olkin measure indicates a statistically acceptable value (KMO = 0,922), confirming the adequacy of the data for a meaningful factor solution.
- Bartlett's test of sphericity is significant (p = 0,000), demonstrating the presence of a non-zero inter-item correlation matrix.
- The quality of representation for the indicators of sustainable involvement is satisfactory, as all observed variables exceed the minimum threshold of 0,5.

Table 11. Exploratory factor analysis of the strategic behavior scale

Items	KMO= 0,922 Bartlett χ^2= 5006,899 ddl = 406 p =0, 000				
	Quality of Representation	Rotated Component Matrix			
		Analyzer	Reactor	Prospector	Defender
Analy2	0,670	0,720	-	-	-
Analy3	0,775	0,797	-	-	-
Analy4	0,610	0,636	-	-	-
Analy5	0,678	0,694	-	-	-
Analy6	0,815	0,739	-	-	-
Analy7	0,773	0,644	-	-	-
Analy8	0,724	0,687	-	-	-
react.2	0,643	-	0,547	-	-
react.3	0,588	-	0,518	-	-
react.4	0,581	-	0,699	-	-
React5	0,588	-	0,592	-	-
Reac6	0,573	-	0.520	-	-
React7	0,573	-	0,514	-	-
React9	0,642	-	0,672	-	-
Prosp1	0,659	-	-	0,678	-
Prosp2	0,597	-	-	0,682	-
Prosp3	0,511	-	-	0,663	-
Prosp4	0,806	-	-	0.797	-

continued on following page

Table 11. Continued

Items	KMO= 0,922 Bartlett χ^2= 5006,899 ddl = 406 p =0, 000				
	Quality of Representation	Rotated Component Matrix			
		Analyzer	Reactor	Prospector	Defender
Prosp5	0,733	-	-	0,790	-
Prosp7	0,585	-	-	0,554	-
Prosp8	0,781	-	-	0,827	-
Prosp9	0,618	-	-	0,671	-
Prosp11	0,715	-	-	0,742	-
def.1	0,837	-		-	0,834
def.2	0,693	-		-	0,758
def.3	0,779	-		-	0,798
def.4	0,762	-		-	0.816
def.5	0.802	-		-	0,837
def.6	0,785	-		-	0.770
Eigenvalues (Kaiser's Rule)		14.318	2.641	1.734	1.210
Cronbach's Alpha		0.882	0.925	0.931	0.938
Total Eigenvalue for Strategic Behavior Dimensions:	19.903%				
Cumulative percentage of variance explained	68,633%				

The percentage of explained variance confirms a multidimensional structure of strategic behavior. All extracted components possess an eigenvalue greater than 1. The items Analy2, Analy3, Analy4, Analy5, Analy6, and Analy7 group together under the expected dimension "Analyzer behavior." The items react.2, react.3, react.4, react.5, react.6, react.7, and react.9 form the expected dimension "Reactor behavior." The items Prosp1, Prosp2, Prosp3, Prosp4, Prosp5, Prosp7, Prosp8, Prosp9, and Prosp11 form the expected dimension "Prospector behavior." Finally, the items def.1, def.2, def.3, def.4, def.5, and def.6 correspond to the expected dimension "Defender behavior." The cumulative eigenvalue of these four components is 19,903, explaining 68,633% of the total variance.

Thus, the strategic behavior measurement instrument relies on the dimensions "Reactor, Analyzer, Prospector, and Defender." In addition, the use of Cronbach's Alpha (α), complementing the exploratory factor analyses, strengthens the assessment of internal reliability and determines the coherence of items within each dimension.

The obtained Alpha coefficients exceed the commonly accepted minimum threshold of 0,6, confirming the reliability of the construct in exploratory research settings.

V. VALIDATION OF THE MEASUREMENT MODEL AND DISCUSSION

In the measurement model, also referred to as the outer model, the objective is to represent the relationships between the latent variables and the observed (manifest) variables. The evaluation of the measurement model relies on three key criteria: item and construct reliability, convergent validity, and discriminant validity.

Data processing was carried out using XLSTAT 2015, which enabled us to verify the overall structure of the measurement model. The descriptive statistics table (see Annexes) presents the characteristics of the model and shows that it includes two latent variables along with their manifest variables. No missing data were observed in the sample of 192 firms, and the mean and standard deviation for each variable are reported.

1. Reliability of the Measurement Model

To ensure the reliability of the measurement model, Chang et al. (2004) state that Cronbach's Alpha and Composite Reliability should be used. Composite Reliability is assessed through Dillon–Goldstein's rho (DG rho) obtained from exploratory factor analysis. For Cronbach's Alpha, the threshold commonly accepted by researchers to determine whether a scale is reliable is 0,70, following the recommendations of Nunnally and Bernstein (1994). As for Dillon–Goldstein's rho, the value must be higher than 0,70. Both indices aim to verify the internal consistency between the measurement items of the construct.

The composite reliability table (see Annexes) presents the factor loadings, Cronbach's Alpha values, and composite reliability associated with the measurement model.

The results presented confirm that the reliability is satisfactory for all the measurement scales used. Indeed, all Cronbach's alphas are above 0,795, thus exceeding the recommended threshold of 0.7 (Chin, 1998). All Dillon–Goldstein's rho coefficients are also greater than 0,8. Finally, we can observe that the first eigenvalue for each scale is higher than 1.

According to Bacon et al. (2014), loadings must be greater than 0,7. The Cross-loadings table (see Annexes) shows that all loadings are significant, since their values exceed the recommended threshold of 0.7 (Chin, 1998). The loadings are presented in the table above in bold type.

The next step concerns the examination of convergent and discriminant validity. After assessing reliability, it appears that all variables are reliable.

We also examined the convergent and discriminant validity of our measurement model. Cowin et al. (2008) state that, to confirm convergent validity, the AVE (Average Variance Extracted), also referred to as the mean extracted variance, must be higher than 0,5.

The table provided in the Annexes reports the AVE values for the latent variables included in the measurement model. All AVE values exceed the recommended threshold of 0,5, which confirms the presence of convergent validity: the items within each construct are strongly and consistently correlated.

Regarding discriminant validity, Fornell and Larcker (1981) propose using the AVE to ensure that each construct shares more variance with its own indicators than with any other construct. In practice, the AVE of a given construct must be greater than the squared correlations between that construct and all others. Our results show that the AVE of every latent variable is above 0,5 and consistently higher than the squared correlations with the other constructs. Discriminant validity is therefore fully confirmed: each construct shares more variance with its own manifest variables than with the remaining constructs in the model (see table in the Annexes).

2. Analysis of the Impact of Business Intelligence on Strategic Behaviors

This section presents the main results regarding the impact of Business Intelligence on strategic behaviors. It highlights how the use of structured information helps shape the orientations adopted by organizations.

Table 12. Influence of business intelligence on strategic behaviors

Analyzed Relationship	Regression Coefficient (β)	p-value	Significance
Business Intelligence → Reactor Behavior	0,1565	0,0046	Positive and significant effect
Business Intelligence → Analyzer Behavior	0,2771	0,0000	Positive and highly significant effect
Business Intelligence → Prospector Behavior	0.2701	0,0005	Positive and highly significant effect
Business Intelligence → Defender Behavior	0.1519	0,0215	Positive and significant effect

The results show that business intelligence has an overall positive and significant effect on all the strategic behaviors studied. The regression coefficients associated with reactor, analyzer, prospector, and defender behaviors are all positive, and their p-values indicate statistical significance. Therefore, the more business intelligence is mobilized within the organization, the more the different strategic profiles tend to be strengthened. This convergence of effects confirms hypotheses H1 to H4 and highlights the transversal role of business intelligence in the strategic dynamics of firms. It emerges as a structuring factor capable of influencing reactive, analytical, exploratory, and defensive behaviors, underscoring its importance in overall strategic functioning.

3. Discussion of the Effect of Business Intelligence on Organizational Strategic Behavior

The demonstration of a positive and significant effect of business intelligence on all strategic behaviors highlights its structuring role in organizational dynamics. The validation of all four hypotheses confirms that this influence operates transversally. The regression coefficients obtained, ranging from 0,1519 to 0,2771, show a variable yet consistent impact depending on the strategic profile. These results align with studies showing that an organization's ability to effectively mobilize information strengthens decision-making and improves environmental understanding.

On one hand, the positive effect of business intelligence on reactor behavior (β = 0,1565) and defender behavior (β = 0,1519) shows that even organizations focused on constrained responsiveness or stability benefit from structured informational support. The validation of H1 and H4 indicates that business intelligence reduces uncertainty, facilitates responses to disruptions, and helps secure the strategic perimeter. These coefficients, although lower than those of innovative profiles, reflect the ability of information to reinforce cohesion and decision-making rigor in strategic models often considered less adaptive.

On the other hand, the higher coefficients observed for analyzer behavior (β = 0,2771) and prospector behavior (β = 0,2701) confirm that business intelligence is a powerful lever for organizations engaged in active monitoring and market exploration. The validation of H2 and H3 shows that the use of relevant information significantly improves the identification of weak signals, trend analysis, and innovation capacity. The magnitude of these coefficients illustrates the essential role of information in strategies based on anticipation and the discovery of opportunities.

Overall, this discussion highlights a transversal phenomenon: regardless of the behavior adopted, business intelligence acts as a strategic catalyst. Variations in coefficients show that it supports stability as much as innovation, reaction as much as exploration. It enables organizations to better align their decisions with environmental dynamics and enhances overall strategic performance. Beyond its technical function, it emerges as a central driver of adaptation, coherence, and competitiveness.

CONCLUSION

This chapter has laid the theoretical, conceptual, and empirical foundations necessary to understand the role of business intelligence in shaping organizational strategic behaviors. The literature review highlighted the core processes of business intelligence: monitoring, information protection, and influence, and demonstrated their importance in adopting a strategic behavior. This informational approach appears essential for enabling organizations to adapt to unstable environments and maintain their competitive position.

The integration of the empirical study into this chapter strengthens these theoretical foundations by providing concrete validation of the proposed conceptual model. The results confirm that business intelligence has a positive and significant effect on the four strategic behaviors identified by Miles and Snow (1978): reactive, analyzer, prospector, and defender, thereby validating the proposed hypotheses. Business intelligence thus goes beyond mere monitoring activities and establishes itself as a true strategic lever directly contributing to the structuring, adjustment, and direction of organizational behaviors.

This chapter makes several major contributions. Theoretically, it proposes an original model linking business intelligence and strategic behaviors. Empirically, it provides recommendations to managers for developing integrated business intelligence systems that go beyond information collection and actively support strategic decision-making. The results suggest that organizations adopting a proactive approach to business intelligence, combining monitoring, analysis, and influence, are better positioned to anticipate market trends and secure their competitiveness.

However, some limitations should be noted. The relationships established are based on a model that, although empirically validated in this context, would benefit from being tested in other organizational environments to strengthen its robustness. Moreover, certain contextual factors such as organizational culture, internal structure, and technological maturity were only partially addressed, even though they may strongly influence the effectiveness of business intelligence. A deeper analysis of these aspects would help better understand why some organizations benefit more from business intelligence than others.

Future research should aim to broaden the empirical evaluation of the model by diversifying the sectors studied and integrating new mediators or moderators. The impact of emerging technologies, such as artificial intelligence, advanced analytics, and automation of informational processes, deserves particular attention, as these innovations profoundly transform the way information is produced, analyzed, and integrated into strategic decision-making. Exploring the links between business intelligence, risk management, organizational performance, and innovation is also a promising avenue for future research.

In summary, this chapter presents a comprehensive and coherent view of the role of business intelligence in shaping strategic behavior. The combination of theoretical foundations, conceptual modeling, and empirical validation strengthens the relevance of this approach and opens avenues for future research aimed at better understanding the complex and rich interactions between information, knowledge, and organizational strategy.

REFERENCES

Ansoff, H. I. (1984). *Implanting strategic management* (2nd ed.). Prentice Hall.

Avci, U., Madanoglu, M., & Okumus, F. (2011). Strategic orientation and performance of tourism firms: Evidence from a developing country. *Tourism Management, 32*(1), 147–157. DOI: 10.1016/j.tourman.2010.01.017

Baaziz, M. (2014). L'intelligence économique et la réactivité stratégique. *Revue Française de Management, 18*(4), 122–136.

Baumard, P. (2020). *Stratégie et organisations: Comprendre les dynamiques de l'intelligence informationnelle.* Presses Universitaires de France.

Bejjani, A. (2024). Analyzing competitive intelligence in a digital age. *Journal of Strategy and Management, 31*(2), 70–85.

Bernard, L. (2008). *La gestion stratégique de l'intelligence économique dans un environnement turbulent.* Éditions Business Insights.

Bernat, J. (2008). *La planification stratégique et la surveillance de l'environnement.* Presses Universitaires de France.

Bisson, C. (2021). Les enjeux de l'intelligence économique dans le secteur concurrentiel. *Revue Française d'Intelligence Économique, 7*(1), 34–45.

Bryman, A. (2021). *Social Research Methods.* Oxford University Press.

Cao, C.. (2013). Agilité et compétitivité dans les entreprises modernes. *Journal of Strategy and Management, 17*(4), 243–258.

Chandler, A. D. (1962). *Strategy and structure: Chapters in the history of the industrial enterprise.* MIT Press.

Chin, W. W. (1998). Commentary: Issues and opinion on structural equation modeling. *Management Information Systems Quarterly*, vii–xvi.

Choo, C. W. (2023). *The knowing organization: How organizations use information to construct meaning, create knowledge, and make decisions* (3rd ed.). Oxford University Press.

Cohen, E., & Amar, A. (2025). *Organizational learning in the age of digital transformation.* Routledge.

Cohen, L. (2007). Les capacités d'apprentissage organisationnel dans les environnements volatils. *Journal of Organizational Behavior, 28*(6), 567–589.

Cowin, L. S., Johnson, M., Craven, R. G., & Marsh, H. W. (2008). Causal modeling of self-concept, job satisfaction, and retention of nurses. *International Journal of Nursing Studies*, *45*(10), 1449–1459. DOI: 10.1016/j.ijnurstu.2007.10.009 PMID: 18242611

Creswell, J. W. (2023). *Educational Research.* Pearson.

Creswell, J. W., & Creswell, J. D. (2018). Research Design: Qualitative, Quantitative, and Mixed Methods Approaches. *Sage (Atlanta, Ga.).*

Dash, G., Ramaswami, S. N., & Singh, R. (2021). CB-SEM vs PLS-SEM methods for research in social science: A comprehensive review and comparison. *Technological Forecasting and Social Change*, *173*, 121092. DOI: 10.1016/j.techfore.2021.121092

DeVellis, R., & Thorpe, C. (2021). Scale Development. *Sage (Atlanta, Ga.).*

Djennas, B.. (2015). Le rôle de l'intelligence économique dans le choix stratégique des PME. *Revue Algérienne de Management*, *12*(3), 54–68.

Dufour, A., & Beaudry, P. (2024). L'intelligence économique à l'ère du numérique et de la stratégie d'innovation. *Innovation & Strategy Review*, *31*(2), 111–124.

Dufour, R., & Lièvre, A. (2023). Transformations organisationnelles et gestion des connaissances dans un environnement digital. *Management et Transformation*, *15*(2), 42–55.

Dyer, J.. (2023). Proactivité et adaptation stratégique dans un monde globalisé. *Journal of Management Studies*, *45*(5), 98–115.

Etikan, I. (2016). Comparison of Convenience Sampling and Purposive Sampling. *American Journal of Theoretical and Applied Statistics*, *5*(1), 1. DOI: 10.11648/j.ajtas.20160501.11

Fissellier, P.. (2018). L'évolution de la fonction veille stratégique dans l'intelligence économique. *Revue de la Veille et de la Stratégie*, *20*(3), 98–113.

Fornell, C., & Larcker, D. F. (1981). Evaluating structural equation models with unobservable variables and measurement error. *JMR, Journal of Marketing Research*, *18*(1), 39–50. DOI: 10.1177/002224378101800104

Freyn, F., & Farley, M. (2020). The impact of intelligence and information sharing in the healthcare industry. *Journal of Healthcare Management*, *34*(5), 243–257.

Gloaguen, A. (2014). L'intelligence économique et son impact sur le management stratégique. *Revue de Gestion Stratégique*, *23*(4), 122–134.

Gloaguen, C. (2012). *L'intelligence économique dans le management stratégique*. L'Harmattan.

Gloaguen, C. (2023). Les dynamiques organisationnelles et l'intelligence économique en pratique. *Revue de Management Stratégique, 24*(3), 211–225.

Goria, F. (2006). *La stratégie informationnelle dans les organisations*. Pearson.

Grant, R. M. (1996). Toward a knowledge-based theory of the firm. *Strategic Management Journal, 17*(S2), 109–122. DOI: 10.1002/smj.4250171110

Gueye, M. (2017). La dimension éthique de l'intelligence économique. *Management et Ethique, 15*(2), 45–60.

Hair, J.. (2022). PLS-SEM: A Primer. *Sage (Atlanta, Ga.)*.

Hair, J. F., Hult, G. T. M., Ringle, C., & Sarstedt, M. (2022). A Primer on Partial Least Squares Structural Equation Modeling (PLS-SEM). *Sage (Atlanta, Ga.)*.

Harbulot, C. (2004). Stratégie et intelligence économique: La quête de compétitivité dans un environnement complexe. *Revue des Sciences de Gestion, 23*(1), 37–45.

Harbulot, C. (2024). *Guerre économique et stratégies d'influence*. VA Press.

Juillet, A., & Racouchot, P. (2012). *L'influence stratégique: Nouveaux enjeux de la compétition informationnelle*. Ellipses.

Kaplan, R. (2022). *Analytics and decision-making: From big data to strategic action*. MIT Press.

Kline, R. (2015). *Principles and Practice of Structural Equation Modeling*. Guilford Press.

Kula, S., & Naktiyok, A. (2021). Strategic intelligence and organizational performance in competitive environments. *Journal of Strategy and Management, 14*(2), 78–91.

Larivert, R. (2006). La contre-intelligence et la protection du patrimoine informationnel. *Revue Internationale de Sécurité, 30*(1), 12–22.

Larivet, C.. (2012). L'intelligence économique et le comportement stratégique des PME. *Review of International Economics, 19*(4), 99–112.

Ledi, A. (2024). Strategic behaviors under the influence of competitive intelligence. *Strategic Management Review, 29*(2), 33–45.

Lemaine, F. (1997). L'intelligence économique: Quelles implications pour les stratégies organisationnelles? *Revue Internationale de Management, 13*(2), 55–68.

Levet, L. (2020). L'intelligence économique et ses apports à la compétitivité des entreprises. *Revue Internationale de Business et Management, 15*(2), 83–100.

Luhn, H. P. (1958). The dimensional analysis of information. *Journal of the American Society for Information Science, 9*(5), 180–188.

Marcon, D. (2011). *Construção do conhecimento pedagógico do conteúdo dos futuros professores de Educação Física* (Doctoral dissertation, Universidade do Porto (Portugal)).

Martre, L. (1994). *L'intelligence économique et la compétitivité des entreprises.* Presses Universitaires de France.

Miles, R. E., & Snow, C. C. (1978). *Organizational strategy, structure, and process.* McGraw-Hill.

Mintzberg, H. (1994). Rethinking strategic planning part I: Pitfalls and fallacies. *Long Range Planning, 27*(3), 12–21. DOI: 10.1016/0024-6301(94)90185-6

Mongereau, P. (2006). L'intelligence économique et son rôle dans la compétitivité. *Revue Internationale de Management, 12*(2), 56–73.

Monino, J. L. (2021). Data value, big data analytics, and decision-making. *Journal of the Knowledge Economy, 12*(1), 256–267. DOI: 10.1007/s13132-016-0396-2

Moustaghfir, K., & Schiuma, G. (2023). L'intelligence économique et l'innovation dans les stratégies organisationnelles. *Journal of Innovation and Knowledge, 8*(1), 59–72.

Nasri, S. (2012). L'intelligence économique et la création d'avantages concurrentiels. *Management et Organisation, 25*(6), 234–245.

Nonaka, I., & Takeuchi, H. (2021). *The knowledge-creating company.* Oxford University Press.

Osei, E. (2023). Competitive strategy in emerging markets: Evidence from Ghana. *Strategic Management Journal, 35*(4), 499–514.

Oubrich, L. (2007). La veille stratégique et ses applications dans l'entreprise moderne. *Revue Européenne de Management, 21*(4), 234–245.

Pupion, P. C. (2018). Une recherche en Management Stratégique Public en quête d'un cadre théorique. *Gestion et management public, 63*(1), 6-13.

Roiron, M. (1999). L'intelligence économique dans le management stratégique. *Revue de Gestion Stratégique, 16*(1), 22–34.

Rouach, D., & Salles, M. (2022). *Competitive intelligence and strategic anticipation in turbulent environments*. Wiley.

Salles, J. (2006). *L'intelligence économique au service du management stratégique*. Presses Universitaires de France.

Salvetat, D. (2011). Les approches théoriques et l'influence sur la sécurité des pratiques d'intelligence économique dans les entreprises européennes de hautes technologies. *Revue française de gestion industrielle, 30*(2), 53-66.

Sarker, F., Hasan, M. M., & Rahman, M. (2024). Why apply SPSS, SmartPLS and AMOS: An essential quantitative data analysis tool for business and social science research investigations. [Journal of Academic Research]. *International Journal of Research and Innovation in Social Science*, *8*(1), 1–9. DOI: 10.47772/IJRISS.2024.8090224

Saunders, M., Lewis, P., & Thornhill, A. (2019). *Research Methods for Business Students*. Pearson.

Sekaran, U., & Bougie, R. (2020). *Research Methods for Business*. Wiley.

Stefanikova, L.. (2015). L'impact de l'intelligence économique sur la compétitivité des entreprises. *International Journal of Business Strategy*, *24*(1), 112–130.

Taherdoost, H. (2022). *Sampling Methods in Research Methodology*. International.

Teece, D. J. (2007). *Dynamic capabilities and strategic management*. Oxford University Press.

Teece, D. J. (2020). *Dynamic capabilities and strategic management*. Oxford University Press.

Ursacescu, M.. (2012). The impact of competitive intelligence on strategic management. *Strategic Management Journal*, *28*(4), 101–115.

Wickramasinghe, D., & Wickramasinghe, V. (2023). Strategic orientation and performance: A study of the impact of Miles & Snow's typology on organizational values. *Journal of Strategy and Management*, *28*(4), 401–420.

Wilensky, H. (1967). The sociology of organizations: A review and appraisal. *Administrative Science Quarterly*, *12*(2), 273–295.

APPENDIX

Table 13. Descriptive statistics

Variable	Observations	Missing Obs.	Complete Obs.	Minimum	Maximum	Mean	Std. Dev.
Mono.1	192	0	192	1	5	4.1615	1.1087
Mono3	192	0	192	1	5	4.3333	0.9483
Mono4	192	0	192	1	5	4.2708	1.0943
protection.1	192	0	192	1	5	4.1927	1.0405
protection.2	192	0	192	1	5	4.1823	1.0523
protection.3	192	0	192	1	5	4.0938	1.0663
influence.1	192	0	192	1	5	4.1615	0.9682
influence.2	192	0	192	1	5	3.9531	1.2132
influence.3	192	0	192	1	5	3.8854	1.0545
influence.4	192	0	192	1	5	4.2656	1.0192
influence.5	192	0	192	1	5	4.2604	1.1479
influence.6	192	0	192	1	5	4.25	1.1456
react.2	192	0	192	1	5	3.7448	1.1422
react.3	192	0	192	1	5	4.1927	1.1362
react.4	192	0	192	1	5	3.974	0.9918
react.5	192	0	192	1	5	3.9323	1.1136
react.6	192	0	192	1	5	3.8177	1.0768
react.7	192	0	192	1	5	3.8333	1.1652
react.9	192	0	192	1	5	3.7031	1.0947
analy.2	192	0	192	1	5	3.9844	1.0728
analy.3	192	0	192	1	5	3.849	1.174
analy.4	192	0	192	1	5	3.8281	1.0189
analy.5	192	0	192	1	5	3.9115	1.2448
analy.6	192	0	192	1	5	3.9896	1.0206
analy.7	192	0	192	1	5	4.0833	1.0223
analy.8	192	0	192	1	5	4.0469	1.1194
prosp.1	192	0	192	1	5	3.9427	1.2466
prosp.2	192	0	192	1	5	3.9115	1.0692
prosp.3	192	0	192	1	5	3.9375	1.0735
prosp.4	192	0	192	1	5	4.1198	1.1416

continued on following page

Table 13. Continued

Variable	Observations	Missing Obs.	Complete Obs.	Minimum	Maximum	Mean	Std. Dev.
prosp.5	192	0	192	1	5	3.8594	1.2188
prosp.7	192	0	192	1	5	3.5469	1.0246
prosp.8	192	0	192	1	5	3.6146	1.2447
prosp.9	192	0	192	1	5	3.5521	1.1307
prosp.11	192	0	192	1	5	4.0365	1.2178
def.1	192	0	192	1	5	3.8646	1.1957
def.2	192	0	192	1	5	3.7083	1.0841
def.3	192	0	192	1	5	4.1406	1.2188
def.4	192	0	192	1	5	3.8333	1.1607
def.5	192	0	192	1	5	3.8646	1.3159
def.6	192	0	192	1	5	3.9167	1.1517

Table 14. Composite reliability

Latent Variable	Dimensions	Cronbach's Alpha	D.G. Rho (EFA)	Condition Number	Critical Value	Eigen values
Monotoring	3	0.8591	0.9142	2.9587	1.0000	2.3413 0.3912 0.2675
Protection	3	0.9149	0.9464	3.9004	1.0000	2.5643 0.2671 0.1686
Influence	6	0.8673	0.9009	4.1208	1.0000	3.6205 0.6540 0.6175 0.5122 0.3826 0.2132
Reacteur	7	0.8820	0.9084	3.6042	1.0000	4.1072 0.6690 0.5970 0.5385 0.3998 0.3723 0.3162

continued on following page

Table 14. Continued

Latent Variable	Dimensions	Cronbach's Alpha	D.G. Rho (EFA)	Condition Number	Critical Value	Eigen values
Analy	7	0.9262	0.9407	5.5262	1.0000	4.8604 0.5512 0.4136 0.3659 0.3491 0.3006 0.1592
Prosp	9	0.9309	0.9427	5.6312	1.0000	5.8313 0.7301 0.5877 0.5101 0.4116 0.3172 0.2398 0.1885 0.1839
Def	6	0.9383	0.9513	5.3300	1.0000	4.5907 0.4494 0.3040 0.2661 0.2281 0.1616

Table 15. Cross-loadings

Construct	Items	Veille	Protection	Influence	Reactor	Analyzer	Prospector	Defender
Intelligence Economique	ville.info.1	0.9051	0.5679	0.4811	0.4524	0.5907	0.5956	0.4859
	ville.info.3	0.8577	0.5088	0.4705	0.4517	0.5002	0.5973	0.4048
	ville.info.4	0.8862	0.5486	0.4455	0.4378	0.5452	0.5248	0.4045
	protection.1	0.5941	0.9046	0.5107	0.5317	0.649	0.6102	0.588
	protection.2	0.5715	0.942	0.5554	0.5475	0.6952	0.6347	0.6483
	protection.3	0.5393	0.9265	0.5079	0.6064	0.6846	0.62	0.5746
	influence.1	0.2248	0.1348	0.6777	0.194	0.1941	0.265	0.2625
	influence.2	0.4706	0.5185	0.8103	0.4817	0.4764	0.5343	0.465
	influence.3	0.4072	0.3561	0.7633	0.231	0.4017	0.3935	0.4084
	influence.4	0.282	0.4243	0.7068	0.2438	0.3739	0.3462	0.4435
	influence.5	0.4596	0.477	0.7846	0.5642	0.5374	0.5635	0.5506
	influence.6	0.5016	0.5684	0.8858	0.3865	0.5306	0.5694	0.5798

continued on following page

Table 15. Continued

Construct	Items	Veille	Protection	Influence	Reactor	Analyzer	Prospector	Defender
Strategic Behaviors	react.2	0.4587	0.5577	0.4789	0.7835	0.5499	0.6462	0.5228
	react.3	0.5379	0.5969	0.4601	0.7589	0.6435	0.5682	0.5342
	react.4	0.393	0.41	0.3295	0.6876	0.4793	0.4539	0.3317
	react.5	0.4953	0.555	0.4349	0.7671	0.5247	0.5975	0.3833
	react.6	0.4811	0.6095	0.4668	0.7574	0.6259	0.5815	0.4474
	react.7	0.4734	0.5633	0.4962	0.8146	0.6209	0.6004	0.5031
	react.9	0.4624	0.6008	0.3747	0.7844	0.5384	0.5431	0.4873
	analy.2	0.5687	0.5244	0.5054	0.5226	0.572	0.811	0.5143
	analy.3	0.4306	0.4691	0.4708	0.5827	0.5291	0.8278	0.4897
	analy.4	0.5254	0.5171	0.388	0.4051	0.5965	0.7686	0.3896
	analy.5	0.51	0.5309	0.5507	0.6109	0.6034	0.8278	0.5424
	analy.6	0.5793	0.6147	0.5252	0.6414	0.6858	0.8942	0.5882
	analy.7	0.5897	0.68	0.5975	0.6767	0.7034	0.8794	0.6752
	analy.8	0.5737	0.5569	0.458	0.5893	0.6512	0.817	0.5021
	prosp.1	0.4109	0.6055	0.5147	0.413	0.673	0.5451	0.8097
	prosp.2	0.2883	0.3915	0.3799	0.3727	0.4882	0.4544	0.7045
	prosp.3	0.2893	0.4237	0.3259	0.3325	0.4965	0.3709	0.6841
	prosp.4	0.4823	0.5916	0.4889	0.3883	0.6633	0.6119	0.8872
	prosp.5	0.4236	0.504	0.4542	0.303	0.6041	0.4971	0.8532
	prosp.7	0.4808	0.5293	0.4388	0.5218	0.6274	0.5981	0.7841
	prosp.8	0.4212	0.4971	0.4971	0.4032	0.5672	0.5362	0.8389
	prosp.9	0.3962	0.4553	0.3693	0.5096	0.5976	0.5514	0.7976
	prosp.11	0.4723	0.4983	0.3973	0.4191	0.6443	0.5264	0.8584
	def.1	0.4183	0.5927	0.5532	0.5433	0.5516	0.6022	0.9116
	def.2	0.4545	0.6009	0.5286	0.4605	0.5124	0.5239	0.8183
	def.3	0.4225	0.5385	0.4759	0.4589	0.5526	0.5667	0.8864
	def.4	0.4426	0.5463	0.4782	0.4882	0.496	0.5123	0.8676
	def.5	0.3904	0.5183	0.5587	0.3744	0.4906	0.5171	0.8816
	def.6	0.4459	0.6196	0.5818	0.5388	0.562	0.6329	0.8793

Table 16. Convergent validity

Latent Variable	Type	Mean (Manifest Variables)	R^2	Adjusted R^2	Average Communalities (AVE)	Average Redundancies	D.G. Rho
Monotoring	Exogenous	0.0000			0.7801		0.9141
Protection	Exogenous	0.0000			0.8547		0.9464
Influence	Exogenous	0.0000			0.5997		0.8992
React	Endogenous	0.0000	0.7404	0.7320	0.5862	0.4340	0.9082
Analy	Endogenous	0.0000	0.6763	0.6658	0.6942	0.4695	0.9407
Prosp	Endogenous	0.0000	0.5338	0.5187	0.6474	0.3456	0.9426
Def	Endogenous	0.0000	0.5419	0.5270	0.7649	0.4145	0.9512
Average					0.6959	0.3541	

Table 17. Discriminant validity

	Monotoring	Protection	Influence	React	Analy	Prosp	Def	Average Communalities (AVE)
Monotoring	1	0.3769	0.2768	0.3829	0.4216	0.2630	0.2409	0.7802
Protection	0.3769	1	0.3214	0.5357	0.4522	0.3944	0.4271	0.8547
Influence	0.2768	0.3214	1	0.3236	0.3619	0.2892	0.3670	0.6003
Reaction	0.3829	0.5357	0.3236	1	0.5592	0.5583	0.3656	0.5862
Analy	0.4216	0.4522	0.3619	0.5592	1	0.4288	0.4118	0.6942
Prosp	0.2630	0.3944	0.2892	0.5583	0.4288	1	0.2748	0.6474
Def	0.2409	0.4271	0.3670	0.3656	0.4118	0.2748	1	0.7649
Average Communalities (AVE)	0.7802	0.8547	0.6003	0.5862	0.6942	0.6474	0.7649	

Conclusion

This book has examined the foundations, adoption processes, and broader implications of human-centered technologies across organizational, industrial, and societal contexts. It demonstrates that intelligent technologies, ranging from privacy-preserving AI and emotionally aligned systems to generative and analytical platforms, are not neutral artifacts, but socio-technical systems whose impact depends on how they are designed, adopted, and governed. The chapters collectively emphasize that successful technological integration requires more than technical efficiency or innovation capability. Human-centered design, ethical considerations, and organizational readiness emerge as essential conditions for technology acceptance, trust, and long-term value creation. Issues such as data privacy, transparency, responsibility, psychological well-being, and sustainability are shown to significantly influence how individuals and organizations respond to intelligent systems.

By addressing technology adoption models, emotional and perceptual intelligence, responsible innovation, and AI-related organizational challenges, the book extends existing frameworks to better reflect the complexity of contemporary digital transformation. It also highlights how human-centered technologies shape strategic behavior, innovation processes, and performance outcomes across diverse sectors, including tourism, international markets, SMEs, and high-technology industries.

From a practical standpoint, the volume offers guidance for managers, policymakers, and innovation leaders seeking to implement technologies in ways that align with human and societal values. The findings underscore that technology-driven transformation must be accompanied by thoughtful governance, inclusive design practices, and a clear understanding of human implications at both individual and collective levels. In conclusion, *Design, Adoption, and Impact of Human-Centered Technologies* positions human-centeredness as a cornerstone of sustainable digital transformation. As intelligent technologies continue to expand their influence, this book calls for approaches that balance innovation with responsibility, ensuring that technological progress enhances human agency, organizational resilience, and societal well-being.

Compilation of References

Abdulquadri, A., Kieu, T. A., & Nguyen, N. P. (2021). Digital transformation in financial services provision: A Nigerian perspective to the adoption of chatbot. *Journal of Enterprising Communities: People and Places in the Global Economy*, *15*(2), 258–281. DOI: 10.1108/JEC-06-2020-0126

Abourokbah, S. H., Mashat, R. M., & Salam, M. A. (2023). Role of Absorptive Capacity, Digital Capability, Agility, and Resilience in Supply Chain Innovation Performance. *Sustainability (Basel)*, *15*(4), 3636. Advance online publication. DOI: 10.3390/su15043636

Abrokwah-Larbi, K., & Awuku-Larbi, Y. (2024). The impact of artificial intelligence in marketing on the performance of business organizations: evidence from SMEs in an emerging economy. In *Journal of Entrepreneurship in Emerging Economies* (Vol. 16, Issue 4, pp. 1090–1117). DOI: 10.1108/JEEE-07-2022-0207

Achmad, F., Prambudia, Y., & Rumanti, A. A. (2023). Sustainable Tourism Industry Development: A Collaborative Model of Open Innovation, Stakeholders, and Support System Facilities. *IEEE Access : Practical Innovations, Open Solutions*, *11*(3), 83343–83363. DOI: 10.1109/ACCESS.2023.3301574

Adner, R. (2016). Ecosystem as Structure: An Actionable Construct for Strategy. *Journal of Management*, *43*(1), 39–58. DOI: 10.1177/0149206316678451

Agarwal, R., & Prasad, J. (1999). Are individual differences germane to the acceptance of new information technologies? *Decision Sciences*, *30*(2), 361–391. DOI: 10.1111/j.1540-5915.1999.tb01614.x

Agudo-Peregrina, Á. F., Hernández-García, Á., & Pascual-Miguel, F. J. (2014). Behavioral intention, use behavior and the acceptance of electronic learning systems: Differences between higher education and lifelong learning. *Computers in Human Behavior*, *34*, 301–314. DOI: 10.1016/j.chb.2013.10.035

Aguinis, H., & Glavas, A. (2012). What we know and don't know about corporate social responsibility: A review and research agenda. *Journal of Management, 38*(4), 932–968. DOI: 10.1177/0149206311436079

Ahmad, R., & Scott, N. (2019). Technology innovations towards reducing hospitality human resource costs in Langkawi, Malaysia. *Tourism Review*, *74*(3), 547–562. DOI: 10.1108/TR-03-2018-0038

Ajzen, I. (1985). From intentions to actions: A theory of planned behavior. In Kuhl, J., & Beckmann, J. (Eds.), *Action control: From cognition to behavior* (pp. 11–39). Springer-Verlag. DOI: 10.1007/978-3-642-69746-3_2

Ajzen, I. (1991). The theory of planned behavior. *Organizational Behavior and Human Decision Processes*, *50*(2), 179–211. DOI: 10.1016/0749-5978(91)90020-T

Ajzen, I. (2020). The theory of planned behavior: Frequently asked questions. *Human Behavior and Emerging Technologies*, *2*(4), 314–324. DOI: 10.1002/hbe2.195

Ajzen, I., & Fishbein, M. (1980). *Understanding attitudes and predicting social behavior*. Prentice-Hall.

Akter, S., McCarthy, G., Sajib, S., Michael, K., Dwivedi, Y. K., D'Ambra, J., & Shen, K. N. (2021). Algorithmic bias in data-driven innovation in the age of AI. *International Journal of Information Management*, *60*, 102387. DOI: 10.1016/j.ijinfomgt.2021.102387

Alami, R., Stachowicz-Stanusch, A., Agarwal, S., & Al Masaeid, T. (2024). Predicting quiet quitting: Machine learning insights into silent resignations in the healthcare industry. *Journal of Ecohumanism*, *3*(4), 3444–3462. DOI: 10.62754/joe.v3i4.3864

Alaql, A. A., AlQurashi, F., & Mehmood, R. (2023). Data-driven deep journalism to discover age dynamics in multi-generational labour markets from LinkedIn media. *Journalism and Media*, *4*(1), 120–145. DOI: 10.3390/journalmedia4010010

Al-azzam, Z. F., Irtaimeh, H. J., & Khaddam, A. A. H. (2017, December). Examining the Mediating Effect of Strategic Agility in the Relationship Between Intellectual Capital and Organizational Excellence in Jordan Service. *International Journal of Management Studies*, *25*. Advance online publication. DOI: 10.32890/ijms.25.1.2018.10496

Al-Emran, M., & Granić, A. (2021). Is it still valid or outdated? A bibliometric analysis of the technology acceptance model and its applications from 2010 to 2020. In A. Al-Emran & M. A. Al-Sharafi (Eds.), Studies in Systems, Decision and Control: Vol. 335.

Al-Gahtani, S. S. (2020). Empirical investigation of e-learning acceptance and assimilation: A structural equation model. *Applied Computing and Informatics*, *12*(1), 27–50. DOI: 10.1016/j.aci.2014.09.001

Alharbi, A., Pandit, A., Rosenberger, P. J.III, & Miah, S. (2025). Understanding AI-enabled conversational agent customer experiences in religious tourism. *Journal of Islamic Marketing*, *16*(August), 2569–2595. Advance online publication. DOI: 10.1108/JIMA-07-2024-0309

Ali, M. A., Hussin, N., Haddad, H., Al-Araj, R., & Abed, I. A. (2021). Intellectual capital and innovation performance: Systematic literature review. *Risks*, *9*(9), 1–19. DOI: 10.3390/risks9090170

Aljaž, T. (2024). Leveraging ChatGPT for enhanced logical analysis in the theory of constraints thinking process. *Organizacija*, *57*(2), 202–214. DOI: 10.2478/orga-2024-0014

Al-Kfairy, M., Mustafa, D., Al-Adaileh, A., Zriqat, S., & Sendaba, O. (2024). User acceptance of AI voice assistants in Jordan's telecom industry. *Computers in Human Behavior Reports*, *16*, 100521. DOI: 10.1016/j.chbr.2024.100521

Al-Khatib, W. (2023). *Drivers of generative artificial intelligence to fostering exploitative and.pdf.*

Allal-Chérif, O. (2022). Intelligent cathedrals: Using augmented reality, virtual reality, and artificial intelligence to provide an intense cultural, historical, and religious visitor experience. *Technological Forecasting and Social Change*, *178*(January), 121604. Advance online publication. DOI: 10.1016/j.techfore.2022.121604

Al-Mamary, Y. H., Al-nashmi, M., Hassan, Y. A. G., & Shamsuddin, A. (2016). A critical review of models and theories in field of individual acceptance of technology. *International Journal of Hybrid Information Technology*, *9*(6), 143–158. DOI: 10.14257/ijhit.2016.9.6.13

Al-Maroof, R. A., Arpaci, I., Al-Emran, M., Salloum, S. A., & Shaalan, K. (2020). Examining the acceptance of WhatsApp stickers through machine learning algorithms. In Al-Emran, M., & Shaalan, K. (Eds.), *Recent Advances in Intelligent Systems and Smart Applications* (pp. 209–221). Springer., DOI: 10.1007/978-3-030-47411-9_12

Al-Nuaimi, M. N., Al Sawafi, O. S., Malik, S. I., Al-Emran, M., & Selim, Y. F. (2022). Evaluating the actual use of learning management systems during the COVID-19 pandemic: An integrated theoretical model. *Interactive Learning Environments*. Advance online publication. DOI: 10.1080/10494820.2022.2055577

Al-Qaysi, N., Mohamad-Nordin, N., & Al-Emran, M. (2020). A systematic review of social media acceptance from the perspective of educational and information systems theories and models. *Journal of Educational Computing Research*, *57*(8), 2085–2109. DOI: 10.1177/0735633118817879

Al-Refai, M., Alzu'bi, A., Yaseen, N. B., & Obeidat, T. (2023). Arabic sentiment analysis with federated deep learning. In *UK Workshop on Computational Intelligence* (pp. 29–38). Springer.

Alsahafi, R., Alzahrani, A., & Mehmood, R. (2023). Smarter Sustainable Tourism: Data-Driven Multi-Perspective Parameter Discovery for Autonomous Design and Operations. *Sustainability (Basel)*, *15*(5), 4166. Advance online publication. DOI: 10.3390/su15054166

Alzeiby, E. A., Islam, N., Shaik, A. S., & Yaqub, M. Z. (2025). AI adoption in enterprises for enhanced strategic human resource management practices: Benefiting the employee engagement and experience. *Journal of Enterprise Information Management*, *38*(5), 1441–1464. DOI: 10.1108/JEIM-05-2024-0249

American Psychological Association. (2023). 2023 Work in America survey. https://www.apa.org/pubs/reports/work-in-america/2023-work-america-ai monitoring

Anand, A., Doll, J., & Ray, P. (2024). Drowning in silence: A scale development and validation of quiet quitting and quiet firing. *The International Journal of Organizational Analysis*, *32*(4), 721–743. DOI: 10.1108/IJOA-01-2023-3600

Anderson, M., Anderson, S. L., Gounaris, A., & Kosteletos, G. (2021). Towards moral machines: A discussion with Michael Anderson and Susan Leigh Anderson. *Conatus: Journal of Philosophy*, *6*(1), 177–202. DOI: 10.12681/cjp.26832

Andrieux, M., Henrio, L., & Radanne, G. (2024). Active objects based on algebraic effects. In *Active Object Languages: Current Research Trends* (pp. 3–36). Springer Nature Switzerland, Cham. DOI: 10.1007/978-3-031-51060-1_1

Ansoff, H. I. (1984). *Implanting strategic management* (2nd ed.). Prentice Hall.

Antal, C., Cioara, T., Anghel, I., Antal, M., & Salomie, I. (2021). Distributed ledger technology review and decentralized applications development guidelines. *Future Internet*, *13*(3), 62. Advance online publication. DOI: 10.3390/fi13030062

Antoun, W., Baly, F., & Hajj, H. (2020). AraBERT: Transformer-based model for Arabic language understanding. *arXiv*. https://arxiv.org/abs/2003.00104

Aouedi, O., Piamrat, K., & Parrein, B. (2021). Performance evaluation of feature selection and tree-based algorithms for traffic classification. In *2021 IEEE International Conference on Communications Workshops (ICC Workshops)* (pp. 1–6). IEEE. DOI: 10.1109/ICCWorkshops50388.2021.9473580

Appel, G., Grewal, L., Hadi, R., & Stephen, A. T. (2020). The future of social media in marketing. *Journal of the Academy of Marketing Science*, *48*(1), 79–95. DOI: 10.1007/s11747-019-00695-1 PMID: 32431463

Aria, M., & Cuccurullo, C. (2017). Bibliometrix: An R-tool for comprehensive science mapping analysis. *Journal of Informetrics*, *11*(4), 959–975. DOI: 10.1016/j.joi.2017.08.007

Arshad, M. Z., Arshad, D., Lamsali, H., Ibrahim Alshuaibi, A. S., Ibrahim Alshuaibi, M. S., Albashar, G., Shakoor, A., & Chuah, L. F. (2023). Strategic resources alignment for sustainability: The impact of innovation capability and intellectual capital on SME's performance. Moderating role of external environment. *Journal of Cleaner Production*, *417*(June), 137884. DOI: 10.1016/j.jclepro.2023.137884

Arthur, W. B. (2009). *The nature of technology: What it is and how it evolves.* Simon & Schuster.

Ascarza, E. (2018). Retention futility: Targeting high-risk customers might be ineffective. *JMR, Journal of Marketing Research*, *55*(1), 80–98. DOI: 10.1509/jmr.16.0163

Au, W., & Tsang, N. (2023). Gig workers' self-protective behaviour against legal risks: An application of protection motivation theory. *International Journal of Contemporary Hospitality Management*, *35*(3), 1376–1397. DOI: 10.1108/IJCHM-12-2021-1537

Avci, U., Madanoglu, M., & Okumus, F. (2011). Strategic orientation and performance of tourism firms: Evidence from a developing country. *Tourism Management*, *32*(1), 147–157. DOI: 10.1016/j.tourman.2010.01.017

Baaziz, M. (2014). L'intelligence économique et la réactivité stratégique. *Revue Française de Management*, *18*(4), 122–136.

Badghish, S., & Soomro, Y. A. (2024). AI adoption by smes to achieve sustainable business performance. *Sustainability*, *16*(5), 1–24. DOI: 10.3390/su16051864 PMID: 38510213

Bae, S., Jung, T., Cho, J., & Kwon, O. (2025). Effects of meta-human characteristics on user acceptance: From the perspective of uncanny valley theory. *Behaviour & Information Technology*, *44*(4), 731–748. DOI: 10.1080/0144929X.2024.2338408

Bagozzi, R. P. (2007). The legacy of the technology acceptance model and a proposal for a paradigm shift. *Journal of the Association for Information Systems*, *8*(4), 244–254. DOI: 10.17705/1jais.00122

Bakker, A. B., & Demerouti, E. (2007). The job demands-resources model: State of the art. *Journal of Managerial Psychology*, *22*(3), 309–328. DOI: 10.1108/02683940710733115

Bandura, A. (1977). Self-efficacy: Toward a unifying theory of behavioral change. *Psychological Review*, *84*(2), 191–215. DOI: 10.1037/0033-295X.84.2.191

Bănescu, C. E., i an, E., & Manea, D. (2022). The impact of E-commerce on the labor market. *Sustainability (Basel)*, *14*(9), 5086. DOI: 10.3390/su14095086

Baporikar, N., & Shikokola, S. (2020). Information technology adoption dynamics for SMEs in the manufacturing sector of Namibia. [IJICTRAME]. *International Journal of ICT Research in Africa and the Middle East*, *9*(2), 60–77. DOI: 10.4018/IJICTRAME.2020070104

Baraghani, N. S. (2008). Factors influencing the adoption of internet banking [Master's thesis, Luleå University of Technology]. DIVA. http://urn.kb.se/resolve?urn=urn:nbn:se:ltu:diva-43300

Barnes, S. J. (2002). The mobile commerce value chain: Analysis and future developments. *International Journal of Information Management*, *22*(2), 91–108. DOI: 10.1016/S0268-4012(01)00047-0

Barney, J. (1991). Firm resources and sustained competitive advantage. *Journal of Management*, *17*(1), 99–120. DOI: 10.1177/014920639101700108

Baron, R. M., & Kenny, D. A. (1986). The moderator–mediator variable distinction in social psychological research: Conceptual, strategic, and statistical considerations. *Journal of Personality and Social Psychology*, *51*(6), 1173–1182. DOI: 10.1037/0022-3514.51.6.1173 PMID: 3806354

Barrena-Martínez, J., Cricelli, L., Ferrándiz, E., Greco, M., & Grimaldi, M. (2020). Joint forces: Towards an integration of intellectual capital theory and the open innovation paradigm. *Journal of Business Research*, *112*(June), 261–270. DOI: 10.1016/j.jbusres.2019.10.029

Barrett, L. F. (2006). Solving the emotion paradox: Categorization and the experience of emotion. *Personality and Social Psychology Review*, *10*(1), 20–46. DOI: 10.1207/s15327957pspr1001_2

Barrett, M., Liyala, S., Oborn, E., & Prince, K. (2024). Building hope for the poor with digital services: Providing prosperity, justice, and dignity for ALL. *Africa Journal of Management, 10*(1), 75–88. DOI: 10.1080/23322373.2024.2316508

Battour, M., Mady, K., Salaheldeen, M., Elsotouhy, M., Elbendary, I., & Boğan, E. (2023). AI-enabled technologies to assist Muslim tourists in Halal-friendly tourism. *Journal of Islamic Marketing, 14*(5), 1291–1309. DOI: 10.1108/JIMA-01-2022-0001

Baumard, P. (2020). *Stratégie et organisations: Comprendre les dynamiques de l'intelligence informationnelle*. Presses Universitaires de France.

Baykov, F. Y., & Ershov, V. S. (2023, October). International trade digital transformation impact on the global digital platforms expansion. In *2023 International Conference on Engineering Management of Communication and Technology (EMCTECH)* (pp. 1-5). IEEE.DOI: 10.1109/EMCTECH58502.2023.10296940

Bejjani, A. (2024). Analyzing competitive intelligence in a digital age. *Journal of Strategy and Management, 31*(2), 70–85.

Benaissa, B., & Kobayashi, M. (2023). The consumers' response to product design: A narrative review. *Ergonomics, 66*(6), 791–820. DOI: 10.1080/00140139.2022.2127919

Bergman, J. Z., Cummings, T. G., & Maher, C. P. (2022). Employee disengagement and organizational responses. *Journal of Organizational Behavior, 43*(2), 145–161.

Bernard, L. (2008). *La gestion stratégique de l'intelligence économique dans un environnement turbulent*. Éditions Business Insights.

Bernat, J. (2008). *La planification stratégique et la surveillance de l'environnement*. Presses Universitaires de France.

Bhalla, R., Chowdhary, N., & Ranjan, A. (2021). Spiritual tourism for psychotherapeutic healing post COVID-19. *Journal of Travel & Tourism Marketing, 38*(8), 769–781. DOI: 10.1080/10548408.2021.1930630

Bietti, E. (2020, January). From ethics washing to ethics bashing: a view on tech ethics from within moral philosophy. In *Proceedings of the 2020 conference on fairness, accountability, and transparency* (pp. 210-219). DOI: 10.1145/3351095.3372860

Bigliardi, B., Filippelli, S., & Tagliente, L. (2022). Industry 4.0 and Open Innovation: Evidence from a case study. *Procedia Computer Science, 200*(2019), 1796–1805. DOI: 10.1016/j.procs.2022.01.380

Bisson, C. (2021). Les enjeux de l'intelligence économique dans le secteur concurrentiel. *Revue Française d'Intelligence Économique*, *7*(1), 34–45.

Blanchard, P., El Mhamdi, E. M., Guerraoui, R., & Stainer, J. (2017). Machine learning with adversaries: Byzantine-tolerant gradient descent. *Advances in Neural Information Processing Systems*, 30.

Blau, P. M. (1964). *Exchange and power in social life*. Wiley.

Blok, V., & Lemmens, P. (2015). The emerging concept of responsible innovation: Three reasons why it is questionable and calls for a radical transformation of the concept of innovation. In Koops, B. (Eds.), *Responsible Innovation 2* (pp. 19–35). Springer. DOI: 10.1007/978-3-319-17308-5_2

Bogers, M., Chesbrough, H., & Moedas, C. (2019). Open innovation: Research, practices, and policies. *California Management Review*, *60*(2), 5–16. DOI: 10.1177/0008125617745086

Bontis, N. (1998). Intellectual capital: An exploratory study that develops measures and models. *Management Decision*, *36*(2), 63–76. DOI: 10.1108/00251749810204142

Boo, H., & Chua, B. (2022). An integrative model of facial recognition check-in technology adoption intention: The perspective of hotel guests in Singapore. *International Journal of Contemporary Hospitality Management*, *34*(11), 4052–4079. DOI: 10.1108/IJCHM-12-2021-1471

Bostrom, N. (2002). Existential risks: Analysing human extinction scenarios and related hazards. *Journal of Evolution and Technology / WTA*, *9*, 1–36.

Bowman, S. R. (2024). Eight things to know about large language models. *Critical AI*, *2*(2). Advance online publication. DOI: 10.1215/2834703X-11556011

Boyack, K. W., & Klavans, R. (2010). Co-citation analysis, bibliographic coupling, and direct citation: Which citation approach represents the research front most accurately? *Journal of the American Society for Information Science and Technology*, *61*(12), 2389–2404. DOI: 10.1002/asi.21419

Breiman, L. (2001). Random forests. *Machine Learning*, *45*(1), 5–32. DOI: 10.1023/A:1010933404324

Brown, S., Davidovic, J., & Hasan, A. (2021). The algorithm audit: Scoring the algorithms that score us. *Big Data & Society*, *8*(1), 2053951720983865. DOI: 10.1177/2053951720983865

Brüggemann, E. R., Monteiro, J. J., & Lunkes, R. J. (2022). The influence of performance measurement systems on organizational agility and open innovation. *Revista de Contabilidade e Organizacoes*, *16*. Advance online publication. DOI: 10.11606/issn.1982-6486.rco.2022.193897

Bryman, A. (2021). *Social Research Methods*. Oxford University Press.

Bryson, J. J. (2018). Patiency is not a virtue: AI and the design of ethical systems. *Ethics and Information Technology*, *20*(1), 15–26. DOI: 10.1007/s10676-018-9448-6

Buhalis, D., Lin, M. S., & Leung, D. (2022). Metaverse as a driver for customer experience and value co-creation: Implications for hospitality and tourism management and marketing. *International Journal of Contemporary Hospitality Management*, *35*(2), 701–716. DOI: 10.1108/IJCHM-05-2022-0631

Buhmann, A. (2016). Corporate social responsibility: Towards new self-regulation in organizational communication. *Management Communication Quarterly*, *30*(3), 283–291.

Buhmann, A., & Fieseler, C. (2021). Corporate responsibility and artificial intelligence: Toward a CSR 4.0 paradigm. *Journal of Business Ethics*, *170*(2), 1–18.

Buhmann, A., Fieseler, C., & Arora, P. (2021). Towards a digital corporate social responsibility. *Journal of Business Research*, *124*, 673–684.

Buttazzo, G. (2008). Artificial consciousness: Hazardous questions (and answers). *Artificial Intelligence in Medicine*, *44*(2), 139–146. DOI: 10.1016/j.artmed.2008.07.004

Cai, R., Cain, L., & Jeon, H. (2022). Customers' perceptions of hotel AI-enabled voice assistants: Does brand matter? *International Journal of Contemporary Hospitality Management*, *34*(8), 2807–2831. DOI: 10.1108/IJCHM-10-2021-1313

Caliskan, A., Özkan Özen, Y. D., & Ozturkoglu, Y. (2021). Digital transformation of traditional marketing business model in new industry era. *Journal of Enterprise Information Management*, *34*(4), 1252–1273. DOI: 10.1108/JEIM-02-2020-0084

Calvo, R. A., & D'Mello, S. (2010). Affect detection: An interdisciplinary review of models, methods, and their applications. *IEEE Transactions on Affective Computing*, *1*(1), 18–37. DOI: 10.1109/T-AFFC.2010.1

Campbell, D. T., & Fiske, D. W. (1959). Convergent and discriminant validation by the multitrait-multimethod matrix. *Psychological Bulletin*, *56*(2), 81–105. DOI: 10.1037/h0046016 PMID: 13634291

Can, H. C., & Alas, D. K. (2025). The silent scream of digital future: Exploring AI awareness and quiet quitting in Turkish teachers. *Acta Psychologica*, *260*, 105589. DOI: 10.1016/j.actpsy.2025.105589

Cannone, G., & Ughetto, E. (2014). Born globals: A cross-country survey on high-tech start-ups. *International Business Review*, *23*(1), 272–283. DOI: 10.1016/j.ibusrev.2013.05.003

Cannon, W. (1927). The James-Lange Theory of Emotions: A Critical Examination and an Alternative Theory. *The American Journal of Psychology*, *39*(1/4), 106–124. DOI: 10.2307/1415404

Cao, S., & Cao, N. (2025). Emotion-Aware Design: Modulating Valence, Arousal, and Dominance in Communication via Design. arXiv preprint arXiv:2502.16038.

Cao, C.. (2013). Agilité et compétitivité dans les entreprises modernes. *Journal of Strategy and Management*, *17*(4), 243–258.

Carrasco-García, P.-M., Frías-Jamilena, D.-M., & Polo-Peña, A.-I. (2025). The Impact of Virtual Reality and Intelligent Virtual Environments on the Tourist Experience: The Moderating Effect of Cognitive Style. *Journal of Travel Research*, 00472875251346933. Advance online publication. DOI: 10.1177/00472875251346933

Carroll, J. M. (2009). Human computer interaction (HCI). Encyclopedia of Human-Computer Interaction. Aarhus: The Interaction Design Foundation, 1, 21-62.

Carroll, A. B. (1999). Corporate social responsibility: Evolution of a definitional construct. *Business & Society*, *38*(3), 268–295. DOI: 10.1177/000765039903800303

Carroll, A. B. (2021). Corporate social responsibility: Perspectives on the CSR construct's development and future. *Business & Society*, *60*(6), 1258–1278. DOI: 10.1177/00076503211001765

Casana, J., Laugier, E. J., Hill, A. C., Reese, K. M., Ferwerda, C., McCoy, M. D., & Ladefoged, T. (2021). Exploring archaeological landscapes using drone-acquired lidar: Case studies from Hawai'i, Colorado, and New Hampshire, USA. *Journal of Archaeological Science, Reports*, *39*(July), 103133. DOI: 10.1016/j.jasrep.2021.103133

Cavusgil, S. T., Knight, G., & Riesenberger, J. R. (2020). *International business: the new realities, global edition. Harlow*. Pearson.

Caza, B. B., & Cortina, L. M. (2007). From insult to injury: Explaining the impact of incivility. *Journal of Management*, *33*(4), 1–29.

Cennamo, C. (2021). Competing in digital markets: A platform-based perspective. *The Academy of Management Perspectives*, *35*(2), 265–291. DOI: 10.5465/amp.2016.0048

Cepeda, G., & Vera, D. (2007). Dynamic capabilities and operational capabilities: A knowledge management perspective. *Journal of Business Research*, *60*(5), 426–437. DOI: 10.1016/j.jbusres.2007.01.013

Chaffey, D., Ellis-Chadwick, F., & Mayer, R. (2009). *Internet marketing: strategy, implementation and practice*. Pearson education.

Chandler, A. D. (1962). *Strategy and structure: Chapters in the history of the industrial enterprise*. MIT Press.

Chaturvedi, P., Sharma, J., & Ranjan, A. (2024). The Role of Souvenir Marketing in Sustaining Handmade Craftsmanship. *ShodhKosh: Journal of Visual and Performing Arts, 5*(3), 278–294. DOI: 10.29121/shodhkosh.v5.i3.2024.1401

Chaudhary, A., Rastogi, R., Mattoo, A., Kumar, P., Kumari, T., & Dubey, D. (2025). Generative adversarial networks (GANs). In Generative AI: Disruptive technologies for innovative applications (pp. 29–55). Wiley. Book DOI: https://doi.org/DOI: 10.1002/9781119963605

Chen, C., Hu, W., & Wei, X. (2024). From anxiety to action: Exploring the impact of artificial intelligence anxiety and artificial intelligence self-efficacy on motivated learning of undergraduate students. *Interactive Learning Environments*, •••, 1–16. DOI: 10.1080/10494820.2024.2371937

Chen, J., Zhao, X., & Wang, Y. (2015). A new measurement of intellectual capital and its impact on innovation performance in an open innovation paradigm. *International Journal of Technology Management, 67*(1), 1–25. DOI: 10.1504/IJTM.2015.065885

Chen, P., Wu, L., & Wang, L. (2023). AI fairness in data management and analytics: A review on challenges, methodologies and applications. *Applied Sciences (Basel, Switzerland), 13*(18), 10258. DOI: 10.3390/app131810258

Chen, T., & Guestrin, C. (2016). XGBoost: A scalable tree boosting system. In *Proceedings of the 22nd ACM SIGKDD International Conference on Knowledge Discovery and Data Mining* (pp. 785–794). DOI: 10.1145/2939672.2939785

Chen, Y., Hsu, T., & Lu, Y. (2018). Impact of flow on mobile shopping intention. *Journal of Retailing and Consumer Services, 41*, 281–287. DOI: 10.1016/j.jretconser.2017.04.004

Chen, Y., Mandler, T., & Meyer-Waarden, L. (2021). Three decades of research on loyalty programs: A literature review and future research agenda. *Journal of Business Research, 124*, 179–197. DOI: 10.1016/j.jbusres.2020.11.057

Chen, Y., Wang, Q., & Zhang, J. (2025). The role of cross-border E-commerce platforms in the digital economy: Empower firms to gain global market insights to increase global competitiveness. *Journal of Digital Management, 1*(1), 1–17. DOI: 10.1007/s44362-024-00003-0

Chesbrough, H. (2006). Open innovation: a new paradigm for understanding industrial innovation. *Open Innovation: Researching a New Paradigm, 400*, 0–19.

Chesbrough, H. (2003). *Open innovation: The new imperative for creating and profiting from technology*. Harvard Business School Press.

Chesbrough, H. (2020). *Open innovation results: Going beyond the hype and getting down to business*. Oxford University Press.

Chesbrough, H., & Crowther, A. K. (2006). Beyond high tech: Early adopters of open innovation in other industries. *Research Management, 36*(3), 229–236.

Chin, W. W. (1998). Commentary: Issues and opinion on structural equation modeling. In *MIS quarterly* (pp. vii–xvi). JSTOR.

Chin, W. W. (1998). Commentary: Issues and opinion on structural equation modeling. *Management Information Systems Quarterly*, vii–xvi.

Chi, O. H., Chi, C. G., Gursoy, D., & Nunkoo, R. (2023). Customers' acceptance of artificially intelligent service robots: The influence of trust and culture. *International Journal of Information Management, 70*, 102623. DOI: 10.1016/j.ijinfomgt.2023.102623

Choe, J. (2025). Religious tourism. *Tourism Geographies, 27*(3–4), 830–839. DOI: 10.1080/14616688.2024.2423168

Choo, C. W. (2023). *The knowing organization: How organizations use information to construct meaning, create knowledge, and make decisions* (3rd ed.). Oxford University Press.

Chuttur, M. Y. (2009). "Overview of the Technology Acceptance Model: Origins, Developments and Future Directions, " Indiana University, USA. *Sprouts: Working Papers on Information Systems*, 9(37). http://sprouts.aisnet.org/9-37

Cimino, at el., 2025. (2025). *Corp Soc Responsibility Env - 2025 - Cimino - Artificial Intelligence Adoption for Sustainable Growth in SMEs An Extended (1).pdf.*

Ciupac-Ulici, M., Beju, D.-G., Bresfelean, V. P., & Zanellato, G. (2023). Which Factors Contribute to the Global Expansion of M-Commerce? *Electronics (Basel), 12*(1), 197. DOI: 10.3390/electronics12010197

Clarke, R. (2019). Why the world wants controls over artificial intelligence. *Computer Law & Security Review, 35*(4), 423–433. DOI: 10.1016/j.clsr.2019.04.006

Coeckelbergh, M. (2020). *AI ethics*. MIT Press. DOI: 10.7551/mitpress/12549.001.0001

Cohen, E., & Amar, A. (2025). *Organizational learning in the age of digital transformation*. Routledge.

Cohen, L. (2007). Les capacités d'apprentissage organisationnel dans les environnements volatils. *Journal of Organizational Behavior, 28*(6), 567–589.

Cohen, L., & Levinthal, D. A. (1990). Absorptive capacity: A new perspective on learning and innovation. *Administrative Science Quarterly, 35*(1), 128–152. DOI: 10.2307/2393553

Conceição, A., & Palma-Moreira, A. (2025). The Relationship Between Occupational Stress, Burnout, and Perceived Performance: The Moderating Role of Work Regime. *Administrative Sciences, 15*(10), 377. DOI: 10.3390/admsci15100377

Constantinides, P., Henfridsson, O., & Parker, G. G. (2018). Introduction—Platforms and infrastructures in the digital age. *Information Systems Research, 29*(2), 381–400. DOI: 10.1287/isre.2018.0794

Coppola, D. (2021). E-commerce worldwide-statistics & facts. *Retrieved,* (Dec), 30.

Costa, A., Crupi, A., De Marco, C. E., & Di Minin, A. (2023). SMEs and open innovation: Challenges and costs of engagement. *Technological Forecasting and Social Change, 194*(June 2022), 122731. DOI: 10.1016/j.techfore.2023.122731

Costa, J., & Castro, R. (2021). SMEs must go online—E-commerce as an escape hatch for resilience and survivability. *Journal of Theoretical and Applied Electronic Commerce Research, 16*(7), 3043–3062. DOI: 10.3390/jtaer16070166

Cowin, L. S., Johnson, M., Craven, R. G., & Marsh, H. W. (2008). Causal modeling of self-concept, job satisfaction, and retention of nurses. *International Journal of Nursing Studies, 45*(10), 1449–1459. DOI: 10.1016/j.ijnurstu.2007.10.009 PMID: 18242611

Cowls, J., Tsamados, A., Taddeo, M., & Floridi, L. (2021). The AI gambit: Leveraging artificial intelligence to combat climate change—Opportunities, challenges, and recommendations. *AI & Society, 36*(3), 1–20.

Cox, D. R. (1958). The regression analysis of binary sequences. *Journal of the Royal Statistical Society. Series B, Statistical Methodology, 20*(2), 215–232. DOI: 10.1111/j.2517-6161.1958.tb00292.x

Creswell, J. W. (2023). *Educational Research.* Pearson.

Creswell, J. W., & Creswell, J. D. (2018). Research Design: Qualitative, Quantitative, and Mixed Methods Approaches. *Sage (Atlanta, Ga.).*

Damaševičius, R., & Sidekerskienė, T. (2024). Virtual worlds for learning in the metaverse: A narrative review. *Sustainability (Basel), 16*(5), 2032. Advance online publication. DOI: 10.3390/su16052032

Das, D. K., Chowdhary, B., Mishra, S. V., & Aditi, A. (2024). Varanasi—The Making of a Smart Heritage City. *Environment & Urbanization Asia*, *15*(1), 141–155. DOI: 10.1177/09754253241230588

Dash, G., Ramaswami, S. N., & Singh, R. (2021). CB-SEM vs PLS-SEM methods for research in social science: A comprehensive review and comparison. *Technological Forecasting and Social Change*, *173*, 121092. DOI: 10.1016/j.techfore.2021.121092

Davis, F. D. (1986). A technology acceptance model for empirically testing new end-user information systems: Theory and results [Doctoral dissertation, Massachusetts Institute of Technology]. MIT Sloan School of Management.

Davis, F. D. (2015). On the relationship between HCI and technology acceptance research. In *Human-computer interaction and management information systems: Foundations* (pp. 409-415). Routledge.

Davis, F. D. (1989). Perceived usefulness, perceived ease of use, and user acceptance of information technology. *Management Information Systems Quarterly*, *13*(3), 319–340. DOI: 10.2307/249008

Davis, F. D., Bagozzi, R. P., & Warshaw, P. R. (1989). User acceptance of computer technology: A comparison of two theoretical models. *Management Science*, *35*(8), 982–1003. DOI: 10.1287/mnsc.35.8.982

Davis, F. D., Bagozzi, R. P., & Warshaw, P. R. (1992). Extrinsic and intrinsic motivation to use computers in the workplace. *Journal of Applied Social Psychology*, *22*(14), 1111–1132. DOI: 10.1111/j.1559-1816.1992.tb00945.x

De Almeida, P. G. R., dos Santos, C. D., & Farias, J. S. (2021). Artificial intelligence regulation: A framework for governance. *Ethics and Information Technology*, *23*(3), 505–525. DOI: 10.1007/s10676-021-09593-z

De Veirman, M., Cauberghe, V., & Hudders, L. (2017). Marketing through Instagram influencers: The impact of number of followers and product divergence on brand attitude. *International Journal of Advertising*, *36*(5), 798–828. DOI: 10.1080/02650487.2017.1348035

Deci, E. L., & Ryan, R. M. (2000). The "what" and "why" of goal pursuits: Human needs and the self-determination of behavior. *Psychological Inquiry*, *11*(4), 227–268. DOI: 10.1207/S15327965PLI1104_01

DeLone, W. H., & McLean, E. R. (2004). Measuring e-commerce success: Applying the DeLone & McLean information systems success model. *International Journal of Electronic Commerce*, *9*(1), 31–47. DOI: 10.1080/10864415.2004.11044317

DemandSage. (2025). *Global Mobile Commerce Statistics 2025.* Retrieved from https://www.demandsage.com/mobile-commerce-statistics/

Demerouti, E., Bakker, A. B., Nachreiner, F., & Schaufeli, W. B. (2001). The job demands-resources model of burnout. *The Journal of Applied Psychology, 86*(3), 499–512. DOI: 10.1037/0021-9010.86.3.499

Desmet, P. (2003). A multilayered model of product emotions. *The Design Journal, 6*(2), 4–13. DOI: 10.2752/146069203789355480

Desmet, P. M. (2012). Faces of product pleasure: 25 positive emotions in human-product interactions. *International Journal of Design, 6*(2).

DeVellis, R., & Thorpe, C. (2021). Scale Development. *Sage (Atlanta, Ga.).*

Di Pietro, L., Guglielmetti Mugion, R., Mattia, G., Renzi, M. F., & Toni, M. (2015). The integrated model on mobile payment acceptance (IMMPA): An empirical application to public transport. *Transportation Research Part C, Emerging Technologies, 56*, 463–479. DOI: 10.1016/j.trc.2015.05.001

Dignum, V. (2019). *Responsible artificial intelligence: Developing and using AI responsibly*. Springer. DOI: 10.1007/978-3-030-30371-6

Dillon, A., & Morris, M. G. (1996). User acceptance of information technology: Theories and models. In Williams, M. (Ed.), *Annual review of information science and technology* (Vol. 31, pp. 3–32). Information Today.

Ding, L., Venditti, M., & Antonucci, G. (2024). Unveiling user responses to AI-powered personalised recommendations: A qualitative study of consumer engagement dynamics on Douyin. *Qualitative Market Research, 28*(2), 234–255. Advance online publication. DOI: 10.1108/QMR-11-2023-0151

Dirks, K. T., & Ferrin, D. L. (2002). Trust in leadership: Meta-analytic findings and implications for research and practice. *The Journal of Applied Psychology, 87*(4), 611–628. DOI: 10.1037/0021-9010.87.4.611

Djennas, B.. (2015). Le rôle de l'intelligence économique dans le choix stratégique des PME. *Revue Algérienne de Management, 12*(3), 54–68.

Donthu, N., Kumar, S., Mukherjee, D., Pandey, N., & Lim, W. M. (2021). How to conduct a bibliometric analysis: An overview and guidelines. *Journal of Business Research, 133*, 285–296. DOI: 10.1016/j.jbusres.2021.04.070

Dufour, A., & Beaudry, P. (2024). L'intelligence économique à l'ère du numérique et de la stratégie d'innovation. *Innovation & Strategy Review, 31*(2), 111–124.

Dufour, R., & Lièvre, A. (2023). Transformations organisationnelles et gestion des connaissances dans un environnement digital. *Management et Transformation, 15*(2), 42–55.

Dwivedi, Y. K., Hughes, L., Ismagilova, E., Aarts, G., Coombs, C., Crick, T., Duan, Y., Dwivedi, R., Edwards, J., Eirug, A., Galanos, V., Ilavarasan, P. V., Janssen, M., Jones, P., Kar, A. K., Kizgin, H., Kronemann, B., Lal, B., Lucini, B., & Williams, M. D. (2021). Artificial intelligence (AI): Multidisciplinary perspectives. *International Journal of Information Management, 57*, 101994. DOI: 10.1016/j.ijinfomgt.2019.08.002

Dyer, J.. (2023). Proactivité et adaptation stratégique dans un monde globalisé. *Journal of Management Studies, 45*(5), 98–115.

Dzenopoljac, V., Senic, V., Labben, T. G., Arici, H. E., & Koseoglu, M. (2025). Intellectual capital in hospitality and tourism: A critical review and future research agenda. *International Hospitality Review, 39*(1), 124–143. DOI: 10.1108/IHR-02-2023-0010

Dziubaniuk, O., & Nyholm, M. (2021). Constructivist approach in teaching sustainability and business ethics: A case study. *International Journal of Sustainability in Higher Education, 22*(1), 177–197. DOI: 10.1108/IJSHE-02-2020-0081

Edmondson, A. C. (1999). Psychological safety and learning behavior in work teams. *Administrative Science Quarterly, 44*(2), 350–383. DOI: 10.2307/2666999

Eisenhardt, K. M., & Martin, J. A. (2017). Dynamic capabilities: what are they? *The SMS Blackwell handbook of organizational capabilities*, 341-363.

Eisenhardt, K. M. (1989). Building theories from case study research. *Academy of Management Review, 14*(4), 532–550. DOI: 10.2307/258557

Ekman, P. (1992). An argument for basic emotions. *Cognition and Emotion, 6*(3-4), 169–200. DOI: 10.1080/02699939208411068

Elkington, J. (1998). *Cannibals with forks: The triple bottom line of 21st century business.* New Society Publishers.

Elmadany, A. A., Mubarak, H., & Magdy, W. (2018). An Arabic speech-act and sentiment corpus of tweets. In *Proceedings of the 3rd Workshop on Open-Source Arabic Corpora and Processing Tools.* European Language Resources Association (ELRA).

Etikan, I. (2016). Comparison of Convenience Sampling and Purposive Sampling. *American Journal of Theoretical and Applied Statistics*, *5*(1), 1. DOI: 10.11648/j.ajtas.20160501.11

European Commission. (2021). *Proposal for a regulation laying down harmonized rules on artificial intelligence (Artificial Intelligence Act)* (COM(2021) 206 final).

Fan, Y., Li, Y., Zhan, M., Cui, H., & Zhang, Y. (2020). IoTDefender: A federated transfer learning intrusion detection framework for 5G IoT. In *2020 IEEE 14th International Conference on Big Data Science and Engineering (BigDataSE)* (pp. 88–95). IEEE. DOI: 10.1109/BigDataSE50710.2020.00023

Feenberg, A. (1999). *Questioning technology*. Routledge.

Feng, G. C., Su, X., Lin, Z., He, Y., Luo, N., & Zhang, Y. (2021). Determinants of technology acceptance: Two model-based meta-analytic reviews. *Journalism & Mass Communication Quarterly*, *98*(1), 83–104. DOI: 10.1177/1077699020952400

Ferguson, S. M., & Henrekson, M. (2019). The long-run performance of born globals in computing: the role of digital platforms. https://ssrn.com/abstract=3229229

Fishbein, M., & Ajzen, I. (1975). *Belief, attitude, intention and behavior: An introduction to theory and research.* Addison-Wesley.

Fissellier, P.. (2018). L'évolution de la fonction veille stratégique dans l'intelligence économique. *Revue de la Veille et de la Stratégie*, *20*(3), 98–113.

Fitrianti, N. G., Hanuun, N. N. P., & Fatmasari, R. R. (2024). Dynamics of customer participation in subscription business models: case analysis and implications for sustainable marketing strategies. *Journal of Economics, Accounting, Business, Management, Engineering and Society,* 1(5), 15-28. https://kisainstitute.com/index.php/kisainstitute/article/view/24

Fix, E. (1985). *Discriminatory analysis: Nonparametric discrimination, consistency properties* (Vol. 1). USAF School of Aviation Medicine.

Floridi, L. (2020). *The logic of information: A theory of philosophy as conceptual design*. Oxford University Press.

Floridi, L., Cowls, J., Beltrametti, M., Chatila, R., Chazerand, P., Dignum, V., Luetge, C., Madelin, R., Pagallo, U., Rossi, F., Schafer, B., Valcke, P., & Vayena, E. (2018). AI4People—An Ethical Framework for a Good AI Society. *Minds and Machines*, *28*(4), 689–707. DOI: 10.1007/s11023-018-9482-5

Formica, S., & Sfodera, F. (2022). The great resignation and quiet quitting paradigm shifts: An overview of current situation and future research directions. *Journal of Hospitality Marketing & Management, 31*(8), 899–907. DOI: 10.1080/19368623.2022.2136601

Fornell, C., & Larcker, D. F. (1981). Evaluating structural equation models with unobservable variables and measurement error. *JMR, Journal of Marketing Research, 18*(1), 39–50. DOI: 10.1177/002224378101800104

Freeman, R. E. (1984). *Strategic management: A stakeholder approach.* Pitman.

Freyn, F., & Farley, M. (2020). The impact of intelligence and information sharing in the healthcare industry. *Journal of Healthcare Management, 34*(5), 243–257.

Frijda, N. H. (1988). The laws of emotion. *The American Psychologist, 43*(5), 349–358. DOI: 10.1037/0003-066X.43.5.349

Fuchs, C. (2017). Social Media: A Critical Introduction. *Sage (Atlanta, Ga.).*

Galanis, P., Katsiroumpa, A., Vraka, I., Siskou, O., Konstantakopoulou, O., Moisoglou, I., & Kaitelidou, D. (2023). The quiet quitting scale: Development and initial validation. *AIMS Public Health, 10*(4), 828–848. DOI: 10.3934/publichealth.2023055

Garriga, E., & Melé, D. (2004). Corporate social responsibility theories: Mapping the territory. *Journal of Business Ethics, 53*(1–2), 51–71. DOI: 10.1023/B:BUSI.0000039399.90587.34

Gavino, M. C., Wayne, S. J., & Erdogan, B. (2012). Discretionary and transactional human resource practices and employee outcomes: The role of perceived organizational support. *Human Resource Management, 51*(5), 665–686. DOI: 10.1002/hrm.21493

Gbadegeshin, S. A., Olaleye, S. A., Ukpabi, D. C., Omokaro, B., Mogaji, E., Ugwuja, A. A., & Adetoyinbo, A. (2021). Female unemployment in an emerging economy: A study of online social support as a coping strategy. In *Technology and Women's Empowerment* (1st ed., pp. 93–106). Routledge. DOI: 10.4324/9781003045946-12

Gebremichael, H. S. (2018). The impact of open innovation practice on innovative performance through intellectual capital: Empirical study on SMEs. *African Journal of Business Management, 12*(20), 609–619. DOI: 10.5897/AJBM2018.8651

Gefen, D., Karahanna, E., & Straub, D. W. (2003). Trust and TAM in online shopping: An integrated model. *Management Information Systems Quarterly, 27*(1), 51–90. DOI: 10.2307/30036519

George, G.. (2021). Digital Sustainability and Entrepreneurship. *Journal of Business Venturing*, *36*(5), 106–120.

George, G., Merrill, R. K., & Schillebeeckx, S. J. D. (2021). Digital sustainability and entrepreneurship: How digital innovations are helping tackle climate change and sustainable development. *Journal of Business Venturing*, *36*(5), 106–120.

Gladilina, I., Degtev, G., Kochetkov, E., Tretyak, E., Stepanova, D., & Mutaliyeva, L. (2023). Development of User Subscription Services in E-Commerce: Effects on Consumer Behavior. *International Journal of Computer Science & Network Security*, *23*(11), 53–58. DOI: 10.22937/IJCSNS.2023.23.11.6

Gloaguen, A. (2014). L'intelligence économique et son impact sur le management stratégique. *Revue de Gestion Stratégique*, *23*(4), 122–134.

Gloaguen, C. (2012). *L'intelligence économique dans le management stratégique*. L'Harmattan.

Gloaguen, C. (2023). Les dynamiques organisationnelles et l'intelligence économique en pratique. *Revue de Management Stratégique*, *24*(3), 211–225.

Gong, J. (2024). Challenges and Countermeasures for China's Cross-Border E-Commerce in International Market Competition under the "Belt and Road" Initiative. *Advances in Economics. Management and Political Sciences*, *111*, 173–179. DOI: 10.54254/2754-1169/2024.17763

Goria, F. (2006). *La stratégie informationnelle dans les organisations*. Pearson.

Gozalo-Brizuela, R., & Garrido-Merchán, E. C. (2023). A survey of generative AI applications. arXiv. https://arxiv.org/abs/2306.02781

Granić, A. (2022). Educational Technology Adoption: A systematic review. *Education and Information Technologies*, *27*(7), 9725–9744. DOI: 10.1007/s10639-022-10951-7

Grant, R. M. (1996). Toward a knowledge-based theory of the firm. *Strategic Management Journal*, *17*(S2), 109–122. DOI: 10.1002/smj.4250171110

Greene, D., Hoffmann, A. L., & Stark, L. (2019). Better, Nicer, Clearer, Fairer: A Critical Assessment of the Movement for Ethical AI. *HICSS Proceedings*.

Guest, D. E. (2011). Human resource management and performance: Still searching for some answers. *Human Resource Management Journal*, *21*(1), 3–13. DOI: 10.1111/j.1748-8583.2010.00164.x

Gueye, M. (2017). La dimension éthique de l'intelligence économique. *Management et Ethique*, *15*(2), 45–60.

Gupta, R., & Banerjee, P. (2025). Can artificial intelligence anxiety lead to quiet quitting intention? A moderated mediation analysis with tech-savviness and technostress. In *Evidence-based HRM: a Global Forum for Empirical Scholarship*. Emerald Publishing Limited.

Gupta, K., & Gulla, A. (2010). Internet deployment in the spiritual tourism industry: The case of Vaishno Devi Shrine. *Worldwide Hospitality and Tourism Themes*, *2*(5), 507–519. DOI: 10.1108/17554211011090120

Gursoy, D., Chi, O. H., Lu, L., & Nunkoo, R. (2019). Consumers acceptance of artificially intelligent (AI) device use in service delivery. *International Journal of Information Management*, *49*, 157–169. DOI: 10.1016/j.ijinfomgt.2019.03.008

Hair, J. F., Hult, G. T. M., Ringle, C., & Sarstedt, M. (2022). A Primer on Partial Least Squares Structural Equation Modeling (PLS-SEM). *Sage (Atlanta, Ga.)*.

Hair, J. F.Jr, Ringle, C. M., & Sarstedt, M. (2013). Partial least squares structural equation modeling: Rigorous applications, better results and higher acceptance. *Long Range Planning*, *46*(1–2), 1–12. DOI: 10.1016/j.lrp.2013.01.001

Hair, J.. (2022). PLS-SEM: A Primer. *Sage (Atlanta, Ga.)*.

Hair, J.Jr, Sarstedt, M., Hopkins, L., & Kuppelwieser, G., V. (. (2014). Partial least squares structural equation modeling (PLS-SEM) An emerging tool in business research. *European Business Review*, *26*(2), 106–121. DOI: 10.1108/EBR-10-2013-0128

Halpern, N., Mwesiumo, D., Budd, T., Suau-Sanchez, P., & Bråthen, S. (2021). Segmentation of passenger preferences for using digital technologies at airports in Norway. *Journal of Air Transport Management*, *91*, 102005. DOI: 10.1016/j.jairtraman.2020.102005

Hambrick, D. C., & Mason, P. A. (1984). Upper echelons: The organization as a reflection of its top managers. *Academy of Management Review*, *9*(2), 193–206. DOI: 10.2307/258434

Hamouche, S., Koritos, C., & Papastathopoulos, A. (2023). Quiet quitting: Relationship with other concepts and implications for tourism and hospitality. *International Journal of Contemporary Hospitality Management*, *35*(12), 4297–4312. DOI: 10.1108/IJCHM-11-2022-1362

Hantono, B. S., Nugroho, L. E., & Santosa, P. I. (2018). Meta-review of augmented reality in education. In *In2018 10th international conference on information technology and electrical engineering (ICITEE)* (pp. 312–315). IEEE. DOI: 10.1109/ICITEED.2018.8534888

Harbulot, C. (2004). Stratégie et intelligence économique: La quête de compétitivité dans un environnement complexe. *Revue des Sciences de Gestion*, *23*(1), 37–45.

Harbulot, C. (2024). *Guerre économique et stratégies d'influence*. VA Press.

Hassan, M. U., & Iqbal, A. (2020). Open Innovation and Innovative Performance of Pakistani SMEs: Moderated Mediation of Knowledge Management Capability and Innovative Climate. *Pakistan Journal of Commerce and Social Science*, *14*(4), 962–990.

Hassan, S. H. (2015). Conceptualizing the Antecedents and Consequences of Religious Travellers Experience and Wellbeing. *International Journal of Business and Management*, *10*(6), 103–112. DOI: 10.5539/ijbm.v10n6p103

Hassan, S. H., Ramayah, T., & Qureshi, M. I. (2023). Elucidating Well-Being Measurement from the Wellness Perspective of Religious Travelers. *WORLD (Oakland, Calif.)*, *4*(1), 171–184. DOI: 10.3390/world4010012

Hatami, M., Qu, Q., Chen, Y., Kholidy, H., Blasch, E., & Ardiles-Cruz, E. (2024). A survey of the real-time metaverse: Challenges and opportunities. *Future Internet*, *16*(10), 379. Advance online publication. DOI: 10.3390/fi16100379

Heidari, A., Yazdani, H. R., Saghafi, F., & Jalilvand, M. R. (2018). The perspective of religious and spiritual tourism research: A systematic mapping study. *Journal of Islamic Marketing*, *9*(4), 747–798. DOI: 10.1108/JIMA-02-2017-0015

Helfat, C. E., & Peteraf, M. A. (2003). The dynamic resource-based view: Capability lifecycles. *Strategic Management Journal*, *24*(10), 997–1010. DOI: 10.1002/smj.332

Hennart, J. (2014). The Accidental Internationalists: A Theory of Born Globals. *Entrepreneurship Theory and Practice*, *38*(1), 117–135. DOI: 10.1111/etap.12076

Henseler, J., Ringle, C. M., & Sarstedt, M. (2015). A new criterion for assessing discriminant validity in variance-based structural equation modeling. *Journal of the Academy of Marketing Science*, *43*(1), 115–135. DOI: 10.1007/s11747-014-0403-8

He, X., & Liu, Y. (2024). Knowledge evolutionary process of Artificial intelligence in E-commerce: Main path analysis and science mapping analysis. *Expert Systems with Applications*, *238*, 121801. DOI: 10.1016/j.eswa.2023.121801

Hidayat, M., Salam, R., Hidayat, Y. S., Sutira, A., & Nugrahanti, T. P. (2022). Sustainable Digital Marketing Strategy in the Perspective of Sustainable Development Goals. Komitmen. *Jurnal Ilmiah Manajemen*, *3*(2), 100–106. DOI: 10.15575/jim.v3i2.22687

Hinson, R. E., Nwoba, A. C., & Nguyen, N. P. (2021). Corporate social responsibility for women's empowerment: A study on Nigerian banks. *International Journal of Bank Marketing, 39*(4), 516–540. DOI: 10.1108/IJBM-04-2020-0195

Ho, A. G., & Siu, K. W. M. G. (2012). Emotion design, emotional design, emotionalize design: A review on their relationships from a new perspective. *The Design Journal, 15*(1), 9–32. DOI: 10.2752/175630612X13192035508462

Hobfoll, S. E. (1989). Conservation of resources: A new attempt at conceptualizing stress. *The American Psychologist, 44*(3), 513–524. DOI: 10.1037/0003-066X.44.3.513

Ho, J. C., Wu, C. G., Lee, C. S., & Pham, T. T. T. (2020). Factors affecting the behavioral intention to adopt mobile banking: An international comparison. *Technology in Society, 63*, 101360. DOI: 10.1016/j.techsoc.2020.101360

Hornung, O., & Smolnik, S. (2022). AI invading the workplace: Negative emotions towards the organizational use of personal virtual assistants. *Electronic Markets, 32*(1), 123–138. DOI: 10.1007/s12525-021-00493-0

Howard, N. L., Marshall, P., & Swatman, P. A. (2010). Reconceptualising motivation in adoption and acceptance research: Back to basics. In Proceedings of the 21st Australasian Conference on Information Systems. Brisbane, Australia. https://aisel.aisnet.org/acis2010/36

Huang, Z., Liu, F., & Zou, Y. (2020). Federated learning for spoken language understanding. In *Proceedings of the 28th International Conference on Computational Linguistics* (pp. 3467–3478).

Hudaefi, F. A., & Beik, I. S. (2020). Digital zakāh campaign in time of Covid-19 pandemic in Indonesia: A netnographic study. *Journal of Islamic Marketing, 12*(3), 498–517. DOI: 10.1108/JIMA-09-2020-0299

Huma, S., Muslim, S., & Ahmed, W. (2024). Understanding the role of organizational intellectual capital on developing absorptive capacity to strategize innovation ambidexterity. *Review of International Business and Strategy*. DOI: 10.1108/RIBS-08-2023-0088

Hussain, S., Ahmad, N. H., & Syed, T. (2025). (2025). *Green and smart sustainable performance of.pdf*. malque.pub.

Hwang, H. G., Chang, I. C., Chen, F. J., & Wu, S. Y. (2008). Investigation of the application of KMS for diseases classifications: A study in a Taiwanese hospital. *Expert Systems with Applications, 34*(1), 725–733. DOI: 10.1016/j.eswa.2006.10.018

Hwang, K., tom Dieck, M. C., Jung, T., & Kwon, O. (2023). The influence of virtual reality on the experience of religious cultural heritage content. *Internet Research*. Advance online publication. DOI: 10.1108/INTR-08-2022-0669

Ikhtiyorov, F. (2023). Navigating AI's Potential in E-Commerce: Legal Regulations, Challenges, and Key Considerations. *Agrobiotexnologiya Va Veterinariya Tibbiyoti Ilmiy Jurnali*, *2*(5), 41–49.

Innocenti, P. (2023). Pilgrim's progress? A field ethnography of multimodal recording, curating and sharing of the Camino de Santiago experience. *The Journal of Documentation*. Advance online publication. DOI: 10.1108/JD-10-2022-0213

International Telecommunication Union (ITU). (2024). *Bridging the gender digital divide: Internet access and skills gap report 2024*. International Telecommunication Union.

Jabarzadeh, Y., Khangah, M. H., Çemberci, M., Cerchione, R., & Sanoubar, N. (2022). Effect of Absorptive Capacity on Strategic Flexibility and Supply Chain Agility: Implications for Performance in Fast-Moving Consumer Goods. *Operations and Supply Chain Management*, *15*(3), 407–423. DOI: 10.31387/oscm0500356

Jacobides, M. G., Cennamo, C., & Gawer, A. (2018). Towards a theory of ecosystems. *Strategic Management Journal*, *39*(8), 2255–2276. DOI: 10.1002/smj.2904

Jankova, L., Auzina, A., & Zvirbule, A. (2023). Regional smart cultural tourism destinations in a region of Latvia. *Worldwide Hospitality and Tourism Themes*, *15*(5), 507–516. DOI: 10.1108/WHATT-06-2023-0082

Jereb, E., & Urh, M. (2024). The use of artificial intelligence among students in higher education. *Organizacija*, *57*(4), 333–345. DOI: 10.2478/orga-2024-0024

Jha, P., Bansal, T., Rawat, P., & Warpa, V. (2025). The holy hues of Amritsar: An inquiry into the interplay of religious tourism and sacred space. *Tourism Recreation Research*, *50*(3), 636–651. DOI: 10.1080/02508281.2023.2294253

Jiao, J. R., Zhang, Y., & Helander, M. (2006). A Kansei mining system for affective design. *Expert Systems with Applications*, *30*(4), 658–673. DOI: 10.1016/j.eswa.2005.07.020

Jobin, A., Ienca, M., & Vayena, E. (2019). The global landscape of AI ethics guidelines. *Nature Machine Intelligence*, *1*(9), 389–399. DOI: 10.1038/s42256-019-0088-2

Johnson, K., & Verdicchio, M. (2019). Reframing AI discourse: AI as socio-technical systems. *Philosophy & Technology*, *32*(3), 331–348.

Jordan, P. W. (2002). *Designing pleasurable products: An introduction to the new human factors*. CRC press.

Jorge, A. (2023). Pilgrimage to Fátima and Santiago after COVID: Dis/connection in the post-digital age. *Mobile Media & Communication, 11*(3), 549–565. DOI: 10.1177/20501579221151041

Juillet, A., & Racouchot, P. (2012). *L'influence stratégique: Nouveaux enjeux de la compétition informationnelle*. Ellipses.

Jutidharabongse, J., Imjai, N., Pantaruk, S., Surbakti, L. P., & Aujirapongpan, S. (2024). Exploring the effect of management control systems on dynamic capabilities and sustainability performance: The role of open innovation strategy amidst COVID-19. *Journal of Open Innovation, 10*(1), 100224. DOI: 10.1016/j.joitmc.2024.100224

Kahn, W. A. (1990). Psychological conditions of personal engagement and disengagement at work. *Academy of Management Journal, 33*(4), 692–724. DOI: 10.2307/256287

Kalleberg, A. L., Marsden, P. V., Reynolds, J., & Knoke, D. (2006). Beyond profit? Sectoral differences in high-performance work practices. *Work and Occupations, 33*(3), 271–302. DOI: 10.1177/0730888406290049

Kang, J. W., & Namkung, Y. (2019). The role of personalization on continuance intention in food service mobile apps: A privacy calculus perspective. *International Journal of Contemporary Hospitality Management, 31*(2), 734–752. DOI: 10.1108/IJCHM-12-2017-0783

Kaplan, R. (2022). *Analytics and decision-making: From big data to strategic action*. MIT Press.

Karrani, M. A., Bani-Melhem, S., & Mohd-Shamsudin, F. (2024). Employee quiet quitting behaviours: Conceptualization, measure development, and validation. *Service Industries Journal, 44*(3–4), 218–236. DOI: 10.1080/02642069.2023.2286604

Katić, M., & Blaće, A. (2023). The geography of pilgrimage: Adriatic maritime pilgrimages and natural features of the landscape. *Landscape Research, 48*(6), 811–826. DOI: 10.1080/01426397.2023.2198203

Kessler, M. M. (1963). Bibliographic coupling between scientific papers. *American Documentation, 14*(1), 10–25. DOI: 10.1002/asi.5090140103

Kevin, I., Wang, K., Zhou, X., Liang, W., Yan, Z., & She, J. (2021). Federated transfer learning–based cross-domain prediction for smart manufacturing. *IEEE Transactions on Industrial Informatics, 18*(6), 4088–4096. DOI: 10.1109/TII.2021.3113025

Khalique, M.. (2018). Intellectual capital and SME performance. *Journal of Intellectual Capital, 19*(1), 1–21.

Khalique, M., & Bontis, N., Abdul Nassir bin Shaari, J., & Hassan Md. Isa, A. (. (2015). Intellectual Capital in Pakistani Small Medium Enterprises. *Journal of Intellectual Capital, 16*(1), 224–238. DOI: 10.1108/JIC-01-2014-0014

Khalique, M., Hina, K., Ramayah, T., & Shaari, J. A. N. (2020). Intellectual capital in tourism SMEs in Azad Jammu and Kashmir, Pakistan. *Journal of Intellectual Capital, 21*(3), 333–355. DOI: 10.1108/JIC-11-2018-0206

Khan, N. A. (2024). Artificial intelligence, self-efficacy and engagement in religious tourism: Evidence from Arbaeen pilgrimage. *Journal of Hospitality and Tourism Insights, 7*(3), 1660–1678. DOI: 10.1108/JHTI-10-2023-0725

Khan, N. U., Anwar, M., Li, S., & Khattak, M. S. (2021). Intellectual capital, financial resources, and green supply chain management as predictors of financial and environmental performance. *Environmental Science and Pollution Research International, 28*(16), 19755–19767. DOI: 10.1007/s11356-020-12243-4 PMID: 33405102

Kholkina, V., Chesnokova, E., & Zelenskaya, E. (2024). Virtual or human? The impact of the influencer type on Gen Z consumer outcomes. *Journal of Product and Brand Management, 34*(1), 104–118. Advance online publication. DOI: 10.1108/JPBM-12-2023-4885

Kim, C., Mirusmonov, M., & Lee, I. (2010). An empirical examination of factors influencing the intention to use mobile payment. *Computers in Human Behavior, 26*(3), 310–322. DOI: 10.1016/j.chb.2009.10.013

Kim, K. T., & Sohn, Y. W. (2024). The impact of quiet quitting on turnover intentions in the era of digital transformation: The mediating roles of job satisfaction and affective commitment, and the moderating role of psychological safety. *Systems, 12*(11), 460. DOI: 10.3390/systems12110460

Kline, R. (2015). *Principles and Practice of Structural Equation Modeling*. Guilford Press.

Klotz, A. C., & Bolino, M. C. (2022). When quiet quitting is worse than the real thing. *Harvard Business Review.* https://hbr.org/2022/09/when-quiet-quitting-is-worse-than-the-real-thing

Koohang, A., Nord, J. H., Ooi, K. B., Tan, G. W. H., Al-Emran, M., Aw, E. C. X., Baabdullah, A. M., Buhalis, D., Cham, T.-H., Dennis, C., Dutot, V., Dwivedi, Y. K., Hughes, L., Mogaji, E., Pandey, N., Phau, I., Raman, R., Sharma, A., Sigala, M., & Wong, L. W. (2023). Shaping the metaverse into reality: A holistic multidisciplinary understanding of opportunities, challenges, and avenues for future investigation. *Journal of Computer Information Systems*, *63*(3), 735–765. DOI: 10.1080/08874417.2023.2165197

Kornowski, R. (2016). Contemporary issues related to STEMI management. *Minerva Cardioangiologica*, *64*(3), 217–218. PMID: 27149504

Korteling, J. E. H., van de Boer-Visschedijk, G. C., Blankendaal, R. A., Boonekamp, R. C., & Eikelboom, A. R. (2021). Human versus artificial intelligence. *Frontiers in Artificial Intelligence*, *4*, 622364. Advance online publication. DOI: 10.3389/frai.2021.622364 PMID: 33981990

Koskinen, I. (2023). *Design, empathy, interpretation: Toward interpretive design research.* MIT Press. DOI: 10.7551/mitpress/14346.001.0001

Kowalkowski, C., & Ulaga, W. (2024). Subscription offers in business-to-business markets: Conceptualization, taxonomy, and framework for growth. *Industrial Marketing Management*, *117*, 440–456. DOI: 10.1016/j.indmarman.2024.01.014

Kozinets, R. (2012). Marketing netnography: Prom/ot (ulgat) ing a new research method. *Methodological Innovations Online*, *7*(1), 37–45. DOI: 10.4256/mio.2012.004

Kraaijenbrink, J. (2011). Human Capital in the Resource-Based View. *The Oxford Handbook of Human Capital, April 2018*, 1–24. DOI: 10.1093/oxfordhb/9780199532162.003.0009

Król, K., & Hernik, J. (2022). Digital Folklore of Rural Tourism in Poland. *Sustainability (Basel)*, *14*(3), 1165. Advance online publication. DOI: 10.3390/su14031165

Kula, S., & Naktiyok, A. (2021). Strategic intelligence and organizational performance in competitive environments. *Journal of Strategy and Management*, *14*(2), 78–91.

Kuppens, P., Tuerlinckx, F., Russell, J. A., & Barrett, L. F. (2013). The relation between valence and arousal in subjective experience. *Psychological Bulletin*, *139*(4), 917–940. DOI: 10.1037/a0030811

Kurland, N. B. (1995). Ethical intentions and the theories of reasoned action and planned behavior. Journal of Applied Social Psychology, *25*(4), 297–313. DOI: 10.1111/j.1559-1816.1995.tb01593.x

Kurzadkar, P., Bawangade, S., & Sathawane, N. (2024). E-Commerce Platform of Online Shopping Consumers. International *Journal of Advanced Research in Science. Tongxin Jishu, 350-354*, 350–354. Advance online publication. DOI: 10.48175/IJARSCT-17853

Kwak, S., Shin, M., Lee, M., & Back, K. (2023). Integrating the reviewers' and readers' perceptions of negative online reviews for customer decision-making: A mixed-method approach. *International Journal of Contemporary Hospitality Management, 35*(12), 4191–4216. DOI: 10.1108/IJCHM-03-2022-0410

Lai, P. C. (2017). The literature review of technology adoption models and theories for the novelty technology. *Journal of Information Systems and Technology Management, 14*(1), 21–38. DOI: 10.4301/S1807-17752017000100002

Landers, R. N., & Marin, S. (2021). Theory and technology in organizational psychology: A review of technology integration paradigms and their effects on the validity of theory. *Annual Review of Organizational Psychology and Organizational Behavior, 8*(1), 235–258. DOI: 10.1146/annurev-orgpsych-012420-060843

Lang, P. J., Bradley, M. M., & Cuthbert, B. N. (2005). International affective picture system (IAPS): Affective ratings of pictures and instruction manual. Technical Report A-6. University of Florida, Gainesville, FL.

Larivert, R. (2006). La contre-intelligence et la protection du patrimoine informationnel. *Revue Internationale de Sécurité, 30*(1), 12–22.

Larivet, C.. (2012). L'intelligence économique et le comportement stratégique des PME. *Review of International Economics, 19*(4), 99–112.

Laudon, K. C., & Traver, C. G. (2021). *E-commerce 2021: Business, technology, and society* (16th ed.). Pearson.

Lazarus, R. S. (1991). Progress on a cognitive-motivational-relational theory of emotion. *The American Psychologist, 46*(8), 819–834. DOI: 10.1037/0003-066X.46.8.819

Ledi, A. (2024). Strategic behaviors under the influence of competitive intelligence. *Strategic Management Review, 29*(2), 33–45.

Lee, C. (2023). *Knowledge sharing and innovation performance: a case study on the impact of organizational culture, structural capital, human resource management practices, and relational capital of real estate agents. 51*. DOI: 10.1057/s41599-023-02185-w

Lei, J., Indiran, L., Kohar, U. H. A., & Liu, H. (2024). Digital Innovation in Emerging Economies: A Comparative Review of India, Malaysia, China, and Indonesia. *International Journal of Academic Research in Business & Social Sciences*, *14*(1), 3207–3227. DOI: 10.6007/IJARBSS/v14-i1/20457

Lemaine, F. (1997). L'intelligence économique: Quelles implications pour les stratégies organisationnelles? *Revue Internationale de Management*, *13*(2), 55–68.

Lestari, N. S., Zainal, V. R., Chan, S., & Nawangsari, L. C. (2024). Impact of career development, job insecurity, and tech awareness on the quiet quitting of hospitality employees in Indonesia. *Problems and Perspectives in Management*, *22*(3), 427–439. DOI: 10.21511/ppm.22(3).2024.33

Levet, L. (2020). L'intelligence économique et ses apports à la compétitivité des entreprises. *Revue Internationale de Business et Management*, *15*(2), 83–100.

Liao, Y., Wu, G., & Huang, J. (2023). The impact of rural e-commerce environment development on orchard expansion from the perspective of tele-coupling: The case of pinghe county in Southeast China. *Land (Basel)*, *12*(11), 1991. DOI: 10.3390/land12111991

Li, J., & Huang, J. S. (2020). Dimensions of artificial intelligence anxiety based on the integrated fear acquisition theory. *Technology in Society*, *63*, 101410. DOI: 10.1016/j.techsoc.2020.101410

Lin, B. Y., He, C., Zeng, Z., Wang, H., Huang, Y., Dupuy, C., Gupta, R., Soltanolkotabi, M., Ren, X., & Avestimehr, S. (2021). FedNLP: Benchmarking federated learning methods for natural language processing tasks. *arXiv*. https://arxiv.org/abs/2104.08815

Liu, Y., Li, Y., & Wu, A. (2023). Ecosystem-specific Advantages of Digital Platform and Emerging Market Firms' International Outcomes. In *Academy of Management Proceedings (Vol.* 2023, No. 1, p. 16406). Briarcliff Manor, NY 10510. *Proceedings - Academy of Management*, *2023*(1), 16406. Advance online publication. DOI: 10.5465/AMPROC.2023.16406abstract

Li, X.-C., Li, L., Zhan, D.-C., Shao, Y., Li, B., & Song, S. (2021). Preliminary steps towards federated sentiment classification. *arXiv*. https://arxiv.org/abs/2107.11956

Lobschat, L., Mueller, B., Eggers, F., Brandimarte, L., Diefenbach, S., Kroschke, M., & Wirtz, J. (2021). Corporate Digital Responsibility. *Journal of Business Research*, *122*, 875–888. DOI: 10.1016/j.jbusres.2019.10.006

Lo, C., Wang, C., & Chen, Y. C. (2020). The mediating role of intellectual capital in open innovation in the service industries. *Sustainability (Basel), 12*(12), 1–12. DOI: 10.3390/su12125220

Longoni, A., & Cagliano, R. (2020). Sustainable innovation and responsible supply chains in the digital era. *International Journal of Operations & Production Management, 40*(9), 1389–1416.

Long, T. B., & Blok, V. (2018). Integrating the management of innovation and responsible research and innovation: A case study of innovation projects in the Dutch agri-food sector. *Journal on Chain and Network Science, 18*(1), 35–52.

Lubberink, R.. (2017). Responsible Innovation in Business. *Journal of Responsible Innovation, 4*(3), 310–332.

Lubberink, R., Blok, V., Van Ophem, J., & Omta, O. (2017). A framework for responsible innovation in the business context: Lessons from responsible research and innovation. *Sustainability, 9*(5), 721. DOI: 10.3390/su9050721

Luhn, H. P. (1958). The dimensional analysis of information. *Journal of the American Society for Information Science, 9*(5), 180–188.

Lu, M., Al Mamun, A., Chen, X., Yang, Q., & Masukujjaman, M. (2023). Quiet quitting during COVID-19: The role of psychological empowerment. *Humanities & Social Sciences Communications, 10*(1), 1–16. DOI: 10.1057/s41599-023-02012-2

Luthans, F., Vogelgesang, G. R., & Lester, P. B. (2007). Developing the psychological capital of resiliency. *Human Resource Development Review, 6*(1), 25–44. DOI: 10.1177/1534484305285335

Lu, Z., Pan, H., Dai, Y., Si, X., & Zhang, Y. (2024). Federated learning with non-IID data: A survey. *IEEE Internet of Things Journal, 11*(11), 19188–19209. Advance online publication. DOI: 10.1109/JIOT.2024.3376548

Ly, B., & Ly, R. (2022). Internet banking adoption under Technology Acceptance Model—Evidence from Cambodian users. *Computers in Human Behavior Reports, 7*, 100224. DOI: 10.1016/j.chbr.2022.100224

Magateshvaren Saras, M. A., Mitra, M. K., & Tyagi, S. (2025). Navigating the multiverse: A hitchhiker's guide to selecting harmonisation methods for multimodal biomedical data. *Biology Methods and Protocols, 10*(1), bpaf028. Advance online publication. DOI: 10.1093/biomethods/bpaf028 PMID: 40308831

Maillet, É., Mathieu, L., & Sicotte, C. (2015). Modeling factors explaining the acceptance, actual use and satisfaction of nurses using an Electronic Patient Record in acute care settings: An extension of the UTAUT. *International Journal of Medical Informatics, 84*(1), 36–47. DOI: 10.1016/j.ijmedinf.2014.09.004

Marangunić, N., & Granić, A. (2015). Technology acceptance model: A literature review from 1986 to 2013. *Universal Access in the Information Society, 14*(1), 81–95. DOI: 10.1007/s10209-014-0348-1

Marcon, D. (2011). *Construção do conhecimento pedagógico do conteúdo dos futuros professores de Educação Física* (Doctoral dissertation, Universidade do Porto (Portugal)).

Mariani, M. M., & Borghi, M. (2019). Industry 4.0 in tourism. *Tourism Management, 72*, 243–256.

Martin Lackéus, 2015. (2015). *No Title.*

Martinuzzi, A., Blok, V., Brem, A., Stahl, B., & Schönherr, N. (2018). Responsible research and innovation in industry: Challenges, insights and perspectives. *Sustainability (Basel), 10*(3), 702. DOI: 10.3390/su10030702

Martre, L. (1994). *L'intelligence économique et la compétitivité des entreprises.* Presses Universitaires de France.

Maslach, C., Schaufeli, W. B., & Leiter, M. P. (2001). Job burnout. *Annual Review of Psychology, 52*(1), 397–422. DOI: 10.1146/annurev.psych.52.1.397

Mathieson, K. (1991). Predicting user intentions: Comparing the technology acceptance model with the theory of planned behavior. *Information Systems Research,* *2*(3), 173–191. https://doi.org/DOI: 10.1287/isre.2.3.173

McCallum, A., & Nigam, K. (1998). A comparison of event models for naive Bayes text classification. In *AAAI-98 Workshop on Learning for Text Categorization* (pp. 41–48).

McCarthy, I., Mikalef, P., & Krogstie, J. (2023). Human-centered AI: A framework for responsible design and implementation. *Information Systems Journal, 33*(1), 74–99.

McClure, P. K. (2018). "You're fired," says the robot: The rise of automation in the workplace, technophobes, and fears of unemployment. *Social Science Computer Review, 36*(2), 139–156. DOI: 10.1177/0894439317698637

McDuff, D., & Czerwinski, M. (2018). Designing emotionally sentient agents. *Communications of the ACM, 61*(12), 74–83. DOI: 10.1145/3186591

McLean, P. D. (1990). *The triune brain in evolution: Role in paleocerebral functions*. Plenum Press.

McMahan, B., Moore, E., Ramage, D., Hampson, S., & Arcas, B. A. (2017). Communication-efficient learning of deep networks from decentralized data. In *Proceedings of the 20th International Conference on Artificial Intelligence and Statistics* (pp. 1273–1282). PMLR.

Mehta, D., Siddiqui, M. F. H., & Javaid, A. Y. (2018). Facial emotion recognition: A survey and real-world user experiences in mixed reality. *Sensors (Basel)*, *18*(2), 416. DOI: 10.3390/s18020416

Ménard, M., Richard, P., Hamdi, H., Daucé, B., & Yamaguchi, T. (2015, February). Emotion Recognition based on Heart Rate and Skin Conductance. In PhyCS (pp. 26-32).

Mendy, J., & Rahman, M. (2019). Supporting SMEs' internationalisation through a deeper understanding of human and technology barriers: Applying effective HRM processes from a developing country. *Journal of Organizational Effectiveness: People and Performance*, *6*(4), 205–226. DOI: 10.1108/JOEPP-12-2018-0121

Meng, J., Lu, H., & She, S. (2024). An analysis of how digital technology impacts trade costs—Based on the empirical data of RCEP member countries. *Financial Economics Letters*, *3*(3), 1–12. DOI: 10.58567/fel03030001

Men, L. R., & Stacks, D. W. (2014). The effects of authentic leadership on strategic internal communication and employee–organization relationships. *Journal of Public Relations Research*, *26*(4), 301–324. DOI: 10.1080/1062726X.2014.908720

Mention, A. L. (2011). Co-operation and co-opetition as open innovation practices in the service sector: Which influence on innovation novelty? *Technovation*, *31*(1), 44–53. DOI: 10.1016/j.technovation.2010.08.002

MercadoLibre. (2024). *Mujeres en Tecnología Report*. MercadoLibre.

Metz, T. (2017). Ubuntu Ethics and AI. *AI & Society*.

Miles, R. E., & Snow, C. C. (1978). *Organizational strategy, structure, and process*. McGraw-Hill.

Milgram, P., & Kishino, F. (1994). A taxonomy of mixed reality visual displays. *IEICE Transactions on Information and Systems*, *77*(12), 1321–1329.

Miller, J., & Khera, O. (2010). Digital library adoption and the technology acceptance model: Across-country analysis. *The Electronic Journal on Information Systems in Developing Countries*, *40*(1), 1–19. DOI: 10.1002/j.1681-4835.2010.tb00288.x

Mintzberg, H. (1994). Rethinking strategic planning part I: Pitfalls and fallacies. *Long Range Planning*, *27*(3), 12–21. DOI: 10.1016/0024-6301(94)90185-6

Mobley, W. H. (1977). Intermediate linkages in the relationship between job satisfaction and employee turnover. *The Journal of Applied Psychology*, *62*(2), 237–240. DOI: 10.1037/0021-9010.62.2.237

Mogaji, E., Viglia, G., Srivastava, P., & Dwivedi, Y. K. (2024). Is it the end of the technology acceptance model in the era of generative artificial intelligence? *International Journal of Contemporary Hospitality Management*, *36*(10), 3324–3339. Advance online publication. DOI: 10.1108/IJCHM-08-2023-1271

Mogaji, E., Wirtz, J., Belk, R. W., & Dwivedi, Y. (2023). Immersive time (ImT): Conceptualising time spent in the metaverse. *International Journal of Information Management*, *72*, 102659. DOI: 10.1016/j.ijinfomgt.2023.102659

Monaghan, S., Tippmann, E., & Coviello, N. (2020). Born digitals: Thoughts on their internationalization and a research agenda. *Journal of International Business Studies*, *51*(1), 11–22. DOI: 10.1057/s41267-019-00290-0

Mongeon, P., & Paul-Hus, A. (2016). The Journal Coverage of Web of Science and Scopus. *Scientometrics*, *106*(1), 213–228. DOI: 10.1007/s11192-015-1765-5

Mongereau, P. (2006). L'intelligence économique et son rôle dans la compétitivité. *Revue Internationale de Management*, *12*(2), 56–73.

Monino, J. L. (2021). Data value, big data analytics, and decision-making. *Journal of the Knowledge Economy*, *12*(1), 256–267. DOI: 10.1007/s13132-016-0396-2

Monö, R. G., Knight, M., & Monö, R. (1997). *Design for product understanding: The aesthetics of design from a semiotic approach*. Liber.

Moore, G. C., & Benbasat, I. (1991). Development of an instrument to measure the perceptions of adopting an information technology innovation. Information Systems Research, *2*(3), 192–222. https://doi.org/DOI: 10.1287/isre.2.3.192

Moors, A., Ellsworth, P. C., Scherer, K. R., & Frijda, N. H. (2013). Appraisal theories of emotion: State of the art and future development. *Emotion Review*, *5*(2), 119–124. DOI: 10.1177/1754073912468165

Moradi, E., Jafari, S. M., Doorbash, Z. M., & Mirzaei, A. (2021). Impact of organizational inertia on business model innovation, open innovation and corporate performance. *Asia Pacific Management Review*, *26*(4), 171–179. DOI: 10.1016/j.apmrv.2021.01.003

Mori, M. (1970). Bukimi no tani [The uncanny valley]. *Energy*, *7*, 33.

Morini, C., Leonardo, F. P., Chaudhary, V., & Hintsa, J. (2024). A Paradigm Shift in Cross-Border E-Commerce Regulatory Compliance: Evidence from Brazil. *World Customs Journal*, *18*(2), 3–19. DOI: 10.55596/001c.123504

Morley, J., Floridi, L., Kinsey, L., & Elhalal, A. (2021). From what to how: An initial review of publicly available AI ethics tools, methods and research to translate principles into practices. *Science and Engineering Ethics*, *27*(4), 1–25.

Morris, M. G., & Venkatesh, V. (2000). Age differences in technology adoption decisions: Implications for a changing workforce. *Personnel Psychology*, *53*(2), 375–403. DOI: 10.1111/j.1744-6570.2000.tb00206.x

Moustaghfir, K., & Schiuma, G. (2023). L'intelligence économique et l'innovation dans les stratégies organisationnelles. *Journal of Innovation and Knowledge*, *8*(1), 59–72.

Muangasame, K., & Tan, E. (2023). Phygital rural cultural heritage: A digitalisation approach for destination recovery and resilience. *Worldwide Hospitality and Tourism Themes*, *15*(1), 8–17. DOI: 10.1108/WHATT-08-2022-0096

Mulyono, H., & Syamsuri, A. R. (2023). Organizational Agility, Open Innovation, and Business Competitive Advantage: Evidence from Culinary SMEs in Indonesia. *International Journal of Social Science and Business*, *7*(2), 268–275. DOI: 10.23887/ijssb.v7i2.54083

Munjal, P. G. (2021). Charting the role of digital platforms for cultural heritage tourism in India. *Worldwide Hospitality and Tourism Themes*, *13*(2), 186–198. DOI: 10.1108/WHATT-10-2020-0126

Musa, H. G., Fatmawati, I., Nuryakin, N., & Suyanto, M. (2024). Marketing research trends using technology acceptance model (TAM): A comprehensive review of researches (2002–2022). *Cogent Business &amp. Cogent Business & Management*, *11*(1), 2329375. Advance online publication. DOI: 10.1080/23311975.2024.2329375

Nagamachi, M. (1995). Kansei engineering: A new ergonomic consumer-oriented technology for product development. *International Journal of Industrial Ergonomics*, *15*(1), 3–11. DOI: 10.1016/0169-8141(94)00052-5

Nagamachi, M., & Lokman, A. M. (2016). *Innovations of Kansei engineering*. CRC Press. DOI: 10.1201/EBK1439818664

Najar, T., Dhaouadi, K., & Ben Zammel, I. (2020). Intellectual capital impact on open innovation: The case of technology-based sectors in Tunisia. *Journal of Innovation Economics and Management*, *32*(2), 75–106. DOI: 10.3917/jie.032.0075

Narver, J. C., Slater, S. F., & MacLachlan, D. L. (2000). *Total market orientation, business performance, and innovation*. Marketing Science Institute.

Nasri, S. (2012). L'intelligence économique et la création d'avantages concurrentiels. *Management et Organisation*, *25*(6), 234–245.

Ndiaye., . . . (2018). *Demystifying small and medium enterprises' (SMEs) performance in emerging and developing economies | Elsevier Enhanced Reader*. https://reader.elsevier.com/reader/sd/pii/S2214845018300280?token=9DA9B61DEE297BFD4628B3B1DBFA5C36C1037960FE9BD6FB93AAB4796BF3DA66AF0180F3289221C0D5B92ECEFCB5A925&originRegion=eu-west-1&originCreation=20211118213959

Neal, T. O. (2015). Evolving a Successful University-Based Incubator. *Lessons Learned From the UCF Technology Incubator.*, *9247*. Advance online publication. DOI: 10.1080/10429247.2005.11415293

Necula, S. C., Dumitriu, F., & Greavu- erban, V. (2024). A systematic literature review on using natural language processing in software requirements engineering. *Electronics (Basel)*, *13*(11), 2055. DOI: 10.3390/electronics13112055

Niyas, M., Jacob, R., Thomas, T. K., Vipin, R., Raju, J. S., Najjim, M., & Saju, V. (2025). Augmented Reality's Impact on Visitor Engagement and Experiential Management in Religious Heritage Sites. In *Technology and Religious Tourism: Emerging Trends, Cases and Futuristic Perspectives* (pp. 61–76). Emerald Publishing Limited. DOI: 10.1108/978-1-83662-260-420251005

Nonaka, I., & Takeuchi, H. (2021). *The knowledge-creating company*. Oxford University Press.

Norman, D. (2007). *Emotional design: Why we love (or hate) everyday things*. Basic books.

Norman, D. (2013). *The design of everyday things: Revised and expanded edition*. Basic books.

Norman, D. A., & Draper, S. W. (1986). *User centered system design: New perspectives on human-computer interaction*. CRC Press. DOI: 10.1201/b15703

Ntumba, C., Aguayo, S., & Maina, K. (2023). Revolutionizing Retail: A Mini Review of E-commerce Evolution. *Journal of Digital Marketing and Communication*, *3*(2), 100–110. DOI: 10.53623/jdmc.v3i2.365

O'Dea, X. (2024). Generative AI: Is it a paradigm shift for higher education? *Studies in Higher Education*, *49*(5), 811–816. DOI: 10.1080/03075079.2024.2332944

Obradović, T., Vlačić, B., & Dabić, M. (2021). Open innovation in the manufacturing industry: A review and research agenda. *Technovation, 102*, 102221. Advance online publication. DOI: 10.1016/j.technovation.2021.102221

Ocón, D. (2023). Low-cost digital tools to preserve cultural heritage 'blind spots': The case of Kubor Kassim in Singapore. *International Journal of Heritage Studies, 29*(9), 961–987. DOI: 10.1080/13527258.2023.2231903

Olsen, D. H., & Timothy, D. J. (2020). The COVID-19 pandemic and religious travel: Present and future trends. *International Journal of Religious Tourism and Pilgrimage, 8*(7), 170–188.

Omerzel, D. G., & Jurdanab, D. S. (2016). The influence of intellectual capital on innovativeness and growth in tourism SMEs: Empirical evidence from Slovenia and Croatia. *Ekonomska Istrazivanja, 29*(1), 1075–1090. DOI: 10.1080/1331677X.2016.1211946

Ortony, A., Clore, G. L., & Collins, A. (1988). *The cognitive structure of emotions*. Cambridge University Press. DOI: 10.1017/CBO9780511571299

Osei, E. (2023). Competitive strategy in emerging markets: Evidence from Ghana. *Strategic Management Journal, 35*(4), 499–514.

Ota, M., & Aoyama, H. (2001). Aesthetic design based on 'Kansei language'. In *10th International Conference on Precision Engineering (ICPE)*, Yokohama, Japan, 917–921.

Oubrich, L. (2007). La veille stratégique et ses applications dans l'entreprise moderne. *Revue Européenne de Management, 21*(4), 234–245.

Owen, R.. (2021). Responsible Innovation: A State-of-the-Art Review. *Science & Public Policy, 50*(1), 104132. Advance online publication. DOI: 10.1016/j.respol.2020.104132

Owen, R., Bessant, J., & Heintz, M. (2013). *Responsible research and innovation: From science in society to science for society, with society*. Wiley-Blackwell. DOI: 10.1002/9781118551424

Öztürk, O., Genç, S. Y., & Akarsu, A. (2024). Bibliometric analysis in digital ethics research: Trends and insights. *Technological Forecasting and Social Change, 198*, 122–179.

Pai, Y., & Kumar, K. N. (2021). E-Commerce to Multinational Conglomerate: Journey of Alibaba Group—A Case Study. International Journal of Case Studies in Business [IJCSBE]. *IT and Education, 25*. Advance online publication. DOI: 10.5281/zenodo.4544394

Palandrani, P. (2020). *E-commerce: Entering the Next Wave of Growth*. NASDAQ.

Park, Y., Son, H., & Kim, C. (2012). Investigating the determinants of construction professionals' acceptance of web-based training: An extension of the technology acceptance model. *Automation in Construction*, *22*, 377–386. DOI: 10.1016/j.autcon.2011.09.016

Patrick, W. S., Thakur, M., & Jha, J. K. (2024). Attachment and attractiveness towards organizations: Reinforcing the intention to stay amidst the 'great resignation'. *Evidence-based HRM: A Global Forum for Empirical Scholarship*, *12*(3), 611–629.

Pavelka, K., Šedina, J., & Matoušková, E. (2018). High resolution drone surveying of the pista geoglyph in palpa, Peru. *Geosciences*, *8*(12), 479. Advance online publication. DOI: 10.3390/geosciences8120479

Pentland, A. (2000). Perceptual user interfaces: Perceptual intelligence. *Communications of the ACM*, *43*(3), 35–44. DOI: 10.1145/330534.330536

Peter, K. A., Schols, J. M., Halfens, R. J., & Hahn, S. (2020). Investigating work-related stress among health professionals at different hierarchical levels: A cross-sectional study. *Nursing Open*, *7*(4), 969–979. DOI: 10.1002/nop2.469

Petter, S., DeLone, W., & McLean, E. R. (2008). Measuring information systems success: Models, dimensions, measures, and interrelationships. *European Journal of Information Systems*, *17*(3), 236–263. DOI: 10.1057/ejis.2008.15

Petter, S., & McLean, E. R. (2009). A meta-analytic assessment of the DeLone and McLean IS success model: An examination of IS success at the individual level. *Information & Management*, *46*(3), 159–166. DOI: 10.1016/j.im.2008.12.006

Picard, R. W. (2000). *Affective computing*. MIT press. DOI: 10.7551/mitpress/1140.003.0008

Pookulangara, S., Wen, H., & Bharath, J. (2023). Consumer attitudes toward ordering from cloud kitchens: A gender and marital status perspective. *International Journal of Contemporary Hospitality Management*, *35*(5), 1859–1879. DOI: 10.1108/IJCHM-03-2022-0310

Porter, M. E., & Kramer, M. R. (2011). Creating shared value. *Harvard Business Review*, *89*(1–2), 62–77.

Posner, J., Russell, J. A., & Peterson, B. S. (2005). The circumplex model of affect: An integrative approach to affective neuroscience, cognitive development, and psychopathology. *Development and Psychopathology*, *17*(3), 715–734. DOI: 10.1017/S0954579405050340

Pradhan, R. K., & Jena, L. K. (2017). Employee resilience and well-being at work. *Management Research Review*, *40*(5), 509–530.

Prasanthi, P., Kaur, M. R., Ilyas, M. M., Natarajan, S., Neelima, S., & Rajalakshmi, M. (2024). The role of social media influencers in shaping e-commerce trends and consumer behavior. *In Obstetrics & Gynaecology Forum* (No. 3s, p. 2278).

Prensky, M. (2001). Digital natives, digital immigrants. *On the Horizon*, *9*(5), 1–6. DOI: 10.1108/10748120110424816

Presbitero, A., & Teng-Calleja, M. (2023). Job attitudes and career behaviors relating to employees' perceived incorporation of artificial intelligence in the workplace: A career self-management perspective. *Personnel Review*, *52*(4), 1169–1187. DOI: 10.1108/PR-02-2021-0103

Puccio, A., Manocchio, M. C., & Di Virgilio, F. (2025). Strategic Application of AI Tools in Enhancing Tourism for SMEs: The Tourist Management in the Seismic Risk Areas.

Pupion, P. C. (2018). Une recherche en Management Stratégique Public en quête d'un cadre théorique. *Gestion et management public, 63*(1), 6-13.

Quinlan, J. R. (1986). Induction of decision trees. *Machine Learning*, *1*(1), 81–106. DOI: 10.1023/A:1022643204877

Qurashi, J., & Sharpley, R. (2018). The impact of SMART media technologies (SMT) on the spiritual experience of Hajj Pilgrims. *International Journal of Religious Tourism and Pilgrimage*, *6*(3), 37–48.

Rahman, N. (2019). Islamic Ethics and Technology Governance. *Journal of Islamic Ethics*. 8, 001-018.

Rahman, S. S., & Dekkati, S. (2022). Revolutionizing Commerce: The Dynamics and Future of E-Commerce Web Applications. *Asian Journal of Applied Science and Engineering*, *11*(1), 65–73. DOI: 10.18034/ajase.v11i1.58

Raj, S., Sampat, B., Behl, A., & Jain, K. (2023). Understanding senior citizens' intentions to use virtual reality for religious tourism in India: A behavioural reasoning theory perspective. *Tourism Recreation Research*, *48*(6), 983–999. Advance online publication. DOI: 10.1080/02508281.2023.2246735

Ramayah, T., & Ignatius, J. (2005). Impact of perceived usefulness, perceived ease of use and perceived enjoyment on intention to shop online. *ICFAI Journal of systems management (IJSM), 3*(3), 36-51.

Ramayah, T., & Jantan, M. (2004). Technology acceptance: An individual perspective current and future research in Malaysia. Review of Business Research, *2*(1), 103–111.

Ramayah, T., & Jantan, M. (2004). Technology acceptance: An individual perspective. Current and future research in Malaysia. *Review of Business Research*, *2*(1), 103–111.

Ramírez-Solis, E. R., Llonch-Andreu, J., & Malpica-Romero, A. D. (2022). Relational capital and strategic orientations as antecedents of innovation: Evidence from Mexican SMEs. *Journal of Innovation and Entrepreneurship*, *11*(1), 42. Advance online publication. DOI: 10.1186/s13731-022-00235-2

Ranjan, A., & Chaturvedi, P. (2023). Digitally Sustaining: The Rural Intangible Cultural Heritage. In *Embracing Business Sustainability Through Innovation and Creativity in the Service Sector* (pp. 14–30). DOI: 10.4018/978-1-6684-6732-9.ch002

Ranjan, A., & Chaturvedi, P. (2025). Creating Meaningful Tourism Experiences With Digital Storytelling. In *Meaningful Tourism* (pp. 127–144). Emerald Publishing Limited., DOI: 10.1108/978-1-83797-837-320251019

Ransbotham, S., Kiron, D., LaFountain, B., & Candelon, F. (2021). Winning with AI: Pioneers combine strategy, organizational structure, and AI capabilities. *MIT Sloan Management Review*.

Ransbotham, S., Kiron, D., & Prentice, P. K. (2021). The future of human-AI collaboration. *MIT Sloan Management Review*, *62*(4), 24–33.

Rautela, S., Sharma, A., & Panackal, N. (2025). Exploring the sacred-unravelling the growth and development of religious tourism in Islamic culture: A bibliometric analysis. *Cogent Business & Management*, *12*(1), 2482020. Advance online publication. DOI: 10.1080/23311975.2025.2482020

Recent Advances in Al-Emran, M., & Teo, T. (2020). Do knowledge acquisition and knowledge sharing really affect e-learning adoption? An empirical study. Education and Information Technologies, 25, 1983–1998. https://doi.org/DOI: 10.1007/s10639-019-10062-w

Rhee, T., & Jin, X. (2021). The effect of job anxiety of replacement by artificial intelligence on organizational members' job satisfaction in the 4th industrial revolution era: The moderating effect of job uncertainty. *Journal of Digital Convergence*, *19*(7), 1–9.

Ritter, C. S. (2023). Gazing from the air: Tourist encounters in the age of travel drones. *Tourism Geographies*, *0*(0), 1–17. DOI: 10.1080/14616688.2023.2264823

Rodrigues, M., Silva, R., Borges, A. P., Franco, M., & Oliveira, C. (2025). Artificial intelligence: Threat or asset to academic integrity? *A bibliometric analysis. Kybernetes*, *54*(5), 2939–2970. DOI: 10.1108/K-09-2023-1666

Rogers, E. M. (2003). *Diffusion of innovations* (5th ed.). Free Press.

Roiron, M. (1999). L'intelligence économique dans le management stratégique. *Revue de Gestion Stratégique*, *16*(1), 22–34.

Rondan-Cataluña, F. J., Arenas-Gaitán, J., & Ramírez-Correa, P. E. (2015). A comparison of the different versions of popular technology acceptance models. *Kybernetes*, *44*(5), 788–805. DOI: 10.1108/K-09-2014-0184

Rosen, L. D., Sears, D. C., & Weil, M. M. (1987). Computerphobia. *Behavior Research Methods, Instruments, & Computers*, *19*(2), 167–179. DOI: 10.3758/BF03203781

Roslan, F. A. B. M., & Ahmad, N. B. (2023). The Rise of AI-Powered Voice Assistants: Analyzing Their Transformative Impact on Modern Customer Service Paradigms and Consumer Expectations. *Quarterly Journal of Emerging Technologies and Innovations*, *8*(3), 33–64.

Rouach, D., & Salles, M. (2022). *Competitive intelligence and strategic anticipation in turbulent environments*. Wiley.

Rúben Pinhal, at el. (2025). *Open_Innovation_in_the_Tourism_Industry_A_Systemat.pdf.*

Russell, J. A. (1980). A circumplex model of affect. *Journal of Personality and Social Psychology*, *39*(6), 1161–1178. DOI: 10.1037/h0077714

Said, G. R. E. (2023). Metaverse-based learning opportunities and challenges: A phenomenological metaverse human–computer interaction study. *Electronics (Basel)*, *12*(6), 1379. Advance online publication. DOI: 10.3390/electronics12061379

Salanova, M., Llorens, S., & Cifre, E. (2013). The dark side of technologies: Technostress among users of information and communication technologies. *International Journal of Psychology*, *48*(3), 422–436. DOI: 10.1080/00207594.2012.680460

Salles, J. (2006). *L'intelligence économique au service du management stratégique*. Presses Universitaires de France.

Salvetat, D. (2011). Les approches théoriques et l'influence sur la sécurité des pratiques d'intelligence économique dans les entreprises européennes de hautes technologies. *Revue française de gestion industrielle, 30*(2), 53-66.

Sampat, B., Mogaji, E., & Nguyen, N. P. (2023). The dark side of FinTech in financial services: A qualitative inquiry into FinTech developers' perspective. *International Journal of Bank Marketing*. Advance online publication. DOI: 10.1108/IJBM-07-2022-0328

Samuel Godadaw. (2025). *Artificial intelligence adoption dynamics and knowledge in SMEs and large.pdf.*

Sánchez-Prieto, J. C., Olmos-Migueláñez, S., & García-Peñalvo, F. J. (2017). MLearning and pre-service teachers: An assessment of the behavioral intention using an expanded TAM model. *Computers in Human Behavior, 72*, 644–654. DOI: 10.1016/j.chb.2016.09.061

Sanders, E. B. N., & Stappers, P. J. (2014). Probes, toolkits and prototypes: Three approaches to making in codesigning. *CoDesign, 10*(1), 5–14. DOI: 10.1080/15710882.2014.888183

Sanders, E. B.-N. (1990). Converging perspectives: Product development research for the 1990s. *Design Management Journal, 3*(4), 49–54. DOI: 10.1111/j.1948-7169.1992.tb00604.x

Sarkar, B., & Dey, B. K. (2023). Is online-to-offline customer care support essential for consumer service? *Journal of Retailing and Consumer Services, 75*, 103474. DOI: 10.1016/j.jretconser.2023.103474

Sarkar, B., Kar, S., Basu, K., & Seo, Y. W. (2023). Is the online-offline buy-online-pickup-in-store retail strategy best among other product delivery strategies under variable lead time? *Journal of Retailing and Consumer Services, 73*, 103359. DOI: 10.1016/j.jretconser.2023.103359

Sarker, F., Hasan, M. M., & Rahman, M. (2024). Why apply SPSS, SmartPLS and AMOS: An essential quantitative data analysis tool for business and social science research investigations. [Journal of Academic Research]. *International Journal of Research and Innovation in Social Science, 8*(1), 1–9. DOI: 10.47772/IJRISS.2024.8090224

Saunders, M., Lewis, P., & Thornhill, A. (2019). *Research Methods for Business Students*. Pearson.

Scherer, A. G., & Palazzo, G. (2011). The new political role of business in a globalized world: A review of a new perspective on CSR and its implications for the firm, governance, and democracy. *Journal of Management Studies, 48*(4), 899–931. DOI: 10.1111/j.1467-6486.2010.00950.x

Scherer, K. R. (2005). What are emotions? And how can they be measured? *Social Sciences Information. Information Sur les Sciences Sociales*, *44*(4), 695–729. DOI: 10.1177/0539018405058216

Scherer, K. R. (2009). The dynamic architecture of emotion: Evidence for the component process model. *Cognition and Emotion*, *23*(7), 1307–1351. DOI: 10.1080/02699930902928969

Scherer, K. R., Schorr, A., & Johnstone, T. (Eds.). (2001). *Appraisal processes in emotion: Theory, methods, research*. Oxford University Press. DOI: 10.1093/oso/9780195130072.001.0001

Scherer, R., Siddiq, F., & Tondeur, J. (2019). The technology acceptance model (TAM): A meta-analytic structural equation modeling approach to explaining teachers' adoption of digital technology in education. *Computers & Education*, *128*, 13–35. DOI: 10.1016/j.compedu.2018.09.009

Scheyett, A. (2023). Quiet quitting. *Social Work*, *68*(1), 5–7. DOI: 10.1093/sw/swac051

Schorr, A. (2020). Skala zur Erfassung der Digitalen Technologieakzeptanz – Weiterentwicklung zum testtheoretisch geprüften Instrument Gesellschaft für Arbeitswissenschaft (Ed.) *Digitaler Wandel, Digitale Arbeit, Digitaler Mensch?* Dokumentation des 66. Arbeitswissenschaftlichen Kongresses, No. 35, B.20.5, pp. 1-6.

Schorr, A. (2023). The Technology Acceptance Model (TAM) and its importance for digitalization research: A review. In Proceedings of the International Symposium on Technikpsychologie (TecPsy) 2023 (pp. 55-65). Technische Universität Darmstadt. https://doi.org/DOI: 10.2478/9788366675896-005

Schorr, A., & Gorovoj, A. (2023). Acceptance of Digital Technology Among Male and Female University Students: With a Focus on STEM Students. *Journal of Humanities, Arts and Social Science, 7*(9).

Seddon, P., & Kiew, M. Y. (1996). A partial test and development of Delone and McLean's model of IS success. *AJIS. Australasian Journal of Information Systems*, *4*(1), 90–109. DOI: 10.3127/ajis.v4i1.379

Sekaran, U., & Bougie, R. (2020). *Research Methods for Business*. Wiley.

Senbeto, D. L. (2023). The Greener, the Better? Probing Green Innovation in Pilgrimage Tourism Destinations. *Journal of Hospitality & Tourism Research (Washington, D.C.)*. Advance online publication. DOI: 10.1177/10963480231151674

Séraphin, H., & Jarraud, N. (2022). COVID-19: Impacts and perspectives for religious tourism events. The case of Lourdes Pilgrimages. *Journal of Convention & Event Tourism, 23*(1), 15–40. DOI: 10.1080/15470148.2021.1906810

Sestino, A., Pino, G., & Guido, G. (2023). The effect of fervid attachment to religious rites on tourism: Evidence from the Holy Week in Southern Italy. *Journal of Cultural Heritage Management and Sustainable Development, 13*(2), 201–218. DOI: 10.1108/JCHMSD-01-2021-0010

Shachak, A., Kuziemsky, C., & Petersen, C. (2019). Beyond TAM and UTAUT: Future directions for HIT implementation research. *Journal of Biomedical Informatics, 100*, 103315. DOI: 10.1016/j.jbi.2019.103315

Shafiee, S., Jahanyan, S., Ghatari, A. R., & Hasanzadeh, A. (2023). Developing sustainable tourism destinations through smart technologies: A system dynamics approach. *Journal of Simulation, 17*(4), 477–498. DOI: 10.1080/17477778.2022.2030656

Shanahan, K. J., & Hyman, M. R. (2010). Motivators and enablers of SCOURing: A study of online piracy in the US and the UK. *Journal of Business Research, 63*(9–10), 1095–1102. DOI: 10.1016/j.jbusres.2009.02.026

Shenoy, M. V. (2023). HFEDDI: A novel privacy-preserving horizontal federated learning–based scheme for IoT device identification. *Journal of Network and Computer Applications, 214*, 103616. DOI: 10.1016/j.jnca.2023.103616

Shinde, K. A. (2010). Entrepreneurship and indigenous enterpreneurs in religious tourism in India. *International Journal of Tourism Research, 12*(5), 523–535. DOI: 10.1002/jtr.771

Shinde, K. A. (2021). Religious theme parks as tourist attraction systems. *Journal of Heritage Tourism, 16*(3), 281–299. DOI: 10.1080/1743873X.2020.1791887

Shinde, K., & Singh, R. P. B. (2023). Still on UNESCO's "Tentative List of World Heritage"? Heritage, Tourism, and Stunted Growth in Sarnath (Varanasi), India. *Heritage, 6*(7), 5051–5065. DOI: 10.3390/heritage6070267

Shmushko, K. (2023). Between the Tibetan Plateau and Eastern China—Religious Tourism, Lay Practice and Ritual Economy during the Pandemic. *Religions, 14*(3), 1–17. DOI: 10.3390/rel14030291

Shneiderman, B. (2022). *Human-centered AI*. Oxford University Press. DOI: 10.1093/oso/9780192845290.001.0001

Shokry, R. B. (2025). Exploring the Impact of Artificial Intelligence on Urban Design. In *Journal of Engineering Sciences* (Vol. 53, Issue 4, pp. 457–473). DOI: 10.21608/jesaun.2025.370145.1459

Shyu, S. H. P., & Huang, J. H. (2011). Elucidating usage of e-government learning: A perspective of the extended technology acceptance model. *Government Information Quarterly*, *28*(4), 491–502. DOI: 10.1016/j.giq.2011.04.002

Simon, B. (2001). *Wissensmedien im Bildungssektor: Eine Akzeptanzuntersuchung an Hochschulen* [Knowledge media in the education system: Acceptance research in universities]. WU Vienna University of Economics and Business.

Simpson, A., Day, C., Goulding, J., & Asha, J. (2022). Australian teachers' perceptions of effectiveness in a performative culture. *Teaching and Teacher Education*, *109*, 103542. DOI: 10.1016/j.tate.2021.103542

Singh, R. (2023). "My contract is breached, and I want to leave, but I am embedded!" How do reluctant stayers respond? *Evidence-based HRM: A Global Forum for Empirical Scholarship, 11*(4), 594–610.

Singh, N., & Matsuo, H. (2004). Measuring cultural adaptation on the Web: A content analytic study of U.S. and Japanese Web sites. *Journal of Business Research*, *57*(8), 864–872. DOI: 10.1016/S0148-2963(02)00482-4

Singh, S., Darwish, T. K., Wood, G., & Mohamed, A. F. (2017). Institutions, complementarity, human resource management and performance in a South-East Asian petrostate: The case of Brunei. *International Journal of Human Resource Management*, *28*(18), 2538–2569. DOI: 10.1080/09585192.2016.1170713

Snyder, H. (2019). Literature review as a research methodology: An overview and guidelines. *Journal of Business Research*, *104*, 333–339. DOI: 10.1016/j.jbusres.2019.07.039

Sobchyshak, O., Berrezueta-Guzman, S., & Wagner, S. (2025). Pushing the boundaries of immersion and storytelling: A technical review of Unreal Engine. arXiv. https://arxiv.org/abs/2507.08142

Soo, C., Tian, A. W., Teo, S. T. T., & Cordery, J. (2017). Intellectual Capital–Enhancing HR, Absorptive Capacity, and Innovation. *Human Resource Management*, *56*(3), 431–454. DOI: 10.1002/hrm.21783

Srivastava, A., Pandey, A., Sharma, D., & Ghosh, K. (2025). Apathy under the surface: Theorizing quiet quitting's impact on organizational learning. *Development and Learning in Organizations*, *39*(2), 15–17. DOI: 10.1108/DLO-03-2024-0080

Stahl, B. C. (2021). *Artificial intelligence for a better future: An ecosystem perspective on the ethics of AI and emerging digital technologies*. Springer. DOI: 10.1007/978-3-030-69978-9

Steen, M. (2015). Upon opening the black box and finding it full: Exploring the ethics in design practices. *Science, Technology & Human Values*, *40*(3), 389–420. DOI: 10.1177/0162243914547645

Stefanikova, L.. (2015). L'impact de l'intelligence économique sur la compétitivité des entreprises. *International Journal of Business Strategy*, *24*(1), 112–130.

Stephen, A. T., & Toubia, O. (2010). Deriving value from social commerce networks. *JMR, Journal of Marketing Research*, *47*(2), 215–228. DOI: 10.1509/jmkr.47.2.215

Stilgoe, J., & Guston, D. H. (2017). Responsible research and innovation. In Fisher, E. (Eds.), *The handbook of science and technology studies* (4th ed., pp. 853–880). MIT Press.

Stilgoe, J., Owen, R., & Macnaghten, P. (2013). Developing a framework for responsible innovation. *Research Policy*, *42*(9), 1568–1580. DOI: 10.1016/j.respol.2013.05.008

Suárez, M. A., Salas, E. L., Franco, I. C., & Sousa, A. Á. (2025). Towards a methodology of good practices for heritage-led rural regeneration: From the main paths to the surrounding areas. *Cities (London, England)*, *161*(February), 105849. Advance online publication. DOI: 10.1016/j.cities.2025.105849

Sundaram, R., Sharma, D. R., & Shakya, D. A. (2020). Digital transformation of business models: A systematic review of impact on revenue and supply chain. *International Journal of Management, 11*(5). https://ssrn.com/abstract=3628963

Szromek, A. R., & Polok, G. (2022). A business model for spa tourism enterprises: Transformation in a period of sustainable change and humanitarian crisis. *Journal of Open Innovation*, *8*(2), 72. DOI: 10.3390/joitmc8020072

Taherdoost, H. (2018). A review of technology acceptance and adoption models and theories. *Procedia Manufacturing*, *22*, 960–967. DOI: 10.1016/j.promfg.2018.03.137

Taherdoost, H. (2022). *Sampling Methods in Research Methodology*. International.

Talukder, M. F., & Prieto, L. (2025). Quiet quitting and job security: Investigating the impacts of employee's capital and habitus. *The International Journal of Organizational Analysis*. Advance online publication. DOI: 10.1108/IJOA-04-2025-5444

Tamilmani, K., Rana, N. P., & Dwivedi, Y. K. (2017). A systematic review of citations of UTAUT2 article and its usage trends. In *Conference on e-Business, e-Services and e-Society* (pp. 38-49). Springer, Cham. DOI: 10.1007/978-3-319-68557-1_5

Tarafdar, M., Cooper, C. L., & Stich, J. F. (2019). The technostress trifecta—Techno eustress, techno distress and design: Theoretical directions and an agenda for research. *Information Systems Journal, 29*(1), 6–42. DOI: 10.1111/isj.12169

Tarafdar, M., Tu, Q., & Ragu-Nathan, A. T. (2010). Impact of technostress on end-user satisfaction and performance. *Journal of Management Information Systems, 27*(3), 303–334. DOI: 10.2753/MIS0742-1222270311

Tarafdar, M., Tu, Q., Ragu-Nathan, B. S., & Ragu-Nathan, T. S. (2007). The impact of technostress on role stress and productivity. *Journal of Management Information Systems, 24*(1), 301–328. DOI: 10.2753/MIS0742-1222240109

Teece, D. J. (2007). *Dynamic capabilities and strategic management.* Oxford University Press.

Teece, D. J. (2007). Explicating dynamic capabilities: The nature and microfoundations of (sustainable) enterprise performance. *Strategic Management Journal, 28*(13), 1319–1350. DOI: 10.1002/smj.640

Teetzen, F., Klug, K., Steinmetz, H., & Gregersen, S. (2023). Organizational health climate as a precondition for health-oriented leadership: Expanding the link between leadership and employee well-being. *Frontiers in Psychology, 14*, 1181599. DOI: 10.3389/fpsyg.2023.1181599

Teodorescu, M. H., Morse, L., Awwad, Y., & Kane, G. C. (2021). Failures of fairness in automation require a deeper understanding of human-ML augmentation. *Management Information Systems Quarterly, 45*(3), 1483–1500. DOI: 10.25300/MISQ/2021/16535

Terzi, R. (2020). An adaptation of artificial intelligence anxiety scale into Turkish: Reliability and validity study. *International Online Journal of Education & Teaching, 7*(4), 1501–1515.

Thakur, A. (2019). Impact of Mood of the Millennial Customers on Purchase of Apparels Online. In Dasgupta, S., & Grover, P. (Eds.), *Optimizing Millennial Consumer Engagement with Mood Analysis* (pp. 240–266). IGI Global Scientific Publishing., DOI: 10.4018/978-1-5225-5690-9.ch011

Thomas, R., & Wood, E. (2015). The absorptive capacity of tourism organisations. *Annals of Tourism Research, 54*, 84–99. DOI: 10.1016/j.annals.2015.06.004

Thompson, R. L., Higgins, C. A., & Howell, J. M. (1991). Personal computing: Toward a conceptual model of utilization. MIS Quarterly, *15*(1), 124–143. https://doi.org/DOI: 10.2307/249443

Topcuoglu, E., Kobanoglu, M. S., Kaygın, E., Karafakıoglu, E., Erdogan, S. U., Torun, B. T., & Oktaysoy, O. (2023). The improving role of digital leadership in the impact of social loafing on job performance. *International Journal of Organizational Leadership*, *12*(1), 22–40. DOI: 10.33844/ijol.2023.60347

Tornatzky, L. G., & Fleischer, M. (1990). *The processes of technological innovation*. Lexington Books.

Truong, B. T. T., & Nguyen, P. V. (2023). Driving business performance through intellectual capital, absorptive capacity, and innovation: The mediating influence of environmental compliance and innovation. *Asia Pacific Management Review*, *xxxx*. Advance online publication. DOI: 10.1016/j.apmrv.2023.06.004

Tschang, T., & Almirall, E. (2021). The technological base of innovation ecosystems: How innovation ecosystems emerge and evolve. *Research Policy*, *50*(2), 104–118.

Tscheligi, M., Tscheligi, A., & Obrist, M. (2020). *Human-centered interactive technologies*. Springer.

Udenia, M. (2025). The Influence of Digital Transformation on Traditional Business Models. [IJARMT]. *International Journal of Advanced Research and Multidisciplinary Trends*, *2*(1), 582–597. https://ijarmt.com/index.php/j/article/view/166

UNCTAD. (2022). *Global E-Commerce Statistics: 2020–2022 Overview*. United Nations.

Upadhyay, A., & Khandelwal, P. (2023). AI literacy programs for employees: Enhancing competence and reducing anxiety. *Journal of Business Research*, *162*, 113–124.

Ur Rehman, S., Elrehail, H., Alsaad, A., & Bhatti, A. (2022). Intellectual capital and innovative performance: A mediation-moderation perspective. *Journal of Intellectual Capital*, *23*(5), 998–1024. DOI: 10.1108/JIC-04-2020-0109

Ursacescu, M.. (2012). The impact of competitive intelligence on strategic management. *Strategic Management Journal*, *28*(4), 101–115.

Uygungil-Erdogan, S., Şahin, Y., Sökmen-Alaca, A. İ., Oktaysoy, O., Altıntaş, M., & Topçuoğlu, V. (2025). Assessing the effect of artificial intelligence anxiety on turnover intention: The mediating role of quiet quitting in turkish small and medium enterprises. *Behavioral Sciences (Basel, Switzerland)*, *15*(3), 249. DOI: 10.3390/bs15030249

Van Gorp, T., & Adams, E. (2012). *Design for emotion*. Elsevier. DOI: 10.1016/B978-0-12-386531-1.00001-6

Van Raaij, E. M., & Schepers, J. J. (2008). The acceptance and use of a virtual learning environment in China. *Computers & Education*, *50*(3), 838–852. DOI: 10.1016/j.compedu.2006.09.001

Vapnik, V. (1995). Support-vector networks. *Machine Learning*, *20*(3), 273–297. DOI: 10.1023/A:1022627411411

Vaska, S., Massaro, M., Bagarotto, E. M., & Dal Mas, F. (2021). The digital transformation of business model innovation: A structured literature review. *Frontiers in Psychology*, *11*, 539363. DOI: 10.3389/fpsyg.2020.539363 PMID: 33584396

Velev, D., & Zlateva, P. (2017). Virtual reality challenges in education and training. *International Journal of Learning and Teaching*, *3*(1), 33–37. DOI: 10.18178/ijlt.3.1.33-37

Venkatesh, V. (2000). Determinants of perceived ease of use: Integrating control, intrinsic motivation, and emotion into the technology acceptance model. Information Systems Research, *11*(4), 342–365. DOI: 10.1287/isre.11.4.342.11872

Venkatesh, V., & Bala, H. (2008). Technology acceptance model 3 and a research agenda on interventions. Decision Sciences, *39*(2), 273–315. https://doi.org/DOI: 10.1111/j.1540-5915.2008.00192.x

Venkatesh, V., & Davis, F. D. (2000). A theoretical extension of the technology acceptance model: Four longitudinal field studies. Management Science, *46*(2), 186–204.

Venkatesh, V., Morris, M. G., Davis, G. B., & Davis, F. D. (2003). User acceptance of information technology: Toward a unified view. *Management Information Systems Quarterly*, *27*(3), 425–478. DOI: 10.2307/30036540

Verhoef, P. C., Broekhuizen, T., Bart, Y., Bhattacharya, A., Dong, J. Q., Fabian, N., & Haenlein, M. (2021). Digital transformation: A multidisciplinary reflection and research agenda. *Journal of Business Research*, *122*, 889–901. DOI: 10.1016/j.jbusres.2019.09.022

Vettoruzzo, A., Bouguelia, M.-R., Vanschoren, J., Rögnvaldsson, T., & Santosh, K. (2024). Advances and challenges in meta-learning: A technical review. *IEEE Transactions on Pattern Analysis and Machine Intelligence*, *46*(7), 4763–4779. DOI: 10.1109/TPAMI.2024.3357847 PMID: 38265905

Vila-Lopez, N., & Kuster-Boluda, I. (2022). Data mining to reposition a religious tourist destination in COVID-19. *International Journal of Contemporary Hospitality Management*. Advance online publication. DOI: 10.1108/IJCHM-03-2022-0390

Vinchon, F., Gironnay, V., & Lubart, T. (2024). GenAI creativity in narrative tasks: Exploring new forms of creativity. *Journal of Intelligence, 12*(12), 125. DOI: 10.3390/jintelligence12120125

von Schomberg, R. (2013). A vision of responsible research and innovation. In Owen, R. (Eds.), *Responsible innovation: Managing the responsible emergence of science and innovation in society* (pp. 51–74). Wiley-Blackwell. DOI: 10.1002/9781118551424.ch3

von Schomberg, R. (2019). Why responsible innovation? *Journal of Responsible Innovation, 6*(2), 191–200.

Vrontis, D.. (2022). Digital transformation and innovation in SMEs. *Journal of Business Research, 145*, 311–322.

Wang, C., Ahmad, S. F., Ayassrah, A. Y. A. B. A., Awwad, E. M., Irshad, M., Ali, Y. A., Al-Razgan, M., Khan, Y., & Han, H. (2023). An empirical evaluation of technology acceptance model for Artificial Intelligence in E-commerce. Heliyon, *9*(8), e18349. https://doi.org/DOI: 10.1016/j.heliyon.2023.e18349

Wang, J. X. (2021). Meta-learning in natural and artificial intelligence. *Current Opinion in Behavioral Sciences, 38*, 90–95. DOI: 10.1016/j.cobeha.2021.01.002

Wang, M. C., Chen, P. C., & Fang, S. C. (2021). How environmental turbulence influences firms' entrepreneurial orientation: The moderating role of network relationships and organizational inertia. *Journal of Business and Industrial Marketing, 36*(1), 48–59. DOI: 10.1108/JBIM-05-2019-0170

Wang, W., Chen, L., Xiong, M., & Wang, Y. (2023). Accelerating AI adoption with responsible AI signals and employee engagement mechanisms in health care. *Information Systems Frontiers, 25*(6), 2239–2256. DOI: 10.1007/s10796-021-10154-4

Wang, Y.-M., Wei, C.-L., Lin, H.-H., Wang, S.-C., & Wang, Y.-S. (2022). What drives students' AI learning behavior: A perspective of AI anxiety. *Interactive Learning Environments, 32*(6), 2584–2600. DOI: 10.1080/10494820.2022.2153147

Wang, Y., Wang, L., & Siau, K. L. (2025). Human-centered interaction in virtual worlds: A new era of generative artificial intelligence and the metaverse. *International Journal of Human-Computer Interaction, 41*(2), 1459–1501. DOI: 10.1080/10447318.2024.2316376

Wang, Y.-Y., & Wang, Y.-S. (2022). Development and validation of an artificial intelligence anxiety scale: An initial application in predicting motivated learning behavior. *Interactive Learning Environments, 30*(4), 619–634. DOI: 10.1080/10494820.2019.1674887

Ware, C. (2019). *Information visualization: perception for design*. Morgan Kaufmann.

Webster, J., & Watson, R. T. (2002). Analyzing the past to prepare for the future: Writing a literature review. *Management Information Systems Quarterly, 26*(2), xiii–xxiii.

Wegner, D., Zuquetto, R. D., & Grisi, F. C. (2024). Decentralized autonomous organizations (DAOs): Field of research and avenues for future studies. BAR – Brazilian Administration Review, 21, Article e230183. https://doi.org/DOI: 10.1590/1807-7692bar2024230183

Wei, L., & Xia, Z. (2022). Big data-Driven Personalization in E-Commerce: Algorithms, Privacy Concerns, and Consumer Be-havior Imp*lications. International Journal of Applied Machine Learning and Computational Intelligence, 12*(4).

Wennberg, K., Wiklund, J., & Wright, M. (2011). The effectiveness of university knowledge spillovers: Performance differences between university spinoffs and corporate spinoffs. *Research Policy, 40*(8), 1128–1143. DOI: 10.1016/j.respol.2011.05.014

Wernerfelt, B. (1984). A resource-based view of the firm. *Strategic Management Journal, 5*(2), 171–180. DOI: 10.1002/smj.4250050207

Wickramasinghe, D., & Wickramasinghe, V. (2023). Strategic orientation and performance: A study of the impact of Miles & Snow's typology on organizational values. *Journal of Strategy and Management, 28*(4), 401–420.

Wilensky, H. (1967). The sociology of organizations: A review and appraisal. *Administrative Science Quarterly, 12*(2), 273–295.

Williams, M., Rana, N., Dwivedi, Y., & Lal, B. (2011). Is UTAUT really used or just cited for the sake of it? A systematic review of citations of UTAUT's originating article. aisel.aisnet.org

Wirtz, B. W., Weyerer, J. C., & Sturm, B. J. (2023). Ethical artificial intelligence: Concepts, applications, and challenges. *Government Information Quarterly, 40*(1), 101–134.

Wu, J. H., & Wang, S. C. (2003). An empirical study of consumers adopting mobile commerce in taiwan: Analyzed by structural equation modeling [Paper presentation]. *Proceedings of the 5th International Conference on Electronic Commerce,* 81–94.

Wu, M., Chou, H., Weng, Y. C., & Huang, Y. (2011). TAM-2 based study of website user behavior-using web 2.0 websites as an example. *WSEAS Transactions on Business and Economics*, *4*(8), 133–151.

Xiao, L., Saleem, A., Tariq, S. M., Ul Haq, J., & Guo, M. (2021). I wish i could be like her/him! how self-congruence stimulates a desire to mimic. *Journal of Theoretical and Applied Electronic Commerce Research*, *16*(7), 3025–3042. DOI: 10.3390/jtaer16070165

Xia, W., Li, Y., Zhang, L., Wu, Z., & Yuan, X. (2021). A vertical federated learning framework for horizontally partitioned labels. *arXiv*. https://arxiv.org/abs/2106.10056

Yadav, R., Sharma, S. K., & Tarhini, A. (2016). A multi-analytical approach to understand and predict the mobile commerce adoption. *Journal of Enterprise Information Management*, *29*(2), 222–237. DOI: 10.1108/JEIM-04-2015-0034

Yang, C., Pang, L., Zhang, J., & Cao, X. (2024). Workload measurement method for manned vehicles in multitasking environments. *Aerospace (Basel, Switzerland)*, *11*(5), 406. DOI: 10.3390/aerospace11050406

Yang, F., Tang, J., Men, J., & Zheng, X. (2021). Consumer perceived value and impulse buying behavior on mobile commerce: The moderating effect of social influence. *Journal of Retailing and Consumer Services*, *63*, 102683. DOI: 10.1016/j.jretconser.2021.102683

Yang, Q., Liu, Y., Cheng, Y., Kang, Y., Chen, T., & Yu, H. (2020). Vertical federated learning. In Yang, Q., Liu, Y., Chen, T., & Tong, Y. (Eds.), *Federated learning* (pp. 69–81). Springer. DOI: 10.1007/978-3-031-01585-4_5

Yang, Q., Liu, Y., Chen, T., & Tong, Y. (2020). Federated learning: Siloed data exploitation via model aggregation. *International Journal of Machine Learning and Cybernetics*, *11*(12), 345–359. DOI: 10.1007/s13042-020-01064-8

Yang, T. T., Ruan, W. Q., Li, Y. Q., & Zhang, S. N. (2023). Virtual tourist motivation: The differences between virtual tourism and on-site tourism. *Tourism Review*, *78*(5), 1280–1297. DOI: 10.1108/TR-07-2022-0331

Yen, D. C., Wu, C. S., Cheng, F. F., & Huang, Y. W. (2010). Determinants of users' intention to adopt wireless technology: An empirical study by integrating TTF with TAM. *Computers in Human Behavior*, *26*(5), 906–915. DOI: 10.1016/j.chb.2010.02.005

Youssef, H. A. H., & Hossam, A. T. A. (2023). Privacy issues in AI and cloud computing in e-commerce setting: A review. *International Journal of Responsible Artificial Intelligence*, *13*(7), 37–46.

Yuan, H., & Li, S. (2022). Cyber security risks of net-zero technologies. In *Proceedings of the 2022 IEEE Conference on Dependable and Secure Computing (DSC)*. IEEE. DOI: 10.1109/DSC54232.2022.9888883

Yuan, S. (2024). The Application and Influence of E-commerce in International Trade — Taking Amazon as an Example. *Advances in Economics. Management and Political Sciences.*, *134*(1), 119–125. DOI: 10.54254/2754-1169/2024.18701

Yuan, Y. (2023). Cross-border e-commerce logistics service challenges and development. *Frontiers in Business, Economics and Management*, *8*(1), 262–265. DOI: 10.54097/fbem.v8i1.6225

Zahra, S. A., Sapienza, H. J., & Davidsson, P. (2006). Entrepreneurship and dynamic capabilities: A review, model and research agenda. *Journal of Management Studies*, *43*(4), 917–955. DOI: 10.1111/j.1467-6486.2006.00616.x

Zarkada, A. K., Kashif, M., & Zainab, Z. (2025). The structure and content of the religious tourism destination image construct: An exploratory netnography of travelers' reviews of Makkah and Medina. *Journal of Islamic Marketing*, *16*(3), 689–712. DOI: 10.1108/JIMA-06-2024-0229

Zhang, H., & He, X. (2025). The effect of awe on tourists' responsible behavioral intention in a mountainous religious tourism destination: Evidence from China. *Journal of Sustainable Tourism*, *33*(7), 1392–1410. DOI: 10.1080/09669582.2024.2354315

Zhao, C. (2022). Variable Interest Entity, Offshore Domesticated Foreign Finance, and the Political Economy of China's Internet Firms: The Case of Alibaba. *Social Sciences (Basel, Switzerland)*, *11*(3), 99. DOI: 10.3390/socsci11030099

Zhou, L. (2022). Cross-Border E-Commerce: Opportunities versus Challenges. *Science Insights*, *40*(5), 489–490. DOI: 10.15354/si.22.co021

Zlatanović, S., Sovilj, R., & Maksimović, M. (2025). The quiet quitting phenomenon in digital workplaces: A legal-theoretical and comparative analysis. *Review of European and Comparative Law*, *62*(3), 133–153. DOI: 10.31743/recl.18618

Zuboff, S. (2023). The age of surveillance capitalism. In *Social Theory Re-wired* (pp. 203–213). Routledge. DOI: 10.4324/9781003320609-27

Zupic, I., & Čater, T. (2015). Bibliometric methods in management and organization. *Organizational Research Methods*, *18*(3), 429–472. DOI: 10.1177/1094428114562629

About the Contributors

Sihem Ben Saad is an Assistant Professor of Marketing at the Higher School of Sciences and Technology of Design in Tunisia. She earned her Ph.D. in Marketing from IHEC – Carthage Institute of Higher Commercial Studies. Dr. Ben Saad has broad expertise across multiple domains and teaches courses in marketing fundamentals, distribution management, digital marketing, branding and consumer behavior, as well as project management, entrepreneurship, and corporate culture. Her research has been published in prestigious journals, including the Journal of Consumer Behaviour, European Journal of Marketing, International Journal of Retail and Distribution Management, Marketing Intelligence and Planning, Journal of Marketing Management, International Journal of Contemporary Hospitality Management, and the Journal of Research in Marketing and Entrepreneurship, reflecting a significant scholarly impact in the field.

Rahmath Nisha, Saveetha School of Management,Saveetha Institute of Medical and Technical sciences,Chennai,India Poonamalle. Driven by her passion for teaching, Rahmath Nisha transitioned into academia, drawing on her background as an Engineer specializing in Electronics and Communication. Her academic achievements include ranking as a Gold Medalist in her MBA (HR and Hospital Management) from Saveetha University, where she was also recognized as the Best Outgoing Student. Rahmath Nisha's aspiration is to equip students with industry-ready skills through real-time teaching methods, thereby bridging the gap between academic knowledge and practical application in the workplace.

A.K. Subramani, Saveetha School of Management, Saveetha Institute of Medical and Technical Sciences,Chennai,India. Poonamalle. Dr. A.K. Subramani is a distinguished academic with a PhD in Business Administration from Manonmaniam Sundaranar University, Tirunelveli, India. With 18 years of teaching experience, he has made significant contributions to the field of human resource management and organisational behaviour. He has an impressive publication record with 80 articles in international journals, including two papers in the ABDC-A category, eight in the ABDC-B category, three in the ABDC-C category, 30 in Scopus-indexed journals, and eight in Web of Science journals. He has served as a resource person for various training workshops on SPSS and AMOS software packages.

Faris Abuhashish received his MSc degree in computer science, and his PhD from Media and Games Innovation Centre of Excellence (MaGIC-X) in Universiti Teknologi Malaysia. He has published numerous articles in international journals, conference proceedings and technical papers, including chapters in books. He is an active keynote speaker in many international conferences. He is reviewer of many conference and international journals. His research interests include computer vision.

Noor Hazlina Ahmad currently serves as the Dean of the School of Management at Universiti Sains Malaysia since 2019. She holds a PhD in Entrepreneurship from the University of Adelaide, Australia, and has devoted more than two decades to teaching, research, and nurturing future leaders. She is also the President of the Asian Academy of Management, having served from 2015 till date. Her expertise also extends to public policy. She serves on the National Education Reform Taskforce under Akademi Sains Malaysia and the Ministry of Economy, and contributes to Malaysia's Innovation Standard Taskforce under ISO56K, Ministry of Investment, Trade and Industry Malaysia.

Belgacem Bchini is an Associate Professor of Management at the Higher Institute of Management of Tunis, University of Tunis. He is the Director of the Department of Management, Human Resources, and Law, and the Head of the Research Master's Program in Business Administration and Strategy. He is a member of the ARBRE Research Laboratory, with research interests in strategy, entrepreneurship, and knowledge management. He has published over forty research papers and continues to contribute actively to academic research in these fields.

Priya Chaturvedi, is a dedicated educator and Senior Research Fellow affiliated with the School of Studies in Travel and Tourism Management at Jiwaji University, Gwalior, India. She has over four years of teaching experience and specializes in Intangible Cultural Heritage, with a strong academic commitment to the preservation and promotion of cultural traditions. Her research explores multiple dimensions of intangible cultural heritage, and she has made notable contributions to the academic community through her research publications and scholarly activities. She has authored several book chapters in edited volumes highlighting the significance of intangible cultural heritage and has presented her work at numerous national and international conferences, fostering academic dialogue and knowledge exchange. Ms. Chaturvedi has also contributed manuscripts to the Encyclopedia of Tourism

Management and Marketing, covering key concepts related to tourism and heritage studies. In addition to her research activities, she is actively involved in teaching a wide range of tourism-related subjects to undergraduate and postgraduate students, demonstrating a strong commitment to education and the development of future professionals in the tourism sector. Her engagement with cultural heritage extends beyond academia. She volunteered with Bakri Chhap Agro Tourism & Natural Products Pvt. Ltd. from January 2023 to June 2023, supporting initiatives aimed at preserving tangible and intangible cultural heritage and promoting rural tourism development in Madhya Pradesh, India. Her contributions were formally recognized through a recommendation and experience letter issued by the organization. Through her research, teaching, and field engagement, Ms. Chaturvedi continues to make valuable contributions to the fields of intangible cultural heritage and tourism, inspiring colleagues and students through her dedication to cultural preservation and sustainable tourism practices.

Gaurav Dhiman is a practicing Chartered Accountant with expertise in the field of accounts and taxation. He is a member of the Institute of Chartered Accountants of India (ICAI). He has professional experience of more than five years, during which he has developed strong competencies in financial accounting, direct and indirect taxation, statutory compliance, auditing, and advisory services. Through his professional practice, he has gained in-depth exposure to handling tax planning, return filings, financial reporting, and compliance matters for individuals and businesses. His practical approach and analytical skills enable him to provide effective and reliable solutions to clients across diverse sectors. He is committed to maintaining high professional and ethical standards and continuously updates his knowledge in line with changing tax laws and regulatory frameworks. He can be contacted at: gauravdhiman.om@gmail.com.

Shallu Dhiman has recently submitted her doctoral thesis in Human Resource Management at Maharishi Markandeshwar (Deemed to be University) and has teaching experience of more than two years. Her research interests include various aspects of Human Resource Management and organizational behavior. She has knowledge of various software's such as SPSS, SmartPLS, Bibexcel, Biblioshiny, Vos Viewer, Pajek, etc. She has published two papers and three papers are under review. She is the corresponding author and can be contacted at: email2shalludhiman@gmail.com

Sudhanshu Dogra is an Associate Professor in the Department of Mechanical Engineering at Lovely Professional University, Punjab, with over 12 years of teaching, research, and academic leadership experience. He holds a Ph.D. in

Mechanical Engineering, an M.Tech in Thermal Engineering, and is currently pursuing an MBA in HR and Operations Management. His core research interests include renewable energy, solar energy technologies, convection heat transfer, and thermal management systems. Dr. Dogra has published extensively in reputed Scopus- and SCI-indexed journals and conferences and holds multiple patents in the areas of energy systems, aerospace, and mechanical design. He has guided numerous undergraduate, postgraduate, and doctoral research scholars. A recipient of the Best Teacher Award, he is also an Associate Member of ASHRAE and an active contributor to academic conferences, faculty development programs, and interdisciplinary research initiatives focused on sustainable engineering solutions.

Faten Hosni, PhD, researcher and a leading voice in in Strategic Foresight and Human- AI Interaction, focuses her work on Emotional and Cognitive Artificial Intelligence, Ethics of AI, and Anticipatory Governance. Her studies and researches cover the long-term evolution and development of cognitive, emotional, and socio-technical systems resulting from the generative and adaptive nature of Artificial Intelligence. Through the application and lens of futures studies, systems thinking, and interdisciplinarity, the author explores the ways in which Strategic Foresight can shape the design, governance, and regulation of emotionally intelligent technologies. Her research work is characterized by a strong focus on diversity and Global Southern perspectives and proposes a systemic vision for the study of the futures of human-AI Emotional Ecology.

Sajjad Hussain is an Assistant Professor at NUST Business School and holds a PhD in Management Sciences. He previously served as an academician at the Virtual University of Pakistan and has published several research articles. With nearly 19 years of combined academic and public-sector experience, including administrative roles, he brings strong expertise to his professional work. For more information you can contact me qazisajjadpk@gmail.com.

Ismahafezi Bin Ismail is an Associate Professor at Universiti Sultan Zainal Abidin (UniSZA), specializing in Digital Media and Interactive Technologies. He holds a Ph.D. from Universiti Teknologi Malaysia (UTM) and a Bachelor's degree in Mechanical Engineering (Manufacturing). Dr. Ismahafezi's research expertise spans 3D character motion deformation, virtual reality (VR) prototyping, augmented reality (AR) for educational purposes, and artificial intelligence (AI) applications such as chatbot intent classification. He is a prolific researcher with numerous publications in high-impact journals, including the International Journal of Advanced Computer Science and Applications and the Journal of Advanced Research in Applied Sciences and Engineering Technology. His work frequently explores the intersection of immersive environments and human-centered design, specifically focusing on enhancing user experiences in gaming, animation, and medical simulations..

Mohamed Khaldi is an Associate Professor at the Private University of Ibn Khaldoun of Tunis and an active member of the Laboratory of Operations Research, Decision, and Control of Processes (LARODEC). His early research contributions include peer-reviewed publications in Natural Language Processing and optimization. His current research interests center on Arabic Natural Language Processing and automated harmful content detection, leveraging state-of-the-art and emerging computational technologies.

Waleed Maqableh is a distinguished academic and researcher with a PhD in Multimedia and AR/VR Technology from Malaysia. he specializes in innovative areas and his areas of interest include, facial expression recognition, education technology, augmented and virtual reality, and gamification, Dr. Maqableh has dedicated his career to teaching at the university level across Saudi Arabia, the United Arab Emirates, and Jordan.

Mariem Balti is an Assistant Professor of Management at the Faculty of Economic Sciences and Management of Tunis (FSEGT), Université de Tunis El Manar. She is a member of the Laboratoire d'Innovation, Stratégie, Entrepreneuriat, Finance et Économie (LISEFE), where she contributes to multidisciplinary research in organizational behavior, leadership, and strategic management. Her research focuses on emotional intelligence, servant leadership, adaptive performance, and the influence of leadership climates on individual and organizational outcomes. Dr. Balti's recent work includes the peer-reviewed article "Employee and Manager's Emotional Intelligence and Individual Adaptive Performance: The Role of Servant Leadership Climate," published in the Journal of Management Development (Emerald). Her scholarly contributions also encompass book chapters, conference communications, and her doctoral dissertation, which examines how emotional competencies interact with leadership environments to shape adaptive behavior in organizations. In addition to her research activities, Dr. Balti teaches courses in management, leadership, and organizational behavior. She is committed to fostering evidence-based management education and to integrating empirical insights into pedagogical practice. Her academic work aims to advance understanding of leadership processes and to support the development of resilient, high-performing organizations.

Aditya Ranjan is an accomplished academic and industry professional specializing in marketing. He currently serves as an Assistant Professor

(Marketing) at the School of Management, ITM University, Gwalior, India. He holds a Ph.D. titled "Deconstructing Rural Tourism in India" from Jamia Millia Islamia. His academic work focuses on consumer behavior and rural tourism, and he has actively contributed to knowledge dissemination through teaching, research, and the organization of international conferences. Prior to his current academic role, Dr. Ranjan served as Head of the Consulting Vertical at Bakri Chhap Agro Tourism and Natural Products Pvt. Ltd., where he led the design and implementation of rural tourism projects across India. He has also held the position of Assistant Professor at Chandigarh University, contributing extensively to undergraduate and postgraduate education. His scholarly contributions include 23 Scopus-indexed publications, book chapters, and editorial roles in academic outlets, reflecting his recognized expertise in rural tourism and marketing.

Nadia Sfar, Ph.D., is a marketing scholar specializing in consumer emotions, digital marketing, and AI-driven customer interactions. She holds a Ph.D. in Marketing and serves as a faculty member at the Faculty of Economics and Management of Mahdia, University of Monastir, Tunisia. Her research focuses on technology acceptance, and the emotional drivers of consumer behavior. Dr. Sfar has authored numerous articles in peer-reviewed journals such as Marketing Intelligence & Planning, International Journal of Quality and Service Sciences, and The TQM Journal, along with several book chapters on AI in marketing. She can be contacted at: nadia.3lisfar@gmail.com.

Parveen Sharma is a Professor in the School of Mechanical Engineering at Lovely Professional University, with over 15 years of rich academic and research experience. He earned his PhD from the Department of Mechanical Engineering at the National Institute of Technology (NIT), Kurukshetra, India. His core research expertise lies in Facility Layout Planning for manufacturing industries, with a strong focus on improving productivity, operational efficiency, and resource optimization. Over the years, Dr. Sharma has developed extensive teaching and research experience across emerging paradigms of Industry 4.0, Industry 5.0, and Industry 6.0, integrating advanced digital technologies such as smart manufacturing systems, automation, data-driven decision-making, and human-centric production models. His work also spans supply chain management, emphasizing resilient, sustainable, and intelligent supply chains aligned with modern manufacturing ecosystems.

Sultan Singh is presently working as Professor of Management at Maharishi Markandeshwar (Deemed to be University) and has teaching experience of 38 years. His research interests encompass various areas within the field of finance, such as Risk Management, Corporate finance, etc. His leading publications are in the journals of National and International repute. He can be contacted at: profsultansingh@gmail.com.

Abir Smiti is currently an Associate Professor at the High School of Economic and Commercial Sciences of Tunis and a member of the Laboratory of Operations Research, Decision, and Control of Processes (LARODEC). She has contributed to numerous research papers published in refereed journals and presented at international conferences, totaling over 35 publications in the areas of Machine Learning. Her research interests include natural language processing, sentiment analysis, and advanced AI applications in the medical field.

Mohd Shahrizal Sunar is the Director of the Institute of Human Centered Engineering (iHumEn) and a Professor in the Faculty of Computing at Universiti Teknologi Malaysia (UTM). A prominent figure in Creative Content Technology, he leads research programs in Augmented Reality, Virtual Reality, and UI/UX, having successfully managed over RM5 million in research and consultancy projects. Beyond academia, he serves as the CEO of MaGICX and has been a fellow in the Ministry of Higher Education CEO@Faculty Programme, where he was attached to Petronas. Dr. Shahrizal is a recognized expert for Malaysian government agencies like MQA and MyRA, and in 2018, he was named a Top 3 Outstanding Entrepreneurship Mentor by the Ministry of Education. He is also highly active in professional societies, serving as the Deputy President of the Malaysian Muslim Scientist Association (PERINTIS) and holding fellowships in international bodies like the European Alliance of Innovation.

Tayyaba Syed is a lecturer in the Management Science Department at the Virtual University of Pakistan. She holds a PhD in Entrepreneurship and Innovation from Universiti Sains Malaysia, USM. In addition, she served as a Graduate Research Assistant (GRA) at Universiti Sains Malaysia (USM) and has published several research articles in high-impact journals. With nearly 19 years of combined academic and public sector experience, including administrative responsibilities, she brings a wealth of knowledge and expertise to her professional endeavours.

Amit Kumar Thakur, Professor and Head of Aerospace Engineering at Lovely Professional University, has over 22 years of academic and research experience. His expertise includes Renewable Energy, Thermal Engineering, Propulsion, and Industry 4.0. He has published 105+Scopus-indexed papers (76 SCI), authored three books, and holds 200+ patents. With 1140+citations and an h-index of 16, he has guided M.Tech and Ph.D. scholars. He contributed to DRDO's SRE project and is a member of SAE, ISTE, and AMeASI.

Nidal Abdulrahman Yousef is an Associate Professor of Computer Science at Zarqa University in Jordan. He holds a Ph.D. in Computer Information Systems and has extensive academic leadership experience, having served as the Head of the Department of Computer Information Systems at Isra University and as a faculty member at King Abdulaziz University. A specialist in Arabic digital content, Dr. Yousef is the founding member and chairman of the Association for Computing the Arabic Language and Enriching Arabic Content on the Internet. His professional contributions include directing the Wikipedia Education Program in Jordan and supervising the development of national computer science curricula for the Jordanian Ministry of Education. His research focuses on Arabic text retrieval, root extraction algorithms, and the integration of AI in mobile shopping.

Latifa Zeddini is an Assistant Lecturer at the University of Tunis El Manar, Faculty of Economic Sciences and Management of Tunis. She teaches courses in management, human resource management, strategy, and project management. She is a member of the LISEFE research laboratory, with research focusing on business intelligence, strategic monitoring, and organizational strategic behavior. She has published in international academic journals and presented at several conferences. She also supervises student research projects and contributes to academic activities.

Index

S

T

V

www.ingramcontent.com/pod-product-compliance
Lightning Source LLC
LaVergne TN
LVHW080910300926
849162LV00003B/634
9798337399584